GERMAN
WARSHIPS

1815–1945

GERMAN

Volume Two:

ERICH GRÖNER

WARSHIPS
1815–1945
U-Boats and Mine Warfare

Drawings by Erich Gröner, Peter Mickel and Franz Mrva

Revised and Expanded by Dieter Jung and Martin Maass

Naval
Institute
Press

© Bernard & Graefe Verlag 1983 and 1985

First published in West Germany under the title *Die deutschen Kriegsschiffe 1815–1945*

First English language edition published 1991 by

Conway Maritime Press Limited
101 Fleet Street
London EC4Y 1DE

Published and distributed in the United States of America
and Canada by the Naval Institute Press, Annapolis, Maryland 21402

Library of Congress Catalog Card No. 89-64112

ISBN 1-55750-301-X

This edition is authorized for sale only in the United States,
its territories and possessions, and Canada.

Manufactured in Great Britain

Contents

Foreword

The first edition of Erich Gröner's work was published in 1936 under the title *Die deutschen Kriegsschiffe 1815–1936* (German Warships 1815–1936). He was the first writer to attempt to document a national fleet in its entirety over a long period of time, presenting the technical and historical information in the form of tables, drawings to a standard scale, and details of the fates of individual ships. His book was founded on years of painstaking study of the carefully maintained stocks of documents and plans belonging to the Imperial and Reichs navies.

Since the book was so unusual at the time, it represented a risky project in publishing terms, and it was thought necessary to restrict the extent of the work and the length of the print run. As a result the full manuscript could not be published: the detailed 'ships' diaries' (careers) were omitted, and the vast mass of auxiliary ships had to be treated in a very cursory manner. In 1944 a second edition became necessary, but because of the war it was not possible to expand the work, and the only changes made were those necessary to correct known errors. The unpublished sections of manuscript were destroyed in the war.

In the meantime Gröner's book had become acknowledged as a classic example of this type of reference work. When he resumed his labours in about 1950, however, he found that the state of the source material had changed entirely. About 110 tons of German naval documents had survived the war, but they had been requisitioned and placed in storage by the Admiralty in London, where they lay for the most part in disorder. There were no longer any carefully compiled indices, which had made it possible to follow the course of technical developments. It was also clear that many documents concerning particular technical areas had been destroyed during the war in aerial bombardments. If the book was to be continued up to the year 1945, there remained only one course open: Gröner had to attempt to collect and re-assemble thousands of dispersed and disparate fragments of data, and try to correlate and analyse them. The process of analysis and selection turned out to be essential as many items of information, taken out of their context, proved to be contradictory, and implacably resisted interpretation. A further difficulty was the clear evidence of deliberately incorrect entries in official documents.

The source material remained in this state until 1965, when the process of returning naval documents to Germany began. In the summer of the same year Gröner died, during one of his annual journeys in search of new data. In 1966 we were able to publish the first volume, *Die deutschen Kriegsschiffe 1815–1945* - German Warships 1815–

1945 - including that part of the work which he had completed, and in 1968 the second volume followed, which we completed from the raw material he had left behind.

In addition to completing Erich Gröner's work, we undertook the task of re-checking critically all the data, using as a reference the documents which had become available in the intervening period. This task was carried out continuously. The overall state of the source material can now be summarised as follows.

In the technical area the sequential and unbroken series of documents, by means of which developments could be followed, no longer exists. This makes it impossible to assess the relative importance of particular projects and ideas. In the great air attack on Berlin on the night of 22–23 November 1943 the following were destroyed:

The 9th storey of the OKM in the Shellhaus, including the plan chamber (in particular the stocks of old documents of the Imperial and Reichs navies)
The Naval Wehramt (Defence Office)
The office of the Technical Information Service
All departments of the Naval Artillery office
The Naval Torpedo office
The Research, Invention and Patent office

When the main office for warship building (K-Amt) moved from Berlin in 1945, the official documents and plans were burned. Even the working documents taken to Schleswig-Holstein were destroyed at the end of the war.

In view of this, it is inevitable that the work will remain what it is today: a mosaic assembled from scraps of data, in which every entry has been checked, assessed and selected as accurately as possible. There is no possibility of producing a standard source work, in the sense of a straight reprint of a continuous series of documents, from which a sense of historical development emerges naturally, with no need for interpretation. The stocks of documents which remain include construction plans, project drawings, tests on alternative solutions to technical problems, even price quotations and trials results, all jumbled up together; inevitably the disorder and confusion has already given rise to wild speculation and hypothesis.

In the current edition, now expanded by about 40 percent, we have attempted to include everything which stands up to serious investigation. In some areas we have included projects which contribute to the understanding of technical developments in shipbuilding, but we have excluded the majority of suggestions and ideas which were an

inevitable part of the design of almost every new ship type. Such a depth of information could only be provided in a monograph on a ship class or a ship type, not in a work which is intended to provide an overview of all vessels of the German fleet over a period of 130 years, in which the ships were to be treated as equally as possible. We estimate the number of these ships at 10,000. This huge figure brings us to one further important point: we were only able to devote a certain amount of space to any one ship – even the largest. In such cases the book includes construction data and details of important refits, but not every individual modification. One example will make this clear: the continual reinforcement of light AA armament during World War II naturally affected ammunition stocks and crew strengths, but it also affected maximum displacement, maximum weight of fuel, maximum range and much more. A book which intends to summarise cannot encompass the details of such complex interactions; these can also only be covered adequately in a monograph.

We also found it necessary to include large quantities of data relating to the Imperial navy in our critical re-examination. Many of the conclusions of this re-examination are given in notes in the Notes and Abbreviations section, which is completely new. In this regard we owe a debt of gratitude to Prof Dr-Ing E Strohbusch, the last chief officer of the building and maintenance department for large warships and tenders (KIG) in the K-Amt, who suggested a number of fundamental changes. In particular he pointed out to us the problematic and contradictory nature of the information on fuel supplies, fuel consumption, range and trials results. Systematic errors were discovered in some areas, which had slipped in at an earlier stage when complex documents were under assessment. Certain of the contradictions could not be resolved. This is why some of the information which was included in the 1936 edition must now be marked as debatable (?). We would like to emphasise this point here: all amendments which we have made in this text are intentional, including the omissions; the text now represents the true state of current knowledge.

New drawings have been prepared wherever we have been able to discover authentic original plans. Our principal aim here has been to plug obvious gaps and eliminate major errors (eg, distortions of proportion). It has also been possible to include series of drawings relating to certain well-known vessels showing the results of refits. Spatial and financial considerations, and not least the limited time available to our stalwart draughtsmen F Mrva and P Mickel, unfortunately meant that we were unable to satisfy all the wishes of our readers. In particular it proved impossible to provide the depth of detailed information which the builders of large scale models crave. For this type of historical modelling it is best to consider the work as no more than an aid; it can never provide the basis for the actual construction drawings.

After twenty years' work we have now decided to bring our work to an end by issuing a completely new edition, even though we have by no means been able to study all the surviving documents. There are two fundamental reasons for this decision:

1. Categorising accurately the many extant documents has only been possible with the help of former leading naval officers and naval construction officials, many of whom have died in recent years. Of those still living, more and more are now unable to recall detail, and can no longer provide useful information relating to difficult technical questions. Thus as time goes on we increasingly lose vital clues, without which we cannot hope to piece together the jigsaw of the documents in our hands.

2. Our work was and is supported by Erich Gröner's circle of friends, whose number is shrinking. The death of Prof Dr-Ing E Strohbusch and Archive Director Dr G Sandhofer hit us particularly hard, as this work would have been inconceivable without their dedication and support on many fronts. Their place can never be filled again. Thus it seems to us that the time is right to present the material once more in a finished form. The work is planned to take 6 years, and we hope that we will be spared to bring it to a conclusion.

We wish to thank Messrs R Wendeler and W Amann of Bernard & Graefe for granting us the opportunity to realise our plans at a time which is by no means easy for publishers. To all those who have supported and continue to support our work, we offer our heartfelt thanks. Their number is so large that we cannot hope to mention everyone individually.

Berlin/Hamburg, July 1982

Dr Dieter Jung

Martin Maass

Notes and abbreviations

Profiles and sectional drawings of vessels in this book are to a constant 1/1250 scale unless marked otherwise, except those of motor minesweeper etc (pages 135–162), which are to 1/625 scale. A number of more detailed drawings showing conning tower modifications for U-boats are also included.

All headings and table entries give the name by which each vessel was best known, or under which it served for the longest period in the German navies; full details of changes of name are given in Career section of the text, and all names and nick-names are cross-referenced in the index.

Major modifications are listed where possible on a separate line in the tables, under the relevant vessel. Where such modifications resulted in changes of specification, the modified figures are listed. Changes to specifications resulting from modifications other than the major modifications listed separately are incorporated in the tables with the specific individual reference 'mod'.

In the text, data relating to modifications are enclosed within square brackets [ ]; in most cases these data may be related directly to modifications noted in the relevant table.

Note that all ommissions of information from the tables are deliberate; a blank entry indicates that the relevant information is not available. Where a category of information is not applicable, this is indicated in the tables by a dash, —. Parentheses ( ) around a figure in the tables indicate a figure which is uncertain or unconfirmed by all available data. Ditto marks " indicate repetition of the figure or group of figures immediately above.

Tables

Building yards are given as an abbreviated form of the contemporary name, with a glossary giving the full name included at the end of this volume, before the index. In some cases no further information is known than the abbreviated name, and these yards (generally very small) are not included in the glossary.

Building times are calculated for individual vessels from the laying of the keel to commissioning. For groups of vessels, the period indicated is that from the laying of the keel of the first vessel to the commissioning of the last; where a date is given with a dash, this indicates that the vessel or vessels were uncompleted (details are generally given in the text under Careers). In German practice, vessels built in naval dockyards were commissioned before the start of running trials, while those built in private yards were commissioned only after the successful conclusion of trials and official acceptance.

Building costs are given in each case in the German currency in use at the time, unless marked otherwise.

Displacement includes outer plating and external fittings, bilge keels, rudders, propellers, shaft brackets, shaft fairings and exposed shafts. The specific weight of water is calculated at 1.105 in German practice. Gross tonnage (gt) is given where possible.

Maximum (max) displacement equals type displacement plus full load fuel oil, diesel oil, coal, reserve boiler feed water, aircraft fuel and special equipment.

Design (des) displacement includes 25 to 50 percent full load as above, and has been used in the German navy since 1882 as a basis for performance and speed calculations.

Standard (std) displacement, as defined in the 1922 Washington Treaty and used after 1927 in the German navy, includes hull, armour, main and auxiliary engines, all weapons, water and oil in the engine installations and pipework, fixed ballast (if carried), contents of roll tanks (if fitted), full munitions load for all weapons, maximum consumables, food, drinking and washing water, crew and effects – but not fuel and reserve feed water.

Up to 1933 the displacement figures given here apply in almost every case to the vessel at completion, and thus also at commissioning, since modifications and additional equipment were kept within narrow limits in the interim. Later additions are generally listed separately under modifications. After 1933 the official displacement figures are up to 20 percent too low. The low official figures arose partly through a deliberate policy of concealing true displacements because of the Washington Treaty, and partly because extra equipment was added after completion to a much greater extent in this period (as in other navies). The additional weight resulted in increased draught, reduced speed, generally inferior stability and poorer seakeeping; in many cases it led to overstressing of the main structural members.

For U-boats, displacement on the surface, submerged displacement and overall or total displacement are all given where possible. Surface displacement includes all pressure-tight tanks and bunkers up to the floating plane only; submerged displacement represents the entire vessel less all flooded tanks and compartments. The overall or total displacement represents the displacement of the entire U-boat including all free-flooding tanks and compartments.

Length is generally given overall (oa) and at the design waterline (CWL). Length between perpendiculars (bp) was used in the German navy only up to about 1908, and is given here only for vessels taken over from foreign navies or merchant fleets.

For U-boats, the length of the pressure hull is given in place of the CWL length.

Breadth is the maximum beam of the hull, over the outer edge of any belt armour or over the bulkhead edges on ships without belt armour (moulded, that is, less the thickness of the outer plating). Removable fittings, bridge wings, etc, are not included.

For U-boats, the maximum breadth of the pressure hull is given as well as the maximum breadth overall.

Draught is generally given forward (fwd) and aft up to about 1920, and as a mean figure for each of the listed displacements after that date. Where one figure only is given, at any period, this is a mean draught at maximum displacement.

For U-boats, the maximum draught when running on the surface is given before the oblique, and the height of the vessel (that is, the height of the upper surface of the conning tower casing above the keel) after.

Horsepower is generally given as maximum (max) and design (des); the former indicates the maximum output of the individual ship under trial conditions, and the latter the design output (generally common to all ships of the class). The design output as given here represents a short-duration forced output; maximum continuous output was about 15 percent less.

Reversing horsepower available from piston steam engines, internal combustion engines and electric motors was approximately equal to forward power, but for steam turbines the figure was only 25 to 35 percent.

Note that where a second horsepower figure is given after a plus sign, this indicates the horsepower of the secondary propulsion machinery (usually diesel engies). Corresponding figures are given where possible in columns ten, eleven and twelve, also with a plus sign.

For U-boats, the figures given represent the design horsepower for surface propulsion (generally by diesel engines) and the design horsepower for underwater propulsion (generally by electric motor, but for later designs by Walter turbine or diesel engines running on a closed-cycle system). Secondary propulsion such as cruising engines, and electric motors designed for silent running at low speed ('creep' motors), are listed separately.

Revolutions per minute as given here relate to the

horsepower and speed figures given in the appropriate columns. Where a single figure only is given, revolutions at maximum horsepower and speed are indicated. For geared installations the figure for primary revolutions of turbines or motors, where known, is given under Propulsion in the text.

Speed is generally given in maximum nautical miles per hour (knots – kts) as achieved on trial (max) and design speed at design engine output (des). The maximum figures vary widely from ship to ship due to the external circumstances of the trials. The trials instructions specified wind not above Force 3, no current, and deep water (at least three times the ship's draught), but these conditions could not always be observed, especially in wartime. Machinery was also not forced in wartime to the levels achieved in peacetime, because of the danger of damage. In frontline service horsepower, speed and range were all reduced substantially.

For U-boats, the figures given represent maximum speed on the surface and maximum speed submerged. Where secondary propulsion is indicated in the Power column, maximum speeds as applicable are generally shown separately.

Range is given in nautical miles at the stated speed with full fuel supply. The documentary evidence for these figures shows many variations and leaves many vital questions unanswered about the circumstances in which tests were carried out, and the tables therefore list only those values which seem reasonably probable. In some cases the stated ranges were impossible because of limitations on consumption imposed for reasons of stability. Note also that average values are given where there were several ships in one class.

Oil (that is, fuel oil in tonnes) for U-boats is generally given in the form design load before the oblique and proportion within the pressure hull after, with the maximum load, where known, listed separately. Other fuel is also listed separately.

Diving time for U-boats is given where possible with the vessel stationary (simple figure) and with the vessel trimmed down (td), that is moving at speed with hydroplanes trimmed for diving and/or with diving tanks partly full in preparation for a crash dive. The time in seconds is measured from the 'dive' command at action stations to the achievement of a minimum depth of 8m above the top surface of the conning tower casing.

Other information, such as **Gross tonnage** and **Owner** (for vessels requisitioned for naval service) is given as appropriate or available in the tables.

Text

Construction gives the name under which the vessel was built, details of the design and type of construction, and various technical specifications where possible. The extent of any double bottom is given as a percentage of the CWL length of the ship; depth is defined as the height of the ship's hull amidships, measured from the keel to the strength deck, above which the superstructure is generally located; trim moment is short for uniform trim moment, ie, the moment which would produce a 1m change in the ship's trim at the CWL.

For U-boats, the construction notes include details of the basic design (double or single hull), number of watertight compartments, number and volume of main tanks (not including fuel bunkers) and details of the diving depth. Where two figures are given for diving depth, the first is the normal maximum diving depth, and the second the 'crush depth' at which the vessel would be destroyed by pressure.

Propulsion gives details of all propulsion equipment. Note that the distribution of engine and boiler rooms is indicated by figures connected by plus signs (eg, 1 + 1 + 1 boiler rooms); compartments are counted from the stern forward, interpolated zeros (eg, 1 + 0 + 1 engine rooms) indicate compartments used for other purposes, and multiple figures (eg, 1 + 2 + 1 boiler rooms) indicate side-by-side compartments. Boilers are always fore-and-aft unless transverse is specified. The distribution of rudders is also indicated: simple numbers, spelt out, indicate parallel rudders, while figures with plus signs indicate rudders in series, counting from the stern. Details of electrical plant are also given in this section.

For U-boats, propulsion notes also include details of batteries, diesel-electric range in nautical miles, the number and position of the hydroplanes, and details of schnorkels (if any).

Armament gives details of all weapons. Torpedo tubes and mines are included, but no details are given of depth charges, minesweeping equipment or weapons such as flamethrowers, rockets, etc. Note that for home duties only about 60 percent of the weapons and munitions was carried.

For U-boats, details of radar and sonar systems are included where possible, and the number and position of periscopes is given. Where vessels were designed or converted for handling special war cargoes, details are also given in this section.

Handling gives details of seakeeping, manoeuvrability and turning characteristics. For all vessels turning characteristics become progressively worse at lower speeds, and manoeuvring in canals and restricted waterways was always difficult; with very few exceptions, all vessels were particularly difficult to control when going astern.

Complement figures are given wherever possible in the form officers before the oblique, men after. These nominal crew strengths were subject to wide variations, particularly in wartime when extra weapons crew, technical personnel or others embarked for special purposes were frequently carried. The figures quoted are design complements.

Notes generally cover type characteristics and refits, but particular attention is paid to the identifying features of individual vessels. Where colour schemes are noted, full details may be found in Volume I.

Career details given here generally relate to the fate of the vessel, rather than to its operational service; no information is given regarding commands or participation in operational groups or formations. The descriptions given of a vessel's operational status indicate the whole period in which the vessel was considered to belong to that type, before it was reduced to lesser duties; no account is taken of time spent out of commission during these periods. Service abroad indicates ships officially on foreign stations; manoeuvres and training cruises, which were frequent, are not included.

Note that where the date of commissioning is not known, the date of acceptance by the German navy is given. Where ships were purchased or taken as prizes, this information is given before the date of commissioning.

A ship belonged to the German navy from the date of its commissioning to the date of its loss, surrender, or the date at which it was officially stricken. Note that the location of the surrender in 1918–19 is only given here if it differed from the main locations (Harwich for submarines, Firth of Forth for other vessels). In the case of U-boats, references to Operation Deadlight are to the organised scuttling of virtually all surviving German U-boats off Scotland and Northern Ireland under Allied supervision in the aftermath of World War II.

In the case of ships sunk, the site of the loss is given where this is reasonably accurately known (not the site of the wreck at that or a later date).

Brief details are given were possible of the later existence of ex-German navy vessels, but the focus of this book is principally on service with the navy.

Particularly in the case of U-boats, readers are advised that major research is still under way into newly-opened archives in the UK, Eastern Europe and the USSR. It is highly likely that many details of sinkings given here may require amendment; the signs are that perhaps as many as one third of the U-boat sinkings identified by Erich Cröner may be modified in some way by this new information when it becomes available in full.

Abbreviations

AA	anti-aircraft
Afag	Akkumulatorenfabrik AG, Berlin
amp/hr	ampère-hour
BBC	Brown, Boveri & Cie
cm	centimetre
cu m	cubic metre
CWL	construction waterline
des	as designed (see notes)
ehp	effective horsepower, the standard unit for motors, including electric motors
fwd	forward
GM/SA	German Minesweeping Administration (Allied control)
gt	gross tonnage, derived from the internal volume of a ship's hull
ihp	indicated horsepower, the standard unit for expansion (piston) steam engines
KM	*Kaiserliche Marine* up to 1918; *Kriegsmarine* 1934–45
kts	knots
kW	kilowatt
m	metre
M	Mark (currency)
max	maximum (see notes)
mm	milimetre
mod	as modified (see notes)
m-t	metre-tonne
nhp	nominal horsepower, a measurement of the internal geometry of an engine by Lloyds formulae

nm	nautical mile	OKM	*Oberkommando der Marine*, the Naval High Command (Kriegsmarine)	SVK	*Sperr-Versuchskommando*, the Barrage Research Command (Reichsmarine/Kriegsmarine)
nt	net tonnage, a measurement for merchant ships derived from gross tonnage (qv)	OMGUS	Office of Military Government (for Germany) of the United States	t	tonne
NVEK	*Netzversuchs und – Erprobungskommando*, the Net Research and Test Command (Reichsmarine/Kriegsmarine)	ph	pressure hull	T	ton
		QF	quick-firing	td	trimmed down (for U-boats); moving at speed with hydroplanes trimmed for diving and diving tanks partly full
		rpg	rounds per gun		
		RM	*Reichsmarine* 1921–34		
NVK	*Nachrichtensmittel-Versuchskommando*, the Communications Research Command (Reichsmarine/Kriegsmarine)	SEK	*Sperr-Erprobungskommando*, the Barrage Test Command (Reichsmarine/Kriegsmarine)	Tk	torpedo-boat mounting for QF guns
				Uk	U-boat mounting for QF guns
				Utof	torpedo-boat/U-boat AA mounting for QF guns
		sf	surface (for U-boats)		
oa	overall	sm	submerged (for U-boats)	V	Volt

The forerunners of the U-boat

Brandtaucher

Name	Type	Builder (construction no)	Built	Cost in Marks (000s)	Displacement (t = tonnes T = tons)	Length (m)	Breadth (m)	Draught/ height (m)	Power (hp)	Revs (rpm)	Speed (kts)	Range (nm/kts)	Oil (t)	Diving time (sec)
Brandtaucher		Hollersche; completed by S & H	1850–51		28.20t sf 30.95t sm	8.07 oa 7.90 ph	2.01 oa	2.63/ 3.51	0.17 for 10 min	60 or 115	c3	0.5/3	—	162

Construction

Laid down as a coastal submersible for Schleswig-Holstein, designed by Wilhelm Bauer in 1850. Single hull; one watertight compartment; transverse frame with vertical stem; made from rivetted wrought iron, 6mm. Conning tower in the bow. The vessel had no flooding tanks or regulating tanks, although the original design had included two flooding tanks and one regulating tank. 20 tonnes of loose iron ballast were carried in the hold, and one adjustable trim weight, 0.5 tonnes.

Propulsion

Two man-powered treadles, 1.58m diameter, with a two-stage gear on one shaft; one 3-bladed propeller, 1.20m diameter. One manual single-plate rudder. Two manual bilge pumps.

Armament

Storage for explosives (50kg gunpowder) was provided in the side walls of the conning tower. A crew member standing inside the conning tower was supposed to wear special gloves and attach the explosive to the target, and it would then be fired galvanically. The vessel had no weapons of its own and no periscope. The conning tower incorporated bulleyes.

Handling

Due to the height of the gear drive and the vessel's reduced scantlings as constructed (see Notes), *Brandtaucher* required over 6.5 tonnes of ballast to remain upright, and 20.13 tonnes of ballast to stay submerged (displacement 28.2 tonnes).

Complement

Crew: 3.

Notes

Colour: black (tar coated). This was the first German submersible designed with the equipment necessary for submarine travel. Due to lack of funds the Naval Technical Commission requested that the structural parts of the hull be reduced in size (to only 50 per cent of the strength specified by the designer), and that the flooding and regulating tanks be omitted. Because of these changes the structural integrity of the vessel would have been seriously threatened at a depth of 4.65 metres; almost certainly fatally at 5.60 metres. The shape of the hull and the ballast water in the hold meant that, when submerged, the trim weight had no significant effect, and the vessel could not travel on an even keel under water. Preserving static equilibrium while firing an explosive charge would have been impossible with the available technology. Calculations made during the reconstruction of this submarine in 1963–5 showed that, if it had been constructed with the rib spacing, scantlings and flooding and regulating tanks for 2.7 tonnes of water as originally envisaged by the designer, it would have been capable of performing its functions, travelling at the specified depth and could have achieved a diving depth of approximately 25 metres.

Career

Launched 18 Dec 1850; sank at approximately 1000hrs on 1 Feb 1851 in Kiel harbour in a diving accident during her acceptance voyage. No fatalities. Accepted by the navy in a sunken state. Unsuccessful attempts were made to raise her in 1851, 1855, 1856 and 1871. The wreck was rediscovered during dredging operations near Ellerbek, and raised on 5 July 1887. She became a museum ship at the Kiel Naval Academy, and was transferred to the Berlin Maritime Museum in 1906. In 1950 she was taken to Rostock (without the tower etc), after the most seriously damaged and corroded parts of the hull had been removed. She was restored by the shipbuilding faculty of VEB Neptune Dockyard, Rostock, 1963–5; transferred to the German Army Museum at Potsdam in 1965, and then to Dresden Army Museum in 1972.

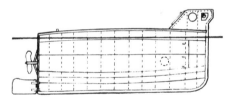

Brandtaucher (1851) (1/156 scale).

Weights (after Bethge)		
Construction members	Weight (tonnes)	% of total weight
Hull (wrought iron)	5.063	18.14
Wooden fittings	0.530	1.90
Equipment on the hull	0.165	0.59
Hull	5.758	20.63
Machinery	0.981	3.51
Equipment and fittings	1.171	4.20
	7.910	28.34
Secured ballast	20.000	71.66
Construction weight	27.910	100.00

Other forerunners of German U-boats

As far as can be ascertained to date, the following reference to the mysterious submarines *W1* and *W2* at the Imperial Dockyards at Kiel and Danzig, which was published in 1888, was the first to appear in any German literature on the subject *(Mitteilungen aus dem Gebiete des Seewesens* XVI, 1888, p357):

German submarine torpedo boats
According to the *Broad Arrow*, trials with a new generation of submarine boats are about to start in Kiel and Danzig.

The 114ft long (34.85m) boats can reach depths of 95 feet (approximately 29m); the machinery to achieve this consists of two horizontal screws set in motion by a 6hp two-cylinder engine.

One cistern holding 51 litres of water serves to control the diving depth. The boat's armaments are said to consist of three McEvoy torpedoes and one quick-fire gun; the crew to be three men strong. The boats can reach a speed of 12 knots and carry enough coal supplies for 200nm. According to the aforementioned source these vessels are merely a modified version of the Nordenfelt boats; . . .

The main source for all subsequent notes on both of these German Nordenfelt submarines is *Submarine Navigation, Past and Present* by Alan H Burgoyne, published in London in 1903. According to Burgoyne, two Nordenfelt submarines, designated *W1* and *W2* (or *U1* and *U2*), which were built in Kiel and Danzig in 1890, participated in naval manoeuvres in Kiel and Wilhelmshaven later that year. The following details are given: length 34.85m; breadth 3.65m; displacement 200 tonnes; diving time 70–80 seconds; range at 'full speed' 2 hours (submerged), 24 hours (surface); propulsion: steam engine.

As yet, no official documentation has been found relating to these boats. The construction number lists of the Imperial Dockyard at Kiel, which attribute numbers even to barges, make no mention of submarines at this time. There is no reference to them in the budgets for the years in question. Torsten Nordenfelt's biography tells us nothing about any German submarines being constructed according to his plans.

The overwhelming impression we are left with is that the *Broad Arrow*'s correspondent and Burgoyne confused the following vessels, which appeared at the same time and had similar dimensions and silhouettes above the water line:

Nordenfelt diving boats
No 1: Length 19.5m; breadth 2.7m; displacement 60 tonnes. Built in 1885 and tested in the Baltic Sea; sold to Greece in 1886.
Nos 2, 3: Length 30.5m; breadth 3.6m; displacement 160 tonnes. Built in England in 1886; delivered to Turkey in sections.
No 4: Length 38m; breadth 3.7m; displacement 200 tonnes. Built in England, 1886–7; ran aground at Jutland while being delivered to Russia, and abandoned.

German trial torpedo boats
W1, 2: Length 34.9m; breadth 3.9m; displacement 91 tonnes. Built at AG Weser in 1884.
A: Length 34.6m; breadth 4.1m; displacement 88 tonnes. Built at the Imperial Dockyard, Danzig; 1888–9.
K: Length 37.6m; breadth 4.8m; displacement 102 tonnes. Built at the Imperial Dockyard, Kiel; 1887–9. (Construction no 13).
Burgoyne also states that a submarine designated *U5* was built by Howaldt, Kiel, in 1891, with the following dimensions: length 30.85m; breadth 3.6m; displacement 180 tonnes. A photograph of a spindle-shaped submersible with prominent long-

itudinal ribs on its hull is provided as evidence. The origins of this vessel remain unclear, but it has substantially smaller dimensions than the Howaldt *U5* boat. The first submarine definitely known to have been built by Howaldt in Kiel was constructed in 1897–8 in accordance with proposals made by Karl Leps, and given the construction number 333. The Leps submersible was 14m long, had a displacement of 40 tonnes, and was powered by electricity. It was built purely on speculation by the dockyard – demonstrations were given to the navy and even, in 1901, to the Kaiser. As it seemed to be a somewhat unreliable vessel, and had not performed any free diving trials, it did not arouse any interest among the German naval authorities and was scrapped in 1902.

The first fully functional submarine built at a German dockyard was the *Forelle*, a purely electrically-powered, spindle-shaped vessel 13m in length, with a displacement of 15.5 tonnes. It had been designed in 1902 by d'Equevilley, the Spanish submarine engineer, and was constructed in 1902–3 at Friedrich Krupp's Germania dockyard in Kiel. It served both to familiarise the shipyard workers with the construction and the special features of a submarine, and as a model to increase interest in submarine production amongst the Germania dockyard's potential domestic and foreign customers. It was also shown to the German naval authorities. Kaiser Wilhelm saw it in 1903, and Prince Heinrich of Prussia even participated in a diving manoeuvre. No orders were placed by the German navy at this stage, however, because of the reluctance shown by Admiral von Tirpitz, the Secretary of State at the Imperial Navy Office. Only when Russia purchased the *Forelle* in 1904, because of its apparent good qualities, and ordered three larger submarines from the Germania yard, did the Imperial German navy decide to set up its own Submarine Construction Office, and ordered one submarine from the Germania yard too.

U-boats up to 1918

U1

Name	Type	Builder (construction no)	Built	Cost in Marks (000s)	Displacement (t = tonnes T = tons)	Length (m)	Breadth (m)	Draught/ height (m)	Power (hp)	Revs (rpm)	Speed (kts)	Range (nm/kts)	Oil (t)	Diving time (sec)
U1		Germania (119)	1904–06	1905	238t sf 283t sm	42.39 oa 32.50 ph	3.75 oa 2.80 ph	3.17/ 6.35	400ehp sf 400ehp sm	500 sf 500 sm	10.8 sf 8.7 sm	1500/10 sf 50/5 sm	22 max	100 50 td

Construction
Laid down as a coastal submersible, designed by Friedrich Krupp at the Germania dockyard, 1904–5. Double hull; seven watertight compartments; adjustable ballast; no trim tanks. Diving depth 30m. Detachable fuel oil container. Constructed with help from d'Equevilley, based on the designs for *Karp*, *Karas* and *Kambala* (which had been built for the Imperial Russian navy in 1904, and had a displacement of 236 tonnes, similar dimensions and fittings). Pressure hull welded by Fitzner, Laurahütte; transverse seams rivetted. Conning tower of 40mm antimagnetic cast nickel steel.

Propulsion
One 6-cylinder 2-stroke Körting petrol engine in compartment 1; two electric motors by Deutsche Elektromotoren Werke, Aachen, in compartment 1; dry batteries by the 'Watt' Akkumulatoren Werke, Zehdenick b. Berlin, in compartments 2

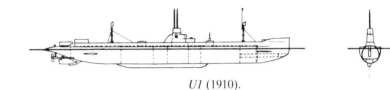

U1 (1910).

and 6 below. Two 3-bladed propellers, 1.30m diameter; two hydroplanes forward and two aft, with stabilisers in front; two rudders.

Armament
One 45cm torpedo tube at the bow, below the waterline - 3 torpedoes; no guns. Two periscopes in the tower, one in the forward hatch.

Handling
Suitable for coastal use only, with limited seafaring capability; average manoeuvrability; not particularly responsive to the helm.

Complement
Crew: 2/10 [3/19]. One dinghy.

Notes
The vessel had an upper deck, formed by a step above the saddle tanks.

Career
Launched 4 Aug 1906; commissioned 14 Dec 1906. Used for trials and submarine training. Stricken 19 Feb 1919. Wreck sold to the Germaniawerft (Kiel) foundation at the Deutsches Museum, Munich, and restored after bomb damage.

U2

Name	Type	Builder (construction no)	Built	Cost in Marks (000s)	Displacement (t = tonnes T = tons)	Length (m)	Breadth (m)	Draught/ height (m)	Power (hp)	Revs (rpm)	Speed (kts)	Range (nm/kts)	Oil (t)	Diving time (sec)
U2		KWD (1*)	1906–08	1548	341t sf 430t sm	45.42 oa 39.30 ph	5.50 oa 3.40 ph	3.05/ 6.62	600ehp sf 630ehp sm	550 sf 685 sm	13.2 sf 9.0 sm	1600/13 sf 50/5 sm	46 max	86 50 td

* The KWD U-boat construction numbers began at 1 and were identified by the prefix DU.

Construction
Laid down as a coastal submersible, official Design Project 7, 1905. Double hull; five watertight compartments; trim and regulating tanks, 6.4cu m; diving depth, 30m; detachable fuel oil container. Rivetted pressure hull.

U2 (1910).

Propulsion

Two Daimler 6-cylinder, 4-stroke petrol engines in compartment 1; two SSW electric motors and 2 SSW double dynamos in compartment 1; 130 Afag (Akkumulatorenfabrik AG, Berlin) large-surface battery cells in compartments 2 and 4 below. Two 3-bladed propellers, 1.0m diameter; two hydroplanes forward and two aft; two rudders.

Armament

Four 45cm torpedo tubes below the waterline, two at the bow and two at the stern - 6 torpedoes; no guns. Two periscopes in the tower, one in the control room.

Handling

Limited seafaring capability; average manoeuvrability; not particularly responsive to the helm.

Complement

Crew: 3/19. One dinghy.

Notes

Trial construction; proved structurally unsound and tended to suffer sea damage. The vessel had an upper deck, formed by a step above the side tank decks.

Career

Launched 18 Jun 1908, commissioned 18 Jul 1908; used for trials and submarine training; stricken 19 Feb 1919, and broken up by Stinnes.

U3 class

Name	Type	Builder (construction no)	Built	Cost in Marks (000s)	Displacement (t = tonnes T = tons)	Length (m)	Breadth (m)	Draught/ height (m)	Power (hp)	Revs (rpm)	Speed (kts)	Range (nm/kts)	Oil (t)	Diving time (sec)
U3, 4		KWD (2, 3)	1907–09	1629	421t sf 510t sm	51.28 oa 45.00 ph	5.60 oa 3.40 ph	3.05/ 6.98	600ehp sf 1030ehp sm	550 sf 600 sm	11.8 sf 9.4 sm	1800/12 sf 55/4.5 sm 3000/9 sf (mod)	48 max	80 47 td
U5–8		Germania (147–150)	1908–11	2540	505t sf 636t sm	57.30 oa 43.10 ph	5.60 oa 3.75 ph	3.55/ 7.28	900ehp sf 1040ehp sm	550 sf 600 sm	13.4 sf 10.2 sm	1900/13 sf 80/5 sm 3300/9 sf (mod)	54 max	65
U9–12		KWD (4–7)	1908–11	2140	493t sf 611t sm	57.38 oa 48.00 ph	6.00 oa 3.65 ph	3.13/ 7.05	600ehp +400ehp sf 1160ehp sm	550 sf 460 sm	14.2 sf 8.1 sm	1800/14 sf 80/5 sm 3250/9 sf (mod)	52 max	90 50 (mod)
(U9 mod)		KWD	1916											
U13–15		KWD (8–10)	1909–12	2101	516t sf 644t sm	57.88 oa 48.50 ph	6.00 oa 3.65 ph	3.44/ 7.25	700ehp +500ehp sf 1160ehp sm	580 sf 440 sm	14.8 sf 10.7 sm	2000/14 sf 90/5 sm 4000/9 sf (mod)	64 max	78 40 (mod)
U16		Germania (157)	1909–11	2539	489t sf 627t sm	57.80 oa 48.50 ph	6.00 oa 3.65 ph	3.36/ 7.25	684ehp +516ehp sf 1160ehp sm	550 sf 470 sm	15.6 sf 10.7 sm	2100/15 sf 90/5 sm 4500/9 sf (mod)	66 max	78 40 (mod)
U17, 18		KWD (11, 12)	1910–12	2333	564t sf 691t sm	62.35 oa 53.00 ph	6.00 oa 3.65 ph	3.40/ 7.30	1400ehp sf 1120ehp sm	580 sf 425 sm	14.9 sf 9.5 sm	6700/8 sf 75/5 sm	74 max	60 70 (mod)
U19–22		KWD (13–16)	1910–13	2450	650t sf 837t sm	64.15 oa 50.50 ph	6.10 oa 4.05 ph	3.58/ 8.10	1700ehp sf 1200ehp sm	320 sm	15.4 sf 9.5 sm	7600/8 sf 80/5 sm 9700/8 sf (mod)	76/54 99/52	90 75 (mod)

Construction

Laid down as submersibles (*U3* and *U4* as official Design Project 12, *U17* and *U18* to official Design Project 20 and to designs by Dr Techel of the Germania yard). Double hull; seven watertight compartments. Diving depth 30m (*U3–8*) or 50m (*U9–22*). Rivetted pressure hull. Trim and regulating tanks 13.3cu m (*U3, 4*), 7.0cu m (*U5–8*), 14.5cu m (*U9–12*), 14.3cu m (*U13, 14*), 14.4cu m (*U15, 16*), 17.1cu m (*U17, 18*) and 18.6cu m (*U19–22*).

Propulsion

Two Körting 8-cylinder 2-stroke petrol engines (or two Körting 6-cylinder plus two Körting 8-cylinder 2-stroke petrol engines, *U9–16*; or two plus two Körting 8-cylinder 2-stroke petrol engines, *U17, 18*; or two MAN 8-cylinder 2-stroke diesel engines, *U19–22*) in compartment 3; two SSW electric motors plus two SSW double dynamos (or two AEG double motor-dynamos, *U19–22*) in compartment 2; two 105 large-surface cell Afag batteries (or tw 106 mass-cell batteries, *U17, 18*; or two 110 mass-cell Afag batteries, *U19–22*) in compartments 5 and 6 below. Two 3-bladed propellers, 1.33m (or 1.30m, *U5–8*; or 1.45m, *U9–12*; or 1.35m, *U13, 14*; or 1.25m, *U15, 16*; or 1.41m, *U17, 18*; or 1.50m, *U19–22*) diameter; two lower hydroplanes forward (or two upper and two lower hydroplanes forward, *U9–12, 19–22*) and two aft; one rudder.

[The after Körting petrol engine on the starboard side of *U9* was replaced in 1916.]

Armament

Four 45cm (or 50cm, *U19–22*) torpedo tubes - 6 torpedoes; one machine gun. The torpedo tubes were laid in pairs, approximately one calibre apart. The stern pair was positioned on the CWL, the forward pair slightly lower. All vessels had two periscopes in the conning tower and one in the control room.

[Before the end of 1914, one 3.7cm machine gun was fitted to *U3–10, 12, 16,* and *17*, one Uk 8.8cm/30 gun - 300 rounds - to *U21*, and one Tk 8.8cm/30 gun - 300 rounds - plus sometimes an additional Uk 8.8cm/30 gun - 300 rounds - to *U22*.

In 1915 all surviving boats except *U21* and *U22* were fitted with one Tk 5cm/40 gun – 72 rounds (or 120 rounds, *U14, 16*; or 180 rounds, *U17*) - (or this weapon plus one 3.7cm machine gun, *U6, 8, 10* and *U17* until 1917 only; or one Uk 8.8cm/30 gun - 300 rounds, *U19, 20*). In 1916 *U19, 20* and *21* were fitted with two Uk 8.8cm/30 guns - 300 rounds. After 1917 *U19*'s 8.8cm guns were replaced by one Tk 10.5cm/45 gun - 200 rounds.

U3's gun was temporarily mounted aft of the conning tower; *U9*'s gun was removed when she was converted to a minelaying boat in 1916; *U10*'s guns were replaced at an unspecified later date by one Uk 8.8cm/40 gun - 80 rounds.

U9 was fitted for minelaying from March to December 1916. She carried 12 P or Tk mines in two rails with semi-circular cross-sections, which ran along either side of the upper deck and met at the stern, approximately 4m forward of the mine-launching position aft. She required extra buoyancy when carrying mines in the Baltic. Trials with net-cutting equipment were also carried out on this boat in 1917.

Handling

Very suitable for surface travel on the high seas in conditions of up to Beaufort 8. The surface steering position had no covering, and therefore became very wet in bad weather. Average manoeuvrability; poor surface steering, especially at slow speed.

U9 required extra buoyancy when carrying mines in the Baltic Sea and 1.5 tonnes of reserve buoyancy in the North Sea.

Complement

Crew: 4/25 (or 3/19, *U3, 4*; or 4/24, *U5, 7*; or 4/31, *U19–22*); one dinghy.

Notes

The petrol-powered boats could be identified from a distance their yellow-white exhaust gases and the noise from their exhausts. The vessels had upper decks, formed by a step above the tank decks.

Careers

U3: launched 27 Mar 1909, commissioned 29 May 1909; used initially for U-boat training, joined a U-boat flotilla in 1911. Sank on 17 Nov 1911, at Kiel, in position 54° 22.5'N, 10° 11.6'E, in an accident; 3 dead. Salvaged using the floating crane *Vulcan*, and used for submarine training. Surrendered 1 Dec 1918, and sank on the way to being broken up at Preston.

U4: launched 18 May 1909, commissioned 1 Jul 1909; used initially for U-boat training, joined a U-boat flotilla in 1911; used for submarine training again in 1913, then for coastal defence 1914–5. Stricken 27 Jan 1919 and broken up at the Imperial

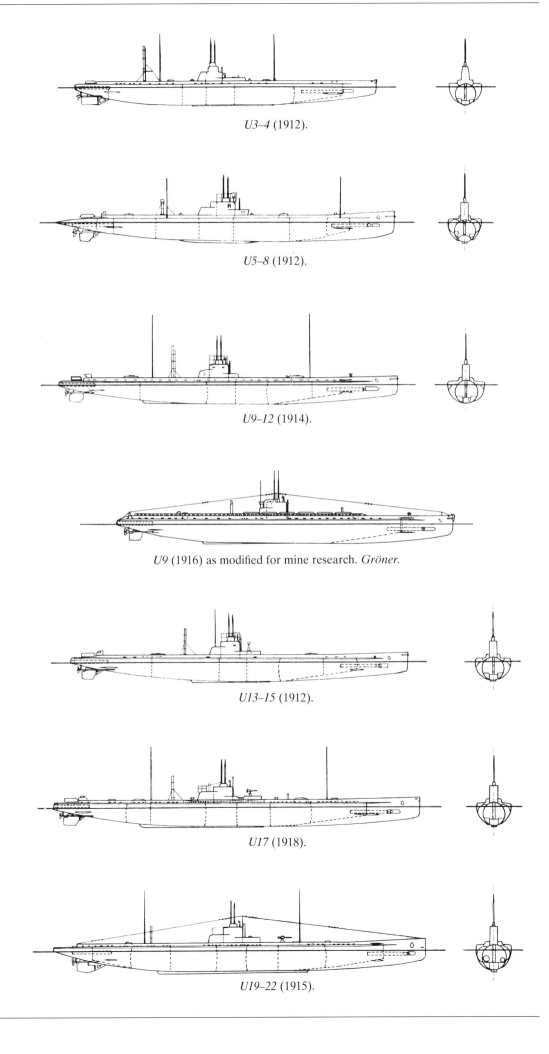

U3–4 (1912).

U5–8 (1912).

U9–12 (1914).

U9 (1916) as modified for mine research. *Gröner.*

U13–15 (1912).

U17 (1918).

U19–22 (1915).

Dockyard, Kiel. Pressure hull sold to Stinnes 3 Feb 1920.

U5: launched 8 Jan 1910, commissioned 2 Jul 1910. Sunk on 18 Dec 1914 in the Channel, approximately in position 51° 23'N, 03° 11'E, possibly mined; 29 dead. Raised and broken up.

U6: launched 18 May 1910, commissioned 12 Aug 1910. Sunk at 1350hrs on 15 Sept 1915 off the Norwegian coast, in position 58° 55'N, 05° 10'E, by a torpedo from the British submarine *E16*; 24 dead.

U7: launched 28 Jul 1910, commissioned 18 Jul 1911. Sunk 21 Jan 1915 in the North Sea, in position 53° 43'N, 06° 02'E, by a torpedo from the German U-boat *U22*; 26 dead.

U8: launched 14 Mar 1911, commissioned 18 Jun 1911. Sunk at 1810 hrs on 4 Mar 1915 in the Channel, in position 50° 41'N, 00° 06'E, by depth charges from the British destroyers *Maori* and *Gurkha*; fatalities not known.

U9: launched 22 Feb 1910, commissioned 18 Apr 1910; used for U-boat training from 20 Apr 1916; surrendered 26 Nov 1918; broken up at Morecambe after 23 Apr 1919.

U10: launched 24 Jan 1911, commissioned 31 Aug 1911. Last voyage 27 May 1916; went missing, presumed sunk, in the Baltic Sea, in position 59° 30'N, 21° 00'E; possibly mined; 29 dead (all crew lost).

U11: launched 2 Apr 1910, commissioned 21 Sep 1910. Sunk on 9 Dec 1914 in the Channel, in position 51° 06'N, 01° 29'E, by a mine; 26 dead.

U12: launched 6 May 1910, commissioned 13 Aug 1911. Sunk on 10 Mar 1915 in the North Sea, in position 56° 07'N, 02° 20'W, after being rammed and depth charged by the British destroyer *Ariel*; 9 dead.

U13: launched 16 Dec 1910, commissioned 25 Apr 1912. Sunk on 9 Aug 1914 in the North Sea, in position 58° 22'N, 01° 16'E after being rammed by a British battleship (identity not known); 23 dead (all crew lost).

U14: launched 11 Jul 1911, commissioned 25 Apr 1912. Sunk on 5 Jun 1915 in the North Sea, in position 57° 16'N, 01° 16'E, after being shelled and rammed by the British steam trawlers *Hawk* and *Oceanis II*; 1 dead.

U15: launched 18 Sept 1911, commissioned 7 Jul 1912. Sunk at approximately 0500hrs on 9 Aug 1914 in the North Sea, in position 58° 22'N, 00° 58'E, after being rammed by the British light cruiser *Birmingham*; 23 dead (all crew lost).

U16: launched 23 Aug 1911, commissioned 28 Dec 1911. Sank on 8 Feb 1919 in the North Sea, in position 58° 59'N, 08° 29'E, in an accident while on passage to surrender.

U17: launched 16 Apr 1912, commissioned 3 Nov 1912; used for U-boat training, 1916. Stricken 27 Jan 1919, and broken up at the Imperial Dockyard, Kiel. Pressure hull sold to Hugo Stinnes, Hamburg, on 3 Feb 1920.

U18: launched 25 Apr 1912, commissioned 17 Nov 1912. Scuttled at 1510hrs on 23 Nov 1914 in the Orkney Isles, in position 58° 42'N, 02° 48'W, following rudder damage etc received while diving under gunfire from the coast; 1 dead.

U19: launched 10 Oct 1912, commissioned 6 Jul 1913; used for U-boat training 1918; surrendered 24 Nov 1918, and broken up at Blyth 1919–20.

U20: launched 18 Dec 1912, commissioned 5 Aug 1913. Scuttled on 5 Nov 1916 after running aground off the coast of Jutland, in position 56° 33'N, 08° 08'E, fatalities not known; wreck blown up 26 Aug 1925.

U21: launched 8 Feb 1913, commissioned 22 Oct 1913; transferred to the Austro-Hungarian Navy in 1915, and served in the Pola U-boat flotilla until 1917; used for U-boat training in 1918. Sunk on 22 Feb 1919 in the North Sea, in position 54° 19'N, 03° 42'W, in an accident while on passage to surrender.

U22: launched 6 Mar 1913, commissioned 25 Nov 1913; used for U-boat training in 1918. Surrendered 1 Dec 1918; renamed *U19*.

U23 class

Name	Type	Builder (construction no)	Built	Cost in Marks (000s)	Displacement (t = tonnes T = tons)	Length (m)	Breadth (m)	Draught/ height (m)	Power (hp)	Revs (rpm)	Speed (kts)	Range (nm/kts)	Oil (t)	Diving time (sec)
U23–26		Germania (177–180)	1911–14	2808	669t sf 864t sm	64.70 oa c52 ph	6.32 oa 4.05 ph	3.45/ 7.70	1800ehp sf 1200ehp sm	450 sf 330 sm	16.7 sf 10.3 sm	7620/8 sf 85/5 sm 9910/8 sf (mod)	85/55 101/57 (mod)	133 85 (mod)
U27–30		KWD (17–20)	1912–14	2636	675t sf 867t sm	,,	,,	3.48/ 7.82	2000ehp sf 1200ehp sm	330 sm	16.7 sf 9.8 sm	9770/8 sf 85/5 sm 8420/8 sf (mod)	87/57 101/57 (mod)	80 45 (mod)
U31–41		Germania (191–201)	1912–15	2891	685t sf 878t sm 971t total	64.70 oa 52.36 ph	,,	3.56/ 7.68 to 8.04	1850ehp sf 1200ehp sm	430 sf 330 sm	16.4 sf 9.7 sm	80/5 sm 8790/8 sf (mod)	110/56	100 50 (mod)

Construction

Laid down as submersibles, to official and Germania Dockyard designs. Double hull; seven watertight compartments; trim and regulating tanks 23.8cu m (or 22.0cu m, *U27–30*; or 27.2cu m, *U31–41*). Diving depth 50m.

Propulsion

Two Germania 6-cylinder 2-stroke diesel engines (or two MAN 6-cylinder 4-stroke diesel engines, *U27–30*) in compartment 3; two SSW double dynamos (or two AEG double dynamos, *U27–30*) in compartment 2; two 110 mass-cell Afag batteries in compartments 5 and 6 below. Two 3-bladed propellers, 1.60m diameter; two hydroplanes forward,

two aft; two [later one] rudders, but one only from *U31* onwards.

Armament

Four 50cm torpedo tubes, two at the bow and two at the stern as for *U3* - 6 [some boats later 9–10] torpedoes; one machine gun. All vessels had periscopes as for *U3*.

[From October 1914 *U25* was fitted with one Uk 8.8cm/30 gun - 300 rounds, and *U35* with one Uk 7.5cm/18 gun - 300 rounds; *U29* and *U31* were sunk before being fitted with guns.

In 1915 all other surviving boats, and also *U35*, were fitted with one (or two, *U27, 28, 36, 37* and sometimes *U25*) Uk 8.8cm/30 gun - 300 rounds (or

200 rounds, *U33, 34*). In 1916–17 all surviving boats except for *U24, 25, 28* and *30* were fitted with one Tk (or Utof, *U32*) 10.5cm/45 gun - 200 rounds. *U30* was fitted with two Uk 8.8cm/30 guns - 300 rounds - after her salvage in 1916, and with one Tk 10.5cm/45 gun - 200 rounds - by the end of 1918.]

Handling

These were very good high seas boats. Average manoeuvrability, good surface steering – unlike their predecessors, which had the rudder situated forward of the propellers!

Complement

Crew: 4/31; one dinghy.

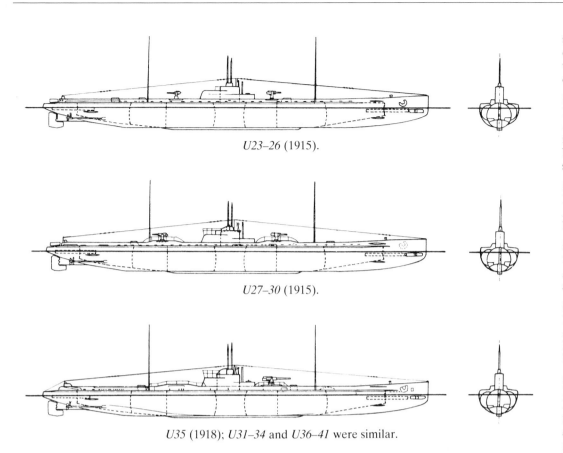

U23–26 (1915).

U27–30 (1915).

U35 (1918); U31–34 and U36–41 were similar.

Notes

Several modifications and conversions were made. The vessels had upper decks, formed by a step above the tank decks.

Careers

U23: launched 12 Apr 1913, commissioned 11 Sept 1913. Sunk at approximately 0900hrs on 20 Jul 1915 in the North Sea, in position 58° 55'N, 00° 14'E, by a torpedo from the British submarine *C27* with the Q-ship *Princess Marie José*; 24 dead.

U24: launched 24 May 1913, commissioned 6 Dec 1913; used for U-boat training from 1917; surrendered on 22 Nov 1918; broken up at Swansea, 1922.

U25: launched 12 Jul 1913, commissioned 9 May 1914; used for U-boat training from 1916; surrendered to France, 23 Feb 1919; broken up at Cherbourg, 1921–2.

U26: launched 16 Oct 1913, commissioned 20 May 1914. Sunk early September 1915 in the Baltic Sea, in approximate position 59° 40'N, 23° 50'E, by mines; 30 dead.

U27: launched 14 Jul 1913, commissioned 8 May 1914. Sunk on 19 Aug 1915 in the Channel, in position 50° 25'N, 08° 15'W, by gunfire from the British Q-ship *Baralong*; 37 dead, of whom 11 were executed by the crew of the *Baralong* (all crew lost).

U28: launched 30 Aug 1913, commissioned 26 Jun 1914. Sunk at 1155hrs on 2 Jul 1917 in the Arctic Sea, in position 72° 34'N, 27° 56'E, by an explosion in the sinking steamship SS *Olive Branch*; 39 dead (all crew lost).

U29: launched 11 Oct 1913, commissioned 1 Aug 1914. Sunk at 1340hrs on 18 Mar 1915 in the North Sea, in position 58° 20'N, 00° 57'E, after being rammed by the British battleship *Dreadnought*; 32 dead (all crew lost).

U30: launched 15 Nov 1913, commissioned 26 Aug 1914. Sank in an accident on 22 Jun 1915 in the Ems estuary, in position 53° 33.7'N, 06° 40.6'E; 31 dead. Raised on 27 Aug 1915; served in a U-boat flotilla; used for U-boat training from 1917; surrendered 22 Nov 1918; broken up at Blyth, 1919–20.

U31: launched 7 Jan 1914, commissioned 18 Sept 1914; went missing Jan 1915 in the North Sea, pre-

sumed sunk; 31 dead (all crew lost). There is no evidence whatever for the story that this boat was washed up on the East Coast of Britain with her entire crew dead from gas poisoning.

U32: launched 28 Jan 1914, commissioned 3 Sept 1914; served in the Mediterranean from 1916 as the Austro-Hungarian *U37*. Sunk on 8 May 1918 northwest of Malta, in position 36° 07'N, 13° 28'E, by depth charges from the British minesweeping sloop *Wallflower*; 41 dead (all crew lost).

U33: launched 19 May 1914, commissioned 27 Sept 1914; served in the Mediterranean from 1915 as the Austro-Hungarian *U33*; surrendered 16 Jan 1919; broken up at Blyth, 1919–20.

U34: launched 9 May 1914, commissioned 5 Oct 1914; served in the Mediterranean from 1915 as the Austro-Hungarian *U34*. Sunk in Oct 1918, cause and location unknown; 41 dead (all crew lost).

U35: launched 18 Apr 1914, commissioned 3 Nov 1914; served in the Mediterranean from 1915 as the Austro-Hungarian *U35*; transferred to the German Mediterranean U-boat flotilla 1918; surrendered 26 Nov 1918; broken up at Blyth, 1919–20.

U36: launched 6 Jun 1914, commissioned 14 Nov 1914. Sunk at 1920hrs on 24 Jul 1915 west of the Rona Isles, in position 59° 05'N, 06° 01'W, by gunfire from the British Q-ship *Prince Charles*; 18 dead.

U37: launched 25 Aug 1914, commissioned 9 Dec 1914. Sunk on 1 Apr 1915 in the Channel, in position 51° 04'N, 01° 48'E, by mines; 32 dead.

U38: launched 9 Sep 1914, commissioned 15 Dec 1914; served in the Mediterranean from 1915 as the Austro-Hungarian *U38*; transferred to the German Mediterranean U-boat flotilla 1918; surrendered 23 Feb 1919 to France; broken up at Brest, July 1921.

U39: launched 26 Sept 1914, commissioned 13 Jan 1915; served in the Mediterranean from 1915 as the Austro-Hungarian *U39*. Disabled by aerial bombing on 18 May 1918 at El Ferrol, in position 43° 29'N, 08° 14'W; interned; surrendered to France, 22 Mar 1919; broken up at Toulon, December 1923.

U40: launched 22 Oct 1914, commissioned 14 Feb 1915. Sunk on 23 June 1915 in the North Sea, in position 56° 35'N, 01° 02'W, by a torpedo from the British Q-ship *Taranaki* and the British submarine *C24*; 29 dead.

U41: launched 10 Oct 1914, commissioned 1 Feb 1915. Sunk at 1000hrs on 24 Sep 1915 in the Channel, in position 49° 10'N, 07° 20'W, by gunfire from the British Q-ships *Wyandra* and *Baralong*; 35 dead.

U42

Name	Type	Builder (construction no)	Built	Cost in Marks (000s)	Displacement (t = tonnes T = tons)	Length (m)	Breadth (m)	Draught/ height (m)	Power (hp)	Revs (rpm)	Speed (kts)	Range (nm/kts)	Oil (t)	Diving time (sec)
U42		San Giorgio	1913–		728t sf 875t sm	65.00 oa	6.05 oa	4.17/	2600ehp sf 900ehp sm		14.0 sf 9.0 sm	3500/10 sf 85/13 sm		150

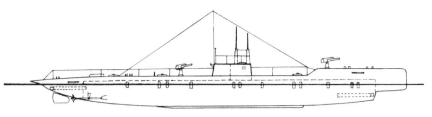

U42, later the Italian submarine *Balilla*.

Construction

Laid down as a submersible for the German navy, to a design by Laurenti, Fiat, 1912–13. Double-hulled, with the pressure hull external; five watertight compartments; diving depth 50m.

Propulsion

Two Fiat 10-cylinder 4-stroke diesel engines; two Savigliano dynamos; number and type of batteries not known. Two 3-bladed propellers (diameter not known); two hydroplanes forward, two aft; one rudder. For safety reasons, the diesel engine's performance was restricted to 1600shp.

Armament

Four 45cm torpedo tubes, two in the bow, two in the stern - number of torpedos not known. Two 7.6cm anti-aircraft guns. Two periscopes.

Complement

Crew: 4/34.

Notes

No step was visible in the cross-section of the vessel above the waterline.

Career

Begun 18 Aug 1913 as the sistership of the Italian vessel *Guglielmo Pacinotti*; delivery delayed until 1914; seized by Italy. Renamed as Italian submarine *Balilla*, 8 Aug 1915; sunk on 14 Jul 1916 off the island of Lissa, by an explosive sweep and gunfire from the Austro-Hungarian torpedo boats *65T* and *66T*; all crew lost.

U43 class mobilisation U-boats

Name	Type	Builder (construction no)	Built	Cost in Marks (000s)	Displacement (t = tonnes T = tons)	Length (m)	Breadth (m)	Draught/ height (m)	Power (hp)	Revs (rpm)	Speed (kts)	Range (nm/kts)	Oil (t)	Diving time (sec)
U43, 44*		KWD (21, 22)	1913–15		725t sf 940t sm 1050t total	65.00 oa c51 ph	6.20 oa 4.18 ph	3.74/ 8.70	2000ehp sf 1200ehp sm	330 sm	15.2 sf 9.7 sm	51/5 sm 11,400/8 sf (mod)	132/57	105 55 td
U45–50		" (23–28)	1914–16	3465	725t sf 940t sm 1059t total	"	"	3.74/ 9.00	"	"	"	"	"	"
U51–56		Germania (233–238)	1914–16	3824	715t sf 902t sm 1060t total	65.20 oa 52.51 ph	6.44 oa 4.05 ph	3.64/ 7.82	2400ehp sf 1200ehp sm	450 sf 330 sm	17.1 sf 9.1 sm	55/5 sm 9400/8 sf (mod)	103/57	105 55 td (mod)
U57–59		Weser (212–214)	1914–16	3924	786t sf 954t sm 1104t total	67.00 oa 54.22 ph	6.32 oa 4.05 ph	3.79/ 8.05	1800ehp sf 1200ehp sm	450 sf 330 sm	14.7 sf 8.4 sm	7730/8 sf 55/5 sm	119/78	49 30 td
U60–62		" (215–217)	"	3946	768t sf 956t sm 1103t total	67.00 oa 54.02 ph	"	3.74/ 8.05	2400ehp sf 1200ehp sm	"	16.5 sf 8.4 sm	49/5 sm 11,400/8 sf (mod)	128/76	50 30 td
U63–65		Germania (247–249)	1915–16	3819	810t sf 927t sm 1160t total	68.36 oa 55.55 ph	6.30 oa 4.15 ph	4.04/ 7.65	2200ehp sf 1200ehp sm	390 sf 300 sm	16.5 sf 9.0 sm	60/5 sm 9170/8 sf (mod)	108/78	50 30 td

* These boats were constructed without a keel.

Construction

Laid down as submersibles under War Contract A (*U43–50* as official Design Project 25, the remainder to Germania Dockyard Mobilisation designs). Double hull; seven watertight compartments in *U43–56* and eight in *U57–65*. The diameter of the pressure hull in compartment 3 of *U57–59* was increased by 0.8m to approximately 6.5m. Trim and regulating tanks 33.7cu m (*U43–50*), 48.4cu m (*U51–56*), 35.5cu m (*U57–59*), 19.3cu m (*U60–62*), and 35.9cu m (*U63–65*); diving depth 50m.

Propulsion

Two MAN (or Germania, *U63–65*) 6-cylinder 4-stroke (or 2-stroke, *U57–59, 63–65*) diesel engines in compartment 3; two SSW double motor-dynamos (or 2 + 2 SSW motor-dynamos, *U63–65*); two 110 mass-cell Afag batteries in compartments 5 and 7 below. Two 3-bladed propellers 1.60m (1.70m, *U51–56, 63–65*; 1.55m, *U57–59*, 1.65m, *U60–62*) diameter; two hydroplanes forward, two aft (*U45–50* were also fitted with hydroplane guards, approximately 7m long, positioned 0.5m above the CWL*); two rudders, but one only from *U51* onwards.

Armament

Four 50cm torpedo tubes, two at the bow and two at the stern, as for *U3 - 6* (or 7, *U57–62*; or 8, *U51–56, 63–65*) torpedoes; one machine gun. *U43–50* were initially fitted with one Uk 8.8cm/30 gun - 400 rounds; U47–50 with one Uk plus one Tk 8.8cm/30 gun - 400/400 rounds; *U51* and 52 with two Uk 8.8cm/30 guns - 276/276 rounds; *U53–55* with two Uk 8.8cm/30 guns - 276/407 rounds; *U56–60* with

*From U51 onwards all new U-boats were designed with the after hydroplanes mounted in the rudder stem so that they operated in the propeller stream, providing stabilising surfaces approximately 3.5m long about 0.5m above the CWL.

one Tk plus one Uk 8.8cm/30 gun – 276/407 rounds; *U61* and *62* with one Tk 10.5cm/45 gun - 200 rounds; and *U63–65* with one unidentified Tk gun – 200 rounds. *U43–50* had one periscope in the conning tower and one in the control room, *U51–62* had two in the conning tower and one in the control room, and *U63–65* had two periscopes in the conning tower only.

[*U43–46* were subsequently refitted with two Uk 8.8cm/30 guns - 400/400 rounds. *U43* and *U44* were fitted with P-mine gear from 1916.

In 1916–17 all surviving boats except *U61–65* were refitted with one Tk 10.5cm/45 gun - 200 rounds (or one Tk 10.5cm/45 gun plus one Uk or Tk 8.8cm/30 gun – 170/270 rounds, *U53–57*; or one Utof 10.5cm/45 gun plus one Uk 8.8cm/30 gun - 200/200 rounds, *U58–60*). *U63–65* were fitted at the end of 1916 with one additional Uk 8.8cm/30 gun - 420 rounds, then refitted from 1917 with one Tk 10.5cm/45 gun plus one Uk 8.8cm/30 gun - 200/240 rounds.]

Handling

Compared to the previous classes, these vessels offered improved ocean-going capability and improved diving and steering qualities; their manoeuvrability was also extremely good.

Complement

Crew: 4/32; one dinghy.

Notes

U43–50 and *U63–65* had upper decks which were enlarged to the full breadth of the vessel, and gently rounded off at the sides. The remaining vessels had upper decks which were formed by a step above the side tanks. The conning towers were of various shapes, as shown in the drawings.

U63–65 were constructed with simplified hulls and converted in approximately 11 months for diesel motors confiscated while under construction for Russia.

Careers

U43: launched 26 Sept 1914, commissioned 30 Apr 1915; surrendered 20 Nov 1918; broken up at Swansea, 1922.

U44: launched 15 Oct 1914, commissioned 7 May 1915. Sunk at 0617hrs on 12 Aug 1917 in the North Sea, in position 58° 51'N, 04° 20'E, after being rammed by the British destroyer *Oracle*; 44 dead (all crew lost).

U45: launched 15 Apr 1915, commissioned 9 Oct 1915. Sunk at 1052hrs on 12 Sep 1917 in the North Channel, in position 55° 48'N, 07° 30'W, by a torpedo from the British submarine *D7*; 43 dead.

U46: launched 18 May 1915, commissioned 17 Dec 1915; surrendered to Japan, 26 Nov 1918. Renamed *O2*; in Japanese service 1920–21. Broken up at Kure, 1922.

U47: launched 16 Aug 1915, commissioned 28 Feb 1916; served in the Mediterranean from 1917 as the Austro-Hungarian *U36*. Scuttled on 28 Oct 1918 during the evacuation of Pola, in position 44° 52'N, 13° 50'E.

U48: launched 3 Oct 1915, commissioned 22 Apr 1916; scuttled at 0430hrs on 24 Nov 1917 after running aground in the Thames estuary, in position 51° 11'N, 01° 31'E; 19 dead.

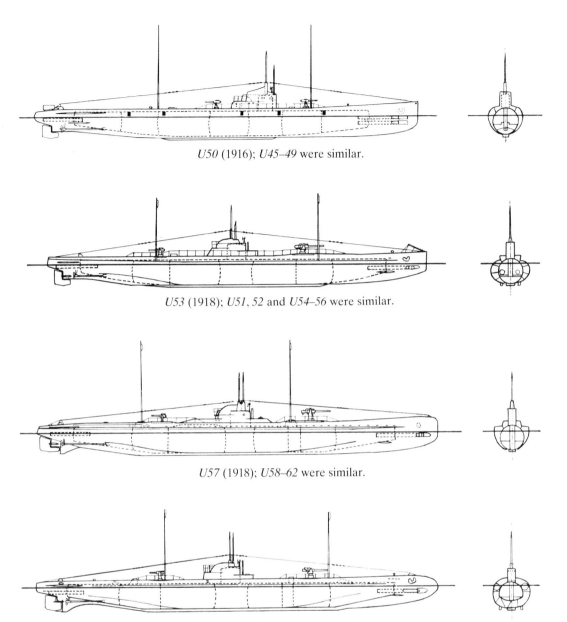

U50 (1916); *U45–49* were similar.

U53 (1918); *U51, 52* and *U54–56* were similar.

U57 (1918); *U58–62* were similar.

U63 (1916); *U64* and *65* were similar.

U49: launched 26 Nov 1915, commissioned 31 May 1916. Sunk at 2120hrs on 11 Sept 1917 west of the southernmost tip of Ireland, in position 46° 17'N, 14° 42'W, after being rammed by the British steamship SS *British Transport*; 43 dead (all crew lost).

U50: launched 31 Dec 1915, commissioned 4 Jul 1916. Sunk on 31 Aug 1917 in the North Sea, in approximate position 55° 15'N, 04° 10'E, by mines; 44 dead (all crew lost).

U51: launched 25 Nov 1915, commissioned 24 Feb 1916. Sunk at 1145 hrs on 14 Jul 1916 in the North Sea, in position 53° 56'N, 07° 55'E, by a torpedo from the British submarine *H5*; 34 dead. Raised in 1968 and broken up.

U52: launched 8 Dec 1915, commissioned 16 Mar 1916. Sunk at 1015hrs on 29 Oct 1917 in the Imperial Dockyard, Kiel, in position 54° 19.5'N, 10° 10'E, after a torpedo exploded in the stern; 5 dead. Raised 31 Oct 1917 with the help of the large Kiel floating crane; repaired and returned to service with a U-boat flotilla, May 1918; surrendered 21 Nov 1918; broken up at Swansea, 1922.

U53: launched 1 Feb 1916, commissioned 22 Apr 1916; surrendered on 1 Dec 1918; broken up at Swansea, 1922.

U54: launched 22 Feb 1916, commissioned 22 May 1916; surrendered to Italy, 24 Nov 1918; broken up at Taranto in May 1919.

U55: launched 18 Mar 1916, commissioned 8 Jun 1916; surrendered to Japan, 26 Nov 1918. Renamed *O3*, and in Japanese service, 1920–21. Broken up at Sasebo, 1922.

U56: launched 18 Apr 1916, commissioned 23 Jun 1916; went missing in the Arctic Sea, 3 Nov 1916; presumed sunk; 35 dead (all crew lost).

U57: launched 29 Apr 1916, commissioned 6 Jul 1916; surrendered to France, 24 Nov 1918; broken up at Cherbourg, 1921.

U58: launched 31 May 1916, commissioned 9 Aug 1916. Sunk on 17 Nov 1917 near Lundy Island in the Bristol Channel, in approximate position 51° 32'N, 05° 21'W, by depth charges from the US cruisers *Fanning* and *Nicholson*; 2 dead.

U59: launched 20 June 1916, commissioned 7 Sept 1916. Sunk at approximately 2300hrs on 14 May 1917 in the North Sea, in position 53° 33'N, 07° 15'E, by a German mine; 37 dead.

U60: launched 5 Jul 1916, commissioned 1 Nov 1916; surrendered 21 Nov 1918; ran aground on the East Coast of Britain while on passage to be broken up, 1921.

U61: launched 22 Jul 1916, commissioned 2 Dec 1916. Sunk at 2232hrs on 2 Dec 1916 east of Waterford, in position 51° 48'N, 05° 32'W, by depth charges from the British patrol boat *PC51*; 42 dead.

U62: launched 2 Aug 1916, commissioned 30 Dec 1916; surrendered 22 Nov 1918; broken up at Bo'ness, 1919–20.

U63: launched 8 Feb 1916, commissioned 11 Mar 1916; served in the Mediterranean from 1916 as the Austro-Hungarian *U63*; surrendered on 16 Jan 1919; broken up at Blyth, 1919–20.

U64: launched 29 Feb 1916, commissioned 15 Apr 1916; served in the Mediterranean from 1916 as the Austro-Hungarian *U64*. Sunk on 17 Jun 1918 southeast of Sardinia, in position 38° 07'N, 10° 27'E, after being rammed and depth charged by the British steam trawler *Partridge II* and sloop *Lychnis*; 38 dead.

U65: launched 21 Mar 1916, commissioned 11 May 1916; served in the Mediterranean from 1916 as the Austro-Hungarian *U65*; scuttled at Pola, 28 Oct 1918 (see *U47*).

U66 class mobilisation U-boats

Name	Type	Builder (construction no)	Built	Cost in Marks (000s)	Displacement (t = tonnes T = tons)	Length (m)	Breadth (m)	Draught/ height (m)	Power (hp)	Revs (rpm)	Speed (kts)	Range (nm/kts)	Oil (t)	Diving time (sec)
U66–70		Germania (203–207)	1913–15	3510	791t sf 933t sm 1150t total	69.50 oa 54.66 ph	6.30 oa 4.15 ph	3.79/ 7.95	2300ehp sf 1240ehp sm	370 sf 300 sm	16.8 sf 10.3 sm	115/5 sm 7370/8 sf (mod)	87/47	100 40 td

Construction
Laid down as submersibles, to a design by Dr Techel of the Germania Dockyard in 1912–13. These vessels were designated *U7-11* for the Austro-Hungarian navy in 1914, and were taken over on 28 Nov 1914 after the amount originally paid (5025 million gold marks or 2 million crowns) had been refunded to Austria-Hungary because of the outbreak of the war. Construction continued as War Contract D, and as Type UD. Double hull; seven watertight compartments; trim and regulating tanks 34.5cu m; diving depth 50m.

Propulsion
Two Germania 6-cylinder 4-stroke diesel engines in compartment 3; 2 + 2 SSW (or Pichler & Co, Vienna, from *U68* onwards) dynamos; two 118 mass-cell Afag batteries in compartments 5 and 7 below. One 3-bladed propeller, 1.80m diameter; two hydroplanes forward and two aft; two rudder guards aft, above; one rudder. These vessels were originally designed to perform at 11 knots underwater!

Armament
Five 45cm torpedo tubes, four at the bow and one at the stern - 12 torpedoes; one Uk 8.8cm/30 gun - 264 rounds. All vessels were fitted with two periscopes, both in the tower.

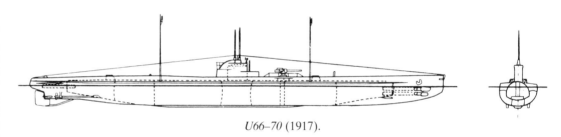

U66–70 (1917).

[In 1916 *U69* was fitted with an additional Tk 8.8cm/30 gun - 200 rounds. In 1916–17 all boats were refitted with one Tk 10.5cm/45 gun - 120 rounds.]

Handling
See the preceding classes.

Complement
Crew: 4/32; one dinghy.

Notes
These vessels had an upper deck, formed by a step above the tank decks.

Careers
U66: launched 22 Apr 1915, commissioned 23 Jul 1915; went missing in the North Sea after 3 Sept 1917; 40 dead (all crew lost).

U67: launched 15 May 1915, commissioned 4 Aug 1915; surrendered 20 Nov 1918; broken up at Fareham, 1921.

U68: launched 1 Jun 1915, commissioned 17 Aug 1915. Sunk at 0715hrs on 22 Mar 1916 off Dunmore Head, in position 51° 54'N, 10° 53'W, by gunfire from the British Q-ship *Q5 (Farnborough)*; 38 dead.

U69: launched 24 Jun 1915, commissioned 4 Sept 1915; went missing in the Irish Sea after 24 Jul 1917; 40 dead (all crew lost).

U70: launched 20 Jul 1915, commissioned 22 Sept 1915; surrendered 20 Nov 1918; broken up at Bo'ness, 1919–20.

U71 class minelayers

Construction
Laid down as submersibles Type UE under War Contract E, official Design Project 38. Single hull with saddle tanks; nine watertight compartments; trim and regulating tanks 21cu m; diving depth 50m.

Propulsion
Two Körting 6-cylinder 2-stroke diesel engines (or two Benz 6-cylinder 4-stroke diesel engines, *U71, 72, 75, 76*) in compartment 5; two SSW double motor-dynamos in compartment 4; two 112 mass-cell Afag batteries in compartments 6 and 7 below.

Two 3-bladed propellers, 1.41m (or 1.38m, *U71, 72, 75, 76*) diameter; two hydroplanes forward and two aft; two rudders.

Armament
Two 50cm torpedo tubes at upper deck level (one

Name	Type	Builder (construction no)	Built	Cost in Marks (000s)	Displacement (t = tonnes T = tons)	Length (m)	Breadth (m)	Draught/ height (m)	Power (hp)	Revs (rpm)	Speed (kts)	Range (nm/kts)	Oil (t)	Diving time (sec)
U71, 72	UEI	Vulcan (H) (55, 56)	1915–16	3153	755t sf 832t sm 980t total	56.80 oa 46.66 ph	5.90 oa 5.00 ph	4.86/ 8.25	900ehp sf 900ehp sm	400 sf 374 sm	10.6 sf 7.9 sm	83/4 sm 7880/7 sf (mod)	90/80	50 40 td
U73, 74	„	KWD (29, 30)	1915		745t sf 829t sm 980t total	„	„	4.84/ 8.25	800ehp sf 800ehp sm	350 sf 324 sm	9.6 sf 7.9 sm	5480/7 sf 83/4 sm	82/69	60 40 td
U75, 76	„	Vulcan (H) (57, 58)	1915–16	3140	755t sf 832t sm 980t total	„	„	4.86/ 8.25	900ehp sf 800ehp sm	400 sf 327 sm	9.9 sf 7.8 sm	83/4 sm 7880/7 sf (mod)	90/80	50 40 td
U77–80	„	„ (59–62)	„	„	„	„	„	„	900ehp sf 900ehp sm	400 sf 374 sm	9.9 sf 7.9 sm	„	„	„

at the bow, port, above the CWL, and one at the stern, starboard, above the CWL) - 4 torpedoes; two 100cm mine-launching tubes at the stern, below the CWL - 38 UE 150 mines; one Uk 8.8cm/30 gun - 170 rounds. One periscope in the conning tower and one in the control room.

[In 1916–17 U73 and 79 (and in 1918 U71, 78 and 80) were refitted with one Tk 10.5cm/45 gun - 130 rounds; in 1917 U72 was refitted with one Tk 10.5cm/45 gun plus one Uk 8.8cm/30 gun - 90/110 rounds.]

Handling
These were poor sea-going vessels, with average manoeuvrability; they had excellent steering, but this was badly affected by bad weather conditions.

Complement
Crew: 4/28; one dinghy.

Notes
These vessels had a very narrow upper deck and an extremely narrow working space in the pressure hull (a 0.6m wide access passage between the mine stores for 3 + 3 + 3 mines on each side of compartment 3 and the mine launch tubes, each holding 1 + 1 + 1 + 1 mines). One storage tube for 2 + 2 + 2 mines was incorporated above the electric motors in compartment 4, below the ceiling.

In order to produce a Type UE sized torpedo U-boat in the shortest possible time, the U-boat Inspectorate suggested, early in 1915, that a Project 38 hull should be fitted out with torpedoes instead of mines. Approval for the construction of six such vessels at the Germania Dockyard and at AG Weser was granted on 27 Feb 1915. They were to be designated Group F, Type UF. However, these UF boats were never built, and War Contract F became instead the order for the MS U-boats U81–92.

Careers
U71: launched 31 Oct 1915, commissioned 10 Dec 1915; used for training, 1918; surrendered to France, 23 Feb 1919; broken up at Cherbourg, 1921.

U72: launched 31 Oct 1915, commissioned 26 Jan 1916; served in the Mediterranean as the Austro-

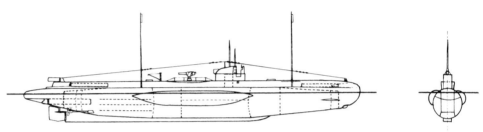

U73, 74 (1916).

U75, 79, 80 (1917).

Hungarian U72. Scuttled in the evacuation of Cattaro on 1 Nov 1918, in position 42° 30'N, 18° 41'E.

U73: launched 16 Jun 1915, commissioned 9 Oct 1915; served in the Mediterranean as the Austro-Hungarian U73. Scuttled at Pola on 30 Oct 1918 (see U47 for details).

U74: launched 10 Aug 1915, commissioned 24 Nov 1915. Sunk at 1255hrs on 27 May 1916 in the North Sea, in position 57° 10'N, 01° 20'E, by gunfire from the British steam trawlers Sea Ranger, Oku, Rodino and Kimberley; 34 dead (all crew lost).

U75: launched 30 Jan 1916, commissioned 26 Mar 1916. Sunk at 2125hrs on 13 Dec 1917 in the North Sea, in position 53° 59'N, 05° 24'E, by mines; 31 dead.

U76: launched 12 Mar 1916, commissioned 11 May 1916. Scuttled at 0300hrs on 27 Jan 1917 in the Arctic Sea, in approximate position 71° 00'N, 23° 00'E, after being rammed by an unknown Russian

steam trawler; 1 dead. Raised July 1971 and broken up.

U77: launched 9 Jan 1916, commissioned 10 Mar 1916. Sunk 7 Jul 1916 in the North Sea, in approximate position 58° 00'N, 03° 00'W, by gunfire from several British steam trawlers; 33 dead (all crew lost).

U78: launched 27 Feb 1916, commissioned 20 Apr 1916. Sunk at 0230hrs on 28 Oct 1918 in the North Sea, in position 56° 02'N, 05° 08'E, by a torpedo from the British submarine G2; 40 dead (all crew lost).

U79: launched 9 Apr 1916, commissioned 25 May 1916; surrendered to France, 21 Nov 1918; renamed Victor Reveille, and served as a French submarine until she was broken up on 29 Jul 1935.

U80: launched 22 Apr 1916, commissioned 6 Jun 1916; surrendered 16 Jan 1919; broken up at Swansea, 1922.

U81 class MS U-boats

Construction

Laid down as submersibles under War Contracts F (*U81–92*), G (*U93–104*), K (*U105–116*), R (*U158–172*), Y (*U201–212*) and AD (*U229–276*), official Design Projects 25 (*U158, 159*) and 43 (*U115, 116, 263–276*) with modifications to the Germania Dockyard Mobilisation designs. Double hull; seven (or six, *U81–86*; or eight, *U99–104*) watertight compartments; trim and regulating tanks 39cu m (or 38.6cu m, *U81–86*; or 39.5cu m, *U87–92*; or 37.3cu m, *U99–104*); diving depth 50m.

Propulsion

Two MAN (or Körting, *U274–276*) 6-cylinder 4-stroke (or Germania 6-cylinder 2-stroke, *U96–98, 112–14, 235–237*) engines in compartment 3; two SSW double dynamos; two 110–112 mass-cell Afag batteries in compartment 5 below or 5 and 6 below (or 4 and 6 below, *U87–92*; or 5 and 7 below, *U99–104*). Two 3-bladed propellers, 1.70m (or 1.66m, *U87–92*; or 1.65m, *U99–104*) diameter; two hydroplanes forward and two aft (with two hydroplane guards just forward of the stern on *U81–92*; one (or two, *U87–92*) rudder.

Armament

Six 50cm torpedo tubes, four at the bow and two at the stern - 12–16 torpedoes (or four 50cm torpedo tubes, two at the bow and two at the stern - 10–12 torpedoes, *U87–92* and *99–104*). *U81–83, 90* and *96–98* were initially fitted with one Tk 10.5cm/45 gun - 140–240 rounds; *U87, 89, 105, 106, 108, 109* and probably *U88* with one Tk 10.5cm/45 gun plus one Uk 8.8cm/30 gun - 140/220 rounds; *U91, 92, 100, 112* and probably *U99* with one Utof 10.5cm/45 gun - 205–240 rounds; *U158, 159, 161–172, 201–212* and *229–276* with one Utof 10.5cm/45 gun - 366–380 rounds; *U107, 110, 111, 113, 115, 116* and probably *U114* with one Utof 10.5cm/45 gun plus one Uk 8.8cm/30 gun - 205/220 rounds; *U93–95* with one Uk 8.8cm/30 gun - 220 rounds; *U84–86* and *101–104* with two Uk 8.8cm/30 guns - 400 rounds; and *U160* with two Utof 10.5cm/45 guns - 340 rounds. Two periscopes in the conning tower and one in the control room (or two periscopes in the conning tower only, *U99–104, 115* and *116*).

[In 1917 *U84–86* were refitted with one Tk 10.5cm/45 gun - 140–240 rounds. In 1918 *U86, 96* and probably *U90–92* were refitted with one Tk 10.5cm/45 gun plus one Uk 8.8cm/30 gun - 140/220 rounds, and *U93, 94* and *100–104* with one Utof 10.5cm/45 gun plus one Uk 8.8cm/30 gun - 205/220 rounds.]

Handling

Good seagoing vessels, with no restrictions on high seas use; manoeuvred and turned extremely well.

Complement

Crew: 4/35 (or 4/31, *U81–86*; or 4/32, *U87–116*).

Notes

Only *U99–104* had an upper deck formed by a step above the side tank decks; all the others had an upper deck which curved towards the sides. These were the most successful MS boats, and became the prototype for numerous later German U-boats (see Type IX) and foreign submarines.

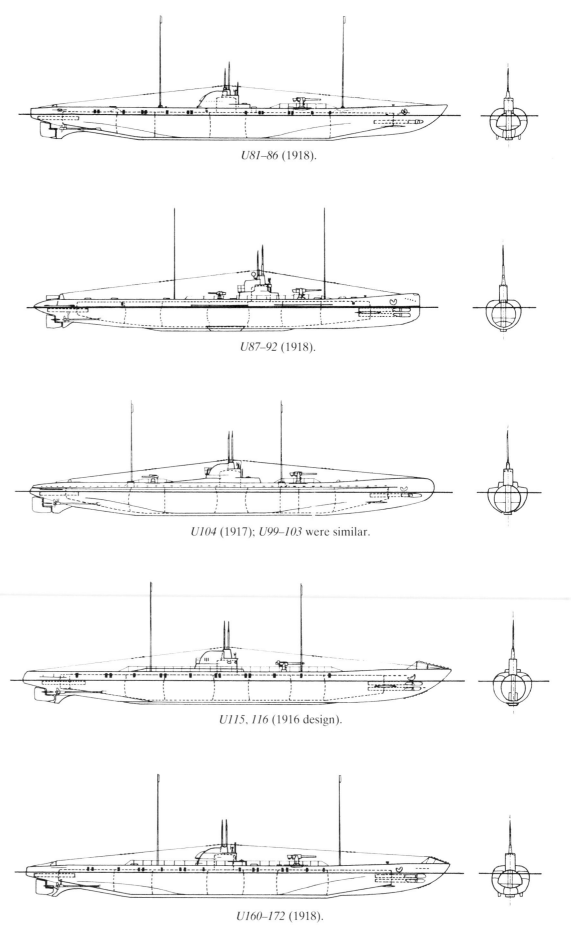

U81–86 (1918).

U87–92 (1918).

U104 (1917); *U99–103* were similar.

U115, 116 (1916 design).

U160–172 (1918).

Name	Type	Builder (construction no)	Built	Cost in Marks (000s)	Displacement (t = tonnes T = tons)	Length (m)	Breadth (m)	Draught/ height (m)	Power (hp)	Revs (rpm)	Speed (kts)	Range (nm/kts)	Oil (t)	Diving time (sec)
U81–86		Germania (251–256)	1915–16	4109	808t sf 946t sm 1160t total	70.06 oa 55.55 ph	6.30 oa 4.15 ph	4.02/ 8.00	2400ehp sf 1200ehp sm	435 sf 335 sm	16.8 sf 9.1 sm	56/5 sm 11,220/8 sf (mod)	119/81	50 45 td
U87–92		KWD (31–36)	1915–17	3680	757t sf 998t sm 1165t total	65.80 oa 50.07 ph	6.20 oa 4.18 ph	3.88/ 9.35	"	"	15.6 sf 8.6 sm	56/5 sm 11,380/8 sf (mod)	133/54	56 45 td
U93–95		Germania (257–259)	1915–17	4398	838t sf 1000t sm 1270t total	71.55 oa 56.05 ph	6.30 oa 4.15 ph	3.94/ 8.25	"	450 sf 330 sm	16.8 sf 8.6 sm	52/5 sm 9020/8 sf (mod)	107/47	66 45 td
U96-98		" (260–262)	1916–17	4415	837t sf 998t sm 1270t total	"	"	"	2300ehp sf 1200ehp sm	390 sf 330 sm	16.9 sf 8.6 sm	8290/8 sf 47/5 sm	104/47	"
U99–104		Weser (250–255)	1916–17	4435	750t sf 952t sm 1100t total	67.60 oa 54.02 ph	6.32 oa 4.05 ph	3.65/ 8.25	2400ehp sf 1200ehp sm	450 sf 379 sm	16.5 sf 8.8 sm	45/5 sm 10,100/8 sf (mod)	114/46	52 45 td
U105–110		Germania (274–279)	1916–17	4792	798t sf 1000t sm 1270t total	71.55 oa 56.05 ph	6.30 oa 4.15 ph	3.90/ 8.25	"	450 sf 330 sm	16.4 sf 8.4 sm	50/5 sm 9280/8 sf (mod)	107/47	66 45 td
U111–114		Germania; hulls by Vulcan (V) (280–283)	1916–18	4807	798t sf 996t sm 1270t total	"	"	3.76/ 8.25	2300ehp sf 1200ehp sm	390 sf 330 sm	"	50/5 sm 8300/8 sf (mod)	104/47	"
U115, 116		Schichau (D) (986, 987)	1916–	4100	882t sf 1233t sm 1305t total	72.30 oa 53.56 ph	6.50 oa 4.22 ph	4.00/ 9.25	2400ehp sf 1200ehp sm	450 sf 330 sm	16.0 sf 9.0 sm	60/4.5 sm 11,470/8 sf (mod)	133/68	30 td
U158, 159		KWD (47, 48)	1917–		811t sf 1034t sm 1243t total	71.15 oa	6.20 oa	3.94/ 8.25	"	450 sf 332 sm	"	12,370/8 sf 55/5 sm	145/58	35 td
U160–172		Vulcan (V) (651–659, from U164)	1917–18 and 1917–	6752	821t sf 1002t sm 1250t total	71.55 oa 56.05 ph	6.30 oa 4.15 ph	3.88/ 8.25	2400ehp sf 1230ehp sm	450 sf 338 sm	16.2 sf 8.2 sm	8500/8 sf 50/5 sm	103/46	45 td
U201–212		" (671-682)	1918–		820t sf 1000t sm 1250t total	"	"	3.87/ 8.25	"	"	16.0 sf 9.0 sm	8500/8 sf 60/4.5 sm	"	"
U229–246		Germania (338–355)	1918–		908t sf 1192t sm	74.00 oa c54 ph	6.70 oa 4.30 ph	4.30/	2900ehp sf 1230ehp sm	480 sf 338 sm	16.5 sf 9.0 sm	11,400/8 sf 50/5 sm	138/71	"
U247–250		Vulcan (V) (691–694)	1919–		940t sf 1205t sm	"	"	"	2400ehp sf 1230ehp sm	450 sf 338 sm	16.0 sf 9.0 sm	"	"	"
U251–262		" (695–706)	"		"	"	"	"	2900ehp sf 1230ehp sm	480 sf 338 sm	16.5 sf 9.0 sm	"	"	"
U263–267		Schichau (D) (1076–1080)	"		882t sf 1233t sm 1305t total	72.30 oa 53.56 ph	6.50 oa 4.22 ph	4.00/ 9.25	2400ehp sf 1230ehp sm	450 sf 338 sm	16.0 sf 9.0 sm	11,470/8 sf 50/5 sm	133/68	30 td
U268–276		" (1081–1089)	"		"	"	"	"	2900ehp sf 1230ehp sm	480 sf 338 sm	16.5 sf 9.0 sm	"	"	"

Careers

U81: launched 24 Jun 1916, commissioned 22 Aug 1916. Sunk at 1600hrs on 1 May 1917 in the Atlantic, in position 51° 25'N, 13° 05'W, by a torpedo from the British submarine *E54*; 31 dead.

U82: launched 1 Jul 1916, commissioned 16 Sept 1916; surrendered on 16 Jan 1919; broken up at Blyth, 1919–20.

U83: launched 13 Jul 1916, commissioned 6 Jun 1916. Sunk on 17 Feb 1917 in the Atlantic, in position 51° 34'N, 11° 23'W, by gunfire from the British Q-ship *Q5* (*Farnborough*); 36 dead (all crew lost).

U84: launched 22 Jul 1916, commissioned 7 Oct 1916. Sunk at 0610hrs on 26 Jan 1918 in the Irish Sea, in position 51° 53'N, 05° 44'W, after being rammed by the British patrol boat *P62*; 40 dead (all crew lost).

U85: launched 22 Aug 1916, commissioned 23 Oct 1916. Sunk at 1530hrs on 12 Mar 1917 in the Channel, in position 50° 02'N, 04° 13'W, by gunfire from the British Q-ship *Q19* (*Privet*); 38 dead (all crew lost).

U86: launched 7 Nov 1916, commissioned 30 Nov 1916; surrendered on 20 Nov 1918; sank in 1921, while en route to being broken up.

U87: launched 22 May 1916, commissioned 26 Feb 1917. Sunk on 25 Dec 1917 in the Irish Sea, in position 52° 56'N, 05° 07'W, after being rammed and depth charged by the British patrol boat *P56*; 44 dead (all crew lost).

U88: launched 22 Jun 1916, commissioned 7 Apr 1916. Sunk on 5 Sept 1917 in the Heligoland Bight, after hitting British mines; 43 dead (all crew lost).

U89: launched 6 Oct 1916, commissioned 21 Jun 1917. Sunk at 0020hrs on 13 Feb 1918 in the Atlantic, in position 55° 38'N, 07° 32'W, after being rammed by the British cruiser *Roxburgh*; 43 dead (all crew lost).

U90: launched 12 Jan 1917, commissioned 2 Aug 1918; surrendered 20 Nov 1918; broken up at Bo'ness, 1919–20.

U91: launched 14 Apr 1917, commissioned 17 Sept 1917; surrendered to France, 26 Nov 1918; broken up at Brest in July 1921.

U92: launched 12 May 1917, commissioned 22 Oct 1917. Sunk on 9 Sep 1918 in the North Sea, position unknown; possibly mined; 42 dead (all crew lost).

U93: launched 15 Dec 1916, commissioned 10 Feb 1916; went missing in the Channel in January 1918; 40 dead (all crew lost).

U94: launched 5 Jan 1917, commissioned 3 Mar 1917; surrendered 20 Nov 1918; broken up at Bo'ness, 1919–20.

U95: launched 20 Jan 1917, commissioned 19 Apr 1917. Sunk at 0415hrs on 7 Jan 1918 in the Channel, in position 49° 59'N, 05° 12'W, after a collision with the British steamship SS *Braenil*; 43 dead (all crew lost).

U96: launched 15 Feb 1917, commissioned 11 Apr 1917; surrendered 20 Nov 1918; broken up at Bo'ness, 1919–20.

U97: launched 4 Apr 1917, commissioned 16 May 1917; used for training from 1918; sunk on 21 Nov 1918 in the North Sea, in position 53° 25'N, 93° 10'E, following an accident while on passage to surrender.

U98: launched 28 Feb 1917, commissioned 31 May 1917; surrendered on 16 Jan 1919; broken up at Blyth, 1919–20.

U99: launched 27 Jan 1917, commissioned 28 Mar 1917. Sunk at 0750hrs on 7 Jul 1917 in the North Sea, in position 58°N, 03° 05'E, by a torpedo from the British submarine *J2*; 40 dead (all crew lost).

U100: launched 25 Feb 1917, commissioned 16 Apr 1917; surrendered 21 Nov 1917; broken up at Swansea, 1922.

U101: launched 1 Apr 1917, commissioned 15 May 1917; surrendered 21 Nov 1918; broken up at Morecambe, from 17 Jun 1920.

U102: launched 12 May 1917, commissioned 18 Jun 1917. Sunk at the end of September 1918 in the North Sea, position unknown, possibly mined; 42 dead (all crew lost).

U103: launched 9 Jun 1917, commissioned 15 Jul 1917. Sunk at 1600hrs on 12 May 1918 in the Channel, in position 49° 16'N, 04° 51'W, after being rammed by the British steam passenger liner *Olympic*; 10 dead.

U104: launched 3 Jul 1917, commissioned 12 Aug 1917. Sunk on 25 Apr 1918 in the Atlantic, in position 51° 59'N, 06° 26'W, after being rammed and depth charged by the British sloop *Jessamine*; 41 dead.

U105: launched 16 May 1917, commissioned 4 Jul 1917; surrendered to France, 20 Nov 1918; served as the French submarine *Jean Autric* until 27 Jan 1937; broken up in 1938.

U106: launched 12 Jun 1917, commissioned 28 Jul 1917. Sunk on 8 Oct 1917 in the North Sea, in approximate position 54° 50'N, 06° 00'E, by mines and net barrage; 41 dead (all crew lost).

U107: launched 28 Jun 1917, commissioned 18 Aug 1917; surrendered 20 Nov 1918; broken up at Swansea, 1922.

U108: launched 11 Oct 1917, commissioned 5 Dec 1917; surrendered to France, 20 Nov 1918; served as the French submarine *Léon Mignot* until 24 Jul 1935; broken up.

U109: launched 25 Sept 1917, commissioned 7 Jul 1917. Sunk at approximately 0800hrs on 26 Jan 1918 in the Channel, in position 50° 54'N, 01° 32'E, by mines and gunfire from the British steam trawler *Beryl III*; 43 dead (all crew lost).

U110: launched 28 Jul 1917, commissioned 25 Sept 1917. Sunk at 1121hrs on 15 Mar 1918 in the Atlantic, in position 54° 49'N, 08° 06'W, by depth charges and gunfire from the British destroyers *Moresby* and *Michael*; 42 dead (all crew lost).

U111: launched 5 Sept 1917, commissioned 30 Dec 1917; surrendered to the USA, 20 Nov 1918; used for exhibitions to raise war loans in harbours along the New England coastline; used for research and sunk by explosives in deep water off Cape Charles, Virginia.

U112: launched 26 Oct 1917, commissioned 30 Jun 1918; surrendered 22 Nov 1918; broken up at Rochester, 1922.

U113: launched 29 Sept 1917, commissioned 23 Feb 1918; surrendered to France, 20 Nov 1918; broken up at Brest in July 1921.

U114: launched 27 Nov 1917, commissioned 19 Jun 1918; surrendered to Italy, 26 Nov 1918; broken up at La Spezia in May 1919.

U115: launched 1918, approximately 95 per cent complete; broken up at the dockyard. Engines used in the conversion of the Third Rate cruiser *Gefion* (see Volume One, pp 98–9) to the MS *Adolf Sommerfeld*.

U116: launched 1918; fate as for *U115*.

U158: launched 16 Apr 1918, approximately 95 per cent complete; broken up in 1919.

U159: launched 25 May 1918, approximately 95 per cent complete; broken up in 1919.

U160: launched 27 Feb 1918, commissioned 26 May 1918; surrendered to France, 24 Nov 1918; broken up at Cherbourg.

U161: launched 23 Mar 1918, commissioned 29 Jun 1918; surrendered 20 Nov 1918; ran aground on the East Coast of Great Britain en route to being broken up, 1921.

U162: launched 20 Apr 1918, commissioned 31 Jul 1918; surrendered to France, 20 Nov 1918; served as the French submarine *Pierre Marrast* until 27 Jan 1937; broken up.

U163: launched 1 Jun 1918, commissioned 21 Aug 1918; surrendered to Italy, 22 Nov 1918; broken up at La Spezia in August 1919.

U164: launched 7 Aug 1918, commissioned 17 Oct 1918; surrendered 22 Nov 1918; broken up at Swansea, 1922.

U165: launched 21 Jun 1918, commissioned 6 Nov 1918. Sank before being surrendered on 18 Nov 1918 in an accident on the Weser, in position 53° 10'N, 08° 35'E; raised and stricken, 21 Feb 1919; broken up.

U166: launched 6 Sept 1918, completed; surrendered to France, 21 Mar 1919; served as the French submarine *Jean Roulier* until 24 Jul 1935; broken up.

U167: launched 28 Sept 1918, completed; surrendered 18 Apr 1919; broken up at Grays, 1921.

U168: launched 19 Oct 1918, approximately 75 per cent completed; broken up in 1919. However the main parts of the machinery were surrendered, and one diesel engine was incorporated in a tandem arrangement on the US submarine *T3* after the original engines had failed.

U169: launched 15 Nov 1918; see *U168*.

U170: launched 1918; see *U168*.

U171: launched 1918; see *U168*.

U172: launched 1918; see *U168*.

U201–209: broken up on the slips; 1919.

U210–276: construction contracts cancelled, 1918–19.

U117 class cruiser minelayers (Project 45)

Name	Type	Builder (construction no)	Built	Cost in Marks (000s)	Displacement (t = tonnes T = tons)	Length (m)	Breadth (m)	Draught/ height (m)	Power (hp)	Revs (rpm)	Speed (kts)	Range (nm/kts)	Oil (t)	Diving time (sec)
U117–121		Vulcan (H) (91–95)	1916–18	6177	1164t sf 1512t sm 1880t total	81.52 oa 61.20 ph	7.42 oa 4.50 ph	4.22/ 10.16	2400ehp sf 1200ehp sm	450 sf 332 sm	14.7 sf 7.0 sm	35.45 sm 13,900/8 sf (mod)	217/95	30 td
U122–126		B & V (299–303)	1916–18	6145	1163t sf 1468t sm 1863t total	82.00 oa 61.32 ph	,,	,,	2400ehp sf 1235ehp sm	450 sf 339 sm	14.7 sf 7.2 sm	11,470/8 sf 35/4.5 sm	191/92	,,

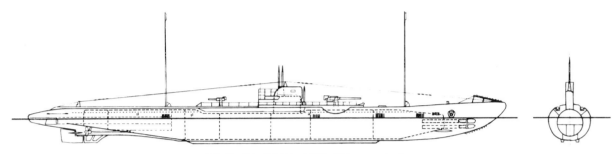

U117–121, (1918); *U122–126* were similar.

Construction

Laid down as submersibles under War Contract L, official Design Project 45, Type UE II. Double hull; seven watertight compartments; trim and regulating tanks 26.6cu m (or 48.6cu m, *U122–126*); diving depth 75m.

Propulsion

Two MAN 6-cylinder 4-stroke diesel engines (constructed under licence by Blohm & Voss in *U124–126*) in compartment 4; two Brown, Boveri & Cie double motor-dynamos (or two SSW double motor-dynamos, *U122–126*); two 124 mass-cell Afag batteries in compartment 6 below. Two 3-bladed propellers, 1.61m diameter; two hydroplanes forward and two aft; one rudder.

Armament

Four 50cm torpedo tubes at the bow, below the CWL - 14 (or 12, *U122–126*) torpedoes; two 100cm mine-launching tubes at the stern, below the CWL - 42 UC 200 mines; a further 2 torpedoes and 30 Tk mines were carried in deck racks, with rails to the stern launching positions. One Utof 15cm/45 gun - 494 rounds (or one such weapon plus one Uk 8.8cm/30 gun - 310 rounds, *U117*; or two Utof 10.5cm/45 guns - 600 rounds, *U123*). Two peri-

scopes in the conning tower and one in the control room.

Handling

Extremely good sea-boats, with average manoeuvrability and responsiveness.

Complement

Crew: 4/36; one dinghy.

Careers

U117: launched 10 Dec 1917; commissioned 23 Mar 1918; surrendered to USA, 21 Nov 1918; used for exhibitions to raise war loans in harbours along the Atlantic coast; sunk on 21 Jun 1921, near Cape Charles, Virginia, after being bombed by a seaplane during tests.

U118: launched 23 Feb 1918, commissioned 8 May 1918; surrendered to France on 23 Feb 1919; broken up at Brest, in July 1921.

U119: launched 4 Apr 1918, commissioned 20 Jun 1918; surrendered to France on 24 Nov 1918; served as the French submarine *René Audry* until 7 Oct 1937; broken up.

U120: launched 20 Jun 1918, commissioned 31 Aug 1918; intended for service in the Mediterra-

nean as the Austro-Hungarian *U83*; surrendered to Italy, 22 Nov 1918; broken up at La Spezia in April 1919.

U121: launched 20 Sept 1918; intended for service in the Mediterranean as the Austro-Hungarian *U84*; surrendered to France, 9 Mar 1919; served as a target ship 1 Jul 1921; sunk near Cherbourg.

U122: launched 9 Dec 1917, commissioned 4 May 1918; surrendered 26 Nov 1918; ran aground on the East Coast of Great Britain while en route to being broken up, 1921.

U123: launched 26 Jan 1918, commissioned 20 Jul 1918; surrendered 22 Nov 1918; ran aground on the East Coast of Great Britain while en route to being broken up, 1921.

U124: launched 28 Mar 1918, commissioned 13 Jul 1918; interned at Karlskrona, Sweden, 13 Nov 1918; surrendered 1 Dec 1918; broken up at Swansea, 1922.

U125: launched 26 May 1918, commissioned 4 Sept 1918; surrendered to Japan, 26 Nov 1918; served as the Japanese submarine, *O1*; broken up at Kure, 1922.

U126: launched 16 Jun 1918, commissioned 7 Oct 1918; surrendered 22 Nov 1918; broken up at Upnor, 1923.

U127 class (U-ship Project 42)

Construction

Laid down as submersibles under War Contract M, official Design Project 42. Double hull; eight watertight compartments. The pressure hull was ellipti-

cal in cross-section, 4.83m wide and 4.35m high (except in *U127–130*, where it was circular in cross-section with external ribs). Trim and regulating tanks 46.4cu m; diving depth 75m.

Propulsion

Two MAN (or Germania, *U129–130*; or Körting, *U134*) 6-cylinder 4-stroke diesel engines in compartment 3 (or 3 and 4, *U134*); two MAN-Brown,

Name	Type	Builder (construction no)	Built	Cost in Marks (000s)	Displacement (t = tonnes T = tons)	Length (m)	Breadth (m)	Draught/ height (m)	Power (hp)	Revs (rpm)	Speed (kts)	Range (nm/kts)	Oil (t)	Diving time (sec)
U127, 128		Germania (290, 291)	1916–		1221t sf 1649t sm 1927t total	82.05 oa 65.15 ph	7.54 oa 4.83 ph	4.21/ 9.46	3500ehp +900ehp sf 1690ehp sm	350 or 400 sf 288 sm	17.0 sf 8.1 sm	c10,000/8 sf 50/4.5 sm	191/53	30 td
U129, 130		„ (292, 293)	„		„	„	„	„	3300ehp +900ehp sf 1690ehp sm	350 or 400 sf 288 sm	„	„	„	„
U131, 132		Weser (272, 273)	„		1160t sf 1527t sm 1792t total	82.50 oa 65.15 ph	7.54 oa 4.83 ph	4.16/ 9.46	3500ehp +900ehp sf 1690ehp sm	380 or 400 sf 288 sm	„	„	„	„
U133, 134		„ (274, 275)	„		„	„	„	„	3400ehp +900ehp sf 1690ehp sm	350 or 400 sf 288 sm	„	„	„	„
U135–138		KWD	1916–18 and 1916–	6438	1175t sf 1534t sm 1880t total	83.50 oa 65.57 ph	7.54 oa 4.85 ph	4.26/ 9.46	„	„	„	„	„	„

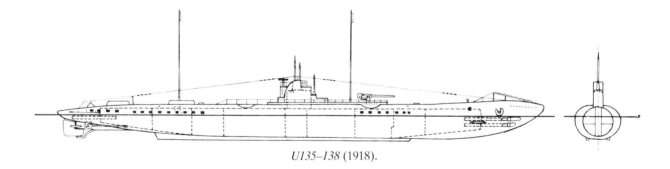

U135–138 (1918).

Boveri & Cie 6-cylinder 4-stroke diesel dynamos (or Germania diesel dynamos, *U129–130*), 900ehp (= 600kW) in compartment 5; two AEG double electric motors in compartment 2; one 124 mass-cell Afag battery in compartment 2 below and two 124 mass-cell Afag batteries in compartment 6 below. Two 3-bladed propellers, 1.85m diameter; two hydroplanes forward and two aft; one rudder.

Armament

Six 50cm torpedo tubes, four at the bow, below the CWL, and two at the stern - 14 torpedoes. One Utof 15cm/45 gun - 540 rounds; two such guns were envisaged in the initial design.

Handling

These vessels were intended for deep sea use; they were very seaworthy, with average manoeuvrability and responsiveness, and relatively comfortable.

Complement

Crew: 4/42; two dinghies.

Careers

U127: launched 8 Jan 1919, 80–85 per cent complete; broken up at Oslebshausen, 1921; all engines surrendered.

U128: launched in 1918, 80–85 per cent complete; broken up at Oslebshausen, 1921.

U129: launched in 1918, 80–85 per cent complete; broken up at Oslebshausen, 1921. Main engines incorporated in the motor tankers *Ostpreussen* and *Oberschlesien* (see *U187, 188* etc).

U130: launched in 1918, 80–85 per cent complete; broken up at Oslebshausen, 1921. Main engines incorporated in the motor tankers *Ostpreussen* and *Oberschlesien* (see *U187, 188* etc).

U131: launched in 1918, 80–85 per cent complete; broken up 1919–20.

U132: launched in 1918, 80–85 per cent complete: broken up 1919–20.

U133: launched in 1918, 80–85 per cent complete; broken up 1919–20.

U134: launched in 1918, 80–85 per cent complete; broken up 1919–20.

U135: launched 8 Sept 1917; commissioned 20 Jun 1918; surrendered 20 Nov 1918; sank off the East Coast of Great Britain while en route to being broken up, 1921.

U136: launched 7 Nov 1917; commissioned 15 Aug 1918; surrendered to France, 23 Feb 1919; broken up at Cherbourg, 1921.

U137: launched 8 Jan 1918, approximately 90 per cent complete; broken up in 1919. Main engines surrendered as compensation for the sinking of *UC48*.

U138: launched 26 Mar 1918; approximately 90 per cent complete; broken up, 1919. Main engines surrendered as compensation for the sinking of *UC48* (*qv*).

U213 class (U-ship Project 42A)

Name	Type	Builder (construction no)	Built	Cost in Marks (000s)	Displacement (t = tonnes T = tons)	Length (m)	Breadth (m)	Draught/ height (m)	Power (hp)	Revs (rpm)	Speed (kts)	Range (nm/kts)	Oil (t)	Diving time (sec)
U213–218		KWD (70–75)	1918–		1335t sf 1830t sm	88.10 oa c68 ph	7.90 oa 4.85 ph	4.00/	3500ehp +900ehp sf 1690ehp sm	380 or 400 sf 288 sm	18.0 or 8.0 sf 9.0 sm	12,000/8 sf 90/4.5 sm	217/53	30 td
U219–224		Weser (364–369)	—		1400t sf 1900t sm	87.60 oa c68 ph	,,	,,	,,	,,	,,	,,	,,	,,
U225–228		B & V (455–458)	—		,,	,,	,,	,,	,,	,,	,,	,,	,,	,,

Construction

Designed as submersibles, to be built under War Contract AE, official Design Project 42A, 1917. Double-hull; eight watertight compartments. Elliptical pressure hulls, 4.83m wide, 4.35m high. Trim and regulating tanks 46.4cu m; diving depth 75m.

Propulsion

Two MAN 6-cylinder 4-stroke diesel engines in compartment 3; two MAN-Brown, Boveri & Cie 6-cylinder 4-stroke diesel dynamos, 900ehp (= 600kW) in compartment 5; two AEG double electric motors in compartment 2; one 124 mass-cell Afag battery in compartment 2 below and two 124 mass-cell Afag batteries in compartment 6 below. Two 3-bladed propellers, 1.85m diameter; two hydroplanes forward and two aft; one rudder.

Armament

Six 50cm torpedo tubes, four at the bow and two at the stern, below the CWL - 16–20 torpedoes; U219–228 were intended to carry two additional 50cm stern tubes above the CWL and one Utof 15cm/45 gun - 800 rounds.

Complement

Crew: 4/42; two dinghies.

Notes

Construction contracts cancelled, 1918.

U139 class U-cruisers (Project 46)

Construction

Laid down as U-cruiser submersibles under War Contracts N (U139–172), U (U173–182) and Z (U183–200), official Design Projects 46 (U139–141) and 46A (U142–200). Double hull; seven watertight compartments; trim and regulating tanks 87.4cu m (or 98cu m from U142); diving depth 75m. Armour: conning tower sides 30mm, roof 60mm, ammunition trunking 25mm.

Propulsion

Two MAN (or MAN-Vulcan, U177, 178; or MAN-Blohm & Voss, U182, 184) 10-cylinder 4-stroke diesel engines in compartment 3, with two additional Germania 2-stroke diesels in U139 and two additional MAN 6-cylinder 4-stroke diesels in U140 and 141; one MAN-Brown, Boveri & Cie 6-cylinder 4-stroke diesel dynamo (or one Germania diesel generator, U173–176 and 183–190), 450ehp (= 300kW), in compartment 4; two AEG double electric motors in compartment 2; two 124 mass-cell Afag batteries in compartments 5 and 6 below. Two 3-bladed propellers, 2.10m diameter; two hydroplanes forward and two aft, with large hydroplane guards; two rudders.

Armament

Six 50cm torpedo tubes, four at the bow below the CWL and two at the stern - 19–24 torpedoes. Two Utof 15cm/45 guns - 980 rounds (or these weapons plus two Uk 8.8cm/30 guns - 200 rounds), U140–147, 173–178; or three Utof 15cm/45 guns - 1050 rounds, U148–150, 183–190, 195–200. Two periscopes in the conning tower.

Handling

Extremely good sea-boats for high seas use, with average manoeuvrability and responsiveness; comfortable accommodation for the crew.

Complement

Crew: 6/56, plus a prize crew of 1/20; one torpedo cutter and one dinghy.

Notes

An upper deck was formed by the step above the side tank decks. In U148–158, 183–190 and 195–200 two of the Utof 15cm/45 guns were mounted en echelon forward.

Careers

U139: launched 3 Dec 1917, commissioned 18 May 1918 as Kapitänleutnant Schwieger; surrendered to France, 24 Nov 1918; served as the French submarine cruiser Halbronn until 24 Jul 1935; broken up.

U140: launched 4 Nov 1917, commissioned 28 Mar 1918 as Kapitänleutnant Weddigen; surrendered to USA, 23 Feb 1919; used for tests; sunk by gunfire from the US destroyer Dickerson at Cape Charles, Virginia, 22 Jul 1921.

U141: launched 9 Jan 1918, commissioned 24 Jun 1918; surrendered 26 Nov 1918; broken up at Upnor, 1923.

U142: launched 4 Mar 1918, commissioned 10 Nov 1918, taken straight back to the dockyard, demilitarised and broken up at Oslebshausen, 1919; main engines surrendered.

U143: launched 20 Apr 1918, approximately 80 per cent complete; broken up at Oslebshausen, 1920; main engines surrendered.

U144: launched 25 May 1918, approximately 80 per cent complete; broken up at Lemwerder, 1920; main engines surrendered.

U145: launched 1 Nov 1918 as Kapitänleutnant Wegener, approximately 75 per cent complete; broken up at Hamburg, 1919–20; main engines surrendered.

U146: (Oberleutnant zur See Saltzwedel) approximately 70–75 per cent complete; broken up, 1919–20.

U147: (Kapitänleutnant Hansen) approximately 70–75 per cent complete; broken up, 1919–20.

U148: launched 22 Jun 1918 as Oberleutnant zur See Pustkuchen, approximately 70–75 per cent complete; broken up, 1919–20.

U149: launched 28 Sept 1918 as Kapitänleutnant Freiherr von Berkheim, approximately 70–75 per cent complete; broken up, 1919–20.

U150: (Kapitänleutnant Schneider); main engines surrendered as compensation for the sinking of UC48.

U173: launched in 1918; broken up at Lemwerder or on the stocks; main engines surrendered.

U174: launched in 1918; broken up at Lemwerder or on the stocks.

U175: Broken up at Lemwerder or on the stocks.

Name	Type	Builder (construction no)	Built	Cost in Marks (000s)	Displacement (t = tonnes T = tons)	Length (m)	Breadth (m)	Draught/ height (m)	Power (hp)	Revs (rpm)	Speed (kts)	Range (nm/kts)	Oil (t)	Diving time (sec)
U139–141		Germania (300–302)	1916–18	10,817 each	1930t sf 2483t sm 3050t total	92.00 oa 71.50 ph	9.12 oa 5.75 ph	5.27/ 11.2	3300ehp or 3500ehp +450ehp sf 1780ehp sm	350 or 380 or 400 sf 266 sm	15.3 or 15.8 or 6.0 sf 7.6 sm	12,630/8 or 17,750/8 sf 53/4.5 sm	386/ 103 or 393/ 103	40 td
U142–144		,, (303–305)	1917–		2158t sf 2785t sm 3350t total	97.50 oa 77.00 ph	9.06 oa 5.70 ph	5.38/ 11.2	6000ehp +450ehp sf 2600ehp sm	390 or 400 sf 268 sm	17.5 or 6.0 sf 8.5 sm	20,000/6 sf 70/4.5 sm	451/ 120	,,
U145–147		Vulcan (H) (101–103)	,,		2173t sf 2789t sm 3358t total	,,	,,	5.36/ 11.2	,,	,,	,,	,,	,,	,,
U148–150		Weser (288–290)	,,		2153t sf 2766t sm 3425t total	,,	,,	,,	,,	,,	,,	,,	467/ 123	,,
U173–176		Germania (306–309)	1918–		2115t sf 2790t sm 3350t total	97.50 oa 77.00 ph	,,	up to 5.36/ 11.2	,,	390 or 400 sf 270 sm	,,	up to 20,700/6 sf 70/4.5 sm	up to 467/ 123	30 td
U177–178		Vulcan (H) (135, 136)	,,		2175t sf 2791t sm 3358t total	,,	,,	,,	,,	,,	,,	,,	,,	,,
U179, 180		Weser (306, 307)	,,		2153t sf 2766t sm 3425t total	,,	,,	,,	,,	,,	,,	,,	,,	,,
U181, 182		B & V (353, 354)	,,		2119t sf 2790t sm 3350t total									
U183–190		Germania (322–329)	,,		2115t sf 2790t sm 3350t total									
U191–194		B & V (361–364)	,,		2119t sf 2790t sm 3350t total				as above					
U195–200		Weser (340–345)	,,		2153t sf 2766t sm 3425t total									

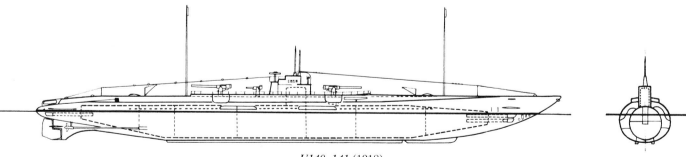

U140, 141 (1918).

U176: Broken up at Lemwerder or on the stocks.

U177–180: launched by order or on the authority of the shipyard; broken up at Lemwerder, 1919–20; main engines surrendered.

U181: launched 19 Oct 1918 by order or on the authority of the shipyard; broken up at Lemwerder, 1919–20; main engines surrendered.

U182: launched by order or on the authority of the

shipyard; broken up at Lemwerder, 1919–20; main engines surrendered.

U183 and 184: launched by order or on the authority of the shipyard; main engines surrendered;

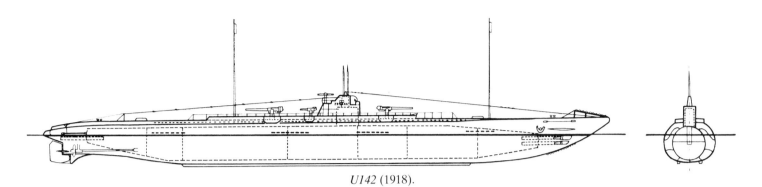

U142 (1918).

hulls incorporated as a pair of tanks in the hull of the motor tanker *Ostpreussen*, which had received the diesel engines from *U129*, and was built for Reederei Hugo Stinnes AG, Hamburg. *Ostpreussen* was sold to A Riebeck-Montan AG in 1923, then to Nereidi Soc. An. di Navig., Genoa; she later operated under the name *Caucaso*.

U185–186: launched by order or on the authority of the shipyard; broken up at Lemwerder, 1919–20; main engines surrendered.

U187 and 188: launched by order or on the authority of the shipyard; incorporated as a pair of tanks in the hull of the motor tanker *Oberschlesien*, which had received the diesel engines from *U130*, and was built for Reederei Hugo Stinnes AG, Hamburg. *Oberschlesien* was sold to A Riebeck-Montan AG in 1923, and to Società Italiana di Navigazione, Genoa, as *Nautilus*; sold to Nautilus Società Anonima di Navigazione in 1931.

U189–195: launched by order or on the authority of the shipyard; broken up at Lemwerder, 1919–20; main engines surrendered.

U196–198: not started.

U199: launched by order or on the authority of the shipyard; broken up at Lemwerder, 1919–20; main engines surrendered.

U200: not started.

Project 47 armoured U-cruiser design

Name	Type	Builder (construction no)	Built	Cost in Marks (000s)	Displacement (t = tonnes T = tons)	Length (m)	Breadth (m)	Draught/ height (m)	Power (hp)	Revs (rpm)	Speed (kts)	Range (nm/kts)	Oil (t)	Diving time (sec)
Project 47	—		—	16,600	4100t sf	110.0 oa 91.95 ph	11.25 oa 7.30 ph	6.60/ 13.90	6000ehp sf 3800ehp sm		18.0 sf 9.0 sm	13200/10 sf 80/4 sm	450 max	

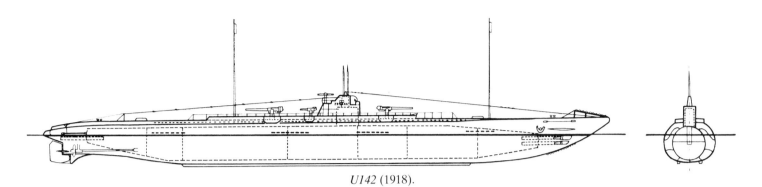

Project 47 (1917).

Construction

Designed as U-cruiser submersibles, official Design Project 47. Double hull; eight watertight compartments; capacity of trim and regulating tanks not known; diving depth 100m. Armour: pressure hull 20mm, casing sides 60mm, casing upper sides 40mm, upper deck 20mm, conning tower casing and periscope support sides 60mm, top 20mm, conning tower 45mm, 15cm gun shields 50mm.

Propulsion

Two MAN 12-cylinder 4-stroke diesel engines in compartment 4; two Man 6-cylinder 4-stroke diesel dynamos, 900 ehp (= 600kW) in compartment 3; two double electric motors, type unknown; two mass-cell Afag batteries (total number of cells not known) in compartments 5 and 6. Two 3-bladed propellers, 2.45m diameter; two hydroplanes forward, above the CWL, and two aft, below the CWL, with four hydroplane guards above the waterline; two rudders.

Armament

Ten 50cm torpedo tubes, four at the bow, below the CWL, four at the sides (in compartment 4, angled at 45° and 60°), below the waterline, and two at the stern - 30 torpedoes. Four Utof 15cm/45 guns - approximately 1800 rounds, and two Uk 8.8cm/30 guns - 440 rounds. 1 + 2 + 1 periscopes in the conning tower.

Complement

Crew: 10/90, plus a prize crew of 2/25; number of dinghies etc not known.

Careers

These U-boats never got beyond the planning stage; no construction contract was ever signed.

UD1 armoured U-cruiser design

Name	Type	Builder (construction no)	Built	Cost in Marks (000s)	Displacement (t = tonnes T = tons)	Length (m)	Breadth (m)	Draught/ height (m)	Power (hp)	Revs (rpm)	Speed (kts)	Range (nm/kts)	Oil (t)	Diving time (sec)
UD1		KWK (44)	1918–		c3800t sf c4500t sm	c125 oa	c10.5 oa c6.0 ph		24,000shp sf 3800ehp sm		25.0 sf 9.5 sm			

Construction

Designed as a U-cruiser submersible, official Design Project 50, 1917; construction begun under War Contract AA. Double-hull; number of compartments not known; diving depth probably 75m. Details of armour not known.

Propulsion

Two sets of steam turbines in compartments 2(?) and 3(?), and four Wölke watertube boilers, two each on either side of compartments 1(?) and 4(?) in pressure-tight diving tanks; two SSW double dynamos between the aft boilers, plus two Brown, Boveri & Cie diesel dynamos, 900ehp, in the aft turbine room; Afag mass-cell batteries were envisaged, but the number, arrangement and the compartments intended for them are not known.

Two 3-bladed propellers, diameter unknown; two hydroplanes forward below the CWL, two adjustable hydroplanes amidships and two fixed hydroplanes aft; one rudder.

Armament

Probably six 50cm torpedo tubes, four at the bow below the CWL and two at the stern below the CWL - number of torpedoes unknown. Three or four Utof 15cm/45 guns - number of rounds unknown. Two periscopes in the conning tower and one in the control room.

Complement

Crew: approximately 9/95; number of boats unknown.

Notes

The original plans, by the engineer H Wölke, were destroyed in 1946, and it is unlikely that any other official documents still exist. Externally, this vessel strongly resembled *U139–141*, and was intended to carry a similar outfit of guns, though the Utof 15cm guns were positioned somewhat further away from the tower.

Career

The construction order was placed in February 1918 after trials with full size boilers; all completed material was broken up or sold after November 1918.

U151 class U-cruisers (converted merchant submarines)

Name	Type	Builder (construction no)	Built	Cost in Marks (000s)	Displacement (t = tonnes T = tons)	Length (m)	Breadth (m)	Draught/ height (m)	Power (hp)	Revs (rpm)	Speed (kts)	Range (nm/kts)	Oil (t)	Diving time (sec)
U151		Hull by Flensburg (381)*	1916–17	5741	1512t sf 1875t sm 2272t total	65.00 oa 57.00 ph	8.90 oa 5.80 ph	5.30/ 9.25	800ehp sf 800ehp sm	390 to 360 sf 360 sm	12.4 sf 5.2 sm	c25,000/ 5.5 sf 65/3 sm	up to 285/ 148	80 50 td
U152–154		Hull by Reiherstieg*	”	”	”	”	”	”	”	”	”	”	”	”
U155		Hull by Flensburg (382)*	”	4135	1503t sf 1880t sm 2272t total	”	”	”	”	”	”	”	”	”
U156		Hull by Atlas (151)*	”	5741	1512t sf 1875t sm 2272t total	”	”	”	”	”	”	”	”	”
U157		Hull by Stülcken*	”	”	”	”	”	”	”	”	”	”	”	”
all vessels as merchant U-boats		see above	1915–16 and 1916–17		1575t sf 1860t sm 2272t total				800ehp sf 750ehp sm	360 sf 360 sm	10.0 sf 6.7 sm	12,000/10 sf	200 max	”

* Final assembly of all boats was undertaken by Germania, under the construction numbers 263 (*U155*) and 294–299.

Construction

Laid down as submersibles for freight transport to designs by Dr Techel of the Germania Dockyard; later converted to U-boat cruisers under War Contract P. Double hull; nine watertight compartments; trim and regulating tanks [63cu m]; diving depth 50m.

Propulsion

Two Germania 6-cylinder 4-stroke diesel engines in compartment 3, originally intended as diesel generators for the battle cruiser *Ersatz Gneisenau* (see Vol One, p59) and the battleship *Sachsen* (see Vol One, p28), non-reversible; two SSW double motor-dynamos in compartment 3; two 118 mass-

cell Afag batteries in compartments 6 and 7 below. Two 3-bladed propellers, 1.60m [1.65m] diameter; two hydroplanes forward and two aft, below the CWL, with hydroplane guards above the CWL.

Armament

Two 50cm torpedo tubes at the bow, below the

CWL - 18 torpedoes. Two Utof 10.5cm/45 guns - 1672 rounds - plus two Uk 8.8cm/30 guns - 764 rounds. One periscope in the conning tower and one in the control room. Until 1918 *U155* was armed only with the so-called 'grid tubes' – six 50cm torpedo tubes arranged in pairs on the upper deck at an angle of 15° to the sides of the vessel - 24 torpedoes; these tubes could only be reloaded when the vessel was on the surface. She was also fitted with two 15cm/40 QF guns from the battleship *Zähringen* (see Vol One, p17).

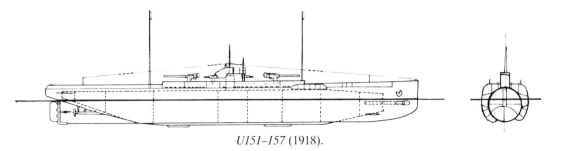

U151–157 (1918).

Handling

Relatively good sea-boats, with stiff motions in heavy seas, so that the conning tower remained comparatively dry. Diving performance was poor.

As the diesel engines were not reversible, the vessel could be manoeuvred only using the electric motors, which started with difficulty. Maximum speed could only be maintained for a short period, and then only with the assistance of the electric motors. All vessels made minimal way in a head sea.

Complement

Crew: 6/50, plus a prize crew of 1/19; one boat plus one dinghy.

Notes

As commercial vessels, these U-boats were registered as 791gt and 414nt.

Careers

Only *Deutschland* and *Bremen* served as merchant submarines. The remainder were all converted into U-boat cruisers after 15 Feb 1917 but before they had made any commercial voyages.

U151: launched 4 Apr 1917, commissioned 12 Jul 1917 (named *Oldenburg* as a commercial submarine); surrendered to France; sunk as a target ship 7 Jun 1921, at Cherbourg.

U152: launched 20 May 1917, commissioned 20 Oct 1917; surrendered 24 Nov 1918; sank en route to being broken up, 1921.

U153: launched 19 Jul 1917, commissioned 17 Nov 1917; surrendered 24 Nov 1918; sank en route to being broken up, 1921.

U154: launched 10 Sept 1917, commissioned 12 Dec 1917; sunk at 1725hrs on 1 May 1918 in the Atlantic Sea, in position 36° 51'N, 11° 50'W, by a torpedo from the British submarine *E35*; 77 dead (all crew lost).

U155: launched 28 Mar 1916, as commercial submarine *Deutschland* (Imperial Navy name *U200*) of the Deutsche Ozean-Reederei company, Bremen; commissioned into the Imperial Navy U-boat fleet 19 Feb 1917; surrendered 24 Nov 1918; exhibited in London and other places; broken up at Morecambe, 1922.

Bremen: launched 1916, and in service as a commercial submarine by the end 1916; went missing off the Orkneys during her first voyage, early in 1917; possibly mined; number of fatalities not known; all crew lost.

U156: launched 14 Apr 1917, commissioned 28 Aug 1917; sank on 25 Sep 1918, in the North Sea, after being mined in the Northern Barrage; 77 dead (all crew lost).

U157: launched 23 May 1917, commissioned 22 Sept 1917; interned at Trondheim, 11 Nov 1918; surrendered to France 8 Feb 1919; broken up at Brest, July 1921.

Coastal and medium U-boats up to 1918

UA (Type UA)

Name	Type	Builder (construction no)	Built	Cost in Marks (000s)	Displacement (t = tonnes T = tons)	Length (m)	Breadth (m)	Draught/ height (m)	Power (hp)	Revs (rpm)	Speed (kts)	Range (nm/kts)	Oil (t)	Diving time (sec)
UA	UA	Germania (202)	1912–14	1729	270t sf 342t sm 380t total	46.70 oa 34.45 ph	4.78 oa 3.15 ph	2.80/ 6.47	700ehp sf 380ehp sm	450 sf 350 sm	14.2 sf 7.3 sm	900/10 sf 76/3.3 sm	13 max	75 67 td

Construction
Laid down as submersibles *A2–4* for Norway, to designs by Dr Techel of the Germania Dockyard (similar to the Italian *Atropo*, but to Norwegian specifications). Construction commenced in October 1912. Double hull; six watertight compartments. Trim and regulating tanks 10.2cu m; diving depth 50m.

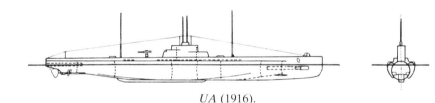

UA (1916).

Propulsion
Two Germania 6-cylinder 4-stroke diesel engines (non-reversing) in compartment 2; two 1.40m diameter; two open SSW motor dynamos in compartment 2, aft; two 70 mass-cell Afag batteries in compartments 5 and 6 below. Two three-bladed rotors, 1.40m diameter; one stern rudder; two hydroplanes forward, above the CWL, two at the stern. The rudder and after hydroplanes were positioned in the propeller stream, the first time this had been done in any navy.

Armament
Three 45cm torpedo tubes, two at the bow, one at the stern, below the CWL - 5 torpedoes. Two periscopes in the conning tower.

[From 1917 she was fitted with one Tk 8.8cm/40 gun -108 rounds - and one machine gun.]

Handling
Limited use on the high seas, otherwise similar to *U5–8*.

Complement
Crew: 3/18; one dinghy.

Career
Launched 9 May 1914 as the Norwegian submarine *A 5*; seized 5 Aug 1914; served in the Imperial navy from 14 Aug 1914, under the serial number *U0*; renumbered *UA* 28 Aug 1914 and served as a coastal defence vessel, then from 1916 as a training boat; surrendered to France 24 Nov 1918; broken up at Toulon, 1920–21.

UB1 class (Type UBI)

Name	Type	Builder (construction no)	Built	Cost in Marks (000s)	Displacement (t = tonnes T = tons)	Length (m)	Breadth (m)	Draught/ height (m)	Power (hp)	Revs (rpm)	Speed (kts)	Range (nm/kts)	Oil (t)	Diving time (sec)
UB1–8	UBI	Germania (229–246)	1914–15	712	127t sf 142t sm 166t total	28.10 oa 23.62 ph	3.15 oa 3.15 ph	3.03/ 7.30	60ehp sf 120ehp sm	550 sf 465 sm	6.47 sf 5.51 sm	1650/5 sf 45/4 sm	3.5 max	33 20 td
UB9–17	"	Weser (218–224, 230–231)	"	711	127t sf 141t sm 166t total	27.88 oa 23.62 ph	"	"	"	450 sf 392 sm	7.45 sf 6.24 sm	1500/5 sf 45/4 sm	3.0 max	33 22 td
(mod)	"	KWB	1916–17		147t sf 161t sm	31.97 oa 26.60 ph	"	2.93/	"	"	"	"	"	"

Construction

Laid down as submersibles under War Contract B, official Design Project 34, 1914. Single hull; four watertight compartments; trim and regulating tanks 4.2cu m (or 5.4cu m, *UB9–17*); diving depth 50m. These vessels were known as Type I.

[In 1917 *UB12* was rebuilt, with compartment 4 of the pressure hull replaced by one which was 3m longer and to the full diameter almost from the bow; a similar modification was planned for *UB10*, *UB16* and *UB17*.]

Propulsion

One Daimler (or Körting, *UB9–17*) 4-cylinder 4-stroke diesel barge engine together with one SSW double motor-dynamo in compartment 2; two 61 mass-cell Afag batteries in the forward part of compartment 3 below, or immediately aft of the mid-ships diving tanks. One 3-bladed propeller, 1.06m (or 1.10m, *UB9–17*) diameter; two hydroplanes forward and two aft; one rudder.

Armament

Two 45cm torpedo tubes at the bow, below the CWL - 2 torpedoes; one machine gun - 1600 rounds. One periscope in the conning tower.

[In the 1917 rebuild undertaken on *UB12* and intended for *UB10*, *16* and *17* the torpedo tubes were replaced by four 100cm mine-launching tubes - 8 Type UC 200 mines. *UB14* was fitted with one 3.7cm machine gun in 1917.]

Handling

These vessels were designed for coastal use, and were poor sea-boats with limited manoeuvrability and only average responsiveness. According to Dr Techel, however, they were 'astonishingly seaworthy'.

Complement

Crew: 1/13; no boats.

Notes

UB1, 3, 7, 8, 14 and *15* were transported in sections by rail to the Austro-Hungarian navy arsenal at Pola and assembled for use in the Mediterranean. *UB4–6, 10, 12, 16* and *17* were similarly transported in sections to the Imperial Dockyard at Hoboken, Antwerp.

UB1–17 (1916).   *UB12* (1918).

Careers

UB1: launched 19 Jan 1915, commissioned 29 Jan 1915 for service in the Mediterranean; transferred to the Austro-Hungarian Navy as *U10*, 12 Jul 1915. Sunk on 9 Jul 1918 near Caorle, by mines; raised 25 Jul 1918; wreck handed over to Italy, 1920, and broken up.

UB2: launched 18 Feb 1915, commissioned 20 Feb 1915; used for U-boat training in Flanders from 1916; stricken 19 Feb 1919; hull broken up by Stinnes, 3 Feb 1920.

UB3: launched 5 Mar 1915; commissioned 14 Mar 1915; served in the Mediterranean as the Austro-Hungarian *U9*; went missing (presumed sunk) in May 1915 in the Mediterranean; 14 dead (all crew lost).

UB4: launch date not known; commissioned 23 Mar 1915; served in Flanders. Sunk at 2025hrs on 15 Aug 1915 in the North Sea, in position 52° 43'N, 02° 18'E, by gunfire from the British Q-ship *Inverlyon*; 15 dead (all crew lost).

UB5: launch date not known; commissioned 25 Mar 1915; served in the Flanders U-flotilla in 1915; used for training, 1916; stricken 19 Feb 1919; broken up by Dräger, Lübeck, 1919.

UB6: launch date not known, commissioned 8 Apr 1915; served in Flanders; ran aground in fog off the Dutch coast, position 51° 53'N, 03° 58'E, 12 Mar 1917, and was then sunk at Hellevoetsluis, 18 Mar 1917, while interned; surrendered to France, 1919; broken up at Brest, July 1921.

UB7: launch date not known; commissioned 6 May 1915; served in the Mediterranean; transferred to Austria-Hungary as *U7*, 4 Jun 1915. Sunk in October 1916 in the Black Sea, in position 44° 30'N, 33° 15'E, by bombs from a Russian aircraft; 15 dead (all crew lost).

UB8: launch date not known; commissioned 23 Apr 1915; served in the Mediterranean as the Austro-Hungarian *U8*; stricken 25 May 1916 and handed over to Bulgaria; renamed Bulgarian submarine *UB8*; surrendered to France 25 Feb 1919; broken up at Bizerta, Aug 1921.

UB9: launched 6 Feb 1915; commissioned 18 Feb 1915; used for training; stricken 19 Feb 1919; broken up by Dräger, Lübeck, 1919.

UB10: launched 20 Feb 1915; commissioned 15 Mar 1915; served in Flanders; scuttled and sunk off the Flanders coast on 5 Oct 1918, in position 51° 21'N, 03° 12'E, during the German evacuation of Belgium.

UB11: launched 2 Mar 1915; commissioned 4 Mar 1915; used for training; stricken 19 Feb 1919; hull broken up by Stinnes, 3 Feb 1920.

UB12: launched 2 Mar 1915; commissioned 29 Mar 1915; served in Flanders. Sunk in the North Sea, 19–31 Aug 1918, in approximate position 51° 20'N, 01° 30'E, by a mine; 19 dead (all crew lost).

UB13: launched 8 Mar 1915; commissioned 6 Apr 1915; served in Flanders. Sunk on the Belgian coast, 24 Apr 1916, in position 51° 33'N, 02° 45'E, after striking a mine net laid by the British Q-ship *Telesia*; 17 dead (all crew lost).

UB14: launched 25 Mar 1915; commissioned 25 Mar 1915; served in the Mediterranean as the Austro-Hungarian *U26*; disarmed at Sevastopol, 25 Nov 1918; surrendered in November 1918 at Malta, broken up 1920.

UB15: launch date not known; commissioned 4 Apr 1915; served in the Mediterranean; transferred to the Austro-Hungarian Navy as *U11*, 18 Jun 1915; broken up at Pola, 1919.

UB16: launched 26 Apr 1915; commissioned 12 May 1915; served in Flanders. Sunk at 2000hrs on 10 May 1918, in the North Sea, in position 52° 06'N, 02° 01'E; after being torpedoed by the British submarine *E 34*; 15 dead (all crew lost).

UB17: launched 21 Apr 1915; commissioned 4 Apr 1915; served in Flanders. Sunk in March 1918, place and cause not known.

UB18 class (Type UBII)

Construction

Laid down as submersibles under War Contract B, official Design Project 39, 1915. Single hull with saddle tanks; six watertight compartments; trim and regulating tanks 8.5cu m/7.9cu m (*UB18, 19, 26, 29, 42–47*), 8.5cu m/8.3cu m (*UB20–23, 36, 38–41*) or 8.2cu m/8.3cu m (*UB24, 25, 27, 28, 30–35, 37*); diving depth 50cm.

Note that the Type name, UBII, of these vessels (normally referred to in naval slang as '*UB-zwoboote*') was sometimes mistakenly written as if the numeral were an exponent, so that they were sometimes referred to as 'UB-squared boats'.

Propulsion

Two Daimler (or Körting, *UB20–23, 36, 38–41*; or Benz, *UB24, 25, 27, 28, 30–35, 37*) 6-cylinder 4-stroke diesel engines together with two SSW double motor-dynamos in compartment 2; two 61 mass-cell Afag batteries in compartment 2 forward

Name	Type	Builder (construction no)	Built	Cost in Marks (000s)	Displacement (t = tonnes T = tons)	Length (m)	Breadth (m)	Draught/ height (m)	Power (hp)	Revs (rpm)	Speed (kts)	Range (nm/kts)	Oil (t)	Diving time (sec)
UB18, 19	UBII	B & V (248, 249)	1915		263t sf 292t sm 324t total	36.13 oa 27.13 ph	4.36 oa 3.85 ph	3.70/ 7.34	284ehp sf 280ehp sm	475 sf 400 sm	9.15 sf 5.81 sm	6650/5 sf 45/5 sm	28/22	45 32 td
UB20–23	,,	,, (250–253)	1915–16	1292	,,	,,	,,	,,	,,	,,	,,	6450/5 sf 45/4 sm	,,	,,
UB24–29	,,	Weser (238–243)	,,	1291	265t sf 291t sm 324t total	,,	,,	3.66/ 7.34	270ehp sf* 280ehp sm	500 sf* 400 sm	8.90 sf* 5.72 sm	7200/5 sf* 45/4 sm	,,	30 22 td
UB30–41	,,	B & V (254–265)	,,	1152	274t sf 303t sm 347t total	36.90 oa 27.90 ph	4.37 oa 3.85 ph	3.69/ 7.34	270ehp sf† 280ehp sm	,,†	9.06 sf† 5.71 sm	7030/5 sf† 45/4 sm	28/21	42 30 td
UB42	,,	Weser (244)	,,		279t sf 305t sm 347t total	,,	,,	3.75/ 7.34	,,	,,	,,	,,	,,	,,
UB43–47	,,	,, (245–249)	,,		272t sf 305t sm 347t total	,,	,,	3.68/ 7.34	284ehp sf 280ehp sm	475 sf 400 sm	8.82 sf 6.22 sm	6940/5 sf 45/4	27/22	37 32 td

* *UB26* and *29* horsepower, revolutions, speed and range figures as for *UB18* and *19*.
† *UB36* and *38–41* horsepower, revolutions, speed and range figures as for *UB20–23*.

and compartment 5 aft. One 3-bladed propeller; two hydroplanes forward and two aft with large hydroplane guards; one rudder.

Armament

Two 50cm torpedo tubes at the bow, below the CWL - 4 [6] torpedoes; one Tk 5cm/40 gun - 200 rounds (or one Uk 8.8cm/30–120 [116] rounds, *UB30–47*).

[*UB21, 22, 27, 34, 35* and *41* were fitted with one 'grid tube' 50cm torpedo tube either side of the conning tower above the CWL, angled at 4°, and the bow tubes were used for launching P-mines - 14 mines carried. *UB18, 21–23, 25* and *27* were refitted from 1916–17 (and *UB24* in 1916–17 only) with one Uk 8.8cm/30 gun - 120, later 116, rounds.]

Handling

These vessels were designed for coastal use only; they were poor sea-boats with limited man-oeuvrability and average responsiveness.

Complement

Crew: 2/21; details of boats unknown.

Notes

Small external differences were evident in the conning towers, wireless masts, etc. *UB43* and *47* were fitted with a breakwater on the forecastle, and had a narrower superstructure deck. *UB42–47* were transported in sections by rail to the Austro-Hungarian naval arsenal at Pola and assembled there.

Careers

UB18: launched 21 Aug 1915, commissioned 11 Dec 1915; served in Flanders. Sank at 0000hrs on 9 Dec 1917 in the west of the Channel, in position 49° 17'N, 05° 47'W, after being rammed by the British trawler *Ben Lawers*; 24 dead (all crew lost).

UB18–27 (1916).

UB41 (1918); *UB21, 22, 27, 34* and *35* were very similar.

UB19: launched 2 Sept 1915, commissioned 17 Dec 1915; served in Flanders. Sunk at 1710hrs on 30 Nov 1916 in the Channel, in position 50° 00'N, 02° 48'W, by gunfire from the British Q-ship Q 7 (*Penshurst*); 8 dead.

UB20: launched 26 Sept 1915, commissioned 10 Feb 1916; served in Flanders from 1917. Sunk on 29 Jul 1917 off the Flanders coast, in approximate position 51° 25'N, 03° 20'E by a mine; 13 dead (all crew lost).

UB21: launched 26 Sept 1915, commissioned 20 Feb 1916; used for training from 1918; surrendered 24 Nov 1918; sank off the East Coast of Britain on the way to being broken up, 1920.

UB22: launched 9 Oct 1915, commissioned 2 Mar 1916. Sunk at 1742hrs on 19 Jan 1918 in the North Sea, in position 54° 40'N, 06° 32'E by a mine; 22 dead (all crew lost).

UB23: launched 9 Oct 1915, commissioned 13 Mar 1916; served in Flanders; interned at Lá Coruña 29 Jul 1917, after sustaining damage from depth charges dropped by the British patrol boat *P 60*; surrendered to France at Cherbourg, 22 Feb 1919; broken up at Brest, July 1912.

UB24: launched 18 Oct 1915, commissioned 18 Nov 1915; used for training; surrendered 24 Nov 1918; fate as for *UB23*.

UB25: launched 22 Nov 1915, commissioned 11 Dec 1915; used for training. Sunk at 2135hrs on 19 Mar 1917 at Kiel, in position 53° 35'N, 10° 12'E, after colliding with *V26*; 16 dead. Raised 22 Mar 1917 by the salvage ship *Vulcan*; used for training; surrendered 26 Nov 1918; broken up at Canning Town, 1922.

UB26: launched 14 Dec 1915, commissioned 7 Jan 1916; served in Flanders. Sunk on 5 Apr 1916 at Le

Havre, in position 49° 28'N, 00° 02'E, in the harbour barrage. Raised on 30 Aug 1917; served as the French submarine *Roland Morillot* until 21 Jan 1925; used for tests; broken up at Cherbourg, 1931.

UB27: launched 10 Feb 1916, commissioned 23 Feb 1916; served in Flanders from 1917. Sank at 1057hrs on 29 Jul 1917 in the North Sea, in position 52° 47'N, 02° 24'E, after being rammed and depth charged by the British sloop *Halcyon*; 22 dead (all crew lost).

UB28: launched 20 Dec 1915, commissioned 27 Dec 1915; used for training; surrendered 24 Nov 1918; broken up at Bo'ness, 1919.

UB29: launched 31 Dec 1915, commissioned 18 Jan 1916; served in Flanders. Sank at 0010hrs on 13 Dec 1916 in the Channel, in position 51° 09'N, 01° 46'E, after being damaged by an explosive sweep and then rammed by the British destroyer *Landrail*; 22 dead (all crew lost).

UB30: launched 16 Nov 1915, commissioned 18 Mar 1916; served in Flanders, 1917; ran aground on 23 Feb 1917 near the island of Walcheren; raised by Dutch ships and interned; released 8 Aug 1917; returned to service in Flanders. Sunk at 1630hrs on 13 Aug 1918 in the North Sea, in position 54° 32'N, 00° 35'W, by depth charges from the British steam trawler *John Gillmann*; 26 dead (all crew lost).

UB31: launched 16 Nov 1915, commissioned 25 Mar 1916; served in Flanders. Sunk at 0805hrs on 2 May 1918 in the Channel, in position 51° 01'N, 01° 16'W, by depth charges from the British steam trawlers *Lord Leitrim*, *Loyal Friend* and *Ocean Roamer*; 26 dead (all crew lost).

UB32: launched 4 Dec 1915, commissioned 11 Apr 1916; served in Flanders from 1917. Sunk on 29 Sept 1917 in the Channel, in position 51° 45'N, 02° 05'W, by bombing; 23 dead (all crew lost).

UB33: launched 4 Dec 1915, commissioned 22 Apr 1916; served in Flanders from 1917. Sunk at 1800hrs on 11 Apr 1918 in the Channel, in position 50° 56'N, 01° 17'E, by a mine; 28 dead (all crew lost).

UB34: launched 28 Dec 1915, commissioned 10 Jun 1916; used for training, 1918; surrendered etc as for *UB25*.

UB35: launched 28 Dec 1915, commissioned 22 Jun 1916; served in Flanders from 1917. Sunk at 1140hrs on 26 Jan 1918 in the Channel, in position 51° 03'N, 01° 46'E, by depth charges from the British destroyer *Leven* and a patrol boat; 21 dead.

UB36: launched 15 Jan 1916, commissioned 22 May 1916; served in Flanders from 1917. Sunk at approximately 0700hrs on 21 May 1917 in the Channel, in position 48° 42'N, 05° 14'W, after being rammed by the French steamship *Molière*; 23 dead (all crew lost).

UB37: launched 28 Dec 1915, commissioned 17 May 1916; served in Flanders from 1917. Sunk at 1630hrs on 14 Jan 1917 in the Channel, in position 50° 07'N 01° 47'E, by gunfire and depth charges from the British Q-ship *Penshurst*; 21 dead (all crew lost).

UB38: launched 1 Apr 1916, commissioned 19 Jul 1916; served in Flanders. Sunk at 2245hrs on 8 Feb 1918 in the Channel, in position 50° 56'N, 01° 25'E by a mine; 27 dead (all crew lost).

UB39: launched 29 Dec 1915, commissioned 29 Apr 1916; served in Flanders. Sunk on about 15 May 1917 in the Channel, in position 50° 20'N, 01° 20'W by a mine; 24 dead (all crew lost).

UB40: launched 25 Apr 1916, commissioned 17 Aug 1916; served in Flanders; scuttled and sunk on 5 Oct 1918 at Ostende, in position 51° 13.5'N, 02°

56'E, during the German evacuation of Belgium.

UB41: launched 6 May 1916, commissioned 25 Aug 1916. Sunk at 0815hrs on 5 Oct 1917 in the North Sea, in position 54° 18'N, 00° 21'W, by a (German ?) mine; 24 dead (all crew lost).

UB42: launched 4 Mar 1916, commissioned 23 Mar 1916; served in Flanders from 1917. Sunk at 1630hrs on 14 Jan 1917 in the Channel, in position 50° 07'N, 01° 47'E, by gunfire and depth charges from the British Q-ship *Penshurst*; 21 dead (all crew lost).

UB43: launched 8 Apr 1916, commissioned 24 Apr 1916; served in the Mediterranean; transferred to the Austro-Hungarian Navy as *U43*, 30 Jul 1917; surrendered at Venice 6 Nov 1918; broken up at Venice, 1919.

UB44: launched 20 Apr 1916, commissioned 11 May 1916; served in the Mediterranean as the Austro-Hungarian *U44*. Sunk on 4 Aug 1916 in the Ionian Sea in position 40° 12'N, 18° 46'E, by depth charges from the British patrol boats *Quarrie*, *Knowe* and *Garrigill*; 24 dead (all crew lost).

UB45: launched 12 May 1916, commissioned 25 May 1916; served in the Mediterranean as the Austro-Hungarian *U45*. Sunk on 6 Nov 1916 in the Black Sea, in position 43° 12'N, 28° 09'E, by a mine; raised in 1936; broken up in Bulgaria.

UB46: launched 31 May 1916, commissioned 12 Jun 1916; served in the Mediterranean as the Austro-Hungarian *U46*. Sunk on 7 Dec 1916 in the Black Sea, in position 41° 26'N, 28° 35'E, by a mine; 20 dead (all crew lost).

UB47: launched 17 Jun 1916, commissioned 4 Jul 1916; served in the Mediterranean; transferred to the Austro-Hungarian Navy as *U47*, 30 Jul 1917; surrendered to France in 1920, and broken up.

UB48 class medium U-boats (Type UBIII)

Construction

Laid down as submersibles under War Contracts J (*UB48–71*), O (*UB72–87*), Q (*UB88–132*), T (*UB133–169*), W (*UB170–205*) and AB (*UB206–249*), official Design Project 44, 1915–16, a smaller version of the MS-boats. Six watertight compartments; trim and regulating tanks 28.2cu m (*UB66–71, 80–87, 133–141, 170–179, 186, 187*), 25.6cu m (*UB60–65, 72–74, 220–249*), 19.2cu m (*UB88–102, 154–169, 194–205*), 24.6cu m (*UB118–132, 180–185, 216–219*), 29.9cu m (*UB142–153, 188–193, 206–215*), 28.4cu m (*UB48–53*), 28.0cu m (*UB54–59*), 28.1cu m (*UB75–79*) and 25.0cu m (*UB103–117*); diving depth 50m (increased to 75m in *UB72–74, 88–102, 154–169* and *172–249*). These vessels were known as Type UB III.

Propulsion

Two 6-cylinder 4-stroke diesel engines coupled with two double motor-dynamos in compartment 2 (engine and motor-dynamo types are given in the table below); two 62 mass-cell Afag batteries in compartments 3 and 5 below. Two 3-bladed propellers, 1.40m diameter; two hydroplanes forward

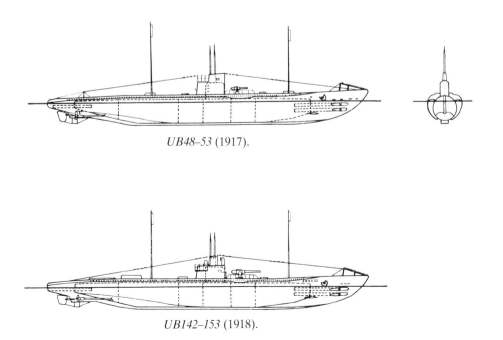

UB48–53 (1917).

UB142–153 (1918).

	Engine type	Motor-dynamo type
UB48–53	MAN	SSW
UB54–59	Körting	SSW
UB60–72	MAN	SSW
UB73–74	Körting	SSW
UB75–79	MAN	SSW
UB80–81	Körting	BB & Cie
UB82–85	Daimler	BB & Cie
UB86–87	Benz	BB & Cie
UB88–99	MAN-Vulcan	SSW
UB100–102	AEG	SSW
UB103–108	MAN-Vulcan	SSW
UB109–114	MAN-Vulcan	Maffei
UB115–117	MAN-Vulcan	AEG
UB118–120	Daimler	SSW
UB121–127	Körting	SSW
UB128–132	Benz	Schiffsunion
UB133–141	MAN-Vulcan	SSW
UB142–148	Benz	Schiffsunion
UB149–153	Körting	SSW
UB154–166	MAN-Vulcan	SSW
UB167–169	Körting	SSW
UB170–177	MAN-Vulcan	SSW
UB178–179	Daimler	SSW
UB180–185	AEG	SSW
UB186–187	MAN-Weser	AEG
UB188–193	Benz	BB & Cie
UB194–205	MAN-Vulcan	Maffei
UB206–215	Benz	BB & Cie
UB216–219	AEG	SSW
UB220–229	Benz	Schiffsunion
UB230–249	MAN	AEG

and two aft, below the CWL, with hydroplane guards above the CWL; two parallel rudders.

Armament

Five 50cm torpedo tubes, four at the bow below the CWL and one at the stern below the CWL - 10 torpedoes; one Uk 8.8cm/30 gun - 160–296 rounds.
[From 1918 UB48–51, 59, 62, 64, 67, 68, 73, 77, 79, 86, 103–105 and 111–113 were refitted with one Utof 10.5cm/45 gun - 108–192 rounds, UB48 and 106 were fitted with one such weapon in addition to their Uk 8.8cm guns, and UB148 was fitted with an additional 8.8cm gun.]

Handling

These vessels were used in coastal areas further afield. Their seakeeping was not as good as that of the MS-boats, but they had good manoeuvrability and were very responsive.

Complement

Crew: 3/31; one dinghy on the upper deck.

Notes

Research was undertaken on these boats into making the conning tower casing free-flooding.

Careers

UB48: launched 6 Jan 1917, commissioned 11 Jun 1917; served in the Mediterranean as the Austro-Hungarian U79; scuttled on 28 Oct 1918 at Pola, in position 44° 52′N, 13° 50′E, on the surrender of Austria-Hungary.

UB49: launched 6 Jan 1917, commissioned 28 Jun 1917; served in the Mediterranean as the Austro-Hungarian U80; surrendered on 16 Jan 1919; broken up at Swansea, 1922.

UB50: launched 6 Jan 1917, commissioned 12 Feb 1917; served in the Mediterranean as the Austro-Hungarian U81; surrendered on 16 Jan 1919; broken up at Swansea, 1922.

UB51: launched 8 Mar 1917, commissioned 26 Jul 1917; served in the Mediterranean as the Austro-Hungarian U82; surrendered on 16 Jan 1919; broken up at Swansea, 1922.

UB52: launched 8 Mar 1917, commissioned 9 Aug 1917; served in the Mediterranean as the Austro-Hungarian U83. Sunk at 2315hrs on 23 May 1918 in the southern Adriatic Sea, in position 41° 36′N, 18° 52′E, by a torpedo from the British submarine H 4; 34 dead.

UB53: launched 9 Mar 1917, commissioned 21 Aug 1917; served in the Mediterranean as the Austro-Hungarian U84; scuttled at approximately 1700hrs on 3 Aug 1918 in the Strait of Otranto, in position 39° 40′N, 18° 40′E, after becoming entangled in the net barrage; 10 dead.

UB54: launched 18 Apr 1917, commissioned 12 Jun 1917; served in Flanders. Sunk on 11 Mar 1918 in the North Sea, in position 53° 15′N, 00° 45′E, by depth charges from the British destroyers Sturgeon, Thruster and Retriever; 36 dead (all crew lost). The details of her loss are not certain.

UB55: launched 9 May 1917, commissioned 1 Jul

Name	Type	Builder (construction no)	Built	Cost in Marks (000s)	Displacement (t = tonnes T = tons)	Length (m)	Breadth (m)	Draught/ height (m)	Power (hp)	Revs (rpm)	Speed (kts)	Range (nm/kts)	Oil (t)	Diving time (sec)
UB48–53	UBIII	B & V (293–298)	1916–17	3276	516t sf 651t sm 730t total	55.30 oa 10.10 ph	5.80 oa 3.90 ph	3.68/ 8.25	1100ehp sf 788ehp sm	450 sf 362 sm	13.6 sf 8.0 sm	9040/6 sf 55/4 sm	75/35	30 td
UB54–59	”	Weser (266–271)	”		516t sf 646t sm 765t total	55.85 oa 40.10 ph	5.80 oa 3.90 ph	3.72/ 8.25	1060ehp sf 788ehp sm	”	13.4 sf 7.8 sm	9020/6 sf 55/4 sm	75/36	”
UB60–65	”	Vulcan (H) (85–90)	”	3279	508t sf 639t sm 725t total	55.52 oa 40.10 ph	5.76 oa 3.90 ph	3.70/ 8.25	1100ehp sf 788ehp sm	”	13.3 sf 8.0 sm	8420/6 sf 55/4 sm	68/32	”
UB66–71	”	Germania (284–289)	”	3276	513t sf 647t sm 730t total	55.83 oa 40.10 ph	5.80 oa 3.90 ph	3.67/ 8.25	”	”	13.2 sf 7.6 sm	9090/6 sf 55/4 sm	75/35	”
UB72–74	”	Vulcan (H) (96–98)	”	3337	508t sf 639t sm 725t total	55.52 oa 40.10 ph	5.76 oa 3.90 ph	3.70/ 8.25	”	”	13.4 sf 7.5 sm	8420/6 sf 55/4 sm	68/32	”
UB75–79	”	B & V (304–308)	”	3338	516t sf 648t sm 730t total	55.30 oa 40.10 ph	5.80 oa 3.90 ph	3.68/ 8.25	”	”	13.6 sf 7.8 sm	8680/8 sf 55/4 sm	73/34	30
UB80–87	”	Weser (280–287)	”	3341	516t sf 647t sm 765t total	55.85 oa 40.10 ph	5.80 oa 3.90 ph	3.72/ 8.25	1060ehp sf 788ehp sm	”	13.4 sf 7.5 sm	8180/6 sf 50/4 sm	68/34	30 td
UB88–102	”	Vulcan (H) (104–118)	1917–18	3654	510t sf 640t sm 760t total	55.52 oa 40.10 ph	5.76 oa 3.90 ph	3.73/ 8.25	1100ehp sf 788ehp sm	”	13.0 sf 7.4 sm	7120/6 sf 55/4 sm	71/32	30

Name	Type	Builder (construction no)	Built	Cost in Marks (000s)	Displacement (t = tonnes T = tons)	Length (m)	Breadth (m)	Draught/ height (m)	Power (hp)	Revs (rpm)	Speed (kts)	Range (nm/kts)	Oil (t)	Diving time (sec)
UB103–117	,,	B & V (309–323)	,,	3714	519t sf* 649t sm* 730t total	55.30 oa 40.10 ph	5.80 oa 3.90 ph	3.70/ 8.25	,,	,,	13.3 sf 7.5 sm	7420/6 sf 55/4 sm	69/24	30 td
UB118–132	,,	Weser (291–305)	,,	3654	512t sf 643t sm 760t total	55.85 oa 40.10 ph	,,	3.72/ 8.25	1060ehp sf 788ehp sm	,,	13.9 sf 7.6 sm	7280/6 sf 55/4 sm	68/34	,,
UB133–141	,,	Germania (310–318)	1917–18 and 1917–	3485	533t sf 656t sm 730t total	55.83 oa 40.10 ph	,,	3.77/ 8.25	1100ehp sf 788ehp sm	,,	13.5 sf 7.5 sm	9090/6 sf 50/4 sm	75/35	,,
UB142–153	,,	Weser (308–319)	,,	4301	523t sf 653t sm 772t total	55.85 oa 40.10 ph	,,	3.75/ 8.25	1060ehp sf 788ehp sm	,,	,,	7280/6 sf 50/4 sm	68/34	,,
UB154–169	,,	Vulcan (H) (119–134)	,,	,,	539t sf 656t sm 775t total	55.52 oa 40.10 ph	,,	3.85/ 8.25	1100ehp or 1060ehp sf 788ehp sm	,,	,,	7120/6 sf 50/4 sm	71/32	,,
UB170–177	,,	Germania (330–337)	1918–		533t sf 656t sm 730t total	56.82 oa 40.10 ph	,,	3.77/ 8.25	1060ehp sf 788ehp sm	,,	,,	9060/6 sf 50/4 sm	75/35	,,
UB178, 179	,,	Weser (346, 347)	,,		555t sf 684t sm 800t total	56.80 oa 40.10 ph	,,	3.66/ 8.25	,,	,,	,,	7280/6 sf 50/4 sm	68/34	,,
UB180–187	,,	,, (348–355)	,,		,,	,,	,,	,,	1100ehp sf 788ehp sm	,,	,,	7120/6 sf 50/4 sm	71/32	,,
UB188–193	,,	Vulcan (H) (137–142)	,,		539t sf 656t sm 775t total	57.80 oa 40.10 ph	,,	3.85/ 8.25	1060ehp sf 788ehp sm	,,	,,	7280/6 sf 50/4 sm	68/34	,,
UB194–205	,,	,, (143–154)	,,		,,	,,	,,	,,	1100ehp sf 788ehp sm	,,	,,	7120/6 sf 50/4 sm	71/32	,,
UB206–215	,,	Weser (370–379)	,,		555t sf 684t sm 800t total	56.80 oa 40.10 ph	,,	3.66/ 8.25	1060ehp sf 788ehp sm	,,	,,	7280/6 sf 50/4 sm	68/34	,,
UB216–219	,,	,, (380–383)	,,		,,	,,	,,	,,	1100ehp sf 788ehp sm	,,	,,	7120/6 sf 50/4 sm	71/32	,,
UB220–229	,,	Vulcan (H) (155–164)	,,		539t sf 656t sm 775t total	57.80 oa 40.10 ph	,,	3.85/ 8.25	1060ehp sf 788ehp sm	,,	,,	7280/6 sf 50/4 sm	68/34	,,
UB230–249	,,	,, (165–184)	,,		,,	,,	,,	,,	1100ehp sf 788ehp sm	,,	,,	7120/6 sf 50/4 sm	71/32	,,

* *UB103, 105* and *109* displacement 510t sf, 629t sm, total unknown.

1917; served in Flanders. Sunk at 0505hrs on 22 Apr 1918 in the Channel, in position 51° 01'N, 01° 20'E, by a mine; 30 dead.

UB56: launched 6 Jun 1917, commissioned 19 Jul 1917; served in Flanders. Sunk at 2342hrs on 19 Dec 1917 in the Channel, in position 50° 58'N, 01° 21'E, by a mine; 37 dead (all crew lost).

UB57: launched 21 Jun 1917, commissioned 30 Jul 1917; served in Flanders. Sunk at 2300hrs on 14 Aug 1918 off the coast of Flanders, in approximate position 51° 56'N, 02° 02'E, by a mine; 34 dead (all crew lost).

UB58: launched 5 Jul 1917, commissioned 10 Aug 1917; served in Flanders. Sunk at 0415hrs on 10 Mar 1918 in the Channel, in approximate position 50° 58'N, 01° 14'E, by a mine; 35 dead (all crew lost).

UB59: launched 21 Jul 1917, commissioned 25 Aug 1917; served in Flanders; scuttled on 5 Oct 1918 at Zeebrugge, in position 51° 19'N, 03° 12'E, during the German evacuation of Belgium.

UB60: launched 14 Apr 1917, commissioned 6 Jun 1917; used for training; surrendered 26 Nov 1918; ran aground on the East Coast of Britain; broken up 1921.

UB61: launched 28 Apr 1917, commissioned 23 Jun 1917. Sunk at approximately 2100hrs on 29 Nov 1917 in the North Sea, in position 53° 20'N, 04° 56'E, by a mine; 34 dead (all crew lost).

UB62: launched 11 May 1917, commissioned 9 Jul 1917; surrendered 21 Nov 1918; broken up at Swansea, 1922.

UB63: launched 26 May 1917, commissioned 23 Jul 1917. Sunk on 28 Jan 1918 in the North Sea, in approximate position 56° 10'N, 02° 00'W, by depth charges from the British steam trawlers *W S Bailey* and *Fort George*; 33 dead (all crew lost).

UB64: launched 9 Jun 1917, commissioned 5 Aug 1917; surrendered 21 Nov 1918; broken up at Fareham, 1921.

UB65: launched 26 Jun 1917, commissioned 18 Aug 1917; sank at 1830hrs on 10 Jul 1918, to the south of Ireland, in position 51° 07'N, 09° 42'W, after an accidental explosion; 37 dead (all crew lost).

UB66: launched 31 May 1917, commissioned 1 Aug 1917; served in the Mediterranean as the Austro-Hungarian *U66*. Sunk on 18 Jan 1918 in the Aegean Sea, in position 38° 30'N, 24° 25'E, by depth charges from the British sloop *Campanula*; 30 dead.

UB67: launched 16 Jun 1917, commissioned 23 Aug 1917; served in the Mediterranean as the Austro-Hungarian *U67*; used for training, 1918; surrendered 24 Nov 1918; broken up at Swansea, 1922.

UB68: launched 4 Jul 1917, commissioned 5 Aug 1917; served in the Mediterranean as the Austro-Hungarian *U68*; scuttled at 0430hrs on 4 Oct 1918 in the Ionian Sea, in position 35° 56'N, 16° 20'E, after being damaged by gunfire from the British sloop *Snapdragon* and steam trawler *Cradosin*; 4 dead.

UB69: launched 7 Aug 1918, commissioned 12 Oct 1917; served in the Mediterranean as the Austro-

Hungarian *U69*; scuttled at 0948hrs on 9 Jan 1918 in the Sicilian Channel, in position 37° 30'N, 10° 38'E, after becoming entangled in a net barrage being towed by the British sloop *Cyclamen*; 31 dead (all crew lost).

UB70: launched 17 Aug 1917, commissioned 29 Oct 1917; served in the Mediterranean as the Austro-Hungarian *U70*. Sunk on 8 May 1918, time and place unknown; 33 dead (all crew lost).

UB71: launched 12 Jul 1917, commissioned 23 Nov 1917; served in the Mediterranean as the Austro-Hungarian *U71*. Sunk at 0402hrs on 21 Apr 1918, southeast of Minorca, in position 35° 58'N, 05° 18'E, by depth charges from the British patrol boat *ML 413*; 32 dead (all crew lost).

UB72: launched 30 Jul 1917, commissioned 9 Sept 1917; served in the Mediterranean. Sunk at 0450hrs on 12 May 1918 in the English Channel, in position 50° 08'N, 02° 41'E, by a torpedo from the British submarine *D 4*; 34 dead.

UB73: launched 11 Aug 1917, commissioned 2 Oct 1917; served in the Mediterranean; surrendered to France, 21 Nov 1918; broken up at Brest in July 1921.

UB74: launched 12 Sept 1917, commissioned 24 Oct 1917; served in Flanders from 1918. Sunk at 2100hrs on 26 May 1918 in the Channel, in position 50° 32'N, 02° 32'W, by depth charges from the British yacht *Lorna*; 35 dead (all crew lost).

UB75: launched 5 May 1917, commissioned 11 Sept 1917. Sunk on 10 Dec 1917 in the North Sea, in position 54° 05'N, 00° 10'E, by a mine; 34 dead (all crew lost).

UB76: launched 5 May 1917, commissioned 23 Sept 1917; used for training; surrendered 12 Feb 1919; broken up at Rochester, 1922.

UB77: launched 5 May 1917, commissioned 2 Oct 1917; surrendered 16 Jan 1919; broken up at Swansea, 1922.

UB78: launched 2 Jun 1917, commissioned 20 Oct 1917; served in Flanders from 1918. Sank at 0050hrs on 9 May 1918, to the west of Cherbourg, in position 49° 49'N, 01° 40'W, after being depth charged and rammed by the British troop transporter *Queen Alexandra*; 35 dead (all crew lost).

UB79: launched 3 Jun 1917, commissioned 27 Oct 1917; used for training, 1918; surrendered 26 Nov 1918; broken up at Swansea, 1922.

UB80: launched 4 Aug 1917, commissioned 8 Sept 1917; served in Flanders from 1918; surrendered to Italy, 26 Nov 1918; broken up at La Spezia in May 1919.

UB81: launched 18 Aug 1917, commissioned 18 Sept 1917; served in Flanders. Sunk at 1745hrs on 2 Dec 1917 in the Channel, in position 50° 27'N, 00° 53'W, by a mine; 29 dead.

UB82: launched 1 Sept 1917, commissioned 2 Oct 1917. Sunk at 1730hrs on 17 Apr 1918 in the Irish Sea, in position 55° 13'N, 05° 55'W, by gunfire and depth charges from the British steam trawlers *Pilot Me* and *Young Fred*; 37 dead (all crew lost).

UB83: launched 15 Sept 1917, commissioned 15 Oct 1917. Sunk at 0624hrs on 10 Sep 1918 in the Orkneys, in position 58° 28'N, 01° 50'W, by depth charges from the British destroyer *Ophelia*; 35 dead (all crew lost).

UB84: launched 3 Oct 1917, commissioned 31 Oct 1917. Sank on 7 Dec 1917 in the Baltic Sea, in position 54° 35'N, 10° 11'E, after a collision; raised by the salvage ship *Vulcan*; used for training; surrendered to France 26 Nov 1918; broken up at Brest, 1921.

UB85: launched 26 Oct 1917, commissioned 24 Nov 1917; scuttled at 1610hrs on 30 Apr 1918 in the Irish Sea, in position 54° 47'N, 05° 23'W, after being damaged by gunfire from the British steam trawler *Coreopsis*; number of fatalities unknown.

UN86: launched 10 Oct 1917, commissioned 10 Nov 1917; surrendered on 24 Nov 1918; broken up at Falmouth, after running aground with *UB97*, *106* and *112* in 1921.

UB87: launched 10 Nov 1917, commissioned 27 Dec 1917; surrendered to France, 20 Nov 1918; broken up at Brest in July 1921.

UB88: launched 11 Dec 1917, commissioned 26 Jan 1918; surrendered to USA, 26 Nov 1918; used for exhibitions to raise War Loans in harbours along the Atlantic coast, the Gulf of Mexico, the coast of Panama and the West Coast as far as the USA's northern border; used for tests; scuttled at San Pedro, California, on 3 Jan 1921, after being used as a gunnery target by the US destroyer *Wilkes*.

UB89: launched 22 Dec 1917, commissioned 25 Feb 1918. Sank at 1908hrs on 21 Oct 1918 at Kiel, in position 54° 21'N, 10° 10'E, after a collision with the cruiser *Frankfurt*; 7 dead. Raised on 30 Oct 1918 by the salvage vessel *Cyclop*; drifted off course while on passage to surrender, 7 Mar 1919, and brought to Ymuiden; broken up at Dordrecht, 1920.

UB90: launched 12 Feb 1918, commissioned 21 Mar 1918. Sunk at 1633hrs on 16 Oct 1918 in the North Sea, in position 57° 55'N, 15° 27'E, by a torpedo from the British submarine *L 12*; 38 dead (all crew lost).

UB91: launched 6 Mar 1918, commissioned 11 Apr 1918; surrendered on 21 Nov 1918; broken up at Briton Ferry, 1921.

UB92: launched 25 Mar 1918, commissioned 27 Apr 1918; surrendered on 21 Nov 1918; broken up at Bo'ness, 1919–20.

UB93: launched 12 Apr 1918, commissioned 15 May 1918; surrendered on 21 Nov 1918; broken up at Rochester, 1922.

UB94: launched 26 Apr 1918, commissioned 1 Jun 1918; surrendered to France, 22 Nov 1918; served as the French submarine *Trinité Schillemans* until 24 Jul 1935; broken up.

UB95: launched 10 May 1918, commissioned 20 Jun 1918; surrendered to Italy, 21 Nov 1918; broken up at La Spezia in August 1919.

UB96: launched 31 May 1918, commissioned 3 Jul 1918; surrendered on 21 Nov 1918; broken up at Bo'ness, 1919–20.

UB97: launched 13 Jun 1918, commissioned 25 Jul 1918; surrendered on 21 Nov 1918; broken up at Falmouth, after running aground with *UB86*, *106* and *112*, 1921.

UB98: launched 1 Jul 1918, commissioned 8 Aug 1918; surrendered on 21 Nov 1918; broken up at Portmadoc, 1922.

UB99: launched 29 Jul 1918, commissioned 4 Sept 1918; surrendered to France, 26 Nov 1918; served as the French submarine *Carissan* until 24 Jul 1935; broken up.

UB100: launched 13 Aug 1918, commissioned 17 Sep 1918; surrendered on 22 Nov 1918; broken up at Dordrecht, 1922.

UB101: launched 27 Aug 1918, commissioned 31 Oct 1918; surrendered on 26 Nov 1918; broken up at Felixstowe, 1919–20.

UB102: launched 13 Sept 1918, commissioned 17 Oct 1918; surrendered to Italy, 22 Nov 1918; broken up at La Spezia in July 1919.

UB103: launched 7 Jul 1917, commissioned 18 Dec 1917; served in Flanders. Sunk on 16 Sept 1918 in the Channel, in position 50° 52′N, 01° 27′E, by depth charges from a British steam trawler and bombs from the airship *SSZ 1*; 37 dead (all crew lost).

UB104: launched 1 Jul 1917, commissioned 15 Mar 1918; served in Flanders. Sunk on 19 Sept 1918 in the North Sea, position not known, by mines in the Northern Barrage; 36 dead (all crew lost).

UB105: launched 7 Jul 1917, commissioned 14 Jan 1918; served in the Mediterranean as the Austro-Hungarian *U97*; surrendered 16 Jan 1919; broken up at Felixstowe, 1922.

UB106: launched 21 Jul 1917, commissioned 7 Feb 1918; served in Flanders. Sank on 15 Mar 1918 in the Baltic Sea, in position 54° 42′N, 10° 09′E, in an accident; 35 dead (all crew lost). Raised on 18 Mar 1918 by the salvage vessel *Vulcan*; surrendered 26 Nov 1918; broken up at Falmouth, after running aground with *UB86, 97* and *112*, 1921.

UB107: launched 21 Jul 1917, commissioned 16 Feb 1918; served in Flanders. Sunk at 2100hrs on 27 Jul 1918 in the North Sea, in position 54° 23′N, 00° 24′W, by depth charges from the British destroyer *Vanessa* and steam trawler *Calvia*; 38 dead (all crew lost).

UB108: launched 21 Jul 1917, commissioned 1 Mar 1918; served in Flanders; went missing in the Channel and presumed sunk, date, place and cause unknown (possibly mined); 36 dead (all crew lost).

UB109: launched 7 Jul 1917, commissioned 31 Dec 1917; served in Flanders. Sunk at 0330hrs on 29 Aug 1918 in the Channel, in position 51° 03′N, 01° 44′E, by a mine; 28 dead.

UB110: launched 1 Sept 1917, commissioned 23 Mar 1918; served in Flanders. Sunk at 1342hrs on 19 Jul 1918 in the North Sea, in position 54° 39′N, 00° 55′W, after being rammed and depth charged by the British destroyer *Garry* and motor boats *ML 49* and *ML 263*; 23 dead. Raised on 4 Oct 1918; broken up in England.

UB111: launched 1 Sept 1917, commissioned 5 Apr 1918; served in Flanders; surrendered on 21 Nov 1918; broken up at Bo'ness, 1919–20.

UB112: launched 15 Sept 1917, commissioned 16 Apr 1918; served in Flanders; surrendered on 24 Nov 1918; broken up at Falmouth, after running aground with *UB86, 97* and *106*, 1921.

UB113: launched 23 Sept 1917, commissioned 15 Apr 1918; served in Flanders. Sunk in September or October 1918, place and cause unknown; 39 dead (all crew lost).

UB114: launched 23 Sept 1917, commissioned 4 May 1918; sank on 13 May 1918 during trimming trials in Kiel harbour; 7 dead. Raised, surrendered 26 Nov 1918; fate as for *UB121*.

UB115: launched 4 Nov 1917, commissioned 28 May 1918; served in Flanders. Sunk on 29 Sept 1918 in the North Sea, in position 55° 13′N, 01° 22′W, by depth charges from the British destroyers *Ouse* and *Star* and six steam trawlers, and by bombs from the airship *R 29*; 39 dead (all crew lost).

UB117: launched 21 Nov 1917, commissioned 6 May 1918; served in Flanders; surrendered 22 Nov 1918; broken up at Felixstowe, 1919–20.

UB118: launched 13 Dec 1917, commissioned 22 Jan 1918; surrendered to France, 20 Nov 1918; sank on 15 Apr 1919, near Hastings, after running aground on a voyage between Harwich and Cherbourg; wreck broken up.

UB119: launched 13 Dec 1917, commissioned 9 Feb 1918; went missing in the North Sea, presumed sunk, in May 1918 (possibly mined); 34 dead (all crew lost).

UB120: launched 23 Feb 1918, commissioned 23 Mar 1918; surrendered 24 Nov 1918; broken up at Swansea, 1922.

UB121: launched 6 Jan 1918, commissioned 10 Feb 1918; surrendered to France, 20 Nov 1918; used for underwater explosions tests; broken up at Toulon, July 1921.

UB122: launched 2 Feb 1918, commissioned 4 Mar 1918; surrendered 24 Nov 1918; ran aground off the East Coast of Britain on the way to being broken up, 1921.

UB123: launched 2 Mar 1918, commissioned 6 Apr 1918. Sunk on 19 Oct 1918 in the North Sea, by mines in the Northern Barrage; 36 dead (all crew lost).

UB124: launched 19 Mar 1918, commissioned 22 Apr 1918. Sunk at 1825hrs on 20 Jul 1918 in the Irish Sea, in position 55° 43′N, 07° 51′W, by depth charges and gunfire from the British destroyers *Marne, Milbrook* and *Pigeon* and over thirty patrol boats; 2 dead.

UB125: launched 16 Apr 1918, commissioned 18 May 1918; surrendered to Japan, 20 Nov 1918; served as Japanese submarine *O 6*; broken up at Kure, 1921.

UB126: launched 12 Mar 1918, commissioned 20 Apr 1918; surrendered to France, 24 Nov 1918; used for underwater explosions tests; broken up at Toulon in July 1921.

UB127: launched 27 Apr 1918, commissioned 1 Jun 1918. Sunk in September 1918 in the North Sea, possibly by mines in the Northern Barrage; 34 dead (all crew lost).

UB128: launched 10 Apr 1918, commissioned 11 May 1918; served in the Mediterranean as the Austro-Hungarian *U54*; surrendered 3 Feb 1919; broken up at Falmouth, 1921.

UB129: launched 11 May 1918, commissioned 11 Jun 1918; served in the Mediterranean as the Austro-Hungarian *U55*; scuttled on 31 Oct 1918 at Fiume, in position 45° 19′N, 14° 26′E, on the surrender of Austria-Hungary.

UB130: launched 27 May 1918, commissioned 28 Jun 1918; intended for use in the Mediterranean as the Austro-Hungarian *U56*; surrendered to France, 26 Nov 1918; used for underwater explosions tests; broken up at Toulon in July 1921.

UB131: launched 4 Jun 1918, commissioned 4 Jul 1918; intended for use in the Mediterranean as the Austro-Hungarian *U57*; surrendered 24 Nov 1918; ran aground near Hastings, 9 Jan 1921; broken up.

UB132: launched 22 Jun 1918, commissioned 25 Jul 1918; intended for use in the Mediterranean as the Austro-Hungarian *U58*; surrendered 21 Nov 1918; broken up at Swansea.

UB133: launched 27 Sept 1918, accepted 20 Apr 1919; intended for use in the Mediterranean as Austro-Hungarian *U133*; surrendered (hull only); broken up at Rochester, 1922.

UB134: launched 1918; intended for use in the Mediterranean as Austro-Hungarian *U134*; broken up, 1919.

UB135: launched 1918; intended for use in the Mediterranean as Austro-Hungarian *U135*; broken up, 1919.

UB136: launched 27 Sept 1918; commissioned 16 Apr 1919; intended for use in the Mediterranean as Austro-Hungarian *U136*; broken up, 1919.

UB137: launched 2 Nov 1918; main engines surrendered; broken up, 1919.

UB138: launched 2 Nov 1918; broken up, 1919.

UB139: launched 2 Nov 1918; broken up, 1919.

UB140: launched 2 Nov 1918, broken up, 1919.

UB141: launched 2 Nov 1918; broken up, 1919.

UB142: launched 23 Jul 1918; commissioned 31 Aug 1918; surrendered to France, 22 Nov 1918; broken up at Landerneau in July 1921.

UB143: launched 21 Aug 1918; commissioned 3 Oct 1918; interned at Karlskrona, 13 Nov 1918; surrendered to Japan, 1 Dec 1918; served as Japanese submarine *O 7*; broken up at Yokosuka, 1921.

UB144: launched 5 Oct 1918; completed; surrendered 27 Mar 1919; broken up at Rochester, 1922.

UB145: launched October 1918; completed; surrendered 27 Mar 1919; broken up at Rochester, 1922.

UB146: launched 1918; intended for use in the Mediterranean as Austro-Hungarian *U146*; broken up.

UB147: launched 1918; intended for use in the Mediterranean as Austro-Hungarian *U147*; broken up.

UB148: launched 7 Aug 1918; commissioned 19 Sept 1918; interned at Karlskrona, 13 Nov 1918; surrendered to USA, 1 Dec 1918; used for exhibitions to raise War Loans in the Atlantic harbours; used for tests; scuttled near Cape Charles, Virginia, after being used as a gunnery target by the US destroyer *Sicard*.

UB149: launched 19 Sept 1918; commissioned 22 Oct 1918; surrendered 22 Nov 1918; broken up at Swansea, 1922.

UB150: launched 19 Oct 1918, commissioned 27

Mar 1919; surrendered (hull only); broken up at Rochester, 1922.

UB151: launched 1918; intended for use in the Mediterranean as Austro-Hungarian *U82*; broken up with *UB152* and *153*.

UB152: launched 1918; broken up with *UB151* and *153*.

UB153: launched 1918; broken up with *UB151* and *152*.

UB154: launched 7 Oct 1918, completed 14 Dec

1918; surrendered to France, 9 Mar 1919; broken up at Brest in July 1921.

UB155: launched 26 Oct 1918, completed 26 Feb 1919; surrendered to France, 9 Mar 1919; served as the French submarine Jean Corre; stricken 7 Oct 1937; broken up.

UB156–175: broken up in 1919 after provisional launching.

UB176, 177: construction contracts cancelled.

UB178–183: broken up in 1919 after provisional launching.

UB184–187: construction contracts cancelled.

UB188, 189: construction contracts cancelled after work had started; broken up.

UB190–195: construction contracts cancelled.

UB196–205: broken up on the slips, 1919.

UB206–249: construction contracts cancelled.

UC1 class coastal minelayers (Type UCI)

Name	Type	Builder (construction no)	Built	Cost in Marks (000s)	Displacement (t = tonnes T = tons)	Length (m)	Breadth (m)	Draught/ height (m)	Power (hp)	Revs (rpm)	Speed (kts)	Range (nm/kts)	Oil (t)	Diving time (sec)
UC1–10	UCI	Vulcan (H) (45–54)	1914–15		168t sf 183t sm 225t total	33.99 oa 29.62 ph	3.15 oa 3.15 ph	3.04/ 6.30	90ehp sf 175ehp sm	550 sf 635 sm	6.20 sf 5.22 sm	780/5 sf 50/4 sm	3 max	36 23 td
UC11–15	,,	Weser (225–229)	,,		168t sf 182t sm 225t total	33.99 oa 29.81 ph	,,	3.06/ 6.30	80ehp sf 175ehp sm	500 sf 585 sm	6.49 sf 5.67 sm	910/5 sf 50/4 sm	,,	45 23 td
(UC12 mod as Italian XI)		Arsenale Taranto	1916–17		171t sf 184t sm 225t total	33.6 oa 29.81 ph	,,	3.15/ 6.30	90ehp sf 175ehp sm	510 sf 585 sm	6.70 sf 5.67 sm	,,	,,	,,

Construction

Laid down as submersibles under War Contract C, official Design Project 34, 1914. Single hull; four watertight compartments; trim and regulating tanks 5.1cu m (*UC1–10*) or 5.6cu m (*UC11–15*); diving depth 50m. These vessels were known as Type UC I.

Propulsion

One Daimler (or Benz, *UC11–15*) 6-cylinder 4-stroke diesel pinnace engine together with one SSW double motor-dynamo in compartnemt 2; one 112 mass-cell Afag battery in compartment 3 below. One 3-bladed propeller, 1.08m (or 1.10m, *UC11–15*) diameter; four hydroplanes forward and two aft, the forward hydroplanes arranged in pairs one above the other directly forward of the forward hydroplane guard; one rudder.

Armament

No torpedo tubes; six 100cm mine-launching tubes - 12 Type UC120 mines; one machine gun - 150 rounds. One periscope in the conning tower.

[From 1916 *UC11* was fitted in addition with one 45cm torpedo tube at the stern above the CWL - 1 torpedo.]

Handling

This class was designed for coastal use only. All were poor sea-boats with limited manoeuvrability and average responsiveness.

Complement

Crew: 1/13; no boats.

Notes

UC12 and *13* were dismantled after trials at Kiel

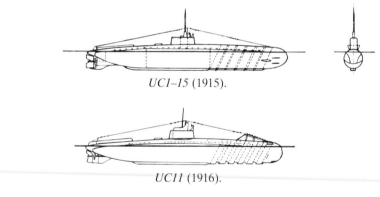

UC1–15 (1915).

UC11 (1916).

and transported in sections by rail to the Austro-Hungarian naval base at Pola for reassembly; *UC14* and *15* were transported to Pola without trials. *UC14* was subsequently returned by rail to the Imperial Dockyard at Ostend.

Careers

UC1: launched 26 Apr 1915, commissioned 7 May 1915; served in Flanders. Sunk in July 1917 off the coast of Flanders, by a mine; 17 dead (all crew lost).

UC2: launched 12 May 1915, commissioned 17 May 1915; served in Flanders. Sunk at 2140hrs on 2 Jul 1917 in the North Sea, in position 52° 28′N, 01° 48′E, after being rammed by the British steamship *Cottingham*; 15 dead (all crew lost). Raised in 1915 by a British salvage company; exhibited on the Thames and in other places; broken up.

UC3: launched 28 May 1915, commissioned 1 Jun 1915; served in Flanders. Sunk at 0500hrs on 27

May 1916 in the North Sea, in position 51° 35′N, 03° 08′E, by a mine; 18 dead (all crew lost).

UC4: launched 6 Jun 1915, commissioned 10 Jun 1915; served mainly in Flanders; scuttled on 5 Oct 1918 off the coast of Flanders, in position 51° 22′N, 03° 12′E, during the German evacuation of Belgium.

UC5: launched 13 Jun 1915, commissioned 19 Jun 1915; served in Flanders; scuttled at 1100hrs on 27 Apr 1916 in the Thames Estuary, in position 51° 59′N, 01° 38′E, after running aground; number of fatalities unknown. Raised and towed in by the British destroyer *Firedrake*; exhibited in British harbours; broken up.

UC6: launched 20 Jun 1915, commissioned 24 Jun 1915; served in Flanders. Sunk on 28 Sept 1917 in the Thames Estuary, in position 51° 30′N, 00° 34′E, by a mine net; 16 dead (all crew lost).

UC7: launched 6 Jul 1915, commissioned 9 Jul

1915; served in Flanders. Sunk on 6 Jul 1916 in the Thames Estuary, in position 51° 22′N, 01° 35′E, by depth charges from a British submarine chaser; 18 dead (all crew lost).

UC8: launched 6 Jul 1915, commissioned 5 Jul 1915; used for training; ran aground on the Dutch coast, 4 Nov 1915, in position 52° 23′N, 05° 05′E, while on passage to Flanders; interned at Nieuwediep and Alkmaar; ceded to the Netherlands; served as the Dutch submarine *M 1*, 13 Mar 1917; broken up 1932.

UC9: launched 11 Jul 1915, commissioned 15 Jul 1915; used for training; served in Flanders. Sunk on 21 Oct 1915 in the North Sea, in position 51° 47′N, 01° 37′E, by one of her own mines; 16 dead (all crew lost).

UC10: launched 15 Jul 1915, commissioned 17 Jul

1915; served in Flanders. Sunk at 1635hrs on 21 Aug 1916 in the North Sea, in position 52° 02′N, 03° 54′E, by a torpedo from the British submarine *E 54*; 18 dead (all crew lost).

UC11: launched 11 Apr 1915, commissioned 23 Apr 1915; served in Flanders. Sunk at 0945hrs on 26 Jun 1918 in the North Sea, in position 51° 55′N, 01° 41′E, by a mine; 19 dead.

UC12: launched 29 Apr 1915, commissioned 2 May 1915; served in the Mediterranean (for a time as the Austro-Hungarian transport U-boat *U24*). Sunk on 16 Mar 1916 near Taranto, in position 40° 27′N, 17° 11′E, by a mine from her own barrage; 15 dead (all crew lost). Raised by an Italian salvage company; converted 9 Dec 1916; served as the Italian submarine *X 1* from 13 Apr 1917; stricken 6 May 1919; broken up.

UC13: launched in May 1915, commissioned 15 May 1915; served in the Mediterranean as the Austro-Hungarian *U25*. Sank on 29 Nov 1915 in the Black Sea, in position 41° 09′N, 30° 30′E, after running aground in a heavy storm; number of fatalities unknown.

UC14: launched 13 May 1915, commissioned 5 Jun 1915; served in the Mediterranean as the Austro-Hungarian *U18*; transported to Flanders in 1916. Sunk on 3 Oct 1917 off the coast of Flanders, in position 51° 19′N, 02° 43′E, by a mine; 17 dead (all crew lost).

UC15: launched 19 May 1915, commissioned 28 Jun 1915; served in the Mediterranean as the Austro-Hungarian *U19*. Sunk on 14 or 15 Nov 1916 in the Black Sea, in position 45° 05′N, 29° 50′E, by a mine; 16 dead (all crew lost).

UC16 class coastal minelayers (Type UCII)

Construction

Laid down as submersibles under War Contracts C (*UC16–23*) and H (*UC34–79*), official Design Project 41, 1915. Double hull; seven watertight compartments; trim and regulating tanks 17.6cu m (*UC25–33, 40–48* and *74–79*), 19.7cu m (*UC16–24*), 20.3cu m (*UC34–39*), 20.7cu m (*UC49–54*), 18.4cu m (*UC55–60*), 18.9cu m (*UC61–64*) or 20.0cu m (*UC65–73*); diving depth 50m. These vessels were known as Type UCII.

Propulsion

Two 6-cylinder 4-stroke diesel engines together with two double motor-dynamos in compartment 2 (engine and motor-dynamo types are given in the table below); two 62 mass-cell Afag batteries in compartments 3 and 5 below. Two 3-bladed propellers (diameters are given in the table below); two hydroplanes forward and two aft in hydroplane guards; two parallel rudders.

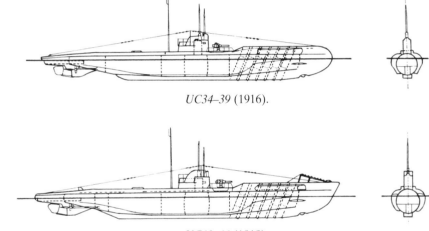

UC34–39 (1916).

UC61–66 (1918).

	Engine type	Motor-dynamo type	Propeller diameter
UC16–21	MAN	BB & Cie	1.23m
UC22–24	MAN-Blohm & Voss	BB & Cie	1.23m
UC25–27	MAN	SSW	1.30m
UC28–30	Daimler	SSW	1.30m
UC31–33	MAN	SSW	1.30m
UC34–36	MAN-Blohm & Voss	BB & Cie	1.24m
UC37–39	MAN	BB & Cie	1.24m
UC40–45	Körting	SSW	1.30m
UC46–48	MAN	SSW	1.29m
UC49–50	Körting	BB & Cie	1.25m
UC51–54	Daimler	BB & Cie	1.25m
UC55–57	Körting	BB & Cie	1.29m
UC58–60	Daimler	BB & Cie	1.29m
UC61–64	MAN	SSW	1.24m
UC65–69	MAN	SSW	1.29m
UC70–73	MAN-Blohm & Voss	SSW	1.29m
UC74–75	Körting	SSW	1.24m
UC76–79	Daimler	SSW	1.24m

Armament

Six 100cm mine-launching tubes - 18 Type UC200 mines; three 50cm torpedo tubes, two at the bow above the CWL and one at the stern below the CWL - 7 torpedoes; one Uk 8.8cm/30 gun - 100–133 rounds - plus one machine gun. One periscope in the conning tower and one in the control room.

[On certain boats in 1918 the gun armament was upgraded to one Utof 10.5cm/45 gun - 120 rounds.]

Handling

These vessels were intended for use on the high seas, but were poor sea-boats with limited manoeuvrability (though this was improved by the modified bow); they were responsive to the helm. The bow torpedo tubes at the sides of the forecastle created a lot of spray.

Complement

Crew: 3/23; one dinghy.

Notes

UC16–45, 55, 56 and *65–73* were completed with a rounded bow; after 1917 they received the shark-shaped bow (fitted on *UC49–54, 57–60* and *74–79*

Name	Type	Builder (construction no)	Built	Cost in Marks (000s)	Displacement (t = tonnes T = tons)	Length (m)	Breadth (m)	Draught/height (m)	Power (hp)	Revs (rpm)	Speed (kts)	Range (nm/kts)	Oil (t)	Diving time (sec)
UC16–24	UCII	B & V (266–274)	1915–16	1729	417t sf 493t sm 545t total	49.35 oa 39.30 ph 52.15 oa (mod)	5.22 oa 3.65 ph	3.68/ 7.46	500ehp sf 460ehp sm	500 sf 365 sm	11.6 sf 7.0 sm	9430/7 sf 55/4 sm	56/41	48 35 td
UC25–27	”	Vulcan (H) (64–66)	”	1727	400t sf 480t sm 550t total	49.45 oa 39.30 ph 51.12 oa (mod)	”	”	500ehp sf 460ehp sm	”	11.6 sf 6.7 sm	9260/7 sf 53/4 sm	55/41	56 48 td
UC28–30	”	” (67–69)	”	”	”	”	”	”	520ehp sf 460ehp sm	450 sf 365 sm	”	9410/7 sf 53/4 sm	”	”
UC31–33	”	” (70–72)	”	”	”	”	”	”	500ehp sf 460ehp sm	500 sf 365 sm	”	10,040/7 sf 53/4 sm	”	”
UC34–39	”	B & V (275–280)	”	1983	427t sf 509t sm c600t total	50.35 oa 40.30 ph 53.15 oa (mod)	”	3.65/ 7.98	600ehp sf 460ehp sm	550 sf 365 sm	11.6 sf 6.8 sm	10,108/7 sf 54/4 sm	55/40	48 35 td
UC40–45	”	Vulcan (H) (73–78)	”	1982	400t sf 480t sm 550t total	49.45 oa 40.30 ph 51.11 oa (mod)	”	3.68/ 7.46	520ehp sf 460ehp sm	”	11.7 sf 6.7 sm	9410/7 sf 60/4 sm	55/41	56 48 td
UC46–48	”	Weser (256–258)	”		420t sf 502t sm 625t total	51.85 oa 39.70 ph	”	3.67/ 7.46	600ehp sf 460ehp sm	”	11.7 sf 6.9 sm	7280/7 sf 54/4 sm	41 max	33
UC49–54	”	Germania (265–270)	1916–17		434t sf 511t sm 600t total	52.69 oa 40.96 ph	”	3.64/ 7.98	580ehp to 600ehp sf 620ehp sm	450 sf 385 sm	11.8 sf 7.2 sm	8820/7 to 9450/7 sf 56/4 sm	56/41	33 30 td
UC55–60	”	KWD (37–42)	”	1935	415t sf 498t sm 594t total	50.52 oa 40.86 ph 51.67 oa (mod)	”	3.61/ 7.98	”	”	11.6 sf 7.3 sm	8660/7 to 9450/7 sf 52/4 sm	”	”
UC61–64	”	Weser (259–262)	”		422t sf 504t sm 625t total	51.85 oa 39.70 ph	”	3.67/ 7.98	600ehp sf 620ehp sm	”	11.9 sf 7.2 sm	8000/7 sf 59.4 sm	43	”
UC65–73	”	B & V (281–289)	1916	2141	427t sf 508t sm c600t total	50.35 oa 40.30 ph 53.15 oa (mod)	”	3.64/ 7.98	”	”	12.0 sf 7.4 sm	10,420/7 sf 52/4 sm	56/41	48 35 td
UC74–79	”	Vulcan (H)	1916–17	2086	410t sf 493t sm 567t total	50.45 oa 40.30 ph 52.11 oa (mod)	”	3.65/ 7.98	600ehp to 580ehp sf 620ehp sm	”	11.8 sf 7.3 sm	10,230/7 to 8660/7 sf 52/4 sm	55/41	33 30 td

from commissioning) shown in the drawings. All these boats had an upper deck formed by a step above the tank decks.

Careers

UC16: launched 1 Feb 1916, commissioned 26 Jun 1916; served in Flanders. Sunk on 23 Oct 1917 in the Channel by a mine; 27 dead (all crew lost).

UC17: launched 19 Feb 1916, commissioned 23 Jul 1916; served in Flanders; surrendered on 26 Nov 1918; broken up at Preston, 1919–20.

UC18: launched 4 Mar 1916, commissioned 15 Aug 1916; served in Flanders. Sunk at 0712hrs on 19 Feb 1917 in the Channel, in position 49° 15'N, 02° 34'W, by gunfire from the British Q-ship *Lady Olive*; 28 dead (all crew lost).

UC19: launched 15 Mar 1916, commissioned 22 Aug 1916; served in Flanders. Sunk on 6 Dec 1916 in the Channel, in position 49° 41'N, 06° 31'W, by depth charges from the British destroyer *Ariel*; 25 dead (all crew lost).

UC20: launched 1 Apr 1916, commissioned 8 Sept 1916; served as a transport boat in the Mediterranean (as the Austro-Hungarian *U60*); surrendered on 16 Jan 1919; broken up at Preston, 1919–20.

UC21: launched 1 Apr 1916, commissioned 15 Sept 1916; served in Flanders. Sunk at the end of September or the beginning of October 1917, place and cause unknown; 27 dead (all crew lost).

UC22: launched 1 Feb 1916, commissioned 1 Jul

1916; served in the Mediterranean as the Austro-Hungarian *U62*; surrendered to France, 3 Feb 1919; broken up at Landerneau in July 1921.

UC23: launched 19 Feb 1916, commissioned 28 Jul 1916; served in the Mediterranean as the Austro-Hungarian *U63*; disarmed and surrendered 25 Nov 1918 at Sevastopol; became a French prize; broken up at Bizerta, in August 1921.

UC24: launched 4 Mar 1916, commissioned 17 Aug 1916; served in the Mediterranean from 1917 as the Austro-Hungarian *U88*. Sunk at 1125hrs on 24 May 1917 in the Adriatic Sea, in position 42° 06'N, 18° 09'E, by a torpedo from the French submarine *Circé*; 24 dead.

UC25: launched 10 Jun 1916, commissioned 28 Jun

1916; served in the Mediterranean from 1917 as the Austro-Hungarian *U89*; scuttled on 28 Oct 1918 at Pola, in position 44° 52′N, 13° 50′E, on the surrender of Austria-Hungary.

UC26: launched 22 Jun 1916, commissioned 18 Jul 1916; served in Flanders. Sunk on 9 May 1917 in the Thames Estuary, in position 51° 03′N, 01° 40′E, after being rammed and depth charged by the British destroyers *Milne*, *Mentor* and *Miranda*; 26 dead.

UC27: launched 28 Jun 1916, commissioned 25 Jul 1916; served in the Mediterranean from 1917 as the Austro-Hungarian *U90*; surrendered to France, 3 Feb 1919; broken up at Landerneau, in July 1921.

UC28: launched 8 Jul 1916, commissioned 6 Aug 1916; used for training; surrendered to France, 12 Feb 1919; broken up.

UC29: launched 15 Jul 1916, commissioned 15 Aug 1916. Sunk at 0830hrs on 7 Jun 1917 in the Atlantic, in position 51° 50′N, 11° 50′W, by gunfire from the British Q-ship *Pargust*; 25 dead.

UC30: launched 27 Jul 1916, commissioned 22 Aug 1916. Sunk on 19 Apr 1917 in the North Sea, in position 55° 20′N, 07° 15′E, by a mine; 27 dead (all crew lost).

UC31: launched 7 Aug 1916, commissioned 2 Sept 1916; surrendered 26 Nov 1918; broken up at Canning Town, 1922.

UC32: launched 12 Aug 1916, commissioned 13 Sept 1916. Sunk at 1800hrs on 23 Feb 1917 in the North Sea, in position 54° 55′N, 01° 20′W, after one of her own mines exploded in the shaft; 22 dead.

UC33: launched 26 Aug 1916, commissioned 25 Sept 1916. Sunk on 26 Sept 1917 off the south coast of Ireland, in position 51° 55′N, 06° 14′W, by ramming and gunfire from the British patrol boat *P 61*; 27 dead.

UC34: launched 6 May 1916, commissioned 26 Sept 1916; served in the Mediterranean as the Austro-Hungarian *U74*; scuttled on 30 Oct 1918 at Pola, in position 44° 52′N, 13° 50′E, on the surrender of Austria-Hungary.

UC35: launched 6 May 1916, commissioned 4 Oct 1916; served in the Mediterranean as the Austro-Hungarian *U75*. Sunk on 16 May 1918 off the SW coast of Sardinia, in position 39° 48′N, 07° 42′E, by gunfire from the French patrol boat *Ailly*; 25 dead.

UC36: launched 25 Jun 1916, commissioned 3 Nov 1916; served in Flanders as the Austro-Hungarian *U76*, as a reserve boat. Sunk on approximately 18 May 1917 in the North Sea, in position 51° 42′N, 03° 03′E, cause unknown; 27 dead (all crew lost).

UC37: launched 5 Jun 1916, commissioned 13 Oct 1916; served in the Mediterranean as the Austro-Hungarian *U77*; disarmed on 25 Nov 1918 in Sevastopol; surrendered in Malta, 1919; broken up, 1920.

UC38: launched 5 Jun 1916, commissioned 19 Oct 1916; served in the Mediterranean as the Austro-Hungarian *U78*. Sunk at 0850hrs on 14 Dec 1917 in the Gulf of Corinth, in position 38° 15′N, 22° 22′E, by gunfire and depth charges from escort vessels (probably ultimately by the destroyer *Lansquenet*) accompanying the French protected cruiser *Chateaurenault*, which *UC38* had just sunk; 9 dead.

UC39: launched 25 Jun 1916, commissioned 29 Oct 1916; served in Flanders. Sunk at 1620 on 8 Feb 1917 in the North Sea, in position 53° 56′N, 00° 06′E, by depth charges and gunfire from the British destroyer *Thrasher*; 7 dead.

UC40: launched 5 Sept 1916, commissioned 1 Oct 1916. Sank on 21 Jan 1919 in the North Sea, in position 54° 55′N, 04° 47′E after an accident while on passage to surrender; 1 dead.

UC41: launched 13 Sept 1916, commissioned 11 Oct 1916. Sunk at 1650hrs on 21 Aug 1917 in the North Sea, in position 56° 25′N, 02° 35′E, by her own mines and by depth charges from the British steam trawlers *Jacinth*, *Thomas Young* and *Chikara*; 27 dead (all crew lost).

UC42: launched 21 Sept 1916, commissioned 18 Nov 1916. Sunk on 10 Sept 1917 off the south coast of Ireland, in position 51° 44′N, 08° 12′W, after running into a barrage she had just laid; 27 dead (all crew lost).

UC43: launched 5 Oct 1916, commissioned 25 Oct 1916. Sunk at 1652hrs on 10 Mar 1917 in the Atlantic in position 60° 57′N 01° 11′W, by a torpedo from the British submarine *G 13*; 26 dead (all crew lost).

UC44: launched 10 Oct 1916, commissioned 4 Nov 1916. Sunk at 0030hrs on 5 Aug 1917 off the south coast of Ireland, in position 52° 07′N, 06° 59′W, by a mine; 29 dead. Raised by the British in July 1917; broken up.

UC45: launched 20 Oct 1916, commissioned 18 Nov 1916. Sank at 1109hrs on 17 Sept 1917 in the North Sea, in position 54° 09′N, 07° 35′E, after a diving accident; 30 dead (all crew lost). Raised 11 Apr 1918 by the salvage vessel *Oberelbe*; in service 24 Oct 1918; surrendered 24 Nov 1918; broken up at Preston, 1919–20.

UC46: launched 15 Jul 1916, commissioned 15 Sept 1916. Sunk at 0400hrs on 8 Feb 1917 in the Channel, in position 51° 07′N, 01° 39′E, by ramming and depth charges from the British destroyer *Liberty*; 23 dead (all crew lost).

UC47: launched 30 Aug 1916, commissioned 13 Oct 1916; served in Flanders. Sunk at 0623hrs on 18 Nov 1917 in the North Sea, in position 54° 03′N, 00° 23′E, by ramming and depth charges from the British patrol boat *P 57*; 28 dead (all crew lost).

UC48: launched 27 Sept 1916, commissioned 6 Nov 1916; served in Flanders; damaged by depth charges off El Ferrol, in position 43° 29′N, 08° 14′W, and interned; scuttled on 15 Mar 1919 near El Ferrol, in position 43° 31′N, 08° 25′W, while on passage to surrender.

UC49: launched 7 Nov 1916, commissioned 2 Dec 1916; served in Flanders. Sunk on 8 Aug 1918 7nm SSW of Berry Head, in approximate position 50° 20′N, 03° 30′E, by depth charges from the British destroyer *Opossum* and from seven motor boats; 31 dead (all crew lost).

UC50: launched 23 Nov 1916, commissioned 21 Dec 1916; served in Flanders. Sunk at 0530hrs on 4 Feb 1918 in the Channel in position 50° 49′N, 00° 59′E, by depth charges from the British destroyer *Zubian*; 29 dead (all crew lost).

UC51: launched 5 Dec 1916, commissioned 6 Jan 1917; served in Flanders. Sunk at 1135hrs on 17 Nov 1917 in the Channel, in position 50° 08′N, 03° 42′W, by a British mine; 29 dead (all crew lost).

UC52: launched 23 Jan 1917, commissioned 15 Mar 1917; served in the Mediterranean as the Austro-Hungarian *U94*; surrendered 16 Jan 1919; broken up at Morecambe, 1919–20.

UC53: launched 27 Feb 1917, commissioned 5 Apr 1917; served in the Mediterranean as the Austro-Hungarian *U95*; scuttled on 28 Oct 1918 at Pola, in position 44° 52′N, 13° 50′E, on the surrender of Austria-Hungary.

UC54: launched 20 Mar 1917, commissioned 10 May 1917; served in the Mediterranean as the Austro-Hungarian *U96*; scuttled on 28 Oct 1918 at Trieste, in position 45° 39′N, 13° 45′E, on the surrender of Austria-Hungary.

UC55: launched 2 Aug 1916, commissioned 15 Nov 1916. Sunk on 29 Sept 1917 near Lerwick, in position 60° 02′N, 01° 02′W, by gunfire and depth charges from the British steam trawler *Moravia* and the destroyers *Sylvia* and *Tyrade* after being damaged by heavy seas; 10 dead.

UC56: launched 26 Aug 1916, commissioned 18 Dec 1916; served in Flanders, 1918; interned 23 May 1918 at Santander, in position 43° 28′N, 03° 48′W, after suffering mechanical damage; surrendered to France at Cherbourg, 26 Mar 1919; broken up at Rochefort, 1923.

UC57: launched 7 Sept 1916, commissioned 22 Jan 1917. Sunk on approximately 19 Nov 1917 in the Gulf of Finland, in position 59°N, 23°E, by a Russian mine; 27 dead. Found on the coast of Estonia after 1918.

UC58: launched 21 Oct 1916, commissioned 12 Mar 1917; surrendered to France, 24 Nov 1918; broken up at Cherbourg, 1921.

UC59: launched 28 Sept 1916, commissioned 12 May 1917; surrendered 21 Nov 1918; broken up at Bo'ness, 1919–20.

UC60: launched 8 Nov 1916, commissioned 25 Jun 1917; used for training, 1918; surrendered 23 Feb 1919; broken up at Rainham, 1921.

UC61: launched 11 Nov 1916, commissioned 13 Dec 1916; served in Flanders; scuttled on 26 Jul 1917 in the Channel, in position 50° 53′N, 53°E, after running aground.

UC62: launched 9 Dec 1916, commissioned 8 Jan 1917; served in Flanders. Sunk in mid-October 1917 near Portland by a British mine; 30 dead (all crew lost).

UC63: launched 6 Jan 1917, commissioned 30 Jan 1917; served in Flanders. Sunk at 0114hrs on 1 Nov 1917 in the Channel, in position 51° 23′N, 02° 00′E, by a torpedo from the British submarine *E 52*; 26 dead.

UC64: launched 27 Jan 1917, commissioned 22 Feb 1917; served in Flanders. Sunk at 0415hrs on 20 Jun 1918 in the Channel, in position 50° 58′N, 01° 23′E, by a mine; 30 dead (all crew lost).

UC65: launched 8 Jul 1916, commissioned 10 Nov 1916; served in Flanders. Sunk at 1610hrs on 3 Nov 1917 in the Channel, in position 50° 31′N, 00° 27′E, by a torpedo from the British submarine *C 15*; 22 dead.

UC66: launched 15 Jul 1916, commissioned 18 Nov 1916; intended for use in the Mediterranean as the Austro-Hungarian *U66*, but remained in Flanders. Sunk on 12 Jun 1917 in the Channel, in position 49° 45′N, 05° 10′W, by depth charges from the British steam trawler *Sea King*; 23 dead.

UC67: launched 6 Aug 1916, commissioned 10 Dec 1916; served in the Mediterranean as the Austro-Hungarian *U91*; surrendered 16 Jan 1919; broken up at Briton Ferry, 1919–20.

UC68: launched 12 Aug 1916, commissioned 17 Dec 1916; served in Flanders. Sunk on 13 Mar 1917 6nm ENE of Star Point, in position 50° 17′N, 03° 32′W, by her own mine while laying a barrage; 27 dead (all crew lost).

UC69: launched 7 Aug 1916, commissioned 23 Dec 1916; intended for use in the Mediterranean as the Austro-Hungarian *U69*, but remained in Flanders. Sank at 2015hrs on 6 Jun 1917 in the Channel in position 49° 57′N, 01° 10′W, after a collision with *U96*; 11 dead.

UC70: launched 7 Aug 1916, commissioned 22 Nov 1916; served in Flanders. Sunk at 0530hrs on 5 Jun 1917 near Ostende, in position 51° 14′N, 02° 55′E, by gunfire from British monitors. Raised and repaired; served in the Flanders U-boat flotilla, from January 1918. Sunk at 1525hrs on 28 Aug 1918 in the North Sea, in position 54° 32′N, 00° 40′W, by depth charges from the British destroyer *Ouse*; 31 dead (all crew lost).

UC71: launched 12 Aug 1916, commissioned 28 Nov 1916; served in Flanders. Sank on 20 Feb 1919 in the North Sea, in position 54° 10′N, 07° 54′E, after an accident while on passage to surrender.

UC72: launched 12 Aug 1916, commissioned 5 Dec 1916; served in Flanders. Sunk on 20 Aug 1919 in the Thames Estuary, in approximate position 46°N, 08° 48′W, by the Q-ship *Acton*; 31 dead (all crew lost).

UC73: launched 26 Aug 1916, commissioned 24 Dec 1916; served in the Mediterranean as the Austro-Hungarian *U92*; occasionally used as a transport boat; surrendered 16 Jan 1919; broken up at Briton Ferry, 1919–20.

UC74: launched 19 Oct 1916, commissioned 26 Nov 1916; served in the Mediterranean as the Austro-Hungarian *U93*; interned at Barcelona, 21 Nov 1918, after running short of fuel oil; surrendered to France, 26 Mar 1919; broken up at Toulon, July 1921.

UC75: launched 6 Nov 1916, commissioned 6 Dec 1916; served in Flanders from 1917. Sunk at 0230hrs on 31 May 1918 in the North Sea, in position 53° 57′N, 00° 09′E, by ramming and gunfire from the British destroyer *Fairy*; 19 dead.

UC76: launched 25 Nov 1916, commissioned 17 Dec 1916. Sunk at 1300hrs on 10 May 1917 near Heligoland, in position 54° 10.5′N, 07° 54′E, by the explosion of one of her own mines in the launching tube; 15 dead. Raised by the salvage vessel *Oberelbe*, 10 May 1917; used for training from 11 Jul 1918; interned at Karlskrona, 13 Nov 1918; surrendered 1 Dec 1918; broken up at Briton Ferry, 1919–20.

UC77: launched 2 Dec 1916, commissioned 29 Dec 1916; served in Flanders from 1917. Sunk in July 1918, in the Channel, place and cause unknown; 30 dead (all crew lost).

UC78: launched 8 Dec 1916, commissioned 10 Jan 1917; served in Flanders. Sunk in May 1918 in the Channel, place and cause unknown; 29 dead (all crew lost).

UC79: launched 19 Dec 1916, commissioned 22 Jan 1917; served in Flanders from 1917. Sunk in April 1918 in the Channel, in approximate position 48° 17′N, 05° 16′W, possibly by a mine; 30 dead (all crew lost).

UC80 class coastal minelayers (Type UCIII)

Name	Type	Builder (construction no)	Built	Cost in Marks (000s)	Displacement (t = tonnes T = tons)	Length (m)	Breadth (m)	Draught/ height (m)	Power (hp)	Revs (rpm)	Speed (kts)	Range (nm/kts)	Oil (t)	Diving time (sec)
UC80–86	UCIII	KWD (49–55)	1917–		474t sf 560t sm 730t total	56.10 oa 42.20 ph	5.54 oa 3.65 ph	3.76/ 7.98	600ehp sf 770ehp sm	450 sf 455 sm	11.5 sf* 6.6 sm*		64/52	15 td
UC87–89	"	Weser (320–322)	"		480t sf 566t sm 735t total	"	"	3.66/ 7.96	580ehp sf 770ehp sm	"	"		67/56	"
UC90–118	"	B & V (324–352)	1917–18 and 1918–	3303	491t sf 571t sm 727t total	56.51 oa 42.20 ph	"	3.77/ 7.98	600ehp sf 770ehp sm	"	"	9850/7 sf* 40/4.5 sm*	"	"
UC119–138	"	B & V (365–384)	1918–		511t sf 582t sm 748t total	57.10 oa 42.20 ph	"	"	"	"	"	"	"	"
UC139–152	"	KWD (56–69)	"		474t sf 564t sm 730t total	56.85 oa 42.20 ph	5.80 oa 3.65 ph	3.76/ 7.98	580ehp sf 770ehp sm	"	"		64/52	30
UC153–192	"	B & V (415–454)	"		511t sf 582t sm 748t total	57.10 oa 42.20 ph	5.54 oa 3.65 ph	3.77/ 7.98	600ehp sf 770ehp sm	"	"	9850/7 sf* 40/4.5 sm*	67/56	15 td

* Design figures only.

Construction

Laid down as submersibles under War Contracts S (*UC80–118*), V (*UC118–152*) and AC (*UC153–192*), official Design Project 41A. Double hull; seven watertight compartments; trim and regulating tanks 28.2cu m; diving depth 75m.

UC80–114 (1918).

Propulsion

Two Benz (or Körting, *UC87-89* and *139–152*; or MAN, *UC90–138* and *153–192*) 6-cylinder 4-stroke diesel engines in compartment 2 forward; two SSW double motor-dynamos; two 62 mass-cell Afag batteries in compartments 3 and 5. Two 3-bladed propellers, 1.29m diameter; two hydroplanes forward and two aft in hydroplane guards; two parallel rudders.

Armament

Six 100cm mine-launching tubes - 14 UC 200 mines; three 50cm torpedo tubes, two at the bow above the CWL (allowing bow launches almost directly ahead) and one at the stern below the CWL - 7 torpedoes; one Uk 8.8cm/30 gun - 230 rounds - or one Utof 10.5cm/45 gun - 150 rounds.

Handling

Intended for use on the high seas, this class offered rather better seakeeping, manoeuvrability and responsiveness than the previous types. The side-mounted torpedo tubes nevertheless caused a broad, clearly visible wake and a reduction in speed during surface travel. Stability when submerged was poorer than on the Type UC II.

Complement

Crew: 3/29; one dinghy.

Notes

This class had an upper deck formed by a step above the tank decks.

Careers

UC80–86: construction not completed; broken up at Helling. *UC83* had been intended for use in the Mediterranean from 21 Nov 1916 (Austro-Hungarian navy number unknown).

UC87–80: launched 1918; broken up.

UC90: launched 19 Jan 1918, commissioned 15 Jul 1918; interned at Karlskrona, 13 Nov 1918; surrendered to Japan, 1 Dec 1918; served as the Japanese submarine *O 4*, 1920–21; broken up at Kure, 1921.

UC91: launched 19 Jan 1918, commissioned 31 Jul 1918. Sank on 5 Sept 1918 in the Baltic Sea, in position 54° 21′N, 10° 10′E, after a collision with the steamship *Alexandra Woermann*; 17 dead. Raised on 6 Sept 1918 by the salvage vessel *Vulcan*, and repaired. Sank on 10 Feb 1919 in the North Sea, in position 54° 15′N, 03° 56′E, after an accident while on passage to surrender.

UC92: launched 19 Jan 1918, commissioned 24 Nov 1918; surrendered 24 Nov 1918; broken up at Falmouth, 1921.

UC93: launched 19 Feb 1918, commissioned 22 Aug 1918; surrendered to Italy, 26 Nov 1918; broken up at La Spezia in August 1919.

UC94: launched 19 Feb 1918, commissioned 31 Aug 1918; surrendered to Italy, 26 Nov 1918; broken up at Taranto in April 1919.

UC95: launched 19 Feb 1918, commissioned 16 Sept 1918; surrendered 22 Nov 1918; broken up at Fareham, 1922.

UC96: launched 17 Mar 1918, commissioned 25 Sept 1918; surrendered 24 Nov 1918; broken up at Morecambe, 1919–20.

UC97: launched 17 Mar 1918, commissioned 6 Sept 1918; surrendered to USA, 22 Nov 1918; used for exhibitions to raise War Loans from New York, via Halifax and the St Lawrence seaway to harbours along the Great Lakes. Sunk on 7 Jun 1921 by gunfire from the US training ship *Willmette*, during tests on Lake Michigan.

UC98: launched 17 Mar 1918, commissioned 10 Sept 1918; surrendered to Italy, 24 Nov 1918; broken up at La Spezia in April 1919.

UC99: launched 17 Mar 1918, commissioned 20 Sept 1918; surrendered to Japan, 22 Nov 1918; served as the Japanese submarine *O 5*, 1920–21; broken up at Sasebo, 1921.

UC100: launched 14 Apr 1918, commissioned 1 Oct 1918; surrendered to France, 22 Nov 1918; broken up at Cherbourg, 1921.

UC101: launched 14 Apr 1918, commissioned 8 Oct 1918; surrendered 24 Nov 1918; broken up at Dordrecht, 1922.

UC102: launched 17 Apr 1918, commissioned 15 Oct 1918; surrendered 22 Nov 1918; broken up at Dordrecht, 1922.

UC103: launched 14 Apr 1918, commissioned 21 Oct 1918; intended for use in the Mediterranean as the Austro-Hungarian *U99*; surrendered to France, 22 Nov 1918; broken up at Cherbourg, 1921.

UC104: launched 25 May 1918, commissioned 18 Oct 1918; surrendered to France, 24 Nov 1918; broken up at Brest in July 1921.

UC105: launched 25 May 1918, commissioned 28 Oct 1918; surrendered 22 Nov 1918; broken up at Swansea, 1922.

UC106: launched 25 May 1918, commissioned 18 Mar 1919; surrendered (without engines and torpedoes) to Britain; broken up at Felixstowe, 1921.

UC107: launched 2 Jun 1918, commissioned 18 Mar 1919; surrendered (without engines and torpedoes) to France; broken up at Brest, 1921.

UC108: launched 2 Jun 1918, commissioned 18 Mar 1919; intended for use in the Mediterranean as the Austro-Hungarian *U100*; surrendered (without engines and torpedoes) to Britain; broken up at Felixstowe, 1921.

UC109: launched 2 Jun 1918, commissioned 24 Apr 1919; surrendered (without engines and torpedoes) to Britain; broken up at Felixstowe, 1921.

UC110: launched 6 Jul 1918, commissioned 18 Mar 1919; surrendered (without engines and torpedoes) to Britain; sank in 1921, while being transferred to Felixstowe.

UC111: launched 6 Jul 1918, commissioned 18 Mar 1919; surrendered (without engines and torpedoes) to Britain; broken up at Felixstowe, 1921.

UC112: launched 6 Jul 1918, commissioned 18 Mar 1919; surrendered (without engines and torpedoes) to Britain; broken up at Felixstowe, 1921.

UC113: launched 6 Jul 1918, commissioned 18 Mar 1919; surrendered (without engines and torpedoes) to Britain; broken up at Newcastle-upon-Tyne, 1921.

UC114: launched 11 Aug 1918, commissioned 18 Mar 1919; surrendered (without engines and torpedoes) to Britain; broken up at Newcastle-upon-Tyne, 1921.

UC115–118: launched 11 Aug 1918; not completed; broken up at the dockyard. *UC116* had been intended for use in the Mediterranean as the Austro-Hungarian *U78*.

UC119: launched 1918; broken up at Hamburg-Moorburg, 1919.

UC120: launched 1918; broken up at Hamburg-Moorburg, 1919. Intended for use in the Mediterranean as Austro-Hungarian *U83*.

UC121: launched 1918; broken up at Hamburg-Moorburg, 1919.

UC122–124: launched 1 Oct 1918; broken up at Hamburg-Moorburg, 1919.

UC125–128: launched 8 Dec 1918; not completed; broken up at the dockyard.

UC129–138: broken up on the slips.

UC139–192: construction contracts cancelled.

UF1 class coastal U-boats (Type UF)

Name	Type	Builder (construction no)	Built	Cost in Marks (000s)	Displacement (t = tonnes T = tons)	Length (m)	Breadth (m)	Draught/ height (m)	Power (hp)	Revs (rpm)	Speed (kts)	Range (nm/kts)	Oil (t)	Diving time (sec)
UF1–92	UF	*	1918–		381t or 364t sf c410t sm 499t total	44.60 oa	4.44 oa	3.95/	600ehp sf 620ehp sm	450 sf 360 sm	11.0 sf 7.0 sm	3500/7 sf 64/4 sm	26/10	

* Builders and construction numbers as follows: *UF1–20* Schichau (E) (1023–1042), *UF21–32* Tecklenborg (323–334), *UF33–38* Atlas (169–174), *UF39–44* Neptun (436–441), *UF45–48* Seebeck (420–423), *UF49–60* Tecklenborg (339–350), *UF61–72* Seebeck (426–437), *UF73–76* Atlas (175–178), *UF77–80* Neptun (444–447) and *UF81–92* Schichau (E) (1064–1075).

Construction

Designed as submersibles for construction under War Contracts X (*UF1–48*) and AF (*UF49–92*), official Design Project 48a, 1917–18. Single hull; probably four watertight compartments; trim and regulating tank capacity unknown; diving depth 75m. These vessels were known as Type UF.

Propulsion

Two Benz, MAN, Körting, Daimler or Linke-Hoffmann-Junkers 6-cylinder 4-stroke diesel engines in compartment 2 forward; two SSW or BB & Cie double motor-dynamos; two 62 mass-cell Afag batteries in compartment 3 below. Two 3-bladed propellers, diameter unknown; two hydroplanes forward and two aft; one rudder.

Armament

Five 50cm torpedo tubes, four at the bow, below the CWL and one at the stern, above the CWL - 7 torpedoes; one Uk 8.8cm/30 gun - (180 rounds); one machine gun.

Handling

These boats were intended for coastal use, mainly in the North Sea.

Complement

Crew: 2/28.

Notes

This design formed the basis for the 1933–4 Type II design (see page 39).

Careers

Those boats on which construction had started were broken up on the stocks; the other contracts were cancelled.

UG1 class coastal U-boats (Type UG)

Name	Type	Builder (construction no)	Built	Cost in Marks (000s)	Displacement (t = tonnes T = tons)	Length (m)	Breadth (m)	Draught/ height (m)	Power (hp)	Revs (rpm)	Speed (kts)	Range (nm/kts)	Oil (t)	Diving time (sec)
UG1–101	UG	*			640t sf	64.0 oa	6.2 oa	4.0/	1900ehp sf 1100ehp sm		14.5 sf 8.0 sm	8000/6 sf 90/3 sm	75 max	

* Construction was planned at the following yards: Vulcan (H), Tecklenborg, Neptun, Atlas, Seebeck, Nordsee and Flensburg.

Construction

Designed as submersibles, as a type design only (with no detailed design work undertaken), official Design Project 51A. Mixed hull type with saddle tanks; seven watertight compartments; trim and regulating tank capacity unknown; diving depth 100m. This design was known as the Type UG.

Propulsion

Similar to the Type UB III, but with more powerful electric motors and supercharged diesel engines; two 62 mass-cell Afag batteries (total battery weight 67t); two hydroplanes forward and two aft; one rudder.

Armament

Six 50cm torpedo tubes, four at the bow above the CWL and two at the stern below the CWL - 12 torpedoes; one Uk 10.5cm/45 gun.

Handling

Suitable for use as for the Type UB III, particularly against convoys in the waters around Great Britain.

Complement

Crew: 3/34.

Notes

See the Type VII (page 43).

Careers

No construction orders were placed. It was intended that these vessels should be built as part of the 1920 construction programme, in conjunction with the Type UF.

U-boats up to 1918: weights and displacements as built

Weight (%)	UB I	UB II	UB III	UF	UC I	UC II	UC III	Proj. 38	Proj. 45	Proj. 46 A
Hull	44.5	44.1	42.6	44.4	46.0	45.0	42.8	43.2	45.2	49.1
Machinery	28.7	31.9	32.4	32.3	22.9	26.0	30.0	27.4	26.0	30.4
Torpedoes	4.8	4.0	5.2	5.4	–	3.5	3.0	0.9	3.3	1.7
Guns	0.2	0.7	1.1	2.4	–	1.0	2.3	1.1	3.2	2.6
Mines	–	–	–	–	7.9	3.5	2.5	4.0	3.3	–
Inventory	1.6	1.9	1.7	1.3		1.6	1.1	0.8	0.7	} 2.9
Materials and lubricating oil	0.4	1.3	1.1	} 3.2	} 8.7	1.4	1.4	1.7	0.9	
Crew, provisions and water	3.1	2.7	2.9			2.8	2.6	4.5	3.2	1.4
Fuel oil (normal load)	2.8	8.4	6.8	2.8		9.2	11.6	8.8	8.0	5.9
Ballast and reserve	13.9	5.0	6.2	8.2	14.5	6.0	2.7	7.6	5.4	6.0
Total weight (t)	127.0	263.0	516.0	359.5	177.0	417.0	480.0	763.0	1172.0	2144.5

Displacement (%)	UB I	UB II	UB III	UF	UC I	UC II	UC III	Proj. 38	Proj. 45	Proj. 46 A
Load-bearing hull volumes	94.0	82.6	75.4		94.9	75.1	70.4	96.0	73.9	
External pressure-tight tanks	–	–	8.6		} 5.1	} 13.7	} 16.4	–	5.2	
Superstructure	7.5	9.7	8.4					} 4.0	11.6	
Fuel oil	–	7.7	7.6		–	11.2	13.2		9.3	
Total displacement submerged, excluding diving tanks, γ = 1.0 (cu m)	127.5	263.5	517.0		178.0	418.0	481.0	764.0	1155.9	
Reserve buoyancy	0.5	0.5	1.0		1.0	1.0	1.0	1.0	1.0*	
Surface stability	0.24	0.39	0.55	0.25†	0.25	0.455	0.53	0.37	0.44	
Submerged stability	0.35	0.23	0.18		0.35	0.18	0.13	0.34	0.19	

* γ = 1.015
† with full auxiliary bunkers (total displacement 380.95t)

Distinguishing features of U-boats, 1914–1918

The following notes on the external appearance of U-boats apply in general to all vessels up to 1918:

The colour scheme was grey overall, occasionally with black decks, but camouflage was applied in wartime.

Fixed bridge protection was eventually fitted on all types, but the older vessels were built merely with guardrails covered in tarpaulins. Numerous other minor modifications were made. At the beginning of 1915 older vessels were fitted with quick-diving equipment, fitted above the tank decks on either side of the conning tower. Other changes included the shortening or removal of air intake masts, radio masts, exhaust pipes and (from 1915) anti-net antennae: see the individual drawings and class notes.

Conning tower ▼	Hull ▶		
forward, no addition	U71–80	U43–50
forward with additional structure	U1	U87–92
aft, no addition	UC1–15, UB12	
aft with additional structure	U2–4, 9–22	U81–86, 93–98, 105–114
amidships, no addition	U139–142, 151–157, UB18–47	U117–126
amidships with additional structure	U5–8, 23–41, 51–56, 66–70, 99–104, UA, UB1–12*, all other UB boats from UB16 onwards	U57–65, 135–138, 160–172

Bow ▼ Stern ▶

			(A)
			(B)
U2, 3–4, 9–12*	(U151–157), (UA), (U9)		
U5–8, 13–18, [23–26], (31–41)	(U51–56), (66–70)		
	U43–50	U87–92	
U1, [19–22], [27–30]			
	(U57–62)	(U99–104)	
[U71–80]*	(U63–65)		UB1–12* (A), 13–17 (A), 18–47 (B) UC1–15 (A)
U139–142, (75), (79)	(U160–172)	(U117–126), (135–138), (UB60–65), (72–75), (88) (UC79)	UB48–59 (B), 66–71 (B), 76–87 (B)
UC16–24*, 25–33*			
UC16–79 as completed, or after modification			

Key:
[ ] modified from two rudders to one.
( ) no upper rudder.
* later rebuilt.

Foreign U-boats (1914–1918)

US1 class (ex-Russian)

Name	Type	Builder (construction no)	Built	Cost in Marks (000s)	Displacement (t = tonnes T = tons)	Length (m)	Breadth (m)	Draught/ height (m)	Power (hp)	Revs (rpm)	Speed (kts)	Range (nm/kts)	Oil (t)	Diving time (sec)
US1, 2		Russud	1915–17		650t sf 785t sm	67.96 oa	4.47 oa	3.86/ —	2640ehp sf 900ehp sm		17 sf 8 sm	900/17 sf 25/8 sm	40 max	150
US3, 4		Baltic; assembly by Nikolayev	1916–17		,,	,,	,,	,,	500 sf 900 sm		10 sf 8.5 sm	3000/10 sf 25/8 sm	40 max	150

Construction
Laid down as Russian submarines of the *Morzh* class (improved *Bars* class), designed by Bubnov. Single hull; diving depth 45m.

Propulsion
Two 250hp diesel engines taken from Amur River gunboats (*US3* and *US4*); two electric motors; two propellers.

Armament
Four 457mm torpedo tubes, two at the bow and two at the stern; four Drzewiecki torpedo drop-collars; one (or two, *US3*, *4*) 7.5cm gun; one 3.7cm Hotchkiss AA gun.

Complement
Crew: 1/13 (from *UB14*).

Careers
US1: launched 1916 as the Russian submarine *Burevestnik*; captured by Germany in Sevastopol, 2 May 1918; renamed *US1*; not used. Renamed as the Russian submarine *Burevestnik*; served in Wrangel's squadron; interned at Bizerta, 29 Dec 1920; broken up.

US2: launched 1917 as the Russian submarine *Orlan*; captured by Germany in Sevastopol, 2 May 1918; renamed *US2*; not used. Scuttled on 6 Apr 1919 by White Russian and Allied troops during the evacuation of Sevastopol. Raised and broken up.

US3: launched 1916 as the Russian submarine *Utka*; captured by Germany in Sevastopol, 2 May 1918; renamed *US3*; trial voyage, 13 Jun 1918; in service, 1 Aug 1918; not used. Renamed as the Russian submarine *Utka* in November 1918, served in Wrangel's squadron; interned at Bizerta, 29 Dec 1920; broken up.

US4: launched 7 Oct 1916, commissioned July 1916 as the Russian submarine *Gargara*; captured by Germany in Sevastopol, 2 May 1918; renamed *US4*; trial voyages, 17 and 25 May 1918; in service, 1 Aug 1918; not used. Renamed as the Russian submarine *Gargara* in November 1918; served in Wrangel's squadron; interned at Bizerta, 29 Dec 1920; broken up.

The submarines *Tyulen* and *Kashalot*; *AG 21* (incomplete); *Kit*, *Narval* and *Karp* (under repair); *Nalim*, *Skat*, *Losos*, *Sudak* and *Karas* (under the independent Ukrainian flag) were also captured in Sevastopol. No German source references have been found regarding the uses to which these vessels were put.

U-boats 1935–1945

Until German submarine construction was officially resumed in 1935, all development work was carried out under the guise of 'Research and development of motor boats'. Types I–VII were thus originally code names for designs, and only later became established Type names for U-boats.

Type I A U-boats

Name	Type	Builder (construction no)	Built	Cost in Marks (000s)	Displacement (t = tonnes T = tons)	Length (m)	Breadth (m)	Draught/ height (m)	Power (hp)	Revs (rpm)	Speed (kts)	Range (nm/kts)	Oil (t)	Diving time (sec)
U25, 26	I A	Deschimag W (903–904)	1935–36	4.5 each	862t sf 983t sm 1200t total	72.39 oa 55.2 ph	6.21 oa 4.28 ph	4.30/	2900ehp to 3080ehp sf 1000ehp sm	470 to 485 sf 310 sm	17.75 to 18.6 sf 8.30 sm	7900/10 6700/12 3300/ 17.75 sf 136/2 78/4 sm	84.6/ 21.8 96.0 max	55 30 td (mod)

Construction

Laid down as ocean-going submersibles, designed c1933–34. Double hull; seven watertight compartments; trim tanks in compartments 1 and 7; diving depth 100/200m. Official displacement 712 tonnes.

Propulsion

Two MAN 8-cylinder 4-stroke M 8 V 40/46 unsupercharged diesel engines; two BBC GG UB 720/8 double electric motors, maximum 530ehp, in compartment 2; two 62-cell AFA 36 MAK 740 batteries (9620 amp/hr) in battery boxes without rubber shock absorbers in compartments 3 and 5 below; diesel-electric range 8100nm at 10kts. Two 3-bladed propellers, 1.65m diameter; two hydroplanes forward and two aft; one rudder. Schnorkels were never fitted to these boats.

Armament

Six 53.8cm torpedo tubes, four at the bow and two at the stern, all below the CWL - 14 torpedoes, or up to 28 TMA (= 42 TMB) mines; one 10.5cm/45

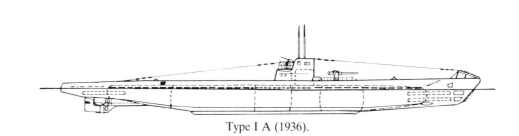
Type I A (1936).

gun - 150 rounds; one 2cm/30–37 AA gun - 200 rounds. One periscope in the tower and one in the control room.

Complement

Crew: 4/39.

Notes

The design history for these submarines stretches back to 1928. The Turkish *Gür* (previously the Spanish *E 1*) can be considered a predecessor.

Careers

U25: launched 14 Feb 1936, commissioned 6 Apr 1936. Sunk 3 Aug 1940 north of Terschelling, in position 54° 00'N, 05° 00'E, by one of her own mines; 49 dead (all crew lost).

U26: launched 14 Mar 1936, commissioned 11 May 1936. Sunk 1 Jul 1940 in the north Atlantic, in position 48° 03'N, 11° 30'W, by the British corvette *Gladiolus* and Australian bombs.

Type II A–D small U-boats

Construction

Laid down as coastal submersibles, 1933–34 design with later improvements. Single hull; three watertight compartments; diving tanks in compartment 2 below, fuel oil bunker immediately aft, trim tanks in compartments 1 and 3; diving depth 80/150m. Official displacement 250 tonnes.

Propulsion

Two MWM RS 127 S 6-cylinder 4-stroke unsupercharged diesel engines in compartment 2 below; two SSW PG VV 332/36 double commutator-type electric motors in compartment 1; one 62-cell AFA 36 MAK 580 battery in battery boxes without rubber shock absorbers (7160amp/hrs) (or one 62-cell AFA 44 MAL 570 battery (8380 amp/hrs), *U2, 6, 8, 11, 17, 57, 58* and *137–152*; or one 62-cell AFA 30 POR 580 battery (6370amp/hrs), with later conversion to type 44 MAL 570 envisaged, *U120* and *121*). Two 3-bladed propellers, 0.85m diameter; hydroplanes and rudders as for the Type IA.

[*U57* and *58* were used as schnorkel trials boats,

and schnorkels were later fitted to a few Type IID boats (for instance, *U149*).]

Armament

Three 53.3cm torpedo tubes at the bow below the CWL - 5 torpedoes or up to 12 TMA (18 TMB) mines; one 2cm/30 AA gun - 1200 rounds. One periscope in the conning tower.

[From 1944 the AA armament was increased to two twin 2cm/30 guns - 1200 rounds.]

Name	Type	Builder (construction no)	Built	Cost in Marks (000s)	Displacement (t = tonnes T = tons)	Length (m)	Breadth (m)	Draught/ height (m)	Power (hp)	Revs (rpm)	Speed (kts)	Range (nm/kts)	Oil (t)	Diving time (sec)
U1–6	II A	DWK (236–241)	1934–35	1.5 each	254t sf 303t sm 381t total	40.90 oa 27.80 ph	4.08 oa 4.00 ph	3.83/ 8.60	700ehp sf 360ehp sm	476 sf 360 sm	13.0 sf 6.9 sm	1600/8 1050/12 sf 35/4 sm	11.61 max	45 25 td (mod)
U7–12	II B	Germania (541–546)	1935		279t sf 328t sm 414t total	42.70 oa 28.20 ph	"	3.90/ 8.60	"	"	13.0 sf 7.0 sm	3100/8 1800/12 sf 35–43/4 sm	21.05 max	35 25 td (mod)
U13–16	"	DWK (248–251)	1935–36		"	"	"	"	"	"	"	"	"	"
U17–24	"	Germania (547–554)	"		"	"	"	"	"	"	"	"	"	"
U120, 121	"	Flender (268, 269)	1939–40		"	"	"	"	"	"	"	"	"	"
U56–63	II C	DWK (254–257 and 259–262)	1937–40	2063	291t sf 341t sm 435t total	43.90 oa 29.60 ph	"	3.82/ 8.40	700ehp sf 410ehp sm	476 sf 375 sm	12.0 sf 7.0 sm	3800/8 1900/12 sf 35–42/4 sm	22.70 max	25 td
U137–152	II D	" (266–281)	1939–40		314t sf 364t sm 460t total	43.97 oa 29.80 ph	4.92 oa 4.00 ph	3.93/ 8.40	"	470 sf 375 sm	12.7 sf 7.4 sm	5650/8 3450/12 sf 100/2 56/4 sm	38.30/ 36.0	"

Complement

Crew: 3/22.

Notes

These submarines were based on the 1918 Type UF vessels; the Finnish submarine *Vesikko* may be considered a prototype. The main external differences between the types were that the Types II A and B had seven flooding slots forward and twelve aft on either side, and the Types II C and D two parallel, stepped rows of flooding slots (10 above, 14 below) and interpolated holes (5 and 19 amidships and 12 in one row aft behind the exhaust).

From 1939–40 the Type IIA had two rows of flooding slots (18 above, 4, 5 and 2 below) running aft from the bows; the Type IIB had flooding slots reaching up to the centreline (43 above, 3 and 13 below).

Black Sea submarines from summer 1943 had enlarged bridges for two 2cm AA guns (later two 2cm twin AA guns). From 1941–2 2cm AA guns were rarely found on board vessels without net cutters.

Type II A (1935).

Type II D (1940).

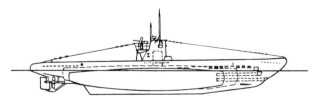

Type II B (1944).

Careers

U1: launched 15 Jun 1935, commissioned 29 Jun 1935. Sunk 16 Apr 1940 in the North Sea southwest of Stavanger, in position 58° 18'N, 05° 47'E, by a torpedo from the British submarine *Porpoise;* 24 dead.

U2: launched 1 Jul 1935, commissioned 25 Jul 1935. Sank 8 Apr 1944 west of Pillau, position not known, after being hit by the steam trawler *Hinrich Freese;* 16 dead. Raised and stricken.

U3: launched 19 Jul 1935, commissioned 6 Aug 1935; stricken 1 Aug 1944 at Gotenhafen; scrapped in 1945.

U4: launched 31 Jul 1935, commissioned 17 Aug 1935; stricken 1 Aug 1944 at Gotenhafen; scrapped in 1945.

U5: launched 14 Aug 1935, commissioned 31 Aug 1935. Sank 19 Mar 1943 west of Pillau, in position 54° 25'N, 19° 50'E, in a diving accident; 21 dead.

U6: launched 21 Aug 1935, commissioned 7 Sept 1935; stricken 7 Aug 1944 at Gotenhafen.

U7: launched 29 Jun 1935, commissioned 18 Jul 1935. Sank 18 Feb 1944 west of Pillau, in position 54° 25'N, 19° 50'E, in a diving accident; 26 dead.

U8: launched 16 Jul 1935, commissioned 5 Aug 1935; scuttled on 2 May 1945 in the Raederschleuse at Wilhelmshaven.

U9: launched 30 Jul 1935, commissioned 21 Aug 1935; in service in the Black Sea, 28 Oct 1942. Sunk at 1030hrs on 20 Aug 1944 at Konstanza, in position 44° 12'N, 28° 41'E, by bombs from Soviet aircraft.

U10: launched 13 Aug 1935, commissioned 9 Sept 1935; stricken 1 Aug 1944 at Danzig; broken up.

U11: launched 27 Aug 1935, commissioned 21 Sept 1935; stricken 5 Jan 1945 at Kiel; scuttled on 3 May 1945 in the Kiel Arsenal; wreck broken up.

U12: launched 11 Sept 1935, commissioned 30 Sept 1935. Sunk 8 Oct 1939 in the Channel near Dover, position not known, by a mine; 27 dead (all crew lost).

U13: launched 9 Nov 1935, commissioned 30 Nov 1935. Sunk 31 May 1940 north of Newcastle, in position 55° 26'N, 02° 02'E, by depth charges from the British sloop *Weston*.

U14: launched 28 Dec 1935, commissioned 18 Jan 1936; scuttled 2 May 1945 at Wilhelmshaven.

U15: launched 15 Feb 1936, commissioned 7 Mar 1936. Sank 31 Jan 1940 at Hoofden, after being rammed in error by the German torpedo boat *Iltis*; 25 dead.

U16: launched 28 Apr 1936, commissioned 16 May 1936. Sunk 25 Oct 1939 in the Channel near Dover, in position 51° 09'N, 01° 28'E, by depth charges from a British submarine chaser; 28 dead (all crew lost).

U17: launched 15 Nov 1935, commissioned 3 Dec 1935; scuttled 2 May 1945 at Wilhelmshaven.

U18: launched 6 Dec 1935, commissioned 4 Jan 1936. Sank at 0954hrs on 20 Nov 1936 in Lübeck Bay in position 54° 07'N, 11° 07'E, after a collision with *T 156*; 8 dead. Raised 28 Nov 1936, in service again 30 Sept 1937; scuttled on 25 Aug 1944 at Konstanza, in position 44° 12'N, 28° 41'E. Raised by the USSR; broken up, 1960.

U19: launched 21 Dec 1935, commissioned 16 Jan 1936; in service in the Black Sea, 9 Dec 1942; scuttled on 10 Sept 1944 off the coast of Turkey, in position 41° 16'N, 31° 26'E.

U20: launched 14 Jan 1936, commissioned 1 Feb 1936; in service in the Black Sea, 27 May 1943; scuttled on 10 Sept 1944 off the coast of Turkey, in position 41° 16'N, 31° 26'E.

U21: launched 13 Jul 1936, commissioned 6 Aug 1936. Sank on 27 Mar 1940 southeast of Mandal, in position 58° 01'N, 07° 29'E, after running aground off Oldknuppen Island following a navigation error; interned by Norway at Kristiansand-Süd. Released to Germany, 9 Apr 1940; stricken 5 Aug 1944 at Pillau; scrapped in February 1945.

U22: launched 28 Jul 1936, commissioned 21 Aug 1936. Sunk before 23 May 1940 in Jammer Bay in the Skagerrak, exact position unknown, by a mine; 27 dead (all crew lost).

U23: launched 28 Aug 1936, commissioned 24 Sept

Conning tower arrangements, Type II

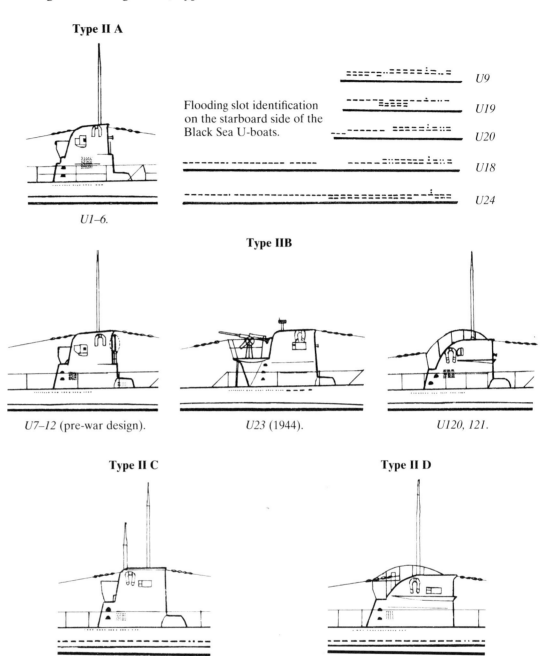

Type II A

U1–6.

Flooding slot identification on the starboard side of the Black Sea U-boats.

U9
U19
U20
U18
U24

Type IIB

U7–12 (pre-war design).   *U23 (1944).*   *U120, 121.*

Type II C

U56–63; note that the bridge of *U61* was similar to those of the Type II D.

Type II D

U137–152.

1936; in service in the Black Sea, 3 Jun 1943; scuttled 10 Sept 1944 off the coast of Turkey, in position 41° 16'N, 31° 26'E.

U24: launched 24 Sept 1936, commissioned 10 Oct 1936; in service in the Black Sea, 14 Oct 1942; scuttled on 25 Aug 1944 at Konstanza, in position 44° 12'N, 28°41'E. Raised by the USSR; broken up, 1960.

U56: Launched 3 Sept 1938, commissioned 26 Nov 1938. Sunk on 28 Apr 1945 at Kiel, in position 54° 19'N, 10° 10'E, by bombs from British aircraft.

U57: launched 3 Sept 1938, commissioned 29 Dec 1938. Sank at 0015 hrs on 3 Sept 1940 at Brunsbüttel, in position 53° 53'N, 09° 09'E, after a collision with the Norwegian steamship *Rona*; 6 dead.

Raised in September 1940; repaired; in service 11 Jan 1941; scuttled 3 May 1945 at Kiel.

U58: launched 14 Oct 1938, commissioned 4 Feb 1939; scuttled 3 May 1945 at Kiel; wreck broken up.

U59: launched 12 Oct 1938, commissioned 4 Mar 1939; stricken in April 1945 at Kiel; scuttled in the Kiel Arsenal; wreck broken up in 1945.

U60: launched 1 Jun 1939, commissioned 22 Jul 1939; scuttled 2 May 1945 at Wilhelmshaven.

U61: launched 15 Jun 1939, commissioned 12 Aug 1939; scuttled on 2 May 1945 at Wilhelmshaven.

U62: launched 16 Nov 1939, commissioned 21 Dec 1939; scuttled 2 May 1945 at Wilhelmshaven.

U63: launched 6 Dec 1939, commissioned 18 Jan 1940. Sunk 25 Feb 1940 south of the Shetland Islands, in position 58° 40'N, 00° 10'W, by depth charges and torpedoes from the British destroyers *Escort, Inglefield* and *Imogen* and the British submarine *Narwhal;* 1 dead.

U120: Originally under construction for China, taken over in 1939; launched 16 Mar 1940, commissioned 20 Apr 1940; scuttled 2 May 1945 at Bremerhaven. Raised October 1949 to November 1950; broken up.

U121: Originally under construction for China, taken over in 1939; launched 20 Apr 1940, commissioned 28 May 1940; scuttled on 2 May 1945 at Wesermünde. Raised October 1949 to November 1950; broken up.

U137: launched 18 May 1940, commissioned 15 Jun 1940; scuttled on 2 May 1945 in the Raederschleuse at Wilhelmshaven; wreck broken up, date unknown.

U138: launched 18 May 1940, commissioned 27 Jun 1940. Sunk 18 Jun 1941 west of Cadiz, in position 36° 04'N, 07° 29'W, by depth charges from the British destroyers *Faulknor, Fearless, Forester, Foresight* and *Foxhound.* Number of fatalities unknown.

U139: launched 28 Jun 1940, commissioned 24 Jul 1940; scuttled 2 May 1945 in the Raederschleuse at Wilhelmshaven; wreck broken up, date unknown.

U140: launched 28 Jun 1940, commissioned 7 Aug 1940; scuttled on 2 May 1945, in the Raederschleuse at Wilhelmshaven; wreck broken up, date unknown.

U141: launched 27 Jul 1940, commissioned 21 Aug 1940; scuttled on 2 May 1945 in the Raederschleuse at Wilhelmshaven; wreck broken up, date unknown.

U142: launched 27 Jul 1940, commissioned 4 Sept 1940; scuttled on 2 May 1945 in the Raederschleuse at Wilhelmshaven; wreck broken up, date unknown.

U143: launched 10 Aug 1940, commissioned 18 Sept 1940; transferred from Wilhelmshaven to Loch Ryan 30 Jun 1945 for Operation Deadlight.

U144: launched 24 Aug 1940, commissioned 2 Oct 1940. Sunk on 9 Aug 1941 north of Dagö, in approximate position 59°N, 23°E, by torpedoes from the Russian submarine *Sc 307;* 28 dead (all crew lost).

U145: launched 21 Sept 1940, commissioned 16 Oct 1940; transferred from Wilhelmshaven to Loch Ryan 30 Jun 1945 for Operation Deadlight.

U146: launched 21 Sept 1940, commissioned 30 Oct 1940; scuttled on 2 May 1945 in the Raederschleuse at Wilhelmshaven; wreck broken up, date unknown.

U147: launched 16 Nov 1940, commissioned 11 Dec 1940. Sunk on 2 Jun 1941 northwest of Ireland, in position 56° 38'N, 10° 24'W, by depth charges from the British destroyer *Wanderer* and the British corvette *Periwinkle;* 26 dead.

U148: launched 16 Nov 1940, commissioned 28 Dec 1940; scuttled on 2 May 1945 in the Raederschleuse at Wilhelmshaven; wreck broken up, date unknown.

U149: launched 19 Oct 1940, commissioned 13 Nov 1940; transferred from Wilhelmshaven to Loch Ryan 30 Jun 1945 for Operation Deadlight.

U150: launched 19 Oct 1940, commissioned 27 Nov 1940; transferred from Wilhelmshaven to Loch Ryan, 30 Jun 1945, in Operation Deadlight; scuttled on 22 Oct 1947 while on manoeuvres with the Canadian navy.

U151: launched 14 Dec 1940, commissioned 15 Jan 1941; scuttled on 2 May 1945 in the Raederschleuse at Wilhelmshaven; wreck broken up, date unknown.

U152: launched 14 Dec 1940, commissioned 29 Jan 1941; scuttled on 2 May 1945 in the Raederschleuse at Wilhelmshaven; wreck broken up, date unknown.

U-boat designs 1934

Name	Type	Builder (construction no)	Built	Cost in Marks (000s)	Displacement (t = tonnes T = tons)	Length (m)	Breadth (m)	Draught/ height (m)	Power (hp)	Revs (rpm)	Speed (kts)	Range (nm/kts)	Oil (t)	Diving time (sec)
—	III	(Project only; construction contracts not granted)	—	4.8	970t sf	79.9 oa 62.7 ph	6.20 oa 4.28 ph	4.35/	3080ehp sf 1000ehp sm	485 sf 310 sm	c18.5 sf c8 sm	12,000/10 sf c75/4 sm		
—	III mod	”	—		c1500t sf c2000t sm	c78 oa 60.8 ph	c7.4 oa 4.28 ph	c5/	”	”	c15.5 sf c7 sm			
—	IV	”	—		c2500t sf									
—	V	”	—		300t sf 320t sm	32 oa	3.2 oa	4.0	4800ehp sf 7500ehp sm*		26 sf 30 sm	2000/15 sf 500/15 sm	36 oil +75 H₂O₂	
—	VI	”	—		c850t sf	c72 oa	6.20 oa 4.28 ph							

* Closed-cycle diesel propulsion.

Type III
Similar to Type I A, with additional storage space aft of the torpedo tubes for a total of 21 T or 42 TMA mines. Two 10.5cm/45 guns, one forward of, and one aft of, the conning tower (mine U-boat).

Type III (modified)
Originally known as Type VII. Similar to Type I A, but with an enlarged outer hull, allowing storage

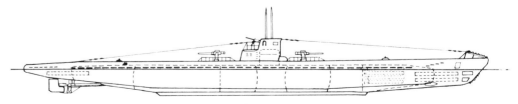

Type III (1934 Project).

for 48 TMA mines. Fitted with a pressure-tight hangar for two 10-tonne LS-boats. This project - transporting S-boats underwater - was soon abandoned due to the great expense and limited operational value.

Type IV
Project for a supply and workshop vessel for front-line U-boats (support U-boat).

Type V
Project for a fast U-boat, based on a suggestion by Hellmuth Walter (see Walter U-boats, below).

Type VI
Reconstruction of Type IA, with steam propulsion, based on a suggestion by Schmidt-Hartmann.

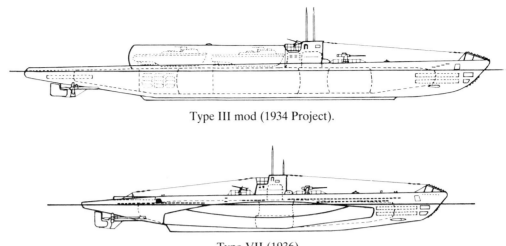

Type III mod (1934 Project).

Type VII (1936).

Type VII–VII C U-boats

Construction
Laid down as ocean-going submersibles, designs 1933–34, 1934–35, 1937–38, 1941. Single hull with saddle tanks; six watertight compartments; trim tanks in compartments 1 and 6; main diving tank and fuel oil bunker under the control room; regulating tanks pressure-tight, apart from the auxiliary tanks etc in the saddle tanks; further diving tanks in the stern. Diving depth 100m, crush depth 200m. Design VII C/41 had a strengthened pressure hull, giving depths of 120/250m; surface displacement was only 759 tonnes and submerged displacement 860 tonnes, due to lighter machinery and ballast – dimensions were otherwise similar to those of the VII C.

Propulsion
Two Germaniawerft F 46 6-cylinder 4-stroke supercharged diesel engines (or two MAN M 6 V 40/46 6-cylinder 4-stroke unsupercharged diesel engines, *U27–36*; or these engines supercharged, *U51–55, 73–82, 85, 86, 88, 90, 101* and *132–136*) in the diesel room in compartment 2; two BBC GG UB 720/8 double electric motors (or two AEG GU 460/8–276 electric motors, *U47, 48, 50, 53, 55, 69–72, 83, 84, 87, 89, 93–98, 101, 102, 201–212, 221–232, 235–300, 331–348, 351–374, 431–450, 731–750, 1051–1058, 1063–1068, 1191–1214, 1271–1285, 1301–1312;* or two GL u Co RP 137/C double electric motors, *U301–330, 375–400, 701–730, 752–782, 1131–1146, 1331–1338, 1401–1404, 1417–1422, 1435–1439, 1801–1804;* or two SSW GU 343/38–8 double electric motors, *U349, 350, 402–430, 453–458, 465–486, 651–698, 901–912, 921–928, 1101–1114, 1161–1190)* in compartment 1.

Batteries were as follows: two 62-cell AFA 27 MAK 740 batteries (6940amp/hrs), *U27, 31–33, 35* and *36*; two 62-cell AFA 33 MAL 740 batteries (8480amp/hrs), *U28–30* and *34*; two 62-cell AFA 33 MAL 800 W batteries (9160amp/hrs), *U46, 48–50, 52, 53–55, 69–72, 74–80, 82–85, 87–90, 93–95, 98–102, 132, 133, 135, 136, 201–212, 221–226, 228–232, 238–240, 244, 245, 248, 251–255, 257–286, 291, 301–304, 306–313, 320, 328–345, 352–366, 372, 374, 376, 378–392, 401–404, 406, 408–412, 414–419, 421, 425, 431–434, 436–440, 442–449, 451, 452, 454–458, 465–472, 474, 551, 553, 556, 557, 559, 560, 562–565, 567–571,* *573–583, 585, 587–591, 594–599, 602–607, 609–617, 619–624, 626–638, 640, 642–668, 670–675, 682, 684–698, 701, 702, 710–713, 715–717, 720, 723–743, 751–757, 759–762, 764, 769–771, 777–782, 905, 907, 922, 951–957, 960, 963, 964, 967–994, 1053, 1104, 1131, 1133–1146, 1166, 1168, 1169, 1171, 1172, 1192, 1194, 1196–1199, 1201–1206, 1208, 1209, 1211–1214, 1272, 1306, 1331–1338, 1401–1404, 1417–1422, 1435–1439;* and two 62-cell AFA 33 MAL 800 E batteries (9160amp/hrs) in all other Type VII C boats, except for the following mixed fits of the 33 MAL 800 cells: 62 type W and 62 type E cells in *U134, 227, 305, 450, 924* and *966*, 6 W + 118 E in *U1170* (later), 7 W + 117 E in *U775*, 12 W + 112 E in *U961*, 16 W + 108 E in *U959*, 24 W + 100 E in *U554* and *714*, 51 W + 73 E in *U681* and *683*, 52 W + 72 E in *U939*, 60 W + 64 E in *U1273*, 61 W + 63 E in *U958* and *1207*, 64 W + 60 E in *U552*, 82 W + 42 E in *U641* and 113 W + 11 E in *U965* (all 9160amp/hrs). All cells were in battery boxes without rubber shock absorbers, except in *U1275, 1277, 1302* and *1303*, where the boxes were of Dynal; all batteries were in compartments 3 and 5 below. Diesel electric range 6800nm at 10kts, 9400nm at 10kts from *U45* (GW diesels) and 9700nm at 10kts from *U51* (MAN diesels).

All boats had two 3-bladed propellers, 1.2m diameter; two hydroplanes forward and two aft; one (or two from the Type VII B onwards) rudder.

Armament
Five 53.3cm torpedo tubes, four at the bow below the CWL and one at the stern above the CWL (or below the CWL, from *U45* onwards) - 11 torpedoes or up to 22 TMA (= 33 TMB) mines, increased to 14 torpedoes or up to 26 TMA (= 39 TMB) mines from *U45*; one Tk 8.8cm/45 gun and one 2cm AA

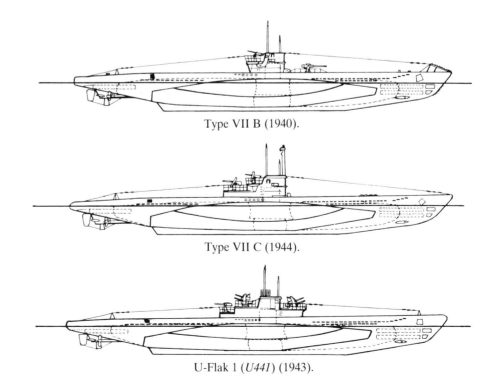

Type VII B (1940).

Type VII C (1944).

U-Flak 1 (*U441*) (1943).

Name	Type	Builder (construction no)	Built	Cost in Marks (000s)	Displacement (t = tonnes T = tons)	Length (m)	Breadth (m)	Draught/ height (m)	Power (hp)	Revs (rpm)	Speed (kts)	Range (nm/kts)	Oil (t)	Diving time (sec)
U27–32	VII	Deschimag (908–913)	1935–37	4189	626t sf 745t sm 915t total	64.51 oa 45.50 ph	5.85 oa 4.70 ph	4.37/ 9.50	2100ehp to 2310ehp sf 750ehp sm	470 to 485 sf 322 sm	16.0 to 17.0 sf 8.0 sm	6200/10 2900/16 sf 73–94/4 sm	67.0/ 58.6	50 td 30 td (mod)
U33–36	"	Germania (556–559)	1935–36	"	"	"	"	"	"	"	"	"	"	"
U45–50	VII B	" (580–585)	1936–37	4439	753t sf 857t sm 1040t total 704t sf*	66.50 oa 48.80 ph	6.20 oa 4.70 ph	4.74/ 9.50	2800ehp to 3200ehp sf 750ehp sm	470 to 485 sf 295 sm	17.2 to 17.9 sf 8.0 sm	8700/10 3850/ 17.2 sf 90/4 sm	99.7/ 57.3 108.3 max	30 td
U51–55	"	" (586–590)	1938–39	"	"	"	"	"	"	"	"	"	"	"
U73–76	"	Vegesack (1–4)	1938–40	4760	"	"	"	"	"	"	"	"	"	"
U83–87	"	Flender (291, 280–283)	1938–41	4714	"	"	"	"	"	"	"	"	"	"
U99–102	"	Germania (593–596)	1937–40	4439	"	"	"	"	"	"	"	"	"	"
U69–72	VII C	" (604, 605, 618 to 619)	1939–41	"	769t sm 871t sm 1070t total 719t sf*	67.10 oa 50.50 ph	6.20 oa 4.70 ph	4.74/ 9.60	"	"	17.0 to 17.7 sf 7.6 sm	8500/10 3250/17 sf 130/2 80/4 sm	105.3/ 62.1 113.5 max	30 td
U77–82	"	Vegesack (5–10)	1939–41	4760	"	"	"	"	"	"	"	"	"	"
U88–92	"	Flender (292–296)	1940–42	4714	"	"	"	"	"	"	"	"	"	"
U93–98	"	Germania (598–603)	1939–40	4439	"	"	"	"	"	"	"	"	"	"

* Light load displacement.
† Construction numbers 839–842 (four numbers) are given in the sources for *U690–692* (three boats); the reasons for this are not known.
‡ From *U575* onwards, the sources give a different sequence of construction numbers for the Blohm & Voss boats, apparently allocated to avoid confusion with the OKM U-numbers of the boats as commissioned. The original construction numbers are given here, since the new numbers are apparently a post-war alteration to the records; they do not appear in documents from the war period.
** The U-boats being built under construction numbers 152 and 153 were severely damaged in an air raid on 27 Jan 1943; new construction numbers were given because of the long delivery delay which this caused.
†† These boats were originally intended for construction by Vulcan (S).

gun. Variations were as follows: only two bow torpedo tubes (*U72, 78, 80, 554* and *555*); no stern torpedo tube (*U83, 203, 331, 351, 401, 431* and *651*); no mine fittings (*U88–92, 333–350, 352–370, 374–401, 404–430, 435–450, 454–458, 657–686, 702–750, 754–782* and all Type VII C/41 boats from *U1271*). [The standard fit of guns from 1944 was one 3.7cm AA gun - 1195 rounds - and two twin 2cm AA guns - 4380 rounds, with the 8.8cm gun landed and deleted from the specification for new boats from about 1942 onwards. Various different fits of AA guns are found from 1943, and certain boats (*U441*, for example) were modified to special Flak U-boats, with one 3.7cm AA gun - 1160 rounds, two quadruple 2cm AA guns - 6000 rounds, various C-42 machine guns, cable rocket launchers and searchlights.]

Handling
Handling was generally similar to that of the Type UB III boats of 1916–18. The special Flak U-boats (see above) tended to be top-heavy, despite reductions in torpedo equipment.

Complement
Crew: 4/40-56. Boats: one to eight (or more) inflatable boats.

Notes
The original Type VII was redeveloped in 1934–35. The hull shape was similar to that of the Type II, but with saddle tanks. Type UG submarines from 1918 may, with certain reservations, be considered precursors.

Various modifications and extensions were made to the conning tower, including for example the addition of splinter protection, fittings for antennae and dipole aerials; see the drawings. From 1943 these boats were fitted with the so-called 'Atlantic stem' - a 13cm extension. From 1944 some boats were fitted with retractable schnorkel masts on the forward port corner of the tower, and with underwater exhausts. Some vessels had GHG balconies, below, hydroplanes forward and 'Alberich' anti-Asdic rubber covering.

Careers
U27: launched 24 Jun 1936, commissioned 12 Aug 1936. Sunk 20 Sept 1939 west of Scotland, in position 58° 35'N, 09° 02'W, by depth charges from the British destroyers *Fortune* and *Forester*.

Name	Type	Builder (construction no)	Built
U201–212	VII C	Germania (630–641)	1940–42
U221–232	,,	,, (651–662)	1941–42
U235–250	,,	,, (665–670, 675–684)	1942–44
U251–267	,,	Vegesack (16–32)	1940–42
U268–291	,,	,, (33–56)	1941–43
U292–300	VII C/41	,, (57–65)	1942–43
U301–308	VII C	Flender (301–308)	1941–42
U309–316	,,	,, (309–316)	1942–43
U317–328	VII C/41	,, (317–328)	1942–44
U329, 330	,,	,, (349, 350)	1943–
U331–340	VII C	Nordsee (203–212)	1940–42
U341–350	,,	,, (213–222)	1941–43
U351–358	,,	Flensburg (470–477)	1940–42
U359–362	,,	,, (480–483)	1941–43
U363–370	,,	,, (484–487, 490–493)	,,
U371–382	,,	Howaldt (K) (2–13)	1939–42
U383–390	,,	,, (14–21)	1941–43
U391–400	,,	,, (23–32)	1942–44
U401–412	,,	Danzig (102–113)	1940–42
U413–420	,,	,, (115–122)	1941–42
U421–430	,,	,, (123–132)	1942–43
U431–438	,,	Schichau (D) (1472–1475, 1477–1480)	1940–41
U439–444	,,	,, (1490–1493, 1498, 1499)	1940–42
U445–450	,,	,, (1505–1508, 1520, 1521)	1941–42

Name	Type	Builder (construction no)	Built
U451–458	,,	DWK (282–289)	1940–41
U465–468	,,	,, (296–299)	1941–42
U469–486	,,	,, (300–311, 316–321)	1941–44
U551–574	,,	B & V (527–550)	1939–41
U575–598	,,	,, (75–98)‡	1940–41
U599–634	,,	,, (99–134)‡	1941–42
U635–650	,,	,, (135–150)‡	,,
U651–662	,,	Howaldt (H) (800–811)	1940–42
U663–674	,,	,, (812–823)	1941–43
U675–686	,,	,, (824–835)	1941–44 and 1943–
U687–698	VII C/41	,, (836–848)†	1943–
U701–706	VII C	Stülcken (760–765)	1940–42
U707–714	,,	,, (771–780)	1941–43
U715–722	,,	,, (781–788)	1942–43
U723–730	VII C/41	,, (793–796, 798–801)	1943–
U731–734	VII C	Schichau (D) (1522–1525)	1941–42
U735–750	,,	,, (1532–1537, 1544–1549, 1557–1560)	1941–43
U751–762	,,	KMW (134–145)	1940–43
U763–776	,,	,, (146–151, 166**, 167**, 154–159)	1941–44
U777–782	,,	,, (160–165)	1943–44
U821–824	,,	Oderwerke (821–824)	1941–44
U825, 826	,,	Schichau (D) (1588, 1589)	1943–44

Name	Type	Builder (construction no)	Built
U827, 828	VII C/41	,, (1590, 1591)	,,
U829–840	,,	,, (1592–1601, 1604, 1605)	—
U901, 902	VII C	Vulcan (S) (14, 15)	1942–44
U903, 904	,,	Flender†† (329, 330)	1942–43
U905–908	,,	Stülcken†† (802–805)	1943–44
U909–912	VII C/41	,, (806–809)	1943–
U921–928	VII C	Neptun (508–515)	1941–44
U929, 930	VII C/41	,, (516, 517)	1943–44
U931–936	,,	,, (518, 519, 524–527)	1943–
U951–994	VII C	B & V (151–194)	1942–43
U995–1006	VII C/41	,, (195–206)	1942–44
U1007–1030	,,	,, (207–230)‡	1943–44 and 1943–
U1031–1050	,,	,, (231–250)‡	1943– and –
U1051–1058	VII C	Germania (685–692)	1943–44
U1063–1065	VII C/41	,, (700–702)	,,
U1066–1068	,,	,, (703–705)	1943–
U1101–1106	VII C	Nordsee (223–228)	1943–44
U1107–1114	VII C/41	,, (229–236)	1943–44 and 1943–
U1131, 1132	VII C	Howaldt (K) (33, 34)	1943–44
U1133–1146	VII C/41	,, (35–48)	1943–
U1161, 1162	VII C	Danzig (133–134)	1942–43
U1163–1170	VII C/41	,, (135–142)	1942–44
U1171–1182	,,	,, (143–154)	1943–44 and 1943–

Name	Type	Builder (construction no)	Built
U1183–1190	,,	,, (155–162)	1943–
U1191–1204	VII C	Schichau (D) (1561–1568, 1573–1578)	1942–44
U1205–1210	,,	,, (1582–1587)	1943–44
U1211–1214	VII C/41	,, (1606–1609)	—
U1271–1279	,,	Vegesack (66–74)	1943–44
U1280–1291	,,	,, (75–86)	1943–
U1301–1308	,,	Flensburg (494–501)	1943–45
U1309–1312	,,	,, (502–505)	1943–
U1331–1338	,,	Flender (351–358)	—
U1401–04, 1417–22	,,	B & V (251–254, 267–272)	—
U1435–1439	,,	,, (285–289)	—
U1801–04, 1823–28	,,	Danzig (163–166, 185–190)	1943–

Conning tower arrangements, Type VII B/C (1/160 scale)

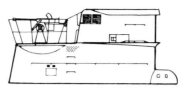

Type VIIC basic conning tower, 1940–43.

AA armament: one 2cm C/30 gun in an LC 30/37 mounting (with four 8mm C/34 machine guns added from mid-1942).

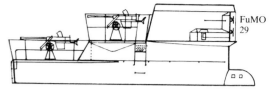

Type VII C with the 'Wintergarden' (bridge modification II, 1943).

AA armament: two 2cm C/38 guns in LC 30/37 mountings.

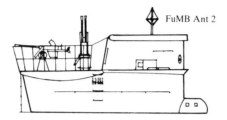

U 81 (Type VII C) with an enlarged bridge, in the Mediterranean in 1943 (*U 453* was similar).

AA armament: two 1.32cm twin Breda machine guns in retractable, pressure-tight mountings; one 2cm C/38 gun in an LC 30/37 mounting.

U 84 (Type VII B) with a raised AA position aft of the bridge (1943).

AA armament: two 2cm C/38 guns in LC 30/37 mountings.

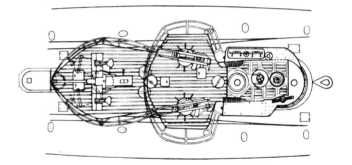

Type VII C (1944–45 design).

AA armament: two 2cm twin 38 M II guns in double LM 43 U mountings; one 3.7cm M 42 U gun in an LM 42 U mounting. In some cases one 2cm quadruple 38/43 U gun with a shield or one 3.7cm twin M 42 in a double LM 42 U mounting was fitted in place of the single 3.7cm gun.

Plan view of the Type VII C bridge (early 1944 design).

Port side, forward to aft: 2-man splinter-proof shelter, FuMB Ant 2 aerial, FuMO 30 aerial; starboard side, ditto: radio direction finder, 3-man splinter-proof shelter.
AA armament: two 2cm twin 38 M II guns in double LM 43 U mountings; one 3.7cm M 42 U gun in an LM 42 U mounting.

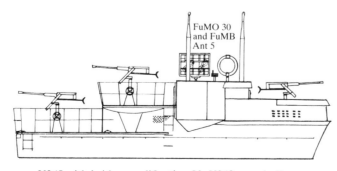

U345 with bridge modification V; *U362* was similar.

AA armament: four 2cm twin 38 M II guns.

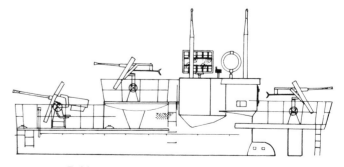

Bridge modification VI (*U673* and *U973*).

AA armament: as Type VII C (1944–45 design), but with one 2cm twin 38 M II gun forward of the bridge.

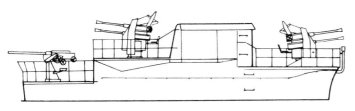

U-flak 1 (*U441*).

AA armament: two 2cm guadruple 38/43 U guns with shields;
one 3.7cm SKC/30 U in an LC/39 mounting.

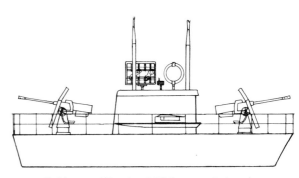

Bridge modification VII (not carried out).

AA armament: four 3.7cm M 42 U guns.

Identification of Germaniawerft Type VII B and C U-boats (after Lennart Lindberg)

Flooding slots Type VII B	Starboard			Port		
	10	15	3	3	19	6
U45	10	15	3	3	19	6
U46	10	15	3	3	19	6
U47	10	15	3	3	19	6
U48	10	15	3	3	19	6
U49	10	15	3	1	17	10
U50	10	15	3	3	15	10
U51	10	15	3	3	19	6
U52	10	15	3	3	19	6
U53	10	15	3			
U54	10	15	3	3	15	10
U55						
U99	10	15	3	3	15	10
U100	10	15	3	3	19	6
U101	10	15	3	0	18	10
U102	10	18	0	0	18	10

Type VII C various identifying features

Slots under the conning tower

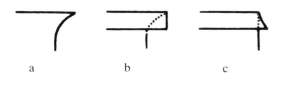

U93, 94, 95

→ Bow

Windshield at upper edge of tower

a   b   c

(a) No windshield as launched:
    U93, 94, 95, 96, 97, 98, 69, 70, 71, 201, 202, 203, 204, 205, 206, 207, 208

(b) Launched with the original tower and added windshield:
    U72, 209, 211

(c) New, straight upper tower with windshield:
    U210, 212, 221 and the following boats.

Exhaust ports at the stern

U-boats at least up to *U207* (possibly also *U208*) had exhaust ports as shown; after this a separate covering plate was added, and this same plate was retro-fitted to some earlier boats (for example, *U203*).

U28: launched 14 Jul 1936, commissioned 12 Sept 1936. Sank 17 Mar 1944 at Neustadt U-boat pier, in position 54° 07'N, 10° 50'E, in an operational accident. Raised in March 1944; stricken 4 Aug 1944.

U29: launched 29 Aug 1936, commissioned 16 Nov 1936. Scuttled 4 May 1945 in Kupfermühlen Bay; wreck broken up c1948.

U30: launched 4 Aug 1936, commissioned 8 Oct 1936. Scuttled 4 May 1945 in Kupfermühlen Bay; wreck broken up c1948.

U31: launched 25 Sept 1936, commissioned 28 Dec 1936. Sunk at 1200hrs on 11 Mar 1940 in the Jadebusen, in position 53° 30'N, 08° 12'E, by British bombs; 58 dead (all crew lost). Raised in March 1940; repaired and returned to service. Sunk 2 Nov 1940 northwest of Ireland, in position 56° 26'N, 10° 18'W, by depth charges from the British destroyer *Antelope* and bombs; 2 dead.

U32: launched 25 Feb 1937, commissioned 15 Apr 1937. Sunk 30 Oct 1940 northwest of Ireland, in position 55° 37'N, 12° 19'W, by depth charges from the British destroyers *Harvester* and *Highlander*; 9 dead.

U33: launched 11 Jun 1936, commissioned 25 Jul 1936. Sunk 12 Feb 1940 in the Firth of Clyde, in position 55° 25'N, 05° 07'W, by depth charges from the British minesweeper *Gleaner*; 25 dead.

U34: launched 17 Jul 1936, commissioned 12 Sept 1936. Sank at 2155hrs on 5 Aug 1943 at Memel, in position 55° 42'N, 21° 09'E, after a collision with the U-boat mother-ship *Lech*; 4 dead. Raised 24 Aug 1943; stricken 8 Sept 1943.

U35: launched 29 Sept 1936, commissioned 3 Nov 1936. Sunk 29 Nov 1939 northwest of Bergen, in position 60° 53'N, 02° 47'E, by depth charges etc from the British destroyers *Kingston*, *Kashmir* and *Icarus*; number of fatalities unknown.

U36: launched 4 Nov 1936, commissioned 16 Dec 1936. Sunk 4 Dec 1939 southwest of Kristiansand, in position 57° 00'N, 05° 20'E, by a torpedo from the British submarine *Salmon*; 40 dead.

U45: launched 27 Apr 1938, commissioned 25 Jun 1938. Sunk 14 Oct 1939 east of Ireland, in position 50° 58'N, 12° 57'W, by depth charges from the British destroyers *Inglefield*, *Ivanhoe* and *Intrepid*; 38 dead (all crew lost).

U46: Launched 10 Sept 1938, commissioned 2 Nov 1938; stricken at Neustadt in October 1943; scuttled 4 May 1945 in Kupfermühlen Bay, in position 54° 50'N, 09° 29'E.

Flooding slots Type VII C	Starboard			Port		
	4	15	3	3	16	2
U93	3	15	3	3	16	2
U94	1	16	3	3	16	1
U95	4	14	3	3	16	1
U96	4	14	3	3	16	1
U97	4	14	3	3	16	1
U98	4	14	3	3	16	1
U69	0	15	3	3	16	1
U70	4	14	3	3	16	1
U71	3	15	3	3	16	1
U72	3	15	3	3	16	1
U201	3	15	3	3	16	1
U202	3	15	3	3	16	1
U203	3	15	3	3	16	1
U204				3	16	1
U205	3	15	3	3	16	1
U206						
U207	3	15	3			
U208						
U209				3	16	1
U210	3	15	3	3	16	1
U211	3	15	3	3	16	1
U212	3	15	3	3	16	1
U221	3	16	2	2	17	1

Type VII C   Bow and sonar array

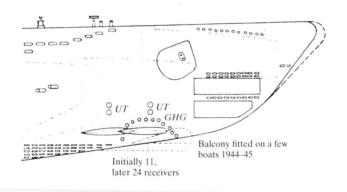

UT   UT   GHG
Balcony fitted on a few boats 1944–45
Initially 11, later 24 receivers

U47: launched 29 Oct 1938, commissioned 17 Dec 1938. Sunk at 0522hrs on 8 Mar 1941 south of Iceland, in position 60° 47'N, 19° 13'W, by depth charges from the British destroyer *Wolverine*; 45 dead (all crew lost).

U48: launched 8 Mar 1938, commissioned 22 Apr 1939; stricken at Neustadt in October 1943; scuttled on 3 May at Neustadt, in position 54° 07'N, 10° 50'E.

U49: launched 24 Jun 1939, commissioned 12 Aug 1939. Sunk 15 Apr 1940 near Narvik, in position 68° 53'N, 16° 59'E, by depth charges from the British destroyers *Fearless* and *Brazen*; 1 dead.

U50: launched 1 Nov 1939, commissioned 12 Dec 1939. Sunk 10 Apr 1940 in the North Sea north of the Shetlands, in position 62° 54'N, 01° 56'W, by depth charges from the British destroyer *Hero*; 44 dead (all crew lost).

U51: launched 11 Jun 1938, commissioned 6 Aug 1938. Sunk 20 Aug 1940 in the Bay of Biscay west of Nantes, in position 47° 06'N, 04° 51'W, by a torpedo from the British submarine *Cachalot*; 43 dead (all crew lost).

U52: launched 21 Dec 1938, commissioned 4 Feb 1939; stricken at Danzig in October 1943; transferred to Kiel; scuttled there 3 May 1945; broken up 1946–47.

U53: launched 6 May 1939, commissioned 24 Jun 1939. Sunk 23 Feb 1940 west of the Orkneys, in position 58° 50'N, 02° 58'W, by depth charges from the British destroyer *Gurkha*; 42 dead (all crew lost).

U54: launched 15 Aug 1939, commissioned 23 Sept 1939. Sunk 23 Feb 1940 off Cape St Vincent, position unknown, by the French destroyer *Simoun*; 41 dead (all crew lost).

U55: launched 11 Oct 1939, commissioned 21 Nov 1939. Sunk 30 Jan 1940 southwest of the Scilly Isles, in position 48° 37'N, 07° 48'W, by depth charges from the British destroyer *Whitshed*, the sloop *Fowey*, the French destroyers *Valmy* and *Guépard*, and by British bombs; 1 dead.

U69: launched 19 Sept 1940, commissioned 2 Nov 1940. Sunk 17 Feb 1943 in the Northwest Atlantic, in position 50° 50'N, 40° 50'W, by depth charges from the British destroyer *Viscount*; 46 dead (all crew lost).

U70: launched 12 Oct 1940, commissioned 23 Nov 1940. Sunk 7 Mar 1941 southeast of Iceland, in position 60° 15'N, 14° 00'W, by depth charges from the British corvettes *Camellia* and *Arbutus*; 20 dead.

U71: launched 30 Oct 1940, commissioned 14 Dec 1940; scuttled 2 May 1945 at Wilhelmshaven.

U72: launched 22 Nov 1940, commissioned 4 Jan 1941; damaged on 30 Mar 1945 at Bremen by US bombs; scuttled there 2 May 1945.

U73: launched 27 Jul 1940, commissioned 30 Sept 1940. Sunk 16 Dec 1943 near Oran, in position 36° 07'N, 00° 50'W, by depth charges and gunfire from the US destroyers *Woolsey* and *Trippe*; 16 dead.

U74: Launched 31 Aug 1940, commissioned 31 Oct 1940. Sunk 2 May 1942 east of Cartagena, in position 37° 32'N, 00° 10'E, by depth charges from the British destroyers *Wishart* and *Wrestler*, and by bombs; 46 dead (all crew lost).

U75: launched 18 Oct 1940, commissioned 19 Dec 1940. Sunk 28 Dec 1941 near Mersa Matruh, in position 31° 50'N, 26° 40'E, by depth charges from the British destroyer *Kipling*; 14 dead.

U76: launched 3 Oct 1940, commissioned 3 Dec 1940. Sunk 5 Apr 1941 south of Iceland, in position 58° 35'N, 20° 20'W, by depth charges from the British destroyer *Wolverine* and the sloop *Scarborough*; 1 dead.

U77: launched 23 Nov 1940, commissioned 18 Jan 1941. Sunk at 0115hrs on 28 Mar 1943 east of Cartagena, in position 37° 42'N, 00° 10'E, by British bombs; 38 dead.

U78: launched 7 Dec 1940, commissioned 15 Feb 1941. Sunk on 16 Apr 1945 at the electricity suppy station at Pillau pier by artillery fire from the Soviet army.

U79: launched 25 Jan 1941, commissioned 13 Mar 1941. Sunk 23 Dec 1941 north of Sollum, in position 32° 15'N, 25° 19'E, by depth charges from the British destroyers *Hasty* and *Hotspur*; number of fatalities unknown.

U80: launched 11 Feb 1941, commissioned 8 Apr 1941. Sunk 28 Nov 1944 west of Pillau, in position 54° 25'N, 19° 50'E, in a diving accident; 50 dead.

U81: launched 22 Feb 1941, commissioned 26 Apr 1941. Sunk at 1130hrs on 4 Jan 1944 at Pola, in position 44° 52'N, 13° 51'E, by US bombs; 2 dead. Raised 22 Apr 1944; broken up.

U82: launched 15 Mar 1941, commissioned 14 May 1941. Sunk 7 Feb 1942 north of the Azores, in position 44° 10'N, 23° 52'W, by depth charges from the British sloop *Rochester* and the corvette *Tamarisk*; 45 dead (all crew lost).

U83: launched 9 Dec 1940, commissioned 8 Feb 1941. Sunk 9 Mar 1943 southeast of Cartagena, in position 37° 10'N, 00° 05'E, by British bombs; 50 dead (all crew lost).

U84: launched 27 Feb 1941, commissioned 29 Apr 1941. Sunk 24 Aug 1943 in the middle of the North Atlantic, in position 27° 09'N, 37° 03'W, by air-dropped torpedoes from aircraft of the US escort carrier *Core;* 46 dead (all crew lost).

U85: launched 10 Apr 1941, commissioned 7 Jun 1941. Sunk 14 Apr 1942 near Cape Hatteras, in position 35° 55'N, 73° 13'W, by gunfire from the US destroyer *Roper;* 45 dead (all crew lost).

U86: launched 10 May 1941, commissioned 8 Jul 1941. Sunk 29 Nov 1943 east of the Azores, in position 39° 33'N, 19° 01'W, by bombs from aircraft of the US escort carrier *Bogue;* 50 dead (all crew lost).

U87: launched 21 Jun 1941, commissioned 19 Aug 1941. Sunk 4 Mar 1943, west of Leixões, in position 41° 36'N, 13° 31'W, by depth charges from the Canadian corvette *Shediac* and the destroyer *St Croix;* 49 dead (all crew lost).

U88: launched 16 Aug 1941, commissioned 15 Oct 1941. Sunk 12 Sept 1942 south of Spitzbergen, in position 75° 40'N, 20° 32'E, by depth charges from the British destroyer *Faulknor;* 46 dead (all crew lost).

U89: launched 20 Sept 1941, commissioned 19 Nov 1941. Sunk 12 May 1943 in the North Atlantic, in position 46° 30'N, 25° 40'W, by bombs from aircraft of the British escort carrier *Biter* and by depth charges from the British destroyer *Broadway* and the frigate *Lagan;* 48 dead (all crew lost).

U90: launched 25 Oct 1941, commissioned 20 Dec 1941. Sunk 24 Jul 1942 east of Newfoundland, in position 48° 12'N, 40° 56'W, by depth charges from the Canadian destroyer *St Croix;* 44 dead (all crew lost).

U91: launched 30 Nov 1941, commissioned 28 Jan 1942. Sunk 25 Feb 1944 in the North Atlantic, in position 49° 45'N, 26° 20'W, by depth charges from the British frigates *Affleck, Gore* and *Gould;* 36 dead.

U92: launched 10 Jan 1942, commissioned 3 Mar 1942. Damaged on 4 Oct 1944 at Bergen, in position 60° 24'N, 05° 19'E, by British bombs; stricken 12 Oct 1944; broken up 1944–45.

U93: launched 8 Jun 1940, commissioned 30 Jul 1940. Sunk 15 Jan 1942 northeast of Madeira, in position 36° 10'N, 15° 52'W, by depth charges from the British destroyer *Hesperus;* 6 dead.

U94: launched 12 Jun 1940, commissioned 10 Aug 1940. Sunk 28 Aug 1942 east of Kingston, in position 17° 40'N, 74° 30'W, after being rammed three times and depth charged by the Canadian corvette *Oakville,* and by US bombs; 19 dead.

U95: launched 18 Jul 1940, commissioned 31 Aug 1940. Sunk 28 Nov 1941 southwest of Almeira, in position 36° 24'N, 03° 20'W, by a torpedo from the Dutch submarine *O 21;* 35 dead.

U96: launched 1 Aug 1940, commissioned 14 Sept 1940. Sunk 30 Mar 1945 at Wilhelmshaven by US bombs; wreck broken up.

U97: launched 15 Aug 1940, commissioned 28 Sept 1940. Sunk 16 Jun 1943 west of Haifa, in position 33°N, 34°E, by Australian bombs; 27 dead.

U98: launched 31 Aug 1940, commissioned 12 Oct 1940. Sunk 19 Nov 1942 west of Gibraltar, in position 35° 38'N, 11° 48'W, by British bombs; 46 dead (all crew lost).

U99: launched 12 Mar 1940, commissioned 18 Apr 1940; scuttled at 0343hrs on 17 Mar 1941 southeast of Iceland, in approximate position 61°N, 12°W, after being depth charged by the British destroyer *Walker;* 3 dead.

U100: launched 10 Apr 1940, commissioned 30 May 1940. Sank at 0318hrs on 17 Mar 1941 southeast of Iceland, in approximate position 61°N, 12°W, after being rammed and depth charged by the British destroyers *Walker* and *Vanoc;* 38 dead.

U101: launched 13 Jan 1940, commissioned 11 Mar 1940; stricken at Neustadt 21 Oct 1943; scuttled there 3 May 1945; wreck broken up.

U102: launched 21 Mar 1940, commissioned 27 Apr 1940; Missing (presumed sunk) on or after 30 Jun 1940 in the North Sea; position unknown; 43 dead (all crew lost).

U132: launched 10 Apr 1941, commissioned 29 May 1941. Sunk at 2345hrs on 3 Nov 1942 southeast of Cape Farewell, in position 58° 07'N, 33° 13'W, by the explosion of the steamship *Empire Lynx;* 47 dead (all crew lost).

U133: launched 28 Apr 1941, commissioned 5 Jul 1941. Sunk at 1900hrs on 14 Mar 1942 near Salamis, in position 37° 59'N, 23° 35'E, by a German mine; 45 dead (all crew lost).

U134: launched 17 May 1941, commissioned 26 Jul 1941. Sunk 24 Aug 1943 in the Bay of Biscay, in position 42° 07'N, 09° 30'W, by a British bomb; 48 dead (all crew lost).

U135: launched 12 Jun 1941, commissioned 16 Aug 1941. Sunk 15 Jul 1943 near Cap Yubi, in position 28° 20'N, 13° 17'W, by depth charges from the British sloop *Rochester,* the corvettes *Mignonette* and *Balsam* and US bombs; 5 dead.

U136: launched 5 Jul 1941, commissioned 30 Aug 1941. Sunk 11 Jul 1942 west of Madeira, in position 33° 30'N, 22° 52'W, by depth charges from the British sloop *Spey,* the frigate *Pelican* and the Free French destroyer *Léopard;* 45 dead (all crew lost).

U201: launched 7 Dec 1940, commissioned 25 Jan 1941. Sunk 17 Feb 1943 east of Newfoundland, in position 50° 36'N, 41° 07'W, by depth charges from the British destroyer *Fame;* 49 dead (all crew lost).

U202: launched 10 Feb 1941, commissioned 22 Mar 1941. Sunk at 0030hrs on 1 Jun 1943 southeast of Cape Farewell, in position 56° 12'N, 39° 52'W, by depth charges and gunfire from the British sloop *Starling;* 18 dead.

U203: launched 4 Jan 1941, commissioned 18 Feb 1941. Sunk 25 Apr 1943 south of Cape Farewell, in position 55° 05'N, 42° 25'W, by bombs and depth charges from aircraft from the British escort carrier *Biter* and by the destroyer *Pathfinder;* 10 dead.

U204: launched 23 Jan 1941, commissioned 8 Mar 1941. Sunk 19 Oct 1941 near Tangier, in position 35° 46'N, 06° 02'W, by depth charges from the British corvette *Mallow* and sloop *Rochester;* 46 dead (all crew lost).

U205: launched 20 Mar 1941, commissioned 3 May 1941. Sunk 17 Feb 1943 near the northernmost point of Cyrene, in position 32° 56'N, 22° 01'E, by bombs and by depth charges from the British destroyer *Paladin;* 8 dead.

U206: launched 4 Apr 1941, commissioned 17 May 1941. Sunk 30 Nov 1941 west of Nantes, in position 46° 55'N, 07° 16'W, by British bombs; 46 dead.

U207: launched 24 Apr 1941, commissioned 17 Jun 1941. Sunk 11 Sept 1941 in the Straits of Iceland southeast of Angmassalik, in position 63° 59'N, 34° 48'W, by depth charges from the British destroyers *Leamington* and *Veteran;* 41 dead (all crew lost).

U208: launched 21 May 1941, commissioned 5 Jul 1941. Sunk 11 Dec 1941 in the Atlantic west of Gibraltar, position unknown, by depth charges from the British corvette *Bluebell;* 45 dead (all crew lost).

U209: launched 28 Aug 1941, commissioned 11 Oct 1941. Sunk 19 May 1943 in the North Atlantic southeast of Cape Farewell, in position 54° 54'N, 34° 19'W, by depth charges from the British frigate *Jed* and the coastguard cutter *Sennen;* 46 dead (all crew lost).

U210: launched 23 Dec 1941, commissioned 21 Feb 1942. Sunk 6 Aug 1942 in the North Atlantic south of Cape Farewell, in position 54° 24'N, 34° 37'W, by ramming, depth charges and gunfire from their Canadian destroyer *Assiniboine;* 6 dead.

U211: launched 15 Jan 1941, commissioned 7 Mar 1942. Sunk 19 Nov 1943 east of the Azores, in position 40° 15'N, 19° 18'W, by a British bomb; 54 dead (all crew lost).

U212: launched 11 Mar 1942, commissioned 25 Apr 1942. Sunk 21 Jul 1944 in the Channel south of Brighton, in position 50° 27'N, 00° 13'W, by depth charges from the British frigates *Curzon* and *Ekins;* 49 dead (all crew lost).

U221: launched 14 Mar 1942, commissioned 9 May 1942. Sunk 27 Sept 1943 southwest of Ireland, in approximate position 47° 00'N, 18° 00'W, by British bombs; 50 dead (all crew lost).

U222: launched 28 Mar 1942, commissioned 23 May 1942. Sank 2 Sept 1944 in the Baltic Sea west of Pillau, in position 54° 25'N, 19° 30'E, after a collision with *U626;* 42 dead.

U223: launched 16 Apr 1942, commissioned 6 Jun 1942. Sunk 30 Mar 1944 north of Palermo, in position 38° 48'N, 14° 10'E, by depth charges from the British destroyers *Laforey* and *Tumult* and the escort destroyers *Hambledon* and *Blencathra;* 23 dead.

U224: launched 7 May 1942, commissioned 20 Jun 1942. Sunk 13 Jan 1943 in the western Mediterranean west of Algiers, in position 36° 28'N, 00° 49'E, by ramming and depth charges from the Canadian corvette *Ville de Quebec;* 45 dead.

U225: launched 28 May 1942, commissioned 11 Jul 1942. Sunk 21 Feb 1943 in the North Atlantic, in position 51° 25'N, 27° 28'W, by depth charges from the US coastguard cutter *Spencer;* 46 dead (all crew lost).

U226: launched 18 Jun 1942, commissioned 1 Aug 1942. Sunk at 0700hrs on 6 Nov 1943 in the North Atlantic east of Newfoundland, in position 44° 49'N, 41° 13'W, by depth charges from the British sloops *Starling, Woodcock* and *Kite;* 51 dead (all crew lost).

U227: launched 9 Jul 1942, commissioned 22 Aug 1942. Sunk 30 Apr 1943 north of the Faroes, in

Flooding slot identification of Type VII B and C U-boats (after Lennart Lindberg)

	A	B	C
Port	Bow slots	Holes under	Small slots
Starboard	(as above, fore to aft)	the gun	under the tower

Type VII B

Type VII B	A	B	C
U83–87	3 14 11	7 × 2	4 8 4 / 8
	3 15 10	7 × 2	8 4 / 8
U54, 99	3 15 10		4 8 4 / 8
	3 15 10		8 4 / 8
U101	0 18 10		4 8 4 / 8
	3 15 10		8 4 / 8
U73–76	3 15 10	6 + 7	· 4 8 4 · · / 8
	3 15 10	6 + 7	· · 8 4 · · / 8
U45–48 U51–52 U100	3 19 6		4 8 4 / 8
	3 15 10		8 4 / 8
U102	0 18 10		4 8 4 / 8
	0 18 10		8 4 / 8

Type VII C

Type VII C	A	B	C
U301	3 14 4	1 + 8 × 2 + 1	4 8 4 / 8
	3 14 4	1 + 8 × 2 + 1	8 4 / 8
U374–377	3 14 4	1 + 10 × 2 + 1	4 8 4 / 8
	3 14 4	1 + 10 × 2 + 1	8 4 / 8
U752–754	3 14 4	18 × 1	4 8 4 / 8
	3 16 6	18 × 1	8 4 / 8
U454–458	3 14 4		4 8 4 / 8
	3 15 8		8 4 / 8

Type VII C

Type VII C	A	B	C
U302–308 U378–379 U465–470 U755–761	3 14 4		4 8 4 / 8
	3 14 4		8 4 / 8
U921–930	3 14 4		4 8 4 / 8
	3 12 6		8 4 / 8
U93–94	3 16 1	27 × 1	2 10 4 / 10
	3 15 3	27 × 1	2 10 4 / 10
U71 U201–202	3 16 1	27 × 1	4 8 4 / 8
	3 15 3	27 × 1	4 8 4 / 4
U371–372	3 16 2	1 + 10 × 2 + 1	4 8 4 / 8
	3 14 8	1 + 10 × 2 + 1	4 8 4 / 8
U551–565	3 16 2	8 + 9	· 2 8 4 / 8
	3 14 10	8 + 9	8 4 / 8
U88–89 U332	3 16 2	1 + 8 × 2 + 1	4 8 4 / 8
	3 14 4	1 + 8 × 2 + 1	8 4 / 8
U90–92; 333–350 U351–370; 404–430 U433–450; 651–659 U702–722; 731–750 U821–826; 1161–1167 U1191–1210; 1301–1308	3 16 2		4 8 4 / 8
	3 14 4		8 4 / 8
U132–136 U251–260	3 16 2	8 + 9	· 4 8 4 · · / 8
	3 14 4	8 + 9	· · 8 4 · · / 8

Type VII C

Type VII C	A	B	C
U451–453	3 14 4		4 8 4 / 8
	3 14 8		4 8 4 / 8
U309–329 U380–40 U762–779 U903–904 U1131–1132	3 14 4		4 8 4 / 8
	3 14 1		8 4 / 8
U96–98 U69–90 U72	3 16 1	27 × 1	4 8 4 / 8
	3 14 4	27 × 1	4 8 4 / 8
U203–212	3 16 1		4 8 4 / 8
	3 15 3		4 8 4 / 8
U331	3 16 2	1 + 8 × 2 + 1	4 8 4 / 8
	3 14 8	1 + 8 × 2 + 1	8 4 / 8
U701	3 16 2		4 8 4 / 8
	3 14 8		8 4 / 8
U401–403 U431–432 U651–659	3 16 2	18 × 1	4 8 4 / 8
	3 14 4	18 × 1	8 4 / 8
U571–574	3 16 2	8 + 9	· 2 8 4 / 8
	3 14 4	8 + 9	8 4 / 8
U575–620	3 16 2		· 2 8 4 / 8
	3 14 4		8 4 / 8
U261–262	3 16 2		· 4 8 4 · · / 8
	3 14 4		· · 8 4 · · / 8

Note: in columns A and C, the first figure indicates the number of slots forward of the double row, the second figure gives the number of slots in the double row, and the third figure indicates the number of slots after the double row. The four echeloned slots at the bow are not counted in column A.

Type VII C	A	B	C
U566–570	3 16 2	8 + 9	· 2 8 4 / 8
	3 16 6	8 + 9	8 4 / 8
U77–82	3 16 2	8 + 9	· 4 8 4 · · / 8
	3 16 6	8 + 9	· · 8 4 · · / 8
U241–250 U1051–1058 U1063–1065	3 16 2		4 8 4 / 8
	3 14 4		4 8 4 / 8
U621–650 U951–1024	3 16 2		· 2 8 4 / 8
	3 14 1		8 4 / 8
U221–231	2 17 1		4 8 4 / 8
	3 16 2		4 8 4 / 8
U235–240	2 17 1		4 8 4 / 8
	2 17 2		4 8 4 / 8
U751	3 16 2	18 × 1	4 8 4 / 8
	3 16 6	18 × 1	8 4 / 8
U373	3 16 2	1 + 8 × 2 + 1	4 8 4 / 8
	3 12 10	1 + 8 × 2 + 1	4 8 4 / 8
U660	3 16 2	18 × 1	4 8 4 / 8
	3 14 4	18 × 1	8 4 / 8
U471–486 U661–683 U905–907 U1101–1110 U1168–1172	3 16 2		4 8 4 / 8
	3 14 1		8 4 / 8
U263–300 U1271–1279	3 16 2		· 4 8 4 · · / 8
	3 14 1		· · 8 4 · · / 8
U232	2 17 1		4 8 4 / 8
	3 15 3		4 8 4 / 8

position 64° 05'N, 06° 40'W, by British bombs; 49 dead (all crew lost).

U228: launched 30 Jul 1942, commissioned 12 Sept 1942; stricken at Bergen 5 Oct 1944; (see *U993*); broken up 1944–45.

U229: launched 20 Aug 1942, commissioned 3 Oct 1942. Sunk 22 Sept 1943 in the North Atlantic southeast of Cape Farewell, in position 54° 36'N, 36° 25'W, by depth charges from the British destroyer *Keppel;* 50 dead (all crew lost).

U230: launched 10 Sept 1942, commissioned 24 Oct 1942; ran aground on 21 Aug 1944 in the Toulon roadsteads, in position 43° 07'N, 20° 38'W; scuttled during the Allied invasion of southern France.

U231: launched 1 Oct 1942, commissioned 14 Nov 1942. Sunk 13 Jan 1944 northeast of the Azores, in position 44° 15'N, 20° 38'W, by British bombs; 7 dead.

U232: launched 15 Oct 1942, commissioned 28 Nov 1942. Sunk 8 Jul 1943 west of Oporto, in position 40° 37'N, 13° 41'W, by US bombs; 46 dead (all crew lost).

U235: launched 4 Nov 1942, commissioned 29 Dec 1942. Sunk 14 May 1943 at the Germania Dockyard, Kiel, by US bombs. Raised, repaired, and returned to service in May 1943. Sunk in error at 0700hrs on 14 Apr 1945 in position 57° 44'N, 10° 39'E, by depth charges from the German torpedo boat *T17*; 46 dead (all crew lost).

U236: launched 24 Nov 1942, commissioned 9 Jan 1943. Sunk 5 May 1945 near Schleimünde, in position 54° 37'N, 10° 03'E, by British bombs; number of fatalities unknown.

U237: launched 17 Dec 1942, commissioned 30 Jan 1943. Sunk 4 Apr 1945 at Deutsche Werke, Kiel, by British bombs; number of fatalities unknown.

U238: launched 7 Jan 1943, commissioned 20 Feb 1943. Sunk 9 Feb 1944 in the North Atlantic southwest of Ireland, in position 49° 45'N, 16° 07'W, by depth charges from the British sloops *Kite*, *Magpie* and *Starling*; 50 dead (all crew lost).

U239: launched 28 Jan 1943, commissioned 13 Mar 1943. Damaged on 24 Jul 1944, at Deutsche Werke, Kiel, by British bombs; stricken 5 Aug 1944; broken up in 1944.

U240: launched 18 Feb 1943, commissioned 3 Apr 1943. Sunk 16 May 1944 northeast of the Faroes, in position 63° 05'N, 03° 10'E, by bombs from a Norwegian aircraft; 50 dead (all crew lost).

U241: launched 25 Jun 1943, commissioned 24 Jul 1943. Sunk 18 May 1944 northeast of the Faroes, in position 63° 36'N, 01° 42'E, by British bombs; 51 dead (all crew lost).

U242: launched 20 Jul 1943, commissioned 14 Aug 1943. Sunk 30 Apr 1945 in the Irish Sea west of Blackpool, in position 53° 42'N, 04° 53'W, by torpedoes from the British destroyers *Hesperus* and *Havelock* and by British bombs; 44 dead (all crew lost).

U243: launched 2 Sept 1943, commissioned 2 Oct 1943. Sunk 8 Jul 1944 in the Bay of Biscay west of Nantes, in position 47° 06'N, 06° 40'W, by British bombs; 11 dead.

U244: launched 2 Sept 1943, commissioned 9 Oct 1943; surrendered at Lisahally, 14 May 1945 (Operation Deadlight).

U245: launched 25 Nov 1943, commissioned 18 Dec 1943; transferred from Bergen to Loch Ryan, 30 May 1945 (Operation Deadlight).

U246: launched 7 Dec 1943, commissioned 11 Jan 1944. Sunk 29 Mar 1945 in the Channel near Lands End, in position 49° 58'N, 05° 25'W, by depth charges from the British frigate *Duckworth*; 48 dead (all crew lost).

U247: launched 23 Sept 1943, commissioned 23 Oct 1943. Sunk 1 Sept 1944 in the Channel near Lands End, in position 49° 54'N, 05° 49'W, by depth charges from the Canadian frigates *St John* and *Swansea*; 52 dead (all crew lost).

U248: launched 7 Oct 1943, commissioned 6 Jun 1943. Sunk 16 Jan 1945 in the North Atlantic in position 47° 43'N, 26° 37'W, by depth charges from the US destroyer escorts *Hayter*, *Otter*, *Varian* and *Hubbard*; 47 dead (all crew lost).

U249: launched 23 Oct 1943, commissioned 20 Nov 1943; surrendered on 8 May 1945 at Portland; transferred to Loch Ryan as the British research vessel *N 86*; scuttled in Operation Deadlight.

U250: launched 11 Nov 1943, commissioned 12 Dec 1943. Sunk 30 Jul 1945 near Koivisto, in position 60° 29'N, 28° 28'E, by depth charges from the USSR guard boat *MO 103* and by USSR bombs; 46 dead. Raised by the USSR, and transferred to Kronstadt, 25 Sept 1944; broken up.

U251: launched 26 Jul 1941, commissioned 20 Sept 1941. Sunk 19 Apr 1945 in the Kattegat south of Göteborg, in position 56° 37'N, 11° 51'E, by British and Norwegian bombs; 39 dead.

U252: launched 14 Apr 1941, commissioned 4 Oct 1941. Sunk at 2230hrs on 14 Apr 1942 in the North Atlantic southwest of Ireland, in approximate position 47° 00'N, 18° 14'W, by depth charges from the British sloop *Stork* and the corvette *Vetch*; 44 dead (all crew lost).

U253: launched 30 Aug 1941, commissioned 21 Oct 1941. Sunk 25 Sept 1942 northwest of Iceland, in approximate position 67° 00'N, 23° 00'W, by a British mine; 45 dead (all crew lost).

U254: launched 20 Sept 1941, commissioned 8 Nov 1941. Sank 8 Dec 1942 in the North Atlantic southeast of Cape Farewell, in approximate position 55° 00'N, 40° 00'W, after a collision with the German U-boat *U221*; 41 dead.

U255: launched 8 Oct 1941, commissioned 29 Nov 1941; transferred to Loch Eriboll, then Loch Ryan, 14 May 1945 (Operation Deadlight).

U256: launched 8 Oct 1941, commissioned 18 Dec 1941; converted to *U-Flak 2* in May 1943; stricken at Bergen on 23 Oct 1942 after sustaining damage in approximate position 60° 24'N, 05° 19'E; transferred to Loch Eriboll, then Loch Ryan, 14 May 1945 (Operation Deadlight).

U257: launched 19 Nov 1941, commissioned 14 Jan 1942. Sunk 24 Feb 1944 in the North Atlantic, in approximate position 47° 19'N, 26° 00'W, by depth charges from the Canadian frigate *Waskesiu* and the British frigate *Nene*; 30 dead.

U258: launched 13 Dec 1941, commissioned 4 Feb 1942. Sunk 20 Apr 1943 in the North Atlantic, in position 55° 18'N, 27° 49'W, by British bombs; 49 dead (all crew lost).

U259; launched 30 Dec 1941, commissioned 18 Feb 1942. Sunk 15 Nov 1942 north of Algiers, in position 37° 20'N, 03° 05'E, by British bombs; 48 dead (all crew lost).

U260: launched 9 Feb 1945, commissioned 14 Mar 1942; scuttled at 2230hrs on 12 Mar 1945 south of Ireland, in position 51° 15'N, 09° 05'W, after being mined.

U261: launched 16 Feb 1942, commissioned 28 Mar 1942. Sunk 15 Sept 1942 west of the Shetlands, in position 59° 50'N, 09° 28'W, by British bombs; 43 dead (all crew lost).

U262: launched 10 Mar 1942, commissioned 15 Apr 1942; bombed at Gotenhafen in December 1944; stricken at Kiel, 2 Apr 1945; broken up in 1947.

U263: launched 18 Mar 1942, commissioned 6 Apr 1942. Sunk 20 Jan 1944 in the Bay of Biscay near La Rochelle, in position 46° 06'N, 01° 36'W, possibly by a mine; 51 dead (all crew lost).

U264: launched 2 Apr 1942, commissioned 22 May 1942. Sunk at 1707hrs on 19 Feb 1944 in the North Atlantic, in position 48° 31'N, 22° 05'W, by depth charges from the British sloops *Woodpecker* and *Starling*.

U265: launched 23 Apr 1942, commissioned 6 Jun 1942. Sunk 3 Feb 1943 south of Ireland, in position 56° 35'N, 22° 49'W, by British bombs; 46 dead (all crew lost).

U266: launched 11 May 1942, commissioned 24 Jun 1942. Sunk 14 May 1943 in the North Atlantic in position 47° 45'N, 26° 57'W, by British bombs; 47 dead (all crew lost).

U267: launched 23 May 1942, commissioned 11 Jul 1942; scuttled on 4 May 1945, in Gelting Bay; wreck broken up.

U268: launched 9 Jun 1942, commissioned 29 Jul 1942. Sunk 19 Feb 1943 west of Nantes, in position 47° 03'N, 05° 56'W, by British bombs; 45 dead (all crew lost).

U269: launched 24 Jun 1942, commissioned 19 Aug 1942. Sunk 25 Jun 1944 in the Channel southeast of Torquay, in position 50° 01'N, 02° 59'W, by depth charges from the British frigate *Bickerton*; 13 dead.

U270: launched 11 Jul 1942, commissioned 5 Sept 1942. Sunk at 0010hrs on 13 Aug 1944 in the Bay of Biscay west of La Rochelle, in position 46° 19'N, 02° 56'W, by Australian bombs.

U271: launched 29 Jul 1942, commissioned 23 Sept 1942. Sunk 28 Jan 1944 west of Limerick, in position 53° 15'N, 15° 52'W, by US bombs; 51 dead (all crew lost).

U272: launched 15 Aug 1942, commissioned 7 Oct 1942. Sank 12 Nov 1942 near Hela, in position 54° 45'N, 18° 50'E, after a collision (other vessel unknown); 28 dead.

U273: launched 2 Sept 1942, commissioned 21 Oct 1942. Sunk 19 May 1943 southwest of Iceland, in position 59° 25'N, 24° 33'W, by British bombs; 46 dead (all crew lost).

U274: launched 19 Sept 1942, commissioned 7 Nov 1942. Sunk 23 Oct 1943 in the North Atlantic southwest of Iceland in position 57° 14'N, 27° 50'W, by depth charges from the British destroyers *Duncan* and *Vedette*, and by British bombs; 48 dead (all crew lost).

U275: launched 8 Oct 1942, commissioned 25 Nov 1942. Sunk 10 Mar 1945 in the Channel south of Newhaven, in position 50° 36'N, 00° 04'E, by a mine; 48 dead (all crew lost).

U276: launched 24 Oct 1942, commissioned 9 Dec 1942; stricken 29 Sept 1944 at Neustadt; used as a floating electricity generating plant; surrendered 1945.

U277: launched 5 Nov 1942, commissioned 21 Dec 1942. Sunk 1 May 1944 in the Arctic southeast of Bear Island, in position 73° 24'N, 15° 32'E, by bombs from aircraft from the British escort carrier *Fencer;* 50 dead (all crew lost).

U278: launched 2 Dec 1942, commissioned 16 Jan 1943; transferred to Loch Eriboll, 19 May 1945 (Operation Deadlight).

U279: launched 16 Dec 1942, commissioned 3 Feb 1943. Sunk 4 Oct 1943 southwest of Iceland, in position 60° 51'N, 28° 26'W, by British bombs; 48 dead (all crew lost).

U280: launched 4 Jan 1943, commissioned 13 Feb 1943. Sunk 16 Nov 1943 southwest of Iceland, in position 49° 11'N, 27° 32'W, by British bombs; 49 dead (all crew lost).

U281: launched 16 Jan 1943, commissioned 27 Feb 1943; at Kristiansand-Süd on 29 May 1945; transferred to Loch Ryan for Operation Deadlight.

U282: launched 8 Feb 1943, commissioned 13 Mar 1943. Sunk 29 Oct 1943 southeast of Greenland, in position 55° 28'N, 31° 57'W, by depth charges from the British destroyers *Vidette* and *Duncan* and the corvette *Sunflower*; 48 dead (all crew lost).

U283: launched 17 Feb 1943, commissioned 31 Mar 1943. Sunk 11 Feb 1944 southwest of the Faeroes, in position 60° 45'N, 12° 50'W, by Canadian bombs; 49 dead (all crew lost).

U284: launched 6 Mar 1943, commissioned 14 Apr 1943; scuttled on 21 Dec 1943 in the North Atlantic southeast of Greenland, in position 55° 04'N, 30° 23'W, after sustaining sea damage.

U285: launched 3 Apr 1943, commissioned 15 May 1943. Sunk 15 Apr 1945 in the North Atlantic southwest of Ireland, in position 50° 13'N, 12° 48'W, by depth charges from the British frigates *Grindall* and *Keats*; 44 dead (all crew lost).

U286: launched 21 Apr 1943, commissioned 5 Jun 1943. Sunk 29 Apr 1945 in the Barents Sea north of Murmansk, in position 69° 29'N, 33° 37'E, by depth charges from the British frigates *Loch Insh*, *Anguilla* and *Cotton*; 51 dead (all crew lost).

U287: launched 13 Aug 1943, commissioned 22 Sept 1943; scuttled on 15/16 May 1945, in the Attenbruch roadsteads; exact position not known.

U288: launched 15 Apr 1943, commissioned 26 Jun 1943. Sunk 3 Apr 1944 in the Barents Sea southeast of Bear Island, in position 73° 44'N, 27° 12'E, by bombs and rockets from aircraft of the British escort carriers *Tracker* and *Activity*; 49 dead (all crew lost).

U289: launched 29 May 1943, commissioned 10 Jul 1943. Sunk 31 May 1944 in the Barents Sea southwest of Bear Island, in position 73° 32'N, 00° 28'E, by depth charges from the British destroyer *Milne;* 51 dead (all crew lost).

U290: launched 16 Jun 1943, commissioned 24 Jul 1943; scuttled in May 1945 in Kupfermühlen Bay, Flensburg Fjord.

U291: launched 30 Jun 1943, commissioned 4 Aug 1943; transferred from Wilhelmshaven to Loch Ryan 24 Jun 1945 for Operation Deadlight.

U292: launched 17 Jul 1943, commissioned 25 Aug 1943. Sunk 27 May 1944 west of Drontheim, in position 62° 37'N, 00° 57'E, by British bombs; 51 dead (all crew lost).

U293: launched 30 Jul 1943, commissioned 8 Sept 1943; surrendered at Loch Ailsh 11 May 1945; transferred to Loch Ryan for Operation Deadlight.

U294: launched 27 Aug 1943, commissioned 6 Oct 1943; at Narvik 19 May 1945; transferred to Loch Eriboll for Operation Deadlight.

U295: launched 13 Sept 1943, commissioned 20 Oct 1943; at Narvik, 19 May 1945; transferred to Loch Eriboll for Operation Deadlight.

U296: launched 25 Sept 1943, commissioned 3 Nov 1943. Sunk 22 Mar 1945 in the north of the Channel, in position 55° 23'N, 06° 40'W, by British aerial torpedoes; 42 dead (all crew lost).

U297: launched 9 Oct 1943, commissioned 17 Nov 1943. Sunk 6 Dec 1944 in Pentland Firth, in positionl 58° 44'N, 04° 29'W, by depth charges from the British frigates *Loch Insh* and *Goodall*; 50 dead (all crew lost).

U298: launched 25 Oct 1943, commissioned 1 Dec 1943; transferred from Bergen to Loch Ryan 29 May 1945 for Operation Deadlight.

U299: launched 6 Nov 1943, commissioned 15 Dec 1943; transferred from Bergen to Loch Ryan 29 May 1945 for Operation Deadlight.

U300: launched 23 Nov 1943, commissioned 29 Dec 1943. Sunk 22 Feb 1945 in the North Atlantic west of Cadiz, in position 36° 29'N, 08° 20'W, by depth charges from the British minesweepers *Recruit*, *Pincher* and the yacht *Evadne*; 9 dead.

U301: launched 25 Mar 1942, commissioned 9 May 1942. Sunk 21 Jan 1943 in the Mediterranean west of Bonifacio, in position 41° 27'N, 07° 04'W, by torpedoes from the British submarine *Sahib;* 45 dead.

U302: launched 25 Apr 1942, commissioned 16 Jun 1942. Sunk 6 Jun 1944 in the North Atlantic northwest of the Azores, in position 45° 05'N, 35° 11'W, by depth charges from the British frigate *Swale;* 51 dead (all crew lost).

U303: launched 16 May 1942, commissioned 7 Jul 1942. Sunk 21 May 1943 in the western Mediterranean south of Toulon, in position 42° 50'N, 06° 00'E, by torpedoes from the British submarine *Sickle;* 19 dead.

U304: launched 13 Jun 1942, commissioned 5 Aug 1942. Sunk 28 May 1943 in the North Atlantic southeast of Cape Farewell, in position 54° 50'N, 37° 20'W, by British bombs; 46 dead (all crew lost).

U305: launched 25 Jul 1942, commissioned 17 Sept

1942. Sunk 17 Jan 1944 in the North Atlantic southwest of Ireland, in position 49° 39'N, 20° 10'W, by depth charges from the British destroyer *Wanderer* and the frigate *Glenarm*; 51 dead (all crew lost).

U306: launched 29 Aug 1942, commissioned 21 Oct 1942. Sunk 31 Oct 1943 in the North Atlantic northeast of the Azores, in position 46° 19'N, 20° 44'W, by depth charges from the British destroyer *Whitehall* and the corvette *Geranium*; 51 dead (all crew lost).

U307: launched 30 Sept 1942, commissioned 18 Nov 1942. Sunk 29 Apr 1945 in the Barents Sea near Murmansk, in position 69° 24'N, 33° 44'E, by depth charges from the British frigate *Loch Insh*; 37 dead.

U308: launched 31 Oct 1942, commissioned 23 Dec 1942. Sunk 4 Jun 1943 in the North Sea northeast of the Faeroes, in position 64° 28'N, 03° 09'W, by torpedoes from the British submarine *Truculent*; 44 dead (all crew lost).

U309: launched 14 Dec 1942, commissioned 27 Jan 1943. Sunk 16 Feb 1945 in the North Sea east of Moray Firth, in position 58° 09'N, 02° 23'W, by depth charges from the Canadian frigate *St John*; 47 dead (all crew lost).

U310: launched 31 Dec 1942, commissioned 24 Feb 1943; used up; at Drontheim 29 May 1945; broken up in March 1947.

U311: launched 1 Feb 1943, commissioned 23 Mar 1943. Sunk 24 Apr 1944 southwest of Ireland, in position 50° 36'N, 18° 36'W, by Canadian bombs; 51 dead (all crew lost).

U312: launched 27 Feb 1943, commissioned 21 Apr 1943; at Narvik, 19 May 1945; transferred to Loch Eriboll for Operation Deadlight.

U313: launched 27 Mar 1943, commissioned 20 May 1943; at Narvik, 19 May 1945; transferred to Loch Eriboll for Operation Deadlight.

U314: launched 17 Apr 1943, commissioned 10 Jun 1943. Sunk 30 Jan 1944 in the Arctic Sea southeast of Bear Island, in position 73° 41'N, 24° 30'E, by depth charges from the British destroyers *White-hall* and *Meteor*; 49 dead (all crew lost).

U315: launched 29 May 1943, commissioned 10 Jul 1943; stricken at Drontheim, 1 May 1945; broken up in March 1947.

U316: launched 19 Jun 1943, commissioned 5 Aug 1943; scuttled on 2 May 1945 near Travemünde, in position 53° 58'N, 10° 53'E.

U317: launched 1 Sept 1943, commissioned 23 Oct 1943. Sunk 26 Jun 1944 northeast of the Shetlands, in position 62° 03'N, 01° 45'E, by British bombs; 50 dead (all crew lost).

U318: launched 25 Sept 1943, commissioned 13 Nov 1943; at Narvik, 19 May 1945; transferred to Loch Eriboll for Operation Deadlight.

U319: launched 16 Oct 1943, commissioned 4 Dec 1943. Sunk 15 Jul 1944 southwest of the Lindesnes Light, in position 57° 40'N, 05° 00'E, by British bombs; 51 dead (all crew lost).

U320: launched 6 Nov 1943, commissioned 30 Dec 1943. Sunk 8 May 1945 in the North Sea west of Bergen, in position 61° 32'N, 01° 53'E, by British bombs.

U321: launched 27 Nov 1943, commissioned 20 Jan 1944. Sunk 2 Apr 1945 southwest of Ireland, in position 50° 00'N, 12° 57'W, by Polish bombs; 41 dead (all crew lost).

U322: launched 18 Dec 1943, commissioned 5 Feb 1944. Sunk 25 Nov 1944 in the North Atlantic west of the Shetlands, in position 60° 18'N, 04° 52'W, by depth charges from the British frigate *Ascension* and by Norwegian bombs; 52 dead (all crew lost).

U323: launched 12 Jan 1944, commissioned 2 Mar 1944; scuttled on 3 May 1945 near Nordenham, in position 53° 30'N, 08° 30'E.

U324: launched 12 Feb 1944, commissioned 5 Apr 1944; at Bergen, 30 May 1945; broken up in March 1947.

U325: launched 25 Mar 1944, commissioned 6 May 1944. Sunk in April 1945 in the Channel, position and cause unknown; 51 dead (all crew lost).

U326: launched 22 Apr 1944, commissioned 6 Jun 1944. Sunk in April 1945 near England; possibly by a mine; 43 dead (all crew lost).

U327: launched 27 May 1944, commissioned 18 Jul 1944. Sunk 27 Feb 1945 in the west of the Channel, in position 49° 46'N, 05° 47'W, by depth charges from the British frigates *Labuan* and *Loch Fada* and the sloop *Wild Goose*; 46 dead (all crew lost).

U328: launched 15 Jul 1944, commissioned 19 Sept 1944; transferred from Bergen to Loch Ryan, 30 May 1945 (Operation Deadlight).

U329: construction suspended, 30 Sept 1943.

U330: construction suspended, 30 Sept 1943.

U331: launched 20 Dec 1940, commissioned 31 Mar 1941. Sunk 17 Nov 1942 in the Mediterranean northwest of Algiers, in position 37° 05'N, 02° 27'E, by bombs and aerial torpedoes from aircraft from the British carrier *Formidable*; 32 dead.

U332: launched 20 Mar 1941, commissioned 7 Jun 1941. Sunk 2 May 1943 north of Cap Finisterre, in position 44° 48'N, 08° 58'W, by Australian bombs; 45 dead (all crew lost).

U333: launched 14 Jun 1941, commissioned 25 Aug 1941. Sunk 31 Jul 1944 in the North Atlantic west of the Scilly Isles, in position 49° 39'N, 07° 28'W, by depth charges from the British sloop *Starling* and the frigate *Loch Killin*; 45 dead (all crew lost).

U334: launched 15 Aug 1941, commissioned 9 Oct 1941. Sunk 14 Jun 1943 in the North Atlantic southwest of Iceland, in position 58° 16'N, 28° 20'W, by depth charges from the British frigate *Jed* and the sloop *Pelican*; 47 dead (all crew lost).

U335: launched 15 Oct 1941, commissioned 17 Dec 1941. Sunk 3 Aug 1942 in the North Sea northeast of the Faeroes, in position 62° 48'N, 00° 12'W, by torpedoes from the British submarine *Saracen*; 43 dead.

U336: launched 1 Dec 1941, commissioned 14 Feb 1942. Sunk 4 Oct 1943 southwest of Iceland, in position 60° 40'N, 26° 30'W, by US bombs; 50 dead (all crew lost).

U337: launched 25 Mar 1942, commissioned 6 May 1942. Sunk 15 Jan 1943 southwest of Iceland, in position 57° 40'N, 27° 10'W, by British bombs; 47 dead (all crew lost).

U338: launched 20 Apr 1942, commissioned 25 Jun 1942. Sunk 20 Sept 1943 southwest of Iceland, in position 57° 40'N, 29° 48'W, by British bombs; 51 dead (all crew lost).

U339: launched 30 Jun 1942, commissioned 25 Aug 1942. Sunk 3 May 1945 near Wilhelmshaven, in position 53° 31'N, 08° 10'E, by British bombs.

U340: launched 20 Aug 1942, commissioned 16 Oct 1942. Sunk at 0430hrs on 2 Nov 1943 near Tangier, in position 35° 33'N, 06° 37'W, by depth charges from the British sloop *Fleetwood*, the destroyers *Active* and *Witherington* and by British bombs; 1 dead.

U341: launched 10 Oct 1942, commissioned 28 Nov 1942. Sunk at 0430hrs on 19 Sept 1943 southwest of Iceland, in position 58° 34'N, 25° 30'W, by Canadian bombs; 50 dead (all crew lost).

U342: launched 10 Nov 1942, commissioned 12 Jan 1943. Sunk 17 Apr 1944 southwest of Iceland, in position 60° 23'N, 29° 20'W, by Canadian bombs; 51 dead (all crew lost).

U343: launched 21 Dec 1942, commissioned 18 Feb 1943. Sunk 10 Mar 1944 in the Mediterranean south of Sardinia, in position 38° 07'N, 09° 41'E, by depth charges from the British anti-submarine trawler *Mull*; 51 dead (all crew lost).

U344: launched 29 Jan 1943, commissioned 26 Mar 1943. Sunk 24 Aug 1944 in the Barents Sea northeast of North Cape, in position 72° 49'N, 30° 41'E, by depth charges from the British sloops *Mermaid* and *Peacock*, the frigate *Loch Dunvegan* and the destroyer *Keppel*; 50 dead (all crew lost).

U345: launched 11 Mar 1943, commissioned 4 Apr 1943; damaged by US bombs, 13 Dec 1943; stricken at Kiel, 23 Dec 1943. Sunk 27 Dec 1945 near Warnemünde, in position 54° 19'N, 12° 01'E, by a mine while on passage to surrender.

U346: launched 13 Apr 1943, commissioned 7 Jun 1943. Sank 20 Sept 1943 in the Baltic Sea near Hela, in position 54° 25'N, 19° 50'E, in a diving accident; 37 dead.

U347: launched 24 May 1943, commissioned 7 Jul 1943. Sunk 17 Jul 1944 west of Narvik, in position 68° 35'N, 06° 00'E, by British bombs; 49 dead (all crew lost).

U348: launched 25 Jun 1943, commissioned 10 Aug 1943. Sunk 30 Mar 1945 near Hamburg, in position 53° 33'N, 09° 57'E, by British bombs; 2 dead.

U349: launched 22 Jul 1943, commissioned 8 Sept 1943; scuttled on 5 May 1945 in Gelting Bay; 1 dead; wreck broken up in 1948.

U350: launched 17 Aug 1943, commissioned 7 Oct 1943. Sunk in March 1945 near Hamburg, in position 53° 33'N, 09° 57'E, by British bombs.

U351: launched 27 Mar 1941, commissioned 20 Jun 1941; scuttled on 5 May 1945 at Hörup Haff; wreck broken up in 1948.

U352: launched 7 May 1941, commissioned 28 Aug 1941. Sunk 9 May 1942 in the North Atlantic south of Cape Hatteras, in position 34° 21'N, 76° 35'W, by depth charges from the US coastguard cutter *Icarus*; 15 dead.

U353: launched 11 Nov 1941, commissioned 31 Mar 1942. Sunk 16 Oct 1942 in the North Atlantic, in position 53° 54'N, 29° 30'W, by depth charges from the British destroyer *Fame*; 6 dead.

U354: launched 6 Jan 1942, commissioned 22 Apr 1942. Sunk 25 Aug 1942 in the Barents Sea northwest of Bear Island, in position 74° 54'N, 15° 26'E, by rockets from aircraft from the British escort carrier *Vindex*; 51 dead (all crew lost).

U355: launched 5 Jul 1941, commissioned 29 Oct 1941. Sunk 1 Apr 1944 in the Barents Sea southwest of Bear Island, in position 73° 07'N, 10° 21'E, by bombs and depth charges from aircraft from the British escort carrier *Tracker* and the destroyer *Beagle*; 52 dead (all crew lost).

U356: launched 16 Sept 1941, commissioned 20 Dec 1941. Sunk 27 Dec 1942 in the North Atlantic north of the Azores, in position 43° 30'N, 25° 40'W, by depth charges from the Canadian destroyer *St Laurent* and the corvettes *Chilliwack*, *Battleford* and *Napanee*; 46 dead (all crew lost).

U357: launched 31 Mar 1942, commissioned 18 Jun 1942. Sunk 26 Dec 1942 in the North Atlantic northwest of Ireland, in position 57° 10'N, 15° 40'W, by depth charges from the British destroyers *Hesperus* and *Vanessa*; 36 dead.

U358: launched 21 Apr 1942, commissioned 15 Aug 1942. Sunk 1 Mar 1944 in the North Atlantic north of the Azores, in position 45° 46'N, 23° 16'W, by depth charges from the British frigates *Gould*, *Affleck*, *Gore* and *Garlies*; 50 dead.

U359: launched 11 Jun 1942, commissioned 5 Oct 1942. Sunk 28 Jul 1943 in the Caribbean south of San Domingo, in position 15° 57'N, 68° 30'W, by US bombs; 47 dead (all crew lost).

U360: launched 9 Sept 1942, commissioned 18 Dec 1942. Sunk 17 Jul 1944 west of Narvik, in position 68° 36'N, 08° 33'E, by British bombs; 52 dead (all crew lost).

U361: launched 21 Oct 1942, commissioned 4 Feb 1943. Sunk 5 Sept 1944 west of Narvik, in position 68° 36'N, 08° 33'E, by British bombs; 52 dead (all crew lost).

U362: launched 21 Oct 1942, commissioned 4 Feb 1943. Sunk 5 Sept 1944 in the Kara Sea, near Krakovka Island, exact position not known, by depth charges from the USSR minesweeper *T-116*; 51 dead (all crew lost).

U363: launched 17 Dec 1942, commissioned 18 Mar 1943; at Narvik, 19 Sept 1945; transferred to Loch Eriboll for Operation Deadlight.

U364: launched 21 Jan 1943, commissioned 3 May 1943. Sunk 30 Jan 1944 west of Bordeaux, in position 45° 25'N, 05° 15'W, by British bombs; 49 dead (all crew lost).

U365: launched 9 Mar 1943, commissioned 8 Jun 1943. Sunk 13 Dec 1944 in the Arctic Ocean east of Jan Mayen, in position 70° 43'N, 08° 07'E, by bombs from aircraft of the British escort carrier *Campania*; 50 dead (all crew lost).

U366: launched 16 Apr 1943, commissioned 16 Jul 1943. Sunk 5 Mar 1944 in the Arctic Ocean northwest of Hammerfest, in position 72° 10'N, 14° 45'E, by rockets from aircraft of the British escort carrier *Chaser*; 50 dead (all crew lost).

U367: launched 11 Jun 1943, commissioned 27 Aug 1943. Sank 15 Mar 1945 in the Baltic Sea near Hela, in position 54° 25'N, 19° 50'E, either in a diving accident or after hitting a mine; 43 dead (all crew lost).

U368: launched 16 Nov 1943, commissioned 7 Jan 1944; at Wilhelmshaven, 23 Jun 1945; transferred to Loch Ryan for Operation Deadlight.

U369: launched 17 Aug 1943, commissioned 15 Oct 1943; transferred from Kirstiansand-Süd to Scapa Flow 29 May 1945 for Operation Deadlight.

U370: launched 24 Sept 1943, commissioned 19 Nov 1943; scuttled in Gelting Bay, 5 May 1945; wreck broken up c1948.

U371: launched 27 Jan 1941, commissioned 15 Mar 1941. Sunk at 0409hrs on 4 May 1944 in the Mediterranean, north of Constantine, in position 37° 49'N, 05° 39'E, by depth charges from the US destroyer escorts *Pride* and *Joseph E Campbell*, the French *Senegalais*, and the British *Blankney*; 3 dead.

U372: launched 8 Mar 1941, commissioned 19 Apr 1941. Sunk 4 Aug 1942 in the Mediterranean near Jaffa, in position 32° 00'N, 34° 00'E, by depth charges from the British destroyers *Sikh* and *Zulu*, and the escort destroyers *Croome* and *Tettcott*, and by British bombs.

U373: launched 5 Apr 1941, commissioned 22 May 1941. Sunk 8 Jun 1944 west of Brest, in position 48° 10'N, 05° 31'W, by British bombs; 4 dead.

U374: launched 10 May 1941, commissioned 21 Jun 1941. Sunk 12 Jan 1942 in the western Mediterranean east of Catania, in position 37° 50'N, 16° 00'E, by torpedoes from the British submarine *Unbeaten*; 42 dead.

U375: launched 7 Jun 1941, commissioned 19 Jul 1941. Sunk 30 Jul 1943 in the western Mediterranean northwest of Malta, in position 36° 40'N, 12° 28'E, by depth charges from the US submarine chaser *PC 24*; 45 dead (all crew lost).

U376: launched 10 Jul 1941, commissioned 21 Aug 1941. Sunk 10 Apr 1943 west of Nantes, in position 46° 48'N, 09° 00'W, by British bombs; 47 dead (all crew lost).

U377: launched 12 Aug 1941, commissioned 2 Oct 1941. Sunk 15 Jan 1944 in the Atlantic, by rockets and depth charges from aircraft of the US escort carrier *Santee;* 52 dead (all crew lost).

U378: launched 13 Sept 1941, commissioned 30 Oct 1941. Sunk 20 Oct 1943 in the North Atlantic, in position 47° 40'N, 28° 27'W, by bombs from aircraft of the British escort carrier *Core*; 48 dead (all crew lost).

U379: launched 16 Oct 1941, commissioned 29 Nov 1941. Sunk 8 Aug 1942 in the North Atlantic southeast of Cape Farewell, in position 57° 11'N, 30° 57'W, by ramming and depth charges from the British corvette *Dianthus*; 40 dead.

U380: launched 15 Nov 1941, commissioned 22 Dec 1941. Sunk at 1200hrs on 11 Mar 1944 near Toulon, in position 43° 07'N, 05° 55'E, by US bombs; 1 dead.

U381: launched 14 Jan 1942, commissioned 25 Feb 1942. Sunk 19 May 1943 in the North Atlantic southeast of Cape Farewell, in position 54° 41'N, 34° 45'W, by depth charges from the British destroyer *Duncan* and the corvette *Snowflake*; 47 dead (all crew lost).

U382: launched 21 Mar 1942, commissioned 25 Apr 1942. Sunk in January 1945 at Entrance 4 at Wilhelmshaven by British bombs. Raised on 20 Mar 1945; stricken; scuttled 3 May 1945.

U383: launched 22 Apr 1942, commissioned 6 Jun 1942. Sunk 1 Aug 1943 west of Brest, in position 47° 24'N, 12° 10'W, by British bombs; 52 dead (all crew lost).

U384: launched 28 May 1942, commissioned 18 Jul 1942. Sunk at 1745hrs on 19 Mar 1943 southwest of Iceland, in position 54° 18'N, 26° 15'W, by British bombs; 47 dead (all crew lost).

U385: launched 8 Jul 1942, commissioned 29 Aug 1942. Sunk 11 Aug 1944 in the Bay of Biscay west of La Rochelle, in position 46° 16'N, 02° 45'W, by depth charges from the British sloop *Starling* and Australian bombs; 1 dead.

U386: launched 19 Aug 1942, commissioned 10 Oct 1942. Sunk 19 Feb 1944 in the North Atlantic in position 48° 51'N, 22° 44'W, by depth charges from the British frigate *Spey*; 33 dead.

U387: launched 1 Oct 1942, commissioned 24 Nov 1942. Sunk 9 Dec 1944 in the Barents Sea near Murmansk, in position 69° 41'N, 33° 12'E, by depth charges from the British corvette *Bamborough Castle*; 51 dead (all crew lost).

U388: launched 12 Nov 1942, commissioned 31 Dec 1942. Sunk 20 Jun 1943 in the North Atlantic southeast of Cape Farewell, in position 57° 36'N, 31° 20'W, by US bombs; 47 dead (all crew lost).

U389: launched 11 Dec 1942, commissioned 6 Feb 1943. Sunk 5 Oct 1943 in the Straits of Denmark southeast of Angmagssalik, in position 62° 43'N, 27° 17'W, by British bombs; 50 dead (all crew lost).

U390: launched 23 Jan 1943, commissioned 13 Mar 1943. Sunk at 1500hrs on 5 Jul 1944 in the Baie de la Seine, in position 49° 52'N, 00° 48'W, by depth charges from the British destroyer *Wanderer* and the frigate *Tavy*; 48 dead.

U391: launched 5 Mar 1943, commissioned 24 Apr 1943. Sunk 13 Dec 1943 northwest of Cap Ortegal, in position 45° 45'N, 09° 38'W, by British bombs; 51 dead (all crew lost).

U392: launched 10 Apr 1943, commissioned 29 May 1943. Sunk 16 Mar 1944 in the Straits of Gibraltar, in position 35° 55'N, 05° 41'W, by depth charges from the British frigate *Affleck*, the destroyer *Vanoc*, and US bombs; 52 dead (all crew lost).

U393: launched 15 Mar 1943, commissioned 3 Jul 1943; scuttled on 4 May 1945 near Holnis, position unknown; after being damaged by British bombs; 2 dead.

U394: launched 19 Jun 1943, commissioned 7 Aug 1943. Sunk 2 Sept 1944 in the North Sea west of Harstad, in position 69° 47'N, 04° 10'E, by bombs and depth charges from aircraft of the British escort carrier *Vindex*, by the destroyers *Keppel* and *Whitehall* and the sloops *Mermaid* and *Peacock*; 50 dead (all crew lost).

U395: launched 17 Jul 1943, bombed while still in the dockyard; never completed.

U396: launched 27 Aug 1943, commissioned 16 Oct 1943. Sunk 23 Apr 1945 in the North Atlantic southwest of the Shetlands, in position 59° 29'N, 05° 22'W, by British bombs; 45 dead (all crew lost).

U397: launched 6 Oct 1943, commissioned 20 Nov 1943; scuttled 5 May 1945 in Gelting Bay.

U398: launched in November 1943, commissioned 18 Dec 1943. Sunk in May 1945 off the British coast, position and cause unknown; 43 dead (all crew lost).

U399: launched in December 1943, commissioned 22 Jan 1944. Sunk 26 Mar 1945 in the Channel near Land's End, in position 49° 56', 05° 22'W, by depth charges from the British frigate *Duckworth*; 46 dead.

U400: launched in January 1944, commissioned 18 Mar 1944. Sunk 17 Dec 1944 in the North Atlantic south of Cork, in position 51° 16'N, 08° 05'W, by depth charges from the British frigate *Nyasaland*; 50 dead (all crew lost).

U401: launched 16 Dec 1940, commissioned 10 Apr 1941. Sunk 3 Aug 1941 in the North Atlantic southwest of Ireland, in position 50° 27'N, 19° 50'W, by depth charges from the British destroyer *Wanderer*, the Norwegian destroyer *St Albans* and the British corvette *Hydrangea*; 44 dead (all crew lost).

U402: launched 28 Dec 1940, commissioned 21 May 1941. Sunk 13 Oct 1943 in the middle of the North Atlantic, in position 48° 56'N, 29° 41'W, by bombs from the aircraft of the US escort carrier *Card*; 50 dead (all crew lost).

U403: launched 26 Feb 1941, commissioned 25 Jun 1941. Sunk 17 Aug 1943 in the mid-Atlantic near Dakar, in position 14° 11'N, 17° 40'W, by British and French bombs; 49 dead (all crew lost).

U404: launched 6 Apr 1941, commissioned 6 Aug 1941. Sunk 28 Jul 1943 in the Bay of Biscay northwest of Cape Ortegal, in position 45° 53'N, 09° 25'W, by US and British bombs; 50 dead (all crew lost).

U405: launched 4 Jun 1941, commissioned 17 Sept 1941. Sunk 1 Nov 1943 in the North Atlantic, in position 49° 00'N, 31° 14'W, by ramming, small arms fire and depth charges from the US destroyer *Borie*, during a storm; 49 dead (all crew lost).

U406: launched 16 Jun 1941, commissioned 22 Oct 1941. Sunk 18 Feb 1944 in the North Atlantic, in position 48° 32'N, 23° 36'W, by depth charges from the British frigate *Spey*; 12 dead.

U407: launched 16 Aug 1941, commissioned 18 Dec 1941. Sunk 19 Sept 1944 in the Mediterranean south of Milos, in position 36° 27'N, 24° 33'E, by depth charges from the British destroyers *Troubridge* and *Terpischore* and the Polish destroyer *Garland*; 5 dead.

U408: launched 16 Jul 1941, commissioned 19 Nov 1941. Sunk 5 Nov 1942 north of Iceland, in position 67° 40'N, 18° 32'W, by US bombs; 45 dead (all crew lost).

U409: launched 23 Sept 1941, commissioned 21 Jan 1942. Sunk 12 Jul 1943 in the Mediterranean northeast of Algiers, in position 37° 12'N, 04° 00'E, by depth charges from the British destroyer *Inconstant;* 11 dead.

U410: launched 14 Oct 1941, commissioned 23 Feb 1942. Sunk at 1200hrs on 11 Mar 1944 near Toulon, in position 43° 07'N, 05° 55'E, by US bombs.

U411: launched 15 Nov 1941, commissioned 18

Mar 1942. Sunk 28 Nov 1942 in the Mediterranean near Bone, in position 37° 05'N, 07° 55'E, by bombs and by depth charges from the Australian destroyer *Quiberon* and the British destroyer *Quentin*; 46 dead (all crew lost).

U412: launched 15 Dec 1942, commissioned 29 Apr 1942. Sunk 22 Oct 1942 northeast of the Faeroes, in position 63° 55'N, 00° 24'E, by British bombs; 47 dead (all crew lost).

U413: launched 15 Jan 1942, commissioned 3 Jun 1942. Sunk on 20 Aug 1944 in the Channel south of Brighton, in position 50° 21'N, 00° 01'W, by depth charges from the British escort destroyer *Wensleydale* and the destroyers *Forester* and *Vidette*; 45 dead.

U414: launched 25 Mar 1942, commissioned 1 Jul 1942. Sunk 25 May 1943 in the western Mediterranean northwest of Ténès, in position 36° 31'N, 00° 40'E, by depth charges from the British corvette *Vetch*; 47 dead (all crew lost).

U415: launched 9 May 1942, commissioned 5 Aug 1942. Sunk at 0915hrs on 14 Jul 1944 near Brest, west of the torpedo net barrier, in position 48° 24'N, 04° 30'W, by a mine; 2 dead.

U416: launched 9 May 1942, commissioned 4 Nov 1942. Sunk 30 Mar 1943 in the Baltic Sea near Bornholm, position unknown, by a mine laid by the USSR submarine *L 3 (Frunzevez)*; number of fatalities unknown. Raised 8 Apr 1943; used for training from 4 Oct 1943; sank on 12 Dec 1944 in the Baltic Sea northwest of Pillau, in position 54° 58'N, 19° 33'E, after a collision with *M 203*; 36 dead.

U417: launched 6 Jun 1942, commissioned 26 Sept 1942. Sunk 11 Jun 1943 southeast of Iceland, in position 63° 20'N, 10° 30'W, by British bombs; 46 dead (all crew lost).

U418: launched 11 Jul 1942, commissioned 21 Oct 1942. Sunk 1 Jun 1943 northwest of Cape Ortegal, in position 47° 05'N, 08° 55'W, by British bombs; 48 dead (all crew lost).

U419: launched 22 Aug 1942, commissioned 18 Nov 1942. Sunk 8 Oct 1943 in the North Atlantic, in position 56° 31'N, 27° 05'W, by British bombs; 48 dead.

U420: launched 12 Aug 1942, commissioned 16 Dec 1942. Sunk 26 Oct 1943 in the North Atlantic, in position 50° 49'N, 41° 01'W, by Canadian bombs; 49 dead (all crew lost).

U421: launched 24 Sept 1942, commissioned 13 Jan 1943. Sunk at 1200hrs on 29 Apr 1944 near Toulon, in position 43° 07'N 05° 55'E, by US bombs.

U422: launched 10 Oct 1942, commissioned 10 Feb 1943. Sunk 4 Oct 1943 in the North Atlantic north of the Azores, in position 43° 18'N, 28° 58'W, by bombs from aircraft of the US escort carrier *Card*; 49 dead (all crew lost).

U423: launched 7 Nov 1942, commissioned 3 Mar 1943. Sunk 17 Jun 1944 northeast of the Faeroes, in position 63° 06'N, 02° 05'E, by Norwegian bombs; 53 dead (all crew lost).

U424: launched 28 Nov 1942, commissioned 7 Apr 1943. Sunk 11 Feb 1944 in the North Atlantic southwest of Ireland, in position 50° 00'N, 18° 14'W, by depth charges from the British sloops

Wild Goose and *Woodpecker*; 50 dead (all crew lost).

U425: launched 19 Dec 1942, commissioned 21 Apr 1943. Sun 17 Feb 1945 in the Barents Sea near Murmansk, in position 69° 39'N, 35° 50'E, by depth charges from the British sloop *Lark* and the corvette *Alnwick Castle*; 52 dead.

U426: launched 6 Feb 1943, commissioned 12 May 1943. Sunk 8 Jan 1944 west of Nantes, in position 46° 47'N, 10° 42'W, by Australian bombs; 51 dead (all crew lost).

U427: launched 6 Feb 1943, commissioned 2 Jun 1943; at Narvik 19 May 1945; transferred to Loch Eriboll for Operation Deadlight.

U428: launched 11 Mar 1943, commissioned 26 Jun 1943; renamed *S 1* after being transferred to Italy in exchange for transport vessels; reverted to Germany, as *U428* after the Italian surrender; scuttled on 3 May 1945 in the Nord-Ostsee canal at Audorf, in position 54° 19'N, 09° 40'E; wreck broken up in 1946.

U429: launched 30 Mar 1943, commissioned 14 Jul 1943; renamed *S 4* after being transferred to Italy in exchange for transport vessels; reverted to Germany as *U429* after the Italian surrender. Sunk 30 Mar 1945 near Wilhelmshaven, in position 53° 31'N, 08° 10'E, by US bombs.

U430: launched 22 Apr 1943, commissioned 4 Aug 1943; renamed *S 6* after being transferred to Italy in exchange for transport vessels; reverted to Germany as *U430* after the Italian surrender. Sunk 30 Mar 1945 near Bremen, in position 53° 08'N, 08° 46'E, by US bombs; 1 dead.

U431: launched 2 Feb 1943, commissioned 5 Apr 1943. Sunk on 30 Oct 1943 in the Mediterranean southeast of Toulon, in position 43° 04'N, 05° 57'E, by a torpedo from the British submarine *Ultimatum*; 52 dead (all crew lost).

U432: launched 3 Feb 1941, commissioned 26 Apr 1941. Sunk 11 Mar 1943, in the North Atlantic, in position 51° 35'N, 28° 20'W, by depth charges and gunfire from the Free French corvette *Aconit*; 26 dead.

U433: launched 15 Mar 1941, commissioned 24 May 1941. Sank at 2155hrs on 16 Nov 1941 in the Mediterranean south of Malaga, in position 36° 13'N, 04° 42'W, after being damaged by depth charges and gunfire 25nm east of Gibraltar by the British corvette *Marigold*; 6 dead.

U434: launched 1 Apr 1941, commissioned 21 Jun 1941. Sunk 18 Dec 1941 in the North Atlantic north of Madeira, in position 36° 15'N, 15° 48'W, by depth charges from the British escort destroyer *Blankney* and the destroyer *Stanley*; 2 dead.

U435: launched 31 May 1941, commissioned 30 Aug 1941. Sunk 9 Jul 1943 west of Figueira, in position 39° 48'N, 14° 22'W, by British bombs; 48 dead (all crew lost).

U436: launched 21 Jun 1941, commissioned 27 Sept 1941. Sunk 26 May 1943 in the North Atlantic west of Cape Ortegal, in position 43° 49'N, 15° 56'W, by depth charges from the British frigate *Test* and the corvette *Hyderabad*; 47 dead (all crew lost).

U437: launched 15 Jun 1941, commissioned 25 Oct

1941; damaged by British bombs at Bergen, 4 Oct 1944, and stricken 5 Oct 1944; broken up in 1946.

U438: launched in July 1941, commissioned 22 Nov 1941. Sunk 6 May 1943 in the North Atlantic northeast of Newfoundland, in approximate position 52° 00'N, 45° 10'W, by depth charges from the British sloop *Pelican*; 48 dead (all crew lost).

U439: launched 10 Aug 1941, commissioned 20 Dec 1941. Sunk at 0030hrs on 4 May 1943 in the North Atlantic west of Cape Ortgal, in position 43° 32'N, 13° 20'W, in a collision with *U659*; 40 dead.

U440: launched 1 Sept 1941, commissioned 24 Jan 1942. Sunk 31 May 1943 in the North Atlantic northwest of Cape Ortegal, in position 45° 38'N, 13° 04'W, by British bombs; 46 dead (all crew lost).

U441: launched 13 Dec 1941, commissioned 21 Feb 1942; refitted and renamed *U-Flak 1*, April–July 1943. Sunk 18 Jun 1944 northwest of Brest, in position 49° 03'N, 04° 48'W, by Polish bombs; 51 dead (all crew lost).

U442: launched 12 Jan 1942, commissioned 21 Mar 1942. Sunk 12 Feb 1943 west of Cape St Vincent, in position 37° 32'N, 11° 56'W, by British bombs; 48 dead (all crew lost).

U443: launched 31 Jan 1942, commissioned 18 Apr 1942. Sunk 23 Feb 1943 in the Mediterranean near Algiers, in position 36° 55'N, 02° 25'E, by depth charges from the British escort destroyers *Bicester*, *Lamerton* and *Wheatland*; 48 dead (all crew lost).

U444: launched 1 Jan 1942, commissioned 9 May 1942. Sunk 11 Mar 1943 in the North Atlantic, in position 51° 14'N, 29° 18'W, by ramming and depth charges from the British destroyer *Harvester* and the Free French corvette *Aconit*; 41 dead.

U445: launched 1 Feb 1942, commissioned 30 May 1942. Sunk 24 Aug 1944 in the Bay of Biscay west of St Nazaire, in position 47° 21'N, 05° 50'W, by depth charges from the British frigate *Louis*; 52 dead (all crew lost).

U446: launched 11 Apr 1942, commissioned 20 Jun 1942. Sunk 21 Sept 1942 near Kallberg in the Gulf of Danzig, exact position unknown, by a mine; 23 dead. Raised 8 Nov 1942; stricken 12 Nov 1942; scuttled 3 May 1945 near Kiel, in position 59° 19'N, 10° 10'E; wreck broken up in 1947.

U447: launched 30 Apr 1942, commissioned 11 Jul 1942. Sunk 7 May 1943 west of Gibraltar, in position 35° 30'N, 11° 55'W, by British bombs; 48 dead (all crew lost).

U448: launched May 1942, commissioned 1 Aug 1942. Sunk 14 Apr 1944 in the North Atlantic northeast of the Azores, in position 46° 22'N, 19° 35'W, by depth charges from the Canadian frigate *Swansea* and the British sloop *Pelican*; 9 dead.

U449: launched 13 Jun 1942, commissioned 22 Aug 1942. Sunk at 1600hrs on 24 Jun 1943 in the North Atlantic, northwest of Cape Ortegal, in position 45° 00'N, 11° 59'W, by depth charges from the British sloops *Wren*, *Woodpecker*, *Kite* and *Wild Goose*; 49 dead (all crew lost).

U450: launched 4 Jul 1942, commissioned 12 Sept 1942. Sunk 10 Mar 1944 in the western Mediterranean south of Ostia, in position 41° 11'N, 12° 27'E, by depth charges from the British escort destroyers *Blankney*, *Blencathra*, *Brecon* and *Exmoor*, and the US destroyer *Madison*.

U451: launched 5 Mar 1941, commissioned 3 May 1941. Sunk 21 Dec 1941 near Tangiers, in position 35° 55'N, 06° 08'W, by British bombs; 44 dead.

U452: launched 29 Mar 1941, commissioned 29 May 1941. Sunk 25 Aug 1941 in the North Sea southeast of Iceland, in position 61° 30'N, 15° 30'W, by depth charges from the British trawler *Vascama* and British bombs; 42 dead (all crew lost).

U453: launched 30 Apr 1941, commissioned 26 Jun 1941. Sunk 21 May 1944 in the Ionian Sea northeast of Cape Spartivento, in position 38° 13'N, 16° 30'E, by depth charges from the British destroyers *Termagant* and *Tenacious* and the escort destroyer *Liddlesdale*; 1 dead.

U454: launched 30 Apr 1941, commissioned 24 Jul 1941. Sunk at 1400hrs on 1 Aug 1943 northwest of Cape Ortegal, in position 45° 36'N, 10° 23'W, by Australian bombs; 32 dead.

U455: launched 21 Jun 1941, commissioned 21 Aug 1941. Sunk 6 Apr 1944 near La Spezia, in position 44° 04'N, 09° 51'E, by a mine, possibly German; 51 dead (all crew lost).

U456: launched 21 Jun 1941, commissioned 18 Sept 1941. Sunk 12 May 1943 in the North Atlantic, in position 47° 00'N, 26° 20'W, by aerial torpedoes and bombs from aircraft of the British escort carrier *Biter* and gunfire from the British destroyer *Pathfinder*; 49 dead (all crew lost).

U457: launched 4 Oct 1941, commissioned 5 Nov 1941. Sunk 16 Sept 1942 in the Barents Sea northeast of Murmansk, in position 75° 05'N, 43° 15'E, by depth charges from the British destroyer *Impulsive*; 45 dead (all crew lost).

U458: launched 4 Oct 1941, commissioned 12 Dec 1941. Sunk 22 Aug 1943 in the Mediterranean southeast of Pantelleria, in position 36° 25'N, 12° 39'E, by depth charges from the British escort destroyer *Easton* and the Greek escort destroyer *Pindos*; 8 dead.

U465: launched 30 Mar 1942, commissioned 20 May 1942. Sunk 5 May 1943 west of St Nazaire, in position 47° 06'N, 10° 58'W, by Australian bombs; 48 dead (all crew lost).

U466: launched 30 Mar 1942, commissioned 17 Jun 1942; scuttled 19 Aug 1944 at Toulon during the Allied invasion of southern France.

U467: launched 16 May 1942, commissioned 15 Jul 1942. Sunk 25 May 1943 southeast of Iceland, in position 62° 25'N, 14° 52'W, by US bombs; 46 dead (all crew lost).

U468: launched 16 May 1942, commissioned 12 Aug 1942. Sunk 11 Aug 1943 near Bathurst, in position 12° 20'N, 20° 07'W, by British bombs; 42 dead.

U469: launched 8 Aug 1942, commissioned 7 Oct 1942. Sunk 25 Mar 1943 south of Iceland, in position 62° 12'N, 16° 40'W, by British bombs; 46 dead (all crew lost).

U470: launched 8 Aug 1942, commissioned 7 Jan 1943. Sunk 16 Oct 1943 southwest of Iceland, in position 58° 20'N, 29° 20'W, by British bombs; 46 dead.

U471: launched 6 Mar 1943, commissioned 5 May 1943. Sunk 6 Aug 1944 near Toulon, in position 43°

07'N, 05° 55'E, by British bombs. Raised in 1945; returned to service as the French submarine *Millé* from 1946; stricken 9 Jul 1963 as *Q 339*.

U472: launched 6 Mar 1943, commissioned 26 May 1943. Sunk 4 Mar 1944 in the Barents Sea southeast of Bear Island, in position 73° 05'N, 26° 40'E, by gunfire and rockets from the British destroyer *Onslaught* and aircraft of the escort carrier *Chaser*; 22 dead.

U473: launched 17 Apr 1943, commissioned 16 Jun 1943. Sunk 5 May 1944 in the North Atlantic west southwest of Ireland, in position 49° 29'N, 21° 22'W, by depth charges from the British sloops, *Starling*, *Wren* and *Wild Goose*; 23 dead.

U474: launched 17 Apr 1943. Sunk in 1943 by bombs while in the dockyard; 95 per cent repaired by 1945; scuttled 3 May 1945; broken up in 1946.

U475: launched 28 May 1943, commissioned 7 Jul 1943; scuttled 3 May 1945 at Kiel-Wik, in position 54° 19'N, 10° 10'E; wreck broken up in 1947.

U476: launched 5 Jun 1943, commissioned 28 Jul 1943; scuttled at 0102hrs on 25 May 1944 northwest of Drontheim, in position 65° 08'N, 04° 53'E, by torpedoes from *U990* after being damaged by British bombs; 33 dead.

U477: launched 3 Jul 1943, commissioned 18 Aug 1943. Sunk 3 Jun 1944 west of Drontheim, in position 63° 59'N, 01° 37'E, by Canadian bombs; 51 dead (all crew lost).

U478: launched 17 Jul 1943, commissioned 8 Sept 1943. Sunk 30 Jun 1944 northeast of the Faeroes, in position 63° 27'N, 00° 50'W, by Canadian and British bombs; 52 dead (all crew lost).

U479: launched 14 Aug 1943, commissioned 27 Oct 1943. Sunk 12 Dec 1944 in the Gulf of Finland, position unknown, by the USSR submarine *Lembit*; 51 dead (all crew lost).

U480: launched 14 Aug 1943, commissioned 6 Oct 1943. Sunk 24 Feb 1945 in the Channel southwest of Land's End, in position 49° 55'N, 06° 08'W, by depth charges from the British frigates *Duckworth* and *Rowley*; 48 dead (all crew lost).

U481: launched 25 Sept 1943, commissioned 10 Nov 1943; at Narvik 19 May 1945; transferred to Loch Eriboll for Operation Deadlight.

U482: launched 25 Sept 1943, commissioned 1 Dec 1943. Sunk 16 Jan 1945 in the northern Channel, in position 55° 30'N, 05° 53'W, by depth charges from the British sloops *Peacock*, *Starling*, *Hart* and *Amethyst* and the frigate *Loch Craggie*; 48 dead (all crew lost).

U483: launched 30 Oct 1943, commissioned 22 Dec 1943; transferred from Drontheim to Scapa Flow, then Loch Ryan, 29 May 1945 (Operation Deadlight).

U484: launched 20 Nov 1943, commissioned 19 Jan 1944. Sunk 9 Sept 1944 south of the Hebrides, in position 56° 30'N, 07° 40'W, by depth charges from the Canadian frigate *Dunver* and the corvette *Hespeler*; 52 dead (all crew lost).

U485: launched 15 Jan 1944, commissioned 23 Feb 1944; surrendered at Gibraltar, 8 May 1945; transferred to Loch Ryan for Operation Deadlight.

U486: launched 12 Feb 1944, commissioned 22

Mar 1944. Sunk 12 Apr 1945 in the North Sea northwest of Bergen, in position 60° 44'N, 04° 39'E, by torpedoes from the British submarine *Tapir*; 48 dead (all crew lost).

U551: launched 14 Sept 1940, commissioned 7 Nov 1940. Sunk 23 Mar 1941 in the North Atlantic southeast of Iceland, in position 62° 37'N, 16° 47'W, by depth charges from the British trawler *Visenda*; 45 dead (all crew lost).

U552: launched 14 Sept 1940, commissioned 4 Dec 1940; scuttled on 2 May 1945 at Wilhelmshaven, in position 53° 51'N, 08° 10'E.

U553: launched 7 Nov 1940, commissioned 23 Dec 1940. Missing, presumed sunk, in the mid North Atlantic in January after going missing in 1943; 47 dead (all crew lost).

U554: launched 7 Nov 1940, commissioned 15 Jan 1941; scuttled on 2 May 1945 near Wilhelmshaven, in position 53° 51'N, 08° 10'E, after being damaged by British bombs in the Kattegat.

U555: launched 7 Dec 1940, commissioned 30 Jan 1941; stricken at Hamburg in May 1945; surrendered to Britain; broken up.

U556: launched 7 Dec 1940, commissioned 6 Feb 1941. Sunk 27 Jun 1941 in the North Atlantic southwest of Iceland, in position 60° 24'N, 20° 00'W, by depth charges from the British corvettes *Nasturtium*, *Celandine* and *Gladiolus*; 5 dead.

U557: launched 22 Dec 1940, commissioned 13 Feb 1941. Sank at 2230hrs on 16 Dec 1941 in the Mediterranean near Salamis, in position 37° 33'N, 23° 14'E, after a collision with the Italian torpedo boat *Orione*; 43 dead (all crew lost).

U558: launched 23 Dec 1940, commissioned 20 Feb 1941. Sunk 20 Jul 1943 northwest of Cape Ortegal, in position 45° 10'N, 09° 42'W, by US bombs; 45 dead.

U559: launched 8 Jan 1941, commissioned 27 Feb 1941. Sunk 30 Oct 1942 in the Mediterranean northeast of Port Said, in position 32° 30'N, 33° 00'E, by depth charges from the British destroyers *Pakenham*, *Petard* and *Hero*, the escort destroyers *Dulverton* and *Hurworth*, and by British bombs; 7 dead.

U560: launched 10 Jan 1941, commissioned 6 Mar 1941. Sank in November 1941 in the Baltic Sea near Memel, position unknown, after a collision; raised in 1941 and stricken; used for training from 1942; scuttled on 3 May 1945 at Kiel; broken up in 1946.

U561: launched 23 Jan 1941, commissioned 13 Mar 1941. Sunk 12 Jul 1943 in the Straits of Messina, in position 38° 16'N, 15° 39'E, by torpedoes from the British *MTB 81*; 42 dead.

U562: launched 24 Jan 1941, commissioned 20 Mar 1941. Sunk 19 Feb 1943 in the Mediterranean northeast of Bengazi, in position 32° 57'N, 20° 54'E, by depth charges from the British destroyer *Isis*, the escort destroyer *Hursley* and two British bombs; 49 dead (all crew lost).

U563: launched 5 Feb 1941, commissioned 27 Mar 1941. Sunk 31 May 1943 southwest of Brest, in position 46° 35'N, 10° 40'W, by British and Australian bombs; 49 dead (all crew lost).

U564: launched 7 Feb 1941, commissioned 3 Apr

1941. Sunk at 1730hrs on 14 Jun 1943 northwest of Cape Ortegal, in position 44° 17'N, 10° 25'W, by British bombs; 28 dead.

U565: launched 20 Feb 1941, commissioned 10 Apr 1941; badly damaged on 24 Sept 1944 near Skaramanga, in position 37° 57'N, 23° 40'E, by US bombs; 5 dead; cannibalised; scuttled on 30 Sept 1944 by three depth charges.

U566: launched 20 Feb 1941, commissioned 17 Apr 1941. Sunk 24 Oct 1943 in the North Atlantic west of Leixões, in position 41° 12'N, 09° 31'W, by British bombs.

U567: launched 6 Mar 1941, commissioned 27 Apr 1941. Sunk 21 Dec 1941 in the North Atlantic northeast of the Azores, in position 44° 02'N, 20° 10'W, by depth charges from the British sloop *Deptford* and the corvette *Samphire*; 47 dead (all crew lost).

U568: launched 6 Mar 1941, commissioned 1 May 1941. Sunk 29 May 1942 in the Mediterranean northeast of Tobruk, in position 32° 42'N, 24° 53'E, by depth charges from the British destroyer *Hero* and the escort destroyers *Eridge* and *Hurworth*.

U569: launched 20 Mar 1941, commissioned 8 May 1941; scuttled on 22 May 1943 in the North Atlantic, in position 50° 40'N, 35° 21'W, after being badly damaged by bombs from aircraft of the US escort carrier *Bogue*; 21 dead.

U570: launched 20 Mar 1941, commissioned 15 May 1941; captured by Britain on 27 Aug 1941 in the North Atlantic south of Iceland, in position 62° 15'N, 18° 35'W, after being damaged by a British aeroplane; towed to Thorlakshafn; became the British submarine *Graph* 29 Sept 1941; out of service in February 1944; stricken 20 Mar 1944 after running aground near Islay; broken up 1961.

U571: launched 4 Apr 1941, commissioned 22 May 1941. Sunk 28 Jan 1944 west of Ireland, in position 52° 41'N, 14° 27'W, by Australian bombs; 52 dead (all crew lost).

U572: launched 5 Apr 1941, commissioned 29 May 1941. Sunk 3 Aug 1943 northeast of Trinidad, in position 11° 35'N, 54° 05'W, by US bombs; 47 dead (all crew lost).

U573: launched 17 Apr 1941, commissioned 5 Jun 1941; damaged by bombs northwest of Algiers; 1 dead; interned at Cartagena, Spain on 2 May 1942; sold to Spain, 2 Aug 1942; became the Spanish submarine *G 7*; in service until c1971.

U574: launched 18 Apr 1941, commissioned 12 Jun 1941. Sunk 19 Dec 1941 in the north Atlantic near Punta Delgada, in position 38° 12'N, 17° 23'W, by depth charges from the British sloop *Stork*; 28 dead.

U575: launched 30 Apr 1941, commissioned 19 Jun 1941. Sunk 13 Mar 1944 in the north Atlantic north of the Azores, in position 46° 18'N, 27° 34'W, by depth charges from the Canadian frigate *Prince Rupert*, the US destroyer *Hobson*, destroyer escort *Haverfield*, and by bombs from British aircraft and aircraft of the US escort carrier *Bogue*; 18 dead.

U576: launched 30 Apr 1941, commissioned 26 Jun 1941. Sunk 15 Jul 1942 in the north Atlantic near Cape Hatteras, in position 34° 51'N, 75° 22'W, by bombs and gunfire from the US motor vessel *Unicoi*; 45 dead (all crew lost).

U577: launched 15 May 1941, commissioned 3 Jul 1941. Sunk 9 Jan 1942 northwest of Mersa Matruh, in position 32° 22'N, 26° 54'E, by British bombs; 43 dead (all crew lost).

U578: launched 15 May 1941, commissioned 10 Jul 1941. Sunk 10 Aug 1942 north of Cape Ortegal, in position 45° 49'N, 07° 44'W, by Czechoslovakian bombs; 49 dead (all crew lost).

U579: launched 28 May 1941, commissioned 17 Jul 1941. Sank in October 1941 in the Baltic Sea in a collision; raised; returned to service in April 1942. Sunk at 0600hrs on 5 May 1945 in the Lille Baelt, in approximate position 55° 30'N, 10° 00'E, by British bombs; 24 dead.

U580: launched 28 May 1941, commissioned 24 Jul 1941. Sank 11 Nov 1941 in the Baltic Sea near Memel, position not known, after a collision with the target ship *Angelburg*; 12 dead.

U581: launched 12 Jun 1941, commissioned 31 Jul 1941. Sunk 2 Feb 1942 in the mid-Atlantic southwest of the Azores, in approximate position 39° 00'N, 30° 00'W, by the British destroyer *Westcott*; 4 dead.

U582: launched 12 Jun 1941, commissioned 7 Aug 1941. Sunk 5 Oct 1942 southwest of Iceland, in position 58° 41'N, 22° 58'W, by US bombs; 46 dead (all crew lost).

U583: launched 26 Jun 1941, commissioned 14 Aug 1941. Sank at 2148hrs on 15 Nov 1941 in the Baltic, position unknown, after a collision with *U153*; 45 dead (all crew lost).

U584: launched 26 Jun 1941, commissioned 21 Aug 1941. Sunk 31 Oct 1943 in the North Atlantic, in position 49° 14'N, 31° 55'W, by bombs from aircraft of the US escort carrier *Card*; 53 dead (all crew lost).

U585: launched 9 Jul 1941, commissioned 28 Aug 1941. Sunk 30 Mar 1942 in the Arctic Ocean north of Murmansk, in position 70° 00'N, 34° 00'E, by a German mine which had drifted from the 'Bantos-A' barrage; 44 dead (all crew lost).

U586: launched 10 Jul 1941, commissioned 4 Sept 1941. Sunk at 1230hrs on 5 Jul 1944 near Toulon, in position 43° 07'N, 05° 55'E, by US bombs.

U587: launched 23 Jul 1941, commissioned 11 Sept 1941. Sunk 27 Mar 1942 in the North Atlantic, in position 47° 21'N, 21° 39'W, by depth charges from the British escort destroyers *Grove* and *Aldenham*, and the destroyers *Volunteer* and *Leamington*; 42 dead (all crew lost).

U588: launched 23 Jul 1941, commissioned 18 Sept 1941. Sunk 31 Jul 1942 in the North Atlantic, in position 49° 59'N, 36° 36'W, by depth charges from the Canadian corvette *Wetaskiwin* and the destroyer *Skeena*; 46 dead (all crew lost).

U589: launched 6 Aug 1941, commissioned 25 Sept 1941. Sunk 14 Sept 1942 in the Arctic Ocean southwest of Spitzbergen, in position 75° 04'N, 04° 49'E, by depth charges from the British destroyer *Onslow*, and bombs from aircraft of the escort carrier *Avenger*; 44 dead (all crew lost).

U589: launched 6 Aug 1941, commissioned 25 Sept 1941. Sunk 14 Sept 1942 in the Arctic Ocean southwest of Spitzbergen, in position 75° 04'N, 04° 49'E, by depth charges from the British destroy *Onslow* and bombs from aircraft of the escort carrier *Avenger;* 44 dead (all crew lost).

U590: launched 6 Aug 1941, commissioned 2 Oct 1941. Sunk on 9 Jul 1943 in the mid-Atlantic near the Amazon estuary, in position 03° 22'N, 48° 38'W, by US bombs; 45 dead (all crew lost).

U591: launched 20 Aug 1941, commissioned 9 Oct 1941. Sunk 30 Jul 1943 near Pernambuco, in position 08° 36'S, 34° 34'W, by US bombs; 19 dead.

U592: launched 20 Aug 1941, commissioned 16 Oct 1941. Sunk at 1000hrs on 31 Jan 1944 in the North Atlantic southwest of Ireland, in position 50° 20'N, 17° 29'W, by depth charges from the British sloops *Starling, Wild Goose* and *Magpie;* 49 dead (all crew lost).

U593: launched 3 Sept 1941, commissioned 23 Oct 1941. Sunk 13 Dec 1943 in the western Mediterranean north of Constantine, in position 37° 38'N, 05° 08'E, by depth charges from the US destroyer *Wainwright* and the British escort destroyer *Calpe.*

U594: launched 3 Sept 1941, commissioned 30 Oct 1941. Sunk 4 Jun 1943 west of Gibraltar, in position 35° 55'N, 09° 25'W, by US bombs; 50 dead (all crew lost).

U595: launched 17 Sept 1941, commissioned 6 Nov 1941. Sunk 14 Nov 1942 in the Mediterranean northeast of Oran, in position 36° 38'N, 00° 30'E, by US bombs.

U596: launched 17 Sept 1941, commissioned 13 Nov 1941. Sunk 24 Sept 1944 in Skaramanga Bay, near Salamis in position 37° 59'N, 23° 34'E, by US bombs; 1 dead; wreck blown up 30 Sept 1944.

U597: launched 11 Oct 1941, commissioned 20 Nov 1941. Sunk 12 Oct 1942 southwest of Iceland, in position 56° 50'N, 28° 05'W, by British bombs; 49 dead (all crew lost).

U598: launched 2 Oct 1941, commissioned 27 Nov 1941. Sunk 23 Jul 1943 in the South Atlantic near Natal, in position 04° 05'S, 33° 23'W, by US bombs; 43 dead.

U599: launched 15 Oct 1941, commissioned 4 Dec 1941. Sunk 24 Oct 1942 northeast of the Azores, in position 46° 07'N, 17° 40'W, by British bombs; 44 dead (all crew lost).

U600: launched 16 Oct 1941, commissioned 11 Dec 1941. Sunk 25 Nov 1943 in the North Atlantic north of Punta Delgada, in position 40° 31'N, 22° 07'W, by depth charges from the British frigates *Bazely* and *Blackwood;* 54 dead (all crew lost).

U601: launched 29 Oct 1941, commissioned 18 Dec 1941. Sunk 25 Feb 1944 northwest of Narvik, in position 70° 26'N, 12° 40'E, by British bombs; 51 dead (all crew lost).

U602: launched 30 Oct 1941, commissioned 29 Dec 1941. Sunk 23 Apr 1943, presumably in the Mediterranean, position and cause not known; 48 dead (all crew lost).

U603: launched 16 Nov 1941, commissioned 2 Jan 1942. Sunk 1 Mar 1944 in the North Atlantic, in position 48° 55'N, 26° 10'W, by depth charges from the US destroyer escort *Bronstein;* 51 dead (all crew lost).

U604: launched 16 Nov 1941, commissioned 8 Jan 1942. Sunk 11 Aug 1943 in the South Atlantic, in position 04° 30'S, 21° 20'W, by US bombs (see also *U185*).

U605: launched 27 Nov 1941, commissioned 15 Jan 1942. Sunk 13 Nov 1942 in the Mediterranean near Algiers, in position 37° 04'N, 02° 55'E, by depth charges from the British corvettes *Lotus* and *Poppy;* 46 dead (all crew lost).

U606: launched 27 Nov 1941, commissioned 22 Jan 1942. Sunk 22 Feb 1943 in the North Atlantic, in position 47° 44'N, 33° 43'W, by depth charges from the US coastguard cutter *Campbell* and the Polish destroyer *Burza;* 36 dead.

U607: launched 11 Dec 1941, commissioned 29 Jan 1942. Sunk at 0800hrs on 13 Jul 1943 northwest of Cape Ortegal, in position 45° 02'N, 09° 14'W, by British bombs; 45 dead.

U608: launched 11 Dec 1941, commissioned 5 Feb 1942. Sunk 10 Aug 1944 in the Bay of Biscay near La Rochelle, in position 46° 30'N, 03° 08'W, by depth charges from the British sloop *Wren,* and by British bombs.

U609: launched 23 Dec 1941, commissioned 12 Feb 1942. Sunk 7 Feb 1943 in the North Atlantic, in position 55° 17'N, 26° 38'W, by depth charges from the Free French corvette *Lobelia;* 46 dead (all crew lost).

U610: launched 24 Feb 1941, commissioned 19 Feb 1942. Sunk 8 Oct 1943 in the North Atlantic, in position 55° 45'N, 24° 33'W, by Canadian bombs; 51 dead (all crew lost).

U611: launched 8 Jan 1942, commissioned 26 Feb 1942. Sunk 10 Dec 1942 south of Iceland, in position 58° 09'N, 22° 44'W, by US bombs; 45 dead (all crew lost).

U612: launched 9 Jan 1942, commissioned 5 Mar 1942. Sank 6 Aug 1942 near Warnemünde, after a collision with *U444;* 1 dead. Raised; returned to service on 31 May 1943 as a training boat; scuttled 2 May 1945 at Warnemünde, in position 54° 11'N, 12° 05'E; wreck broken up in 1946.

U613: launched 29 Jan 1942, commissioned 12 Mar 1942. Sunk 23 Jul 1943 in the mid-Atlantic south of the Azores, in position 35° 32'N, 28° 36'W, by depth charges from the US destroyer *Badger;* 48 dead (all crew lost).

U614: launched 29 Jan 1942, commissioned 19 Mar 1942. Sunk 29 Jul 1943 northwest of Cap Finisterre, in position 46° 42'N, 11° 03'W, by British bombs; 49 dead (all crew lost).

U615: launched 8 Feb 1942, commissioned 26 Mar 1942. Sunk 7 Aug 1943 in the Caribbean southeast of Curaçao, in position 12° 38'N, 64° 15'W, by British bombs; 4 dead.

U616: launched 8 Feb 1942, commissioned 2 Apr 1942. Sunk 17 May 1944 in the Mediterranean east of Cartagena, in position 36° 46'N, 00° 52'E, by depth charges from the US destroyers *Nields, Gleaves, Ellyson, Macomb, Hambleton, Rodman* and *Emmons,* and by British bombs, in a day-long action.

U617: launched 19 Feb 1942, commissioned 9 Apr 1942. Ran aground under British aerial attack 12 Sept 1943 in the Mediterranean near Melilla, in position 35° 38'N, 03° 27'W; wreck destroyed by gunfire from the British corvette *Hyacinth* and the Australian minesweeper *Woollongong.*

U618: launched 20 Feb 1942, commissioned 16 Apr 1942. Sunk 14 Aug 1944 in the Bay of Biscay west of St Nazaire, in position 47° 22'N, 04° 39'W, by depth charges from the British frigates *Duckworth* and *Essington,* and by bombs; 61 dead (all crew lost).

U619: launched 9 Mar 1942, commissioned 23 Apr 1942. Sunk c6 Oct 1942 southwest of Iceland, position unknown, by bombs; 44 dead (all crew lost).

U620: launched 9 Mar 1942, commissioned 30 Apr 1942. Sunk 14 Feb 1943 northwest of Lisbon, in position 39° 27'N, 11° 34'W, by British bombs; 46 dead (all crew lost).

U621: launched 29 Mar 1942, commissioned 7 May 1942; refitted as *U-Flak 3,* 7 Jul 1943. Sunk 18 Aug 1944 in the Bay of Biscay near La Rochelle, in position 45° 52'N, 02° 36'W, by depth charges from the Canadian destroyers *Ottawa, Kootenay* and *Chaudière;* 56 dead (all crew lost).

U622: launched 29 Mar 1942, commissioned 14 May 1942. Sunk at 1400hrs on 24 Jul 1943 near Drontheim, in position 63° 27'N, 10° 23'E, by US bombs.

U623: launched 31 Mar 1942, commissioned 21 May 1942. Sunk 21 Feb 1943 in the Atlantic, position unknown, by British bombs; 46 dead (all crew lost).

U624: launched 31 Mar 1942, commissioned 28 May 1942. Sunk 7 Feb 1943 in the North Atlantic, in position 55° 42'N, 26° 17'W, by British bombs; 45 dead (all crew lost).

U625: launched 15 Apr 1942, commissioned 4 Jun 1942. Sunk 10 Mar 1944 west of Ireland, in position 52° 35'N, 20° 19'W, by Canadian bombs; 53 dead (all crew lost).

U626: launched 15 Apr 1942, commissioned 11 Jun 1942. Sunk 15 Dec 1942 in the North Atlantic, in position 56° 46'N, 27° 12'W, by depth charges from the US coastguard cutter *Ingham;* 47 dead (all crew lost).

U627: launched 29 Apr 1942, commissioned 18 Jun 1942. Sunk 27 Oct 1942 south of Iceland, in position 59° 14'N, 22° 49'W, by US bombs; 44 dead (all crew lost).

U628: launched 29 Apr 1942; commissioned 25 Jun 1942. Sunk 3 Jul 1943 northwest of Cape Ortegal, in position 44° 11'N, 08° 45'W, by US bombs; 49 dead (all crew lost).

U629: launched 12 May 1942, commissioned 2 Jul 1942. Sunk 8 Jun 1944 in the Channel west of Brest, in position 48° 27'N, 05° 47'W, by British bombs; 51 dead (all crew lost).

U630: launched 12 May 1942, commissioned 9 Jul 1942. Sunk 4 May 1943 south of Cape Farewell, in position 56° 38'N, 42° 38'W, by Canadian bombs; 47 dead (all crew lost).

U631: launched 27 May 1942, commissioned 16 Jul 1942. Sunk 17 Oct 1943 in the North Atlantic southeast of Cape Farewell, in position 58° 13'N, 32° 29'W, by depth charges from the British corvette *Sunflower;* 53 dead (all crew lost).

U632: launched 27 May 1942, commissioned 23 Jul 1942. Sunk 6 Apr 1943 southwest of Iceland, in position 58° 02'N, 28° 42'W, by British bombs; 48 dead (all crew lost).

U633: launched 10 Jun 1942, commissioned 30 Jul 1942. Sunk 7 Mar 1943 in the North Atlantic, in position 57° 14'N, 26° 30'W, by British bombs; 43 dead (all crew lost).

U634: launched 10 Jun 1942, commissioned 6 Aug 1942. Sunk 30 Aug 1943, in the North Atlantic east of the Azores, in position 40° 13'N, 19° 24'W, by depth charges from the British sloop *Stork* and the corvette *Stonecrop*; 47 dead (all crew lost).

U635: launched 24 Jun 1942, commissioned 13 Aug 1942. Sunk 6 Apr 1943 in the North Atlantic southwest of Iceland, in position 58° 25'N, 29° 22'W, by depth charges from the British frigate *Tay*; 47 dead (all crew lost).

U636: launched 25 Jun 1942, commissioned 20 Aug 1942. Sunk 21 Apr 1945 in the North Atlantic west of Ireland, in position 55° 50'N, 10° 31'W, by depth charges from the British frigates *Bazely*, *Drury* and *Bentinck*; 42 dead.

U637: launched 7 Jul 1942, commissioned 27 Aug 1942; at Stavanger 29 May 1945; transferred to Loch Ryan for Operation Deadlight.

U638: launched 8 Jul 1942, commissioned 3 Sept 1942. Sunk 5 May 1943 in the North Atlantic northeast of Newfoundland, in position 53° 06'N, 45° 02'W, by depth charges from the British corvette *Loosestrife*; 44 dead.

U639: launched 22 Jul 1942, commissioned 10 Sept 1942. Sunk 30 Aug 1943 in the Arctic Ocean north of Mys Zhelaniya, in approximate position 77° 00'N, 74° 00'E, by torpedoes from the USSR submarine *S 101*; 47 dead.

U640: launched 23 Jul 1942, commissioned 17 Sept 1942. Sunk 17 May 1943 in the North Atlantic near Cape Farewell, in position 58° 54'N, 42° 33'W, by depth charges from the British frigate *Swale*; 49 dead (all crew lost).

U641: launched 6 Aug 1942, commissioned 24 Sept 1942. Sunk 19 Jan 1944 in the North Atlantic southwest of Ireland, in position 50° 25'N, 18° 49'W, by depth charges from the British corvette *Violet*; 50 dead (all crew lost).

U642: launched 6 Aug 1942, commissioned 1 Oct 1942. Sunk 5 Jul 1944 near Toulon, in position 43° 07'N, 05° 55'E, by US bombs.

U643: launched 20 Aug 1942, commissioned 8 Oct 1942. Sunk 8 Oct 1943 in the North Atlantic, in position 56° 14'N, 26° 55'W, by British bombs; 30 dead.

U644: launched 20 Aug 1942, commissioned 15 Oct 1942. Sunk 7 Apr 1944 in the North Sea northwest of Narvik, in position 69° 38'N, 05° 40'W, by torpedoes from the British submarine *Tuna*; 45 dead (all crew lost).

U645: launched 3 Sept 1942, commissioned 22 Oct 1942. Sunk 24 Dec 1943 in the North Atlantic northeast of the Azores, in position 45° 20'N, 21° 40'W, by depth charges from the US destroyer *Schenck*; 55 dead (all crew lost).

U646: launched 3 Sept 1942, commissioned 29 Oct 1942. Sunk 17 May 1943 southeast of Iceland, in position 62° 10'N, 14° 37'W, by British bombs; 46 dead (all crew lost).

U647: launched 16 Sept 1942, commissioned 5 Nov 1942. Sunk 3 Aug 1943 east of the Shetlands, position unknown, possibly mined; 48 dead (all crew lost).

U648: launched 17 Sept 1942, commissioned 12 Nov 1942. Sunk 23 Nov 1943 in the North Atlantic northeast of the Azores, in position 42° 40'N, 20° 37'W, by depth charges from the British frigates *Bazely*, *Blackwood* and *Drury*; 50 dead (all crew lost).

U649: launched 30 Sept 1942, commissioned 19 Nov 1942. Sank 24 Feb 1943 in the Baltic Sea, position unknown, after a collision with *U232*; 35 dead.

U650: launched 11 Oct 1942, commissioned 26 Nov 1942. Sunk in December 1944 in the North Atlantic, position unknown; 47 dead (all crew lost).

U651: launched 21 Dec 1940, commissioned 12 Feb 1941. Sunk 29 Jun 1941 south of Iceland, in position 59° 52'N, 18° 36'W, by depth charges from the British destroyers *Malcolm* and *Scimitar*, the corvettes *Arabis* and *Violet* and the minesweeper *Speedwell*.

U652: launched 7 Feb 1941, commissioned 3 Apr 1941; badly damaged by British bombs and scuttled on 2 Jun 1942 in the Mediterranean in the Gulf of Solum, in position 31° 55'N, 25° 13'E, by torpedoes from *U81*.

U653: launched 31 Mar 1941, commissioned 25 May 1941. Sunk 15 Mar 1944 in the North Atlantic, in position 53° 46'N, 24° 35'W, by bombs from aircraft of the British escort carrier *Vindex*, and by depth charges from the British sloops *Starling* and *Wild Goose*; 51 dead (all crew lost).

U654: launched 3 May 1941, commissioned 5 Jul 1941. Sunk 22 Aug 1942 in the Caribbean Sea north of Colón, in position 12° 00'N, 79° 56'W, by US bombs; 44 dead (all crew lost).

U655: launched 5 Jun 1941, commissioned 11 Aug 1941. Sank 24 Mar 1942 in the Barents Sea, in approximate position 73° 00'N, 21° 00'E, after being rammed by the British minesweeper *Sharpshooter*; 45 dead (all crew lost).

U656: launched 8 Jul 1941, commissioned 17 Sept 1941. Sunk 1 Mar 1942 south of Cape Race, in position 46° 15'N, 53° 15'W, by US bombs; 45 dead (all crew lost).

U657: launched 12 Aug 1941, commissioned 8 Oct 1941. Sunk 14 May 1943 east of Cape Farewell, in position 60° 10'N, 31° 52'W, by US bombs; 47 dead (all crew lost).

U658: launched 11 Sept 1941, commissioned 5 Nov 1941. Sunk 30 Oct 1942 east of Newfoundland, in position 50° 32'N, 46° 32'W, by Canadian bombs; 48 dead (all crew lost).

U659: launched 14 Oct 1941, commissioned 9 Dec 1941. Sank at 0030hrs on 4 May 1943 in the North Atlantic west of Cap Finisterre, in position 43° 32'N, 13° 20'W, after a collision with *U439*; 44 dead.

U660: launched 17 Nov 1941, commissioned 8 Jan 1942. Sunk 12 Nov 1942 in the Mediterranean near Oran, in position 36° 07'N, 01° 00'W, by depth charges from the British corvettes *Lotus* and *Starwort*; 2 dead.

U661: launched 11 Dec 1941, commissioned 12 Feb 1942. Sank 15 Oct 1942 in the North Atlantic, in position 53° 42'N, 35° 56'W, after being rammed by the British destroyer *Viscount*; 44 dead (all crew lost).

U662: launched 22 Jan 1942, commissioned 9 Apr 1942. Sunk 21 Jul 1943 in the Amazon Estuary, in position 03° 56'N, 48° 46'W, by US bombs; 44 dead (all crew lost).

U663: launched 26 Mar 1942, commissioned 14 May 1942. Sunk 7 May 1943 west of Brest, in position 46° 33'N, 11° 12'W, by British bombs; 49 dead (all crew lost).

U664: launched 28 Apr 1942, commissioned 17 Jun 1942. Sunk 9 Aug 1943 in the North Atlantic west of the Azores, in position 40° 12'N, 37° 29'W, by bombs from aircraft of the US escort carrier *Card*; 7 dead.

U665: launched 9 Jun 1942, commissioned 22 Jul 1942. Sunk 22 Mar 1943 west of Nantes, in position 46° 47'N, 09° 58'W, by British bombs; 46 dead (all crew lost).

U666: launched 18 Jul 1942, commissioned 26 Aug 1942. Sunk 10 Feb 1944 in the North Atlantic west of Ireland, in position 53° 56'N, 17° 16'W, by bombs from aircraft of the British escort carrier *Fencer;* 51 dead (all crew lost).

U667: launched 29 Aug 1942, commissioned 20 Oct 1942. Sunk 25 Aug 1944 in the Bay of Biscay near La Rochelle, position unknown, by a mine; 45 dead (all crew lost).

U668: launched 5 Oct 1942, commissioned 14 Nov 1942; at Narvik 19 May 1945; transferred to Loch Eriboll for Operation Deadlight.

U669: launched 15 Dec 1942, commissioned 16 Dec 1942. Sunk 7 Sept 1943 in the Bay of Biscay northwest of Cape Ortegal, in position 45° 36'N, 10° 13'W, by Canadian bombs; 52 dead (all crew lost).

U670: launched 15 Dec 1942, commissioned 26 Jan 1943. Sank at 2230hrs on 20 Aug 1943 in the Gulf of Danzig, position unknown, after a collision with the target ship *Bolkoburg*; 21 dead.

U671: launched 27 Feb 1942, commissioned 3 Mar 1943. Sunk at 0200hrs on 5 Aug 1944 in the Channel south of Brighton, in position 50° 23'N, 00° 06'E, by depth charges from the British frigates *Stayner* and *Wensleydale*; 47 dead.

U672: launched 27 Feb 1943, commissioned 6 Apr 1943. Sunk 18 Jul 1944 in the Channel north of Guernsey, in position 50° 03'N, 02° 30'W, by depth charges from the British frigate *Balfour*.

U673: launched 8 May 1943, commissioned 18 May 1943. Sank at 0115hrs on 24 Oct 1944 in the North Sea north of Stavanger, in position 59° 20'N, 05° 53'E, after running aground near Smaaskjär following a collision with *U382*; raised 9 Nov 1944; moved to Stavanger; surrendered to Norway; broken up.

U674: launched 8 May 1943, commissioned 15 Jun 1943. Sunk 2 May 1944 in the Arctic Ocean northwest of Narvik, in position 70° 32'N, 04° 37'E, by bombs from aircraft of the British escort carrier *Fencer;* 49 dead (all crew lost).

U675: launched 6 Jul 1943, commissioned 14 Jul 1943. Sunk 24 May 1944 west of Ålesund, in position 62° 27'N, 03° 04'E, by British bombs; 51 dead (all crew lost).

U676: launched 6 Jul 1943, commissioned 6 Aug 1943. Sunk on 19 Feb 1945 in the Gulf of Finland, position unknown, by a USSR mine; 57 dead (all crew lost).

U677: launched 18 Sept 1943, commissioned 20 Sept 1943. Sunk 5 Apr 1945 at the Howaldtswerke yard, Hamburg, by British bombs.

U678: launched 18 Sept 1943, commissioned 25 Oct 1943. Sunk 7 Jul 1944 in the Channel southwest of Brighton, in position 50° 32'N, 00° 23'W, by depth charges from the Canadian destroyers *Ottawa* and *Kootenay* and the British corvette *Statice*; 52 dead (all crew lost).

U679: launched 20 Nov 1943, commissioned 29 Nov 1943. Sunk 9 Jan 1945 in the Baltic Sea, position unknown, by depth charges from the USSR anti-submarine vessel *Mo 124*; 51 dead (all crew lost).

U680: launched 20 Nov 1943, commissioned 23 Dec 1943; at Wilhelmshaven 24 Jun 1945; transferred to Loch Ryan for Operation Deadlight.

U681: launched January 1944, commissioned 3 Feb 1944. Sunk at 0930hrs on 10 Mar 1945 near Bishopsrock, in position 49° 53'N, 06° 31'W, by US bombs; 11 dead.

U682: launched 7 Mar 1944, commissioned 17 Apr 1944. Sunk at 0115hrs on 11 Mar 1945 at the Howaldtswerke yard, Hamburg, by US bombs.

U683: launched 7 Mar 1944, commissioned 30 May 1944. Sunk 12 Mar 1945 in the Channel near Land's End, in position 49° 52'N, 05° 52'W, by depth charges from the British frigate *Loch Ruthven* and the sloop *Wild Goose;* 49 dead (all crew lost).

U684–686: laid down 6 Nov 1943; incomplete on the stocks in May 1945; broken up.

U687–698: construction halted 30 Sept 1943; later cancelled.

U701: launched 16 Apr 1941, commissioned 16 Jul 1941. Sunk 7 Jul 1942 near Cape Hatteras, in position 34° 50'N, 74° 55'W, by US bombs; 39 dead.

U702: launched 24 May 1941, commissioned 3 Sept 1941. Sunk in April 1942 in the North Sea, position unknown, possibly mined; 44 dead (all crew lost).

U703: launched 16 Jul 1941, commissioned 16 Oct 1941. Sunk in September 1944 east of Greenland, position unknown, by sea damage; 54 dead (all crew lost).

U704: launched 29 Aug 1941, commissioned 18 Nov 1941. Scuttled 3 May 1945 at Vegesack; wreck broken up in 1947.

U705: launched 23 Oct 1941, commissioned 30 Dec 1941. Sunk 3 Sept 1942 west of Brest, in position 47° 55'N, 10° 04'W, by US bombs; 45 dead (all crew lost).

U706: launched 24 Nov 1911, commissioned 16 Mar 1942. Sunk at 0630hrs on 3 Aug 1943 northwest of Cape Ortegal, in position 46° 15'N, 10° 25'W, by US bombs; 42 dead.

U707: launched 18 Dec 1941, commissioned 1 Jul 1942. Sunk 9 Nov 1943 east of the Azores, in position 40° 31'N, 20° 17'W, by US bombs; 51 dead (all crew lost).

U708: launched 24 Mar 1942, commissioned 24 Jul 1942. Scuttled on 3 May 1945 at Wilhelmshaven; wreck broken up in 1947.

U709: launched 14 Apr 1942, commissioned 12 Aug 1942. Sunk 1 Mar 1944 north of the Azores, in approximate position 49° 10'N, 26° 00'W, by depth charges from the US destroyer escorts *Thomas*, *Bostwick* and *Bronstein*; 52 dead (all crew lost).

U710: launched 11 May 1942, commissioned 2 Sept 1942. Sunk 24 Apr 1943 south of Iceland, in position 61° 25'N, 19° 48'W, by US bombs; 49 dead.

U711: launched 25 Jun 1942, commissioned 26 Sept 1942. Sunk 4 May 1945 near Harstad, in position 68° 48'N, 16° 38'E, by bombs from aircraft of the British escort carriers *Searcher*, *Trumpeter* and *Queen*; 32 dead.

U712: launched 10 Aug 1942, commissioned 5 Nov 1942; at Kristiansand 31 May 1945; transferred to Loch Ryan; used for tests by the British; broken up at Hayle in 1950.

U713: launched 23 Sept 1942, commissioned 29 Dec 1942. Sunk 24 Feb 1944 in the North Sea northwest of Narvik, in position 69° 27'N, 04° 53'E, by depth charges from the British destroyer *Keppel*; 50 dead.

U714: launched 12 Nov 1942, commissioned 10 Feb 1943. Sunk 14 Mar 1945 in the North Sea near the Firth of Forth, in position 55° 57'N, 01° 57'W, by depth charges from the South African frigate *Natal* and the British destroyer *Wivern*; 50 dead.

U715: launched 14 Dec 1942, commissioned 17 Mar 1943. Sunk at 0930hrs on 13 Jun 1944 northeast of the Fareoes, in position 62° 55'N, 02° 59'W, by British bombs; 36 dead.

U716: launched 15 Jan 1943, commissioned 15 Apr 1943; at Narvik 16 May 1945; transferred to Loch Ryan for Operation Deadlight.

U717: launched 19 Feb 1943, commissioned 19 May 1943; scuttled on 2 May 1945 in the Wasserslebenbucht, in position 54° 49'N, 09° 27'E, after being damaged by British bombs.

U718: launched 26 Mar 1943, commissioned 25 Jun 1943. Sank 18 Nov 1943 in the Baltic Sea northeast of Bornholm, in position 55° 21'N, 15° 24'E, after a collision with *U476;* 43 dead.

U719: launched 28 Apr 1943, commissioned 27 Jul 1943. Sunk 26 Jun 1944 in the North Atlantic northwest of Ireland, in position 55° 33'N, 11° 02'E, by depth charges from the British destroyer *Bulldog*; 52 dead (all crew lost).

U720: launched 5 Jun 1943, commissioned 17 Sept 1943; at Wilhelmshaven 24 Jun 1945; transferred to Loch Ryan for Operation Deadlight.

U721: launched 22 Jul 1943, commissioned 8 Nov 1943; scuttled 4 May 1945 in Gelting Bay; wreck broken up.

U722: launched 18 Sept 1943, commissioned 15 Dec 1943. Sunk 27 Mar 1945 in the North Atlantic near the Hebrides, in position 57° 09'N, 06° 55'W, by depth charges from the British frigates *Fitzroy*, *Redmill* and *Byron*; 44 dead (all crew lost).

U722–730: construction halted 30 Sept 1943. *U725–730* cancelled 22 Jul 1944.

U731: launched 25 Jul 1942, commissioned 3 Oct 1942. Sunk 15 Apr 1944 in the mid-Atlantic near Tangier, in position 35° 54'N, 05° 45'W, by depth charges from the British patrol vessel *Kilmarnock* and the anti-submarine trawler *Blackfly* and by US bombs; 54 dead (all crew lost).

U732: launched 25 Aug 1942, commissioned 24 Oct 1942. Sunk 31 Oct 1943 in the mid-Atlantic near Tangier, in position 35° 54'N, 05° 52'W, by depth charges from the British anti-submarine trawler *Imperialist* and the destroyer *Douglas*; 31 dead.

U733: launched 5 Sept 1942, commissioned 14 Nov 1942. Sank 8 Apr 1943 at Gotenhafen after a collision with an unidentified U-boat; raised; scuttled 5 May 1945 in Flensburg Fjord, in position 54° 48'N, 09° 49'E, after being damaged by bombs and gunfire; broken up in 1948.

U734: launched 19 Sept 1942, commissioned 5 Dec 1942. Sunk 9 Feb 1944 in the North Atlantic southwest of Ireland, in position 49° 43'N, 16° 23'W, by depth charges from the British sloops *Wild Goose* and *Starling*; 49 dead (all crew lost).

U735: launched 10 Oct 1942, commissioned 28 Dec 1942. Sunk at 1921hrs on 28 Dec 1944 near Horton, in position 59° 24'N, 10° 28'E, by British bombs; 39 dead (all crew lost).

U736: launched 31 Oct 1942, commissioned 16 Jan 1943. Sunk 6 Aug 1944 in the Bay of Biscay west of St Nazaire, in position 47° 19'N, 04° 16'W, by depth charges from the British frigate *Loch Killin*; 28 dead.

U737: launched 21 Nov 1942, commissioned 30 Jan 1943. Sank at 0050hrs on 19 Dec 1944 in the Vestfjorden, in position 68° 09'N, 15° 39'E, after a collision with *MRS 25*; 31 dead.

U738: launched 12 Dec 1942, commissioned 20 Feb 1943. Sank 14 Feb 1944 in the Baltic Sea near Gotenhafen, in position 54° 31'N, 18° 33'E, after a collision with the steamship *Erna*; 22 dead; raised 3 Mar 1944 and stricken; broken up in 1944.

U739: launched 23 Dec 1942, commissioned 6 Mar 1943; at Wilhelmshaven 30 Jun 1945; transferred to Loch Ryan for Operation Deadlight.

U740: launched 23 Dec 1942, commissioned 27 Mar 1943. Sunk 9 Jun 1944 southwest of the Scilly Isles, in position 49° 09'N, 08° 37'W, by British bombs; 51 dead (all crew lost).

U741: launched 4 Feb 1943, commissioned 10 Apr 1943. Sunk 15 Aug 1944 in the Channel northwest of Le Havre, in position 50° 02'N, 00° 36°W, by depth charges from the British corvette *Orchis*; 48 dead.

U742: launched 4 Feb 1943, commissioned 1 May 1943. Sunk 18 Jul 1944 west of Narvik, in position 68° 24'N, 09° 51'E, by British bombs; 52 dead (all crew lost).

U743: launched 11 Mar 1943, commissioned 15 May 1943. Sunk 9 Sept 1944 in the North Atlantic northwest of Ireland, in position 55° 45'N, 11° 41'W, by depth charges from the British corvette *Porchester Castle* and the frigate *Helmsdale*; 50 dead (all crew lost).

U744: launched 11 Mar 1943, commissioned 5 Jun 1943. Sunk at 1830hrs on 6 Mar 1944 in the North Atlantic, in position 52° 01'N, 22° 37'W, after being torpedoed by the British destroyer *Icarus*, then, after unsuccessful attempts at towing, by depth charges from *Icarus*, the Canadian frigate *St Catherines*, corvettes *Fennel* and *Chilliwack* and destroyers *Chaudière* and *Gatineau*, and the British corvette *Kenilworth Castle*; 12 dead.

U745: launched 16 Apr 1943, commissioned 19 Jun 1943; renamed *S 11* after being transferred to Italy, in exchange for transport vessels; reverted to Germany as *U 745* after the Italian capitulation. Sunk in February 1945 in the Gulf of Finland, position unknown, by a mine; 48 dead (all crew lost).

U746: launched 16 Apr 1943, commissioned 4 Jul 1943; renamed *S 2* after being transferred to Italy in exchange for transport vessels; reverted to Germany as *U746* after the Italian capitulation; scuttled on 5 May 1945 in Gelting Bay after being bombed; broken up in 1948.

U747: launched 13 May 1943, commissioned 17 Jul 1943; renamed *S 3* after being transferred to Italy in exchange for transport vessels; reverted to Germany as *U747* after the Italian capitulation. Sunk 1 Apr 1945 in Hamburg, by US bombs.

U748: launched 13 May 1943, commissioned 31 Jul 1943; renamed *S 5* after being transferred to Italy in exchange for transport vessels; reverted to Germany as *U748* after the Italian capitulation; scuttled on 3 May 1945 in Rendsburg.

U749: launched 10 Jun 1943, commissioned 14 Aug 1943; renamed *S 7* after being transferred to Italy in exchange for transport vessels; reverted to Germany as *U749* after the Italian capitulation. Sunk 4 Apr 1945 at the Germania Dockyard (4), Kiel, by US bombs; 2 dead.

U750: launched 10 Jun 1943, commissioned 26 Aug 1943; renamed *S 9* after being transferred to Italy in exchange for transport vessels; reverted to Germany as *U750* after the Italian capitulation; scuttled 5 May 1945 in Flensburg Fjord, in position 54° 50'N, 09° 30'E.

U751: launched 16 Nov 1940, commissioned 31 Jan 1941. Sunk 17 Jul 1942 northwest of Cape Ortegal, in position 45° 14'N, 12° 22'W, by British bombs; 48 dead (all crew lost).

U752: launched 29 Mar 1941, commissioned 24 May 1941. Sunk 23 May 1943 in the North Atlantic, in position 51° 40'N, 29° 49'W, by rockets from aircraft of the British escort carrier *Archer*; 29 dead.

U753: launched 26 Apr 1941, commissioned 18 Jun 1941. Sunk 13 May 1943 in the North Atlantic, in position 48° 37'N, 22° 39'W, by depth charges from the Canadian frigate *Drumheller*, the British frigate *Lagan* and British bombs; 47 dead (all crew lost).

U754: launched 5 Jul 1941, commissioned 28 Aug 1941. Sunk 31 Jul 1942 northeast of Boston, in position 43° 02'N, 64° 52'W, by Canadian bombs; 43 dead (all crew lost).

U755: launched 23 Aug 1941, commissioned 3 Nov 1941. Sunk 28 May 1943 northwest of Mallorca, in position 39° 58'N, 01° 41'E, by British bombs; 40 dead.

U756: launched 18 Oct 1941, commissioned 30 Dec 1941. Sunk 3 Sept 1942 southwest of Iceland, in approximate position 57° 30'N, 29° 00'W, by British bombs; 43 dead (all crew lost).

U757: launched 14 Dec 1941, commissioned 28 Feb 1942. Sunk 8 Jan 1944 in the North Atlantic southwest of Ireland, in position 50° 33'W, 18° 03'W, by depth charges from the British frigate *Bayntun* and the Canadian corvette *Camrose*; 49 dead (all crew lost).

U758: launched 1 Mar 1942, commissioned 5 May 1942; stricken at Kiel 16 Mar 1945 after being badly damaged by British bombs; broken up 1946–47.

U759: launched 30 May 1942, commissioned 15 Aug 1942. Sunk 26 Jul 1943 east of Jamaica, in approximate position 18° 06'N, 75° 00'W, by US bombs; 47 dead (all crew lost).

U760: launched 21 Jun 1942, commissioned 15 Oct 1942. Damaged by British bombs near vigo. Sunk 8 Sept 1943, in position 42° 14'N, 08° 40'W, and interned at El Ferrol; transferred to Loch Ryan 23 Jul 1945 for Operation Deadlight.

U761: launched 26 Sept 1942, commissioned 3 Dec 1942. Sunk 24 Feb 1944 in the mid-Atlatnic, near Tangier, in position 35° 55'N, 05° 45'W, by depth charges from the British destroyers *Anthony* and *Wishart*, and by British and US bombs; 9 dead.

U762: launched 21 Nov 1942, commissioned 30 Jan 1943. Sunk 8 Feb 1944 in the North Atlantic, in position 49° 02'N, 16° 58'W, by depth charges from the British sloops *Woodpecker* and *Wild Goose*; 51 dead (all crew lost).

U763: launched 16 Jan 1943, commissioned 13 Mar 1943; scuttled 24 Jan 1945 at Königsberg after being damaged by USSR bombs.

U764: launched 13 Mar 1943, commissioned 6 May 1943; surrendered 14 May 1945 at Lisahally; transferred to Loch Eriboll for Operation Deadlight.

U765: launched 22 Apr 1943, commissioned 19 Jun 1943. Sunk 6 May 1944 in the North Atlantic, in position 52° 30'N, 28° 28'W, by bombs and depth charges from aircraft of the British escort carrier *Vindex* and the frigates *Bickerton*, *Bligh* and *Aylmer*; 37 dead.

U766: launched 29 May 1943, commissioned 30 Jul 1943; stricken 21 Aug 1944 near La Pallice, in position 46° 10'N, 01° 14'W, when unable to put to sea, and surrendered to France; became the French submarine *Laubie* in 1947; stricken 11 Mar 1963 as *Q 335*; broken up.

U767: launched 10 Jul 1943, commissioned 11 Sept 1943. Sunk 18 Jun 1944 in the Channel southwest of Guernsey, in position 49° 03'N, 03° 13'W, by depth charges from the British destroyers *Fame*, *Inconstant* and *Havelock*; 48 dead.

U768: launched 22 Aug 1943, commissioned 14 Oct 1943. Sank 20 Nov 1943 in the Gulf of Danzig, position unknown, after a collision.

U769, 770: construction halted 27 Jan 1943, after damage from British bombs while on the building slips at Wilhelmshaven.

U771: launched 26 Sept 1943, commissioned 18 Nov 1943. Sunk 11 Nov 1944 in the Andfjord near Harstad, in position 69° 17'N, 16° 28'E, by torpedoes from the British submarine *Venturer*; 51 dead (all crew lost).

U772: launched 31 Oct 1943, commissioned 23 Dec 1943. Sunk 30 Dec 1944 south of Weymouth, in position 50° 05'N, 02° 31'W, by Canadian bombs; 48 dead (all crew lost).

U773: launched 8 Dec 1943, commissioned 20 Jan 1944; at Drontheim 29 May 1945; transferred to Loch Ryan for Operation Deadlight.

U774: launched 23 Dec 1943, commissioned 17 Feb 1944. Sunk 8 Apr 1945 in the North Atlantic southwest of Ireland, in position 49° 58'N, 11° 51'W, by depth charges from the British frigates *Calder* and *Bentinck*; 44 dead.

U775: launched 11 Feb 1944, commissioned 23 Mar 1944; at Drontheim 29 May 1945; transferred to Loch Ryan for Operation Deadlight.

U776: launched 4 Mar 1944, commissioned 13 Apr 1944; surrendered at Loch Ryan 20 May 1945; became the British submarine *N 65* for tests; scuttled in Operation Deadlight.

U777: launched 25 Mar 1944, commissioned 9 May 1944. Sunk at 2002hrs on 15 Oct 1944 near Wilhelmshaven, in position 53° 51'N, 08° 10'E, by British bombs.

U778: launched 6 May 1944, commissioned 7 Jul 1944; at Bergen 31 May 1945; transferred to Loch Ryan for Operation Deadlight.

U799: launched 17 Jun 1944, commissioned 24 Aug 1944; at Wilhelmshaven 24 Jun 1945; transferred to Loch Ryan for Operation Deadlight.

U780–U782: construction suspended.

U821: launched 26 Jun 1943, commissioned 11 Oct 1943. Sunk at 1145hrs on 10 Jun 1944 in the Bay of Biscay, near Brest, in position 48° 31'N, 05° 11'W, by British bombs; 50 dead.

U822: launched 20 Feb 1944, commissioned 1 Jul 1944; scuttled 3 May 1945 in the Wesermünde, in position 53° 32'N, 08° 35'E; wreck broken up in 1948.

U823–U824: construction suspended.

U825: launched 27 Feb 1944, commissioned 4 May 1944; surrendered at Portland 10 May 1945; transferred to Lisahally for Operation Deadlight.

U826: launched 9 Mar 1944, commissioned 11 May 1944; surrendered at Loch Eriboll, 11 May 1945; transferred to Loch Ryan for Operation Deadlight.

U827: launched 9 Mar 1944, commissioned 25 May 1944; scuttled 5 May 1945 in Flensburg Fjord; wreck broken up in 1948.

U828: launched 16 Mar 1944, commissioned 17 Jun 1944; scuttled 3 May 1945 in the Wesermünde, in position 53° 32'N, 08° 35'E; wreck broken up 1948.

U829–U840: construction suspended.

U901: launched 9 Oct 1943, commissioned 29 Apr 1944; transferred from Stavanger to Lisahally 29 May 1945 for Operation Deadlight.

U902: construction halted because of bomb damage.

U903: launched 17 Jul 1943, commissioned 4 Sept 1943; scuttled 3 May 1945 at Kiel; wreck broken up 1947.

U904: launched 7 Aug 1943, commissioned 25 Sept 1943. Sunk 4 May 1945 at Eckenförde by British bombs.

U905: launched 20 Nov 1943, commissioned 8 Mar 1944. Sunk 20 Mar 1945 southeast of the Faeroes, in position 59° 42'N, 04° 55'W, by British air-launched homing torpedoes; 45 dead (all crew lost).

U906: launched 28 Jun 1943, commissioned 15 Jul 1944. Sunk 31 Dec 1944 in the dockyard by British bombs.

U907: launched 1 Mar 1944, commissioned 18 May 1944; transferred from Bergen to Loch Ryan 29 May 1945 for Operation Deadlight.

U908: launched 27 Apr 1944. Sunk 31 Dec 1944 in the dockyard by British bombs.

U909–U912: construction suspended.

U921: launched 3 Apr 1943, commissioned 30 May 1943. Sunk 30 Sept 1944 in the Arctic Ocean northwest of Hammerfest, in position 72° 32'N, 12° 55'E, by bombs from aircraft of the British escort carrier *Campania*; 51 dead (all crew lost).

U922: launched 1 Jun 1943, commissioned 1 Aug 1943; scuttled on 3 May 1945 at Kiel; wreck broken up in 1947.

U923: launched 7 Aug 1943, commissioned 4 Oct 1943. Sunk 9 Feb 1945 in Kiel Bay, in position 54° 31'N, 10° 18'E, by a mine; 48 dead. Raised in January 1953 and broken up.

U924: launched 25 Sept 1943, commissioned 20 Nov 1943; scuttled on 3 May 1945 at Kiel; wreck broken up in 1947.

U925: launched 6 Nov 1943, commissioned 30 Dec 1943. Sunk c18 Sept 1944 near the Faeroes, position unknown; 51 dead (all crew lost).

U926: launched 28 Dec 1943, commissioned 29 Feb 1944; stricken 5 May 1945 at Bergen; transferred to Loch Ryan, 30 May 1945; became a Norwegian prize in October 1948, and put into service as the Norwegian submarine *Kya*, 10 Jan 1949; stricken in March 1964; broken up.

U927: launched 3 May 1944, commissioned 27 Jun 1944. Sunk 24 Feb 1945 southeast of Falmouth, in position 49° 54'N, 04° 45'W, by British bombs; 47 dead (all crew lost).

U928: launched 15 Apr 1944, commissioned 11 Jul 1944; transferred from Bergen to Loch Ryan 30 May 1945 for Operation Deadlight.

U929: launched June 1944, commissioned 6 Sept 1944; scuttled 3 May 1945 north of Warnemünde, in position 54° 15'N, 12° 04'E. Raised in 1956 and broken up.

U930: launched September 1944, commissioned 6 Dec 1944; transferred from Bergen to Lisahally 30 May 1945 for Operation Deadlight.

U931–U936: construction halted 30 Sept 1943.

U951: launched 14 Oct 1942, commissioned 3 Dec 1942. Sunk 7 Jul 1943 northwest of Cape St Vincent, in position 37° 40'N, 15° 30'W, by US bombs; 46 dead (all crew lost).

U952: launched 14 Oct 1942, commissioned 10 Dec 1942. Sunk 6 Aug 1944 near Toulon, in position 43° 07'N, 05° 55'E, by US bombs.

U953: launched 28 Oct 1942, commissioned 17 Dec 1942; transferred from Drontheim to Scapa Flow, 29 May 1945; became a British N series submarine; used for tests; broken up in June 1949.

U954: launched 28 Oct 1942, commissioned 23 Dec 1942. Sunk 19 May 1943 southeast of Cape Farewell, in position 55° 09'N, 35° 18'W, by British bombs; 47 dead (all crew lost).

U955: launched 13 Nov 1942, commissioned 31 Dec 1942. Sunk 7 Jun 1944 north of Cape Ortegal, in position 45° 13'N, 08° 30'W, by British bombs; 50 dead (all crew lost).

U956: launched 14 Nov 1942, commissioned 6 Jan 1943; surrendered at Loch Eriboll 13 May 1945; transferred to Loch Ryan for Operation Deadlight.

U957: launched 21 Nov 1942, commissioned 7 Jan 1943; badly damaged 19 Oct 1944 near Lofoten, in approximate position 68° 00'N, 15° 00'E, in a collision with a German steamship; stricken at Drontheim, 21 Oct 1944; transferred to Loch Ryan 29 May 1945; broken up.

U958: launched 21 Nov 1942, commissioned 14 Jan 1943; scuttled 3 May 1945 at Kiel; raised in 1947 and broken up.

U959: launched 3 Dec 1942, commissioned 21 Jan 1943. Sunk 2 May 1944 in the North Sea southeast of Jan Mayen, in position 69° 20'N, 00° 20'W, by bombs from aircraft of the British escort carrier *Fencer*; 53 dead (all crew lost).

U960: launched 3 Dec 1942, commissioned 28 Jan 1943. Sunk 19 May 1944 in the western Mediterranean northwest of Algiers, in position 37° 20'N, 01° 35'E, by depth charges from the US destroyers *Niblack* and *Ludlow*, and by British bombs; 31 dead.

U961: launched 17 Dec 1942, commissioned 4 Feb 1943. Sunk 29 Mar 1943 in the North Sea east of Iceland, in position 64° 31'N, 03° 19'W, by depth charges from the British sloop *Starling*; 49 dead (all crew lost).

U962: launched 17 Dec 1942, commissioned 11 Feb 1943. Sunk 8 Apr 1944 in the north Atlantic northwest of Cap Finisterre, in position 45° 43'N, 19° 57'W, by depth charges from the British sloops *Crane* and *Cygnet*; 50 dead (all crew lost).

U963: launched 30 Dec 1942, commissioned 17 Feb 1943; scuttled at 1000hrs on 20 May 1945 off the west coast of Portugal near Nazaré, in position 39° 36'N, 09° 05'W.

U964: launched 30 Dec 1942, commissioned 18 Feb 1943. Sunk at 1930hrs on 16 Oct 1943 southwest of Iceland, in position 57° 27'N, 28° 17'W, by British bombs; 47 dead.

U965: launched 14 Jan 1943, commissioned 25 Feb 1943. Sunk 27 Mar 1945 in the North Sea north of Scotland, in position 58° 34'N, 05° 46'W, by depth charges from the British frigate *Conn*; 51 dead (all crew lost).

U966: launched 14 Jan 1943, commissioned 4 Mar 1943. Sunk at 0800hrs on 10 Nov 1943 in the Bay of Biscay near Cape Ortegal, in approximate position 44° 00'N, 08° 30'W, by US and Czechoslovakian bombs; 8 dead.

U967: launched 28 Jan 1943, commissioned 11 Mar 1943; scuttled 19 Aug 1944 at Toulon, after being damaged by US bombs on 6 Aug 1944; 2 dead.

U968: launched 28 Jan 1943, commissioned 18 Mar 1943; surrendered at Loch Eriboll 19 May 1945; transferred to Loch Ryan for Operation Deadlight.

U969: launched 11 Feb 1943, commissioned 24 Mar 1943. Sunk 6 Aug 1944 at Toulon, by US bombs.

U970: launched 11 Feb 1943, commissioned 25 Mar 1943. Sunk 8 Jun 1944 in the Bay of Biscay north of El Ferrol, in position 45° 15'N, 04° 10'W, by British bombs; 38 dead.

U971: launched 22 Feb 1943, commissioned 1 Apr 1943. Sunk at 1917hrs on 24 Jun 1944 in the Channel south of Land's End, in position 49° 01'N, 05° 35'W, by depth charges from the Canadian destroyer *Haida* and the British destroyer *Eskimo*, and by Czechoslovakian bombs; 1 dead.

U972: launched 22 Feb 1943, commissioned 8 Apr 1943. Sunk in January 1944 in the Atlantic, position unknown; 49 dead (all crew lost).

U973: launched 10 Mar 1943, commissioned 15 Apr 1943. Sunk 6 Mar 1944 in the Arctic Ocean northwest of Narvik, in position 70° 04'N, 05° 18'E, by air-launched rockets from aircraft of the British escort carrier *Chaser*; 51 dead.

U974: launched 11 Mar 1943, commissioned 22 Apr 1943. Sunk at 0710hrs on 19 Apr 1944 near Karsmund, in position 59° 08'N, 05° 23'E, by torpedoes from the Norwegian submarine *Ula*; 42 dead.

U975: launched 24 Mar 1943, commissioned 29 Apr 1943; transferred from Horten to Loch Ryan, 29 May 1945 for Operation Deadlight; sunk at 1610hrs on 10 Feb 1942; in position 55° 42'N, 09° 01'W, by the British vessel *Loch Arkaig*.

U976: launched 25 Mar 1943, commissioned 5 May 1943. Sunk 25 Mar 1944 southwest of St Nazaire, in position 46° 48'N, 02° 43'W, by gunfire from British aircraft; 4 dead.

U977: launched 31 Mar 1943, commissioned 6 May 1943; interned at Mar del Plata on 17 Aug 1945, in position 38° 01'S, 57° 32'W, after a 66-day underwater voyage; surrendered to USA at Boston, Mass, on 13 Nov 1946; scuttled off Cape Cod, after being used for torpedo trials, by USS *Atule*.

U978: launched 1 Apr 1943, commissioned 12 May 1943; transferred from Drontheim to Loch Ryan 29 May 1945 for Operation Deadlight.

U979: launched 15 Apr 1943, commissioned 20 May 1943; scuttled 24 May 1945 north of Amrum, in position 54° 38'N, 08° 23'E, after running aground.

U980: launched 15 Apr 1943, commissioned 27 May 1943. Sunk 11 Jun 1944 northwest of Bergen, in position 63° 07'N, 00° 26'E, by Canadian bombs; 52 dead (all crew lost).

U981: launched 29 Apr 1943, commissioned 3 Jun 1943. Sunk at 0600hrs on 12 Aug 1944 near La Rochelle, in position 45° 41'N, 01° 25'W, by British bombs; 12 dead.

U982: launched 29 Apr 1943, commissioned 10 Jun 1943. Sunk at 1400hrs on 9 Apr 1945 near Hamburg, in position 53° 33'N, 09° 59'E, by US bombs.

U983: launched 12 May 1943, commissioned 16 Jun 1943. Sank 8 Sept 1943 north of Leba, in position 54° 56'N, 17° 14'E, after a collision with *U988*; 5 dead.

U984: launched 12 May 1943, commissioned 17 Jun 1943. Sunk 20 Aug 1944 in the Bay of Biscay west of Brest, in position 48° 16'N, 05° 33'W, by depth charges from the Canadian destroyers *Ottawa*, *Chaudière* and *Kootenay*; 45 dead (all crew lost).

U985: launched 20 May 1943, commissioned 24 Jun 1943; damaged by mines near Lister 23 Oct 1944; stricken 15 Nov 1944 at Kristiansand; transferred to Loch Ryan 29 May 1945 for Operation Deadlight.

U986: launched 20 May 1943, commissioned 1 Jul 1943. Sunk 17 Apr 1944 in the north Atlantic southwest of Ireland, in position 50° 09'N, 12° 51'W, by depth charges from the US minesweeper *Swift* and the submarine chaser *PC 619*; 50 dead (all crew lost).

U987: launched 2 Jun 1943, commissioned 8 Jul 1943. Sunk 15 Jun 1944 in the North Sea west of Narvik, in position 68° 01'N, 05° 08'E, by torpedoes from the British submarine *Satyr*; 52 dead (all crew lost).

U988: launched 3 Jun 1943, commissioned 15 Jul 1943. Sunk 29 Jun 1944 in the Channel west of Guernsey, in position 49° 37'N, 03° 41'W, by depth charges from the British frigates *Essington*, *Duckworth*, *Dommett* and *Cooke*; 50 dead (all crew lost).

U989: Launched 16 Jun 1943, commissioned 22 Jul 1943. Sunk 14 Feb 1945 near the Faeroes, in position 61° 36'N, 01° 35'W, by depth charges from the British frigates *Bayntun*, *Braithwaite*, *Loch Eck* and *Loch Dunvegan*; 47 dead.

U990: launched 16 Jun 1943, commissioned 28 Jul 1943. Sunk at 0735hrs on 25 May 1944 in the North Sea west of Bodö in position 65° 05'N, 07° 28'E, by British bombs; 20 dead.

U991: launched 24 Jun 1943, commissioned 29 Jul 1943; transferred from Bergen to Loch Ryan 29 May 1945 for Operation Deadlight.

U992: launched 24 Jun 1943, commissioned 2 Aug 1943; at Narvik 19 May 1945; surrendered at Loch Eriboll; transferred to Loch Ryan for Operation Deadlight.

U993: launched 5 Jul 1943, commissioned 19 Aug 1943. Sunk at 0930hrs on 4 Oct 1944 at Laksevaag Dockyard, Bergen, by British bombs; 2 dead. Raised and stricken; broken up.

U994: launched 6 Jul 1943, commissioned 2 Sept 1943; transferred from Drontheim to Loch Ryan 29 May 1945 for Operation Deadlight.

U995: launched 22 Jul 1943, commissioned 16 Sept 1943; stricken at Drontheim 8 May 1945; surrendered to Britain; transferred to Norway in October 1948; became the Norwegian submarine *Kaura* 6 Dec 1952; stricken 1965; returned to Germany, and became a museum ship at Laboe in October 1971.

U996: launched 22 Jul 1943; sunk in the dockyard in August 1944 by British bombs.

U997: launched 18 Aug 1943, commissioned 23 Sept 1943; at Narvik 11 May 1945; surrendered at Loch Eriboll; transferred to Loch Ryan for Operation Deadlight.

U998: launched 18 Aug 1943, commissioned 7 Oct 1943; damaged by Norwegian bombs 16 Jun 1944 near the Shetlands; stricken at Bergen 27 Jun 1944; broken up in 1944.

U999: launched 17 Sept 1943, commissioned 21 Oct 1943; scuttled in the Flensburg Fjord 5 May 1945; wreck broken up in 1945.

U1000: launched 17 Sept 1943, commissioned 4 Nov 1943; damaged by mines 16 Jun 1944 in the western Baltic, position unknown; stricken at Kiel, 29 Aug 1944; broken up.

U1001: launched 6 Oct 1943, commissioned 18 Nov 1943. Sunk 8 Apr 1945 in the N Atlantic southwest of Land's End, in position 49° 19'N, 10° 23'W, by depth charges from the British frigates *Fitzroy* and *Byron*; 45 dead (all crew lost).

U1002: launched 27 Oct 1943, commissioned 30 Nov 1943; transferred from Bergan to Loch Ryan 30 May 1945 for Operation Deadlight.

U1003: launched 6 Oct 1943, commissioned 9 Dec 1943; scuttled on 23 Mar 1945 in the north of the Channel, in position 55° 25'N, 06° 53'W, after a collision with the Canadian frigate *New Glasgow*; 17 dead.

U1004: launched 27 Oct 1943, commissioned 16 Dec 1943; transferred from Bergen to Loch Ryan 30 May 1945 for Operation Deadlight.

U1005: launched 17 Nov 1943, commissioned 30 Dec 1943; transferred from Bergen to Loch Ryan 30 May 1945 for Operation Deadlight.

U1006: launched 17 Nov 1943, commissioned 11 Jan 1944. Sunk 16 Oct 1944 in the North Sea southwest of the Faeroes, in position 60° 59'N, 04° 49'W, by depth charges and gunfire from the Canadian frigate *Annan*; 6 dead.

U1007: launched 8 Dec 1943, commissioned 18 Jan 1944. Sunk 2 May 1945 north of Wismar, in position 53° 54'N, 11° 28'E, by mines and British bombs; 1 dead. Raised and broken up in May 1946.

U1008: launched 8 Dec 1943, commissioned 1 Feb 1944. Sunk 6 May 1945 in the Kattegat near Skagens Horn, in position 57° 52'N, 10° 49'E, by British bombs.

U1009: launched 5 Jan 1944, commissioned 10 Feb 1944; surrendered at Loch Eriboll 10 May 1945; transferred to Loch Ryan for Operation Deadlight; scuttled 7 Jan 1946.

U1010: launched 5 Jan 1944, commissioned 22 Feb 1944; surrendered at Loch Eriboll 14 May 1945; transferred to Lishally for Operation Deadlight; scuttled 7 Jan 1946.

U1011: damaged by British bombs in July 1943 while on the building slips, and not rebuilt; broken up.

U1012: damaged by British bombs in July 1943 while on the building slips, and not rebuilt; broken up.

U1013: launched 19 Jan 1944, commissioned 2 Mar 1944. Sank at 2040hrs on 17 Mar 1944 in the Baltic Sea east of Rügen, in position 55° 36'N, 13° 58'E, after a collision with *U286*; 25 dead.

U1014: launched 30 Jan 1944, commissioned 14 Mar 1944. Sunk 4 Feb 1945 in the North Minch in position 58° 17'N, 06° 44'W, by depth charges from the British frigates *Scavaig*, *Nyasaland*, *Papua* and *Loch Shin*; 48 dead (all crew lost).

U1015: launched 7 Feb 1944, commissioned 23 Mar 1944. Sank 19 May 1944 west of Pillau, in position 54° 25'N, 19° 50'E, after a collision with *U1014*; 36 dead.

U1016: launched 8 Feb 1944, commissioned 4 Apr 1944; scuttled 5 May 1945 in Lübeck Bay, position unknown.

U1017: launched 1 Mar 1944, commissioned 13 Apr 1944. Sunk 29 Apr 1945 northwest of Ireland, in position 56° 04'N, 11° 06'W, by British bombs; 34 dead.

U1018: launched 1 Mar 1944, commissioned 25 Apr 1944. Sunk 27 Feb 1945 in the Channel south of Penzance, in position 49° 56'N, 05° 20'W, by depth charges from the British frigate *Loch Fada*; 51 dead.

U1019: launched 22 Mar 1944, commissioned 4 May 1944; transferred from Drontheim to Scapa Flow and Loch Ryan 29 May 1945 for Operation Deadlight.

U1020: launched 22 Mar 1944, commissioned 17 May 1944; went missing in January 1945 off the east coast of Scotland; 52 dead (all crew lost).

U1021: launched 13 Apr 1944, commissioned 25 May 1944. Sunk 30 Mar 1945 in the North Minch, in position 58° 19'N, 05° 31'W, by depth charges from the British frigates *Rupert* and *Conn*; 43 dead (all crew lost).

U1022: launched 13 Apr 1944, commissioned 7 Jun 1944; transferred from Bergen to Lisahally 30 May 1945 for Operation Deadlight.

U1023: launched 3 May 1944, commissioned 15 Jun 1944; surrendered at Weymouth 10 May 1945; transferred to Lisahally (Operation Deadlight), and became the British submarine *N 83*; used for tests; scuttled 7 Jan 1946.

U1024: launched 3 May 1944, commissioned 28 Jun 1944; captured 12 Apr 1945 and sunk on 13 Apr 1945 in the Irish Sea south of the Isle of Man, in position 53° 39'N, 05° 03'W, by depth charges from the British frigate *Loch Glendhu* while under tow by the frigate *Loch More*; 9 dead.

U1025: launched 24 May 1944, commissioned 12 Apr 1945; scuttled 5 May 1945 in the Flensburg Fjord; position unknown.

U1026: launched 25 May 1944; transferred to Flensburg Dockyard 19 Sept 1944 for a refit; scuttled there in May 1945.

U1027: launched 27 Nov 1944; transferred to Flensburg Dockyard 28 Nov 1944 for a refit, then to Germania Dockyard, Kiel; scuttled there 3 May 1945 in Dock 14.

U1028: launched 28 Nov 1944; fate as for *U1026*.

U1029: launched 5 Jul 1944; fate as for *U1026*.

U1030: launched 5 Jul 1944; fate as for *U1026*.

U1031: launched 12 Jul 1944; fate as for *U1027*.

U1032: construction halted 12 Jul 1944.

U1033–U1050: construction halted 30 Sept 1943; cancelled 22 Jul 1944.

U1051: launched 3 Feb 1944, commissioned 4 Mar 1944. Sunk 26 Jan 1945 south of the Isle of Man, in position 53° 39'N, 05° 23'W, by ramming and depth charges from the British frigates *Aylmer*, *Calder*, *Bentinck* and *Manners*; 47 dead (all crew lost).

U1052: launched 16 Dec 1943, commissioned 20 Jan 1944; transferred from Bergen to Loch Ryan 29 May 1945 for Operation Deadlight.

U1053: launched 17 Jan 1944, commissioned 12 Feb 1944. Sank 15 Feb 1945 in the North Sea near Bergen, in position 60° 22'N, 05° 10'E, after an accident during deep diving trials; 45 dead (all crew lost).

U1054: launched 24 Feb 1944, commissioned 25 Mar 1944; stricken at Kiel 16 Sept 1944, after a collision; used as a hospital ship; surrendered to Britain; broken up.

U1055: launched 9 Mar 1944, commissioned 8 Apr 1944. Sunk 30 Apr 1945 west of Brest, in appoximate position 48° 00'N, 06° 30'W, by US bombs; 49 dead (all crew lost).

U1056: launched 30 Mar 1944, commissioned 29 Apr 1944; scuttled 5 May 1945 in Gelting Bay; wreck broken up.

U1057: launched 20 Apr 1944, commissioned 20 May 1944; stricken at Bergen 10 May 1945; transferred to Loch Ryan 30 May 1945; became USSR submarine *S 81* in Novmber 1945.

U1058: launched 11 Apr 1944, commissioned 10 Jun 1944; surrendered at Loch Foyle 10 May 1945; became USSR submarine *S 82* in November 1945.

U1063: launched 8 Jun 1944, commissioned 8 Jul 1944. Sunk 15 Apr 1945 in the Channel west of Land's End, in position 50° 08'N, 05° 52'W, by depth charges from the British frigate *Loch Killin*; 29 dead.

U1064: launched 22 Jun 1944, commissioned 29 Jul 1944; transferred from Drontheim to Loch Ryan 29 May 2945; became USSR submarine *S 83* in November 1945.

U1065: launched 3 Aug 1944, commissioned 23 Sept 1944. Sunk 9 Apr 1945 northwest of Göteborg, in position 57° 48'N, 11° 26'E, by British air-launched rockets; 45 dead.

U1066–U1068: construction suspended.

U1101: launched 15 Sept 1943, commissioned 10 Nov 1943; scuttled 5 May 1945 in Gelting Bay; wreck broken up.

U1102: launched 15 Jan 1944, commissioned 22 Feb 1944; transferred from Kiel to Loch Ryan 23 Jun 1945 for Operation Deadlight.

U1103: launched 12 Oct 1943, commissioned 8 Jan 1944; transferred from Wilhelmshaven to Loch Ryan 23 Jun 1945 for Operation Deadlight.

U1104: launched 7 Dec 1943, commissioned 15 Mar 1944; transferred from Bergen to Loch Ryan 30 May 1945 for Operation Deadlight.

U1105: launched 20 Apr 1944, commissioned 3 Jun 1944; surrendered at Loch Eriboll 10 May 1945; became the British submarine *N 16*; transferred to USA in 1946; sunk during explosives trials in Chesapeake Bay 18 Nov 1948.

U1106: launched 26 May 1944, commissioned 5 Jul 1944. Sunk 29 Mar 1945 northeast of the Faeroes, in position 61° 46'N, 02° 16'W, by British bombs; 46 dead (all crew lost).

U1107: launched 30 Jun 1944, commissioned 8 Aug 1944. Sunk 25 Apr 1945 in the Bay of Biscay west of Brest, in position 48° 12'N, 05° 42'W, by US air-dropped acoustic homing torpedoes; 36 dead.

U1108: launched 5 Sept 1944, commissioned 18 Nov 1944; transferred from Horten to Lisahally 31 May 1945; became a British N type submarine; used for tests; broken up at Briton Ferry in May 1949.

U1109: launched 19 Jun 1944, commissioned 31 Aug 1944; transferred from Horten to Lisahally 31 May 1945 (Operation Deadlight); sunk 6 Jan 1946 by torpedoes from the British submarine *Templar*.

U1110: launched 12 Jun 1944, commissioned 24 Sept 1944; transferred from Wilhelmshaven to Loch Ryan 24 Jun 1945 for Operation Deadlight.

U1111–U1114: construction suspended; cancelled 22 Jul 1944.

U1131: Launched 1944, commissioned 20 May 1944; scuttled 29 Mar 1945 and 1 Apr 1945 at Hamburg-Finkenwärder, after being damaged by British bombs.

U1132: launched 1944, commissioned 24 Jun 1944; scuttled at 2200hrs on 4 May 1945 near Flensburg, Kupfermühlen Bay; wreck broken up.

U1133–U1140: construction suspended 30 Sept 1943.

U1141–U1146: cancelled 30 Sept 1943.

U1161: launched 8 May 1943, commissioned 25 Aug 1943; renamed *S 8* after being transferred to Italy in exchange for transport vessels; reverted to Germany as *U1161* after the Italian capitulation; scuttled at 2200hrs on 4 May 1945 near Flensburg, in Kupfermühlen Bay; wreck broken up.

U1162: launched 29 May 1943, commissioned 15 Sept 1943; renamed *S 10* after being transferred to Italy in exchange for transport vessels; reverted to Germany as *U1162* after the Italian capitulation; scuttled 5 May 1945 in Gelting Bay; wreck broken up.

U1163: launched 12 Jun 1943, commissioned 6 Oct 1943; transferred from Kristiansand-Süd to Loch Ryan 29 May 1945 for Operation Deadlight.

U1164: launched 3 Jul 1943, commissioned 27 Oct 1943; stricken at Kiel 24 Jul 1944 after being damaged by British bombs; broken up.

U1165: launched 20 Jul 1943, commissioned 17 Nov 1943; transferred from Narvik to Loch Eriboll 19 May 1945 for Operation Deadlight.

U1166: launched 28 Aug 1943, commissioned 8 Dec 1943; damaged by a torpedo explosion on 28 Jul 1944 at Eckernförde; stricken at Kiel 28 Aug 1944; scuttled in May 1945 at Deutsche Werke, Kiel (Dock 2).

U1167: Launched 28 Aug 1943, commissioned 29 Dec 1943. Sunk 30 Mar 1945 near the Deutschewerke yard, Hamburg-Finkenwärder, after being damaged by British bombs; 1 dead.

U1168: launched 2 Oct 1943, commissioned 19 Jan 1944; scuttled 4 May 1945 in Gelting Bay, in position 54° 48'N, 09° 48'E, after running aground.

U1169: launched 2 Oct 1943, commissioned 9 Feb 1944. Sunk 5 Apr 1945 in St George's Channel, in position 52° 03'N, 05° 53'W, by a mine; 49 dead (all crew lost).

U1170: launched 14 Oct 1943, commissioned 1 Mar 1944; scuttled 3 May 1945 at Travemünde; wreck broken up.

U1171: launched 23 Nov 1943, commissioned 12 Jan 1944; returned to the dockyard (finally in service 22 Mar 1944); transferred from Stavanger to Loch Ryan 29 May 1945; became the British submarine *N 19*; broken up at Sunderland in April 1949.

U1172: launched 3 Dec 1943, commissioned 20 Apr 1944. Sunk 27 Jan 1945 in St George's Channel, in position 52° 24'N, 05° 42'W, by depth charges from the British frigates *Tyler, Keats* and *Bligh*; 52 dead (all crew lost).

U1173: construction suspended 18 Dec 1943.

U1174: construction suspended 21 Oct 1943.

U1175: construction suspended 28 Oct 1943.

U1176: construction suspended 6 Nov 1943.

U1177–U1179: construction suspended 6 Nov 1943.

U1180–U1190: construction suspended 30 Sept 1943; cancelled 22 Jul 1944.

U1191: launched 6 Jul 1943, commissioned 9 Sept 1943. Sunk 25 Jun 1944 in the Channel southeast of Torquay, in position 50° 03'N, 02° 59'W, by depth charges from the British frigates *Affleck* and *Balfour*; 50 dead (all crew lost).

U1192: launched 16 Jul 1943, commissioned 23 Sept 1943; scuttled 3 May 1945 at Kiel; wreck broken up.

U1193: launched 5 Aug 1943, commissioned 7 Oct 1943; scuttled 5 May 1945 in Gelting Bay; wreck broken up.

U1194: launched 5 Aug 1943, commissioned 21 Oct 1943; transferred from Wilhelmshaven to Loch Ryan 24 Jun 1945 for Operation Deadlight.

U1195: launched 2 Sept 1943, commissioned 4 Nov 1943. Sunk 7 Apr 1945 in the Channel on the roadsteads at Spithead, in position 50° 33'N, 00° 55'W, by depth charges from the British destroyer *Watchman*; 32 dead; salvage attempts abandoned in April 1945.

U1196: launched 2 Sept 1943, commissioned 18 Nov 1943; stricken in August 1944 after a torpedo explosion; scuttled 3 May 1945 at Travemünde; wreck broken up.

U1197: launched 20 Sept 1943, commissioned 2 Dec 1943; damaged by bombs at Bremen and stricken at Wesermünde, 25 Apr 1945; transferred from Wilhelmshaven to Britain 24 Jun 1945 for Operation Deadlight.

U1198: launched 30 Sept 1943, commissioned 9 Dec 1943; transferred from Wilhelmshaven to Loch Ryan 24 Jun 1945 for Operation Deadlight.

U1199: launched 12 Oct 1943, commissioned 23 Dec 1943. Sunk 21 Jan 1945 in the Channel near the Scilly Isles, in position 49° 57'N, 05° 42'W, by depth charges from the British destroyer *Icarus* and the corvette *Mignonette*; 48 dead.

U1200: launched 4 Nov 1943, commissioned 5 Jan 1944. Sunk 11 Nov 1944 south of Ireland, in position 50° 24'N, 09° 10'W, by depth charges from the British corvettes *Pevensey Castle, Lancaster Castle,*

Porchester Castle and *Kenilworth Castle*; 53 dead (all crew lost).

U1201: launched 4 Nov 1943, commissioned 13 Jan 1944; transferred from Hamburg to Loch Ryan 3 May 1945 for Operation Deadlight.

U1202: launched 11 Nov 1943, commissioned 27 Jan 1944; stricken Bergen 10 May 1945; surrendered to Britain; transferred to Norway in October 1948; became the Norwegian submarine *Kinn* 1 Jul 1951; stricken 1 Jun 1961; transferred to Hamburg and broken up in 1963.

U1203: launched 9 Dec 1943, commissioned 10 Feb 1944; transferred from Drontheim to Loch Ryan(?) 29 May 1945 for Operation Deadlight.

U1204: launched 9 Dec 1943, commissioned 17 Feb 1944; scuttled 5 May 1945 in Gelting Bay; wreck broken up.

U1205: launched 30 Dec 1943, commissioned 2 Mar 1944; scuttled 3 May 1945 at Kiel; broken up.

U1206: launched 30 Dec 1943, commissioned 16 Mar 1944. Sank 14 Apr 1945 in the North Sea near Peterhead, in position 57° 21'N, 01° 39'W, in a diving accident; 4 dead.

U1207: launched 6 Jan 1944, commissioned 23 Mar 1944; scuttled 5 May 1945 in Gelting Bay; wreck broken up.

U1208: launched 13 Jan 1944, commissioned 6 Apr 1944. Sunk 20 Feb 1945 south of Waterford, in position 51° 48'N, 07° 07'W, by depth charges from the British sloop *Amethyst*; 49 dead (all crew lost).

U1209: launched 9 Feb 1944, commissioned 13 Apr 1944; scuttled 18 Dec 1944 in the Channel near the Scilly Isles, in position 49° 57'N, 05° 47'W, after hitting Wolf Rock; 9 dead.

U1210: launched 9 Feb 1944, commissioned 22 Apr 1944. Sunk 3 May 1945 near Eckernförde, in position 54° 28'N, 09° 54'E, by British bombs.

U1211–U1214: construction suspended 30 Sept 1943.

U1271: launched 8 Dec 1943, commissioned 12 Jan 1944; transferred from Bergen to Loch Ryan 30 May 1945 for Operation Deadlight.

U1272: launched 23 Dec 1943, commissioned 28 Jan 1944; transferred from Bergen to Loch Ryan 30 May 1945 for Operation Deadlight.

U1273: launched 10 Jan 1944, commissioned 16 Feb 1944. Sunk 17 Feb 1945 in the Oslofjord near Horten, in position 59° 24'N, 10° 28'E, by a mine; 43 dead.

U1274: launched 25 Jan 1944, commissioned 1 Mar 1944. Sunk 16 Apr 1945 in the North Sea north of Newcastle, in position 55° 36'N, 01° 24'W, by depth charges from the British destroyer *Viceroy*; 44 dead (all crew lost).

U1275: launched 8 Feb 1944, commissioned 22 Mar 1944; transferred from Bergen to Loch Ryan (?) 30 May 1945 for Operation Deadlight.

U1276: launched 25 Feb 1944, commissioned 6 Apr 1944. Sunk 3 Apr 1945 northwest of Bergen, in position 61° 42'N, 00° 24'W, by British bombs; 49 dead (all crew lost).

U1277: launched 18 Mar 1944, commissioned 3 May 1944; scuttled 3 Jun 1945 in the north Atlantic west of Oporto, in position 41° 09'N, 08° 41'W; details unknown.

U1278: launched 15 Apr 1944, commissioned 31 May 1944. Sunk 17 Feb 1945 in the North Sea northwest of Bergen, in position 61° 32'N, 01° 36'E, by depth charges from the British frigates *Bayntun* and *Loch Eck*; 48 dead (all crew lost).

U1279: launched May 1944, commissioned 5 Jul 1944. Sunk 3 Feb 1945 in the North Sea northwest of Bergen, in approximate position 61° 21'N, 02° 00'E, by depth charges from the British frigates *Bayntun*, *Braithwaite* and *Loch Eck*; 48 dead (all crew lost).

U1280–U1282: construction suspended 6 Nov 1943.

U1283–U1285: construction suspended 30 Sept 1943; cancelled 22 Jul 1944.

U1286–U1291: reassigned as Type VII C/42 S 22 Mar 1943; cancelled 30 Sept 1943.

U1301: launched 22 Dec 1943, commissioned 11 Feb 1944; transferred from Bergen to Loch Ryan 30 May 1945 for Operation Deadlight.

U1302: launched 4 Apr 1944, commissioned 25 May 1944. Sunk 7 Mar 1945 in St George's Channel, in position 52° 19'N, 05° 23'W, by depth charges from the Canadian frigates *La Hulloise*, *Strathadam* and *Thetford Mines*; 48 dead (all crew lost).

U1303: launched 10 Feb 1944, commissioned 5 Apr 1944; scuttled at 2200hrs on 4 May 1945 near Flensburg, in Kupfermühlen Bay; wreck broken up.

U1304: launched 4 Aug 1944, commissioned 6 Sept 1944; scuttled at 2200hrs on 4 May 1945 near Flensburg, in Kupfermühlen Bay; wreck broken up.

U1305: launched 10 Jul 1944, commissioned 13 Sept 1944; surrendered at Loch Eriboll 10 May 1945; became USSR submarine *S 84* in November 1945.

U1306: launched 25 Oct 1944, commissioned 20 Dec 1944; scuttled 5 May 1945 in Gelting Bay; wreck broken up.

U1307: launched 29 Sept 1944, commissioned 17 Nov 1944; transferred from Bergen to Loch Ryan (?) 30 May 1945 for Operation Deadlight.

U1308: launched 22 Nov 1944, commissioned 17 Jan 1945; scuttled 2 May 1945 northwest of Warnemünde, in position 54° 13'N, 12° 03'E. Raised in October 1952; broken up at Neptun Dockyard, Rostock.

U1309–U1312: construction suspended 30 Sept 1943; cancelled 22 Jul 1944.

U1331–U1338: construction suspended 30 Sept 1943; cancelled 22 Jul 1944.

U1401–U1404: construction suspended 30 Sept 1943; cancelled 22 Jul 1944.

U1417–U1422: construction suspended 30 Sept 1943; cancelled 22 Jul 1944.

U1435–U1439: construction suspended 30 Sept 1943; cancelled 22 Jul 1944.

U1801–U1804: construction suspended 30 Sept 1943; cancelled 22 Jul 1944.

U1823–U1828: cancelled 30 Sept 1943.

Type VII C/42 U-boats

Name	Type	Builder (construction no)	Built	Cost in Marks (000s)	Displacement (t = tonnes T = tons)	Length (m)	Breadth (m)	Draught/ height (m)	Power (hp)	Revs (rpm)	Speed (kts)	Range (nm/kts)	Oil (t)	Diving time (sec)
U699, 700	VII C/42	Howaldt (H) (849, 850)	1943–		999t sf 1099t sm 1363t total	68.7 oa 50.9 ph	6.85 oa 5.00 ph	5.00/ 10.00	4400ehp sf 750ehp sf	295 sm	18.6 sf 7.6 sm	12,600/10 sf 80/4 sm	159 max	

Construction

Laid down as ocean-going submersibles, designed 1942–43. Single hull as for the Type VII C, but with a stronger pressure hull (plating thickness up to 28mm); diving depth, with armour plating, 200/400m. Two periscopes in the tower, as per the Type IX.

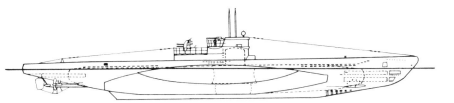

Type VII C/42 (1943 design).

Propulsion

Two MAN 6-cylinder 4-stroke MGV 40/46 highly supercharged diesel engines in compartment 2; two SSW electric motors, as per the Type VII C; similar batteries to Type VII D; rudders as for Type VII C.

Armament

Torpedo armament as for the Type VIIC, but with 16 torpedoes; two twin 2cm AA guns; one quad 2cm AA gun; armour-plated bridge.

Complement

Crew: 4/41.

Notes

In external appearance these boats were very similar to the Type VII C/41.

Careers

All contracts were cancelled in favour of the Type XXI on 30 Sept 1943.

Name	Type	Builder (construction no)	Built
U783–790	VII C/42	KMW (168–175)	1943–
U913–918	”	Stülcken (810–815)	”
U937–942	”	Neptun (529–534)	”
U1069–1080, 1093–1100	”	Germania (706–717, 732–739)	1942– and 1943–
U1115–1120	”	Nordsee (237–242)	1943–
U1147–1152	”	Howaldt (K) (49–54)	”
U1215–1220	”	Schichau (1610–1615)	”
U1292–1297	”	Vegesack (87–92)	”

Name	Type	Builder (construction no)	Built
U1313–1318	”	Flensburg (509–514)	”
U1339–1350	”	Flender (359–370)	”
U1423–1434, 1440–1463	”	B & V (273–284, 290–313)*	”
U1805–1822	”	Danzig (167–184)	”
U1901–1904	”	KMW (176–179)	”
U2001–2004	”	Howaldt (H) (851–854)	”
U2101–2104	”	Germania (740–743)	”
U2301–2318	”	Schichau (1616–1633)	”

Type VII D U-boats

Name	Type	Builder (construction no)	Built	Cost in Marks (000s)	Displacement (t = tonnes T = tons)	Length (m)	Breadth (m)	Draught/ height (m)	Power (hp)	Revs (rpm)	Speed (kts)	Range (nm/kts)	Oil (t)	Diving time (sec)
U213–218	VII D	Germania (645–650)	1940–42		965t sf 1080t sm 1285t total 919t* sf	76.90 oa 59.80 ph	6.38 oa 4.70 ph	5.01/9.70	280ehp to 3200ehp sf 750ehp sm	470 to 490 sf 285 sm	16.0 to 16.7 sf 7.3 sm	11200/10 sf 5050/16 sf 127/2 sm 69/4 sm	155.2/ 115.3 169.4 max	c 30 td

* Light load displacement.

Construction

Laid down as ocean-going submersibles, designed 1939–40. Single hull with saddle tanks; eight watertight compartments (one additional compartment compared with the standard Type VII, behind the conning tower and control room, with a row of mine tubes arranged vertically through the hull); trim tanks in compartments 1 and 8; main diving tank and negative buoyancy tank below the control room; pressurised regulating tanks and bunkers except in the saddle tanks; additional diving tanks in the forecastle and stern; diving depth 100/200m.

Propulsion

Two Germaniawerft 6-cylinder 4-stroke F46 supercharged diesel engines in compartment 2; two AEG GU 460/8–276 double electric motors in compartment 1; 1 + 1 62-cell AFA 33 MAL 800 E (or W, U217) batteries (9160 amp/hr) in compartments 3 and 6 below; diesel-electric range 13,000nm at 10kts. Two 3-bladed propellers, 1.23m diameter; rudders and hydroplanes as for the Type VII C. [A hinged schnorkel was fitted on the port edge of the conning tower casing.]

Armament

Five 53.3cm torpedo tubes, four at the bow and one at the stern, all below the CWL - 12 torpedoes or 26 TMA (= 39 TMB) mines; five mine tubes - 15 SMA mines; one Tk 8.8cm/45 gun - 220 rounds; one 2cm AA gun [two twin 2cm AA guns on bridge extensions from 1943].

Complement

Crew: 4/40. Boats: one inflatable dinghy.

Notes

These vessels were basically a variant of the Type VII C, enlarged for the SMA mine shafts. Hinged schnorkels were fitted to the port forward edge of the conning tower casing on U214 and U218.

Type VII D (1942).

Careers

U213: launched 24 Jul 1941, commissioned 30 Aug 1941. Sunk 31 Jul 1942 in the North Atlantic west of Punta Delgada, in position 36° 45'N, 22° 50'W, by depth charges from the British sloops *Erne*, *Rochester* and *Sandwich*; 50 dead (all crew lost).

U214: launched 18 Sept 1941, commissioned 1 Nov 1941. Sunk 26 Jul 1944 in the Channel southeast of Eddystone, in position 49° 58'N, 03° 30'W, by depth charges from the British frigate *Cooke*; 48 dead (all crew lost).

U215: launched 9 Oct 1941, commissioned 22 Nov 1941. Sunk 3 Jul 1942 in the North Atlantic east of

Boston, in position 41° 48'N, 66° 38'W, by depth charges from the British yacht *Le Tigre*; 48 dead (all crew lost).

U216: launched 23 Oct 1941, commissioned 15 Dec 1941. Sunk 20 Oct 1942 southwest of Ireland, in position 48° 21'N, 19° 25'W, by British bombs; 45 dead (all crew lost).

U217: launched 15 Nov 1941, commissioned 31 Jan 1942. Sunk 5 Jun 1943 in the mid-Atlantic, in approximate position 30° 18'N, 42° 50'W, by bombs from the US escort carrier *Bogue*; 50 dead (all crew lost).

U218: launched 5 Dec 1941, commissioned 24 Jan 1942; transferred from Bergen to Loch Ryan 30 May 1945 for Operation Deadlight.

Type VII F U-boats

Name	Type	Builder (construction no)	Built	Cost in Marks (000s)	Displacement (t = tonnes T = tons)	Length (m)	Breadth (m)	Draught/ height (m)	Power (hp)	Revs (rpm)	Speed (kts)	Range (nm/kts)	Oil (t)	Diving time (sec)
U1059–1062	VII F	Germania (693-696)	1941–43		1084t sf 1181t sm 1345t total	77.63 oa 60.4 ph	7.30 oa 4.70 ph	4.91/9.6	2880ehp to 3200ehp sf 750ehp sm	470 to 490 sf 295 sm	16.9 to 17.6 sf 7.9 sm	14700/10 sf 5350/16.9 sf 130/2 sm 75/4 sm	198.8 max	c 35 td

Construction

Laid down as ocean-going submersibles, designed in 1941. Single hull with saddle tanks; eight watertight compartments (one additional compartment as for the Type VII D, allowing stowage for torpedoes in compartment 4); trim tanks in compartments 1 and 8; main diving tank and negative buoyancy tank below the control room; enlarged saddle tanks by comparison with the Type VII D containing larger diving and fuel oil tanks, pressurised regulating tanks and bunkers; additional diving tanks in the forecastle and stern; diving depth 100/200m.

Propulsion

Two Germaniawerft 6-cylinder 4-stroke F46 supercharged diesel engines in compartment 2; two AEG GU 460/8–276 double electric motors in compartment 1; 1 + 1 62-cell AFA 33 MAL 800 E (or W, *U1059*) batteries (9160 amp/hr); in compartments 3 and 6 below; diesel electric range 13,950nm at 10kts. Two 3-bladed propellers, 1.23m diameter; rudders and hydroplanes as for the Type VII C. [A hinged schnorkel was fitted on the forward port edge of the conning tower casing.]

Armament

Five 53.3cm torpedo tubes, four at the bow and one at the stern, all below the CWL - 14 torpedoes; no mine shafts. One 3.7cm AA gun - 1195 rounds;

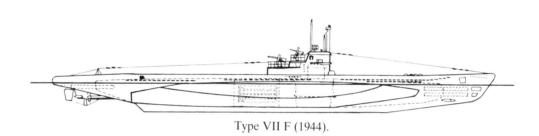
Type VII F (1944).

two 2cm AA guns - 4380 rounds. Two periscopes. Up to twenty-one torpedoes could be carried in the torpedo stowage area, plus five in pressurised containers on the upper deck.

Complement

Crew: 4/42. Boats: one rubber dinghy.

Notes

Hinged schnorkels were fitted at the port forward edge of the conning tower casing on these vessels.

Careers

U1059: launched 12 Mar 1943, commissioned 1 May 1943. Sunk 19 Mar 1944 in the mid-Atlantic southwest of the Cape Verde Islands, in position 13° 10'N, 33° 44'W, by bombs from aircraft of the US escort carrier *Block Island*; 47 dead (all crew lost).

U1060: launched 8 Apr 1943, commissioned 15 May 1943. Sunk 27 Oct 1844 in the North Sea south of Brônnôysund, in position 65° 24'N, 12° 00'E, by bombs from aircraft of the British carrier *Implacable* and by Czechoslovakian bombs; 12 dead.

U1061: launched 22 Apr 1943, commissioned 25 Aug 1943; transferred from Bergen to Loch Ryan 30 May 1945 for Operation Deadlight.

U1062: launched 8 May 1943, commissioned 19 Jun 1943. Sunk 30 Sept 1944 in the mid-Atlantic southwest of the Cape Verde Islands, in position 11° 36'N, 34° 44'W, by depth charges from the US destroyer escort *Fessenden*; 55 dead (all crew lost).

Type IX–IX D large U-boats

Construction

Laid down as ocean going submersibles, designed 1935–36. Double hull; five watertight compartments; trim tanks in compartments 1 and 5; diving tanks and main fuel oil bunkers in the outer hull, with pressure-tight regulating tanks and fuel oil bunkers in way of the control room and additional diving tanks in the forecastle and stern; diving depth 100/200m. 2 + 2 + 2 pressure-tight torpedo containers were fitted at the stern and 2 + 2 at the bow, on the sides of the upper deck.

Propulsion

Two MAN 9-cylinder 4-stroke M 9 V 40/46 supercharged diesel engines in compartment 2; two Siemens-Schuckert 2 GU 345/34 double electric motors in compartment 2; 1 + 1 62-cell AFA 36 MAK 740 W batteries (9260amp/hr) (or one 62-cell AFA 36 MAK 740 W battery (4630amp/hr) plus one 62-cell AFA 44 MAL 740 W battery (5650amp/hr), *U38*; or 1 + 1 62-cell AFA 44 MAL 740 W batteries (11,300amp/hr), *U37, 43* and all subsequent boats), all battery cells in battery boxes with soft rubber shock absorbers in compartment 4 be-

Name	Type	Builder (construction no)	Built	Cost in Marks (000s)	Displacement (t = tonnes T = tons)	Length (m)	Breadth (m)	Draught/ height (m)	Power (hp)	Revs (rpm)	Speed (kts)	Range (nm/kts)	Oil (t)	Diving time (sec)
U37–44	IX	Deschimag W (942–949)	1937–39	6448	1032t sf 1153t sm 1408t total 939t* sf	76.50 oa 58.75 ph	6.51 oa 4.40 ph	4.70/9.40	4400ehp sf 1000ehp sm	470 sf 275 sm	18.2 sf 7.7 sm	10,500/10, 3800/18.2 sf 65–78/4 sm	121/ 53.3 154 max	c 35 td
U64	IX B	,, (952)	1938–39	6163	1051t sf 1178t sm 1430t total 952t* sf	76.50 oa 58.75 ph	6.76 oa 4.40 ph	4.70/9.60	,,	,,	18.2 sf 7.3 sm	12,000/10, 3800/18.2 sf 64/4 sm	129/ 55.3 165 max	,,
U65, 122–124	,,	,, (953–956)†	1938–40	,,	,,	,,	,,	,,	,,	,,	,,	,,	,,	,,
U103–111	,,	,, (966–973, 976)	1939–40	,,	,,	,,	,,	,,	,,	,,	,,	,,	,,	,,
U66–68	IX C	,, (985–987)	1940–41	6448	1120t sf 1232t sm 1540t total 983t* sf	76.76 oa 58.75 ph	,,	,,	,,	,,	18.3 sf 7.3 sm	13,450/10, 5000/18.3 sf 128/2, 63/4 sm	152/ 64.3 208 max	,,
U125–131	,,	,, (988–994)	,,	,,	,,	,,	,,	,,	,,	,,	,,	,,	,,	,,
U153–160, 171–176	,,	,, (995–1000) 1009–1016)	,,	,,	,,	,,	,,	,,	,,	,,	,,	,,	,,	,,
U161–166	,,	Deschimag S (700–705)	1940–42	,,	,,	,,	,,	,,	,,	,,	,,	,,	,,	,,
U501–512	,,	DWA (219–296, 303–308)	1940–41	,,	,,	,,	,,	,,	,,	,,	,,	,,	,,	,,
U513–524	,,	,, (309–339)	1941–42	,,	,,	,,	,,	,,	,,	,,	,,	,,	,,	,,
U167–170	IX C/40	Deschimag S (706–709)	1941–43		1144t sf 1257t sm 1545t total 999t* sf	,,	6.86 oa 4.44 ph	4.67/9.60	,,	,,	,,	13,850/10, 5100/18.3 sf 128/2, 63/4 sm	160/ 63.4 214 max	,,

* Light load displacement.
† U-numbers 122–124 were exchanged with 66–68 at the outbreak of the war.

low; diesel-electric range 11,350, 12,400, 16,300 or 16,800nm at 10kts. Two 3-bladed propellers, 1.92m diameter; hydroplanes and rudders as for the Type VII C.

U193 was fitted with 1 + 1 62-cell 50 MAL 760 E batteries (12,430amp/hr) for trials, and *U844* with 117 type W cells and 7 type E cells. [*U38–41* were refitted with AFA 44 MAL 740 W batteries after a reappraisal of their performance with the original battery outfits. Collapsible schnorkels were fitted on the starboard side at 37m (41m for the Type IX B)].

Armament

Six 53.3cm torpedo tubes, four at the bow and two at the stern, all below the CWL - 22 torpedoes or 44 TMA (= 66 TMB) mines; one Utof 10.5cm/45 gun - 110 rounds; one 3.7cm AA gun - 2625 rounds; one 2cm AA gun - 4250 rounds. One periscope in the control room (deleted from the Type IX C onwards) and two in the tower.

U162–170 and *505–550* were not fitted for mines;

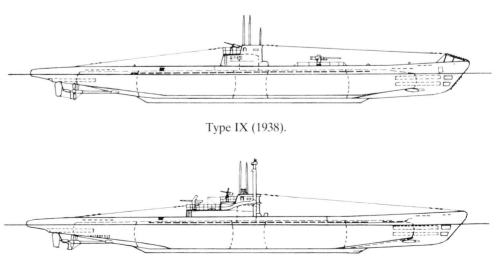

Type IX (1938).

Type IX C (1944).

Conning tower arrangements, Type IX C/D (1/160 scale)

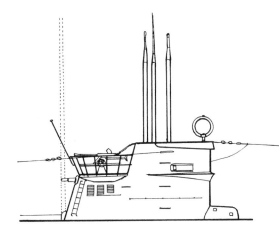

Type IX C basic conning tower, 1941–43.

AA armament: one 2cm C/30 gun in an LC 30/37 mounting; hinged schnorkel on *U183–185* and *U187* only.

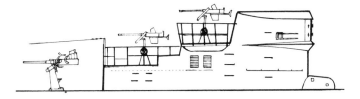

Type IX C with small 'Wintergarden', 1943.

AA armament: two 2cm C/38 guns in LC 30/37 mountings; one 3.7cm SK C/30 U gun in an LC/39 mounting.

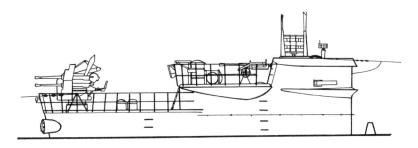

Type IX D 2 with large 'Wintergarden' (bridge modification IV, 1944).

AA armament: two twin 2cm C/38 II guns in double LM 43 U mountings; one quadruple 2cm 38/43 U gun with a shield.

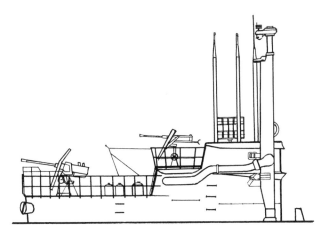

Type IX C with large 'Wintergarden' (bridge modification IV with schnorkel, 1945).

AA armament: two twin C/38 II guns in double LM 43 U mountings; one twin 3.7cm M 42 U gun in a double LM 42 U mounting.

U66–68, 103, 104, 124–131 and *153–158* were fitted as communications boats. [From 1943–44 the 10.5cm gun was removed and two twin 2cm AA guns were fitted in place of the original single.]

Complement

Crew: 4/44. Boats: 1 inflatable boat.

Notes

The Type IX was a development of the Type I A U-boat. Internal arrangements were approximately the same as those of the *U81* class (1915) - see page 12. A collapsible radio mast was initially fitted to *U183–185* and *187*, 15m high and mounted on the port side abaft the bridge; this was shortened after the first operational cruise and removed altogether after the second.

[Various modifications were made to the conning tower casing, including the addition of splinter shields, radar antennae and vent holes. A hinged schnorkel was fitted to the starboard side of the tower casing, and three pressure-tight torpedo containers on the starboard side were removed to allow stowage of the schnorkel in its lowered position. On *U170, 190, 516, 530, 539, 804, 858, 866–868, 1232* and *1233* the upper deck between 48.5m and 63.5m was sharply reduced in width to improve diving speed.]

Careers

U37: launched 14 May 1938, commissioned 4 Aug 1938. Scuttled 8 May 1945 in Sonderburg Bay, in position 54° 55′N, 09° 47′E; later broken up.

U38: launched 9 Aug 1938, commissioned 24 Oct 1938. Scuttled 5 May 1945 at Wesermünde; broken up in 1948.

U39: launched 22 Sept 1938, commissioned 10 Dec 1938. Sunk 14 Sept 1939 northwest of Ireland, in position 58° 32′N, 11° 49′W, by depth charges from the British destroyers *Faulknor, Foxhound* and *Firedrake*.

U40: launched 9 Nov 1938, commissioned 11 Feb 1939. Sunk 13 Oct 1939 in the Channel, position not known, by mines; 45 dead.

U41: launched 20 Jan 1939, commissioned 22 Apr 1939. Sunk 5 Feb 1940 south of Ireland, in position 49° 20′N, 10° 04′W, by depth charges from the British destroyer *Antelope*; 49 dead (all crew lost).

U42: launched 16 Feb 1939, commissioned 15 Jul 1939. Sunk 13 Oct 1939 southwest of Ireland, in position 49° 12′N, 16° 00′W, by depth charges from the British destroyers *Imogen* and *Ilex*; 26 dead.

U43: launched 23 May 1939, commissioned 26 Aug 1939. Sunk 30 Jul 1943 southwest of the Azores, in

position 34° 57′N, 35° 11′W, by bombs and aerial torpedoes from aircraft of the US escort carrier *Santee*; 55 dead (all crew lost).

U44: launched 5 Aug 1939, commissioned 4 Nov 1939. Sunk 20 Mar 1940 southwest of Narvik, in position 67° 33′N, 12° 10′E, by depth charges from the British destroyer *Fortune*; 47 dead (all crew lost).

U64: launched 20 Sept 1939, commissioned 16 Dec 1939. Sunk 13 Apr 1940 in the Herjangs Fjord near Narvik, in approximate position 68° 29′N, 17° 30′E, by bombs from an aircraft carried on the British battleship *Warspite*; 8 dead. Raised in August 1957 and broken up.

U65: launched 6 Nov 1939, commissioned 15 Feb 1940. Sunk 28 Apr 1941 southeast of Iceland, in position 60° 04′N, 15° 45′W, by depth charges from the British corvette *Gladiolus*; 50 dead (all crew lost).

U66: launched 10 Oct 1940, commissioned 2 Jan 1941. Sunk 1 May 1944 west of the Cape Verde Islands, in position 17° 17′N, 32° 29′W, by bombs from aircraft of the US escort carrier *Block Island* and by the destroyer escort *Buckley*; 24 dead.

U67: launched 30 Oct 1940, commissioned 22 Jan 1941. Sunk 16 Jul 1943 in the Sargasso Sea, in posi-

Name	Type	Builder (construction no)	Built
U183–194	IX C/40	Deschimag W (1023–1028, 1035–1040)	1941–43
U525–532	"	DWA (340–347)	1941–42
U533–550	"	" (351–357, 360–371)	1942–43
U801–806	"	Deschimag S (710–715)	1941–44
U807–816, 1501–1506	"	" (716–731)	1943–
U841–846, 853–858	"	Deschimag W (1047–1052, 1059–1064)	1942–43
U865–870, 877–882, 899	"	" (1073–1078, 1085–1090, 1098)	1943–44
U890–894, 1507–1530	"	" (1098–1102, 1121–1144	1943–
U1221–1235	"	DWA (384–398)	1942–44
U1236–1238	"	" (399–401)	1943–
U1239–1262	"	" (402–413, 434–445)	"

tion 30° 05'N, 44° 17'W, by bombs from aircraft of the US escort carrier *Core*; 48 dead.

U68: launched 22 Nov 1940, commissioned 11 Feb 1941. Sunk 10 Apr 1944 northwest of Madeira, in position 33° 24'N, 18° 59'W, by bombs from aircraft of the US escort carrier *Guadalcanal*; 56 dead.

U103: launched 12 Apr 1940, commissioned 5 Jul 1940. Sunk 15 Apr 1945 at Kiel, by bombs; 1 dead.

U104: launched 25 May 1940, commissioned 19 Aug 1940. Sunk 21 Nov 1940 northwest of Ireland, in position 56° 28'N, 14° 13'W, by depth charges from the British corvette *Rhododendron*; 49 dead (all crew lost).

U105: launched 15 Jun 1940, commissioned 10 Sept 1940. Sunk 2 Jun 1943 near Dakar, in position 14° 15'N, 17° 35'W, by French bombs; 53 dead (all crew lost).

U106: launched 17 Jun 1940, commissioned 24 Sept 1940. Sunk 2 Aug 1943 northwest of Cape Ortegal, in position 46° 35'N, 11° 55'W, by British and Australian bombs; 22 dead.

U107: launched 2 Jul 1940, commissioned 8 Oct 1940. Sunk 18 Aug 1944 west of La Rochelle, in position 46° 46'N, 03° 49'W, by British bombs; 58 dead (all crew lost).

U108: launched 15 Jul 1940, commissioned 22 Oct 1940. Sunk 11 Apr 1944 at Stettin, by bombs;

raised; taken out of service at Stettin 17 Jul 1944; scuttled there 24 Apr 1945.

U109: launched 14 Sept 1940, commissioned 5 Dec 1940. Sunk 7 May 1943 south of Ireland, in position 47° 22'N, 22° 40'W, by British bombs; 52 dead.

U110: launched 25 Aug 1940, commissioned 21 Nov 1940; captured 9 May 1941 and taken in tow by the British destroyer *Bulldog*; sunk on 11 May 1941 east of Cape Farewell, in position 60° 22'N, 33° 12'W, by depth charges from the British corvette *Aubretia* and the destroyers *Bulldog* and *Broadway*; 14 dead.

U111: launched 6 Sept 1940, commissioned 19 Dec 1940. Sunk 4 Oct 1941 southwest of Teneriffe, in position 27° 15'N, 20° 27'W, by depth charges from the British anti-submarine trawler *Lady Shirley*; 8 dead.

U122: launched 30 Dec 1939, commissioned 30 Mar 1940; went missing on 22 Jun 1940 between the North Sea and the Bay of Biscay; 48 dead (all crew lost).

U123: launched 2 Mar 1940, commissioned 30 May 1940; taken out of service at Lorient 17 Jun 1944; scuttled there 19 Aug 1944; surrendered to France in 1945 and became the French submarine *Blaison*; stricken 18 Aug 1959 as *Q165*.

U124: launched 9 Mar 1940, commissioned 11 Jun 1940. Sunk 3 Apr 1943 west of Oporto, in position 41° 02'N, 15° 39'W, by depth charges from the British corvette *Stonecrop* and the sloop *Black Swan*; 53 dead (all crew lost).

U125: launched 10 Dec 1940, commissioned 3 Mar 1941. Sunk 6 Apr 1943 east of Newfoundland, in position 52° 13'N, 44° 50'W, by gunfire and ramming by the British destroyer *Oribi* and the corvette *Snowflake*; 54 dead (all crew lost).

U126: launched 31 Dec 1940, commissioned 22 Mar 1941. Sunk 3 Jul 1943 northwest of Cape Ortegal, in position 46° 02'N, 11° 23'W, by British bombs; 55 dead (all crew lost).

U127: launched 4 Feb 1921, commissioned 24 Apr 1941. Sunk 15 Dec 1941 west of Gibraltar, in position 36° 28'N, 09° 12'W, by depth charges from the British destroyer *Nestor*; 51 dead (all crew lost).

U128: launched 20 Feb 1921, commissioned 12 May 1941. Sunk 17 May 1943 south of Pernambuco, in approximate position 10° 00'N, 35° 35'W, by gunfire from the US destroyers *Moffett* and *Jouett*, and by bombs from two aircraft; 7 dead.

U129: launched 28 Feb 1941, commissioned 21 May 1941; taken out of service at Lorient 4 Jul 1944; scuttled there 18 Aug 1944; raised and stricken in 1946, and broken up.

U130: launched 14 Mar 1941, commissioned 11 Jun 1941. Sunk 12 Mar 1943 west of the Azores, in position 37° 10'N, 40° 21'W, by depth charges from the US destroyer *Champlin*; 53 dead (all crew lost).

U131: launched 1 Apr 1941, commissioned 1 Jul 1941. Sunk 17 Dec 1941 northeast of Madeira, in position 34° 12'N, 13° 35'W, by depth charges and gunfire from the British escort destroyers *Exmoor* and *Blankney*, the destroyer *Stanley*, the corvette *Pentstemon* and the sloop *Stork*, and by bombs from aircraft of the British escort carrier *Audacity*.

U153: launched 5 Apr 1941, commissioned 19 Jul 1941. Sunk 13 Jul 1942 near Colon, in position 09° 46'N, 81° 29'W, by depth charges from the US destroyer *Landsdowne*; 52 dead (all crew lost).

U154: launched 21 Apr 1941, commissioned 2 Aug 1941. Sunk 3 Jul 1944 west of Madeira, in approximate position 34° 00'N, 19° 30'W, by depth charges from the US destroyer escorts *Inch* and *Frost*; 57 dead (all crew lost).

U155: launched 12 May 1941, commissioned 23 Aug 1941; transferred from Wilhelmshaven to Loch Ryan 30 Jun 1945 for Operation Deadlight.

U156: launched 21 May 1941, commissioned 4 Sept 1941. Sunk at 1315hrs on 8 Mar 1943 east of Barbados, in position 12° 38'N, 54° 39'W, by US bombs; 52 dead (all crew lost).

U157: launched 5 Jun 1941, commissioned 15 Sept 1941. Sunk at 1600hrs on 13 Jun 1942 northeast of Havana, in position 24° 13'N, 82° 03'W, by depth charges from the US coastguard cutter *Thetis*; 52 dead (all crew lost).

U158: launched 21 Jun 1941, commissioned 25 Sept 1941. Sunk 30 Jun 1942 west of the Bermudas, in position 32° 50'N, 67° 28'W, by US bombs; 54 dead (all crew lost).

U159: launched 1 Jul 1941, commissioned 4 Oct 1941. Sunk 15 Jul 1943 south of Haiti, in position 15° 58'N, 73° 44'W, by US bombs; 53 dead (all crew lost).

U160: launched 12 Jul 1941, commissioned 16 Oct 1941. Sunk 14 Jul 1943 south of the Azores, in position 33° 54'N, 27° 13'W, by aerial torpedoes from aircraft of the US escort carrier *Santee*; 57 dead (all crew lost).

U161: launched 1 Mar 1941, commissioned 8 Jul 1941. Sunk 27 Sept 1943 near Bahia, in position 12° 30'S, 35° 35'W, by US bombs; 53 dead (all crew lost).

U162: launched 1 Mar 1941, commissioned 9 Sept 1941. Sunk 3 Sept 1942 near Trinidad, in position 12° 21'N, 59° 29'W, by depth charges from the British destroyers *Vimy*, *Pathfinder* and *Quentin*; 2 dead.

U163: launched 1 May 1941, commissioned 21 Oct 1941. Missing, presumed sunk, in the Bay of Biscay, position not known; 57 dead (all crew lost).

U164: launched 1 May 1941, commissioned 28 Nov 1941. Sunk 6 Jan 1943 northwest of Pernambuco, in position 01° 58'S 39° 22'W, by US bombs; 54 dead (all crew lost).

U165: launched 15 Aug 1941, commissioned 3 Feb 1942. Sunk 27 Sept 1942 in the Bay of Biscay, in position 47° 50'N, 03° 22'W, probably by mines; 51 dead (all crew lost).

U166: launched 1 Nov 1941, commissioned 23 Mar 1942. Sunk 1 Aug 1942 in the Gulf of Mexico, in position 28° 37'N, 09° 45'W, by US bombs; 52 dead (all crew lost).

U167: launched 5 Mar 1942, commissioned 4 Jul 1942. Sunk 6 Apr 1943 near the Canary Islands, in approximate position 27° 47'N, 15° 00'W, by British bombs. Raised in 1951 and transferred to Spain; used commercially for filming etc; broken up.

U168: launched 5 Mar 1942, commissioned 10 Sept 1942. Sunk at 0130hrs on 6 Oct 1944 in the Java

Flooding slot identification of Type IX A, B, C and D U-boats (after Lennart Lindberg)

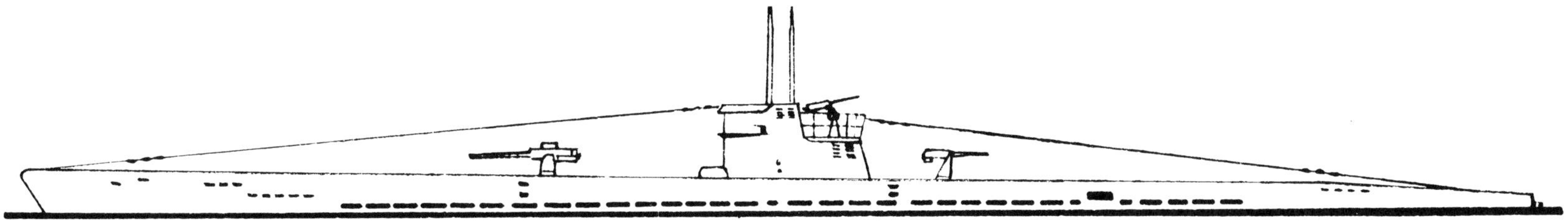

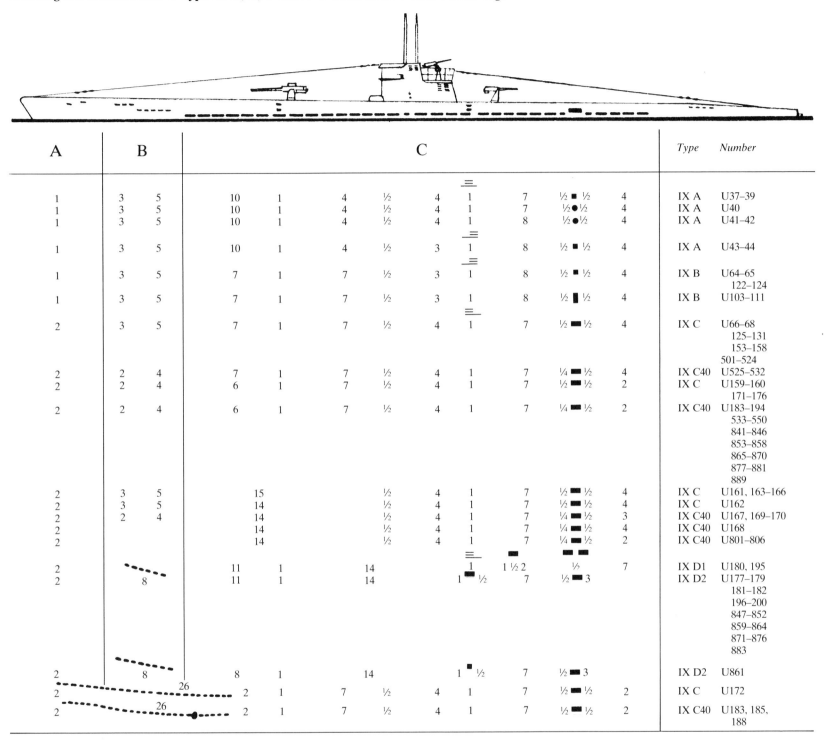

A	B	B	C	C	C	C	C	C	C	C	C	*Type*	*Number*
1	3	5	10	1	4	½	4	≡ 1	7	½ ■ ½	4	IX A	U37–39
1	3	5	10	1	4	½	4	1	7	½●½	4	IX A	U40
1	3	5	10	1	4	½	4	1	8	½●½	4	IX A	U41–42
1	3	5	10	1	4	½	3	≡ 1	8	½ ■ ½	4	IX A	U43–44
1	3	5	7	1	7	½	3	≡ 1	8	½ ■ ½	4	IX B	U64–65 122–124
1	3	5	7	1	7	½	3	1	8	½ ▮ ½	4	IX B	U103–111
2	3	5	7	1	7	½	4	≡ 1	7	½ ▬ ½	4	IX C	U66–68 125–131 153–158 501–524
2	2	4	7	1	7	½	4	1	7	¼ ▬ ½	4	IX C40	U525–532
2	2	4	6	1	7	½	4	1	7	½ ▬ ½	2	IX C	U159–160 171–176
2	2	4	6	1	7	½	4	1	7	¼ ▬ ½	2	IX C40	U183–194 533–550 841–846 853–858 865–870 877–881 889
2	3	5	15			½	4	1	7	½ ▬ ½	4	IX C	U161, 163–166
2	3	5	14			½	4	1	7	½ ▬ ½	4	IX C	U162
2	2	4	14			½	4	1	7	¼ ▬ ½	3	IX C40	U167, 169–170
2			14			½	4	1	7	¼ ▬ ½	4	IX C40	U168
2			14			½	4	1	7	¼ ▬ ½	2	IX C40	U801–806
2			11	1	14			≡ 1	▬ 1 ½ 2	▬ ▬ ½	7	IX D1	U180, 195
2	8		11	1	14			1 ▬ ½	7	½ ▬ 3		IX D2	U177–179 181–182 196–200 847–852 859–864 871–876 883
2	8		8	1	14			1 ■ ½	7	½ ▬ 3		IX D2	U861
2	26		2	1	7	½	4	1	7	½ ▬ ½	2	IX C	U172
2	26		2	1	7	½	4	1	7	½ ▬ ½	2	IX C40	U183, 185, 188

Sea, in position 06° 20′S, 111° 28′E, by a torpedo from the Dutch submarine *Zwaardvisch*; 23 dead.

U169: launched 6 Jun 1942, commissioned 16 Nov 1942. Sunk 27 Mar 1943 south of Iceland, in position 60° 54′N, 15° 25′W, by British bombs; 54 dead (all crew lost).

U170: launched 6 Jun 1942, commissioned 19 Jan 1943; transferred from Horten to Loch Ryan 29 May 1945 for Operation Deadlight.

U171: launched 22 Jul 1941, commissioned 25 Oct 1941. Sunk at 1300hrs on 9 Oct 1941 near Lorient, in position 47° 30′N, 03° 30′W, by mines; 22 dead.

U172: launched 5 Aug 1941, commissioned 5 Nov 1941. Sunk 13 Dec 1943 west of the Canary Islands, in position 26° 29′N, 24° 58′W, by bombs from aircraft of the US escort carrier *Bogue* and by depth charges from the US destroyers *George E Badger*, *Clemson*, *George W Ingram* and *Dupont*; 13 dead.

U173: launched 11 Aug 1941, commissioned 15 Nov 1941. Sunk 16 Nov 1942 at Casablanca, by depth charges from the US destroyers *Woolsey*, *Swanson* and *Quick*; 57 dead (all crew lost).

U174: launched 21 Aug 1941, commissioned 26 Nov 1941. Sunk 27 Apr 1943 south of Newfoundland, in position 43° 35′N, 56° 18′W, by US bombs; 53 dead (all crew lost).

U175: launched 2 Sept 1941, commissioned 5 Dec 1941. Sunk 17 Apr 1943 southwest of Ireland, in position 47° 53′N, 22° 04′W, by depth charges and gunfire from the US coastguard cutter *Spencer* and by bombs; 13 dead.

U176: launched 12 Sept 1941, commissioned 15 Dec 1941. Sunk 15 May 1943 northeast of Havana, in position 23° 21′N, 80° 18′W, by US bombs and the Cuban patrol boat *SC 13*; 53 dead (all crew lost).

U183: launched 9 Jan 1942, commissioned 1 Apr 1942. Sunk at 1300hrs on 23 Apr 1945 in the Java Sea, in position 04° 50′S, 112° 52′E, by a torpedo from the US submarine *Besugo*; 54 dead.

U184: launched 21 Feb 1942, commissioned 29 May 1942. Sunk 20 Nov 1942 in the mid-Atlantic, in position 24° 25′N, 45° 25′W, by depth charges from the Norwegian corvette *Pontentilla*; 50 dead (all crew lost).

U185: launched 2 Mar 1942, commissioned 13 Jun 1942. Sunk 24 Aug 1943 in the mid-Atlantic, in position 27° 00′N, 37° 06′W, by bombs from aircraft of the US escort carrier *Core*; 29 dead, plus 14 dead from *U604*.

U186: launched 11 Mar 1942, commissioned 10 Jul 1942. Sunk 12 May 1945 north of the Azores, in position 41° 54′N, 31° 49′W, by depth charges from the British destroyer *Hesperus*; 53 dead (all crew lost).

U187: launched 16 Mar 1942, commissioned 23 Jul 1942. Sunk 4 Feb 1943 in the North Atlantic, in position 50° 12′N, 36° 35′W, by depth charges from the British destroyers *Vimy* and *Beverley*; 9 dead.

U188: launched 31 Mar 1942, commissioned 5 Aug 1942; scuttled 26 Aug 1944 at Bordeaux when unable to escape the Allied advance; broken up in 1947.

U189: launched 1 May 1942, commissioned 15 Aug 1942. Sunk 23 Apr 1943 east of Cape Farewell, in position 59° 50′N, 34° 43′W, by British bombs; 54 dead (all crew lost).

U190: launched 8 Jun 1942, commissioned 24 Sept 1942; surrendered to Canada on 12 May 1945 at Halifax, and used for tests; sunk 21 Oct 1947 southwest of Newfoundland by bombs and gunfire from the Canadian destroyers *Nootka* and *New Liskeard*.

U191: launched 3 Jul 1942, commissioned 20 Oct 1942. Sunk 23 Apr 1943 southeast of Cape Farewell, in position 56° 45′N, 34° 25′W, by depth charges from the British destroyer *Hesperus*; 55 dead.

U192: launched 31 Jul 1942, commissioned 16 Nov 1942. Sunk 5 May 1943 south of Cape Farewell, in position 54° 56′N, 43° 44′W, by depth charges from the British corvette *Pink*; 55 dead (all crew lost).

U193: launched 24 Aug 1942, commissioned 10 Dec 1942. Sunk 28 Apr 1944 west of Nantes, in position 45° 38′N, 09° 43′W, by British bombs; 59 dead (all crew lost).

U194: launched 22 Sept 1942, commissioned 8 Jan 1943. Sunk 24 Jun 1943 south of Iceland, in position 58° 15′N, 25° 25′W, by British bombs; 54 dead (all crew lost).

U501: launched 25 Jan 1941, commissioned 30 Apr 1941. Sunk at 2330hrs on 10 Sept 1941 in the Denmark Straits south of Angmagsalik, in position 62° 50′N, 37° 50′W, by depth charges from the Canadian corvettes *Chambly* and *Moosejaw*; 11 dead.

U502: launched 18 Feb 1941, commissioned 31 May 1941. Sunk 5 Jul 1942 west of La Rochelle, in position 46° 10′N, 06° 40′W, by British bombs; 52 dead (all crew lost).

U503: launched 5 Apr 1941, commissioned 10 Jul 1941. Sunk 15 Mar 1942 in the North Atlantic

southeast of Newfoundland, in position 45° 50′N, 48° 50′W, by US bombs; 51 dead (all crew lost).

U504: launched 24 Apr 1941, commissioned 30 Jul 1941. Sunk at 1543hrs on 30 Jul 1943 in the North Atlantic northwest of Cape Ortegal, in position 45° 33′N, 10° 56′W, by depth charges from the British sloops *Kite*, *Woodpecker*, *Wren* and *Wild Goose*; 53 dead (all crew lost).

U505: launched 24 May 1941, commissioned 26 Aug 1941. Left sinking at 1120hrs on 4 Jun 1944 northwest of Dakar, in position 21° 30′N, 19° 20′W, after being damaged by bombs, gunfire and depth charges from aircraft of the US escort carrier *Guadalcanal* and the destroyer escort *Pillsbury*; 1 dead. Salvaged and taken to Port Royal Bay, Bermuda; renamed as USS *Nemo* and used for tests; converted to a museum ship in Chicago in 1954.

U506: launched 20 Jun 1941, commissioned 15 Sept 1941. Sunk at 1550hrs on 12 Jul 1943 in the North Atlantic west of Vigo, in position 42° 30′N, 16° 30′W, by US bombs; 48 dead (all crew lost).

U507: launched 15 Jul 1941, commissioned 8 Oct 1941. Sunk 13 Jan 1943 northwest of Natal, in position 01° 38′S, 39° 52′W, by US bombs; 54 dead (all crew lost).

U508: launched 30 Jul 1941, commissioned 20 Oct 1941. Sunk 12 Nov 1943 north of Cape Ortegal, in position 46° 00′N, 07° 30′W, by US bombs; 57 dead (all crew lost).

U509: launched 19 Aug 1941, commissioned 4 Nov 1941. Sunk 15 Jul 1943 in the mid-Atlantic northwest of Madeira, in position 34° 02′N, 26° 01′W, by aerial torpedoes from aircraft of the US escort carrier *Santee*; 54 dead (all crew lost).

U510: launched 4 Sept 1941, commissioned 25 Nov 1941; taken out of service 10 May 1945 at St Nazaire; surrendered to France 12 May 1945; renamed as the French submarine *Bouan*; stricken 1 May 1959 as *Q176*; broken up in 1960.

U511: launched 22 Sept 1941, commissioned 8 Dec 1941; sold to Japan 16 Sept 1943 and became the Japanese submarine *RO 500*; surrendered at Maizuru in August 1945; scuttled in the Gulf of Maizuru by the US Navy, 30 Apr 1946.

U512: launched 9 Oct 1941, commissioned 20 Dec 1941. Sunk 2 Oct 1942 north of Cayenne, in position 06° 50′N, 52° 25′W, by US bombs; 51 dead.

U513: launched 29 Oct 1941, commissioned 10 Jan 1942. Sunk 19 Jul 1943 southeast of São Francisco do Sul, in position 27° 17′S, 47° 32′W, by US bombs; 46 dead.

U514: launched 18 Nov 1941, commissioned 24 Jan 1942. Sunk 8 Jul 1943 northeast of Cap Finisterre, in position 43° 37′S, 08° 59′W, by British bombs; 54 dead (all crew lost).

U515: launched 2 Dec 1941, commissioned 21 Feb 1942. Sunk at 1510hrs on 9 Apr 1944 in the mid-Atlantic north of Madeira, in position 34° 35′N, 19° 18′W, by bombs from aircraft of the US escort carrier *Guadalcanal* and depth charges from the destroyer escorts *Pope*, *Pillsbury*, *Chatelain* and *Flaherty*; 16 dead.

U516: launched 16 Dec 1941, commissioned 10 Mar 1942; surrendered at Loch Foyle; transferred to Liahally 14 May 1945 for Operation Deadlight.

U517: launched 30 Dec 1941, commissioned 21 Mar 1942. Sunk 21 Nov 1942 in the North Atlantic southwest of Ireland, in position 46° 16′N, 17° 09′W, by bombs from aircraft of the British carrier *Victorious*; 1 dead.

U518: launched 11 Feb 1942, commissioned 25 Apr 1942. Sunk 22 Apr 1945 in the North Atlantic northwest of the Azores, in position 43° 26′N, 38° 23′W, by depth charges from the US destroyer escorts *Carter* and *Neal A Scott*; 56 dead (all crew lost).

U519: launched 12 Feb 1942, commissioned 7 May 1942. Sunk 10 Feb 1943 southwest of Ireland, in position 47° 05′N, 18° 34′W, by US bombs; 50 dead (all crew lost).

U520: launched 2 Mar 1942, commissioned 19 May 1942. Sunk 30 Oct 1942 east of Newfoundland, in position 47° 47′N, 49° 50′W, by Canadian bombs; 53 dead (all crew lost).

U521: launched 17 Mar 1942, commissioned 3 Jun 1942. Sunk 2 Jun 1943 in the North Atlantic southeast of Baltimore, in position 37° 43′N, 73° 16′W, by depth charges from the US submarine chaser *PC 565*; 51 dead.

U522: launched 1 Apr 1942, commissioned 11 Jun 1942. Sunk 23 Feb 1943 in the mid-Atlantic southwest of Madeira, in position 31° 27′N, 26° 22′W, by depth charges from the British coastguard cutter *Totland*; 51 dead (all crew lost).

U523: launched 15 Apr 1942, commissioned 25 Jun 1942. Sunk 25 Aug 1943 in the North Atlantic west of Vigo, in position 42° 03′N, 18° 02′W, by depth charges from the British destroyer *Wanderer* and the corvette *Wallflower*; 17 dead.

U524: launched 30 Apr 1942, commissioned 8 Jul 1942. Sunk 22 Mar 1943 south of Madeira, in position 30° 15′N, 18° 13′W, by US bombs; 52 dead (all crew lost).

U525: launched 20 May 1942, commissioned 30 Jul 1942. Sunk 11 Aug 1943 in the North Atlantic northwest of the Azores, in position 41° 29′N, 38° 55′W, by bombs and aerial torpedoes from aircraft of the US escort carrier *Card*; 54 dead.

U526: launched 3 Jun 1942, commissioned 12 Aug 1942. Sunk at 1036hrs on 14 Apr 1943 in the Bay of Biscay near Lorient, in position 47° 30′N, 03° 45′W, by mines; 42 dead.

U527: launched 3 Jun 1942, commissioned 2 Sept 1942. Sunk 23 Jul 1943 in the mid-Atlantic south of the Azores, in position 35° 25′N, 27° 56′W, by bombs from aircraft of the US escort carrier *Bogue*; 40 dead.

U528: launched 1 Jul 1942, commissioned 16 Sept 1942. Sunk 11 May 1943 in the North Atlantic southwest of Ireland, in position 46° 55′N, 14° 44′W, by British bombs and by depth charges from the British sloop *Fleetwood*; 11 dead.

U529: launched 15 Jul 1942, commissioned 30 Sept 1942. Sunk 15 Feb 1943 in the North Atlantic, in position 55° 45′N, 31° 09′W, by British bombs; 48 dead (all crew lost).

U530: launched 28 Jul 1942, commissioned 14 Oct 1942; surrendered in the Rio de la Plata 10 Jul 1945; transferred to USA; used for tests; scuttled during tests 28 Nov 1947 northeast of Cape Cod, by a torpedo.

U531: launchd 12 Aug 1942, commissioned 28 Oct 1942. Sunk 6 May 1943 in the North Atlantic northeast of Newfoundland, in position 52° 31′N, 44° 50′W, by depth charges from the British destroyer *Vidette*; 54 dead (all crew lost).

U532: launched 26 Aug 1942, commissioned 11 Nov 1942; surrendered at Liverpool 10 May 1945; transferred to Loch Ryan for Operation Deadlight.

U533: launched 11 Sept 1942, commissioned 25 Nov 1942. Sunk 16 Oct 1943 in the Gulf of Oman, in position 25° 28′N, 56° 50′E, by British bombs; 52 dead.

U534: launched 23 Sept 1942, commissioned 23 Dec 1942. Sunk 5 May 1945 in the Kattegat northwest of Helsingör, in position 56° 39′N, 11° 48′E, by British bombs; 3 dead.

U535: launched 8 Oct 1942, commissioned 23 Dec 1942. Sunk 5 Jul 1943 northeast of Cap Finisterre, in position 43° 38′N, 09° 13′W, by British bombs; 55 dead (all crew lost).

U536: launched 21 Oct 1942, commissioned 13 Jan 1943. Sunk 20 Nov 1943 in the North Atlantic northeast of the Azores, in position 43° 50′N, 19° 39′W, by depth charges from the British frigate *Nene* and the Canadian corvettes *Snowberry* and *Calgary*; 38 dead.

U537: launched 7 Nov 1942, commissioned 27 Jan 1943. Sunk 9 Nov 1944 in the Java Sea east of Surabaya, in position 07° 13′S, 115° 17′E, by torpedoes from the US submarine *Flounder*; 58 dead (all crew lost).

U538: launched 20 Nov 1942, commissioned 10 Feb 1943. Sunk 21 Nov 1943 in the North Atlantic southwest of Ireland, in position 45° 40′N, 19° 35′W, by depth charges from the British frigate *Foley* and the sloop *Crane*; 55 dead (all crew lost).

U539: launched 4 Dec 1942, commissioned 24 Feb 1943; transferred from Bergen to Loch Ryan 30 May 1945 for Operation Deadlight.

U540: launched 18 Dec 1942, commissioned 10 Mar 1943. Sunk 17 Oct 1943 east of Cape Farewell, in position 58° 38′N, 31° 56′W, by British bombs; 55 dead (all crew lost).

U541: launched 5 Jan 1943, commissioned 24 Mar 1943; surrendered at Gibraltar 14 May 1945; transferred to Lisahally for Operation Deadlight.

U542: launched 19 Jan 1943, commissioned 7 Apr 1943. Sunk 28 No 1943 north of Madeira, in position 39° 03′N, 16° 25′W, by British bombs; 56 dead (all crew lost).

U543: launched 3 Feb 1943, commissioned 21 Apr 1943. Sunk 2 Jul 1944 in the mid-Atlantic southwest of Teneriffe, in position 25° 34′N, 21° 36′W, by bombs from aircraft of the US escort carrier *Wake Island*; 58 dead (all crew lost).

U544: launched 17 Feb 1943, commissioned 5 May 1943. Sunk 17 Jan 1944 in the North Atlantic northwest of the Azores, in position 40° 30′N, 37° 20′W, by bombs from aircraft of the US escort carrier *Guadalcanal*; 57 dead (all crew lost).

U545: launched 3 Mar 1943, commissioned 19 May 1943. Sunk 11 Feb 1944 west of the Hebrides, in position 58° 17′N, 13° 22′W, by British bombs; 1 dead.

U546: launched 17 Mar 1943, commissioned 2 Jun 1943. Sunk 24 Apr 1945 northwest of the Azores, in position 43° 53′N, 40° 07′W, by depth charges from the US destroyer escorts *Flaherty*, *Neunzer*, *Chatelain*, *Varian*, *Hubbard*, *Janssen*, *Pillsbury* and *Keith*; 25 dead.

U547: launched 3 Apr 1943, commissioned 16 Jun 1943; damaged by mines in the Gironde near Pauillac 13 Aug 1944; taken out of service at Stettin, 31 Dec 1944.

U548: launched 14 Apr 1943, commissioned 30 Jun 1943. Sunk 30 Apr 1945 east of Cape Hatteras, in position 36° 34′N, 74° 00′W, by depth charges from the US patrol frigate *Natchez* and the destroyer escorts *Coffman*, *Bostwick* and *Thomas*; 58 dead (all crew lost).

U549: launched 28 Apr 1943, commissioned 14 Jul 1943. Sunk 29 May 1944 in the mid-Atlantic southwest of Madeira, in position 31° 13′N, 23° 03′W, by depth charges from the US destroyer escorts *Eugene E Elmore* and *Ahrens*; 57 dead (all crew lost).

U550: launched 12 May 1943, commissioned 28 Jul 1943. Sunk 16 Apr 1944 in the North Atlantic east of New York, in position 40° 09′N, 69° 44′W, by depth charges and gunfire from the US destroyer escorts *Gandy*, *Joyce* and *Peterson*; 44 dead.

U801: launched 31 Oct 1942, commissioned 24 Mar 1943. Sunk 17 Mar 1944 in the mid-Atlantic near the Cape Verde Islands, in position 16° 42′N, 30° 28′W, by bombs from aircraft of the US escort carrier *Block Island* and depth charges from the destroyer escort *Bronstein*; 10 dead.

U802: launched 31 Oct 1942, commissioned 12 Jun 1943; surrendered at Loch Eriboll 11 May 1945; transferred to Lisahally for Operation Deadlight.

U803: launched 1 Apr 1943, commissioned 7 Sept 1943. Sunk 27 Apr 1944 in the baltic Sea near Swinemünde, in position 53° 55′N, 14° 17′E, by a mine; 9 dead. Raised 9 Aug 1944 and taken out of service; fate unknown.

U804: launched 1 Apr 1943, commissioned 4 Dec 1943. Sunk 9 Apr 1945 in the Kattegat in position 57° 58′N, 11° 15′E, by British rockets; 55 dead (all crew lost).

U805: launched in 1943, commissioned 12 Feb 1944; surrendered on 14 May 1945 near Portsmouth, New Hampshire, in position 43° 04′N, 70° 43′W; used for 'Victory Visits' to the east coast of the USA; scuttled 4 Feb 1946 on the east coast of the USA.

U806: launched in 1943, commissioned 29 Apr 1944; transferred from Wilhelmshaven to Loch Ryan 22 Jun 1945 for Operation Deadlight.

U807–808: construction suspended 30 Sept 1943.

U809–812: construction suspended 30 Sep 1943; cancelled 22 Jul 1944.

U813–816: cancelled 30 Sept 1943.

U841: launched 21 Oct 1942, commissioned 6 Feb 1943. Sunk 17 Oct 1943 in the North Atlantic east of Cape Farewell, in position 59° 57′N, 31° 06′W, by depth charges from the British frigate *Byard*; 26 dead.

U842: launched 14 Nov 1942, commissioned 1 Mar 1943. Sunk at 1400hrs on 6 Nov 1943 in the western North Atlantic, in position 43° 42′N, 42° 08′W, by depth charges from the British sloops *Starling* and *Wild Goose*; 56 dead (all crew lost).

U843: launched 15 Dec 1942, commissioned 24 Mar 1943. Sunk 9 Apr 1945 in the Kattegat west of Gothenberg, in position 57° 58′N, 11° 15′E, by British bombs; 44 dead. Raised 22 Aug 1958 and broken up near Gothenberg, 1958–59.

U844: launched 30 Dec 1942, commissioned 7 Apr 1943. Sunk 16 Oct 1943 southwest of Iceland, in position 58° 30′N, 27° 16′W, by British bombs; 53 dead (all crew lost).

U845: launched 22 Jan 1943, commissioned 1 May 1943. Sunk 10 Mar 1944, in the North Atlantic, in position 48° 20′N, 20° 33′W, by depth charges from the British destroyer *Forester*, the Canadian destroyer *St Laurent*, the corvette *Owensound* and the frigate *Swansea*; 10 dead.

U846: launched 17 Feb 1943, commissioned 29 May 1943. Sunk 4 May 1944 north of Cape Ortegal, in position 46° 04′N, 09° 20′W, by Canadian bombs; 57 dead (all crew lost).

U853: launched 11 Mar 1943, commissioned 25 Jun 1943. Sunk 6 May 1945 in the North Atlantic southeast of New London, in position 41° 13′N, 71° 27′W, by depth charges from the US destroyer escort *Atherton* and the patrol frigate *Moberly*; 55 dead (all crew lost).

U854: launched 5 Apr 1943, commissioned 19 Jul 1943. Sunk at 1157hrs on 4 Feb 1944 in the Baltic Sea north of Swinemünde, in position 54° 44′N, 14° 16′E, by mines; 51 dead (all crew lost). Raised on 18 Nov 1968.

U855: launched 17 Apr 1943, commissioned 2 Aug 1943. Sunk 24 Sept 1944 west of Bergen, in position 61° 00′N, 04° 07′E, by British bombs; 56 dead (all crew lost).

U856: launched 11 May 1943, commissioned 19 Aug 1943. Sunk 7 Apr 1944 in the North Atlantic east of New York, in position 40° 18′N, 62° 22′W, by depth charges from the US destroyer *Champlin* and the destroyer escort *Huse*; 27 dead.

U857: launched 23 May 1943, commissioned 16 Sept 1943. Sunk 7 Apr 1945 in the North Atlantic east of Boston, in position 42° 22′N, 69° 46′W, by depth charges from the US destroyer escort *Gustafson*; 59 dead (all crew lost).

U858: launched 17 Jun 1943, commissioned 30 Sep 1943; surrendered at Portsmouth, New Hampshire, on 14 May 1945; scuttled at the end of 1947 after being used for torpedo trials near New England.

U865: launched 11 Jul 1943, commissioned 25 Oct 1943. Sunk 19 Sept 1944 northwest of Bergen, in position 62° 20′N, 02° 30′E, by British bombs; 59 dead (all crew lost).

U866: launched 29 Sept 1943, commissioned 17 Nov 1943. Sunk 18 Mar 1945 in the North Atlantic northeast of Boston, in position 43° 18′N, 61° 08′W, by depth charges from the US destroyer escorts *Lowe*, *Menges*, *Pride* and *Mosley*; 55 dead.

U867: launched 24 Aug 1943, commissioned 11 Dec 1943. Sunk 19 Sept 1944 northwest of Bergen, in position 62° 15′N, 01° 50′E, by British bombs; 60 dead.

U868: launched 18 Sept 1943, commissioned 23 Dec 1943; taken out of service at Bergen 5 May

1945; transferred to Loch Ryan 30 May 1945 for Operation Deadlight.

U869: launched 5 Oct 1943, commissioned 26 Jan 1944. Sunk 28 Feb 1945 in the mid-Atlantic near Rabat, in position 34° 30′N, 08° 13′W, by depth charges from the US destroyer escort *Fowler* and the French submarine chaser *L'Indiscret*; 56 dead (all crew lost).

U870: launched 29 Oct 1943, commissioned 3 Feb 1944. Sunk 30 Mar 1945 at Bremen by US bombs.

U877: launched 10 Dec 1943, commissioned 24 Mar 1944. Sunk 27 Dec 1944 in the North Atlantic northwest of the Azores, in position 46° 25′N, 36° 38′W, by depth charges from the Canadian corvette *St Thomas*.

U878: launched 6 Jan 1944, commissioned 14 Apr 1944. Sunk 10 Apr 1945 west of St Nazaire, in position 47° 35′N, 10° 33′W, by depth charges from the British destroyer *Vanquisher* and the corvette *Tintagel Castle*; 51 dead (all crew lost).

U879: launched 11 Jan 1944, commissioned 19 Apr 1944. Sunk 19 Apr 1945 in the North Atlantic east of Boston, in position 42° 19′N, 61° 45′W, by depth charges from the US destroyer escorts *Buckley* and *Reuben James*; 52 dead (all crew lost).

U880: launched 10 Feb 1944, commissioned 11 May 1944. Sunk 16 Apr 1945 in the North Atlantic, in position 47° 53′N, 30° 26′W, by depth charges from the US destroyer escorts *Stanton* and *Frost*; 49 dead (all crew lost).

U881: launched 4 Mar 1944, commissioned 27 May 1944. Sunk 6 May 1945 in the North Atlantic southeast of Newfoundland, in position 43° 18′N, 47° 44′W, by depth charges from the US destroyer escort *Farquhar*; 53 dead (all crew lost).

U882: launched 29 Apr 1944; badly damaged on about 30 Mar 1945 by US bombs in the dockyard harbour; construction work suspended.

U889: launched in 1944, commissioned 4 Aug 1944; surrendered on 15 May 1945 at Shelburne, Nova Scotia, in position 43° 32′N, 65° 12′W; transferred to Halifax; transferred to the US Navy 10 Jan 1946; scuttled at the end of 1947, after being used for torpedo trials off New England.

U890: launched in 1944. Badly damaged on 29 Jul 1944 by British bombs; no further construction; broken up in 1944.

U891: launched in 1944. Badly damaged in 29 Jul 1944 by British bombs; no further construction; broken up in 1944.

U892–894: construction suspended 30 Sept 1943.

U1221: launched 2 May 1943, commissioned 11 Aug 1943. Sunk 3 Apr 1945 at Kiel Buoy A 7 by British bombs; 7 dead.

U1222: launched 9 Jun 1943, commissioned 1 Sept 1943. Sunk 11 Jul 1944 west of La Rochelle, in position 46° 31′N, 05° 29′W, by British bombs; 56 dead (all crew lost).

U1223: launched 16 Jun 1943, commissioned 6 Oct 1943; taken out of service in April 1945 and sunk 28 Apr 1945 near Wesermünde, in position 53° 32′N, 08° 35′E, by British bombs; 7 dead.

U1224: launched 7 Jul 1943, commissioned 20 Oct 1943; served as *RO 501* in Japanese service from 15 Feb 1944. Sunk 13 Apr 1945 in the mid-Atlantic northwest of the Cape Verde Islands, in position 18° 08′N, 33° 13′W, by depth charges from the US destroyer escort *Francis M Robinson*.

U1225: launched 21 Jul 1943, commissioned 10 Nov 1943. Sunk 24 Jun 1944 northwest of Bergen, in position 63° 00′N, 00° 50′W, by Canadian bombs; 56 dead (all crew lost).

U1226: launched 21 Aug 1943, commissioned 24 Nov 1943. Sank 28 Oct 1944 in the Atlantic, position not known; possibly because of a schnorkel defect; 56 dead.

U1227: launched 18 Sept 1943, commissioned 10 Dec 1943; damaged by British bombs 9 Apr 1945 and taken out of service at Kiel 10 Apr 1945; scuttled 3 May 1945; broken up.

U1228: launched 2 Oct 1943, commissioned 22 Dec 1943; surrendered at Portsmouth, New Hampshire, 9 May 1945; scuttled 5 Feb 1946 off the east coast of the USA.

U1229: launched 22 Oct 1943, commissioned 13 Jan 1944. Sunk 20 Aug 1944 in the North Atlantic southeast of Newfoundland, in position 42° 20′N, 51° 39′W, by bombs from aircraft of the US escort carrier *Bogue*; 18 dead.

U1230: launched 8 Nov 1943, commissioned 26 Jan 1944; transferred from Wilhelmshaven to Loch Ryan 24 Jun 1945 for Operation Deadlight.

U1231: launched 18 Nov 1943, commissioned 9 Feb 1944; surrendered at Loch Foyle 14 May 1945; became the USSR submarine *N 25*; broken up in 1960.

U1232: launched 20 Dec 1943, commissioned 8 Mar 1944; taken out of service at Wesermünde in April 1945; possibly blown up at the end of the war.

U1233: launched 23 Dec 1943, commissioned 22 Mar 1944; transferred from Wilhelmshaven to Loch Ryan 24 Jun 1945 for Operation Deadlight.

U1234: launched 7 Jan 1944, commissioned 19 Apr 1944. Sank at 2300hrs on 14 May 1944 at Gotehafen, after colliding in fog with the steam tug *Anton*; 13 dead. Raised and repaired, placed in service 17 Oct 1944; scuttled 5 May 1945 at Hörup Haff; broken up.

U1235: launched 25 Jan 1944, commissioned 17 May 1944. Sunk 15 Apr 1945 in the North Atlantic, in position 42° 54′N, 30° 25′W, by depth charges from the US destroyer escorts *Stanton* and *Frost*; 57 dead (all crew lost).

U1236: launched 7 Feb 1944; construction suspended.

U1237: launched 22 Feb 1944; construction suspended.

U1238: launched 23 Feb 1944; construction suspended.

U1239–1241: construction suspended 30 Sept 1943.

U1242–1250: construction suspended 30 Sept 1943; cancelled 22 Jul 1944.

U1251–1262: cancelled 30 Sept 1943.

U1501–1506: construction suspended 30 Sept 1943; cancelled 22 Jul 1944.

U1513–1515: construction suspended 30 Sept 1943; cancelled 22 Jul 1944.

U1507–1512: cancelled 30 Sept 1943.

U1516–1530: cancelled 30 Sept 1943.

Type XI D1, D2 and D/42 large U-boats

Construction

Laid down as ocean-going submersibles, designed 1939–40. Double hull; seven watertight compartments; trim tanks in compartments 1 and 7; diving tanks and main fuel oil bunkers in the outer hull, with pressure-tight regulating tanks and fuel oil bunkers in way of the control room and additional diving tanks in the forecastle and stern; diving depth 100/200m. 2 + 2 pressure-tight torpedo containers were fitted at the stern and 1 + 1 + 2 at the bow [1 + 2 at the bow only in the Type D1 after modification].

Propulsion

The Type D1 was initially fitted with two sets of three parallel Daimler-Benz 20-cylinder 4-stroke MB 501 unsupercharged diesel S-boat engines with a Vulcan drive for each set, together giving 9000shp at 1600rpm, in engine rooms in compartments 3 and 6 [these were replaced after the first operational cruise by two Germaniawerft 6-cylinder 4-stroke F 46 supercharged diesel engines]; the Type D2 and D/42 were fitted with two MAN 9-cylinder 4-stroke M 9 V 40/46 supercharged diesel engines plus two MWM 6-cylinder 4-stroke RS 34.5 S unsupercharged diesel engines for cruising, with the whole installation arranged 2 + 2 in a large engine room in compartment 3; the Types D1 and D2 were fitted with two Siemens-Schuckert 2 GU 345/34 double electric motors in compartment 2;

the Types D1 (initially) and D2 were fitted with 1 + 1 62-cell AFA 44 MAL 740 W batteries (11,300amp/hr) in compartments 6 or 5 and 6 below [as modified, the Type D1 battery capacity was doubled by combining compartments 5 and 6 and installing 1 + 1 + 1 + 1 62-cell AFA 44 MAL 740 W batteries in this and the former forward engine room below, giving a total of 22,600amp/hr and effectively doubling the underwater range; a hinged schnorkel was also fitted during this modification on the forward starboard side of the conning tower casing]; diesel electric range 13,000nm at 10kts for the Type D1 as modified, 32,000nm at 10kts for the Type D2 and D/42. Two 3-bladed propellers, 1.90m diameter in the Type

Name	Type	Builder (construction no)	Built	Cost in Marks (000s)	Displacement (t = tonnes T = tons)	Length (m)	Breadth (m)	Draught/ height (m)	Power (hp)	Revs (rpm)	Speed (kts)	Range (nm/kts)	Oil (t)	Diving time (sec)
U180, 195	IX D1	Deschimag W (1020, 1041)	1941–42		1610t sf 1799t sm 2150t total 1365t* sf	87.58 oa 68.50 ph	7.50 oa 4.40 ph	5.35/ 10.2	9000ehp sf 1000ehp sm 2800 to 3200ehp sf (mod)	540 sf 260 sm 470 to 490 sf (mod)	20.8 sf 6.9 sm 15.8 to 16.5 sf (mod)	9500/14 sf 121/2 sm 12,750/10, 5600/15.8 sf 245/2, 115/4 sm (mod)	203 max	c 35 td
U177–179, 181, 182	IX D2	,, (1017–1019, 1021, 1022)	1940–42		,,	,,	,,	,,	,,	,,	,,	,,	,,	,,
U196–200	,,	,, (1042–1046)	1941–42		,,	,,	,,	,,	,,	,,	,,	,,	,,	,,
U847–852, 859–864	,,	,, (1053–1058, 1065–1070)	1941–43		,,	,,	,,	,,	,,	,,	,,	,,	,,	,,
U871–876	,,	,, (1079–1084)	1942–44		,,	,,	,,	,,	,,	,,	,,	,,	,,	,,
U883–888	IX D/42	,, (1091–1096)	1943–		1616t sf 1804t sm 2150t total 1366t* sf	,,	,,	,,	4400ehp +1000ehp sf 1000ehp sm	495 +750 sf 260 sm	19.2 sf 6.9 sm	31,500/10, 8500/19.2 sf 121/2, 57/4 sm	413/ 182 441 max	,,
U895–900	,,	,, (1103–1108)	,,		,,	,,	,,	,,	,,	,,	,,	,,	,,	,,
U1531–1542	,,	,, (1145–1156)	,,		,,	,,	,,	,,	,,	,,	,,	,,	,,	,,

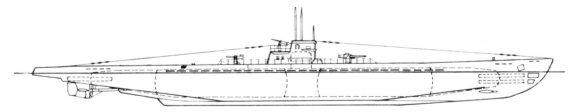

Type IX D 2 (1942).

D1 and 1.85m diameter in the Type D2 and D/42; hydroplanes and rudders as for the Type VII C.

Armament

Six 53.3cm torpedo tubes, four at the bow and two at the stern, all below the CWL - 24 torpedoes or 48 TMA (= 72 TMB) mines; one (or two, *U196*) Utof 10.5cm/45 gun - 150 (or 240, *U196*) rounds; one 3.7cm AA gun - 2575 rounds; one 2cm AA gun - 4100 rounds. Two periscopes as for the Type IX C.

[In 1943–44 the torpedo tubes were removed from the Type D1 boats when they were converted for freight transport, and the gun armament was reduced on the Type D2 boats to one 3.7cm AA gun - 2575 rounds - and two twin 2cm AA guns (8100 rounds).]

Complement

Crew: 4/51 to 7/57. Boats: two inflatable dinghies.

Notes

The Type IX D was developed from the Type IX C, with a lengthened pressure hull and enlarged outer casing. The 'Monsoon' boats, intended for co-operation with the Japanese navy in Far Eastern waters, carried one Focke-Achgelis FA 'Bachstelze' (Water-wagtail) FA 330 tethered autogiro kite for aerial reconnaissance. No net cutters were fitted. The schnorkel and conning tower casing modifications were as for the Type IX. *U195*, *864*, *873–875* and *883* had the upper deck reduced in width and tapered at the bow in order to reduce diving time. As a transport boat the Type D1 could carry 252t of freight.

Careers

U177: launched 1 Oct 1941, commissioned 14 Mar 1942. Sunk 6 Feb 1944 west of Ascension Island, in position 10° 35'S, 23° 15'W, by US bombs; 50 dead.

U178: launched 28 Oct 1941, commissioned 14 Feb 1942; scuttled 25 Aug 1944 at Bordeaux as she was not seaworthy in time to escape the Allied advance; broken up in 1947.

U179: launched 18 Nov 1941, commissioned 7 Mar 1942. Sunk 8 Oct 1942 near Cape Town, in position 33° 28'S, 17° 05'W, by depth charges from the British destroyer *Active*; 61 dead (all crew lost).

U180: launched 10 Dec 1941, commissioned 16 May 1942. Sunk 22 Aug 1944 west of Bordeaux, in approximate position 44° 00'N, 02° 00'W, by mines; 56 dead.

U181: launched 30 Dec 1941, commissioned 9 May 1942; taken over by Japan in May 1945 and became the Japanese submarine *I 501*, 15 Jul 1945; surrendered in Singapore in August 1945; scuttled there on 12 Feb 1946.

U182: launched 3 Mar 1942, commissioned 30 Jun 1942. Sunk 16 May 1943 north of Tristan da Cunha, in position 33° 55'S, 20° 35'W, by depth charges from the US destroyer *Mackenzie*; 61 dead (all crew lost).

U195: launched 8 Apr 1942, commissioned 5 Sept 1942; taken over by Japan in May 1945 and became the Japanese submarine *I 506*, 15 Jul 1945; surrendered at Djakarta in August 1945; broken up in 1947.

U196: launched 24 Apr 1942, commissioned 11 Sept 1942. Sank on approximately 30 Nov 1944 near the Sunda Straits, exact position unknown, possibly because of a diving accident; 65 dead (all crew lost).

U197: launched 21 May 1942, commissioned 10 Oct 1942. Sunk 10 Oct 1942 south of Madagascar, in position 28° 40′S, 42° 36′E, by British bombs; 67 dead (all crew lost).

U198: launched 15 Jun 1942, commissioned 3 Nov 1942. Sunk 12 Aug 1944 near the Seychelles, in position 03° 35′S, 52° 49′E, by depth charges from the British frigate *Findhorn* and the Indian sloop *Godavari*; 66 dead (all crew lost).

U199: launched 12 Jul 1942, commissioned 28 Nov 1942. Sunk 31 Jul 1943 east of Rio de Janeiro, in position 23° 54′S, 42° 54′W, by bombs from one US and two Brazilian aircraft; 49 dead.

U200: launched 20 Aug 1942, commissioned 22 Dec 1942. Sunk 24 Jun 1943 southwest of Iceland, in position 59° 00′N, 26° 18′W, by US bombs; 62 dead (all crew lost).

U847: launched 5 Sept 1942, commissioned 23 Jan 1943. Sunk 27 Aug 1943 in the Sargasso Sea, in position 28° 19′N, 37° 58′W, by air-launched torpedoes from aircraft of the US escort carrier *Card*; 62 dead (all crew lost).

U848: launched 6 Oct 1942, commissioned 10 Feb 1943. Sunk 5 Nov 1943 southwest of Ascension Island, in approximate position 10° 09′S, 18° 00′W, by US bombs; 63 dead (all crew lost).

U849: launched 31 Oct 1942, commissioned 11 Mar 1943. Sunk 25 Nov 1943 in the South Atlantic west of the Congo estuary, in position 06° 30′S, 05° 40′W, by US bombs; 63 dead (all crew lost).

U850: launched 7 Dec 1942, commissioned 17 Apr 1943. Sunk 20 Dec 1943 in the mid-Atlantic west of Madeira, in position 32° 54′N, 37° 01′W, by bombs from aircraft of the US escort carrier *Bogue*; 66 dead (all crew lost).

U851: launched 15 Jan 1943, commissioned 21 May 1943; missing, presumed sunk, in the North Atlantic in March or April 1944; 70 dead (all crew lost).

U852: launched 28 Jan 1943, commissioned 15 Jun 1943; scuttled on 3 May 1944 in the Arabian Sea off the east coast of Somalia, in position 09° 32′N, 50° 59′E, after running aground during a British air attack; 7 dead.

U859: launched 2 Mar 1943, commissioned 8 Jul 1943. Sunk 23 Sept 1944 near Penang in the Straits of Malacca, in position 05° 46′N, 100° 04′E, by torpedoes from the British submarine *Trenchant*; 47 dead.

U860: launched 23 Mar 1943, commissioned 12 Aug 1943. Sunk 15 Jun 1944 in the South Atlantic south of St Helena, in position 25° 27′S, 05° 30′W, by bombs from aircraft of the US escort carrier *Solomons*; 44 dead.

U861: launched 29 Apr 1943, commissioned 2 Sept 1943; taken out of service at Drontheim 6 May 1945; transferred to Lisahally 29 May 1945 for Operation Deadlight.

U862: launched 5 Jun 1943, commissioned 7 Oct 1943; taken over by Japan at Singapore in May 1945, and became the Japanese submarine *I 502*, 15 Jul 1945; surrendered at Singapore in August 1945; scuttled there on 13 Feb 1946.

U863: launched 29 Jun 1943, commissioned 3 Nov 1943. Sunk 29 Sept 1944 east-southeast of Recife, in position 10° 45′S, 25° 30′W, by US bombs; 69 dead (all crew lost).

U864: launched 12 Aug 1943, commissioned 15 Dec 1943. Sunk 9 Feb 1945 in the North Sea west of Bergen, in position 60° 46′N, 04° 35′E, by torpedoes from the British submarine *Venturer*; 73 dead (all crew lost).

U871: launched 7 Sept 1943, commissioned 15 Jan 1944. Sunk 26 Sept 1944 northwest of the Azores, in position 43° 18′N, 36° 28′W, by British bombs; 69 dead (all crew lost).

U872: launched 20 Oct 1943, commissioned 10 Feb 1944; badly damaged on 29 Jul 1944 at Bremen by US bombs; 1 dead; taken out of service 10 Aug 1944; broken up.

U873: launched 16 Nov 1943, commissioned 1 Mar 1944; surrendered at Portsmouth, New Hampshire, 16 May 1945; broken up in 1948.

U874: launched 21 Dec 1943, commissioned 8 Apr 1944; transferred from Horten to Lisahally 29 May 1945 for Operation Deadlight.

U875: launched 16 Feb 1944, commissioned 21 Apr 1944; transferred from Bergen to Lisahally 30 May 1945 for Operation Deadlight.

U876: launched 29 Feb 1944, commissioned 24 May 1944; damaged by British bombs 9 Apr 1945; scuttled at Eckernförde 3 May 1945; broken up in 1947.

U883: launched 28 Apr 1944, commissioned 27 Mar 1945; transferred from Wilhelmshaven to Lisahally 21 Jun 1945 for Operation Deadlight.

U884: launched 17 May 1944. Badly damaged 30 Mar 1945 in the dockyard harbour by US bombs; further construction work suspended.

U885, 886: construction suspended 30 Sept 1943.

U887, 888: construction suspended 30 Sept 1943.

U895–900: contracts cancelled 30 Sept 1943.

U1531–1542: contracts cancelled 30 Sept 1943.

Type X A minelayer project

Name	Type	Builder (construction no)	Built	Cost in Marks (000s)	Displacement (t = tonnes T = tons)	Length (m)	Breadth (m)	Draught/ height (m)	Power (hp)	Revs (rpm)	Speed (kts)	Range (nm/kts)	Oil (t)	Diving time (sec)
–	X A	Project only	–	–	c2500t sf	103 oa	9.5 oa	4.4/			14 sf			

Construction
A design for an ocean-going submersible, 1937. Double hull.

Armament
Four mine shafts on each side (see the Type X B), with additional dry storage for mines and two mine launching tubes in the stern for SMA mines; four 53.3cm torpedo tubes, all at the bow below the CWL - number of torpedoes unknown; one Utof 10.5cm/45 gun; one 3.7cm AA gun; one 2cm AA gun.

Notes
Developed from the World War I design for *U117–126*. The design was abandoned in favour of the Type X B, with purely wet storage for mines.

Type X B minelayers

Construction
Laid down as ocean-going submersibles, designed 1938. Double hull; seven watertight compartments; trim tanks in compartments 1 and 7; diving tanks and fuel oil bunkers in the outer hull (which was almost square in section) as were pressure-tight regulating tanks and fuel oil bunkers amidships; additional diving tanks in the bow and stern; diving depth 100/200m. 2 + 2 + 2 pressure-tight torpedo containers were fitted on the outer hull, under the upper deck.

Propulsion
Two Germaniawerft 9-cylinder 4-stroke F46 a 9 pu supercharged diesel engines in an engine room in compartment 3; two AEG GU 720/8–287 double electric motors in compartment 2; 1 + 1 124-cell AFA 33 MAL 800 W (or 1 type W and one type E,

Name	Type	Builder (construction no)	Built	Cost in Marks (000s)	Displacement (t = tonnes T = tons)	Length (m)	Breadth (m)	Draught/ height (m)	Power (hp)	Revs (rpm)	Speed (kts)	Range (nm/kts)	Oil (t)	Diving time (sec)
U116–119	X B	Germania (615–617, 624)	1939–42	6350	1763t sf 2177t sm 2710t total 1695t* sf	89.80 oa 70.90 ph	9.20 oa 4.75 ph	4.71/ 10.2	4200ehp to 4800 ehp sf 1100ehp sm	470 to 490 sf 275 sm	16.4 to 17.0 sf 7.0 sm	18450/10, 6750/16.9 sf 188/2, 93/4 sm	338/ 130.6 368 max	
U219, 220	,,	,, (625, 626)	1941–43	,,	,,	,,	,,	,,	,,	,,	,,	,,	,,	
U233, 234	,,	,, (663, 664)	1941–44	,,	,,	,,	,,	,,	,,	,,	,,	,,	,,	

* Light load displacement.

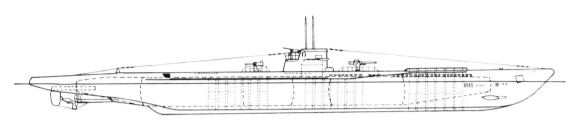

Type X B (1942).

U220; or 1 + 1 type E, *U234*) accumulator batteries (1960 amp/hr) in compartments 4 and 6 below. [A hinged schnorkel was fitted on the starboard side at 45m.]

Armament

Two groups of six mine shafts each side of the outer hull, making twenty-four in all - 48 SMA mines; six further mine shafts in the forward outer hull - 18 SMA mines; two 53.3cm torpedo tubes, both at the stern below the CWL - 15 torpedoes; one Utof 10.5cm/45 gun - 200 rounds; one 3.7cm AA gun - 2500 rounds; one 2cm AA gun - 4000 rounds. [The 10.5cm gun was deleted from 1943–44, and the AA armament increased to one 3.7cm - 2500 rounds - and two twin 2cm - 8000 rounds. As transport boats these vessels carried freight containers in the mine shafts.]

Complement

Crew: 5/47. Boats: two inflatable dinghies.

Notes

Modifications to the conning tower were as for the

Type IX and Type VII. A hinged schnorkel was fitted from mid-1944 on the starboard after edge of the conning tower casing. *U219* and *U220* each had an additional torpedo container on either side of the 10.5cm gun.

Careers

U116: launched 3 May 1941, commissioned 26 Jul 1941. Sunk in October 1942 in the North Atlantic; details and position not known; 55 dead (all crew lost).

U117: launched 26 Jul 1941, commissioned 25 Oct 1941. Sunk 7 Aug 1943 in the North Atlantic, in position 39° 42′N, 38° 21′W, by bombs from aircraft of the US escort carrier *Card*; 62 dead (all crew lost).

U118: launched 23 Sept 1941, commissioned 6 Dec 1941. Sunk 12 Jun 1943 west of the Canary Islands, in position 30° 49′N, 33° 49′W, by bombs from aircraft of the US escort carrier *Bogue*; 43 dead (all crew lost).

U119: launched 6 Jan 1942, commissioned 2 Apr

1942. Sunk 24 Jun 1943 northwest of Cape Ortegal, in position 44° 59′N, 12° 24′W, by ramming and depth charges from the British sloop *Starling*; 57 dead (all crew lost).

U219: launched 6 Oct 1942, commissioned 12 Dec 1942; taken over by Japan in May 1945 and became the Japanese submarine *I 505*; surrendered at Djakarta in August 1945; broken up in 1948.

U220: launched 16 Jan 1943, commissioned 27 Mar 1943. Sunk 28 Oct 1943 in the North Atlantic, in position 48° 53′N, 33° 30′W, by bombs from aircraft of the US escort carrier *Block Island*; 56 dead (all crew lost).

U223: launched 8 May 1943, commissioned 22 Sept 1943. Sunk 5 Jul 1944 in the North Atlantic east of Halifax, in position 42° 16′N, 59° 49′W, by ramming, depth charges and gunfire from the US destroyer escorts *Baker* and *Thomas*; 32 dead.

U234: launched 23 Dec 1943, commissioned 2 Mar 1944; surrendred at Portsmouth, New Hampshire, 16 May 1945; sunk during trials off Cape Cod in November 1946, position not known.

Type XI U-cruisers

Name	Type	Builder (construction no)	Built	Cost in Marks (000s)	Displacement (t = tonnes T = tons)	Length (m)	Breadth (m)	Draught/ height (m)	Power (hp)	Revs (rpm)	Speed (kts)	Range (nm/kts)	Oil (t)	Diving time (sec)
U112–115	XI	Deschimag W (977–980)	1939–	17,410	3140t sf 3930t sm 4650t total	114.96 oa 91.25 ph	9.50 oa 6.80 ph	6.17/	17600ehp sf 2200ehp sm	470 sf 275 sm	23.25 sf 7.0 sm	20600/10, 4000/22.7 sf 140/2, 50/4 sm	500/ 169	

Construction

Laid down as U-cruiser submersibles, designed 1937–38. Double hull; ten watertight compartments; trim tanks in compartments 1 and 10; diving tanks and main fuel oil bunkers in the outer hull, which also contained pressurised regulating tanks and bunkers etc amidships; diving depth 120/240m.

Propulsion

Eight MWM 12-cylinder 4-stroke RS 38 Zw diesel engines coupled to four Vulcan drives in compartments 4 and 6; two Brown, Boveri & Cie GG UB 1200/8 double electric motors in compartment 3; 1 + 1 124-cell AFA 28 MAL 1000W batteries, giving approximately 24,000 amp/hr, in compartments 8 and 10 below; diesel electric range 24,000nm at 10kts. Two 3-bladed propellers, 2.18m diameter; two rudders; two hydroplanes forward and two aft; three periscopes.

Armament

Six 53.3cm torpedo tubes, two at the stern, four at the bow, all below the CWL - 12 torpedoes; no mines; four 12.7cm QF guns - 940 rounds; two 3.7cm AA guns - 4000 rounds; one 2cm AA gun - 2000 rounds; one small Arado Ar 231 aircraft in a watertight and pressure-tight vertical shaft 2.6m in diameter between compartments 7 (control room) and 8.

Complement

Crew 7–8/103–104. Boats: inflatable dinghies (number unknown).

Notes

Aft of the conning tower the pressure hull resembled a compressed, horizontal figure 8 in section, with a vertical diameter of 5.4m and a maximum horizontal diameter of 6.8m.

Careers

U112–115: order placed 17 Jan 1939; construction contract cancelled at the outbreak of war.

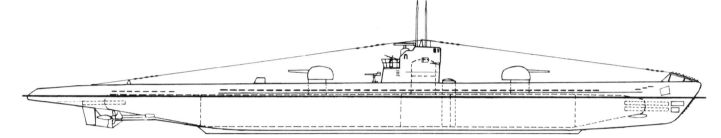

Type XI (1939 design).

Type XII large U-boat project

Name	Type	Builder (construction no)	Built	Cost in Marks (000s)	Displacement (t = tonnes T = tons)	Length (m)	Breadth (m)	Draught/ height (m)	Power (hp)	Revs (rpm)	Speed (kts)	Range (nm/kts)	Oil (t)	Diving time (sec)
–	XII	Project only	–		2041t sf	92.4 oa	8.5 oa	5.4/	7000ehp sf 1680ehp sm		22.0 sf 10.0 sm	20000/12 sf		

Construction

A fleet U-boat design project, 1938. Double hull design.

Propulsion

Two Germaniawerft diesel engines; two double electric motors; accumulator batteries; other details unknown.

Armament

Eight 53.3cm torpedo tubes, six at the bow and two at the stern, all below the CWL - 20 torpedoes; no mines; gun armament as for the Type IX.

Notes

This design was a development of the Type IX design. Nine vessels were to be constructed at Deschimag, Bremen, for completion by 1945.

Type XIII small U-boat project

Name	Type	Builder (construction no)	Built	Cost in Marks (000s)	Displacement (t = tonnes T = tons)	Length (m)	Breadth (m)	Draught/ height (m)	Power (hp)	Revs (rpm)	Speed (kts)	Range (nm/kts)	Oil (t)	Diving time (sec)
–	XIII	Project only	–		400t sf						15 sf			

Construction

Single-hull design, proposed in a 1939 project.

Propulsion

Two diesel engines; two double electric motors; other details unknown.

Armament

Four 53.3cm torpedo tubes, all at the bow, below the CWL; one 2cm AA gun.

Notes

This design was a further development of the Type II design.

Type XIV tanker U-boats

Name	Type	Builder (construction no)	Built	Cost in Marks (000s)	Displacement (t = tonnes T = tons)	Length (m)	Breadth (m)	Draught/ height (m)	Power (hp)	Revs (rpm)	Speed (kts)	Range (nm/kts)	Oil (t)	Diving time (sec)
U459–464	XIV	DWK (290–295)	1940–42		1688t sf 1932t sm 2300t total	67.10 oa 48.51 ph	9.35 oa 4.90 ph	6.51/ 11.7	2800 to 3200ehp sf 750ehp sm	470 to 490 sf 280 sm	14.4 to 14.9 sf 6.2 sm	12,350/10, 5500/14.4 sf 120/2, 55/4 sm	203 max	
U487–493	"	" (312–315, 322–324)	1941–43 and 1943–		"	"	"	"	"	"	"	"	"	
U494–500, 2201–2204	"	Germania* (744–754)	1943–		"	"	"	"	"	"	"	"	"	

* Contracts originally granted to DWK 22 Sept 1942 and 17 Apr 1943 (construction numbers 325–329 and 332–337), but transferred to Germania in 1943.

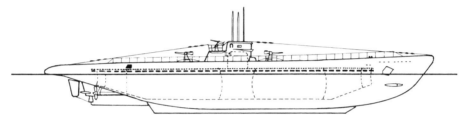

Type XIV (1942).

Construction

Laid down as ocean-going tanker submersibles, designed 1939–40. Ten watertight compartments, of which compartments 1 and 10 were used as trim tanks; diving tanks and fuel oil bunkers were in the wide outer hull, which also contained pressurised regulating tanks, bunkers etc amidships, with additional diving tanks in the bow and stern; diving depth 120/240m.

Propulsion

Two Germaniawerft 6-cylinder 4-stroke supercharged diesel engines in compartment 4; two Siemens-Schuckert GU 343/38–8 double electric motors in compartment 3; 1 + 1 62-cell AFA 28 MAL 1000W batteries (12,000amp/hr); diesel electric range 12,300nm at 10kts. Two 3-bladed propellers, diameter unknown; two rudders; two hydroplanes at the bow and two at the stern.

Armament

No weapons were fitted apart from two 3.7 AA guns - 2500 rounds - and one 2cm AA gun - 3000 rounds). Four torpedoes were carried as replenishment cargo in pressurised containers aft of the conning tower, 2 + 1 on the starboard side and 1 + 0 on the port side, and bunkers in the outer hull held 432t of diesel oil. [From 1943–44 the 2cm AA armament was reinforced as per the Type VIIC.]

Complement

Crew: 6/47. Boats: two inflatable dinghies.

Notes

These vessels were developed from the Type IX D, with the length reduced to that of Type VII C. No net cutters were fitted. A hinged schnorkel was later added to the aft port edge of the conning tower casing. The breadth and bulk of these vessels, together with their intended purpose, resulted in the nickname 'Sea Cows'.

Careers

U459: launched 13 Sept 1941, commissioned 15 Nov 1941. Sunk 24 Jul 1943 northwest of Cape Ortegal, in position 45° 53′N, 10° 38′W, by British bombs; 19 dead.

U460: launched 13 Sept 1941, commissioned 24 Dec 1941. Sunk 4 Oct 1943 in the North Atlantic north of the Azores, in position 43° 13′N, 28° 58′W, by bombs from aircraft of the US escort carrier *Card*; 62 dead (all crew lost).

U461: launched 8 Nov 1941, commissioned 30 Jan 1942. Sunk at 1206hrs on 30 Jul 1943 northwest of Cape Ortegal, in position 45° 33′N, 10° 47′W, by Australian bombs; 53 dead.

U462: launched 29 Nov 1941, commissioned 5 Mar 1942. Sunk at 1214hrs on 30 Jul 1943 northwest of Cape Ortegal, in position 45° 33′N, 10° 48′W, by British bombs and gunfire from the British sloops *Kite*, *Wren*, *Woodpecker*, *Wild Goose* and *Woodcock*; 1 dead.

U463: launched 20 Dec 1941, commissioned 2 Apr 1942. Sunk 15 May 1943 southwest of the Scilly Isles, in position 48° 28′N, 10° 20′W, by British bombs; 56 dead (all crew lost).

U464: launched 20 Dec 1941, commissioned 30 Apr 1942. Sunk 20 Aug 1942 in the North Sea southeast of Iceland, in position 61° 25′N, 14° 40′W, by US bombs; 2 dead.

U487: launched 17 Oct 1942, commissioned 21 Dec 1942. Sunk 13 Jul 1943 in the mid-Atlantic, in position 27° 15′N, 34° 18′W, by bombs from aircraft of the US escort carrier *Core*; 31 dead.

U488: launched 17 Oct 1942, commissioned 1 Feb 1943. Sunk 26 Apr 1944 in the mid-Atlantic northwest of the Cape Verde Islands, in position 17° 54′N, 38° 05′W, by depth charges from the US destroyer escorts *Frost*, *Huse*, *Barber* and *Snowden*; 64 dead (all crew lost).

U489: launched 24 Dec 1942, commissioned 8 Mar 1943. Sunk 4 Aug 1943 southeast of Iceland, in position 61° 11′N, 14° 38′W, by Canadian bombs; 1 dead.

U490: launched 24 Dec 1942, commissioned 27 Mar 1943. Sunk 11 Jun 1944 northwest of the Azores, in position 42° 47′N, 40° 08′W, by bombs from aircraft of the US escort carrier *Croatan* and depth charges from the destroyer escorts *Frost*, *Inch* and *Huse*.

U491: laid down 31 Jul 1943; construction halted with the vessel 75 per cent complete in 1944; broken up.

U492: laid down 28 Aug 1943; construction halted with the vessel 75 per cent complete in 1944; broken up.

U493: laid down 25 Sept 1943; construction halted with the vessel 75 per cent complete in 1944; broken up.

U494–U500: construction suspended 27 May 1944.

U2201–U2204: construction suspended 27 May 1944.

Type XV and XVI large transport and repair U-boat projects

Name	Type	Builder (construction no)	Built	Cost in Marks (000s)	Displacement (t = tonnes T = tons)	Length (m)	Breadth (m)	Draught/ height (m)	Power (hp)	Revs (rpm)	Speed (kts)	Range (nm/kts)	Oil (t)	Diving time (sec)
–	XV	Project only	–	–	5000 sf				2800ehp sf 750ehp sm					
–	XVI	Project only	–	–	3000t sf				2800ehp sf 750ehp sm					

Construction

A preliminary design for a double-hulled submersible for transport and repair work, with a pressure hull consisting of three horizontally interlocking cylinders.

Propulsion

Two Germaniawerft diesel engines and two double electric motors etc, as per the Type VIIC.

Armament

These vessels were intended to carry torpedoes, food and fuel oil as cargo.

Research U-boat V 80

Name	Type	Builder (construction no)	Built	Cost in Marks (000s)	Displacement (t = tonnes T = tons)	Length (m)	Breadth (m)	Draught/ height (m)	Power (hp)	Revs (rpm)	Speed (kts)	Range (nm/kts)	Oil (t)	Diving time (sec)
V 80	–	Germania (597)	1939–40		73t sf 76t sm 85.5t total	22.05 oa 16.9 ph	2.10 oa 2.10 ph	3.20/ 5.65	2600ehp sm		28 sm	50/28 sm	21 (H_2O_2)	

Construction

Laid down as a research boat, designed by Germaniawerft and Hellmuth Walter GmbH, 1938–39. Single hull; three watertight compartments with a separate casing for the fuel bunkers etc below the pressure hull ('Walter-type' hull); no conning tower.

Propulsion

One Germaniawerft Walter turbine (20,000rpm) in

compartment 1; one accumulator battery for auxiliary equipment in compartment 3.

Armament

No armament was fitted.

Complement

Crew: 4.

Career

Launched 19 Apr 1940; used for trials in April

1940; taken out of service at the end of 1942; scuttled at Hela in March 1945.

V80 (1940).

Type V 300, Wa 201 and Wk 202 research U-boats

Construction

Designed as submersibles by Germaniawerft and Hellmuth Walter GmbH in 1940–41. Single hull; nine watertight compartments; the design was based on the Walter-type hull of *V 80*, but with a conning tower.

Propulsion

Two MWM 6-cylinder 4-stroke RS 125 Su diesel engines in compartment 2; two Germaniawerft-Walter turbines in compartment 1; two Garbe, Lahmeyer & Co RP 813 single commutator motors

in compartment 2; one 62-cell AFA 29 MAL 740 W battery (7460amp/hr) in compartment 4. One 3-bladed propeller; rudder and stabilisers arranged in a cross at the stern; hydroplanes forward.

Armament

Two 53.3cm torpedo tubes, 7m long, at the bow below the CWL - 6 torpedoes; no guns. One periscope in the tower and one in the control room.

Complement

Crew: 25 men.

Career

Contract granted 18 Feb 1942; construction suspended in summer 1942 in favour of *Wk 202*.

Types Wa 201 and Wk 202

Construction

Laid down as submersibles, designed by the building yards and Hellmuth Walter GmbH in 1942. Single Walter-type hull; three watertight compartments; no conning tower.

Name	Type	Builder (construction no)	Built	Cost in Marks (000s)	Displacement (t = tonnes T = tons)	Length (m)	Breadth (m)	Draught/ height (m)	Power (hp)	Revs (rpm)	Speed (kts)	Range (nm/kts)	Oil (t)	Diving time (sec)
U791	V 300	Germania (698)	1942–		610t sf 655t sm c725t total	52.08 oa 40.00 ph	4.03 oa 4.00 ph	5.49/	300 to 330ehp sf 150ehp sm 4360ehp sm*	735 sm 2000 sm*	9.33 sf 9.6 sm 19.0 sf sm*	5000/5.5, 2330/9.33 sf 150/2 sm 205/19, 450/10 sm*	34 max +98 (H$_2$O$_2$)	
U792, 793	Wa 201	B & V (455, 456)	1942		277t sf 309 sm 373t total	39.05 oa 26.15 ph	4.50 oa 3.30 ph	4.30/	210 to 230ehp sf 77.5ehp sm 5000ehp sm*	208 to 214 sf 170 sm 580 sm*	9.0 sf 5.0 sm 24–25 sm*	2910/8.5 sf 50/2 sm 127/20 sm*	18 max +34 (H$_2$O$_2$)	
U794, 795	Wk 202	Germania (718, 719)	"		236t sf 259 sm 312t total	34.60 oa	4.50 oa 3.40 ph	4.55/	"	"	"	1840/9 sf 76.2 sm 117/20 sm*	14 max +40 (H$_2$O$_2$)	

* Walter turbine drive.

Propulsion
One Deutz 8-cylinder 4-stroke SAA 8 M 517 diesel engine in compartment 2; two BKC or Germaniawerft-Walter turbines with Kanis-Roeder transmission (or only one Walter turbine, giving reduced performance, *U793, 795*) in compartment 1; one AEG AWT 97 single commutator motor in compartment 2; one 62-cell AFA 17 MAL 570 E battery (3240 amp/hr) in compartment 3. One 3-bladed propeller, 2.0m diameter; rudder and hydroplanes as for the Type XVII B and G (see below).

Armament
Two 53.3cm torpedo tubes, 5m long, at the bow below the CWL - 4 torpedoes; no guns; 1 + 1 periscopes in the control room.

Complement
Crew: 12.

Notes
These vessels were constructed purely for research purposes.

Careers
U792 (Type Wa 201): launched 28 Sept 1943, commissioned 16 Nov 1943; used for trials; sunk at 0130hrs on 4 May 1945 in the Audorfer See, near Rendsburg; later raised and taken as a British prize; used for trials; fate unknown.

U793 (Type Wa 201): launched 4 Mar 1944, commissioned 24 Apr 1944; sunk at 0130hrs on 4 May 1945 in the Audorfer See, near Rendsburg; later raised, taken as a British prize; used for trials; fate unknown.

U794 (Type Wk 202): launched 7 Oct 1943, commissioned 14 Nov 1943; used for trials; scuttled 5 May 1945 in Gelting Bay; raised and broken up.

U795 (Type Wk 202): launched 21 Mar 1944, commissioned 22 Apr 1944; used for trials; scuttled 3 May 1945 at Germaniawerft, Kiel; broken up.

Wk 202 (1943).

Type XVII B and G research U-boats

Name	Type	Builder (construction no)	Built	Cost in Marks (000s)	Displacement (t = tonnes T = tons)	Length (m)	Breadth (m)	Draught/ height (m)	Power (hp)	Revs (rpm)	Speed (kts)	Range (nm/kts)	Oil (t)	Diving time (sec)
U1405–1409	XVII B	B & V (255–259)	1943–44 and 1943–		312t sf 337t sm 415t total	41.45 oa 27.30 ph	4.50 oa 3.30 ph	4.30/	210 to 230ehp sf 77.5ehp sm 2500ehp sm* 5000ehp sm* (planned)	1350 to 1390 sf 170 sm 14,500/ 580 sm*	8.5† to 8.8 sf 5.0 sm 25.0 sm*	3000/8 sf† 76/2 sm 163/15, 123/25 sm*	20.2 max +52 (H$_2$O$_2$)	
U1410–1416	"	" (260–266)	1943–		"	"	"	"	"	"	"	"	"	"	
U1081–1092	XVII G	Germania (720–731)	"		314t sf 345t sm 385t total	39.51 oa	4.50 oa 3.30 ph	4.72/ 9.20	"	"	"	2850/8.8 sf 50/2 sm 84/25 sm*	22.3 max +39.2 (H$_2$O$_2$)	

* Walter turbine drive.
† Project figures only.

Construction

Laid down as submersibles, designed by the construction yards and H Walter GmbH in 1942–43. Single Walter-type hull; three watertight compartments; pressure-tight regulating tanks amidships; fuel (H_2O_2) containers made from Mipolam below compartment 1; diving tanks forward, aft and immediately forward of the regulating tanks; no pressure-tight conning tower; hull breadth 3.30m or 3.43m; diving depth approximately 80/150m.

Propulsion

One Deutz 8-cylinder 4-stroke SAA 8 M 517 supercharged diesel engine in compartment 2; one (although initial plans were for two) Brückner & Kanis or Germaniawerft-Walter turbine with Kanis-Roeder transmission in compartment 1; one AEG AT 98 single commutator motor in compartment 1; one 62-cell AFA 26 MAL 570 E battery (3240amp/hr) in compartment 3 below. One 3-bladed propeller, 1.75m or 1.90m diameter; rudder and hydroplanes at the stern arranged in a stabilising cross; no hydroplanes forward, but adjustable stabilisers were fitted in the forecastle.

Armament

Two 53.3cm torpedo tubes, 5m long, at the bow, below the CWL - 4 torpedoes; no guns. One periscope, with a schnorkel in place of the second periscope.

Complement

Crew: 3/16.

Notes

These designs were further developments of the Types Wa 201 and Wk 202 respectively.

Careers

U1081–U1092: contracts granted 4 Jan 1943; construction suspended in autumn 1943 in favour of the Type XXI; cancelled.

U1405: launched 1 Dec 1944, commissioned 21 Dec 1944; scuttled 5 May 1945 in Eckernförd Bay; broken up.

U1406: launched 2 Jan 1945, commissioned 8 Feb 1945; scuttled 5 May 1945 at Cuxhaven; raised and transported to the USA on the deck of the US transport ship *Shoemaker*; used for trials; broken up at New York after 18 May 1948.

U1407: launched in February 1945, commissioned 29 Mar 1945; scuttled on 5 May 1945 at Cuxhaven; raised and taken as a British prize; became the UK submarine *Meteorite* 1946–49; broken up at Barrow in 1949.

U1408: scuttled at the construction yard before completion; later broken up; no further details known.

U1409: scuttled at the construction yard before completion; later broken up; no further details known.

U1410: contract granted 4 Jan 1943; construction suspended 10 Mar 1944 in favour of the Type XVII K.

U1411–U1416: contracts granted Jan 1943; cancelled 30 Sept 1943 in favour of the Type XXI.

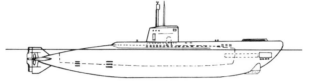

Type XVII B (1945).

Type XVII K research U-boat

Name	Type	Builder (construction no)	Built	Cost in Marks (000s)	Displacement (t = tonnes T = tons)	Length (m)	Breadth (m)	Draught/ height (m)	Power (hp)	Revs (rpm)	Speed (kts)	Range (nm/kts)	Oil (t)	Diving time (sec)
U798	XVII K	Germania (787)	1944–		308t sf 340t sm 425t total	40.71 oa 27.90 ph	4.50 oa 3.40 ph	c4.9/	1500ehp sf 500ehp sm 1500ehp sm*	1500/ 500 sf 90 sm 1600/ 535 sm*	14.0 sf† 2.0 sm 16.0 sm*	2600/10,† 1100/14 sf 30/6 sm 115/16 sm*	23.4 max +9.2 (O_2)	

* Walter turbine drive.
† Project figures only.

Construction

Laid down as a trials boat for the closed-cycle diesel propulsion system. Three watertight compartments; sixteen oxygen flasks under compartments 2 and 3 instead of fuel bunkers.

Propulsion

One Daimler-Benz 20-cylinder 4-stroke MB 501 diesel engine in compartment 3, operating in a closed-cycle system; one AEG GU 720/8 single commutator motor modified for slow speeds; one 62-cell AFA 26 MAL 570 E battery (4940amp/hr) in compartment 3. One 3-bladed propeller, 1.80m

diameter; rudder and hydroplanes as for the Type XVII G, but with forward hydroplanes.

Armament

No armament fitted. One periscope; a hinged schnorkel was fitted amidships, forward of the bridge.

Complement

Crew: 3/16.

Notes

The closed-cycle diesel system was developed at

the Propulsion and Motor Vehicle Engine Development Institute at the Technische Hochschule, Stuttgart, between 1941 and 1944. It was supported, somewhat erratically, by the OKM, but more strongly towards the end of the war because of the lack of fuel (H_2O_2) for the Walter submarines.

Career

U798: contract granted 15 Feb 1944; abandoned unfinished 16 Feb 1945; scuttled in May 1945, and later broken up.

Type XVIII Walter U-boats

Name	Type	Builder (construction no)	Built	Cost in Marks (000s)	Displacement (t = tonnes T = tons)	Length (m)	Breadth (m)	Draught/ height (m)	Power (hp)	Revs (rpm)	Speed (kts)	Range (nm/kts)	Oil (t)	Diving time (sec)
U796, 797	XVIII	Germania (755, 756)	1943–		1485t sf 1652t sm 1887t total	71.50 oa	8.00 6.20 oa 5.30 ph	6.36/	4000 to 4400ehp sf 396ehp sm 15,000ehp sm*	352 to 364 sf 187 sm 500 sm*	17.0 to 18.5 sf 7.0 sm 24.0 sm*	7000/10,† 3000/17 sf 45/4 sm 350/16, 202/24 sm*	124 max +204 (H$_2$O$_2$)	

* Walter turbine drive.
† Project figures only.

Construction

Laid down as submarines, designed by Deutsche Werke, Kiel, and H Walter GmbH, 1942–43; similar to the Type XXI, but with six fuel (H$_2$O$_2$) bunkers below the cylindrical pressure-hull to give a Walter-type hull.

Propulsion

Two MWM 12-cylinder 4-stroke RS 12 V 26/34 supercharged diesel engines in compartment 3; two Brückner, Kanis & Co-Walter turbines with Kanis-Roeder transmission in compartment 2; two Siemens-Schuckert 2 GU 355/22 double electric motors in compartment 3; 1 + 1 62-cell AFA 33 MAL 800 W batteries (9160amp/hr) in compartment 5. Two 3-bladed propellers, 1.90m diameter; rudder and hydroplanes as for the Type XXI.

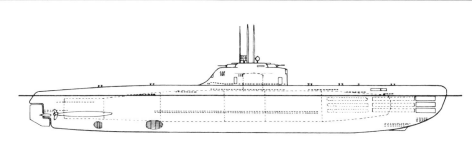

Type XVIII (1943 design).

Armament

As per the Type XXI, but with four 3cm AA guns - 4188 rounds.

Complement

Crew: 5/47.

Careers

U796, 797: contract granted to Deutsche Werke, Kiel, 4 Jan 1943 (construction nos 330, 331); transferred to Germaniawerft 14 Dec 1943; construction suspended in favour of the Type XXVI 28 Mar 1944.

Type XIX ocean-going freighter U-boat project

Name	Type	Builder (construction no)	Built	Cost in Marks (000s)	Displacement (t = tonnes T = tons)	Length (m)	Breadth (m)	Draught/ height (m)	Power (hp)	Revs (rpm)	Speed (kts)	Range (nm/kts)	Oil (t)	Diving time (sec)
–	XIX	Project only	–		2000t total						14.5* sf 6.5 sm			

* Project figures only.

Construction

A design for ocean-going submersibles for freight transport, developed by the OKM from the Type XB design at the end of 1942.

Propulsion

Two supercharged diesel engines in compartment 2; two 3-bladed propellers, diameter not known; see the Type XB for details of dynamos, batteries, rudders and hydroplanes.

Armament

No weapons; these vessels were intended for transporting supplies of rubber and precious metals.

Notes

This was a preliminary design for the Type XX, with a revised diesel installation.

Type XX ocean-going freighter U-boats

Construction

Laid down as ocean-going submersibles for the transport of freight to and from the Far East, designed by the OKM and AG Weser in 1943 (based on the Type X B design). Double hull; nine watertight compartments; trimming tanks in compartments 1 and 9; regulating tanks and bunkers were pressure-tight tanks sickle-shaped in section amidships above the pressure hull; diving tanks, bunkers and cargo holds were in the outer hull, which was almost square in cross section; one diving tank in the bow.

Name	Type	Builder (construction no)	Built	Cost in Marks (000s)	Displacement (t = tonnes T = tons)	Length (m)	Breadth (m)	Draught/ height (m)	Power (hp)	Revs (rpm)	Speed (kts)	Range (nm/kts)	Oil (t)	Diving time (sec)
U1601–1615	XX	Germania (760–762, 766–768, 772–774, 778–780, 784–786)	1943–		2708t sf 2962t sm 3425t total	77.10 oa 58.50 ph	9.15 oa 5.10 ph	6.60/ 11.4	2800 to 3200ehp sf 750ehp sm	470 to 490 sf 295 sm	12.5* to 12.7 sf 5.8 sm	18900/10,* 11000/12.5 sf 110/2, 49/4 sm	471 max	
U1701–1715	,,	,, (757–759, 763–765, 769–771, 775–777, 781–783)	1943–		,,	,,	,,	,,	,,	,,	,,	,,	,,	

* Project figures only.

Propulsion

Two Germaniawerft 6-cylinder, 4-stroke F 46 supercharged diesel engines in compartment 4; two Garbe, Lahmeyer & Co RP 137c double electric motors in compartment 3; 1 + 1 62-cell AFA 28 MAL 1000 W batteries (1200amp/hr) in compartments 5 and 7. Two 3-bladed propellers, 1.55m diameter; one rudder; two hydroplanes forward and two aft; one schnorkel.

Armament

No torpedo tubes; one 3.7cm AA gun - 2500 rounds; two twin 2cm AA guns - 8000 rounds; 1 + 1 periscopes. The vessel's payload was 800 tonnes, which included 50 tonnes of dry cargo in compartment 8.

Complement

Crew: 6/52. Boats: two inflatable dinghies.

Notes

Rectangular hatches were fitted in the upper tank deck.

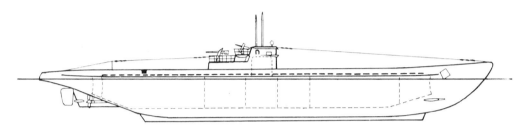

Type XX (1943 design).

Careers

U1601–1615: contract granted to Deutsche Werft, Hamburg-Finkenwerder, (construction nos 452–466) 3 Mar 1943; transferred to Germaniawerft, Kiel, 14 Dec 1943; construction halted in favour of the Type XXI 27 May 1944.

U1616–1700: contracts not granted.

U1701–1715: contract granted to Vegesacker Werft, Vegesack, (construction nos 93–107) 3 Mar 1943; transferred to Germaniawerft, Kiel, 14 Dec 1943; construction halted in favour of the Type XXI 27 May 1944. On 15 ASug 1944 it was decided that *U1701–1703* should be constructed as H_2O_2 transporters; construction was finally halted at the beginning of 1945.

U1716–1800: contracts not granted.

Type XXI U-boats

Construction

Laid down as submarines with very high underwater performance, official design 1943, with preliminary construction work by AG Weser and the 'Glückauf' Engineering Office, Blankenburg, Harz. Mass production was organised by the Shipbuilding Commission, working directly under the Reichs Ministry for Armaments. The schnorkel, streamlined hull shape and high underwater power made the Type XXI the first true submarine, intended principally for service underwater, in the world.

Double hull, with a very streamlined outer casing; the upper pressure hull was circular in section, with the smaller semi-circular and intersecting to form an unequal figure eight; hull maximum breadth 6.60m; seven watertight compartments. The hull was built in eight sections, as follows:

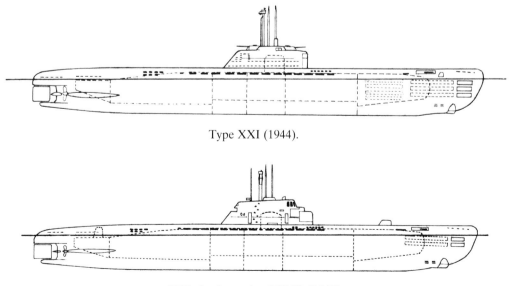

Type XXI (1944).

Wilhelm Bauer (ex *U2540*) (1968).

Section	Description	Weight
1	stern	65t
2	electric motor room	130t
3	diesel engine room	140t
4	crew quarters	70t
5	central command room	140t
6	forward quarters	165t
7	reload torpedo stowage	92t
8	bow	110t

Type XXI C (1944 design).

Thirty-two steel works were involved in the production of the 'raw' sections, which were then fitted out at eleven U-boat yards. The completed sections were assembled into U-boats at three major shipyards, as follows:

Section yard	Section	Assembly yard
Bremer Vulkan, Vegesack	3, 5, 6	AG Weser, Bremen
KM Werft, Wilhelmshaven	2	AG Weser, Bremen, and Blohm & Voss, Hamburg
Howaldtswerke, Kiel	1	„
Deutsche Werke, Kiel	8	„
Flender-Werke, Lübeck	4	„
Seebeck, Wesermünde	7	„
Howaldtswerke, Hamburg	5	Blohm & Voss, Hamburg
Deutsche Werft, Hamburg	3, 6	„
Danziger Werft	1, 2, 3, 8	Schichau, Danzig
Schichau, Danzig	4, 5	„
Deutsche Werke, Gotenhafen	6, 7	„

Construction of these vessels was expected to take approximately 6 months, as follows:

Production of sections	56 days
Fitting out of sections	50 days
Transportation	9 days
Assembly	50 days
Fitting out, etc	6 days
Shipyard trials	5 days

Diving depth 120/240m (originally intended to be 135/270m).

Propulsion

Two MAN 6-cylinder 4-stroke M6V 40/46 diesel engines with BBC superchargers in compartment 3; two Siemens-Schuckert 2 Gu 365/30 double electric motors in compartment 2, for normal underwater use; two Siemens-Schuckert GV 323/28 single commutator electric motors, occasionally constructed under licence at AEG or BBC, for silent running underwater, in compartment 2. 1 + 1 + 1 124-cell AFA 44 MAL 740 E batteries (33,900amp/hr) in compartments 4 and 6 in the lower part of the upper (larger) pressure hull, and in the lower (smaller) pressure hull. Two 3-bladed propellers, 2.15m diameter; one rudder; two hydroplanes at the stern, below the CWL; two swivelling hydroplanes at the bow, above the CWL; two large stabilisers aft. A schnorkel was fitted in the conning tower, allowing underwater running at 5 to 6kts.

Armament

Six 53.3cm torpedo tubes at the bow, below the waterline - 23 torpedoes, or 14 torpedoes and 12 TMC mines; stowage for 17 torpedoes was provided immediately abaft the torpedo tubes with an automatic system for rapid loading (first reload 11–15 mins, second reload 15¾–18¾mins). Four 2cm AA guns - 16,000 rounds - (originally planned as four 3cm AA guns with 14,000 rounds) in flak turrets forward and aft of the bridge. Two periscopes

Name	Type	Builder (construction no)	Built	Cost in Marks (000s)	Displacement (t = tonnes T = tons)	Length (m)	Breadth (m)	Draught/ height (m)	Power (hp)	Revs (rpm)	Speed (kts)	Range (nm/kts)	Oil (t)	Diving time (sec)
U2501–2564	XXI	B & V (2501–2564)	1944–45 and 1944–	5750 each	1621t sf 1819t sm 2100t total	76.70 oa 60.50 ph	8.00 oa 5.30 ph 3.50	6.32/ 11.30	4000ehp sf 4200ehp sm 226ehp sm*	315 sf 330 sm 122 sm*	15.6 sf 17.2 sm 6.1 sm*	15,500/10, 5100/15.6 sf 340/5, 110/10, 30/15 sm	250/ 228	20
U2565–2762	„	„ (2565–2762)	–	„	„	„	„	„	„	„	„	„	„	„
U3001–3063	„	Deschimag W (1160–1222)	1944–45 and 1944–	„	„	„	„	„	„	„	„	„	„	„
U3064–3100	„	„ (1223–1259)	–	„	„	„	„	„	„	„	„	„	„	„
U3101–3295	„	Vegesack 'Valentin'	–	„	„	„	„	„	„	„	„	„	„	„
U3501–3538	„	Schichau (D) (1646–1683)	1944–45 and 1944–	„	„	„	„	„	„	„	„	„	„	„
U3539–3595	„	„ (1684–1841)	–	„	„	„	„	„	„	„	„	„	„	„

* Silent-running motors only.

Conning tower casings on surrendered Type XXI U-boats (1/320 scale)

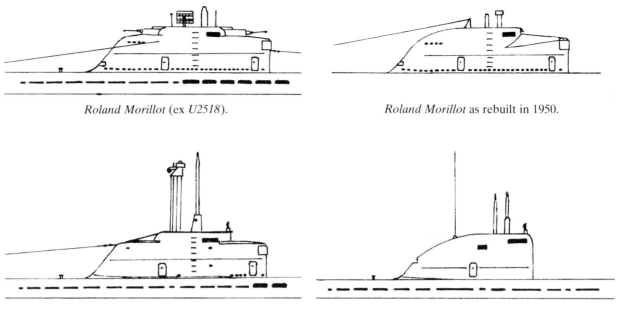

Roland Morillot (ex *U2518*).   *Roland Morillot* as rebuilt in 1950.

U2513 as rebuilt in the USA.   *U3008* as rebuilt in the USA.

(a wide angle periscope was not included); one retractable antenna mast; one retractable FuMO 'Hohentwiel' radar aerial in the port bridge bulwark; one FuMB 'Bali' aerial and an improved 'Naxos' direction finder; passive sonar equipment consisted of a GHG array in a specially constructed balcony at the bow, and active sonar was provided by SU 'Nibelung' equipment on the forward side of the conning tower. 'Ursel' rocket launching tubes with an SP guidance system for use against shadowing aircraft were planned at the stern.

Handling
Though the turning circle on the surface was larger than intended, the Type XXI's surface performance was otherwise very good. The bridge became known as the 'bathtub' because it was easily flooded in rough seas.

Complement
Crew: 5/52. Boats: six inflatable dinghies.

Notes
The overall form of these boats, and some of the fittings, were derived from the Type XVIII. The earliest boats to be constructed required several modifications to the flooding slots. The Type XXIs had (relatively) generous accommodation: sleeping areas were separated off from the machinery, there were three WCs with a waste tank, the washroom had three basins and a shower, and ultra-violet lamps were provided. The trial period was prolonged due to the many technical innovations incorporated in the design. When the Allies occupied the shipyards there were sixteen U-boats on the stocks at AG Weser, fourteen at Blohm & Voss and five at Schichau; a large numbr of fully-fitted sections also stood ready for assembly. The Type XXI design significantly influenced the construction of post-war submarines worldwide.

The following modified versions of the Type XXI reached project stage only:

Type XXI B: six lateral torpedo tubes angled aft (the so-called 'Schnee organ', after its inventor, Korv-Kpt Schnee) in place of the torpedo stowage space.

Type XXI C: two rows of six lateral torpedo tubes angled aft, fitted by increasing the length of the boat to 83m. This version had no reserve torpedoes - undesirable in so large a vessel.

Type XXI D: an oil-fuel replenishment boat, with 430 additional tonnes of oil in an enlarged outer hull; surface displacement 1949t; the torpedo armament was reduced to two 53.3cm tubes at the bow, below the CWL - two torpedoes; conning tower as per the basic Type XXI.

Type XXI E: a transport version, with 800 additional tonnes payload in an enlarged outer hull; surface displacement 2809t; torpedo armament reduced as per the Type XXI D; conning tower as per the basic Type XXI.

Type XXI V: an oil fuel replenishment version, with a smaller payload than the Type XXI D; outer hull as per the basic Type XXI, but with an enlarged upper deck to allow the crew space to work the refuelling equipment; only half the battery capacity of the Type XXI; armament as per the Type XXI D.

Type XXI T: a transport version with 275 tonnes payload; outer hull as per the Type XXI V; only half the battery capacity of the Type XXI; armament as per the Type XXI D.

Careers
U2501: launched 12 May 1944, commissioned 28 Jun 1944; scuttled at 0708hrs on 3 May 1945 at Hamburg; wreck broken up.

U2502: launched 15 Jun 1944, commissioned 19 Jul 1944; transferred from Horten to Lisahally 29 May 1945 for Operation Deadlight.

U2503: launched 29 Jun 1944, commissioned 1 Aug 1944. Sunk 4 May 1945 in the Lille Baelt off the North coast of Fyn, in position 55° 37′N, 10° 00′E, by British bombs; 13 dead.

U2504: launched 18 Jul 1944, commissioned 12 Aug 1944; scuttled at 0700hrs on 3 May 1945 near Hamburg, position not known; wreck broken up.

U2505: launched 27 Jul 1944, commissioned 7 Nov 1944; scuttled at 0700hrs on 3 May 1945 near Hamburg, position not known; wreck broken up.

U2506: launched 5 Aug 1944, commissioned 31 Aug 1944; transferred from Bergen to Lisahally 30 May 1945 for Operation Deadlight.

U2507: launched 14 Aug 1944, commissioned 8 Sept 1944; scuttled 5 May 1945 in Gelting Bay; wreck broken up.

U2508: launched 19 Aug 1944, commissioned 26 Sept 1944; scuttled 3 May 1945 at Kiel; wreck broken up.

U2509: launched 27 Aug 1944, commissioned 21 Sept 1944. Sunk 8 Apr 1945 near Hamburg, by bombs.

U2510: launched 29 Aug 1944, commissioned 29 Sept 1944; scuttled 2 May 1945 at Travemünde; wreck broken up.

U2511: launched 2 Sept 1944, commissioned 29 Sept 1944; transferred from Bergen to Lisahally 30 May 1945 for Operation Deadlight; scuttled 7 Jan 1946.

U2512: launched 7 Sept 1944, commissioned 10 Oct 1944; scuttled 3 May 1945 at Eckernförde; wreck broken up.

U2513: launched 14 Sept 1944, commissioned 12 Oct 1944; at Horten on 29 May 1945; transferred to USA in 1946; used for trials; sunk off Key West during rocket tests 7 Oct 1951.

U2514: launched 17 Sept 1944, commissioned 17 Oct 1944. Sunk 8 Apr 1945 at Hamburg by bombs; wreck broken up.

U2515: launched 22 Sept 1944, commissioned 19 Oct 1944. Sunk 17 Jan 1945 in Dock III, Hamburg, by bombs while damaged sections were being replaced; wreck broken up.

U2516: launched 27 Sept 1944, commissioned 24 Oct 1944. Sunk 9 Apr 1945 at Kiel, by bombs; wreck broken up.

U2517: launched 4 Oct 1944, commissioned 31 Oct 1944; scuttled 5 May 1945 in Gelting Bay; wreck broken up.

U2518: launched 4 Oct 1944, commissioned 4 Nov 1944; transferred to Britain from Horten, 29 May 1945; transferred to France in 1947; became the French submarine *Roland Morillot*; stricken 17 Oct 1967 as Q426; broken up in 1968.

U2519: launched 18 Oct 1944, commissioned 15 Nov 1944; scuttled 3 May 1945 at Kiel; wreck broken up.

U2520: launched 16 Oct 1944, commissioned 14 Nov 1944; scuttled 3 May 1945 at Kiel; wreck broken up.

U2521: launched 18 Oct 1944, commissioned 31 Oct 1944. Sunk 4 May 1945 in the Kattegat east of Aarhus, in position 56° 11′N, 11° 08′E, by British bombs; 44 dead.

U2522: launched 22 Oct 1944, commissioned 22 Nov 1944; scuttled 5 May 1945 in Gelting Bay; wreck broken up.

U2523: launched 25 Oct 1944, commissioned 26 Dec 1944. Sunk 17 Jan 1945 at Hamburg (Position 4), by bombs; wreck broken up.

U2524: launched 30 Oct 1944, commissioned 9 Jan 1945. Sunk 3 May 1945 southeast of the island of Fehmarn, by bombs; 2 dead.

U2525: launched 30 Oct 1944, commissioned 12 Dec 1944; scuttled 5 May 1945 in Gelting Bay; wreck broken up.

U2526: launched 30 Nov 1944, commissioned 15 Dec 1944; scuttled 2 May 1945 at Travemünde; wreck broken up.

U2527: launched 30 Nov 1944, commissioned 23 Dec 1944; scuttled 2 May 1945 at Travemünde; wreck broken up.

U2528: launched 18 Nov 1944, commissioned 9 Dec 1944; scuttled 2 May 1945 at Travemünde; wreck broken up.

U2529: launched 18 Nov 1944, commissioned 22 Feb 1945; transferred from Kristiansand-Süd to Loch Ryan 29 May 1945; became the British submarine *N 27*; transferred to the USSR in 1947; further details unknown.

U2530: launched 23 Nov 1944, commissioned 30 Dec 1944. Sunk 31 Dec 1944 at Hamburg, by bombs; raised in January 1945; sunk again during air attacks on Dock V on 17 Jan 1945, 20 Feb 1945 and 11 Mar 1945; wreck broken up.

U2531: launched 5 Dec 1944, commissioned 10 Jan 1945; scuttled 2 May 1945 at Travemünde; wreck broken up.

U2532: launched 7 Dec 1944; sunk 31 Dec 1945 at Hamburg (Position 5); sunk again on 17 Jan 1945, along with *Hiev* and *Griep*, by an air attack during attempts to raise her; wreck broken up.

U2533: launched 7 Dec 1944, commissioned 18 Jan 1945; scuttled 3 May 1945 at Travemünde; wreck broken up.

U2534: launched 11 Dec 1944, commissioned 17 Jan 1945. Sunk 6 May 1945 south of Göteborg, in position 57° 08′N, 11° 52′E, by British bombs; 1 dead.

U2535: launched 16 Dec 1944, commissioned 28 Jan 1945; scuttled 3 May 1945 at Travemünde; wreck broken up.

U2536: launched 16 Dec 1944, commissioned 6 Feb 1945; scuttled 3 May 1945 at Travemünde; wreck broken up.

U2537: launched 22 Dec 1944, commissioned 21 Mar 1945. Sunk 31 Dec 1944 at Hamburg (Position 1), by bombs.

U2538: launched 6 Jan 1945, commissioned 16 Feb 1945; scuttled at 0445hrs on 8 May 1945 off the southwest coast of the island of Aerø near Marstel, in position 54° 53.5′N, 10° 15.7′E; wreck broken up in 1975.

U2539: launched 6 Jan 1945, commissioned 21 Feb 1945; scuttled 3 May 1945 at Kiel; wreck broken up.

U2540: launched 13 Jan 1945, commissioned 24 Feb 1945; scuttled 4 May 1945 near the Flensburg lightship; raised in 1957; became the research vessel *Wilhelm Bauer* in the Bundesmarine, 1 Sept 1960; transferred to the *Deutsches Schiffahrtsmuseum* (German Maritime Museum) at Bremerhaven in 1984.

U2541: launched 13 Jan 1945, commissioned 1 Mar 1945; scuttled 5 May 1945 in Gelting Bay; wreck broken up.

U2542: launched 22 Jan 1945, commissioned 5 May 1945. Sunk 3 Apr 1945 at the Hindenburg bank at Kiel, by bombs; wreck broken up.

U2543: launched 9 Feb 1945, commissioned 7 Mar 1945; scuttled 3 May 1945 at Kiel; wreck broken up.

U2544: launched 9 Feb 1945, commissioned 10 Mar 1945. Sunk 5 May 1945 east-southeast of Aarhus, in position 56° 06.5′N, 10° 27.9′E; raised in 1952 and broken up.

U2545: launched 12 Feb 1945, commissioned 26 Mar 1945; scuttled 3 May 1945 at Kiel; wreck broken up.

U2546: launched 19 Feb 1945, commissioned 28 Feb 1945; scuttled 3 May 1945 at Kiel; wreck broken up.

U2547: launched 9 Mar 1945; bombed while being fitted out 11 Mar 1945; broken up.

U2548: launched 9 Mar 1945, commissioned 31 Mar 1945; scuttled 3 May 1945 at Kiel; wreck broken up.

U2549: bombed while being assembled 11 Mar 1945 and 2 May 1945; broken up.

U2550: bombed while being assembled 11 Mar 1945 and 8 Apr 1945; broken up.

U2551: launched 31 Mar 1945, commissioned in April 1945. Sunk 5 May 1945 near Flensburg-Solitude, position not known; wreck broken up.

U2552: launched 31 Mar 1945, commissioned 20 Apr 1945. Sunk 3 May 1945 near Kiel-Wik, position not known; wreck broken up.

U2553–2564: broken up 1945–46, whil on the building slips, almost complete.

U2565–2608: sections partially completed; keels never laid.

U2609–2643: contract placement postponed 1 Dec 1944.

U2644–2762: orders cancelled 1 Dec 1944.

U3001: launched 30 May 1944, commissioned 20 Jul 1944; scuttled 3 May 1945 northwest of Wesermünde; wreck broken up.

U3002: launched 9 Jul 1944, commissioned 6 Aug 1944; scuttled 2 May 1945 at Travemünde; wreck broken up.

U3003: launched 18 Jul 1944, commissioned 22 Aug 1944. Sunk 4 Apr 1945 at Kiel, by bombs; wreck broken up.

U3004: launched 26 Jul 1944, commissioned 30 Aug 1944; scuttled 2 May 1945 at Hamburg; wreck broken up.

U3005: launched 18 Aug 1944, commissioned 20 Sept 1944; scuttled 3 May 1945 at Kiel; wreck broken up.

U3006: launched 25 Aug 1944, commissioned 5 Oct 1944; scuttled at 0700hrs on 1 May 1945 at Wilhelmshaven; wreck broken up.

U3007: launched 4 Sept 1944, commissioned 22 Oct 1944. Sunk 24 Feb 1945 near Bremen, by bombs; wreck broken up.

U3008: launched 15 Sept 1944, commissioned 19 Oct 1944; transferred to the USA in June 1945; used for tests until at least 1954, then broken up at Puerto Rico.

U3009: launched 30 Sept 1944, commissioned 10 Nov 1944; scuttled 1 May 1945, near Wesermünde; wreck broken up.

U3010: launched 20 Oct 1944, commissioned 11 Nov 1944; scuttled 3 May 1945 at Kiel; wreck broken up.

U3011: launched 20 Oct 1944, commissioned 21 Dec 1944; scuttled 3 May 1945 at Travemünde; wreck broken up.

U3012: launched 13 Oct 1944, commissioned 4 Dec 1944; scuttled 3 May 1945 at Travemünde; wreck broken up.

U3013: launched 19 Oct 1944, commissioned 22 Nov 1944; scuttled 3 May 1945 at Travemünde; wreck broken up.

U3014: launched 25 Oct 1944, commissioned 17 Dec 1944; scuttled 3 May 1945 near Neustadt, position not known; wreck broken up.

U3015: launched 27 Oct 1944, commissioned 17 Dec 1944; scuttled 5 May 1945 in Gelting Bay; wreck broken up.

U3016: launched 2 Nov 1944, commissioned 5 Jan 1945; scuttled 2 May 1945 at Travemünde; wreck broken up.

U3017: launched 5 Nov 1944, commissioned 5 Jan 1945; at Horten in May 1945, and transferred to Britain; became the British submarine *N 41*; used for tests; broken up at Newport in November 1949.

U3018: launched 29 Nov 1944, commissioned 6 Jan 1945; scuttled 2 May 1945 at Travemünde; wreck broken up.

U3019: launched 15 Nov 1944, commissioned 23 Dec 1944; scuttled 2 May 1945 at Travemünde; wreck broken up.

U3020: launched 16 Nov 1944, commissioned 23 Dec 1944; scuttled 2 May 1945 at Travemünde; wreck broken up.

U3021: launched 27 Nov 1944, commissioned 12 Jan 1945; scuttled 2 may 1945 at Travemünde; wreck broken up.

U3022: launched 30 Nov 1944, commissioned 25 Jan 1945; scuttled 5 May 1945 in Gelting Bay; wreck broken up.

U3023: launched 2 Dec 1944, commissioned 22 Jan 1945; scuttled 3 May 1945 at Travemünde; wreck broken up.

U3024: launched 6 Dec 1944, commissioned 13 Jan 1945; scuttled 3 May 1945 near Neustadt, position not known; wreck broken up.

U3025: launched 9 Dec 1944, commissioned 20 Jan 1945; scuttled 3 May 1945 at Travemünde; wreck broken up.

U3026: launched 14 Dec 1944, commissioned 22 Jan 1945; scuttled 3 May 1945 at Travemünde; wreck broken up.

U3027: launched 18 Dec 1944, commissioned 25 Jan 1945; scuttled 3 May 1945 at Travemünde; wreck broken up.

U3028: launched 22 Dec 1944, commissioned 27 Jan 1945. Sunk 3 May 1945 in the Great Belt, position not known, by bombs.

U3029: launched 28 Dec 1944, commissioned 5 Feb 1945; scuttled 3 May 1945 in the Aussenförde at Kiel.

U3030: launched 31 Dec 1944, commissioned 14 Feb 1945. Sunk 3 May 1945 east of Frederica, in position 55° 30′N, 10° 00′E, by British bombs.

U3031: launched 6 Jan 1945, commissioned 28 Feb 1945; scuttled 3 May 1945 at Kiel; wreck broken up.

U3032: launched 10 Jan 1945, commissioned 12 Feb 1945. Sunk 3 May 1945 east of Frederica, in position 55° 30′N, 10° 00′E, by British bombs; 28 dead.

U3033: launched 20 Jan 1945, commissioned 27 Feb 1945; scuttled 4 May 1945 in Wasserleben Bay; wreck broken up.

U3034: launched 21 Jan 1945, commissioned 1 Mar 1945; scuttled on 4 May 1945 in Wasserleben Bay; wreck broken up.

U3035: launched 24 Jan 1945, commissioned 1 Mar 1945; transferred from Stavanger to Loch Ryan 1 Jun 1945; became the British submarine *N 28*; transferred to the USSR in 1947; further details unknown.

U3036: launched 27 Jan 1945, commissioned 6 Feb 1945. Sunk 3 Mar 1945 in the shipyard at Bremen, by bombs.

U3037: launched 31 Jan 1945, commissioned 3 Mar 1945; scuttled 3 May 1945 at Travemünde; wreck broken up.

U3038: launched 7 Feb 1945, commissioned 4 Mar 1945; scuttled 3 May 1945 at Kiel; wreck broken up.

U3039: launched 14 Feb 1945, commissioned 8 Mar 1945; scuttled 3 May 1945 at Kiel; wreck broken up.

U3040: launched 10 Feb 1945, commissioned 7 Mar 1945; scuttled 3 May 1945 at Kiel; wreck broken up.

U3041: launched 23 Feb 1945, commissioned 10 Mar 1945; transferred from Horten to Loch Ryan 29 May 1945; became the British submarine *N 29*; transferred to the USSR in 1947; further details unknown.

U3042: badly damaged by bombs on the building slips at Bremen in February 1945; broken up.

U3043: badly damaged by bombs on the building slips at Bremen in February 1945; broken up.

U3044: launched 1 Mar 1945, commissioned 27 Mar 1945; scuttled 5 May 1945 in Gelting Bay; wreck broken up.

U3045: launched 6 May 1945; sunk 30 Mar 1945 by British bombs while still in the shipyard at Bremen; wreck broken up.

U3046: launched 10 Mar 1945; sunk 30 Mar 1945 by British bombs while still in the shipyard at Bremen; wreck broken up.

U3047: launched 11 Apr 1945; scuttled 5 May 1945 west of Wesermünde; wreck broken up.

U3048: broken up on the building slips.

U3049: broken up on the building slips.

U3050: launched 18 Apr 1945; scuttled 5 May 1945 west of Wesermünde; wreck broken up.

U3051: launched 20 Apr 1945; scuttled on 5 May 1945 west of Wesermünde; wreck broken up.

U3052–3063: broken up on the building slips.

U3064–3088: sections partially completed; keels never laid.

U3089–3100: construction not started.

U3101–3295: contract granted to U-boat construction bunker 'Valentin'; construction not started.

U3296–3500: contracts not placed.

U3501: launched 19 Apr 1944, commissioned 29 Jul 1944; scuttled 5 May 1945 at the west side of the Weser estuary; wreck broken up.

U3502: launched 6 Jul 1944, commissioned 19 Aug 1944; taken out of service at Hamburg on 3 May 1945, after bomb damage to the stern and the electricity plant; broken up.

U3503: launched 27 Jul 1944, commissioned 9 Sept 1944; scuttled 8 May 1945 west of Göteborg, in position 57° 39′N, 11° 44′E; raised in 1946 and broken up.

U3504: launched 16 Aug 1944, commissioned 23 Sept 1944; scuttled 2 May 1945 at Wilhelmshaven; wreck broken up.

U3505: launched 25 Aug 1944, commissioned 7 Oct 1944. Sunk at 1730hrs on 3 May 1945 at Kiel, by bombs; 1 dead; wreck broken up.

U3506: launched 28 Aug 1944, commissioned 14 Oct 1944; scuttled 2 May 1945 at Hamburg; wreck broken up.

U3507: launched 16 Sept 1944, commissioned 19 Oct 1944; scuttled 3 May 1945 at Travemünde; wreck broken up.

U3508: launched 22 Sept 1944, commissioned 2 Nov 1944. Sunk 4 Mar 1945 at Wilhelmshaven, by bombs.

U3509: launched 27 Sept 1944; damaged by bombs in September 1944 in an air raid on the building slips; repaired and completed; commissioned 29 Jan 1945; scuttled 3 May 1945 in the western Weser estuary.

U3510: launched 4 Oct 1944, commissioned 11 Nov 1944; scuttled 5 May 1945 in Gelting Bay; wreck broken up.

U3511: launched 11 Oct 1944, commissioned 18 Nov 1944; scuttled on 3 May 1945 at Travemünde; wreck broken up.

U3512: launched 11 Oct 1944, commissioned 27 Nov 1944. Sunk 8 Apr 1945 at Kiel, by bombs; wreck broken up.

U3513: launched 21 Oct 1944, commissioned 2 Dec 1944; scuttled 3 May 1945 at Travemünde; wreck broken up.

U3514: launched 21 Oct 1944, commissioned 9 Dec 1944; transferred from Bergen to Loch Ryan 29 May 1945 for Operation Deadlight; scuttled at 1004hrs on 12 Feb 1946, in position 56° 00′N, 10° 05′W, the last vessel to be scuttled in the operation.

U3515: launched 4 Nov 1944, commissioned 14 Dec 1944; transferred from Horten to Loch Ryan 30 May 1945; became the British submarine *N 30*; transferred to the USSR in 1946; further details unknown.

U3516: launched 4 Nov 1944, commissioned 18 Dec 1944; scuttled 2 May 1945 at 1945 at Travemünde; wreck broken up.

U3517: launched 6 Dec 1944, commissioned 22 Dec 1944; scuttled 2 May 1945 at Travemünde; wreck broken up.

U3518: launched 11 Dec 1944, commissioned 29 Dec 1944; scuttled 3 May 1945 at Kiel; wreck broken up.

U3519: launched 23 Nov 1944, commissioned 15 Dec 1944. Sunk 5 Mar 1945 north of Warnemünde, in position 54° 11′N, 12° 05′E, by mines; 65 dead.

U3520: launched 23 Nov 1944, commissioned 23 Dec 1944. Sunk 31 Jan 1945 northeast of Bülk, in position 54° 28′N, 10° 12′E, by mines; 80 dead.

U3521: launched 3 Dec 1944, commissioned 14 Jan 1945; scuttled 2 May 1945 at Travemünde; wreck broken up.

U3522: launched 3 Dec 1944, commissioned 21 Jan 1945; scuttled 2 May 1945 at Travemünde; wreck broken up.

U3523: launched 14 Dec 1944, commissioned 29 Jan 1945. Sunk 5 May 1945 east of Aarhus, in position 56° 06′N, 11° 06′E, by British bombs; 57 dead.

U3524: launched 14 Dec 1944, commissioned 26 Jan 1945; scuttled 5 May 1945 in Gelting Bay; wreck broken up.

U3525: launched 23 Dec 1944, commissioned 31

Jan 1945; damaged by bombs on 30 Apr 1945 in the western Baltic; taken to Kiel, and scuttled there, 1 May 1945; wreck broken up.

U3526: launched 23 Dec 1944, commissioned 22 Mar 1945; scuttled 5 May 1945 in Gelting Bay; wreck broken up.

U3527: launched 10 Jan 1945, commissioned 10 Mar 1945; scuttled 5 May 1945 in the western Weser estuary; wreck broken up.

U3528: launched 10 Jan 1945, commissioned 18

Mar 1945; scuttled 5 May 1945 in the western Weser estuary; wreck broken up.

U3529: launched 26 Jan 1945, commissioned 22 Mar 1945; scuttled 5 May 1945 in Gelting Bay; wreck broken up.

U3530: launched 26 Jan 1945, commissioned 22 Mar 1945; scuttled 3 May 1945 at Kiel; wreck broken up.

U3531–3538: towed to Wesermünde shortly before completion, and broken up.

U3539–3542: scuttled at Schichau dockyard over 80 percent complete; taken as USSR prizes and probably completed there; further details unknown.

U3543–3571: sections partially completed; keels never laid.

U3572–4000: construction contracts suspended or never actually placed.

Most of the scuttled boats were raised between 1946 and 1953 and broken up.

Type XXII coastal U-boats

Name	Type	Builder (construction no)	Built	Cost in Marks (000s)	Displacement (t = tonnes T = tons)	Length (m)	Breadth (m)	Draught/ height (m)	Power (hp)	Revs (rpm)	Speed (kts)	Range (nm/kts)	Oil (t)	Diving time (sec)
U1153, 1154	XXII	Howaldt (K)† (55, 56)	1943–		155t sf c170t sm c200t total	27.10 oa 18.60 ph	3.00 oa 3.00 ph	4.20/ 6.90	210ehp sf 77 ehp sm 1850ehp sm*	208 sf 170 sm*	7.0 sf 20.1 sm*	1550/6.5 sf 96/20 sm*	12 max +30 (H$_2$O$_2$)	

* Walter turbine drive.
†A further 34 boats were ordered from Howaldtswerke, Kiel (all contracts cancelled 6 Nov 1943), and preliminary contracts for 36 more were placed on 6 Jul 1943 with Howaldtswerke, Hamburg (cancelled 30 Sept 1943).

Construction

Laid down as U-boats for coastal and Mediterranean use, designed by H Walter GmbH. Walterform hull (see *V 80*, etc), but with a stern tapering to a large vertical rudder, instead of the stabilising cross of *V 80*; three watertight compartments; a low bridge was provided, but no conning tower.

Propulsion

One Deutz 12-cylinder 4-stroke R 12 V 26/340 supercharged diesel engine in compartment 2; one Brückner, Kanis & Co Walter turbine with an exhaust condenser; electric motor and batteries as

Type XXII (1943 design).

per the Type XVII. One 3-bladed propeller, 1.90m diameter; a schnorkel was incorporated in the bridge casing.

Armament

Three 53.3cm torpedo tubes (5m long), two at the bow, below the CWL and one abaft the bridge, above the CWL - 3 torpedoes; no other armament. One periscope in the control room.

Complement

Crew: 2/10.

Careers

Original plans were for 72 of these U-boats. In autumn 1943 construction was suspended and contracts cancelled in favour of the Type XXIII.

Type XXIII coastal U-boats

Name	Type	Builder (construction no)	Built	Cost in Marks (000s)	Displacement (t = tonnes T = tons)	Length (m)	Breadth (m)	Draught/ height (m)	Power (hp)	Revs (rpm)	Speed (kts)	Range (nm/kts)	Oil (t)	Diving time (sec)
U2321–2331	XXIII	DWA (475–485)	1944	0.76	234t sf 258t sm 275t total	34.68 oa 26.0 ph	3.02 oa 3.00 ph 2.80	3.66/ 7.70	575 to 630ehp sf 580ehp sm 35ehp sm*	850/300 to 880/310 sf 850/300 sm 100 sm*	9.7 sf 12.5 sm 4.5 sm*	4450/6, 2600/8 sf 35/10, 194/4 sm	20 max	14
U2332, 2333	”	Germania (941, 942)	1944	”	”	”	”	”	”	”	”	”	”	”

Construction

Laid down as U-boats for use in the Mediterranean and in coastal waters, official design 1943, with preliminary work by the 'Glückauf' Engineering Office (see the Type XXI). Single hull; three watertight compartments; the pressure hull was figure-eight shaped in section forward, and pressure-tight regulating tanks and (non-pressure-

tight) diving tanks and fuel oil bunkers were arranged in a separate casing aft, below a cylindrical pressure hull. These boats were constructed in sections, assembled at the same yards. Section 1

Name	Type	Builder (construction no)	Built
U2334–2371	XXIII	DWA (488–525)	1944–45
U2372–2392	„	Germania (1189–1209)	–
U2393–2400	„	DWA (547–554)	–
U2401–2430	„	Ansaldo (GS) (804–833)	1944–
U2431–2445	„	CRDA (M) (656–670)	1944–
U2446–2460	„	Linz	1944–
U4001–4120	„	DWA (555–674)	–
U4701–4748, 4751–4780	„	Germania (943–990, 1210–1329)	1944–45, 1945– and –

(stern) weighed 11.3 tonnes; section 2 (engine room) 14 tonnes; section 3 (control room and forward living quarters) 18.2 tonnes; section 4 (bow) 16.5 tonnes. Diving depth 80/160m (originally planned as 100/200m). The design included a conning tower.

Propulsion
One MWM 6-cylinder 4-stroke RS 34 S un-supercharged diesel engine in compartment 1, forward of amidships; one AEG GU 4463-8 double electric motor for normal underwater propulsion and one BBC GCR 188 single-commutator electric motor for silent running underwater, in compartment 1; one 62-cell AFA 2 × 21 MAL 740 E battery (5400 amp/hr) in the lower pressure hull forward of amidships vessel at ¼ of the boat's length. One 3-bladed propeller, 1.78m diameter; one rudder; two hydroplanes aft and two at the bow (not included in the original design); one pair of horizontal stabilisers at the bow and one pair at the stern; a schnorkel was incorporated in the conning tower casing, allowing underwater travel at speeds of up to 10.75 kts.

Armament
Two 53.3cm torpedo tubes at the bow, below the CWL - 2 torpedoes; no other armament. One periscope in the tower.

Handling
Good underwater performance; poor surface seakeeping.

Construction
Crew: 2/12. Boats: one inflatable dinghy.

Notes
This Type was a development of the Type XXII design. The shipyards initially intended for their construction were as follows: *U2321–2370*, Deutsche Werft, Hamburg; *U2371–2400*, Deutsche Werft, Toulon Naval Dockyard; *U2446–2460*, Deutsche Werft, Nikolayev.

Careers
U2321: launched 17 Apr 1944, commissioned 12 Jun 1944; transferred from Kristiansand S to Loch Ryan 29 May 1945 for Operation Deadlight.

U2322: launched 30 Apr 1944, commissioned 1 Jul 1944; transferred from Stavanger to Loch Ryan 31 May 1945 for Operation Deadlight.

U2323: launched 31 May 1944, commissioned 18 Jul 1944. Sunk at 1635hrs on 26 Jul 1944 west of Möltenort, in position 54° 23′N, 10° 11′E, by a mine; 2 dead.

U2324: launched 16 Jun 1944, commissioned 25 Jul 1944; transferred from Stavanger to Loch Ryan 29 May 1945 for Operation Deadlight.

U2325: launched 13 Jul 1944, commissioned 3 Aug 1944; transferred from Kristiansand S to Loch Ryan 29 May 1945 for Operation Deadlight.

U2326: launched 17 Jul 1944, commissioned 10 Aug 1944; surrendered at Loch Foyle, 14 May 1945; became the British submarine *N 35*; transferred to France in 1946; sank 6 Dec 1946 at Toulon in an accident; 17 dead. Raised and broken up.

U2327: launched 29 Jul 1944, commissioned 19 Aug 1944; scuttled 2 May 1945 at Hamburg; wreck broken up.

U2328: launched 17 Aug 1944, commissioned 25 Aug 1944; transferred from Bergen to Loch Ryan 30 May 1945 for Operation Deadlight.

U2329: launched 11 Aug 1944, commissioned 1 Sept 1944; transferred from Stavanger to Loch Ryan in June 1945 for Operation Deadlight.

U2330: launched 19 Aug 1944, commissioned 7 Sept 1944; scuttled 3 May 1945 at Kiel; wreck broken up.

U2331: launched 22 Aug 1944, commissioned 12 Sept 1944. Sank 10 Oct 1944 near Hela, in approximate position 54° 00′N, 18° 00′E, in an accident; 15 dead. Raised and towed to Gotenhafen; further details unknown.

U2332: launched 18 Oct 1944, commissioned 13 Nov 1944; scuttled 3 May 1945 at Hamburg; wreck broken up.

U2333: launched 16 Nov 1944, commissioned 18

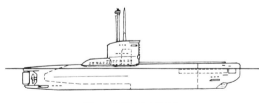

Type XXIII (1944).

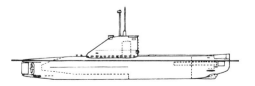

Hai (ex *U2365*) and *Hecht* (ex *U2367*) after their 1965 rebuild.

Dec 1944; scuttled 5 May 1945 in Gelting Bay; wreck broken up.

U2334: launched 26 Aug 1944, commissioned 21 Sept 1944; transferred from Kristiansand S to Loch Ryan 29 May 1945 for Operation Deadlight.

U2335: launched 31 Aug 1944, commissioned 27 Sept 1944; transferred from Kristiansand S to Loch Ryan 29 May 1945 for Operation Deadlight.

U2336: launched 10 Sept 1944, commissioned 30 Sept 1944; transferred from Wilhelmshaven to Lisahally 21 Jun 1945 for Operation Deadlight.

U2337: launched 15 Sept 1944, commissioned 4 Oct 1944; transferred from Kristiansand S to Loch Ryan 29 May 1945 for Operation Deadlight.

U2338: launched 18 Sept 1944, commissioned 9 Oct 1944. Sunk 4 May 1945 east-northeast of Frederica, in position 55° 34′N, 09° 49′E, by British bombs; 12 dead. Raised in 1952 and broken up.

U2339: launched 22 Sept 1944, commissioned 16 Nov 1944; scuttled 5 May 1945 in Gelting Bay; wreck broken up.

U2340: launched 28 Sept 1944, commissioned 16 Oct 1944. Sunk 30 Mar 1945 at Hamburg by British bombs; wreck broken up.

U2341: launched 3 Oct 1944, commissioned 21 Oct 1944; transferred from Wilhelmshaven to Lisahally 21 Jun 1945 for Operation Deadlight.

U2342: launched 13 Oct 1944, commissioned 1 Nov 1944. Sunk at 2240hrs on 26 Dec 1944 north of Swinemünde, in position 54° 01.8′N, 14° 15.20′E, by a mine; 7 dead. Wreck still in this location, in August 1953.

U2343: launched 18 Oct 1944, commissioned 6 Nov 1944; scuttled at 1300hrs on 5 May 1945 in or near Gelting Bay; wreck broken up.

U2344: launched 24 Oct 1944, commissioned 10 Nov 1944. Sank 18 Feb 1945 north of Heiligendamm, in position 54° 16.5′N, 11° 48.5′E, after a collision with *U2336*; 7 dead. Raised in June 1956; measured and conserved, but not restored; broken up at Rostock in 1958.

U2345: launched 28 Oct 1944, commissioned 15 Nov 1944; transferred from Stavanger to Loch Ryan 30 Jun 1945 for Operation Deadlight.

U2346: launched 31 Oct 1944, commissioned 20 Nov 1944; scuttled 5 May 1945 in Gelting Bay; wreck broken up.

U2347: launched 6 Nov 1944, commissioned 2 Dec 1944; scuttled 5 May 1945 in Gelting Bay; wreck broken up.

U2348: launched 11 Nov 1944, commissioned 4 Dec 1944; transferred from Stavanger to Loch Ryan 30 Jun 1945 for Operation Deadlight; broken up at Belfast in April 1949.

U2349: launched 20 Nov 1944, commissioned 11 Dec 1944; scuttled 5 May 1945 in Gelting Bay; wreck broken up.

U2350: launched 22 Nov 1944, commissioned 23 Dec 1944; transferred from Kristiansand S to Loch Ryan 29 May 1945 for Operation Deadlight.

U2351: launched 25 Nov 1944, commissioned 30 Dec 1944; taken out of service at Kiel in April 1945, after being bombed; transferred to Lisahally for Operation Deadlight.

U2352: launched 5 Dec 1944, commissioned 11 Jan 1945; scuttled 5 May 1945 at Hörup Haff; wreck broken up.

U2353: launched 6 Dec 1944, commissioned 9 Jan 1945; transferred from Kristiansand S to Loch Ryan 29 May 1945 for Operation Deadlight; became the British submarine *N 37*; transferred to the USSR in 1947; broken up in 1963.

U2354: launched 10 Dec 1944, commissioned 11 Jan 1945; transferred from Kristiansand S to Loch Ryan 29 May 1945 for Operation Deadlight.

U2355: launched 13 Dec 1944, commissioned 12 Jan 1945; scuttled 3 May 1945 northwest of Laboe, in position 54° 24.4′N, 10° 12′E.

U2356: launched 19 Dec 1944, commissioned 12 Jan 1945; transferred from Wilhelmshaven to Lisalhally 21 Jun 1945 for Operation Deadlight.

U2357: launched 19 Dec 1944, commissioned 13 Jan 1944; scuttled 5 May 1945 in Gelting Bay; wreck broken up.

U2358: launched 20 Dec 1944, commissioned 16 Jan 1945; scuttled 5 May 1945 in Gelting Bay; wreck broken up.

U2359: launched 23 Dec 1944, commissioned 16 Jan 1945. Sunk 2 May 1945 in the Kattegat, in position 57° 29′N, 11° 24′E, by British and Norwegian bombs; 12 dead.

U2360: launched 29 Dec 1944, commissioned 23 Jan 1945; scuttled 5 May 1945 in Gelting Bay; wreck broken up.

U2361: launched 3 Jan 1945, commissioned 3 Feb 1945; transferred from Kristiansand S to Loch Ryan 29 May 1945 for Operation Deadlight.

U2362: launched 11 Jan 1945, commissioned 5 Feb 1945; scuttled 5 May 1945 in Gelting Bay; wreck broken up.

U2363: launched 18 Jan 1945, commissioned 5 Feb 1945; transferred from Kristiansand S to Loch Ryan 29 May 1945 for Operation Deadlight (scuttled in November 1945).

U2364: launched 23 Jan 1945, commissioned 14 Feb 1945; scuttled 5 May 1945 in Gelting Bay; wreck broken up.

U2365: launched 26 Jan 1945, commissioned 2 May 1945; scuttled 8 May 1945 in the Kattegat, in position 56° 51′N, 11° 49′E. Raised in June 1956; renamed *UW 20* (later *Hai*) in the German Federal

Navy 15 Aug 1957; sank at 1854hrs on 14 Sept 1966 in the North Sea, in position 55° 15′N, 04° 22′E, after taking in water; 19 dead. Raised 24 Sept 1966 and broken up.

U2366: launched 17 Feb 1945, commissioned 10 Mar 1945; scuttled 5 May 1945 in Gelting Bay; wreck broken up.

U2367: launched 23 Feb 1945, commissioned 17 Mar 1945. Sank 5 May 1945 near Schleimünde, in approximate position 55° 00′N, 11° 00′E, after a collision with an unidentified German U-boat. Raised in August 1956; renamed *Hecht* and served in the German Federal Navy from 1 Oct 1957; broken up at Kiel in 1969.

U2368: launched 19 Mar 1945, commissioned 10 Apr 1945; scuttled 5 May 1945 in Gelting Bay; wreck broken up.

U2369: launched 24 Mar 1945, commissioned 30 Mar 1945; scuttled 5 May 1945 in Gelting Bay; wreck broken up.

U2370: launched in March 1945, commissioned 15 Apr 1945; scuttled 2 May 1945 at Hamburg; wreck broken up.

U2371: launched 18 Apr 1945, commissioned 24 Apr 1945; scuttled at 0200hrs on 3 May 1945 at Hamburg; wreck broken up.

U2372–2377: sections constructed at Deutsche Werft, Hamburg (construction nos 526–531) and delivered to Germaniawerft, Kiel.

U2378–2389: sections partially completed at Deutsche Werft, Hamburg (Construction nos 532–543), and assembly started.

U2390–2400: orders cancelled 1 Dec 1944.

U2401–2403: construction halted in July 1944; further details unknown.

U2404–2430: construction not started.

U2431–2432: construction halted in July 1944; blown up and destroyed on the slips 1 May 1945.

U2433–2460: construction not started.

U2461–2500: orders not placed.

U4001–4120: orders placed, 23 Nov 1944, but no details found in the shipyard documents.

U4121–4500: orders not placed.

U4701: launched 14 Dec 1944, commissioned 10 Jan 1945; scuttled 5 May 1945 at Hörup Haff; wreck broken up.

U4702: launched 20 Dec 1944, commissioned 22 Jan 1945; scuttled 5 May 1945 at Hörup Haff; wreck broken up.

U4703: launched 3 Jan 1945, commissioned 21 Jan 1945; scuttled 5 May 1945 in Gelting Bay; wreck broken up.

U4704: launched 13 Feb 1945, commissioned 14 Mar 1945; scuttled 5 May 1945 at Hörup Haff; wreck broken up.

U4705: launched 11 Jan 1945, commissioned 2 Feb 1945; scuttled 3 May 1945 at Kiel; wreck broken up.

U4706: launched 19 Jan 1945, commissioned 7 Feb 1945; transferred from Kristiansand S to Loch Ryan 29 May 1945; given a British pennant number; transferred to Norway in October 1948; became the Norwegian submarine *Knerter*; used for storage by the Royal Norwegian Yacht Club from 14 Apr 1950; stricken in 1954 and broken up.

U4707: launched 25 Jan 1945, commissioned 20 Feb 1945; scuttled 5 May 1945 in Gelting Bay; wreck broken up.

U4708: launched 26 Mar 1945. Sunk 9 Apr 1945 at Germaniawerft, Kiel, by British bombs, before completion.

U4709: launched 8 Feb 1945; commissioned 3 Mar 1945; scuttled 4 Apr 1945 at Germaniawerft, Kiel; wreck broken up.

U4710: launched 14 Apr 1945, commissioned 1 May 1945; scuttled 5 May 1945 in Gelting Bay; wreck broken up.

U4711: launched 21 Feb 1945; commissioned 21 Mar 1945; scuttled 4 Apr 1945 at Germaniawerft, Kiel; wreck broken up.

U4712: launched 1 Mar 1945; commissioned 3 Apr 1945; scuttled 4 Apr 1945 at Germaniawerft, Kiel; wreck broken up.

U4713: launched 19 Apr 1945; broken up at Germaniawerft, Kiel, 95 percent complete.

U4714: launched 26 Apr 1945; broken up at Germaniawerft, Kiel 95 percent complete.

U4715–4718: broken up at Germaniawerft, Kiel, up to 95 percent complete.

U4719–4750: assembly not started.

U4751–4871: not started.

U4872–5000: orders not placed.

Type XXIV Walter U-boat project

Construction
A 1943 design for an ocean-going U-boat. Double hull, similar to that of the Type XVIII.

Propulsion
Two MWM 6-cylinder 4-stroke supercharged diesel engines; two Walter-drive turbines; two AEG electric motors and two SSW silent-running electric motors; 1 + 1 62-cell AFA 44 MAL 740 batteries. Two 3-bladed propellers; schnorkel.

Armament
Fourteen 53.3cm torpedo tubes below the CWL, six at the bow and four each side trained aft (this arrangement of the lateral tubes was known as the 'Schnee-organ' after its inventor, Korv-Kpt Schnee) - 14 torpedoes; AA guns as per the Type XXI.

Complement
Crew: approximately 58.

Notes
The conning tower and casing were as for the Type XXI. This Walter U-boat design was intended for long-distance operations, but the torpedo provision was insufficient for such a large vessel (see the Type XXI C).

Careers
No construction orders were ever placed for these U-boats.

Name	Type	Builder (construction no)	Built	Cost in Marks (000s)	Displacement (t = tonnes T = tons)	Length (m)	Breadth (m)	Draught/ height (m)	Power (hp)	Revs (rpm)	Speed (kts)	Range (nm/kts)	Oil (t)	Diving time (sec)
–	XXIV	Project only	–	–	c1800t sf			5.40 ph	2000ehp sf 396ehp sm 15,000ehp sm* 140ehp sm*	187 sm 500 sm*	14.0 sf 7.0 sm 22.0 sm* 3.0 sm†	15,000/10 sf		

* Walter turbine drive.
† Silent running motors only.

Type XXV small coastal U-boat project

Name	Type	Builder (construction no)	Built	Cost in Marks (000s)	Displacement (t = tonnes T = tons)	Length (m)	Breadth (m)	Draught/ height (m)	Power (hp)	Revs (rpm)	Speed (kts)	Range (nm/kts)	Oil (t)	Diving time (sec)
	XXV	Project only	–	–	160t sf	28 oa	3.0 oa 3.0 ph		160ehp sm		9.0 sm	400/6 sm		

Construction
A design for a pure U-boat with full electric propulsion only, for coastal use, designed in 1943. The hull form was similar to that of the Type XXIII, but no conning tower was included.

Propulsion
Two SSW GV 323/28 single-commutator electric motors; 1 + 1 62-cell AFA 2 × 21 MAL 740 E batteries (5400amp/hr).

Armament
Two 53.3cm torpedo tubes at the bow, below the CWL - 2 torpedoes; no other armament. One periscope in the control room.

Notes
These vessels were disproportionately large for their range of operation.

Careers
No construction orders were ever placed for these submarines.

Type XXVI Walter U-boats

Name	Type	Builder (construction no)	Built	Cost in Marks (000s)	Displacement (t = tonnes T = tons)	Length (m)	Breadth (m)	Draught/ height (m)	Power (hp)	Revs (rpm)	Speed (kts)	Range (nm/kts)	Oil (t)	Diving time (sec)
U4501–4600	XXVI W	B & V (4501–4600)	1944–		842t sf 926t sm 1160t total	56.20 oa 40.50 ph	5.45 oa 5.40 ph	5.9/	580ehp sf 265ehp sf* 536ehp sm 7500ehp sm† 71ehp sm‡	245 sf* 208 sm 500 sm† 106 sm‡	11.0 sf* 10.0 sm 24.0 sm† 5.0 sm‡	7300/10 sf* 45/6 sm 158/22 sm† 107/4‡	65 +97 (H$_2$O$_2$)	

* Diesel-electric drive.
† Walter turbine drive.
‡ Silent running motors only.

Construction
Laid down as high-seas U-boats, designed by H Walter GmbH with preliminary work by the 'Glückauf' Engineering Office, as for the Type XXI. Walter-form hull similar to the Type XXII, but with the pressure hull assembled in sections because of complications arising from the lateral torpedo tubes; four watertight compartments; diving depth 135/270m.

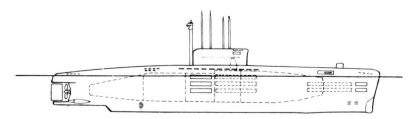

Type XXVI W (1944 design).

Propulsion

One MWM 6-cylinder 4-stroke diesel engine and one MAN 8-cylinder 4-stroke diesel generator, in compartment 2; one AEG single commutator electric motor and one SSW single commutator silent-running motor also in compartment 2; one Brückner-Kanis & Co Walter turbine with exhaust condenser in compartment 1; 1 + 1 62-cell 2 × 21 MAL 40 E batteries (5400amp/hr) in compartment 4. One 3-bladed propeller, 2.15m diameter; one rudder; one pair of hydroplanes at the stern, with large stabilisers immediately forward; one pair of swivelling hydroplanes forward. A collapsible schnorkel was fitted on the aft edge of the bridge casing.

Armament

Ten 53.3 torpedo tubes, four at the bow and three each side trained aft in the so-called 'Schnee-organ' battery - 10 torpedoes; no AA guns. Two periscopes in the control room; a retractable radio antenna and various radar (FuMO and FuMB) aerials were fitted.

Complement

Crew: 3/30.

Notes

These vessels had no conning tower, only a high casing round the tower hatch for the periscopes

and other pieces of equipment. The design was based on the Type XVII, with a tapered stern and lateral torpedo tubes (Type XVII A), then lengthened and given a new type of bridge casing as the Type XXVI; the OKM produced parallel designs as the Type XXVI A and XXVI B, and the Type XXVI E was an alternative project with more powerful electric motors.

Careers

U4501–4504: the sections for these vessels were under construction when the war came to an end; orders for the other vessels in the contract had already been cancelled.

Type XXVII and XXVII B mini U-boats

Name	Type	Builder (construction no)	Built	Cost in Marks (000s)	Displacement (t = tonnes T = tons)	Length (m)	Breadth (m)	Draught/ height (m)	Power (hp)	Revs (rpm)	Speed (kts)	Range (nm/kts)	Oil (t)	Diving time (sec)
U2111–2113, U2251–2300*	XXVII 'Hecht'	Germania (788–840)	1944		11.85 to 12.25 total	10.40 to 10.50 oa	1.30 oa	1.40/	12ehp sf and sm	1300/ 300	5.6 to 6.0 sf and sm	45–78/3 38–70/4 25–40/6	–	
U5001–5003	XXVII B 'See-hund'	Howaldt (K)	1944		14.9 sf 17.0 sm	11.90 oa 9.67 ph	1.84 oa 1.30 ph	1.74/ 2.30	60ehp sf 12ehp sm	300 sf 260 sm	7.7 sf 6.0 sm	300/7 sf 63/3 sm	0.5	2
U5004–5187, 5194–5250, 6201–6243	"	Germania (844–923, 941–1080, 1089–1188)	1944–		"	"	"	"	"	"	"	"	"	"
U5251–5750, 6253–6442	"	Schichau (E)	1944–		"	"	"	"	"	"	"	"	"	"
U5751–6170	"	Klöckner	–		"	"	"	"	"	"	"	"	"	"
U6172–6200	"	CRDA (M)	–		"	"	"	"	"	"	"	"	"	"

* Originally intended for CRDA (M) with assembly at Simmering, Graz, and Pauker, Vienna.

Construction

The Type XXVII 'Hecht' (Pike) was designed as a mini U-boat for tactical use, originally intended for attaching limpet mines to ships at anchor. The requirement to perform other tasks led to changes in the design, most of which proved unsatisfactory.

The Type XXVII BS 'Seehund' (Seal) was the last in a long line of Type XXVII B developments, with the addition of a diesel engine. It was an official 1944 design, with preliminary design work and production planning by the 'Glückauf' Engineer-

ing Office. The official type designation finally adopted for the Seehund was Type 127.

Single hull; transverse frame construction; two watertight compartments. The 'Hecht' design included no diving tanks, one regulating tank in compartment 1 and a trim weight. The 'Seehund' design included one regulating tank in compartment 1, two trim tanks in compartment 2, and one diving tank in the free-flooding forecastle; a cylindrical extension to the keel, between the torpedoes, contained the fuel oil bunker (forward),

two battery troughs (amidships) and the after diving tanks. Diving depth 30/60m (56m was the deepest dive recorded).

Propulsion

One AEG-AV 76-Eto electric torpedo motor (plus one Büssing 4-cylinder 4-stroke NAG-LD6 diesel engine, 'Seehund'); five troughs with four 32-cell 8 MAL 210 batteries (or eight troughs with six 32-cell 8 MAL 210 batteries, 'Hecht' without the mine holder; or eight troughs with six 32-cell 8 MAL 210

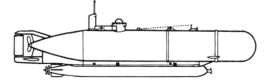

Type XXVII 'Hecht' (1944) (1/156 scale).

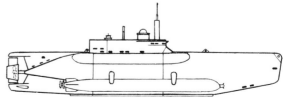

Type 127 'Seehund' (1944) (1/156 scale).

'Hecht' and 'Seehund' commissioning dates

'Hecht'					
U211	23 May 1944	U5012	24 Oct 1944	U5081	20 Jan 1945
U2112	7 Jun 1944	U5013	20 Oct 1944	U5082	1 Jan 1945
U2113	9 Jun 1944	U5014	21 Oct 1944	U5083	23 Jan 1945
U2114–2220	suspended/cancelled	U5015	23 Oct 1944	U5084	24 Jan 1945
U2251	15 Jul 1944	U5016	24 Oct 1944	U5085	25 Jan 1945
U2252	17 Jul 1944	U5017	3 Nov 1944	U5086	26 Jan 1945
U2253	19 Jul 1944	U5018	4 Nov 1944	U5087	27 Jan 1945
U2254	20 Jul 1944	U5019	15 Nov 1944	U5088	28 Jan 1945
U2255	31 Jul 1944	U5020	17 Nov 1944	U5089	30 Jan 1945
U2256	22 Jul 1944	U5021	8 Nov 1944	U5090	31 Jan 1945
U2257	28 Jul 1944	U5022	12 Nov 1944	U5091	1 Feb 1945
U2258	2 Aug 1944	U5023	28 Nov 1944	U5092	2 Feb 1945
U2259	4 Aug 1944	U5024	30 Nov 1944	U5093	3 Feb 1945
U2260	3 Aug 1944	U5025	17 Nov 1944	U5094	5 Feb 1945
U2261	4 Aug 1944	U5026	17 Nov 1944	U5095	6 Feb 1945
U2262	7 Aug 1944	U5027	11 Nov 1944	U5096	7 Feb 1945
U2263	5 Aug 1944	U5028	19 Nov 1944	U5097	8 Feb 1945
U2264	7 Aug 1944	U5029	22 Nov 1944	U5098	9 Feb 1945
U2265	8 Aug 1944	U5030	20 Nov 1944	U5099	10 Feb 1945
U2266	5 Aug 1944	U5031	17 Nov 1944	U5100	13 Feb 1945
U2267	7 Aug 1944	U5032	18 Nov 1944	U5101	14 Feb 1945
U2268	8 Aug 1944	U5033	14 Nov 1944	U5102	15 Feb 1945
U2269	9 Aug 1944	U5034	15 Nov 1944	U5103	16 Feb 1945
U2270	10 Aug 1944	U5035	17 Nov 1944	U5104	19 Feb 1945
U2271	9 Aug 1944	U5036	18 Nov 1944	U5105	20 Feb 1945
U2272	10 Aug 1944	U5037	20 Nov 1944	U5106	21 Feb 1945
U2273	11 Aug 1944	U5038	23 Nov 1944	U5107	21 Feb 1945
U2274	12 Aug 1944	U5039	24 Nov 1944	U5108	22 Feb 1945
U2275	14 Aug 1944	U5040	25 Nov 1944	U5109	22 Feb 1945
U2276	12 Aug 1944	U5041	27 Nov 1944	U5110	24 Feb 1945
U2277	14 Aug 1944	U5042	29 Nov 1944	U5111	26 Feb 1945
U2278	15 Aug 1944	U5043	30 Nov 1944	U5112	27 Feb 1945
U2279	16 Aug 1944	U5044	13 Dec 1944	U5113	28 Mar 1945
U2280	17 Aug 1944	U5045	2 Dec 1944	U5114	28 Mar 1945
U2281	15 Aug 1944	U5046	5 Dec 1944	U515	2 Mar 1945
U2282	15 Aug 1944	U5047	7 Dec 1944	U5116	5 Mar 1945
U2283	16 Aug 1944	U5048	16 Dec 1944	U5117	6 Mar 1945
U2284	16 Aug 1944	U5049	7 Dec 1944	U5118	7 Mar 1945
U2285	17 Aug 1944	U5050	8 Dec 1944	U5119–5121	cancelled
U2286	20 Aug 1944	U5051	9 Dec 1944	U5122–5147	partially completed
U2287	22 Aug 1944	U5052	12 Dec 1944	U5148–5187	on order
U2288	25 Aug 1944	U5053	13 Dec 1944	U5194–5250	on order
U2289	25 Aug 1944	U5054	14 Dec 1944	U5251	10 Oct 1944
U2290	25 Aug 1944	U5055	15 Dec 1944	U5252	3 Oct 1944
U2291	19 Aug 1944	U5056	21 Dec 1944	U5253	11 Oct 1944
U2292	23 Aug 1944	U5057	20 Dec 1944	U5254	18 Oct 1944
U2293	21 Aug 1944	U5058	21 Dec 1944	U5255	13 Oct 1944
U2294	22 Aug 1944	U5059	22 Dec 1944	U5256	21 Oct 1944
U2295	25 Aug 1944	U5060	23 Dec 1944	U5257	15 Oct 1944
U2296	24 Aug 1944	U5061	26 Dec 1944	U5258	15 Oct 1944
U2297	25 Aug 1944	U5062	28 Dec 1944	U5259	17 Oct 1944
U2298	23 Aug 1944	U5063	29 Dec 1944	U5260	19 Oct 1944
U2299	23 Aug 1944	U5064	30 Dec 1944	U5261	20 Oct 1944
U2300	25 Aug 1944	U5065	30 Dec 1944	U5262	22 Oct 1944
		U5066	3 Dec 1944	U5263	24 Oct 1944
		U5067	4 Jan 1945	U5264	25 Oct 1944
		U5068	5 Jan 1945	U5265	31 Oct 1944
'Seehund'		U5069	6 Jan 1945	U5266	31 Oct 1944
U5001	5 Sept 1944	U5070	7 Jan 1945	U5267	1 Nov 1944
U502	19 Sept 1944	U5071	9 Jan 1945	U5268	3 Nov 1944
U5003	13 Sept 1944	U5072	10 Jan 1945	U5269	3 Nov 1944
U5004	30 Oct 1944	U5073	11 Jan 1945	U5270–5352	1944
U5005	23 Oct 1944	U5074	12 Jan 1945	U5353–5394	1945
U5006	30 Oct 1944	U5075	13 Jan 1945	U5395–5450	suspended/cancelled
U5007	21 Oct 1944	U5076	15 Jan 1945	U5451–5750	on order
U5008	27 Oct 1944	U5077	16 Jan 1945	U5751–6170	suspended/cancelled
U5009	27 Oct 1944	U5078	18 Jan 1945	U6171–620	suspended/cancelled
U5010	31 Oct 1944	U5079	18 Jan 1945	U6201–6243	on order
U5011	31 Oct 1944	U5080	19 Jan 1945	U6301–6442	on order

A total of 1000 'Seehund' mini U-boats was planned from 1 June 1944.

batteries of which two were in the keel extension, 'Seehund'). One 3-bladed propeller, 0.45m diameter; one pair of hydroplanes aft; one rudder. The 'Hecht' had one pair of stabilisers forward. In place of the single rudder, the 'Seehund' was sometimes fitted with a Kort nozzle or a box rudder.

Armament

One (or two, 'Seehund') G 7 e surface-running torpedo, carried beneath the hull (or one magnetic mine carried in a mine holder, three 'Hecht' boats only - no active service). The 'Seehund' was fitted with a passive sonar array beneath the hull, with six receivers.

Handling

Both types had a limited operational range. The limpet-mine attack capability of the 'Hecht' was never tested in action, due to lack of suitable opportunities, and its range and speed, both on the surface and submerged, were too limited to permit successful torpedo attacks. The 'Seehund' was capable of surface attacks in conditions up to Beaufort 4, but had to be almost stationary for submerged attacks.

Complement

Crew: 2. Escape gear was fitted.

Notes

Both types had a fixed periscope and air circulation equipment. The 'Hecht' had a gyro compass, while the 'Seehund' had a periscope compass. Approximately fifty 'Seehunds' constructed in 1944 had a bulge amidships for an additional fuel oil bunker; their radius of action was thus increased to about 500m/7kts. These were tested, to a limited extent, in an attack on Dungeness.

Careers

At present it is not possible to give details of the individual careers of these submarines. Identifiable commissioning dates are shown in the table.

Project K and Type 227 mini U-boat projects

Name	Type	Builder (construction no)	Built	Cost in Marks (000s)	Displacement (t = tonnes T = tons)	Length (m)	Breadth (m)	Draught/ height (m)	Power (hp)	Revs (rpm)	Speed (kts)	Range (nm/kts)	Oil (t)	Diving time (sec)
Project K		Project only	–		16.4 sf	11.70 oa 9.70 ph	1.84 oa 1.40 ph	2.0/	95ehp sf 8ehp sm	567 sf 240 sm	9.5 sf 10 sm* 5.2 sm	180/9.5 sf 60/10* 34/5	0.48 +0.62 (O$_2$)	
	227 'Kreis-lauf See-hund'	Germania	1944–		17.0 sf	13.60 oa	1.68 oa 1.28 ph	1.7/	100ehp sf 80ehp sm* 25 ehp	660 sf 345 sm ,	8.0 sf 10.3 sm* 6.9 sm	340/8 sf 71/10 sm* 17/4.4 sm	0.6 +0.72 (O$_2$)	

* Closed-cycle diesel operation with O$_2$ fuel.

Construction

Designed as small submersibles for tactical use, but with an increased underwater range through use of closed-cycle diesel propulsion. Both were official designs from summer 1944, with preliminary design work and production planning for the Type 227 by the 'Glückauf' engineering office. The hull shape was based on the Seehund.

Propulsion

One MWM 6-cylinder 4-stroke GS 145 diesel engine (or one DB 6-cylinder 4-stroke OM 67/4 diesel engine as planned for the Type 227, replaced for production reasons by the Büssing NAG-LD6 Seehund diesel engine, which was less powerful) operating on the closed-cycle principle for underwater propulsion, with an O$_2$ supply; one SSW G 107m silent-running electric motor (or one AEG AW 77 electric torpedo motor, Type 227); four 7 MAL 210 battery troughs.

Armament

Two G 7 e surface-running torpedoes below the hull, those on the Project K design half-covered by saddle tanks. One fixed periscope with a periscope compass.

Complement

Crew: 2.

Notes

The Project K design carried oxygen for closed-cycle diesel oxygen operation in gas form in pressurised flasks (400atm); the Type 227 carried oxygen in liquid form in the forecastle.

Careers

U5188–5190: (Construction nos 938–940) construction started at Germaniawerft, Kiel; broken up incomplete.

U5191–5193: (Construction nos 1083–1085) order placed at Germaniawerft, Kiel; suspended.

U6244–6248: (Construction nos 1081–1082, 1086–1088) order placed at Germaniawerft, Kiel; suspended.

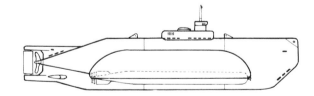

Project K (*Kurzak*) (1944) (1/156 scale).

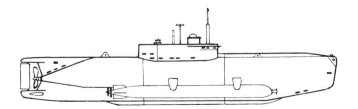

Type 227 (closed-cycle 'Seehund') (1944) (1/156 scale).

Electric 'Seehund' project

Name	Type	Builder (construction no)	Built	Cost in Marks (000s)	Displacement (t = tonnes T = tons)	Length (m)	Breadth (m)	Draught/ height (m)	Power (hp)	Revs (rpm)	Speed (kts)	Range (nm/kts)	Oil (t)	Diving time (sec)
U6251, 6252	'See-hund'*	Schichau (E)	1944–											

* 'Seehund' with battery primary drive.

Construction
At present no details are available on these vessels, which were presumably based on the 'Seehund' (Type 127).

Propulsion
One 20kW zinc-chloride battery (1000kW/hr) for primary propulsion, consisting of four battery blocks each of thirty elements with connecting ter-minals (1.26m long); these were available by the beginning of 1945.

Type XXVII F and Schwertwal 1 mini U-boats

Name	Type	Builder (construction no)	Built	Cost in Marks (000s)	Displacement (t = tonnes T = tons)	Length (m)	Breadth (m)	Draught/ height (m)	Power (hp)	Revs (rpm)	Speed (kts)	Range (nm/kts)	Oil (t)	Diving time (sec)
	XXVII F	Project only	–		9.2t sf	11.2 oa		1.0 oa 1.0 ph	200ehp sm*		22.6 sm		–	
Schwertwal 1 (SW1)	–	Walter	1944–45		11.3t sf	11.2 oa		2.4 oa 1.3 ph	500ehp sm*		25 sm	108/15 sm 27/22 sm	5 (H$_2$O$_2$)	

* Walter torpedo turbine drive.

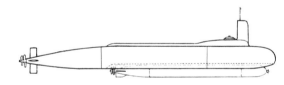

Type XXVII F (1944 design) (1/156 scale). 'Schwertwal' (1945) (1/156 scale).

Construction
Designed as mini U-boats for tactical use, with high underwater speed provided by Walter propulsion; the Type XXVII F was an official design of summer 1944, the 'Schwertwal' (Killer-whale) was designed by H Walter GmbH in 1944. Both designs featured a torpedo-shaped hull with rudder steering. Type XXVII F had a tower-like casing for the periscope and periscope compass; the 'Schwertwal' had no periscope, only a plexiglas hood for observation while on the surface and a Patin aircraft compass-autopilot on the rudder.

Propulsion
The Walter torpedo turbine with fresh water injection as used in the 'Steinbut' torpedo was intended for the Type XXVII F, and the modified Walter torpedo turbine with seawater injection, as used in the 'Steinwal' torpedo, for the 'Schwertwal'.

Armament
One surface-running G7 torpedo in a moulding beneath the hull on the Type XXVII F; two G7 'K-Butt' surface-running torpedoes beneath the hull or a 'Grimsche' towed mine on the 'Schwertwal'. Neither design was expected to exceed 22kts when carrying torpedoes.

Complement
Crew: Type XXVII F, 1; 'Schwertwal', 2.

Careers
Development of the Type XXVII F began in the autumn of 1944. Only a prototype 'Schwertwal' had been completed by the end of the war; it was scuttled in the Größer Plöner See before trials began, then later raised and broken up.

The 'Neger', 'Marder', 'Hai', 'Biber', 'Molch', 'Delphin' and 'Seeteufel' mini U-boats will be covered in a future volume.

U-boat projects (Type XXVI to Type XXXVI) 1943–1944

Type XXVI A–E U-boat projects

Name	Type	Builder (construction no)	Built	Cost in Marks (000s)	Displacement (t = tonnes T = tons)	Length (m)	Breadth (m)	Draught/ height (m)	Power (hp)	Revs (rpm)	Speed (kts)	Range (nm/kts)	Oil (t)	Diving time (sec)
–	XXVI A	Project only	–		950t sf	58.00 oa 40.20 ph	6.70 oa 5.10 ph	6.5/	2200ehp sf 100ehp sf 7500ehp sm* 1670ehp sm 75ehp sm†		15.0 sf 22.5 sm*			
–	XXVI B	”	–		c1050t sf 1124 sm	61.30 oa 43.50 ph	”	”	”		14.5 sf 21.5 sm* 13.0 sm	8000/10 sf 130/21.5 sm* 85/6	115 +83 (H$_2$O$_2$)	
–	XXVI E1	”	–		c785t sf 865t sm	60.0	5.00 oa 5.00 ph	6.4/	1400ehp sf 100ehp sf 2500ehp sm* 50ehp sm†		13.0 sf 16.5 sm*	6000/10 sf 175/6 sm	70	
–	XXVI E2	”	–		c900t sf 1000t sm	58.00 oa	6.50 oa 5.10 ph	6.5/	2200ehp sf 100ehp sf 2500ehp sm* 113ehp sm†		15.0 sf 15.8 sm*	8900/10 sf 150/6	115	

* Walter turbine drive.
† Silent-running motors only.

Construction
Alternative designs to the Type XXVI W; Types XXVI A, B and E2 were official designs, and Type XXVI E1 by Oelfken.

Propulsion
Propulsion systems were as follows:
Designs A and B: one Deutz 16-cylinder 2-stroke diesel engine and one diesel generator; one Walter turbine; one main electric motor and one silent-running electric motor; 1 + 1 62-cell 44 MAL 740 E batteries. One 3-bladed propeller.

Design E1: one MAN 6-cylinder 4-stroke M6V 40/46 unsupercharged diesel engine and one diesel generator; one SSW 2 GU 365/30 double electric motor and one BBC GCR 188 silent-running electric motor; 1 + 1 + 1 62-cell 44 MAL 740 E batteries. One 3-bladed propeller.

Design E2: one Deutz 16-cylinder 2-stroke diesel engine and one diesel generator; one SSW 2 GU 365/30 double electric motor and one SSW GV 323/28 silent-running electric motor; 1 + 1 + 1 62-cell 44 MAL 740 E batteries. One 3-bladed propeller.

Armament
Armament fits were as follows:

Designs A, B and *E2:* twelve 53.3cm torpedo tubes, six at the bow and three each side, below the CWL - 12 torpedoes. Conning tower and AA armament as per the Type XXI.

Design E1: eight 53.3cm torpedo tubes, four at the bow and four at the stern, below the CWL - 12 torpedoes. No conning tower or AA guns.

Careers

Following a decision taken by the OKM on 22 Apr 1944, no orders were ever placed. Types XXVI E1 and E2 were, however, the basis for Project XXIX.

Type XXVIII U-boat project

Name	Type	Builder (construction no)	Built	Cost in Marks (000s)	Displacement (t = tonnes T = tons)	Length (m)	Breadth (m)	Draught/ height (m)	Power (hp)	Revs (rpm)	Speed (kts)	Range (nm/kts)	Oil (t)	Diving time (sec)
–	XXVIII	Project only	–		c200t sf	32.00 oa			250ehp sm* 70ehp sm†		10.0 sm* 5.0 sm†	2000/6 sm* 250/5 sm†	–	

* Walter turbine drive.
† Silent-running motor only.

Construction

A design for a true U-boat for use in the Mediterranean, designed 1943–44. The hull form was similar to that of the Type XXIII, without the conning tower.

Propulsion

One small turbine (indirect Walter process); one

SSW GV 323/28 silent-running electric motor; batteries as per the Type XXIII. One 3-bladed propeller.

Armament

Four 53.3cm torpedo tubes at the bow, below the CWL - 4 torpedoes; no anti-aircraft armament.

Careers

The project was abandoned on 27 Mar 1944 as the indirect Walter process had not been sufficiently developed.

Type XXIX A–H U-boat projects

Construction

Design studies for medium-sized U-boats with half the machinery of the Type XXI, designed in summer 1944 (Type XXIX A–D as official designs; F, GK and H by the 'Glückauf' Engineering Office).

Propulsion

One MWM 6-cylinder 4-stroke RS 34 supercharged diesel engine (Type XXIX A–C) or one MAN 6-cylinder 4-stroke MGV 40/46 supercharged diesel engine (Type XXIX B2–D) or two MWM 6-cylinder 4-stroke RS 34 supercharged diesel engines (Type XXIX F, GK and H); one cruising diesel (F, GK and H); one MAN W 8 V diesel generator (A–C and B2–D) or one unspecified diesel generator (F, GK and H); one SSW 2 GU 365/30 double electric motor and one SSW GV 323/28 single-commutator silent-running electric motor (all designs); 1 + 1 62-cell (A and H) or 1 +

1 + 1 62-cell (B, D and F) or 1 + 1 + 1 70-cell (B2) or 1 + 1 + 1 + 1 62-cell (C and GK) 44 MAL 740 E batteries. One 3-bladed propeller. All designs featured a collapsible schnorkel; Types XXIX GK and H also had a retractable periscope schnorkel.

Armament

Eight 53.3cm torpedo tubes at the bow - 8 torpedoes (Type XXIX A–C) or twelve such tubes, eight at the bow and four at the sides - 12 torpedoes (Type XXIX D) or eight such tubes, four at the bow and four at the sides - 8 torpedoes (Type XXIX F) or twelve such tubes, six at the bow and six at the sides - 17 torpedoes (Type XXIX GK) or six such tubes at the bow - 10 torpedoes (Type XXIX H), all below the CWL. No AA guns. Detection systems included the GHG, SU, TAG, Berlin, Lessing, Athos and Siegmund systems.

Complement

Crew: 35 (Type XXIX GK); 27 (Type XXIX H).

Notes

These designs had no conning tower, only an access hatch to the bridge casing. Types XXIX A–D and H were to have pressure hulls with a circular cross-section, but it was to be figure eight shaped in cross section near the bow tubes on A–D. Types XXIX F and GK were to have pressure hulls with a figure eight shaped cross-section as for the Type XXI. Types XXIX GK and H were to have pressure hulls that were lens-shaped in cross-section.

Careers

Type XXIX B 2 was judged the most successful at a meeting of the Naval Construction Office on 29 Aug 1944. The question of issuing construction orders was, however, deferred.

Type XXIX H (1944 Project).

Name	Type	Builder (construction no)	Built	Cost in Marks (000s)	Displacement (t = tonnes T = tons)	Length (m)	Breadth (m)	Draught/ height (m)	Power (hp)	Revs (rpm)	Speed (kts)	Range (nm/kts)	Oil (t)	Diving time (sec)
–	XXIX A	Project only	–		681t sf	53.70 oa	4.80 oa 4.80 ph	5.10/	750ehp sf 265ehp sf 1400ehp sm 70ehp sm*		12.0 sf 13.8 sm 4.8 sm*	7100/10 sf 125/6 sm 215/4 sm*		
–	XXIX B	„	–		753t sf	57.50 oa	„	„	750ehp sf 265ehp sf 2100ehp sm 110ehp sm*		11.9 sf 15.4 sm 5.4 sm*	7100/10 sf 175/6 sm 305/4 sm*		
–	XXIX B2	„	–		790t sf	57.00 oa	„	5.6/ 10.3	1400ehp sf 265ehp sf 2400ehp sm 120ehp sm*		15.3 sf 16.6 sm 5.8 sm*	7100/6 sf 235/6 sm 345/4 sm*		
–	XXIX C	„	–		825t sf	61.30 oa	„	5.10/	750ehp sf 265ehp sf 2800ehp sm 140ehp sm*		11.8 sf 16.7 sm	7100/10 sf 250/6 sm 380/4 sm*		
–	XXIX D	„	–		1035t sf	66.70 oa	5.40 oa 5.40 ph	5.30/	2000ehp sf 265ehp sf 2100ehp sm 110ehp sm*		15.0 sf 14.8 sm	7100/10 sf 150/6 sm 275/4 sm*		
–	XXIX F	„	–		880t sf	57.00 oa	5.40 oa 5.40 ph 3.60	6.00/	750ehp sf 750ehp sf 2100ehp sm 110ehp sm*		13.5 sf 15.0 sm	6500/10 sf		
–	XXIX GK	„	–		c1000t sf 1100t sm	57.80 oa 43.20 ph	6.70 oa 5.40 ph 3.60	6.00/	750ehp sf 750ehp sf 2800ehp sm 140ehp sm*		12.0 sf 16.5 sm 6.0 sm*	10,000/10 sf 225/6 sm 320/4 sm*	150	
–	XXIX H	„	–		c630t sf c700t sm c860t total	52.00 oa 37.0 ph	6.40 oa 5.30 ph	4.60/	580ehp sf 580ehp sf 1400ehp sm 70ehp sm*		13.0 sf 15.5 sm 5.3 sm*	9000/10 sf 120/6 sm 225/4 sm*	89	

* Silent-running motors only.

Type XXIX K1–4 U-boat projects

Construction

Designs for true U-boats with closed-cycle diesel propulsion, similar to the Type XXIX A–D (official designs produced in the summer of 1944).

Propulsion

Two MWM 6-cylinder 4-stroke RS 34 super-charged diesel engines (K 1) or four such engines (K 2) or four Daimler-Benz 20-cylinder 4-stroke MB 501 diesel engines (K 3) or two MWM 12-cylinder 4-stroke RS 12 26/34a diesel engines, all designed for closed-cycle operation with an O_2 supply for underwater propulsion; one electric motor; one 62-cell battery. One 3-bladed propeller. All designs featured a collapsible schnorkel.

Armament

Ten 53.3cm torpedo tubes, eight at the bow and two at the stern - 18 torpedoes (K 1, 2 and 4) or eight such tubes, all at the bow - 8 torpedoes, all tubes below the CWL; no AA armament.

Name	Type	Builder (construction no)	Built	Cost in Marks (000s)	Displacement (t = tonnes T = tons)	Length (m)	Breadth (m)	Draught/ height (m)	Power (hp)	Revs (rpm)	Speed (kts)	Range (nm/kts)	Oil (t)	Diving time (sec)
–	XXI K1	Project only	–		915t sf	57.8 oa			2200ehp sf 2040ehp sm* 110ehp sm		16.7 sf 14.8 sm* 5.8 sm	7200/10 sf 694/6 sm* 69/5.8 sm		
–	XXIX K2	,,	–		1060t sf	64.5 oa			4400ehp sf 4080ehp sm* 127ehp sm		18.0 sf 18.2 sm* 5.8 sm	7200/10 sf 800/6 sm* 58/5.8 sm		
–	XXIX K3	,,	–		930t sf	51.8 oa			6000ehp sf 6000ehp sm* 127ehp sm		17.6 sf 21.5 sm* 6.1 sm	7200/10 sf 1000/6 sm	41 (O_2)	
–	XXIX K4	,,	–		c1060t sf	c64 oa			4000ehp sf 4000ehp sm* 127ehp sm			7200/10 sf		

* Closed-cycle diesel operation with O_2 fuel.

Notes

In designs K 1 and K 2 the O_2 supply was from pressurised flasks, while in K 3 and K 4 the O_2 was partly stored in liquid form. The K 3 design was produced as a study for maximising underwater speed.

Careers

These designs were produced only as studies: no construction orders were ever placed.

Type XXX and XXXI U-boat projects

Name	Type	Builder (construction no)	Built	Cost in Marks (000s)	Displacement (t = tonnes T = tons)	Length (m)	Breadth (m)	Draught/ height (m)	Power (hp)	Revs (rpm)	Speed (kts)	Range (nm/kts)	Oil (t)	Diving time (sec)
–	XXX A	Project only	–		1180t sf	68.90 oa 56.40 ph	5.40 oa 5.40 ph	6.2/	2000ehp sf 265ehp sf 2800ehp sm 140ehp sm*		14.6 sf 15.6 sm 5.6 sm*	15,500/10 sf 210/6 sm 320/4 sm*		
–	XXX B	,,	–		1170t sf	65.70 oa 48.00 ph	,,		,,		14.6 sf 15.8 sm 5.6 sm*	15,500/10 sf 215/6 sm 340/4 sm*		
–	XXXI	,,	–		1200 sf	54.00 oa 35.20 ph	6.20 oa 5.00 ph 5.00		,,		14.3 sf 16.4 sm 5.9 sm*	15,500/10 sf 245/6 sm 380/4 sm*		

* Silent-running motors only.

Construction

Designs for large U-boats similar to the Type XXI, but with half the propulsion machinery and other differences in form and armament (official designs, summer 1944).

Propulsion

One MAN 6-cylinder 4-stroke M6V 40/46 diesel engine; one MAN W 8 V diesel generator; one SSW 2 GU 365/30 double electric motor and one SSW GV 323/28 single-commutator silent-running motor; 1 + 1 + 1 + 1 62-cell 44 MAL 740 W batteries. One 3-bladed propeller. All designs featured a collapsible schnorkel abaft the bridge.

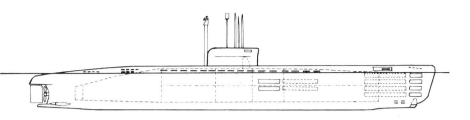

Type XXX A (1944 design).

Armament

Twelve 53.3cm torpedo tubes, eight at the bow and four at the sides - 12 torpedoes (Type XXX A) or eight such tubes, all at the bow – 16 torpedoes (Type XXX B) or twelve such tubes as for the Type XXX A - 24 torpedoes (Type XXXI), all tubes below the CWL; no AA armament.

Notes

The Type XXX A and B featured a pressure hull which was circular in cross-section for most of its length, but figure eight shaped in cross section in way of the torpedo tubes. The Type XXXI pressure hull was figure eight shaped in cross-section for its entire length, thus allowing a much shorter overall length. Neither design included a conning tower, and the bridge casing on the Type XXXI was very low.

Careers

These designs were produced as studies, and the Type XXXI was judged the best. No construction orders were placed.

Type XXXII mini U-boat project

Name	Type	Builder (construction no)	Built	Cost in Marks (000s)	Displacement (t = tonnes T = tons)	Length (m)	Breadth (m)	Draught/ height (m)	Power (hp)	Revs (rpm)	Speed (kts)	Range (nm/kts)	Oil (t)	Diving time (sec)
–	XXXII	Project only	–		c20t sf				25ehp sm					–

Construction

A design for a mini U-boat similar to the Type XXVII B, but with larger batteries and no diesel engine, designed in summer 1944.

Propulsion

One AG-AV 76 electric torpedo motor; one battery.

Armament

Two G 7 e surface-running torpedos, mounted on the hull; one extended periscope in a conning tower.

Complement

Crew: 2.

Notes

Operational endurance was four days.

Careers

No construction orders were placed for these boats.

Type XXXIII coastal U-boat project

Name	Type	Builder (construction no)	Built	Cost in Marks (000s)	Displacement (t = tonnes T = tons)	Length (m)	Breadth (m)	Draught/ height (m)	Power (hp)	Revs (rpm)	Speed (kts)	Range (nm/kts)	Oil (t)	Diving time (sec)
–	XXXIII	Project only	–		360t sf	40 oa	4.00 oa 4.00 ph	4.20/	580ehp sf 580ehp sm* 30ehp sm†		9.5 sf 11.5 sm* 3.0 sm†	1550/9.5 sf 1600/6 sm* 52/3 sm†	24 +26 (O$_2$)	

* Closed-cycle diesel operation with O$_2$ fuel.
† Silent-running motor only.

Construction

A design for a coastal U-boat with closed-cycle diesel propulsion, designed in autumn 1944. The external appearance was similar to that of the Type XXIII, but the conning tower was flatter and the armament increased. Diving depth 180m.

Propulsion

One MWM 6-cylinder 4-stroke RS 34 diesel engine, designed for closed-cycle operation with an O$_2$ supply for underwater operation; one silent-running electric motor; one 62-cell AFA MAL 570 E battery. A collapsible schnorkel was included abaft the bridge.

Armament

Four 53.3cm torpedo tubes at the bow, below the waterline - 4 torpedoes; no AA armament.

Notes

The O$_2$ supply was in liquid form.

Career

This design was produced as a study for increased underwater endurance; no construction orders were placed.

Type XXXIV coastal U-boat project

Name	Type	Builder (construction no)	Built	Cost in Marks (000s)	Displacement (t = tonnes T = tons)	Length (m)	Breadth (m)	Draught/ height (m)	Power (hp)	Revs (rpm)	Speed (kts)	Range (nm/kts)	Oil (t)	Diving time (sec)
–	XXXIV	Project only	–		90t sf	23.00 oa	2.50 oa 2.50 ph	2.6/	1500ehp sf 1500ehp sm* 16ehp sm†		12 sf 21 sm* 6 sm†	over 1000/12 sf 80/21 sm*	4 +6 (O_2)	

* Closed-cycle diesel operation with O_2 fuel.
† Silent-running motor only.

Construction
A design for a coastal U-boat with closed-cycle diesel propulsion, designed in autumn 1944. The external appearance was similar to that of the Type XXIII, but no conning tower was included. Diving depth 100m.

Propulsion
One Daimler-Benz 20-cylinder 4-stroke MB 501 diesel engine, designed for closed-cycle operation with an O_2 supply for underwater propulsion; one silent-running electric motor; seven battery troughs with 7 MAL 210 batteries, One 3-bladed propeller.

Armament
Two G 7 2 surface-running torpedoes, mounted on the hull; one collapsible periscope.

Complement
Crew: 3.

Notes
The O_2 supply was in liquid form.

Career
This design was produced as a study for high underwater speed; no construction orders were placed.

Type XXXV and XXXVI U-boat projects

Name	Type	Builder (construction no)	Built	Cost in Marks (000s)	Displacement (t = tonnes T = tons)	Length (m)	Breadth (m)	Draught/ height (m)	Power (hp)	Revs (rpm)	Speed (kts)	Range (nm/kts)	Oil (t)	Diving time (sec)
–	XXXV	Project only	–		c1000t sf	c50 oa			2000ehp sf 7500ehp sm* 175ehp sm†		22.0 sm*	7000/10 sf 160/22 sm*	65 (O_2)	
–	XXXVI	„	–		„	61.20 oa	5.40 oa 5.40 ph	6.0/ 11.2	580ehp sf 265ehp sf 7500ehp sm* 536ehp sm 71ehp sm†		22.0 sm*	7000/10 sf 110/22*		

* Walter turbine drive.
† Silent-running motor only.

Construction
Designs for true U-boats with pure oxygen Walter turbine propulsion, designed at the end of 1944. The Type XXXV was similar in appearance to the Type XXIX B2, and the Type XXXVI to the Type XXVI, but both dsigns were 5m longer to allow for the oxygen tank.

Propulsion
The Type XXXV design included one MWM 12-cylinder 4-stroke RS 12 26/34a diesel engine; one Walter turbine; one silent-running electric motor; one 62-cell 2 × 21 MAL 740 E battery and one 3-bladed propeller. The Type XXXVI propulsion machinery was the same as that of the Type XXVI W.

Armament
Eight 53.3cm torpedo tubes at the bow, below the waterline - 12 torpedoes; no anti-aircraft guns (Type XXXV). Armament for the Type XXXVI was as for the Type XXVI W.

Notes
The oxygen supply was partially in liquid form.

Career
These designs were produced as studies; no construction orders were placed.

Foreign U-boats (1939–1945)

UA (ex-Turkish)

Name	Type	Builder (construction no)	Built	Cost in Marks (000s)	Displacement (t = tonnes T = tons)	Length (m)	Breadth (m)	Draught/ height (m)	Power (hp)	Revs (rpm)	Speed (kts)	Range (nm/kts)	Oil (t)	Diving time (sec)
UA		Germania (575)	1936–39		1128t sf 1284t sm	86.65 oa	6.80 oa 4.35 ph	4.12/	4200ehp to 4600ehp sf 1300ehp sm	460 to 480 sf 285 sm	18.0 sf 8.4 sm	13100/10 sf 4900/18 sf 146/2 sm 75/4 sm	250 sf 113 sm	

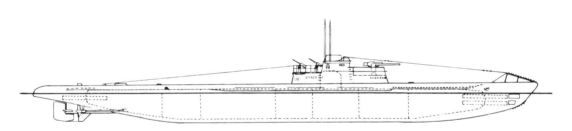

UA (ex *Batiray*) (1940).

Construction
Laid down for Turkey as the ocean-going submersible *Batiray*. Double hull; five watertight compartments; trim tanks in compartments 1 and 5; diving tanks and fuel bunkers in the outer hull; diving depth 100/200m.

Propulsion
Two Burmeister & Wain 2-stroke diesel engines (number of cylinders not known) in an engine room in the forward part of compartment 2; two BBC GGUB 721/8 double electric motors in the aft part of compartment 2; 1 + 1 62-cell AFA 28 MAD 865 batteries (11,540amp/hr) in compartment 4; diesel electric range maximum 16,400nm at 10kts. Two 3-bladed propellers, 1.92 diameter; rudder and hydroplanes as for the Type VII C.

Armament
Six 53.3cm torpedo tubes, four at the bow and two at the stern, all below the CWL - 12 torpedoes; one 10.5cm/45 gun - 185 rounds; two 2cm AA guns (2500 rounds); no mines.

Complement
Crew: 4/41.

Notes
Various alterations were made to the conning tower and the bridge.

Career
Launched 28 Mar 1939, ready for service as *Batiray* 28 Sept 1939; requisitioned on the outbreak of war and temporarily renamed *Optimist* in German service; renamed *UA* 21 Sept 1939; taken out of service in May 1944 at Neustadt, Holstein. Scuttled 2 May 1945 at the Kiel Arsenal; wreck broken up.

UB (ex-British)

Name	Type	Builder (construction no)	Built	Cost in Marks (000s)	Displacement (t = tonnes T = tons)	Length (m)	Breadth (m)	Draught/ height (m)	Power (hp)	Revs (rpm)	Speed (kts)	Range (nm/kts)	Oil (t)	Diving time (sec)
UB		Chatham	1939–39	£430.9	1770t sf 2113t sm	89.30 oa	7.74 oa 5.79 ph	5.18/	3300ehp sf 1630 ehp sm	400 sf 330 sf 272 sm	16.0 sf 14.75 sf 8.7 sm	6500/10, 4950/14.7 sf	138	
(mod)			1940											

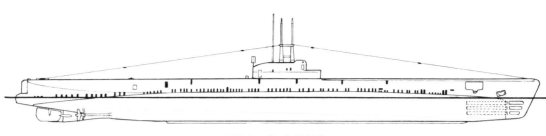

UB (ex *Seal*) (1941).

Construction

Laid down as a British ocean-going submersible of the *Porpoise* class, designed at the Admiralty, London. Double hull; six watertight compartments; the pressure hull had an elliptical cross-section amidships; diving depth 60/120m.

Propulsion

Two 4-stroke diesel engines with air injection (number of cylinders not known) in an engine room in compartment 2; two double-armature electric motors; 1 + 1 + 1 112-cell MI 33 batteries (4560amp/hr with a 10hr discharge); diesel-electric range 7600nm at 10kts. Two 3-bladed propellers,

diameter unknown; one pair of hydroplanes forward and one pair aft; one rudder.

Armament

Six 53.3cm torpedo tubes at the bow, below the waterline - 12 torpedoes. The original armament comprised one 10.2cm/40 gun and 120 mines. The latter were mounted on double rails amidships, forward, abeam and aft of the conning tower, and were launched clear of the stern.

Complement

Crew: 4/43 (55 in total in British service).

Notes

Minor alterations only were made to the vessel's appearance.

Career

Launched as the British minelaying submarine *Seal* 27 Sept 1938, commissioned at Chatham, 24 May 1939; captured by a German aircraft and taken as a prize after being damaged by mines and suffering engine failure 4 May 1940 east of Laesoe, in position 57° 12′N, 10° 44′E; commissioned as *UB* 30 Nov 1940 for training and trials purposes; taken out of service 31 Jul 1941 and cannibalised; scuttled 3 May 1945 in Heikendorf Bay, in position 54° 22′N, 10° 11′E; wreck broken up.

UC1 class (ex-Norwegian)

Name	Type	Builder (construction no)	Built	Cost in Marks (000s)	Displacement (t = tonnes T = tons)	Length (m)	Breadth (m)	Draught/ height (m)	Power (hp)	Revs (rpm)	Speed (kts)	Range (nm/kts)	Oil (t)	Diving time (sec)
UC1, 2		Hovedwerft (116, 117)	1914–29 and 1915–30		427t sf 554t sm	51.00 oa	5.34 oa c3.70 ph	3.50/	900ehp sf 710ehp sm	425 sf 375 sm	14.5 sf 10.5 sm		19.0 max	

Construction

Laid down as 'Holland' type submersibles by the Electric Boat Co of the USA. Single hull with saddle tanks; four watertight compartments; diving depth approximately 50m.

Propulsion

Two Sulzer-Horten 6-cylinder 2-stroke diesel engines; two General Electric Co motor-dynamos; one 140-element 19 MA 780/5 battery (4500amp/hr). Two 3-bladed propellers, 1.42m diameter; one rudder.

Armament

Four 45cm torpedo tubes two at the bow and two at the stern, below the CWL - 6 torpedoes.

Complement

Crew: 3/22.

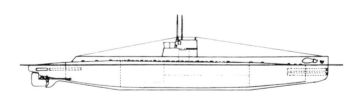

UC1 (ex *B5*) (1941), *UC2* (ex *B6*).

Careers

UC1: launched as the Norwegian submarine *B 5* 17 Jun 1929; commissioned 1 Oct 1929; taken as a German prize at Kristiansand, 20 Nov 1940; found to be unsuitable for reserve training use; broken up in 1942.

UC2: launched as the Norwegian submarine *B 6* 24

Sept 1929; commissioned 1 May 1930; taken as a German prize at Florö, 20 Nov 1940; used for training; taken out of service at Bergen in October 1944. Sunk by sabotage or bombs; raised and broken up in 1945.

The U-number *UC3* is given in some sources as the designation for the Norwegian submarine *A 3*, but this seems highly unlikly.

UD1 (ex-Dutch)

Construction

Laid down as a 'Holland' type submersible by the Electric Boat Co of the USA, designed 1913–14 as the British H-class. Single hull; four watertight compartments; diving depth approximately 50m.

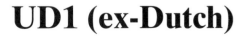

UD1 (ex *O 8*) (1941).

Name	Type	Builder (construction no)	Built	Cost in Marks (000s)	Displacement (t = tonnes T = tons)	Length (m)	Breadth (m)	Draught/ height (m)	Power (hp)	Revs (rpm)	Speed (kts)	Range (nm/kts)	Oil (t)	Diving time (sec)
UD1		Vickers C	1914–16		359t sf 429t sm	46.20 oa 44.68 ph	4.86 oa c4.65 ph	3.87/	480ehp sf 320ehp sm	375 sf 8.5 sm	11.5 sf 8.5 sm	1350/12 sf	19.8 max	
(mod)			1940											

Propulsion

Two Nelseco (New London Ship and Engine Co, Groton, Connecticut) 8-cylinder 4-stroke Sulzer diesel engines; two General Electric Co motor-dynamos; one 60-cell 44 MAL 740 W battery. Two 3-bladed propellers, 1.395m diameter; one pair of hydroplanes forward above the CWL and one pair aft below the CWL; one rudder.

Armament

Four 45cm torpedo tubes at the bow, below the CWL - 8 torpedoes.

Complement

Crew: 3/22.

Career

Launched as the British submarine *H 6* in August 1915; in service in 1915; interned after running aground at Schiermonnikoog, 18 Jan 1916, and subsequently purchased by the Netherlands; became the Dutch submarine *O 8*; taken as a German prize at Den Helder 14 May 1940 and commissioned as *UD1* 21 Nov 1940; taken out of service at Kiel 23 Nov 1943; scuttled at Kiel 3 May 1945; wreck broken up.

UD2 (ex-Dutch)

Name	Type	Builder (construction no)	Built	Cost in Marks (000s)	Displacement (t = tonnes T = tons)	Length (m)	Breadth (m)	Draught/ height (m)	Power (hp)	Revs (rpm)	Speed (kts)	Range (nm/kts)	Oil (t)	Diving time (sec)
UD2		De Schelde (186)	1929–31		555t sf 715t sm	60.50 oa	5.38 oa c3.85 ph	3.55/	1800ehp sf 600ehp sm	450 sf 290 sm	15.0 sf 8.0 sm	3500/10 sf 26/8 sm	93.0/ 22.6	
(mod)		Wilton	1943											

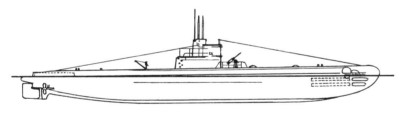

UD2 (ex *O 12*) (1941).

Construction

Laid down as a submersible of the *O 12–15* class for use in European waters, designed by the Royal Dutch Navy, 1928–29. Double hull; six watertight compartments; diving depth 80m.

Propulsion

Two Sulzer–de Schelde 6-cylinder 4-stroke diesel engines; two W Schmitt double-armature electric motors; 1 + 1 60-cell 28 MAD 860 batteries (8000amp/hr). Two 3-bladed propellers, 1.60m diameter; hydroplanes as for *UD1*; one rudder.

Armament

Five 53.3cm torpedo tubes, four at the bow and one at the stern, all below the CWL - 10 torpedoes; initially two 4cm AA guns (600 rounds) in retractable mounts on the conning tower [one 2cm AA gun - 1000 rounds - from 1941]. Two periscopes.

Handling

For technical reasons this vessel was not suitable for front line operations.

Complement

Crew: 3/31.

Notes

[The conning tower was modified in accordance with German standards.]

Career

Launched as the Dutch submarine *O 12* 8 Nov 1930; in service 20 Jul 1931; scuttled at Den Helder 14 May 1940; raised and taken as a German prize; commissioned as *UD2* 28 Jan 1941; taken out of service at Kiel 6 Jul 1944; scuttled at Kiel 3 May 1945; wreck broken up.

UD3 class (ex-Dutch)

Construction

Laid down as submersibles of the *O 21–27* class (improved *O 19* class) for operation in European waters, designed by the Royal Dutch Navy in 1937. Double hull; six watertight compartments; diving depth 100m.

Propulsion

Two Sulzer–de Schelde 7-cylinder 2-stroke diesel engines with Buchi superchargers two W Schmitt double-armature G 2 74/79 electric motors; one 192-cell 26 POR 730 battery (6900amp/hr); diesel-electric range 7700nm at 10kts. Two 3-bladed pro-

pellers, 1.88m diameter; rudder and hydroplanes as for *UD2*.

Armament

Eight 53.3cm torpedo tubes, four at the bow and two at the stern, all below the CWL, and two deck

Name	Type	Builder (construction no)	Built	Cost in Marks (000s)	Displacement (t = tonnes T = tons)	Length (m)	Breadth (m)	Draught/ height (m)	Power (hp)	Revs (rpm)	Speed (kts)	Range (nm/kts)	Oil (t)	Diving time (sec)
UD3		Wilton (667)	1938–41		949t sf 1054t sm 1372t total	77.53 oa	6.55 oa 4.25 ph	3.90/ –	5300ehp to 580ehp sf 1000ehp sm	430 to 450 sf 240 sm	19.3 to 20.3 sf 8.0 sm	7100/10 sf 2500/19 sf	137.0/ 45.3	
UD4, 5		Rotterdam DD (209, 210)	"		"	"	"	"	"	"	"	"	"	

mounted tubes, above the CWL - 14 torpedos; initially designed to carry 40 mines; the Dutch design included one 8.8cm/45 gun, two 4cm AA guns and two periscopes [in German service, UD3 and UD5 were equipped with one 8.8cm/45 gun - 125 rounds - and two 2cm AA guns - 2000 rounds - and UD4 with two 2cm AA guns - 2000 rounds - only; all were fitted with a schnorkel.

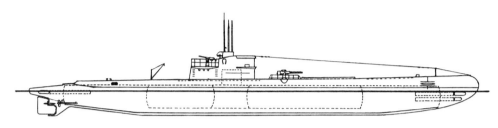

UD3–5 (ex O 25–27) (1943).

Complement
Crew: 4/41.

Notes
[The conning tower was modified in accordance with German standards.]

Careers
UD3: launched 1 May 1940 as the Dutch submarine (*Onderzeeboot*) *O 25*, and scuttled at the dockyard; taken as a German prize 14 May 1940; raised in June 1940; commissioned as *UD3* 8 Jun

1941; in service from 1 Mar 1942; taken out of service at Kiel 13 Oct 1944 after suffering bomb damage; broken up.

UD4: built as the Dutch submarine *O 26* and taken as a German prize at the dockyard in Rotterdam 14 May 1940; launched 23 May 1940; commissioned as *UD4* 28 Jan 1941. Scuttled 3 May 1945 at the Kiel Arsenal; wreck broken up.

UD5: built as the Dutch submarine *O 27* and taken as a German prize at the dockyard in Rotterdam 14 May 1940; launched 26 Sept 1941; commissioned as *UD5* 30 Jan 1942; transferred from Bergen to UK in May 1945; returned from Dundee to the Netherlands 13 Jul 1945; recommissioned as the Dutch submarine *O 27*; stricken 14 Nov 1959; broken up in 1961.

UF1 class (ex-French)

Name	Type	Builder (construction no)	Built	Cost in Marks (000s)	Displacement (t = tonnes T = tons)	Length (m)	Breadth (m)	Draught/ height (m)	Power (hp)	Revs (rpm)	Speed (kts)	Range (nm/kts)	Oil (t)	Diving time (sec)
UF1		Worms	1937		818t sf 928t sm 1078t total	73.50 oa 68.15 ph	6.50 oa 4.45 ph	4.57/ –	300ehp sf 1400ehp sm	475 sf 325 sm	15.5 sf 10.0 sm	2250/15 sf 80/5 sm	101	
UF2		"	1937–42		"	"	"	"	"	"	"	"	"	
UF3		Dubigeon	1938–		"	"	"	"	"	"	"	"	"	

Construction
Laid down as French ocean-going submersibles of the improved *Aurore* class, designed by Fuzier and Roquebert, 1937–38. Double hull; six watertight compartments; diving depth 100m.

Propulsion
Two Schneider (Le Creusot) or Sulzer 6-cylinder 2-stroke supercharged diesel engines in compartment 3; two Schneider Westinghouse double-armature electric motors 1 + 1 97-cell French 'D'-type batteries. Two 3-bladed propellers, 1.42m diameter; one pair of hydroplanes forward and one pair aft; one rudder.

Armament
Nine 55.0cm torpedo tubes, four at the bow and

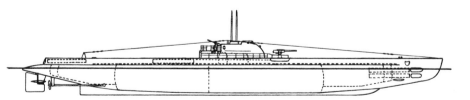

UF2 (ex La Favorite) (1942), UF1, 3.

two at the stern, all below the CWL, and three trainable tubes on the deck, above the CWL - number of torpedoes unknown; one 2cm AA gun - 2000 rounds. Two periscopes.

Complement
Crew: 3/37.

Careers

UF1: under construction as the French submarine *L'Africaine* when taken as a German prize at the dockyard in June 1940; commissioned as *UF1* 13 May 1941; not completed during the German occupation of France; launched 7 Dec 1946; in service as the French submarine *L'Africaine* from October 1949; taken out of service in 1961; stricken 28 Feb 1963 as *Q 334*.

UF2: launched as the French submarine *La Favorite* in September 1938; taken as a German prize at the dockyard in June 1940; commissioned as *UF2* 13 May 1941; completed 5 Nov 1942; taken out of service at Gotenhafen 5 Jul 1944; scuttled at Gotenhafen in 1945.

UF3: under construction as the French submarine *L'Astrée* when taken as a German prize at the dockyard in June 1940; launched in 1940; commissioned as *UF3* 13 May 1941 but never operational; taken back to the building yard in 1946 and re-launched 3 May 1946; in service as the French submarine *L'Astrée* from April 1949; taken out of service in 1962; stricken 27 Nov 1965 as *Q 404*; broken up.

UIT1 class (ex-Italian)

Name	Type	Builder (construction no)	Built	Cost in Marks (000s)	Displacement (t = tonnes T = tons)	Length (m)	Breadth (m)	Draught/ height (m)	Power (hp)	Revs (rpm)	Speed (kts)	Range (nm/kts)	Oil (t)	Diving time (sec)
UIT1–3		OTO (M)	1943–		1300t sf 2220t sm 2616t total	86.50 oa 70.70 ph	7.86 oa 6.28 ph	5.34/ 11.5	2600ehp sf 900ehp sm	400 sf	14.0 sf 6.5 sm	12,000/9 sf 90/4 sm	(610 max)	
UIT4–6		CRDA (M)	1943–		"	"	"	"	"	"	"	"	"	

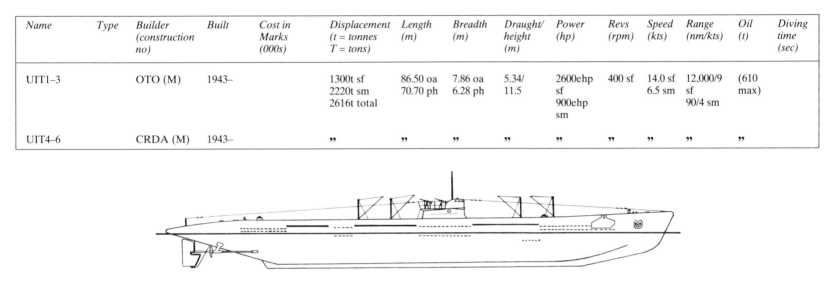

UIT1–6 (ex R class) (1943).

Construction

Laid down as large Italian ocean-going freighter submersibles (*sommergibili trasporti oceanici*) of the *Romolo* class, designed in 1941–42. Double hull; thirteen watertight compartments; diving depth 100m.

Propulsion

Two Tosi 4-stroke diesel engines (number of cylinders unknown); two Marelli electric motor-dynamos; four 42-cell batteries. Two 3-bladed propellers, 1.85m diameter.

Armament

Three 2cm AA guns. Transport of up to 600cu m of freight was possible in cargo holds in compartments 1–6 forward and aft of the control room; each hold had a 1.4m diameter hatch.

Complement

Crew while in Italian service: 7/56.

Careers

Construction of these vessels was to be continued, under German orders, after the surrender of Italy on 8 Sept 1943. However, none was actually completed.

UIT1: launched 12 Jul 1943; scuttled at the East Mole, La Spezia, 9 Sept 1943; raised under German orders and transferred to Genoa; fitting out commenced 13 Sept 1944. Sunk 4 Oct 1944 at Genoa, by British bombs; wreck broken up in 1946.

UIT2: launched 6 Aug 1943; taken over by Germany 9 Sept 1943; fitting out commenced 13 Sept 1944. Sunk 24 Apr 1945 at Genoa; raised in 1946; stricken in 1947; used as floating oil tank *GR 522*.

UIT3: launched 29 Sept 1943; completed under German orders 9 Sept 1943; scuttled near the East Mole, La Spezia, 24 Apr 1945; raised in 1946; stricken 27 Mar 1947; used as floating oil tank *GR 523*.

UIT4: launched 21 Oct 1943; sunk 25 May 1944 at Monfalcone, by British bombs; raised 31 May 1946; broken up in 1948.

UIT5: launched 28 Dec 1943; sunk 20 Apr 1944 at Monfalcone, by British bombs; raised 3 Jun 1946; broken up in 1948.

UIT6: launched 27 Feb 1944; fitted out 13 Sept 1944; sunk 16 Mar 1945 at Monfalcone, by British bombs; raised in 1946; broken up in 1948.

UIT7 class (ex-Italian)

Construction

Laid down as Italian medium cruiser submersibles (*sommergibili di media crociera*) of the *Tritone* class, second and first groups, designed by Cantieri Riuniti del Adriatico in 1941. Double hull; five watertight compartments; diving depth 130m.

Propulsion

Two Fiat 6-cylinder 4-stroke diesel engines; two Cantieri Riuniti del Adriatico electric motor dynamos; Tudor Ironclad-SGIAE, Melzo batteries (10,000amp/hr). Two 4-bladed propellers, 1.28m diameter.

Armament

Six 53.3cm torpedo tubes, four at the bow and two at the stern, all below the CWL - 12 torpedoes; one 10cm/47 gun; two to four 2cm or lighter AA guns. In German hands, these vessels were intended for use as freight transporters (tonnage not known), and were to have no armament other than two AA guns. Two periscopes.

Complement

Crew (while in Italian service): 5/44

Notes

These vessels were shorter and broader than the German Type VIIC U-boats.

Career

Construction of these vessels was continued, under German orders, after the surrender of Italy on 8 Sept 1943.

Name	Type	Builder (construction no)	Built	Cost in Marks (000s)	Displacement (t = tonnes T = tons)	Length (m)	Breadth (m)	Draught/ height (m)	Power (hp)	Revs (rpm)	Speed (kts)	Range (nm/kts)	Oil (t)	Diving time (sec)
UIT7–14		CRDA (M)	1943–		928t sf 1131t sm	64.19 oa	6.98 oa 4.32 ph	4.93/ 10.7	2400ehp sf 800ehp sm	450 sf	16.0 sf 8.0 sm	5400/8 sf 80/4 sm	82 max	
UIT15, 16, 20		OTO (M)	1942–43		905t sf 1070t sm	63.15 oa	6.98 oa 4.38 ph	4.87/10.7	,,	,,	,,	,,	,,	
UIT19		CRDA (M)	1942–43		,,	,,	,,	,,	,,	,,	,,	,,	,,	

UIT7 (ex Bario): launched 23 Jan 1944; sunk 16 Mar 1945 at the dockyard by British bombs; construction recommenced; scuttled on 1 May 1945. Raised in 1945; recommissioned as the Italian submarine *Bario* in 1946; modernised, etc, 1957–59; relaunched 21 Jun 1959; renamed *Pietro Calvi* 16 Dec 1961.

UIT8 (ex Litio): launched 19 Feb 1944; sunk 16 Mar 1945 at the dockyard by British bombs; construction recommenced; scuttled 1 May 1945.

UIT9 (ex Sodio): launched 16 Mar 1944; sunk 16 Mar 1945 at the dockyard by British bombs; construction recommenced; scuttled 1 May 1945.

UIT10 (ex Potassio): launched 22 Nov 1943; scuttled incomplete 1 May 1945 at Monfalcone.

UIT11 (ex Rame): launched 4 Nov 1943; scuttled incomplete 1 May 1945 at Monfalcone.

UIT12 (ex Ferro): launched 22 Nov 1943; scuttled incomplete 1 May 1945 at Monfalcone.

UIT13 (ex Piombo): launched 4 Nov 1943; scuttled incomplete 1 May 1945 at Monfalcone.

UIT14 (ex Zinco): launched 4 Nov 1943; scuttled incomplete 1 May 1945 at Monfalcone.

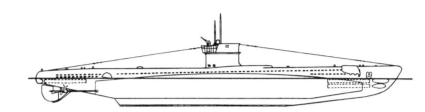

UIT7–16, 19, 20 (ex Tritone class) (1943).

UIT15 (ex Sparide): launched 21 Feb 1943; commissioned 7 Aug 1943; scuttled 9 Sept 1943 at La Spezia. Raised; repairs commenced under German orders 18 Mar 1944. Sunk 6 Sept 1944 at Genoa by British bombs; raised in March 1947 and broken up.

UIT16 (ex Murena): launched 11 Apr 1943, commissioned 25 Aug 1943; scuttled 9 Sept 1943 at La Spezia. Raised; repairs commenced under German orders 18 Mar 1944. Sunk 4 Sept 1944 at Genoa by British bombs; raised in March 1947 and broken up.

UIT19 (ex Nautilo): launched 20 Mar 1943, commissioned 26 Jul 1943; taken over by German forces 9 Sept 1943. Sunk 9 Jan 1944 at Pola, by British bombs; raised in 1944; wreck taken as a prize by Yugoslavia; repaired in 1949; commissioned as the Yugoslav submarine *Sava*; taken out of service in 1971.

UIT20 (ex Grongo): launched 6 May 1943, commissioned in 1943; scuttled 9 Sept 1943. Raised; taken over by German forces; repairs commenced 18 Mar 1944. Sunk 4 Sept 1944 at Genoa, by British bombs.

UIT17 class (ex-Italian)

Name	Type	Builder (construction no)	Built	Cost in Marks (000s)	Displacement (t = tonnes T = tons)	Length (m)	Breadth (m)	Draught/ height (m)	Power (hp)	Revs (rpm)	Speed (kts)	Range (nm/kts)	Oil (t)	Diving time (sec)
UIT17, 18		CRDA (M)	1943–45		92t sf 114t sm	32.95 oa	2.89 oa 2.55 ph	2.77/ 5.16	660ehp sf 120ehp sm		14.0 sf 6.0 sm	2000/9 sf 70/4 sm		

Construction
Laid down as small submersibles of the Italian *CM 1* class with planned increase in size, Bernardis-type designs 'con doppio fondi resistenti interni'. Single hull; probably three watertight compartments. The lens-shaped diving and regulating tanks were mounted amidships on the pressurized outer casing.

Propulsion
Two Fiat Spa diesel engines; two Cantieri Riuniti del Adriatico electric motors; details of the batteries unknown. Two 3-bladed propellers, 0.98m diameter; two pairs of hydroplanes, below the waterline; one rudder.

UIT17, 18 (ex CM 1, 2) (1945).

Armament
Two 54cm torpedo tubes at the bow angled diagonally across one another - two torpedoes; one 45cm torpedo tube at the stern - 1 torpedo; two machine guns.

Complement
Crew: 2/6.

Careers
UIT17 (ex CM 1): launched 5 Sept 1943; taken over by German forces 8 Sept 1943; commissioned 4 Jan 1945; captured by Italian partisans in April 1945; returned to the Italian navy in ports under allied occupation; disarmed; stricken 1 Feb 1948.

UIT18 (ex CM 2): launched in February 1944; taken over by German Forces 4 Jan 1945; bombed while still at the dockyard 25 May 1944; later scuttled at Monfalcone. Raised in October 1950 and parts of the vessel displayed in the Musea Navale, Trieste.

UIT21 (ex-Italian)

Name	Type	Builder (construction no)	Built	Cost in Marks (000s)	Displacement (t = tonnes T = tons)	Length (m)	Breadth (m)	Draught/ height (m)	Power (hp)	Revs (rpm)	Speed (kts)	Range (nm/kts)	Oil (t)	Diving time (sec)
UIT21		OTO (M)	1934–36		1550t sf 2060t sm	84.30 oa	7.71 oa 5.55 ph	5.21/ 12.9	4400ehp sf 1800ehp sm	380 sf 256 sm	17.1 sf 7.9 sm	11400/8 sf 80/4 sm 120/3 sm	248.5 max	

Construction

Laid down as an Italian ocean-going submersible (*sommergibile oceanice*) of the *Pietro Calvi* class, designed by Odro-Terni-Orlando in 1933–34. Double hull; six watertight compartments; diving depth 100/200m.

Propulsion

Two Fiat 8-cylinder 4-stroke diesel engines; two San Giorgio electric motor-dynamos; one battery manufactured by Cantonodo-Marelli, Milan (20,000amp/hr). Two 4-bladed propellers, 1.86m diameter.

Armament

Eight 53.3cm torpedo tubes, four at the bow and four at the stern, all below the CWL - 16 torpedoes; two 12cm/45 guns; four machine guns.

Complement

Crew (in Italian service): 7/65.

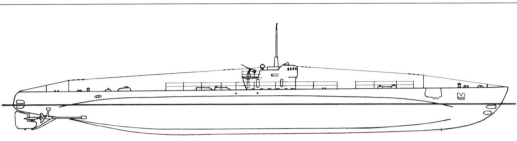

UIT21 (ex Giuseppe Finzi) (1943).

Career

Launched as the Italian *Giuseppe Finzi* 29 Jun 1935, commissioned 8 Jun 1936; taken over by German Forces while at Bordeaux 9 Sept 1943; taken out of service, then scuttled 25 Aug 1944.

UIT22–25 (ex-Italian)

Name	Type	Builder (construction no)	Built	Cost in Marks (000s)	Displacement (t = tonnes T = tons)	Length (m)	Breadth (m)	Draught/ height (m)	Power (hp)	Revs (rpm)	Speed (kts)	Range (nm/kts)	Oil (t)	Diving time (sec)
UIT22		Tosi	1938–39		1166t sf 1484t sm	76.10 oa	7.12 oa 5.25 ph	4.55/ 13.1	3500ehp sf 1400ehp sm	400 sf	17.7 sf 8.5 sm	13,000/8 sf 108/4 sm	134.5 max	
UIT23		,,	1938–40		,,	,,	,,	,,	,,		,,	,,	,,	
UIT24		OTO (M)	1938–39		1060t sf 1313t sm	73.10 oa	8.15 oa 6.00 ph	5.12/ 12.6	3000ehp sf 1300ehp sm	450 sf	17.4 sf 8.0 sm	9500/8 sf 80/4 sm	c108 max	
UIT25		,,	1938–40		1191t sf 1489t sm	76.04 oa	7.91 oa 6.38 ph	4.72/ 11.95	3600ehp sf 1500ehp sm	450 sf	18.0 sf 8.0 sm	10500/8 sf 110/3 sm	117.5 max	

Construction

Laid down as Italian ocean-going submersibles (*sommergibili oceanici*) of the *Console Generale Liózzi* and *Marcello/Marconi* classes, designed in 1937–38 by Carallini, Odero-Terni-Orlando and Bernardis. Six watertight compartments; diving depth 100m.

Propulsion

UIT22 and *23*: two Tosi 6-cylinder 4-stroke diesel engines; two Ansaldo motor-dynamos; one Tudor Ironclad-SGIAE (Melzo) battery (9000amp/hr). Two 4-bladed propellers, 1.86m diameter.

UIT24: two Fiat 8-cylinder 4-stroke diesel engines; two Cantiere Riuniti del Adriatico motor-dynamos; one Catanodo-Marelli (Milan) battery (7375 amp/hr). Two 4-bladed propellers, 1.20m diameter.

UIT25: two Cantieri Riuniti del Adriatico 6-cylinder 4-stroke diesel engines; two Catanodo-Marelli motor-dynamos; one Deutsche Kriegsmarine (Hensemberger) battery (7375amp/ hr). Two 3-bladed propellers.

Armament

Eight 53.3cm torpedo tubes, four at the bow and four at the stern, all below the CWL - 12 torpedoes); one 10cm/45 gun; four twin 1.32cm AA guns.

Complement

Crew (Italian): 7/50.

Notes

Various modifications were made to the conning towers. No torpedoes or guns were shipped when these submarines were used as freight transporters, and only one periscope was fitted.

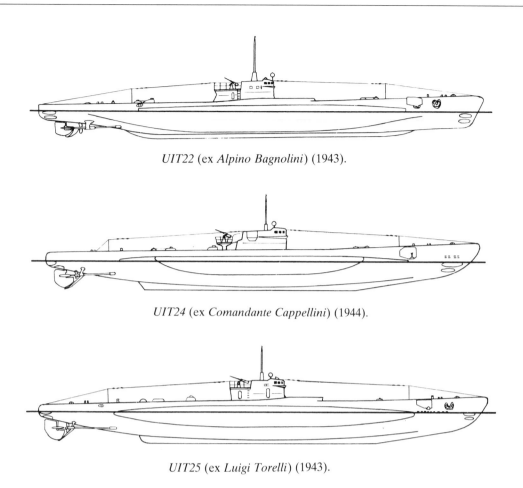

UIT22 (ex *Alpino Bagnolini*) (1943).

UIT24 (ex *Comandante Cappellini*) (1944).

UIT25 (ex *Luigi Torelli*) (1943).

Careers

UIT22: launched as the Italian *Alpino Bagnolini* 28 Oct 1939; commissioned 22 Dec 1939; taken over by German forces at Bordeaux and commis-

sioned as *UIT22* 10 Sept 1943. Sunk 11 Mar 1944 south of the Cape of Good Hope, in position 41° 28′N, 17° 40′E, by a South African bomb; 43 dead.

UIT23: launched as the Italian *Reginaldo Giuliani*

13 Mar 1939; commissioned 3 Feb 1940; taken over by Germany at Singapore and commissioned as *UIT23* 10 Sept 1943. Sunk 14 Feb 1944 in the Straits of Malacca, in position 04° 27′N, 100° 11′E, by torpedoes from the British submarine *Tallyho*; 26 dead.

UIT24: launched as the Italian *Comandante Capellini* 14 May 1939; commissioned 23 Sept 1939; taken over by Germany at Sabang and commissioned as *UIT24* 10 Sept 1943; taken over by Japan at Kobe and recommissioned as *I504* 10 May 1945; in Kobe at the time of the Japanese surrender, 2 Sept 1945; scuttled at Kii Suido 16 Apr 1946 by the US Navy.

All Italian submarine types, apart from *UIT17* and *18*, had one rudder and four hydroplanes (one pair forward, one pair aft), which could be folded upwards together with the hydroplane guards. The main differences between Italian and German submarines were as follows:

Bernardis-type submarines had a pressurised hull, which was only 3.00 to 3.25m in diameter amidships, near the pressurised conning tower. Here unpressurised lens-shaped tanks were positioned above the diving and regulating tanks, which tapered sharply towards the ends of the vessel. The submarine was thus double-hulled amidships, but single-hulled at the bow and stern.

Capellin-type submarines were similar to the German double-hulled vessels. Occasionally the unpressurised tank hull was constructed with such sharp angles (see *R 1–6*) that it formed a bilge keel.

Submarines constructed at Cantieri Riuniti del Adriatico had a sealed tank hull below the pressure hull, following its contours. As with German U-boats, the superstructure formed the second hull on the upper part of the vessel.

Comparison of the weight distribution and construction hours of various Kriegsmarine U-boats

Weights (%)	II B	VII C	IX C	XIV	XXI	XXIII	XVII B	XXVI
Hull	44.7	41.5	36.1	33.6	40.2	40.8	35.6	42.6
Machinery	29.5	28.3	26.9	16.1	30.0	36.0	21.8	20.9
Armament	8.1	7.5	7.8	1.3	4.7	6.3	3.4	6.4
Fuel	7.5	14.7	17.9	38.7	14.9	8.2	6.8 oil	7.4 oil
							16.6 H_2O_2	12.4 H_2O_2
Other weights	5.0	3.9	4.0	5.6	3.6	4.1	6.2	7.2
Effective ballast	5.2	4.1	7.3	4.7	6.6	4.6	9.6	3.1
Total weight (t)	291	761	1120	1763	1621	228	316	869
*Surface stability**	0.30	0.43	0.57	0.74	0.35	0.19	0.25	0.21
Submerged stability†	0.31	0.32	0.23	0.32	0.40	0.33	0.33	0.31
Construction hours 1943–44‡		(B & V)	(Weser)	(Germania)	(B & V)	(DWA)	(B & V)	(B & V)
Steel manufacturing		35,000	40,000	–	80,000	20,000	–	
Ship construction		147,000	200,500	400,000	252,000	42,000	115,000	180,000
Machinery construction		107,000	141,300	164,000		34,100	85,000	
Total hours		289,000	381,800	564,000	332,500	96,100	200,000	

* Metacentric height in metres.
† The distance between the centre of buoyancy and the centre of gravity in metres.
‡ Excluding time expended on the production of the main motors and Walker installations, and unproductive (office) work. The last amounted to approximately 26.3 percent of the time taken to build the Type VII C at B & V and 30.3 percent of the time taken to build the Type IX C at Weser.

Minesweepers 1914–1918

M 1 class

Name	Builder (construction no)	Built	Cost in Marks (000s)	Displacement (t = tonnes T = tons)	Length (m)	Breadth (m)	Draught (m)	Power (hp)	Revs (rpm)	Speed (kts)	Range (nm/kts)	Coal (t)	Oil (t)
M 1–6 (M1 mod)	Seebeck (359–364)	1914–15	515	456t max 425t des 466t max 435t des	55.10 oa 53.50 cwl 56.50 oa	7.30	2.00	1400ihp des	220 des	16.3 des	1680/14 1350/16	100 +12	—
M 7–12, 18–20	Neptun (348–356)	1914–15	515 to 570	476t max 450t des	56.40 oa 54.80 cwl	7.30	2.00	1600ihp des	220 des	16.2 des	1680/14 1350/16	100 +12	—
M 13, 14	Nordsee (63, 64)	1914–16	,,	,,	,,	,,	,,	,,	,,	,,	,,	,,	—
M 15–17	Seebeck (365–367)	1915–16	,,	,,	,,	,,	,,	,,	,,	,,	,,	,,	—
M 21, 22	Frerichs	1915	,,	,,	,,	,,	,,	,,	,,	,,	,,	,,	—
M 23–26	Tecklenborg (279–282)	1915–16	,,	,, .	,,	,,	,,	,,	,,	,,	,,	,,	—
M 27–30	Neptun (363–366)	1915–16	725 to 735	507t max* 480t des	58.41 oa 56.10 cwl	7.30	2.25	1800ihp des	230 des	16.5 des	2000/14	115 +30	—
M 31–34	Seebeck (381–384)	,,	,,	,,	,,	,,	,,	,,	,,	,,	,,	,,	—
M 35–38	Tecklenborg (279–282)	,,	,,	,,	,,	,,	,,	,,	,,	,,	,,	,,	—
M 39–42	Vulkan (601–604)	,,	,,	,,	,,	,,	,,	,,	,,	,,	,,	,,	—
M 43, 44	Atlas (141, 142)	,,	,,	,,	,,	,,	,,	,,	,,	,,	,,	,,	—
M 45–49	Neptun (367–371)	1916	725	513t max 486t des	58.30 oa 56.00 cwl	7.33	2.25	1800ihp des	240 des	16.3 des	2000/14	115 +30	—
M 54–56	Vulkan (605–607)	,,	,,	,,	,,	,,	,,	,,	,,	,,	,,	,,	—
M 50–53 M 50 mod as *Brommy*	Seebeck (385–388)	1916 1936–37	725 —	503t max 476t des 497t des	58.20 oa 55.00 cwl 58.38 oa 57.30 cwl	7.30 8.01	2.25 2.25	1890ihp des 1440ehp des		16.5 des 14.0	2000/14	115 +30 —	—
M 57–62	Seebeck (400–405)	1916–18	715	535t max* 506t des	59.28 oa 57.78 cwl	7.30	2.20	1750ihp des		c16 des	2000/14	130 +20	—
M 63–66	Tecklenborg (288–291)	1916–17	715 to 750	539t max* 500t des	59.30 oa 56.00 cwl	7.40	2.15	1850ihp des	240 des	16.0 des	2000/14	120 +30	—
M 67–70	Neptun (381–384)	,,	,,	,,	,,	,,	,,	,,	,,	,,	,,	,,	—
M 71–74	Vulkan (622–625)	1917–18		553t max 515t des	58.20 oa 55.00 cwl	7.30	2.25	1790ihp des		c16 des	2000/14	115 +20	—

Name	Builder (construction no)	Built	Cost in Marks (000s)	Displacement (t = tonnes, T = tons)	Length (m)	Breadth (m)	Draught/ height (m)	Power (hp)	Revs (rpm)	Speed (kts)	Range (nm/kts)	Coal (t)	Oil (t)
(M 72 mod)		1935		668T max 554t des 526T std	58.20 oa 56.10 cwl	8.10	2.25	1790ihp des				144 +30	—
M 75–78, 87–90 (M 89 mod)	Tecklenborg (294–301)	1916–18	900	505t des* 653T max 513t des	59.30 oa 56.00 cwl 59.30 oa 56.00 cwl	7.30 7.40	2.15 2.23	1870ihp des		16.5 des	2000/14	115 +20	—
M 79–82 (M 81, 82 mod)	Seebeck (406–409)	1918–19	715	553t max 515t des 630T to 652T max	59.30 oa 56.00 cwl	7.40	2.23 2.58	1850ihp des ,,	240 des ,,	16.0 des 15.0 des	2000/14 3200/10	120 +30 130 +10	— —
M 83, 84, 95–96 (M 84 mod)	Atlas (152–155)	1917–18	750	553t max 515t des 630T to 652T max	59.30 oa 56.00 cwl	7.40	2.23 2.58	1850ihp des ,,	240 des ,,	16.0 des 15.0 des	2000/14 3200/10	120 +30 130 +10	— —
M 85, 86 (M85 mod)	Nordsee (110, 111)	1917–18	750	553t max 515t des 630T to 652T max	59.30 oa 56.00 cwl	7.40	2.23 2.58	1850ihp des 1800ihp des	240 des ,,	16.0 des 15.0 des	2000/14 3200/10	120 +30 130 +10	— —
M 91–94	Neptun (385–388)	1917–18	750	553t max 515t des	59.30 oa 56.00 cwl	7.40	2.23	1850ihp des	240 des	16.0 des	2000/14	120 +30	—
M 97–100, 107–112, 137–140, 163–166	Tecklenborg (304–307, 317–322, 335–338, 351–354)	1917–19	1050 to 1250	548t max* 508t des	59.60 oa 56.10 cwl	7.30	2.15	1840ihp des	250 des	16.0 des	2000/14	115 +20	—
(M 98 mod)	Mützelfeld	1941		671T max 535t des	59.28 oa 57.78 cwl	,,	2.58	1840ihp des	,,	15.5 des		130 +20	—
(M 108 mod as *Delphin*)				631T max 511t des	59.59 oa 56.10 cwl	8.09		1825ihp des				120 +90	—
(M 109 mod as *Sundevall*)				,,	,,	,,		,,				134 +90	—
(M 110 mod)				651T max 532t des	59.28 oa 56.10 cwl	8.25	2.20	1850ihp des				152 +30	
(M 111 mod)				661T max 532t des	59.58 oa 56.10 cwl	8.25	2.20	1600ihp des				140 +20	
M 101, 102, 115–118 (M 115 mod as M 515)	Atlas (156, 157, 160–163)	1917–19	1050 to 1250	564t max* 525t des 662T max	59.30 oa 56.00 cwl	7.40	2.28	1850ihp des 1860ihp des	240 des 245 des	16.0 des 15.0 des	2000/14 3400/10	120 +30 65 +10	— 75
M 103–104, 119–122, 144, 145 (M 145 mod)	Neptun (395–396, 432–435, ...)	1917–19	1050 to 2590	560t max* 632T max	59.63 oa 56.10 cwl 59.28 oa 57.78 cwl	7.30 7.30	2.15 2.20	1850ihp des ,,	240 des ,,	16.0 des ,,	2000/14 ,,	115 +20 128 +30	— —
M 105, 106, 129–132, 161, 162 (M 129 mod as *Otto Braun*) (M 130 mod as *Fuchs*)	Reiherstieg (515, 517, 529–532, ...)	1918–19	1180 and more	550t max* 508t des 630T max 532t des ,,	59.58 oa 56.10 cwl 59.28 oa 56.10 cwl ,,	7.30 8.25 ,,	2.15 2.20 ,,	1850ihp des ,, ,,	240 des ,, ,,	16.0 des ,, ,,	2000/14 ,, ,,	115 +20 139 +30 ,,	— — —
M 113, 114 141–143	Stülcken (545, 546, ...)	1918–	1250	590t max*	59.30 oa 56.10 cwl	7.40	2.23	1850ihp des	240 des	16.0 des	2000/14	120 +30	—
M 123, 124	Seebeck (416, 417)	1918–	1250	560t max 525t des	59.30 oa 56.10 cwl	7.30	2.15	1850ihp des	240 des	16.0 des	2000/14	115 +30	
M 125, 126, 146–149	Flensburg (379, 380, 384–385, ...)	1918–	1180	550t max 508t des	59.63 oa 52.10 cwl	7.30	2.15	1850ihp des	240 des	16.0 des	2000/14	115 +20	—
(M 146 mod as *Taku*, M 126 mod as *Alders*)		1933		633T max 532t des	59.28 oa	8.25	2.20	,,	,,	,,	,,	130	—

Name	Builder (construction no)	Built	Cost in Marks (000s)	Displacement (t = tonnes T = tons)	Length (m)	Breadth (m)	Draught/ height (m)	Power (hp)	Revs (rpm)	Speed (kts)	Range (nm/kts)	Coal (t)	Oil (t)
(M 146 mod as *Von der Lippe*)		1941–42		804T max	64.78 oa 61.60 cwl	"	2.60	"	245 des	15.0 des		120	—
M 127, 128, 159–160	Union ((194–197))	1918–		560t max 525t des	59.30 oa 56.10 cwl	7.40	2.28	1800ihp des				120 +30	—
M133–136, 153–156	Frerichs	1918–20	over 2000	550t max 508t des	59.50 oa 56.10 cwl	7.30	2.15	1600ihp des		15.0 des		115 +20	—
(M 133 mod as *Raule*, M 135 mod as *Gazelle*)		1938–39		737T max 635t des	59.28 oa 57.78 cwl		2.50	"		"		127	—
(M 134 mod as *Frauen-lob*, M 136 mod as *Havel*)		"		644T max 526t des	59.50 oa 56.10 cwl	8.10	2.78	"				145	—
M 157, 158	Nordsee	1918–20	2665	550t max 508t des	59.63 oa 56.10 cwl	7.30	2.15	1850ihp des	240 des	16.0 des	2000/14	115 +20	—
M 150–152	Hansa	—	—	560t max	59.30 oa	7.40	2.28	1850ihp des	240 des	16.0 des	2000/14	120 +30	—
M 167,168	Frerichs	—	—	"	"	"	"	"	"	"	"	"	—
M 169, 170	Unterweser	—	—	"	"	"	"	"	"	"	"	"	—
M 171, 172	Koch (244, 245)	—	—	"	"	"	"	"	"	"	"	"	—
M 173, 174	J & S	—	—	"	"	"	"	"	"	"	"	"	—
M 175, 176	Nüscke	—	—	"	"	"	"	"	"	"	"	"	—
UT 1–3	San Rocco	1918–	—	576t max 525t des	59.30 oa 56.00 cwl	7.40	2.30	1850ihp des	240 des	16.0 des	2000/14	120 +30	—
(UT 4–7 as mod)	L & B	—	—	"	"	"	"	"	"	"	"	"	—
Reconstruction as R-escort boats													
Hille (ex M 60), *Alders* (ex M 126), *Juningen* (ex M 134)	Mützelfeld	1942–43		785T max 721T std	64.20 oa 61.20 cwl	8.30	2.60 max 2.00 des	1860ihp des	245 des	15.7 des			—
Von der Groeben (ex M107)		1938–39		"	"	"	"	'	"	"			—
Nettelbeck (ex M 138)	KMW	"		"	"	"	"	1680ehp des	390 des	14.1 des	2600/11	—	90

* New displacements were recorded for the following boats after their later rebuilds: *M 28* (668T), *M 61* (677T), *M 66* (668T, later 735T), *M 75* (662T), *M 102* (628T), *M 104* (633T), *M 107* (785T), *M 113* (634T), *M 117* (623T), *M 122* (652T), *M 126* (644T) and *M 132* (630T).

Construction

Laid down as minesweepers (official design 1914, official design 1915 after *M 27*, adapted 1916 after *M 57*) and U-boat flotilla tenders (*U-Flottillen-Tender*) for the Mediterranean and U-cruiser groups (official design 1918). Transverse frame steel construction, with a box keel after *M 57*. Depth 3.27–3.50m; immersion increased by 1cm per 3.09–3.11t; [after conversion per 3.20–3.57t].

Propulsion

Two vertical 3-cylinder triple expansion engines (merchant ship design) in one engine room (two 3-bladed screws, 1.70m diameter; 1.80m diameter after *M 7*, 1.90m diameter after *M 57*). Two Marine-type boilers (four fireboxes, 16 atmospheres forced, 186sq m; four fireboxes, 16.5 atmospheres forced, 195sq m after *M 27*) in one boiler room [in two boiler rooms in *M 1*, *M 9–11*, *M 16*, *M 18–21*] and in two boiler rooms after *M 27*. [Later machinery fits were as follows:

M 138 (*Zieten*) had two 6-cylinder four-stroke diesel engines, by Germania to starboard, and by MAN to port (one 3-bladed screw, 1.97m diameter); *Brommy* (ex-*M 50*) had two MWM R 43 SU diesel engines in two engine rooms.]

Electrical installation details not known. One rudder.

Armament

M 1–26 were initially fitted with one 8.8cm/30 QF gun (100 rounds) and one 3.7cm machine cannon; they were subsequently fitted with two 8.8cm/30 QF guns (160 rounds) and thirty mines. *M 67–74* and *M 85–96* were fitted with two 8.8cm/45 QF guns (260 rounds) and thirty mines, *M 43–56* and *M 75–84* with three 8.8cm/45 QF guns (300 rounds) and thirty mines, *M 27–42* and *M 57–66* with two 10.5cm/45 guns (210 rounds) and thirty mines, *M 97–176* with two 10.5cm/45 Utof guns (240 rounds) and thirty mines, and *UT 1–7* were designed for two 8.8cm/45 Utof guns (300 rounds) and mounts for twelve type G7 V torpedoes. [In Reichsmarine and Kriegsmarine service some vessels were fitted with one 10.5cm/45 Utof gun (150 rounds) forward or aft and one or two (in some cases later three) 2cm AA guns (2000–6000 rounds) in place of the standard armament.]

Handling

Good seaboats, responsive and with a good turning circle. With sweeping gear extended, maximum speed was approximately 12.5 to 13kts. [An extension to the stern improved steering and stability and reduced the tendency for the screws to come out of the water.]

Complement

Crew: 1/39 or 0/40 (plus 2/12 as hq boat) [after 1919, approximately 1/50 or 0/51 (plus 2/13); after 1938 0/49 or 1/58 depending on use]. Boats: two yawls; after 1933 one motor pinnace, one yawl and one dinghy.

Notes

Colour scheme grey or black overall, in some cases black below yellow rubbing strake only; *Hela* (ex *M 135*) until her conversion was black overall with a narrow white stripe on the top edge of her forecastle and bulwark. [Subsequent variations were tried for experimental purposes.] *M 1–26* were built with a slight whaleback forecastle, approximately as that of the torpedo boats. The drawings give details of the differences between the main series boats and later conversions. *M 57–62* were fitted with a folding lattice foremast, telescopic mainmast and folding funnel for service on the Danube. [Most vessels were given an extended stern and widened stern bulge in 1937–38; details are as follows:] *M 98* and *M 104* stern bulge only; *M 82*, *M 84*, *M 85*, *M 113 Acheron*, *M 115 Arkona*, *M 117*, *M 145* and *M 157* stern extension only; *M 89*, *M 110*, *M 111*, *M 122*, *M 126 Alders*, *M 129 Otto Braun*, *M 130 Fuchs*, *M 134 Frauenlob* and *M 146 Taku* widening without stern extension; *M 109 Sundevall* widening with stern extension; *M 102*, *M 108 Delphin*, *M 132* and *M 136 Havel* widening with stern bulge; *M 107 Von der Groeben* and *M 135 Gazelle* lengthening and widening; *M 133 Raule* and *M 138 Nettelbeck* lengthening and widening with stern extension. Widening of these vessels gave an increase in fuel load of about 10t of were also undertaken: a planned conversion to *UT 1–7*, for example, envisaged an enlarged poop, the after bulwark reduced by 0.4m, and a thicker mainmast with two derricks.]

Careers

Documentary evidence on these vessels is very incomplete, especially concerning vessels which en-

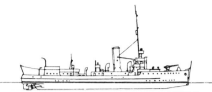

M 1–26 (1918).

M 45–56 (1918).

M57–62 (1918).

M 98 (1920).

M-boats with the extended stern (*M 82, 84, 85, 117, 145, 157*) (1936–37).

Research boat *Pelikan* (ex *M 28*) (1936).

R-escort boat *Brommy* (ex *M 50*) (1938).

Research boat *Hecht* (ex *M 60*) (1938).

Research boat *Hille* (ex *Hecht*, ex *M 60*) (1943).

R-escort boat *Raule* (ex *M 133*) (1940).

tered private ownership; no detailed information is available on the following vessels: two M-boats possibly named *Castor* and *Pollux* sold to Turkey after 1921 as passenger steamers; one M-boat sold in about 1922 to southern Norway, possibly used for liquor smuggling; one M-boat sold in about 1923 to Romania (Braila) for conversion; one M-boat sold as a post and passenger steamer to Cattaro, Yugoslavia, perhaps renamed *Jakljan*; and one M-boat sold as a passenger steamer (30 cabins) to Cartagena, Spain.

M 1: launched 26 May 1915, commissioned* 17 Jul 1915. Stricken 17 Mar 1920; sold 28 Jun 1922 for 1,200,000M; broken up at Wilhelmshaven.

M 2: launched 3 Jun 1915, commissioned* 8 Aug 1915. Stricken 24 Oct 1921; sold 29 Mar 1922 for 1,750,000M to Victor Biotin of Berlin, for conversion at German dockyards for sale abroad; further details unknown.

M 3: launched 19 Sept 1915, commissioned* 28 Sept 1915. Subsequent fate as for *M 2*.

M 4: launched 19 Sept 1915, commissioned* 2 Oct 1915. Subsequent fate as for *M 2*.

U-boat tender *Acheron* (ex *M 113*) (1936).

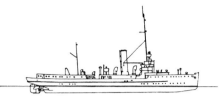

Fleet tender *Hela* (ex *M 135*) (1933).

TF-boat *M 517* (ex *M 117*) (1945).

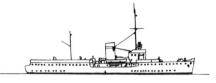

Fleet tender *Gazelle* (ex *Hela*, ex *M 135*) (1939).

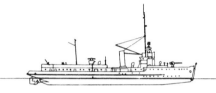

Anti-aircraft training boat *Fuchs* (ex *M 130*)
(1936).

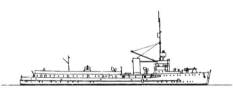

Station tender *Zieten* (ex *M 138*) (1936).

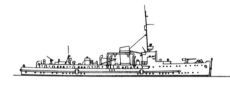

R-escort boat *von der Groeben* (ex *M 107*) (1940).

R-escort boat *Nettelbeck* (ex *Zieten*, ex *M 138*)
(1939).

M 5: launched 19 Sept 1915, commissioned* 25 Oct 1915. Subsequent fate as for *M 2*.

M 6: launched 19 Sept 1915, commissioned* 13 Nov 1915. Sunk at 1400hrs on 31 Jul 1918 in the North Sea, position 55° 18′N, 04° 35′E, by a mine; five dead.

M 7: launched 1915, commissioned* 29 Jul 1915. Stricken 24 Oct 1921; sold 28 Jun 1922 for 1,100,000M; broken up at Wilhelmshaven.

M 8: launched 18 Jun 1915, commissioned* 15 Aug 1915. Stricken 21 Nov 1920. Subsequent career as for *M 7*.

M 9: launched 1915, commissioned* 4 Sept 1915. Sunk 18 Jun 1917 in the North Sea, position 53° 36′N, 06° 05′E, by a mine; two dead.

M 10: launched 1915, commissioned* 24 Sept 1915. Stricken 17 Mar 1920; sold 19 Mar 1920 for 80,000 Dutch guilders to Athens; served from 1922 as the Greek auxiliary cruiser *Aktion*, otherwise owned by the Hellenic Co of Maritime Enterprises, Piraeus. Sold 1930 to Canadian National SS Ltd of Halifax and renamed *Prince William*; sold again 1939 to Armour Salvage & Towing Co of Halifax, retaining the name *Prince William*. Still in existence 1945, fate unknown.

M 11: launched 21 Jun 1915, commissioned* 13 Oct 1915. Sunk at 1630hrs on 28 Dec 1917 in the North Sea, position 53° 57′N, 05° 38′E, by a mine; twenty dead.

M 12: launched 27 Jul 1915, commissioned* 31 Oct 1915. Sunk 27 Jul 1916 in the North Sea, position 53° 42′N, 06° 46′E, by a mine; four dead.

M 13: launched 26 May 1915, commissioned* 23 Nov 1915. Stricken 17 Mar 1920; sold 28 Apr 1922 for 1,300,000M to Victor Biotin of Berlin for conversion at a German dockyard for sale abroad; fate unknown.

M 14: launched 21 Nov 1915, commissioned* 4 Feb 1916. Sunk at 2015hrs on 16 May 1917 in the North Sea, position 55° 33′N, 07° 15′E, by a mine; number of casualties not known.

M 15: launched 19 Sept 1915, commissioned* 13 Dec 1915. Sunk 30 Mar 1917 in the North Sea, position 55° 33′N, 08° 03′E, by a mine; sixteen dead.

M 16: launched 14 Nov 1915, commissioned* 10 Jan 1916. Sunk 21 Mar 1917 in the North Sea, position 55° 08′N, 08° 06′E, by a mine; three dead.

M 17: launched 19 Dec 1915, commissioned 29 Jan 1916; converted to a training and experimental boat. Stricken 17 Mar 1920; sold 28 Apr 1922 as for *M 13*; fate unknown.

M 18: launched 25 Aug 1915, commissioned* 18 Nov 1915. Stricken 13 Jul 1920; sold 30 Jun 1922 for 1,200,000M; broken up at Wilhelmshaven.

M 19: launched 10 Sept 1915, commissioned* 15 Dec 1915. Stricken 13 Jul 1921; sold 4 Apr 1922 for 1,300,000M; broken up at Wilhelmshaven.

M 20: launched 30 Sept 1915, commissioned* 23 Dec 1915. Stricken 13 Jul 1921; sold 28 Apr 1922 as for *M 13*; fate unknown.

M 21: launched in October 1915, commissioned* 17 Dec 1915. Stricken 13 Jul 1921; sold 28 Apr 1922 as for *M 13*; fate unknown.

M 21: launched in October 1915, commissioned* 17 Dec 1915. Stricken 17 Mar 1920; sold 22 Jun 1922 for 1,250,000M; broken up at Wilhelmshaven.

M 22: launched in December 1915, commissioned* 31 Jan 1916. Sunk at 1602hrs on 14 Oct 1918 in the North Sea, position 55° 59′N, 05° 33′E, by a mine; eleven dead.

M 23: launched 29 Jul 1915, commissioned* 27 Aug 1915. Sunk at 0639hrs on 4 Jun 1917 in the North Sea, position 53° 48′N, 06° 39′E, by a mine; two dead.

M 24: launched 11 Aug 1915, commissioned* 13 Sept 1915. Sunk 16 Mar 1917 in the North Sea, position 55° 06′N, 08° 07′E, by a mine; three dead.

M 25: launched 28 Aug 1915, commissioned* 8 Oct 1915. Stricken 13 Jul 1921; sold 29 Apr 1922 for 1,100,000M; broken up at Wilhelmshaven.

M 26: launched 9 Sept 1915, commissioned* 18 Oct 1915. Sunk 21 Mar 1917 in the North Sea, position 55° 07′N, 08° 07′E, by a mine; seven dead.

M 27: launched 15 Apr 1916, commissioned* 31 May 1916 for use as a training boat. Sunk 11 Aug 1916 in the western Baltic, position 54° 56′N, 13° 51′E, after a collision the previous day with the German ss *Paranagua*; number of casualties not known.

M 28: launched 6 May 1916, commissioned 24 Jun 1916 as an escort boat; reverted to minesweeping duties in 1917*. Renamed *Pelikan* 11 Mar 1929 and served as an experimental mine vessel in the SVK (Barrage Research Command); renamed *M 528* 1 Oct 1940. Taken as a US prize 1945, and served in the GM/SA; transferred to OMGUS 28 Oct 1947; used at Seebeck dockyard as a barrack ship from 29 Sept 1947; returned to OMGUS 10 Mar 1949; transferred to the US Army Sept 1949; broken up during the 1950s.

M 29: launched 27 May 1916, commissioned 15 Jul 1916 as an escort boat; reverted to minesweeping duties in 1917*. Stricken 24 Oct 1921. Subsequent fate as for *M 2*.

M 30: launched 17 Jun 1916, commissioned 4 Aug 1916. Career and fate as for *M 29*.

M 31: launched 30 Apr 1916, commissioned 6 Jun 1916 as an escort boat; reverted to minesweeping

*These M-boats carried out active minesweeping duties at some stage in their careers.

duties 7 Oct 1917*. Sunk at 1820hrs on 7 Oct 1917 off the Courland coast, position 57° 31′N, 21° 34′E, by a mine; one dead.

M 32: launched 14 May 1916, commissioned 29 Jun 1916 as an escort boat; reverted to minesweeping duties in 1917*. Stricken 17 Mar 1920; sold in 1922 to Paul Selinger of Dortmund; broken up.

M 33: launched 25 Jun 1916, commissioned 20 Jul 1916 as an escort boat; reverted to minesweeping duties in 1917*. Stricken 17 Mar 1920; sold in 1922 to a Berlin company; broken up.

M 34: launched 25 Jun 1916, commissioned 10 Aug 1916 as an escort boat; reverted to minesweeping duties in 1917*. Stricken 17 Mar 1920; subsequent fate as for *M 32.*

M 35: launched 18 May 1916, commissioned 18 Jun 1916 as an escort boat; reverted to minesweeping duties in 1917*. Stricken 24 Oct 1921; subsequent fate as for *M 33.*

M 36: launched 3 Jun 1916, commissioned 16 Jun 1916 as an escort boat; reverted to minesweeping duties in 1917*. Sunk 23 Mar 1918 in the North Sea, position 53° 40′N, 06° 14′E, by a mine; three dead.

M 37: launched 24 Jun 1916, commissioned 6 Aug 1916 as an escort boat; reverted to minesweeping duties in 1917*. Stricken 17 Mar 1920; sold 10 May 1922 for 1,100,000M; broken up at Wilhelmshaven.

M 38: launched 13 Jul 1916, commissioned 20 Aug 1916 as an escort boat; reverted to minesweeping duties in 1917*. Stricken 20 Feb 1922 and reduced to the barrack hulk *K 103 Wb*; taken 25 Apr 1946 as a USSR prize; fate unknown.

M 39: launched 27 May 1916, commissioned 17 Jul 1916 as an escort boat; reverted to minesweeping duties in 1917*. Sunk 20 Apr 1918 in the North Sea, position 53° 49′N, 04° 57′E, by a mine; seven dead.

M 40: launched 15 Jun 1916, commissioned 10 Aug 1916 as an escort boat; reverted to minesweeping duties in 1917*. Sunk at 1223hrs on 23 Mar 1918 in the North Sea, position 53° 51′N, 04° 57′E, by a mine; number of casualties not known.

M 41: launched 5 Aug 1916, commissioned 1 Sept 1916 as an escort boat; reverted to minesweeping duties in 1917*. Sunk 6 Sept 1918 in the North Sea, position 53° 57′N, 05° 38′E, by her own mine; three dead.

M 42: launched 11 Aug 1916, commissioned 22 Sept 1916 as an escort boat; reverted to minesweeping duties in 1917*. Stricken 17 Mar 1920; sold 11 Aug 1920 for 2,300,000M to a Berlin company, then in 1922 to the Vicomte le Gualès de Mezaubran at Nice as *La Nymphe*; sold in 1923 to Norddeutscher Lloyd and converted to the steam ferry *Nymphe*; sold in 1928 to SA des Bains de Mer et du Cercle des Etrangers de Monaco. Served 1939–40 as the French minesweeper *AD 204*; conversion planned to submarine hunter training ship *Nymphe* in April 1944; became the mineship *Nymphe* in the Kriegsmarine in May 1944. Sunk in April 1945, position unknown.

M 43: launched 7 May 1916, commissioned 28 Jun 1916 as an escort boat; reverted to minesweeping duties in 1917*. Stricken 24 Oct 1921; sold 5 May 1922 for 1,250,000M; broken up.

M 44: launched 4 Jun 1916, commissioned 8 Aug 1916 as an escort boat; reverted to minesweeping duties in 1917. Stricken 24 Oct 1921; sold 29 Apr 1922 to a Berlin company for 1,100,000M; fate unknown.

M 45: launched 8 Jul 1916, commissioned 27 Aug 1916 as an escort boat; reverted to minesweeping duties in 1917. Stricken 24 Oct 1921; sold 1922 to a Berlin company; fate unknown.

M 46: launched 19 Aug 1916, commissioned* 16 Sept 1916. Stricken 1 Dec 1922, free from 10 Sept 1923; fate unknown.

M 47: launched 19 Aug 1916, commissioned* 7 Oct 1916. Sunk 8 Jun 1917 in the North Sea, position 53° 27′N, 04° 51′E, by a mine; five dead.

M 48: launched 9 Sept 1916, commissioned* 28 Oct 1916. Stricken 24 Sept 1921; sold 18 Mar 1922 for 1,650,000M to Hugo Stinnes of Hamburg, then to Argentina under the name *Maria*; became the Argentinian minesweeper *M 1*; renamed *Bathurst* after 1936. Stricken 16 Dec 1946; used as a target hulk on the Rio Santiago; broken up in 1951.

M 49: launched 30 Sept 1916, commissioned* 19 Nov 1916. Sunk 7 May 1917 in the North Sea, position 55° 17′N, 07° 43′E, by a mine; six dead.

M 50: launched 19 Aug 1916, commissioned 19 Sept 1916 as an escort boat*; served in the Reichsmarine and the Kriegsmarine (from 26 Nov 1937 as the R-escort *Brommy*); from 1 Oct 1940 as *M 550*. Sunk at 2300hrs on 15 Jun 1944 at Boulogne, by British bombers.

M 51: launched 10 Sept 1916, commissioned 12 Oct 1916 as an escort boat*. Stricken 24 Sept 1921; sold 18 Mar 1922 as for *M 48* under the names *Martha*, *M 2* and *Fourner*. Stricken 5 Apr 1937 and sold as a hulk to Yacimientos Petroliferos Fiscales, Argentina; broken up in 1943.

M 52: launched 22 Nov 1916, commissioned* 26 Nov 1916. Stricken 24 Sept 1921; sold 18 Mar 1922 as for *M 48*, under the name *Jorge*; became the aviso *Cormoran* 26 Jan 1940. Stricken 26 Aug 1946.

M 53: launched 22 Nov 1916, commissioned* 16 Dec 1916. Stricken 24 Sept 1921; sold 18 Mar 1922 as for *M 48*, under the names *Minna*, *M 4* and *King*. Stricken 27 Jul 1937; recommissioned in November 1941 as the torpedo training ship *Teniente de la Sota*. Stricken 16 Dec 1946; sold in 1948 for breaking up.

M 54: launched 14 Sept 1916, commissioned 14 Oct 1916 as an escort boat*. Stricken 13 Jul 1921; sold 29 Apr 1922 to a Hamburg company for 1,100,000M; fate unknown.

M 55: launched 7 Oct 1916, commissioned* 5 Nov 1916. Sunk 19 Nov 1917 in the North Sea, position 54° 27′N, 08° 22′E, during a towing operation after stranding; six dead.

M 56: launched 4 Nov 1916, commissioned* 12 Dec 1916. Sunk 9 Feb 1917 in the North Sea, position 54° 12′N, 06° 58′E, by a mine; six dead.

M 57: launched 1 Jul 1917, commissioned* 16 Sept 1917; reduced 1 Dec 1922 to a barrack boat at the Kiel arsenal and the Blucher bridge; fate unknown.

M 58: launched 4 Aug 1917, commissioned* 23 Oct 1917. Stricken 13 Jul 1921; sold 10 May 1922 for 1,100,000M; broken up at Wilhelmshaven.

M 59: launched 31 Oct 1917, commissioned* 30 Nov 1917. Stricken 24 Oct 1921; sold 2 Aug 1922 to a Paris company for 1,000,000M; sold in 1927 to Lithuania and became the Lithuanian patrol boat *Prezidentas A. Smetona*; taken as a USSR prize 1940, renamed *Otlichnik*, then *Korall*; stricken about 1955.

M 60: launched 28 Nov 1917, commissioned* 15 Jan 1918. Served in the Reichsmarine and the Kriegsmarine, from 29 Aug 1938 as the experimental boat *Hecht*, and from 1 Oct 1940 as *M 560*; converted in 1942 to an R-escort boat; renamed *Hille* 21 Jan 1943. Taken over by the GM/SA in 1945; taken as a USSR prize 17 Nov 1945; fate unknown.

M 61: launched 13 Apr 1918, commissioned* 20 Apr 1918. Served in the Reichsmarine and the Kriegsmarine, from 1 Nov 1938 as a torpedo recovery boat. Sunk 26 Jul 1940 off Hook of Holland, position 51° 25′N, 04° 04′E, by a mine.

M 62: launched 13 Apr 1918, commissioned* 29 Apr 1918. Sunk at 2323 hrs on 9 Aug 1918 in the North Sea, position 55° 54′N, 05° 49′E, by a mine; eighteen dead.

M 63: launched 27 Mar 1917, commissioned* 6 May 1917. Sunk 28 Jun 1917 in the North Sea, position 53° 29′N, 05° 20′E, by a mine; three dead.

M 64: launched 21 Apr 1917, commissioned* 20 May 1917. Sunk 20 Apr 1918 in the North Sea, position 53° 49′N, 04° 57′E, by a mine; twenty-nine dead.

M 65: launched 12 May 1917, commissioned* 10 Jun 1917. Stricken 13 Jul 1921; sold 5 Jul 1922; broken up at Wilhelmshaven.

M 66: launched 2 Jul 1917, commissioned 1 Jul 1917. Served in the Reichsmarine and the Kriegsmarine, from November 1937 as the experimental boat *Störtebeker*, and after 1 Oct 1940 as the experimental boat *M 566* for the NVK - Communications Research Command. Taken as a US prize in 1945 and transferred to the GM/SA; taken over by OMGUS 1 Dec 1947; sold 18 Jun 1948 to Ostdeutsche Dampfschiff & Transport AG; reverted to OMGUS control 12 Sept 1949 and transferred 13 Sept 1949 to the US Army. Broken up during the 1950s.

M 67: launched 30 Jun 1917, commissioned* 4 Sept 1917. Sunk at 1230hrs on 25 Apr 1918 in the North Sea, position 55° 13′N, 06°E by a mine; seven dead.

M 68: launched 25 Jul 1917, commissioned* 6 Oct 1917. Sunk at 1430hrs on 29 Oct 1917 off Dunamunde, position 57° 04′N, 24° 01′E, by a mine; one dead. Raised 1920 by Latvia; commissioned 10 Nov 1921 as the Latvian gunboat *Virsaitis*; taken as a USSR prize in 1940, renamed *T–297 Virsaitis*; sunk 3 Dec 1941 in the vicinity of Hango, by a mine.

M 69: launched 16 Aug 1917, commissioned* 3 Nov 1917. Stricken 24 Oct 1921; sold 2 Aug 1922 for 1,000,000M to the Paris company Moinet; fate unknown.

M 70: launched 28 Sept 1917, commissioned* 7 Dec 1917. Stricken 23 Jun 1921; sold in 1922 to a Hamburg company; fate unknown.

M 71: launched 11 Jan 1918, commissioned* 14 Apr 1918. Stricken 24 Oct 1921; sold in 1922 to a Dortmund company; fate unknown.

M 72: launched 20 Feb 1918, commissioned* 28 Apr 1918. Served in the Reichsmarine and the Kriegsmarine, from 1 Oct 1940 as *M 572*, and from May 1942 as a barrage training boat. Taken as a US prize in 1945, and transferred to the GM/SA; taken over by OMGUS 25 Oct 1946; became a police barrack ship at Bremen 11 Jun 1947; broken up in March 1953 in Belgium.

M 73: launched 20 Feb 1918, commissioned* 18 Jul 1918. Stricken 24 Oct 1921; sold 1 May 1922 for 1,115,000M to Ing B Plage of Berlin; fate unknown.

M 74: launched 26 Apr 1918, commissioned* 18 Jun 1918. Stricken 13 Jul 1921; sold 18 Mar 1922 as for *M 48*, under the names *Meta*, *M 5* and *Murature*. Became the aviso *Cormoran* in 1938; became a museum ship in about 1940; still in existence in 1966.

M 75: launched 21 Jul 1917, commissioned* 16 Aug 1917. Served in the Reichsmarine and the Kriegsmarine, from 1940 as *M 575*. Capsized and sunk on 2 Mar 1945 off Oresund.

M 76: launched 15 Aug 1917, commissioned* 9 Sept 1917. Stricken 13 Jul 1921; sold 5 May 1922 for 1,250,000M; broken up.

M 77: launched 4 Sept 1917, commissioned* 30 Sept 1917. Stricken 13 Jul 1921; sold in 1922 to a Berlin company for conversion to a Rhine tug under the name *Luwen 3*, at Duisburg; sold in 1928 to the Hafen-Dampfschiffahrt AG of Hamburg, as a steam harbour ferry, under the name *Reichspräsident*; sold in 1935 to Blohm & Voss of Hamburg for use as a dockyard aircraft salvage ship under the name *Kranich*; became an auxiliary aircraft recovery vessel for the Luftwaffe in 1941; taken as a British prize in 1945; later sold to Alex Schmidt of Hamburg as the salvage ship *Kranich*; broken up 1961–62 at Bremerhaven.

M 78: launched 20 Nov 1917, commissioned* 13 Dec 1917. Stricken 13 Jul 1921; sold 1 May 1922 for 1,200,000M to Ing B Plage of Berlin; fate unknown.

M 79: launched 15 Jan 1919, commissioned 18 Mar 1919. Stricken 24 Sept 1921; sold 18 Mar 1922 as for *M 48*, under the names *Melittam*, *M 6* and *Pinedo*. Stricken 25 Jul 1951; sold to the Club Nautico Azoparto, San Nicolas, as a barrack ship; sold in 1956 to the Escuela de Gremetos 'Juan Bautista Azopardo', Santa Fe, as a barrack ship; sold in 1969 for 1,350,000 Pesos to Fa Alfredo S Mufarrege.

M 80: launched 15 Jan 1919, commissioned 1 Apr 1919. Stricken 12 Sept 1921; sold 18 Mar 1922 as for *M 48*, under the names *Margot*, *M 7* and *PY*; fell over in drydock in 1936; stricken 13 Jan 1937 and finally used as a pontoon at the La Plata central dock.

M 81: launched 8 Sept 1919, commissioned 13 Oct 1919; served in the Reichsmarine and the Kriegsmarine, after 11 Mar 1929 for mine experiments under the name *Nautilus* for the SVK; became *M 581* 1 Oct 1940; converted to a torpedo recovery boat in 1941. Taken as a US prize in 1945, and transferred to the GM/SA; taken over by OMGUS 25 Oct 1946; sold 5 Dec 1947 to Schuchmann as a barrack ship; reverted to OMGUS 10 Mar 1949; transferred to the US Army 13 Sept 1949; broken up during the 1950s.

M 82: launched 8 Sept 1919, commissioned 8 Nov 1919. Served in the Reichsmarine and the Kriegsmarine, from 11 Mar 1929 as the *Jagd*, after 1 Oct 1940 as *M 582*, and after 1941 as a torpedo recovery boat. Taken as a US prize in 1945 and was transferred to the GM/SA; taken over by OMGUS 10 Dec 1947; used from 15 Jun 1948 by Erfurter Samenversand of Bremerhaven, as a barrack boat; sold 5 Oct 1954 to A Sonnenberg of Bremen for breaking up.

M 83: launched 19 Sept 1917, commissioned* 13 Nov 1917. Sunk at 0100hrs on 1 Jul 1918 in the North Sea, position 56° 03'N, 06° 36'E, by a mine; fourteen dead.

M 84: launched 10 Oct 1917, commissioned* 16 Dec 1917. Served in the Reichsmarine and the Kriegsmarine, from 1 Oct 1940 as *M 584*, and from 21 Feb 1942 as a torpedo recovery boat. Sunk at 0920hrs on 30 Nov 1944 in the Kattegat, position 56° 53'N, 10° 48'E, by a mine; one dead.

M 85: launched 10 Apr 1918, commissioned* 3 Aug 1918. Served in the Reichsmarine and the Kriegsmarine. Sunk at 1430hrs on 1 Oct 1939 northeast of Heisternest, by a mine; twenty-four dead.

M 86: launched 10 Oct 1917, commissioned* 21 Mar 1918. Stricken 13 Jul 1921; sold 5 May 1922 for 1,250,000M; broken up at Kiel.

M 87: launched 30 Oct 1917, commissioned* 23 Nov 1917. Stricken 13 Jul 1921; sold in 1922 to a Berlin company; fate unknown.

M 88: launched 26 Sept 1917, commissioned* 14 Oct 1917. Stricken 13 Jul 1921; fate as for *M 78*.

M 89: launched 11 Dec 1917, commissioned* 1 Jan 1918; served in the Reichsmarine and the Kriegsmarine. Sunk 26 Jul 1940 off Hook of Holland, position 51° 59'N, 04° 04'E, by a mine.

M 90: launched 29 Dec 1917, commissioned* 23 Jan 1918. Stricken 24 Sept 1921; sold 18 Mar 1922 as for *M 48*, under the names *Marianne*, *M 8* and *Segui*, salvage ship from 1934. Stricken 29 Apr 1950; used from 1951 as a divers' club ship on the Rio Uruguay; sunk 18 Aug 1963 on the Rio Uruguay.

M 91: launched 1 Nov 1917, commissioned* 10 Jan 1918. Sunk at 0500hrs on 10 Mar 1918 in the North Sea, position 55° 05'N, 05° 25'E, by a mine; eight dead.

M 92: launched 8 Dec 1917, commissioned* 21 Feb 1918. Sunk at 0200hrs on 1 Jul 1918 in the North Sea, position 56° 04'N, 06° 42'E, by a mine; fifteen dead.

M 93: launched 18 Jan 1918, commissioned* 14 Mar 1918. Stricken 24 Oct 1921; sold 15 Aug 1922 for 1,650,000M to Paul Diete & Co of Kiel; fate unknown.

M 94: launched 20 Feb 1918, commissioned* 15 Apr 1918. Stricken 17 Mar 1921; sold 1 May 1922 for 1,200,000M to Ing B Plage of Berlin; fate unknown.

M 95: launched 21 Dec 1917, commissioned 5 Mar 1918. Sunk at 0010hrs on 20 Apr 1918 in the North Sea, position 54° 49'N, 04° 57'E, by a mine; thirty-seven dead.

M 96: launched 22 Feb 1918, commissioned* 15 Apr 1918; served after 1921 as a hospital ship at Stettin. Sunk there at 1015hrs on 15 Mar 1922 after capsizing during the Kapp Putsch. Raised 21 Aug 1922; stricken 29 Aug 1922; broken up.

M 97: launched 28 Mar 1918, commissioned* 21 Apr 1918. Stricken 24 Oct 1921; sold 20 Jul 1921 for 1,400,000M to Yugoslavia (via a Hamburg company) as a tug – became instead the Yugoslav minelayer *Orao*; taken as an Italian prize in April 1941 and renamed *Vergada*; repaired at Malta 7 Dec 1943 and reverted to Yugoslav service as *Orao*; renamed *Pionir* in August 1945; renamed *Zelengora* in 1955; stricken in 1962.

M 98: launched 16 Apr 1918, commissioned* 7 May 1918. Served in the Reichsmarine and the Kriegsmarine, from 1 Oct 1940 as *M 598*, and from 1941 as a torpedo recovery boat. Taken as a US prize in 1945 and transferred to the GM/SA; taken over by OMGUS 26 Oct 1946; used as a police barrack boat at Bremen from 28 May 1947; returned to OMGUS in August 1948; broken up in March 1949.

M 99: launched 8 May 1918, commissioned* 26 May 1918. Stricken 24 Oct 1921; sold in 1922 to a Berlin company; broken up at Hamburg-Moorburg.

M 100: launched 23 May 1918, commissioned* 16 Jun 1918. Stricken 3 Mar 1921; sold 20 Jul 1921 as for *M 97* under the name *Galeb*; taken as an Italian prize in 1941 and renamed *Selve* 22 May 1941. Set on fire and sunk at 1500hrs on 6 Nov 1942 in Benghazi Bay by British aircraft; wreck broken up in 1948.

M 101: launched 20 Apr 1918, commissioned* 19 Jun 1918. Stricken 13 Jul 1921; sold 18 Mar 1922 as for *M 48* under the names *M 9* and *Thorne*. Stricken 16 Dec 1946; recommissioned 17 Jul 1947 as the aviso *Petrel*. Stricken 8 Aug 1948 and reduced to a hulk at the Base Naval de Rio Santiago; sold 20 Jul 1959 to Idoeta, Reboratti & Cia; fate unknown.

M 102: launched 31 May 1918, commissioned* 24 Jul 1918. Served in the Reichsmarine and the Kriegsmarine, from 1 Oct 1940 as *M 502*, from 1941 as a torpedo recovery boat and from Sept 1941 as a leader boat for barrage training. Taken as a US prize in 1945 and transferred to the GM/SA; taken over by the OMGUS 25 Oct 1946; broken up in March 1949 at Ghent.

M 103: launched 27 Mar 1918, commissioned* 25 May 1918. Stricken 24 Oct 1921; fate as for *M 78*.

M 104: launched 27 Apr 1918, commissioned* 29 Jun 1918. Served in the Reichsmarine and the Kriegsmarine, from 1 Oct 1940 as *M 504*. Sunk 9 Apr 1945 in the Deutsche Werke dock VII at Kiel, by British aircraft.

M 105: launched 6 Jul 1918, commissioned* 10 Oct 1918. Stricken 9 Feb 1921; sold 18 Mar 1922 as for *M 48*, under the names *Mecha* and *M 10*, then in 1925 became the Argentinian President's yacht *Golondrina*. Stricken 20 Aug 1958; sold to Arenera 'Yapeyu'.

M 106: launched 8 Jul 1918, commissioned 21 Mar 1919. Stricken 24 Oct 1921 as for *M 97*, under the names *Gavran* and *Labud* (from 1923); taken as an Italian prize 21 Apr 1941; served from 29 May 1941

*These M-boats carried out active minesweeping duties at some stage in their careers.

as the Italian *Zuri*; renamed *Oriole* 1 Jun 1942. Scuttled and sunk at 2015hrs on 10 Jul 1943 in Augusta harbour, after an air attack.

M 107: launched 3 Jul 1918, commissioned* 30 Jul 1918. Served in the Reichsmarine and the Kriegsmarine, from 15 Apr 1939 as the R-escort boat *Von der Groeben*, and from 1 Oct 1940 as *M 507*. Stranded 18 Aug 1940 in the vicinity of Boulogne, after hitting a mine. Raised, repaired, and finally sunk at 2300hrs on 15 Jun 1944 at Boulogne, during an air attack.

M 108: launched 17 Jul 1918, commissioned* 10 Aug 1918. Served in the Reichsmarine and the Kriegsmarine, from 15 Nov 1925 as a gunnery school rangefinder tender and target tug, from 24 Oct 1936 as the gunnery training boat *Delphin*, and from 1 Oct 1940 as *M 508*. Taken over in 1945 by the GM/SA; taken as a USSR prize 17 Nov 1945; fate unknown.

M 109: launched 7 Aug 1918, commissioned* 29 Aug 1918. Served in the Reichsmarine and the Kriegsmarine, from 29 Aug 1938 as the *Johann Wittenborg* with the SVK, from 2 Dec 1938 as *Sundevall*, and from 1 Oct 1940 as *M 509*. Taken as a US prize in 1945, and served with the GM/SA; transferred to OMGUS 25 Oct 1946, and served from 23 Mar 1948 as a barrack ship for D G Neptun; returned to OMGUS 7 Apr 1949; transferred to the US Army in September 1949; broken up in August 1950.

M 110: launched 27 Aug 1918, commissioned 19 Sept 1918. Served in the Reichsmarine and the Kriegsmarine, from 1 Oct 1940 as *M 510*, and from November 1941 as a torpedo recovery boat. Taken as a US prize in 1945 and served with the GM/SA; transferred to OMGUS 25 Oct 1946; served from 19 Sept 1947 as a barrack ship at Seebeck dockyard; returned to OMGUS in March 1949; transferred to the US Army in September 1949; broken up in 1950 at Ghent.

M 111: launched 17 Sept 1918, commissioned* 11 Oct 1918. Served in the Reichsmarine and the Kriegsmarine, from 1 Oct 1940 as *M 511* and from 1941 as a torpedo recovery boat. Sunk 3 Nov 1941 at the approach to Kolberg, by a mine in the German harbour barrage.

M 112: launched 12 Nov 1918, commissioned 31 Oct 1919. Stricken 24 Oct 1921 as for *M 97*, under the name *Jastreb*; converted to oil firing in 1938–39; taken as an Italian prize 17 Apr 1941 at Kumbor, and became the Italian *Irona* 20 May 1941. Stranded at 0200hrs on 25 Nov 1941 at Benghazi during an air attack; wreck scuttled during the evacuation of Benghazi 18 Nov 1942; raised in 1948; broken up.

M 113: launched 27 May 1919, commissioned* 28 Apr 1920. Served in the Reichsmarine and the Kriegsmarine, from 20 Jun 1936 as a guard boat for the UAK - U-boat Acceptance Commission, from 8 Oct 1936 as the submarine tender *Acheron*, and from 1 Oct 1940 as *M 513*; taken as a US prize in 1945; transferred to OMGUS 25 Oct 1946.

M 114: stricken 24 Jun 1919 and sold incomplete 26 Jun 1919 for 710,000M to a Hamburg company for conversion; launched 28 Sept 1920 as the motor vessel *Leopold David* for the Leopold David Shipping Co. Sunk 9 Jan 1922 at Cuxhaven, after an explosion of her petrol cargo.

M 115: launched 12 Jul 1918, commissioned* 19 Sept 1918. Served in the Reichsmarine and the Kriegsmarine, from 1 Oct 1935 as the experimental boat *Arkona*, from 28 Jun 1941 as *M 515*, and from May 1942 as a barrage training boat. Sunk 22 May 1944 west of Fehmarn, position 54° 34′N, 10° 45′E, by a land mine; later broken up.

M 116: launched 10 Aug 1918, commissioned* 15 Oct 1918. Used in 1920 as a transport for POWs, and in 1922 as the barrack boat *W 1 Wb*; still in existence in 1934.

M 117: launched 20 Sept 1918, commissioned during 1919. Served in the Reichsmarine and the Kriegsmarine, from 1 Oct 1940 as *M 517*, and from November 1941 as a torpedo recovery boat. Taken as a US prize in 1945 and transferred to the GM/SA; transferred to OMGUS 28 Oct 1947; fate unknown.

M 118: launched 12 Oct 1918, commissioned 1 Apr 1919. Stricken 13 Jul 1921; sold in 1922 to a Berlin company.

M 119: launched 22 Jun 1918, commissioned* 17 Aug 1918. Stricken 9 Mar 1921; sold to Italy 15 Dec 1921 as the Italian minesweeper *Meteo*; renamed *Vieste* in 1925. Severely damaged 11 Sept 1943 in the vicinity of Naples and no longer serviceable; scuttled in 1944 during the evacuation of Naples; broken up after 1945.

M 120: launched 24 Jul 1918, commissioned* 20 Sept 1918. Stricken 9 Mar 1921; sold 15 Dec 1921 to Italy as the Italian minesweeper *Abastro*; renamed *Cotrone* in 1925; became the minelayer *Crotone* in 1931. Taken over by German forces at La Spezia 9 Sept 1943; sunk there in dock 4 in an air attack. Raised in March 1947; repaired; became the Italian merchant navy training ship *Garaventa*. Stricken in September 1968; broken up.

M 121: launched 10 Sept 1918, commissioned 25 Oct 1918. Stricken 13 Jul 1921; sold 20 Jul 1921 as for *M 97*, under the name *Kobac*; taken as an Italian prize 10 Apr 1941 at Sebenico, and became the Italian *Unie* 30 Nov 1941. Sunk at 1405hrs on 30 Jan 1943 at the Bizerta arsenal quay, during an air attack.

M 122: launched 21 Sept 1918, commissioned* 27 Feb 1919. Served in the Reichsmarine and the Kriegsmarine, from 1 Nov 1938 as an S-boat escort vessel, from 1 Oct 1940 as *M 522*, and from November 1941 as a torpedo recovery boat. Sunk 20 Mar 1945 at Kiel, by an aircraft bomb. Raised, repaired; handed over to the GM/SA. Scuttled at 0507hrs on 18 May 1946 in the Skagerrak, position 58° 10′N, 10° 42′E.

M 123, 124: construction halted before completion.

M 125: launched 26 Oct 1918, commissioned* 24 Apr 1919; used in 1920 as a POW transport, then as the barrack boat *W 2 Wb*; still in existence in 1934; fate unknown.

M 126: launched 21 Dec 1918, commissioned* 1 Jul 1919. Served in the Reichsmarine and the Kriegsmarine, from 1 Oct 1940 as *M 526*, and from 27 Apr 1943 as the R-escort boat *Alders*; taken as a US prize 1945, transferred to the GM/SA; transferred to OMGUS 25 Oct 1946; fate unknown.

M 127, 128: construction halted before completion.

M 129: launched 15 Jan 1919, commissioned* 20 May 1919. Served in the Reichsmarine and the Kriegsmarine from 29 Aug 1938 as the *Otto Braun*, and from 28 Jun 1941 as *M 529*. Sunk 2 Dec 1941 at the entrance to Kolberg, by a mine in the German harbour barrage; ten dead.

M 130: launched 13 Feb 1919, commissioned* 29 Jul 1919. Served in the Reichsmarine and the Kriegsmarine, from 12 May 1928 as the AA training boat *Fuchs*, from 1 Oct 1940 as *M 530*, and from 1944 as *M 3800*; taken over by the GM/SA in 1945; taken as a USSR prize 17 Nov 1945; fate unknown.

M 131: launched 7 Jun 1919. Stricken 24 Jun 1919; converted to a steam passenger launch; sold 4 Nov 1919 for £22,000 to Alberto A Dodero of Montevideo; fate unknown.

M 132: launched 14 Jan 1919, commissioned 14 Nov 1919. Served in the Reichsmarine and the Kriegsmarine. Sunk on 13 Nov 1939 in the Lister Tief, by a depth charge from an M-boat steaming ahead; casualties not known.

M 133: launched in 1919, commissioned* 15 Dec 1919. Served in the Reichsmarine and the Kriegsmarine, from 11 Mar 1929 as the tender *Wacht*, from 24 Aug 1939 as the R-escort boat *Raule*, and from 1 Oct 1940 as *M 533*. Sunk 9 May 1942 northwest of Boulogne in a collision with *R 45*.

M 134: launched 28 Jul 1919, commissioned* 12 Mar 1920. Served in the Reichsmarine and the Kriegsmarine, from 11 Mar 1929 as the tender *Frauenlob* and from 1 Oct 1940 as *M 534*. Sunk 9 May 1940 at Bergen, by an aircraft bomb; three dead. Raised, repaired and converted; recommissioned 27 Sept 1943 as the R-escort boat *Jungingen*; taken as a US prize in 1945 and transferred to the GM/SA; fate unknown.

M 135: launched 15 Mar 1919, commissioned* 31 Oct 1919. Served in the Reichsmarine and the Kriegsmarine, from 5 Feb 1923 as the fleet tender *Hela*, renamed *Gazelle* 2 Jan 1939, and from 1 Oct 1940 as *M 535*. Transferred to the GM/SA in 1945; taken as a USSR prize 8 Feb 1946 and became the Soviet *Desna*; renamed *Venta* (245) in 1951; broken up in the 1960s.

M 136: launched during 1919, commissioned* 15 Nov 1919. Served in the Reichsmarine and the Kriegsmarine, from 1939 as the U-boat tender *Havel*, later *M 89*. Sunk 26 Jul 1940 in the vicinity of the Hook of Holland, position 51° 59′N, 04° 04′E, by a mine.

M 137: launched 15 Jan 1919, commissioned* 20 Mar 1919. Stricken 5 Jul 1921; sold 10 May 1922 for 1,180,000M; subsequently broken up.

M 138: launched 17 Feb 1919, commissioned* 21 Mar 1919. Served in the Reichsmarine, from 11 Sept 1924 as the fisheries protection boat *Zieten* and from 4 Oct 1932 as a station tender; served as an R-escort boat from 5 Mar 1936; renamed *Nettelbeck* 10 May 1939 and *M 538* from 1 Oct 1940. Damaged 21 June 1944 in the vicinity of Vyborg, by an aircraft bomb; towed in to Königsberg and repaired; stranded 26 Jan 1945 in the vicinity of Hela during a storm; finally stricken 3 Feb 1945.

M 139: launched 12 Mar 1919. Stricken 24 Jun 1919; sold 19 Jun 1919 for 800,000M to Hapag, and converted to the steam ferry *Helgoland*; sold in 1922 to the Tonsberg & Hortens D/S, Tönsberg, as the Norwegian *Tönsberg I*; sold in 1931 to Colombia and became the Colombian patrol boat *Bogota*; sunk in 1946, details unknown.

M 140: launched 15 Apr 1919. Stricken 24 Jun 1919; sold 19 Jun 1919 for 750,000M to Hapag, and converted to the steam ferry *Hörnum* for the first service to East Prussia; sold in 1922 to the Liverpool and North Wales SS Co, Liverpool, as the British *St Elian*; sold in 1927 to Soc. Partenopea Anon di Nav, Naples, as the Italian *Partenope*; renamed *Ischia* in 1949; sold in 1972 under the same name to Carmine Lauri of Salerno; still in service in 1982.

M 141–143: construction halted before completion.

M 144: launched 19 Mar 1919, commissioned* 20 Jun 1919. Stricken 17 Jun 1921; sold 20 Jul 1921 as for *M 97*, under the name *Sokol*; taken as an Italian prize at Split in April 1941, and became the Italian *Eso* 1 Feb 1942. Sunk at 2100hrs on 19 Jan 1943 at Djerba Island, position 33° 26′N, 11° 06′E, by an aircraft torpedo, while on escort duty with the destroyer *San Martino* and two other vessels.

M 145: launched 22 May 1918, commissioned* 20 Jun 1919. Served in the Reichsmarine and the Kriegsmarine, from 1 Oct 1940 as *M 545*, and from May 1942 as a barrage training boat. Taken as a US prize in 1945 and transferred to the GM/SA; transferred to OMGUS 28 Oct 1947; sold 19 Mar 1948 to Reinecke & Brehmer of Hamburg as a barrack ship; wrecked in September 1949; broken up.

M 146: launched 21 Dec 1918, commissioned* 11 Aug 1919. Served in the Reichsmarine and the Kriegsmarine, from 26 Aug 1933 to 1 Jul 1934 as the fleet tender *Taku*, from 28 Oct 1935 as *M 146*, and from May 1940 as *M 546*; converted 29 Aug

1941 to the R-escort boat *Von der Lippe*. Sunk at 2300hrs on 15 Jun 1944 at Boulogne, by an aircraft bomb.

M 147: stricken 24 June 1919 and sold incomplete 26 Jun 1919 as for *M 114*; launched in May 1920 as the motor vessel *Erna David*; sold in 1922 to Th Lechelt & Co, Hamburg, as *Principio*; sold in 1928 to Occidental Transportation, Manzanillo, as the Mexican *Zaragoza*; renamed *Appollo* during the early 1930s, then reverted to the name *Principio*; sold in 1932 to South Sea Traders, St Johns, Newfoundland, as *Tooya*; sold in 1935 to E Rougier, Papeete, Tahiti, then in 1938 to Boleo-Estudios e Inversiones Minas SA, Santa Rosalia, as the Mexican *Korrigan IV*; sold in 1956 to Impulsora Minera e Industrial de Baja California, Santa Rosalia, under the same name. Sunk on 28 Nov 1966 90nm southeast of Cezalbo Island, Gulf of California, after capsizing during a storm.

M 148, 149: construction halted before completion; materials used for the lighters *FSG I* and *FSG II*.

M 150: launched in May 1920. Stricken 24 Jun 1919; sold 11 Aug 1920 for 2,300,000M to H Klinck of Kiel, and converted to the motor vessel *Julius*. Sunk on 14 Nov 1920 off Farö Island, position 57° 55′N, 10° 08′E, after grounding.

M 151: launched in September 1920. Stricken 24 Jun 1919; sold 26 Jun 1919 for 710,000M for conversion, and became the motor vessel *Kosmos I* for Krull & Mais, Hamburg; sold in 1925 to W M P Angione, Corinto, as the Nicaraguan *Kosmos*; sold in 1930 to the Standard Fruit & SS Co, Ceiba, as the Honduran *Kosmos I*; sold in 1941 to Cia de Nav y Tierras . . . 'Elliot' as the Panamanian *Baranquilla*; sold in 1945 to the Cia Continental de Navigacion SA de CV, Mexico, as *Presidente Madero*; sold in 1948 to Hermanos Ayo, Puerto

Limon, as the Costa Rican *Florita*. Sunk on the Quita Sueno Bank, position 14° 13′N, 81° 06′W, after grounding.

M 152: launched in June 1920. Stricken 24 Jun 1919 and sold incomplete on 26 Jun 1919 for 710,000M to a Hamburg company for conversion, and became the motor vessel *Silbo* for W Boelstler & Co, Hamburg. Sunk at Scharhorn on 19 Jan 1923, during a storm.

M 153–156: not completed.

M 157: launched 9 Apr 1919, commissioned* 8 Dec 1919. Served in the Reichsmarine and the Kriegsmarine, from 28 Jun 1941 as *M 557*. Sunk at 2305hrs on 27 Dec 1941 northeast of Rugen after hitting a mine during a snowstorm; all crew lost.

M 158: launched during 1920. Stricken 14 Jun 1919 and sold 11 Aug 1920 as for *M 42*, under the name *Grille*; sold in 1923 to the Vicomte le Guales de Mezaubran, St Brieux, as the French *Dinard*; sold in 1933 to Colombia and became the Colombian patrol boat *Cordova*. Sunk in 1946, no details known.

M 159, 160: contract with Union-Giesserei, Königsberg, cancelled.

M 161, 162: under construction at Reiherstieg Schiffswerfte, Hamburg; not completed.

M 163–176: contracts cancelled (see the list of dockyards for contract details).

UT 1–3: contracts granted 25 Aug 1918, but building preparations only were undertaken.

UT 4–7: conversion of four standard M-boats, then under construction, was planned using these designations; the conversions were never carried out.

*These M-boats carried out active minesweeping duties at some stage in their careers.

FM 1 class

Name	Builder (construction no)	Built	Cost in Marks (000s)	Displacement (t = tonnes T = tons)	Length (m)	Breadth (m)	Draught (m)	Power (hp)	Revs (rpm)	Speed (kts)	Range (nm/kts)	Coal (t)	Oil (t)
FM 1–36	*		640	193t max 170t des	43.00 oa 41.80 cwl	6.00	1.68 fwd 1.40 aft	600ihp des	310 des	14.0 des	650/14	32	—
FM 37–66	*		640	205t max 185t des	45.50 oa 44.20 cwl	6.00	1.71 fwd 1.40 aft	750ihp des	330 des	14.3 des	640/14	35	—

* Builders and construction numbers as follows: *FM 1, 2* Seebeck (412–3); *FM 3, 4* Tecklenborg (302–3); *FM 5–7* Frerichs (303–5); *FM 8–10* Stülcken (538–40); *FM 11, 12* Sachsenberg (800–1); *FM 13,14* Union (189–90); *FM 15, 16* Übigau; *FM 17, 18* Meyer (332–3); *FM 19, 20* Tecklenborg (308–9); *FM 21, 22* Seebeck (414–5); *FM 23, 24* Frerichs; *FM 25, 26* Unterweser (162–3); *FM 27, 28* Wollheim; *FM 29* Nobiskrug (90); *FM 30, 31* LMG (143–4); *FM 32* Sachsenberg (802); *FM 33,34* Nordsee (113–4); *FM 35* Union (191); *FM 36* Oderwerke (682); *FM 37–41* Unterweser (171–5); *FM 42–44* Rickmers (185–7); *FM 45–47* Koch (249–51); *FM 48–50* Meyer (335–6); *FM 51–53* Janssen; *FM 54, 55* Kremer (482–3); *FM 56, 57* Wollheim; *FM 58, 59* Übigau; *FM 60, 61* Nobiskrug (93–4); *FM 62* Thormählen; *FM 63, 64* Klawitter; *FM 65, 66* Nüscke.

Construction

Laid down as shallow draught minesweepers (*Flachgehende Minensuchboote*), official design 1917, adapted 1918. Transverse frame steel construction (four watertight compartments) built to merchant ship standards. Depth 2.29m.

Propulsion

Two vertical 3-cylinder triple expansion engines (two 3-bladed screws, 1.40m diameter) in the engine room, in some cases supplied by companies other than the dockyard. One Marine-type boiler (16 atmospheres forced, four fireboxes, 160sq m) in

FM 1–36 (1918); *FM 37–66* were similar.

the boiler room, in some cases supplied by companies other than the dockyard. Electrical installation details not known. One rudder.

Armament

Fitted with one torpedo boat gun or one 8.8cm/30 QF gun (100 rounds).

Handling

Seagoing capability up to about Beaufort 5–6, manoeuvring not as good as for M boats, moderate turning circle.

Complement

Crew: 0/35. Boats: two yawls.

Notes

Colour scheme grey or black overall. In 1918 nineteen boats remained incomplete after the development of a new bow defence system for M boats, due to their poor seakeeping, inadequate structural strength and other faults.

Careers

FM 1: launched 15 Jun 1918, commissioned 18 Jul 1918; served in the Reichsmarine for submarine training. Stricken 7 Dec 1920; sold 16 Jan 1922 for 475,000M to East Prussia/Latvia, renamed *Tepscora* and used in liquor smuggling; transferred 1924 to J B Hermann of Elbing, and in 1925 to O Karczinowsky of Königsberg for use as the steam harbour ferry *Siegfried*; became a motor harbour ferry in 1938–39; became the *H 521* flagship in 1939, used 27 Jun 1942 as the navigation training boat *Nordpol*. Sunk 9 Oct 1943 at Gotenhafen, by an aircraft bomb. Raised, returned 3 Mar 1947 to Karczinowsky at Kappeln for use as the barrack ship *Siegfried*, used again as a motor harbour ferry in 1950 and at Urdingen in about 1960; later broken up.

FM 2: launched 6 Jul 1918, commissioned* 24 Aug 1918; served in the Reichsmarine for submarine training. Stricken 10 Mar 1920; sold for 1,000,000M to Kiel and later to Poland for use as the minesweeper *Czaika*. Stricken 1935, later became ss *Czaika*; scuttled in September 1939 at Gdynia; raised, broken up.

FM 3: launched 17 Jan 1918, commissioned* 13 Feb 1918; used for submarine training. Stricken 8 May 1919; sold for 300,000M to Berlin, then in the 1920s to Cie Continentale Belge de Nav, Antwerp, renamed *Cecedena IV*, transferred 1925 to

Notes: FM 9, 15 and 48, sold at Berlin, were presumably inland vessels since they have no individual record; the same applies to FM 10, 14, 30 and 32, which were sold at Breslau.

The subsequent allocation of names to vessels sold at Bucharest (FM 4, 16, 20, 23, 33 and 36) is by no means certain. It is likely that all six had a fairly long life, working in the Balkan region until about 1939, but official records are completely lacking. One vessel out of FM 4, 20 and 23 was transferred to the Hungarian navy in 1928 as the minesweeper Körös; she was taken as a US prize in 1945, transferred to Passau in 1951, and later broken up.

Those vessels sold at Hamburg are not covered by official records; some hulls were subsequently used as barges, lighters or similar.

One unidentified FM boat was sold to Greece as Cecedena 1, later became Megaris under the ownership of K Kastanis of Piraeus, then Cecedena II, and finally Cecedena III, serving as a lighter at Apatin in the 1930s. One further unidentified FM boat subsequently became the ss Assaje.

Leonhardt & Blumberg of Hamburg for use as the steam tug *Cecedena 4*; transferred to G Joos, renamed *Minna*; transferred 1930 to J Knaack, and 1931 to F Mützelfeld; sold in 1935 and broken up at Harburg.

FM 4: launched 23 Feb 1918, commissioned* 27 Feb 1918; served in the Reichsmarine for submarine training. Stricken 10 Mar 1920; sold to a Bucharest bank.

FM 5: launched in 1918, commissioned* 5 Aug 1918; served in the Reichsmarine for submarine training. Stricken 8 May 1919; sold 14 Oct 1919 to Greece for use as the steam harbour ferry *Georgios Galeos*, later renamed *Maria K* and . . . *Kalydon*, taken by Germany in 1941, renamed *10 V 1*; sunk (details not known).

FM 6: launched in 1918, commissioned 21 Oct 1918; served in the Reichsmarine for submarine training. Stricken 31 Dec 1919; sold 22 Jul 1920 to Luwen of Duisburg-Ruhrort for use as an inland ship; fate unknown.

FM 7: launched 1918. Stricken 8 May 1919; sold for 200,000M to Gerhard Hulskens & Co of Wesel for use as an inland ship; fate unknown.

FM 8: launched 26 Jul 1918, commissioned 19 Oct 1918. Stricken; fate as for *FM 7*.

FM 9: launched 3 Dec 1918, commissioned 14 Jan 1919. Stricken 8 May 1919; sold for 300,000M to Berlin; fate unknown.

FM 10: launched 16 Jan 1919, commissioned 1 Apr 1919; served in the bay and river flotilla. Stricken 26 Nov 1919; sold to Bieber of Memel; fate unknown.

FM 11: launched 1918, commissioned 13 Sept 1918; used for submarine training. Stricken; fate as for *FM 9*.

FM 12: launched 1918. Stricken 8 May 1919; sold as a lighter to Fa Fentsch & Laeisz; fate unknown.

FM 13: launched 20 Jul 1918, commissioned 7 Oct 1918. Stricken 8 May 1919; sold for 300,000M to Antwerpener Schiffs- & Maschinenbau-Ges. of Hamburg; fate unknown.

FM 14: launched 28 Oct 1918, commissioned* 23 Jan 1919; served in the bay and river flotilla. Stricken 26 Nov 1919; fate as for *FM 10*.

FM 15: launched 1918, commissioned* 1918 and used in submarine training. Stricken 8 May 1919; sold 14 Oct 1919; fate unknown.

FM 16: launched 1919. Stricken, as for *FM 4*; used in Albania as the gunboat *Squpnia*; sunk in 1935, details not known.

FM 17: launched 18 May 1918, commissioned 10 Sept 1918; used for submarine training; fate as for *FM 9*.

FM 18: launched 1918, commissioned 1918. Stricken 8 May 1919; fate as for *FM 13*.

FM 19: launched 23 Feb 1918, commissioned* 14 Mar 1918; served in the Reichsmarine for submarine training; converted in the Hansa dockyard at Tönning in 1922; transferred to Portugal as part of war reparations, commissioned 26 Oct 1922 as the motor ferry *Raul Cascais* at Tejo; became the Portuguese fisheries protection boat *Raoul Cascais* 13 Oct 1924. Stricken 4 Sept 1936; broken up 1937.

FM 20: launched 9 Mar 1918, commissioned* 27 Mar 1918; served in the Reichsmarine for submarine training. Stricken 10 Mar 1920; fate as for *FM 4*.

FM 21: launched 14 Dec 1918, commissioned 1 Apr 1919; named *Peilboot III* in 1920. Stricken 1 Oct 1928; sold 7 Aug 1930 for 15,600RM to F Mützelfeld of Cuxhaven, 1935 to SA Bremerhaven. Sunk 24 Oct 1944 at Bremerhaven by British bombs.

FM 22: launched 19 Feb 1919, commissioned 9 May 1919; named *Peilboot IV* in 1920. Stricken 22 Jul 1927; broken up 1928 at Hamburg-Moorburg.

FM 23: launched 1918, commissioned 25 Dec 1918. Stricken 31 Dec 1919, as for *FM 4*; became the Albanian gunboat *Sqenderbeg*; sunk in 1935.

FM 24: launched 1918, commissioned 15 Mar 1919; served in the Reichsmarine. Stricken 29 Apr 1922; sold 7 Apr 1922 for 650,000M to Hamburg; became the Persian gunboat *Fatiya* in 1923, *Pahlavi* in 1926 and *Shahin* 1935–41; broken up.

FM 25: launched 10 May 1918, commissioned* 3 Aug 1918; served in the Reichsmarine submarine school. Stricken 29 Apr 1922; sold 7 Apr 1922 for 650,000M to Hamburg, transferred 1925 to P Mestermann of Rostock for use as the steam harbour ferry *Bismarck*; transferred 1927 to Alands Angbaats OY of Finland, renamed *Alands-Express*, then to Aabolands Angf in 1930; renamed *Express*; transferred to Italy in 1933, renamed *S Constanzo Express*, used in 1935 at the Nav a Vapore municipalazzata at Trieste, renamed *Gianpaolo I*; broken up in 1954.

FM 26: launched 19 Jul 1918, commissioned* 1 Oct 1918; used in submarine training; became *Peilboot VII* in 1920. Stricken 22 Jul 1927; broken up 1928 at Hamburg-Moorburg.

FM 27: launched 1918. Stricken 10 Oct 1919; sold 20 Sept 1920 for 1,000,000M, renamed *Jaskolka*; stricken again 1935, broken up.

FM 28: launched 1918; transferred to Kiel and later to Poland as the minesweeper *Mewa*; became the survey ship *Pomorzamin* in 1934. Sunk 1 Sept 1939 at *Jastarnia*; raised in 1946, broken up.

FM 29: launched 1919; served in the Reichsmarine. Stricken 8 Jun 1925; sold to Heidmann of Stettin for use as the steam harbour ferry *Westfalen*; sold 1928 to C Wollheim of Stettin, and 1932 to the Soc Maritima de Transportes Ltda of Barreiro, Portugal, renamed *Montijense*; still in existence in 1958, sunk (details not known).

FM 30: launched 1919; served in the bay and river flotilla. Stricken 26 Nov 1919; sold 3 May 1921 to Breslauer Dampfer Cie as an inland ship.

FM 31: launched 1919, commissioned 11 Jun 1919. Stricken 10 Mar 1920, as for *FM 27*; used in Poland as the minesweeper *Rybitwa*; stricken again in 1935; broken up.

FM 32: launched 1919; served in the bay and river flotilla. Stricken 26 Nov 1919; remaining career as for *FM 30*.

FM 33: launched 1919, commissioned 18 Jun 1919. Stricken 10 Oct 1919; remaining career as for *FM 4*.

FM 34: launched 1919. Stricken 31 Dec 1919; remaining career as for *FM 6*.

FM 35: launched 1919. Stricken 10 Oct 1919; sold 23 Feb 1920 for 650,000M to Memel, transferred 1922 to Otwiwerke of Bremen as ss *Baltic*; fate unknown.

FM 36: launched 1919; served in the bay and river flotilla. Stricken 31 Dec 1919; as for *FM 4*, also served as the steam harbour ferry *Socrates*; purchased 5 Oct 1941 in the Danube area, commissioned 18 Oct 1941 into the German minesweeper teaching command at Constanta as *Xanten*; renamed *UJ 116* in 1942; scuttled 25 Aug 1944 in Constanta.

FM 37: launched 1919. Stricken 22 Aug 1921; sold for 325,000M to Berlin, and in 1923 to the Costiera SA di Nav. Marittima at Fiume, and in 1939 to the Soc Fiumana di Nav. as *Fiumana I*; renamed *Arco Azurro* in 1939; sunk 23 Oct 1942 at Genoa by an aircraft bomb; broken up.

FM 38: launched 1919. Remaining career as *FM 37*; also named *Lurana* in 1938 and *Fiumana II* in 1945; fate unknown.

FM 39: commissioned summer 1918. Stricken 16 Sept 1919; sold for 270,000M to Berlin, later to Regensburg; fate unknown.

FM 40, 41: turned down by the Kriegsmarine before completion; broken up.

FM 42: launched 1918, commissioned 18 Nov 1919. Stricken 29 Apr 1922; sold 7 Apr 1922 for 550,000M to Aug Bolten of Hamburg as ss *Pionier*. She was the first ship to sail from the Baltic through the Russian canals and rivers to the Volga and Caspian Sea; sold to Russia.

FM 43: launched 1919. No other details.

FM 44–47: turned down by the Kriegsmarine before completion; broken up.

FM 48: launched 1919. Stricken 29 Aug 1921; sold in November 1921 to Berlin[1].

FM 49: launched 1919; converted to a steam ferry after summer 1918. Stricken 8 May 1919; sold for 300,000M 14 Oct 1919 to a Berlin company, as for *FM 37* from 1922; also named *Albona*; broken up in 1939.

FM 50: launched 1919; as for *FM 49*; also sold 1922 to Smyrna International Ferry Services Ltd of Greece as the steam harbour ferry *Eleine*; fate unknown.

FM 51–53: turned down by the Kriegsmarine before completion; broken up.

FM 54: launched 1919; sold in March 1920 to B Plage of Berlin, converted by D W Kremer Sohn; commissioned 15 Apr 1920 as the steam harbour ferry *Freiheit*; sold 1922 to Rinkjöbing Dampskip-S of Denmark as the *Vestjyden*, 1925 to Seebäderdienst Memel as the *Memelland*, 1927 to G Hermann of Elbing, 1930 to O Karczinowsky of Königsberg; renamed *Brunhilde*; sold 1935 to Polska Zegluga Rzeczna Vistula of Gdynia as the *Carmen*; sunk 1939 (no details).

FM 55: launched 1918; construction interrupted before completion; underwent further work in 1922 as ss *King Albert*; sold 1930 to D Dekker of Wildervink, Netherlands, as *Wilhelmina*; sold 1931 to SA des Bateaux Belges of Antwerp, Belgium, as *Miramar*, taken 1940 as a German prize, served as the service vessel *Eider* at Helgoland; fate unknown.

FM 56, 57: commissioned summer 1918. Stricken 16 Sept 1919, sold 1920–21 for 270,000M each via Berlin to Regensburg; fate unknown.

FM 58–61, 63–66: turned down by the Kriegsmarine before completion; broken up.

FM 62: launched 1919; converted to a steam ferry after summer 1918. Stricken 6 Jun 1919; sold for 240,000M to Bremerhaven as the *Vaterland*; sold in about 1935 to the Soc Marittima de Transportes Ltda of Barreiro, Portugal, and converted to the motor harbour ferry *Ribatejo Primeiro*; still in existence in 1947.

*These FM boats took part in active mineseeking service after completion. Some of the boats known to have sunk are not listed in Lloyd's Register Book after 1935–36. Despite their design and production shortcomings, it is likely that they continued working for a while, unclassified, or as inland ships.

M-boats 1935–1943

M 1 class (1935/39 Type)

Name	Builder (construction no)	Built	Cost in Marks (000s)	Displacement (t = tonnes T = tons)	Length (m)	Breadth (m)	Draught (m)	Power (hp)	Revs (rpm)	Speed (kts)	Range (nm/kts)	Coal (t)	Oil (t)
M 1–3, 10	Stülcken (710–712, 718)		5452	874T max 772t des 682T std 894t max (mod)	68.10 oa 66.00 cwl	8.70 8.30	2.65 max 2,12 des 2.70 max (mod)	3500ihp des 3200shp des		18.3 max 18.2 des	5000/10 1000/17	–	143
M 4–6, 11	Oderwerke (787–789, 798)		,,	,,	,,	,,	,,	,,		,,	,,	—	,,
M 7–9, 12	Flender (242–244, 249)		,,	,,	,,	,,	,,	,,		,,	,,	—	,,
M 13–16	Stülcken (727–30)		4952	,,	,,	,,	,,	,,		,,	,,	–	,,
M 17–19	Oderwerke (803–805)		,,	,,	,,	,,	,,	,,		,,	,,	—	,,
M 20–24	Flender (257–261)		,,	,,	,,	,,	,,	,,		,,	,,	—	,,
M 37–39	Atlas (366–368)		3452	878T max 785t des 685T std 898t max (mod)	68.40 oa 66.60 cwl	8.70 8.30	2.65 max 2,12 des 2.70 max (mod)	3700ihp des					
M 81–100	LMG (427–431, –)		,,	,,	,,	,,	,,	,,					
M 101–130	Rickmers (229–232, –)		,,	,,	,,	,,	,,	,,					
M 131–150	Lindenau (79–81, –)		,,	,,	,,	,,	,,	,,					
M 151–200	Oderwerke (829–834, –)		,,	,,	,,	,,	,,	,,					
M 201–250	Neptun (494–499, –)		,,	,,	,,	,,	,,	,,					
M 251–260	DWA (285–290, –)		,,	,,	,,	,,	,,	,,					

Construction

Laid down as minesweepers in 1935, mobilising 1936, official design by Marine ObBrt Driessen in 1935; various modifications were incorporated in 1939 at the start of construction including a sharper stem, built-in roll keels, extended deadwood, and a greater slope in the foreship frames. Construction plans were taken up in 1939 by H C Stülcken Sohn of Hamburg. Longitudinal and transverse frame steel construction, partly welded (twelve watertight compartments, double bottom 87 per cent), light alloy superstructure, bridge bulwarks armoured with 10mm Ww (soft) steel, transom stern. Depth 3.75m, 3.90m after 1939 mobilisation. The stem was ice reinforced in 1943.

Propulsion

Two Lentz uniform expansion engines[1] (two

3-bladed 1.75m diameter screws, *M 1* and *M 2* each with two Voith-Schnieder 6-bladed 2.50m diameter propellers) in one engine room. Two Wagner or M . . . La Mont high pressure boilers (35 atmospheres forced, 450 degrees, size unknown) in 1 + 1 boiler rooms; fuel oil consumption 1.3kg per shp/hr. Electrical system included two diesel 40kW generators, one 100kW turbo-generator, making a total output of 220V, 180kW, and a mine protection and KFRG (*Kabel Fern Raum Gerät* – magnetic sweeping gear) system including two diesel 60V, 20kW generators. All boats had two rudders, except *M 1* and *M 2* which had Voith-Schnieder propellers; after *M 25* some boats had Kort nozzles for 3-bladed screws. Active roll damping was removed after 1939/40.

Armament

Two, formerly one, 10.5cm/45 QF guns (480 rounds); two, formerly one, 3.7cm AA gun (3000 rounds); two 2cm AA guns (4000 rounds); in addition four 2cm AA guns (6000 rounds) were fitted in 1942. Thirty mines (62 tons extra load).

Handling

Excellent seaboats, manoeuvred well with a good turning circle, but the class was crank at high speed, so a rudder deflection restriction was imposed after 1935 (after *M 24*); the same measure was taken on a few Kriegsmarine ships for stability reasons. *M 1* had a KFRG system, remote control sweeping, towed loop gear of 27t fixed ballast and a limitation on water/oil consumption, leaving a residue of 40t. The transom stern limited both seakeeping and speed.

Complement

Crew: 3/81 in 1935, 5/90 up to 2/116 (flotilla flagship 3/8) in 1939. Boats: one motor pinnace, one yawl, one dinghy.

Notes

Colour scheme grey overall with camouflage. The design was complex, with long building times, and was demanding of the engine crew. The armament' was generous compared with the initial barrage weapons equipment, which were not taken into account sufficiently for the boat's design and weight. After 1939 the central deck was not timber clad and the mast was later shortened. For differences in appearance, see the drawings; the wide boat supports for the motor pinnace after *M 25* are clearly seen; some ships such as *M 81* have standard davits. The boats were re-equipped and rearmed for DT, and a folding bulwark for the forward bridge was installed after 1942. The boats were delivered from the dockyard as leader boat, medical boat and similar:

Type A: flotilla leader boat (*M 22, M 32, M33*)
Type B: *Bojenboot mit Ingenieur* (*M 11, M 17, M 25–28, M 34, M 39*)
Type C: *Bojenboot mit Feuerwerker*, etc (*M 13, M 14, M 23, M 30*)
Type D: *Bojenboot* with administrative officer (*M 15*)
Type E: medical boat (*M 35, M 37*)
Type F: administration boat (*M 24, M 29, M 31*)
Type G: senior administrator's boat (*M 19*)
Type H: *Schuhmacher* boat, etc (*M 16, M 20, M 21, M 36, M 38*)

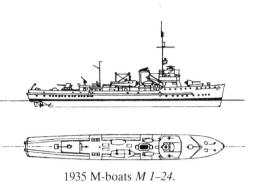

1935 M-boats *M 1–24*.   1939 mobilisation M-boats *M 25–260. Mrva.*

Careers

M 1: launched 5 Mar 1937, commissioned * 1 Sept 1938; tactical designation *C 5501* given in 1941, *M 5201* in 1942/43. Sunk at 1252hrs on 12 Jan 1945 at Nordbyfjord in the vicinity of Bergen, by six torpedoes and aircraft bombs; twenty dead.

M 2: launched 20 May 1937, commissioned* 25 Mar 1939; tactical designation *M 5202* given in 1942/43. Sunk 11 Mar 1945 at Fedjefjord by aircraft rockets.

M 3: launched 28 Sept 1937, commissioned* 10 Dec 1938; taken 15 Nov 1945 as a Russian prize, transferred to the Black Sea fleet as a *T 9* class minesweeper; fate unknown.

M 4: launched 16 Oct 1937, commissioned* 10 Nov 1938; taken 1945 as a US prize, transferred to the GM/SA; transferred 9 Oct 1947 to France. Stricken 7 Aug 1948, used as the hulk *Q 108*, still in existence in 1972 at Lorient.

M 5: launched 16 Oct 1937, commissioned* 14 Jan 1939. Sunk at 0339hrs on 18 Jun 1940 at Ramsoyfjord, position 63° 30′N, 08° 09′E, by two mines; twenty-eight dead.

M 6: launched 8 Jan 1938, commissioned* 6 Jun 1939. Sunk at 1245hrs on 23 Oct 1941 south of Lorient, position 47° 18′N, 04° 20′E, by a mine; twenty-one dead.

M 7: launched 29 Sept 1937, commissioned* 21 Oct 1938; taken 15 Nov 1945 as a USSR prize and transferred to the Black Sea fleet as a *T 9* class minesweeper; fate unknown.

M 8: launched 29 Sept 1937, commissioned* 11 Jan 1939. Sunk at 0400hrs on 14 May 1943 in the vicinity of the Hook of Holland, position 52° 03′ 0″N, 03° 51′ 5″E, by two torpedoes from British MTBs; fifty-three dead.

M 9: launched 16 Nov 1937, commissioned* 5 May 1939; taken 1945 as a US prize, transferred to the GM/SA; transferred 9 Oct 1947 to France as the *Somme*; stricken 8 Mar 1960, became the hulk *Q 204*, broken up in 1966.

M 10: launched 9 Aug 1938, commissioned* 30 May 1939. Sunk in action near Lorient after July 1943.

M 11: launched 23 Aug 1938, commissioned* 7 Aug 1939. Sunk at 1045hrs on 6 Jun 1940 southwest of Feiestein in the vicinity of Hellestø, by a mine; five dead.

M 12: launched 6 Aug 1938, commissioned* 21 Aug 1939; taken 1945 as a US prize, transferred to the GM/SA; transferred 9 Oct 1947 to France, used as a barrack boat at Lorient; broken up.

M 13: launched 28 Feb 1939, commissioned* 7 Sept 1939. Sunk at 1240hrs on 31 May 1944 in the Gironde estuary, by her own mine after rudder failure.

M 14: launched 25 Apr 1939, commissioned* 1 Dec 1939. Sunk 3 May 1945 in the vicinity of Swinemünde, by a mine. Raised, repair planned for DDR sea police.

M 15: launched 4 Sept 1939, commissioned* 22 Feb 1940. Sunk 20 Mar 1945 at Kohlenhof arsenal, Kiel, by an aircraft bomb; broken up.

M 16: launched 15 Nov 1939, commissioned* 1 Jun 1940; severely damaged at 1300hrs on 4 Nov 1943, by an aircraft bomb in Kotka timber harbour, towed to Kiel, stricken; bombed again 20 Mar 1945, wreck scuttled 18 May 1946, position 58° 10′N, 10° 42′E.

M 17: launched 29 Jul 1939, commissioned* 17 Jan 1940; taken out of service 22 Aug 1944 at Rochefort during retreat; taken 15 Nov 1945 as a USSR prize, transferred to the Black Sea fleet as a *T 9* class minesweeper.

M 18: launched 16 Sept 1939, commissioned* 19 Mar 1940. Scuttled at Deutsche Werke Kiel, blown up during repairs; broken up.

M 19: launched 28 Oct 1939, commissioned* 8 May 1940. Sunk 9 Apr 1945 in Kiel bay, by an aircraft bomb, stranded.

M 20: launched 16 Jun 1939, commissioned* 11 Dec 1939. Sunk at 2330hrs on 21 Jul 1944 in Narva

---

[1] Fitted with two twin double-acting expansion engines because gudgeon pins, connecting rods and crankshaft were lubricated in an oil-tight housing by sprayed and forced oil, a new concept for the time.

*Service as a minesweeper in active flotillas

Bay, off Vainupa, position 59° 35′ 9″N, 26° 16′ 4″E, by Soviet aircraft bombs together with *M 413*; five dead.

M 21: launched 6 Sept 1939, commissioned* 18 Apr 1940; taken 1945 as a US prize, transferred to the GM/SA; transferred to France 9 Oct 1947, used as a barrack boat at Lorient; broken up.

M 22: launched 20 Mar 1940, commissioned* 30 Jul 1940. Scuttled and sunk 7 May 1945 in the vicinity of Achterwehr (Kiel canal), position 54° 19′N, 09° 58′E; raised and broken up.

M 23: launched 11 Jul 1940, commissioned* 26 Oct 1940. Beached after hitting a mine 11 Jul 1941 in the vicinity of Pernau; one dead. Raised in 1941, recommissioned 22 Apr 1943; taken as a British prize, transferred to the GM/SA; broken up in Britain.

M 24: launched 12 Oct 1940, commissioned* 22 Feb 1941; taken 1945 as a British prize, transferred to the GM/SA; transferred 9 Oct 1947 to France as the *Ailette*; stricken 22 Nov 1956, used as the hulk *Q 76*; transferred 28 Feb 1957 to the German Federal navy as *Wespe*; taken out of service 20 Sept 1963, used as the target ship *Z 4*, severely damaged 22 Oct 1973 45nm northwest of Helgoland; scuttled 25 Oct 1973 in the North Sea, position 54° 21′ 8″N, 06° 42′ 2″E.

M 37: launched 12 Oct 1940, commissioned* 16 Jun 1941. Sunk at 0110hrs on 4 Jun 1944 in Narva bay, position 59° 30′ 5″N, 27° 36′E, by torpedoes from Soviet MTBs; thirteen dead.

M 38: launched 28 Feb 1941, commissioned* 13 Dec 1941; taken 1945 as a British prize, transferred to the GM/SA; transferred 9 Oct 1947 to France as the *Oise*; stricken 24 Feb 1958, used as the hulk *Q 90*, broken up.

M 39: launched 8 Aug 1941, commissioned* 5 May 1942. Sunk at 0330hrs on 24 May 1944 northwest of Ouistreham, position 49° 21′N, 00° 19′W, by torpedoes from a British MTB; approximately seventy dead.

M 40–80: contracts not granted.

M 81: launched 20 Dec 1940, commissioned* 17 Jul 1941; taken 1945 as a US prize, transferred to the GM/SA; transferred 9 Oct 1947 to France as the *Laffaux*; stricken 22 Nov 1956, used as the hulk *Q 75*; transferred 29 Feb 1957 to the German Federal navy as the *Hummel*; taken out of service 5 Oct 1963, used as a target ship. Stranded in December 1966 at Fano-Weststrand in a storm and sunk; raised in April/May 1967, broken up after 19 Mar 1976 at Kiel.

M 82: launched 23 Mar 1941, commissioned* 17 Nov 1941; taken 1945 as a British prize, transferred to the GM/SA; served in Britain in 1948, broken up.

M 83: launched 5 Jun 1941, commissioned* 9 Mar 1942. Sunk 14 Jun 1944 in the vicinity of Jersey, position 49° 44′ 8″N, 01° 56′ 9″W, by torpedoes from British MTBs; approximately seventy dead.

M 84: launched 3 Sept 1941, commissioned* 9 Jun 1942. Scuttled 11 Aug 1944 in the dock at Le Havre.

M 85: launched 6 Dec 1941, commissioned* 18 Sept 1942; taken 1945 as a British prize, transferred

to the GM/SA; transferred 9 Oct 1947 to France as the *Yser*; stricken 21 Dec 1956, used as the hulk *Q 78*; transferred 12 Feb 1957 to the German Federal navy as the *Brummer*; taken out of service 5 Oct 1963, used as a navigation training boat; used 9 Jun 1966 as a hulk; transferred 8 Apr 1974 to Kiel for breaking up.

M 86–100: contracts not granted.

M 101: launched 15 Mar 1941, commissioned* 22 Sept 1941. Sunk at 1810hrs on 25 Nov 1942 west of Namsos, position 64° 09′N, 10° 07′E, in a collision with the motor vessel *Levante*.

M 102: launched 1 Aug 1941, commissioned* 28 Apr 1942; taken 1945 as a British prize, transferred to the GM/SA; served in Britain in 1948, broken up.

M 103: launched 3 Dec 1941, commissioned* 6 Aug 1942. Sunk at 0705hrs on 15 Jun 1944 in the vicinity of the Ems estuary, position 53° 35′N, 06° 10′E, by an aircraft torpedo and gunfire, together with *Gustav Nachtigal* and *Amerskerk*; three dead.

M 104: launched 1 Apr 1942, commissioned* 7 Nov 1942; taken 1945 as a British prize, transferred to the GM/SA; served in Britain in 1948, broken up.

M 105–130: contracts not granted.

M 131: launched 20 Dec 1941, commissioned* 31 Aug 1942; taken 1945 as a British prize, transferred to the G/SA; served in Britain in 1948, broken up.

M 132: launched 7 Apr 1941, commissioned* 20 Jan 1942. Sunk at 2355hrs on 20 Sept 1944 in the vicinity of Egeroy, position 58° 23′ 5″N, 05° 34′E, by torpedoes from a British submarine; eleven dead.

M 133: launched 3 Aug 1942, commissioned* 26 Mar 1943. Sunk 6 Aug 1944 at St Malo, during an air attack.

M 134–150: contracts not granted.

M 151: launched 19 Oct 1940, commissioned* 5 May 1941; taken 15 Nov 1945 as a USSR prize, transferred to the Black Sea fleet as a *T 9* class minesweeper; fate not known.

M 152: launched 16 Nov 1940, commissioned* 30 Jun 1941. Sunk at 1513hrs on 23 Jul 1943 in the Gironde estuary, by a mine; approximately fifty dead.

M 153: launched 4 Jan 1941, commissioned* 1 Sept 1941. Capsized and sunk after engine failure at about 1800hrs on 10 Jul 1943 off the coast of Vizcaya, approximately 14 hours after an engagement with a destroyer and an MGB; eighteen dead.

M 154: launched 3 May 1941, commissioned* 1 Nov 1941; taken 1945 as a US prize, transferred to the GM/SA; taken 13 Feb 1946 as a USSR prize; became a *T 9* class minesweeper; fate unknown.

M 155: launched 19 Jul 1941, commissioned* 27 Jan 1942; taken 15 Nov 1945 as a USSR prize, transferred to the Black Sea fleet as a *T 9* class minesweeper; fate unknown.

M 156: launched 4 Oct 1941, commissioned* 28 Apr 1942. Damaged 5 Feb 1944 during engagement with British destroyers off Brittany coast; arrived L'Abervrach 6 Feb and sunk during air attack 1045hrs.

M 157–200: contracts not granted.

M 201: launched 18 May 1940, commissioned* 20 Dec 1940. Badly damaged 10 Jul 1941 in the Irben straits, by a mine. Repaired in the 1940s and recommissioned; taken 1945 as a British prize, transferred to the GM/SA; served in Britain in 1948, broken up.

M 202: launched 29 Sept 1940, commissioned* 3 Apr 1941; taken 1945 as a US prize, transferred to the GM/SA; transferred 9 Oct 1947 to France as the *Craonne*; stricken 27 Jun 1951, broken up.

M 203: launched 29 Sept 1940, commissioned* 3 Jun 1941; taken 15 Nov 1945 as a USSR prize, transferred to the Black Sea fleet as a *T 9* class minesweeper; fate unknown.

M 204: launched 21 Dec 1940, commissioned* 24 Aug 1941; remaining career as for *M 203*.

M 205: launched 3 May 1941, commissioned* 4 Nov 1941; taken 1945 as a US prize, transferred to the GM/SA; transferred 9 Oct 1947 to France as the *Belfort*; stricken 22 Nov 1956, used as the hulk *Q 74*; transferred 28 Feb 1957 to the German Federal navy as the *Biene*, taken out of service 20 Sept 1963, used 28 May 1968 as a training hulk, transferred 8 Jul 1974 to Kiel for breaking up.

M 206: launched 5 May 1941, commissioned* 21 Dec 1941. Scuttled and sunk 6 Aug 1944 at St Malo, position 48° 39′N, 02° 02′W.

M 207–250: contracts not granted.

M 251: launched 12 Jul 1940, commissioned* 16 Dec 1940; taken 1945 as a US prize, transferred to the GM/SA; transferred 9 Oct 1947 to France as the *Peronne*; stricken 27 Jun 1951, broken up.

M 252: launched 27 Sept 1940, commissioned* 15 Feb 1941; taken 1945 as a US prize, transferred to the GM/SA; transferred 9 Oct 1947 to France, served 8 Dec 1947 as the navigation training boat *Ancre*; stricken 28 Jul 1960, used as the hulk *Q 199*, at the breakwater off Brest.

M 253: launched 23 Nov 1940, commissioned* 21 Apr 1941; taken 1945 as a US prize, renamed *V 5502*, transferred to the GM/SA; transferred 9 Oct 1947 to France as the *Vimy*; stricken 22 Nov 1956, used as the hulk *Q 77*; transferred 12 Feb 1957 to the German Federal navy as the *Bremse*; taken out of service 5 Oct 1963, used as a target ship, sent 24 Aug 1976 to Wilhelmshaven for breaking up.

M 254: launched 17 Feb 1941, commissioned* 16 Jun 1941; taken 1945 for the GM/SA; taken 3 Feb 1946 as a USSR prize, transferred to the Black Sea fleet as a *T 9* class minesweeper; fate unknown.

M 255: launched 1 Apr 1941, commissioned* 11 Oct 1941; taken 15 Nov 1945 as a USSR prize, transferred to the Black Sea fleet as a *T 9* class minesweeper; fate unknown.

M 256: launched 31 May 1941, commissioned* 19 Jan 1942. Sunk at 1753hrs on 15 May 1942 in Cherbourg outer harbour during a towing operation after an aircraft bombing at 1400hrs. Raised, recommissioned in May 1944, transferred 1945 to the GM/SA; taken 29 Nov 1945 as a USSR prize, transferred to the Black Sea fleet as a *T 9* class minesweeper; fate unknown.

M 257–260: contracts not granted.

M 25 class (1938 Type)

Name	Builder (construction no)	Built	Cost in Marks (000s)	Displacement (t = tonnes T = tons)	Length (m)	Breadth (m)	Draught/ height (m)	Power (hp)	Revs (rpm)	Speed (kts)	Range (nm/kts)	Oil (t)
M 25–28	Stülcken (741–744)			908T max 713T des	71.00 oa 68.60 cwl	9.20 8.80	2.12 des	3200shp des		18.1 des	5000/10	—	155
M 29–32	Oderwerke (813–816)			”	”	”	”	”		”	”	—	”
M 33, 34	LMG* (432, 433)			”	”	”	”	”		”	”	—	”
M 35, 36	Schichau (1437, 1438)			”	”	”	”	”		”	”	—	”

* Construction of these vessels was originally allocated to Flender-Werft, Lübeck, but the contracts were taken over by LMG on 20 January 1941. The original Flender construction numbers were 278 and 279.

Construction
Laid down in 1938 as minesweepers, official design 1938–39 from 1935. Longitudinal and transverse frame steel construction, welded (thirteen 89 per cent watertight compartments), with a transom stern. Depth 3.90m.

Propulsion
Two Lentz uniform expansion engines (two 6-bladed, 3.00m diameter Voith-Schneider propellers), as for 1935 M boats. No rudders.

Armament
Two 10.5cm/45 QF guns (480 rounds), three 2cm AA guns (6000 rounds). Thirty mines.

Complement
5/92. Boats: one motor pinnace, one yawl, one dinghy.

Notes
M 25–36 construction contracts were changed from the 1935–36 mobilisation type M boats at the outbreak of war, due to supply difficulties with the Voith-Schneider drive system, as the complex 1938 design placed excessive demands on the dockyards, and demanded new standards compared with the 1935 design.

Careers
M 25: launched 19 Mar 1940, commissioned* 16 Nov 1940. Sunk in September 1944 in western France, scuttled.

M 26: launched 21 May 1940, commissioned* 21 Dec 1940. Sunk at 1405hrs on 15 May 1942 in the Channel, in the vicinity of Cap de la Hague, by aircraft bombs, together with *M 256*.

M 27: launched 20 Nov 1940, commissioned* 10 Feb 1941. Sunk at 1955hrs on 11 Aug 1944 in the Gironde estuary, position 45° 15′N, 00° 44′ 6″W, by a mine; forty-one dead.

M 28: launched 29 Jul 1940, commissioned* 22 May 1941; taken out of service 16 Jan 1945 at St Nazaire; taken 1945 as a British prize, transferred to the GM/SA; transferred 9 Oct 1947 to France as the *Meuse*; stricken 14 Jan 1957, used as the hulk *Q 79* at the breakwater off Brest.

M 29: launched 18 May 1940, commissioned* 4 Sept 1940; taken 15 Nov 1945 as a USSR prize, transferred to the Black Sea fleet as a *T 9* class minesweeper; fate unknown.

M 30: launched 1 Jun 1940, commissioned* 31 Oct 1940; remaining career as for *M 29*.

M 31: launched 13 Jul 1940, commissioned* 19 Dec 1940. Sunk at 0226hrs on 21 Oct 1944 in the vicinity of Honningsvaag, by torpedoes from Soviet MTBs.

M 32: launched 24 Aug 1940, commissioned* 8 Mar 1941; taken 1945 as a US prize, transferred to the GM/SA; transferred 1 Nov 1947 to the OMGUS, then 18 Jun 1948 to the Ostdeutsche Dampfschiff & Transport Ges (DSTG) of Hamburg for conversion to a motor ferry, but considered unsuitable; returned 12 Sept 1949 to the US Navy; broken up at Ghent in 1950.

M 33: launched 1 Apr 1942, commissioned* 18 Dec 1942; taken 1945 as a British prize, transferred to the GM/SA; used as a barrack boat for wreck salvage, broken up.

M 34: launched 7 Aug 1942, commissioned* 26 Jun 1943; transferred to the GM/SA; taken 3 Feb 1946 as a USSR prize, transferred to the Black Sea fleet as a *T 9* class minesweeper; fate unknown.

M 35: launched 9 Nov 1940, commissioned* 6 Sept 1941; taken 1945 as a US prize, transferred to the GM/SA; transferred 9 Oct 1947 to France as the *Bapaume*; stricken 23 Jul 1952, broken up.

M 36: launched 21 Dec 1940, commissioned* 2 Jan 1942. Sunk 4 May 1945 in the Great Belt, by bombs from British aircraft.

*Service as a minesweeper in active flotillas

M 261 class (1940 Type)

Construction
Laid down in 1940 as minesweepers, official design by MarOBrt Driessen in 1939–40, which showed similarity to the official 1915 designs and their improvements. Preparatory work and detail drawings were by Deutsche Werke Kiel AG; adaptations in November–December 1941 effectively increased displacement by approximately 8t to 543t and 774t respectively. Transverse frame steel construction, welded (eleven watertight compartments, double bottom 87 per cent), with hard chine foreship and tug stern. Bridge bulwark armoured with 10mm Ww (soft) steel. Transverse and lateral bunkers for coal. Depth 3.65m.

Propulsion
Two vertical 3-cylinder triple expansion engines of 900hp each, with switchable Bauer-Wach exhaust steam turbines of 450hp each (two 3-bladed screws, 2.15m diameter) in one engine room. Two coal-fired Marine type boilers using the Schulz system (four fireboxes, 16.5 atmospheres forced, 320 degrees, 288sq m, 13t/hr) in 1 + 1 boiler rooms. The electricity station between the engine and boiler

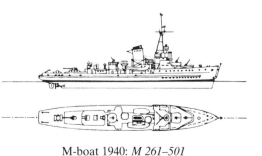

M-boat 1940: *M 261–501*

Name	Builder (construction no)	Built	Cost in Marks (000s)	Displacement (t = tonnes T = tons)	Length (m)	Breadth (m)	Draught (m)	Power (hp)	Revs (rpm)	Speed (kts)	Range (nm/kts)	Coal (t)	Oil (t)
M 261–501	*			775T max 637t des 543T std	62.30 oa 57.60 cwl	8.90 8.50	2.82 max 2.34 des 2.10 std	2615ihp max 2400ihp des 2150shp des	251 max 230 des	17.2 max 16.8 des	4000/10	156 +10	

* Builders and construction numbers (where construction was begun) as follows: *M 261–270* Atlas (369–375, –), *M 271–290* Rickmers (233–242, –), *M 291–300* Lindenau (82–88, –), *M 301–320* Unterweser (298–304, –), *M 321–328* Oderwerke (835–842), *M 329–340* LMG (434, 435, –), *M 341–360* Neptun (500–507, –), *M 361–380* Schichau (1494–1497, 1509–1512, 1550–1553, 1579, 1580, 1455–1460), *M 381–400* Elsfleth (244–263), *M 401–410* Rotterdam DD ((229–236, –), or (230–237, –)), *M 411–420* De Schelde (218–223, –), *M 421–430* Wilton (677–684, –), *M 431–40* Nederland SB (284–288, 302–304, –), *M 441–450* Smit, P (552–557, –), *M 451–458* Gusto (796–801, –), *M 459–463* Nederland Dok (97–101), *M 467–474* v d Giessen (675–679, –), *M 475–482* Smit, J & K (783, 784, –), *M 483–485* Boele's (903, 904, –), *M 486–488* Verschure (238, –), *M 489–494* Smit, L (905,–), *M 495–501* Gebr Pot (888, 889,–).

room II had two diesel generators of 20kW each, with a total output of 220V, 40kW; later boats had one 20kW and one 50kW, with a total output of 220V, 70kW; the MES or KFRG system had one 60V, 30kW diesel generator. One rudder, two after mid-1943.

Armament
One 10.5cm/45 Utof gun (120 rounds), one 3.7cm AA gun (2000 rounds), two 2cm AA guns (4000 rounds), increased in 1941 to seven 2cm AA guns (1400 rounds); no mines. After June 1943 the TS boats (torpedo boat versions) had two 53.3cm TT (rounds unknown) on the forecastle, one on each side. The 'combat' boats in the Front flotillas, such as *M 294* and *M 328*, had two 10.5cm/45 QF guns (300 rounds), three to four 3.7cm or Bofors 4cm AA guns (1500 rounds each), and up to eight 2cm AA guns. The MES system was in operation after 1943.

Handling
Excellent seaboats with good manoeuvrability but a poor turning circle, satisfactory double rudder. Metacentric height 0.87m, but 0.62–0.65m after AA reinforcement.

Complement
Originally 4/64, later up to 5/65, finally 2/73 (flagship 3/8); TS boats had 2/71. Boats: one motor pinnace, one yawl and two inflatables.

Notes
Colour scheme grey overall with camouflage. After completion of the preliminary boat *M 381*, the number of 2cm AA guns was increased to meet Front requirements, the tripod mast moved forward and the after mast removed. The increase in crew reduced living space to 1.28sq m per man.

Careers
In 1942 the construction of twenty-seven boats (later only twelve) was halted due to the shortage of copper. Building contracts planned for 1943 were not granted in favour of 1943 M boats, or were changed to that type. Six boats already under construction at Galatz with Santierde Navale Galati SA, with German materials intended for Romania, were completed after 1945 and named *Demokratia*, *Descatusaria*, *Desrobirea*, and *Dreptatea*.

M 261: launched 10 Apr 1941, commissioned* 10 Sept 1942; taken 1945 as a British prize, transferred to the GM/SA; transferred 19 Nov 1947 to Norway, broken up.

M 262: launched 25 Jun 1942, commissioned* 30 Dec 1942. Sunk 25 Aug 1944 at Bordeaux, together with *M 304*, *M 363* and *M 463*.

M 263: launched 17 Dec 1942, commissioned* 18 May 1943. Sunk 6 Aug 1944 north of Ile d'Yeu, position unknown, by gunfire from the British cruiser *Bellona* and destroyers *Tartar, Ashanti, Haida* and the Canadian destroyer *Iroquois*, together with *M 486*, *SG 3* and *V 414* on escort duties.

M 264: launched 19 May 1943, commissioned* 21 Sept 1943. Sunk 8 Jul 1944 at 0630hrs west of Helgoland, by aircraft rockets.

M 265: launched 21 Sept 1943, commissioned* 15 Jan 1944; taken 1945 into the GM/SA; taken 28 Dec 1945 as a USSR prize; became a *T 7* class minesweeper; fate unknown.

M 266: launched 18 Mar 1944, commissioned* 15 Aug 1944. Sunk 26 Aug 1944 at the Hindenburg bank, Kiel, by an aircraft bomb. Raised in 1944; sunk 11 Mar 1945 at Kiel by an aircraft bomb, broken up.

M 267: launched 13 Jun 1944, commissioned* 8 Mar 1945; completed at Rickmers dockyard; transferred 1945 to the GM/SA; taken 20 Nov 1945 as a USSR prize; became a *T 7* class minesweeper; fate unknown.

M 268–270: contracts not granted; *M 268–269* replaced by *M 621–622*.

M 271: launched in 1942, commissioned* 30 Jan 1943. Sunk at 1915hrs on 5 Aug 1944 at Pauillac coal jetty, by an aircraft bomb, together with *M 325* and *V 725*.

M 273: launched in 1943, commissioned* 15 May 1943. Sunk 11 Jan 1945 in the vicinity of Egersund, position 58° 20′N, 05°E, by gunfire from the British cruisers *Norfolk* and *Bellona*, and the destroyers *Onslow*, *Orwell* and *Onslaught*.

M 274: launched in 1943, commissioned* 12 Jun 1943. Scuttled at 1710hrs on 5 Sept 1944 in the Schelde estuary, near Doel, after serious engine problems.

M 275: launched 25 May 1943, commissioned* 4 Sept 1943; taken 1945 as a British prize, transferred to the GM/SA; transferred 7 Jul 1947 to France as the navigation training boat *Ancre*; stricken 8 Dec 1947; used 7 Apr 1952 as the training hulk *Lucifer*; sold 12 May 1960; fate unknown.

M 276: launched in 1943, commissioned* 30 Oct 1943. Scuttled at 1630hrs on 5 Sept 1944 in the Schelde estuary 400 metres northeast of Buoy 60, after serious engine problems.

M 277: launched in 1943, commissioned* 5 Feb 1944; taken 1945 as a British prize, transferred to the GM/SA; transferred 1946 to France; stricken 7 Apr 1948, used as the hulk *Q 109*; used 12 May 1960 as the training hulk *Lucifer*; sold 4 Oct 1967 for breaking up.

M 278: launched 25 Jan 1944, commissioned 20 Apr 1944 as the *TS 4*; taken 1945 as a US prize; transferred to the GM/SA; transferred 1 Apr 1948 to Paulsen & Ivers of Kiel for conversion to a motor ferry, but replaced by *M 607*; served in February 1951 in the US Labor Service Unit B as *M 202*; transferred 15 Aug 1956 to the German Federal navy, renamed *Seestern*; taken out of service 14 Jan 1960, used as the barrack boat *WBM 1* in the late 1960s, broken up.

M 279: launched 4 Jul 1944, commissioned 21 Oct 1944 as the *TS 9*; taken 1945 into the GM/SA; taken 20 Nov 1945 as a USSR prize; became a *T 7* class minesweeper; fate unknown.

M 280: launch date unknown. Remained incomplete as *TS 14*; broken up in 1946.

M 281–290: construction contracts not granted.

M 291: launched 27 Mar 1943, commissioned* 5 Aug 1943; taken 1945 into the GM/SA; taken 24 Nov 1945 as a USSR prize; became a *T 7* class minesweeper; fate unknown.

M 292: launched 19 Jun 1943, commissioned* 24 Nov 1943. Sunk 21 Aug 1944 at 1730hrs in the Gironde estuary, by British aircraft.

M 293: launched in 1943, commissioned* 26 Apr 1944. Sunk 2 May 1945 in the Kattegat by aircraft.

M 294: launched 4 Mar 1944, commissioned* 28 Aug 1944; taken 1945 as a US prize, transferred to the GM/SA; transferred 8 Oct 1947 to the OMGUS; transferred 4 Jun 1948 to Paulsen & Ivers of Kiel for conversion to a motor ferry but proved unsuitable; served in February 1951 in the US Labor Service Unit B as *M 201*; transferred 30 Aug 1956 to the German Federal navy as the *Seepferd*; taken out of service 11 Feb 1960, used as the barrack boat *WBM VI*; broken up in 1966.

M 295: launched in 1944; remained incomplete in 1945 at Gotenhafen, scuttled. Raised, served 1949 as the Polish steam ferry *Panna Wodna*, and in the 1970s with the diving club at Gdansk; still in existence in 1979.

M 296: commissioned 23 Mar 1945; scuttled on the stocks.

M 297: scuttled as *TS 15* shortly after construction commenced.

M 298–300: construction contracts not granted.

M 301: launched 9 Apr 1941, commissioned* 11 Oct 1941. Sunk 4 May 1945 in the Skagerrak, position 57° 56′N, 07° 34′E, by an aircraft bomb.

M 302: launched 28 Jul 1941, commissioned* 18 Apr 1942; taken 1945 as a British prize, transferred to the GM/SA; transferred 19 Nov 1947 to Norway; fate unknown.

M 303: launched 29 Dec 1941, commissioned* 5 Sept 1942. Sunk at 2300hrs on 11 Oct 1944 in the vicinity of Kiberg, northern Norway, by a torpedo from the Soviet *TKA 205* and *TKA 219*.

M 304: launched 30 Apr 1942, commissioned* 17 Nov 1942. Scuttled 25 Aug 1944 at Bordeaux, together with *M 262*, *M 363*, and *M 463*.

M 305: launched 20 Oct 1942, commissioned* 15 Feb 1943. Capsized and sank at 1130hrs on 17 Jan 1945 in the vicinity of Brüsterort, through rudder failure in a sever storm; forty dead.

M 306: launched 19 Dec 1942, commissioned* 4 May 1943; taken 1945 as a British prize, transferred to the GM/SA; transferred 19 Nov 1947 to Norway; fate unknown.

M 307: launched 16 Jun 1943, commissioned* 11 Oct 1943. Sunk at 2125hrs on 21 Jul 1944 north of Langeoog, position 53° 30′N, 07° 36′E, by an aircraft bomb and gunfire.

M 308–320: construction contracts not granted.

M 321: launched 29 Mar 1941, commissioned* 19 Sept 1941; taken 1945 as a British prize, transferred to the GM/SA; transferred 19 Nov 1947 to Norway; fate unknown.

M 322: launched 31 May 1941, commissioned 6 Dec 1941. Stranded and burnt at 1445hrs on 10 Jan 1945 near Lepsoey; taken 1945 as a British prize, transferred to the GM/SA; transferred 19 Nov 1947 to Norway and in 1953 to Denmark; broken up.

M 323: launched 9 Aug 1941, commissioned* 11 Jun 1942; taken 1945 as a British prize, transferred to the GM/SA; transferred 19 Nov 1947 to Norway; fate unknown.

M 324: launched 20 Sept 1941, commissioned* 28 Nov 1942; taken 26 Oct 1945 as a USSR prize; became a *T 7* class minesweeper; fate unknown.

M 325: launched 31 Oct 1942, commissioned* 18 Jun 1943. Sunk 5 Aug 1944 at 1915hrs in the vicinity of Pauillac, by an aircraft bomb, together with *M 271* and *V 725*.

M 326: launched 30 Jan 1943, commissioned* 23 Oct 1943; taken 1945 as a British prize, transferred to the GM/SA; transferred 19 Nov 1947 to Norway; fate unknown.

M 327: launched 12 Jun 1943, commissioned* 4 Mar 1944; taken 1945 as a US prize, transferred to the GM/SA; served 18 Jun 1948 in the East German Dampfschiff & Transport Ges, Hamburg, taken 1949 as a USSR prize, became a *T 7* class minesweeper; fate unknown.

M 328: launched 12 Jun 1943, commissioned* 18 Aug 1944; taken 1945 as a US prize, transferred to the GM/SA 1945–47; served in August 1948 as a barrack ship with the Bremerhaven police, transferred 20 Jul 1949 to Italy as the *Antilope*, broken up in 1959.

M 329: launched 27 May 1943, commissioned* 24 Mar 1944. Sunk 30 Mar 1945 at Wilhelmshaven, by an aircraft bomb.

M 330: launched 7 Feb 1944, commissioned* 21 Oct 1944; taken 1945 into the GM/SA; taken 29 Nov 1945 as a USSR prize; became a *T 7* class minesweeper; fate unknown.

M 331–340: construction contracts not granted; *M 331–332* replaced by *M 751–752*.

M 341: launched 10 Jun 1941, commissioned* 19 Apr 1942; taken 1945 into the GM/SA; taken 3 Feb 1946 as a USSR prize; became a *T 7* class minesweeper; fate unknown.

M 342: launched 11 Jun 1941, commissioned* 7 Jun 1942; taken 1945 into the GM/SA; taken 26 Oct 1945 as a USSR prize; became a *T 7* class minesweeper; fate unknown.

M 343: launched 6 Dec 1941, commissioned* 20 Sept 1942. Sunk at 0130hrs on 14 Jun 1944 in the vicinity of Jersey, in an engagement with the British destroyer *Ashanti* and the Polish *Piorun*.

M 344: launched 13 Dec 1941, commissioned* 14 Dec 1942. Scuttled 23 Aug 1944 at Rochefort.

M 345: launched 27 Jun 1942, commissioned* 24 Jan 1943. Sunk at 0010hrs on 18 May 1943 between Calais and Dunkirk, position 51° 03′ 5″N, 02° 07′ 6″E, by aircraft bombs; six dead.

M 346: launched 27 Jun 1942, commissioned* 18 Apr 1943. Sunk at 0135hrs on 17 Jul 1943 in Tanafjord, by torpedoes from the Soviet submarine *SC 403*; thirty-two dead.

M 347: launched 7 Nov 1942, commissioned* 4 Jul 1943. Sunk at 2100hrs on 25 Aug 1944 off Hubert Gat, position 53° 34′N, 06° 01′E, by a rocket from a British Beaufighter.

M 348: launched 7 Nov 1942, commissioned* 19 Sept 1943; taken 24 Nov 1945 as a USSR prize; became a *T 7* class minesweeper; fate unknown.

M 349–360: construction contracts not granted.

M 361: launched 5 Mar 1941, commissioned* 24 Jul 1942; taken 1945 as a British prize, transferred to the GM/SA; fate unknown.

M 362: launched 1 Apr 1941, commissioned* 26 Oct 1942; taken 1945 as a British prize, transferred to the GM/SA; transferred 19 Nov 1947 to Norway and in 1952 to Denmark, broken up.

M 363: launched 31 May 1941, commissioned* 5 Jan 1943. Scuttled 25 Aug 1944 at Bordeaux, together with *M 262*, *M 304* and *M 463*.

M 364: launched 9 Aug 1941, commissioned* 4 Mar 1943; taken 1945 as a British prize, transferred to the GM/SA; transferred 19 Nov 1947 to Norway; fate unknown.

M 365: launched 25 Jul 1942, commissioned* 20 Apr 1943; remaining career and fate as for *M 364*.

M 366: launched 5 Sept 1942, commissioned* 11 Jun 1943. Sunk at 1840hrs on 8 Aug 1944 in the vicinity of Noirmoutier, by fighter-bombers, together with *M 428* and *M 438*.

M 367: launched 23 Dec 1942, commissioned* 5 Jul 1943; fate as for *M 366*.

M 368: launched 15 Feb 1943, commissioned* 14 Aug 1943. Sunk 15 Apr 1945 in southern Norway in a collision with a U-boat.

M 369: launched 18 Jun 1943, commissioned* 21 Sept 1943; taken 1945 into the GM/SA; taken 20 Nov 1945 as a USSR prize; became a *T 7* class minesweeper; fate unknown.

M 370: launched 17 Jul 1943, commissioned* 3 Nov 1943. Stranded and sunk at 1020hrs on 12 Aug 1944 in the vicinity of Royan after and air attack.

M 371: launched 31 Jul 1943, commissioned as *TS 1*; taken 1945 as a US prize, transferred to the GM/SA; sold 5 May 1948 to P Zocke as the barrack ship *Fehmarn*; sold 5 May 1955 to Walter Riede of Lübeck for sale abroad; fate unknown.

M 372: launched 25 Sept 1943, commissioned as *TS 3*. Sunk 12 May 1944 in the vicinity of Swinemünde, position 54° 41′N, 12° 33′E, by an aircraft bomb.

M 373: launched 30 Nov 1943, commissioned as *TS 5*; taken 1945 as a US prize, transferred 4 Oct 1945 to the GM/SA; transferred 23 Jun 1948 to M Scharpagge of Düsseldorf for conversion to a hotel ship; returned 11 May 1949 to the US Navy; fate unknown.

M 374: launched 18 Dec 1943, commissioned as *TS 6*; taken 1945 as a US prize, transferred 17 Oct 1945 to the GM/SA; transferred 7 Apr 1948 as a barrack and salvage ship to Eisen & Metall of Hamburg; returned 29 Aug 1949 to the US Navy; broken up at Ghent in 1950.

M 375: launched 10 Mar 1944, commissioned 25 Jul 1944 as *TS 8*; taken 1945 as a US prize, transferred 15 Oct 1945 to the GM/SA; transferred 22 Jun 1948 to H Schammel of Glücksburg as a barrack ship; returned 7 Sept 1949 to the US Navy; fate unknown.

M 376: launched 19 Apr 1944, commissioned as *TS 10*. Sunk 11 Apr 1945 in the vicinity of Hela, by a Soviet aircraft bomb.

M 377: launched 27 Jun 1944, commissioned 27 Oct 1944 as *TS 11*; taken 1945 into the GM/SA; taken 20 Nov 1945 as a USSR prize; became a *T 7* class minesweeper; fate unknown.

M 378: launched in 1944 incomplete (approx 90 per cent) as *TS 13*; towed in April 1945 to Rostock; taken as a USSR prize; became a *T 7* class minesweeper; fate unknown.

M 379 and *M 380:* scuttled on the stocks together in 1945.

M 381: launched 15 Feb 1941, commissioned* 9 Aug 1941. Sunk 12 Feb 1945 at Kristiansand N, position 63° 07′N, 07° 32′E, by a torpedo from the British submarine *Venturer*.

*These M-boats carried out active minesweeping duties at some stage in their careers.

M 382: launched 28 Jun 1941, commissioned* 20 Dec 1941. Sunk at 2132 hrs on 31 Jan 1945 north of Molde, position 63° 06′N, 07° 32′E, by a mine; twenty-two dead.

M 383: launched 22 Nov 1941, commissioned* 20 Jun 1942. Sunk at 0620hrs on 13 Aug 1944 north of Spiekeroog, position 53° 50′N, 07° 45′E, by a rocket.

M 384: launched 12 Sept 1942, commissioned* 19 Dec 1942. Scuttled 10 Aug 1944 at Pier Basse-Indre, Nantes.

M 385: launched in 1943, commissioned* 17 May 1943 as *TS 12*. Sunk 15 Aug 1944 at 1112hrs north of Les Sables d'Olonne, in an engagement with the British cruiser *Mauritius*, the destroyer *Ursa*, and the Canadian destroyer *Iroquois*.

M 386: launched 1 Jul 1943, commissioned* 9 Oct 1943; used as an experimental boat in a barrage group, transferred 1945 to the GM/SA; taken 15 Oct 1945 as a USSR prize; became a *T 7* class minesweeper; fate unknown.

M 387: launched in 1943, commissioned 11 Feb 1944 as *TS 2*, Scuttled, sunk 2 May 1945 at Lübeck, broken up.

M 388: launched 22 Apr 1944, commissioned 22 Jul 1944 as *TS 7*; taken 1945 as a US prize, transferred to the GM/SA; transferred 1 Apr 1948 to Paulsen & Ivers of Kiel for conversion to a motor ferry, but found unsuitable; served in February 1951 in the US Labor Service Unit B as *M 203*; transferred 17 Jul 1956 to the German Federal navy as the *Seehund*; taken out of service 4 Jan 1960 and used as the barrack boat *WBM V*; stricken 25 Apr 1968, planned to scuttle as a target hulk in 1973, broken up at Leer in May–June 1975.

M 389: launched 22 Jul 1944, commissioned 20 Dec 1944 as *TS 12*; taken 1945 as a US prize, transferred to the GM/SA; transferred 28 Apr 1948 to Schmidt GmbH of Flensburg for conversion to a hotel ship; returned 8 Sept 1949 to the US Navy; fate unknown.

M 390–400: construction contract not granted, *M 390–391* replaced by *M 661–662*.

M 401: launched 4 Apr 1942, commissioned* 30 Nov 1942; taken 26 Oct 1945 as a USSR prize; became a *T 7* class minesweeper; fate unknown.

M 402: launched 4 Apr 1942, commissioned* 3 Jan 1943. Sunk at 2300hrs on 15 Jun 1944 at Boulogne, in an air attack, together with the *Von der Groeben*, *Brommy*, *Von der Lippe* and others.

M 403: launched 15 Sept 1942, commissioned* 27 Feb 1943. Sunk 19 Apr 1945 southwest of Gothenberg, position 56° 36′N, 11° 49′E, by an aircraft bomb and gunfire.

M 404: launched 14 Oct 1942, commissioned* 26 Mar 1943; taken 1945 as a British prize; transferred to the GM/SA; transferred in 1948 to France; stricken 7 Aug 1948, used as the hulk *Q 110* and a pontoon at Lorient; sold in November 1972.

M 405: launched 14 Nov 1942, commissioned* 29 Apr 1943; taken 1945 into the GM/SA; taken 20 Nov 1945 as a USSR prize; became a *T 7* class minesweeper; fate unknown.

M 406: launched 30 Dec 1942, commissioned* 2 Jun 1943; taken 1945 into the GM/SA; taken 15 Oct 1945 as a USSR prize; became a *T 7* class minesweeper; fate unknown.

M 407: launched 15 Feb 1943, commissioned* 19 Jun 1943; taken 20 Nov 1945 as a USSR prize; became a *T 7* class minesweeper; fate unknown.

M 408: launched 25 Mar 1943, commissioned* 3 Jul 1943; taken 1945 as a British prize, transferred to the GM/SA; transferred in 1948 to France; stricken 7 Aug 1948.

M 409, 410: construction contracts not granted.

M 411: launched 22 Aug 1942, commissioned* 29 Oct 1942; taken 26 Oct 1945 as a USSR prize; became a *T 7* class minesweeper; fate unknown.

M 412: launched 5 Sept 1942, commissioned* 9 Dec 1942. Grounded in shallow water at Granville 9 Mar 1945 and blown up.

M 413: launched 26 Oct 1942, commissioned* 13 Jan 1943. Sunk 21 Jul 1944 at 0126hrs in Narva bay, in the vicinity of Vainupa, by a Soviet aircraft bomb.

M 414: launched 9 Nov 1942, commissioned* 7 Feb 1943. Sunk at 2110hrs on 17 May 1943 west of Texel, position 53° 09′N, 04° 38′E, by aircraft torpedoes.

M 415: launched 16 Jan 1943, commissioned* 15 Mar 1943; taken 1945 into the GM/SA; taken 20 Nov 1945 as a USSR prize; became a *T 7* class minesweeper; fate unknown.

M 416: launched 13 Feb 1943, commissioned* 7 Apr 1943. Sunk 12 Nov 1944 at 2330hrs in the vicinity of Egersund, position 58° 20′N, 06° 00′E, in an engagement with the British destroyers *Myngs*, *Verulam*, *Zambesi* and cruisers *Kent* and *Bellona*, together with *M 427*, *UJ 1221*, *UJ 1713*, and *UJ 1223*.

M 417–420: construction contracts not granted.

M 421: launched 29 Nov 1941, commissioned* 10 Sept 1942. Sunk 17 Feb 1945 at 1457hrs in the entrance to Kolberg, approximately 1000 metres north-northeast point lb, route 53, by a mine from a German harbour barrage.

M 422: launched 6 Aug 1942, commissioned* 28 Oct 1942. Sunk 4 Aug 1944 at 1815hrs in St Malo roads, by an aircraft bomb.

M 423: launched 18 Oct 1942, commissioned* 29 Nov 1942; taken 1945 into the GM/SA; taken 26 Oct 1945 as a USSR prize; became a *T 7* class minesweeper; fate unknown.

M 424: launched 18 Oct 1942, commissioned* 22 Dec 1942. Sunk 4 Aug 1944 in St Malo roads, Rance estuary, by an aircraft bomb; taken as a British prize, raised in July 1946; served in the GM/SA; transferred in 1947 to France; cannibalised.

M 425: launched 18 Oct 1942, commissioned* 31 Jan 1943; taken 1945 into the GM/SA; taken 20 Nov 1945 as a USSR prize; became a *T 7* class minesweeper; fate unknown.

M 426: launched 18 Oct 1942, commissioned* 5 Mar 1943. Sunk at 1550hrs on 12 Sept 1944 in the west entrance to Kristiansand S, by an aircraft bomb; twenty-two dead.

M 427: launched 18 Oct 1942, commissioned* 14 Apr 1943. Stranded, capsized and sunk at 1300 hrs

on 13 Nov 1944 at Rekkefjord, position 58° 20′N, 06° 13′E; see also *M 416*.

M 428: launched 18 Oct 1942, commissioned* 29 May 1943. Sunk at 1840hrs on 8 Aug 1944 in the vicinity of Noirmoutier, by fighter-bombers, together with *M 366*, *M 367* and *M 438*.

M 429, 430: construction contracts not granted.

M 431: launched 7 Mar 1942, commissioned* 29 Sept 1942; taken 1945 into the GM/SA; taken 4 Nov 1945 as a USSR prize; became a *T 7* class minesweeper; fate unknown.

M 432: launched 7 Mar 1942, commissioned 27 Oct 1942; taken 1945 as a British prize; served in the GM/SA; transferred in October 1947 to France as the *Suippe*; stricken 15 Jun 1953, broken up.

M 433: launched 11 Apr 1942, commissioned* 24 Nov 1942. Sunk 26 Oct 1944 at Vegefjord, position 65° N′12″E, by an aircraft bomb.

M 434: launched 11 Apr 1942, commissioned* 23 Dec 1942; taken 1945 as a British prize, transferred to the GM/SA; transferred October 1947 to France; stricken 7 Aug 1948, broken up.

M 435: launched 27 Jun 1942, commissioned* 8 Feb 1943. Capsized during towing by the *M 369* after a fighter-bomber rocket hit at 1315hrs; sunk at 1620hrs on 14 May 1944 northeast of Ameland, position 53° 34′ 8″N, 06° 04′ 5″E; four dead.

M 436: launched 27 Jun 1942, commissioned* 6 Mar 1943; taken 1945 as a British prize, transferred to the GM/SA; transferred 19 Nov 1947 to Norway; fate unknown.

M 437: launched 27 Jun 1942, commissioned* 28 Apr 1943; taken 24 Nov 1945 as a USSR prize; became a *T 7* class minesweeper; fate unknown.

M 438: launched 27 Jun 1942, commissioned* 10 Jun 1943. Sunk 8 Aug 1944 at 1840hrs in the vicinity of Noirmoutier, by fighter-bombers, together with *M 366*, *M 367* and *M 428*.

M 439, 440: construction contracts not granted.

M 441: launched 19 Jun 1942, commissioned* 26 Nov 1942; taken 1945 as a British prize, transferred to the GM/SA; transferred 20 May 1947 to Schichau as a barrack boat; served 24 Oct 1947 in the US Labor Service Unit B as *M 205*; transferred 17 Jul 1956 to the German Federal navy as *Seelöwe*, taken out of service 4 Jan 1960, used as the barrack boat *WBM III*; stricken 8 Jan 1969, broken up in 1970.

M 442: launched 17 Aug 1942, commissioned* 31 Dec 1942; taken 1945 as a US prize, transferred to the GM/SA; transferred October 1947 to France as the *Marne*; stricken 19 Jun 1957, used as the hulk *Q 93* and as a pontoon.

M 443: launched 14 Sept 1942, commissioned* 1 Feb 1943; taken 1945 into the GM/SA; taken 28 Dec 1945 as a USSR prize; became a *T 7* class minesweeper; fate unknown.

M 444: launched 30 Nov 1942, commissioned* 4 Apr 1943. Sunk 14 Aug 1944 in the vicinity of Brest, by a mine and aircraft bombs.

M 445: launched 12 Dec 1942, commissioned* 8 May 1943. Sunk 31 Dec 1944 at Hamburg, in a US air attack.

M 446: launched 3 Feb 1943, commissioned* 8 Jun

1943; taken 1945 into the GM/SA; taken 20 Nov 1945 as a USSR prize; became a *T 7* class minesweeper; fate unknown.

M 447–450: construction contracts not granted.

M 451: launched 24 Dec 1941, commissioned 4 Jan 1943. Stranded in a storm 30 Jan 1944 at 1710hrs north of Porkkala, ship abandoned, wreck sunk 31 Jan 1944.

M 452: launched 19 Dec 1942, commissioned* 7 Feb 1943; taken 1945 as a British prize, transferred into the GM/SA; transferred in October 1947 to France as the *Aisne*; stricken 7 Apr 1952, used as the hulk *Q 109*, still in existence in 1958.

M 453: launched 15 Dec 1942, commissioned* 20 Mar 1943; taken 1945 as a US prize, transferred 4 Oct 1945 into the GM/SA; transferred 24 Feb 1948 to DDG Hansa of Bremen for conversion to a motor ferry but found unsuitable; returned February 1949 to the US Navy; broken up March 1949 at Ghent.

M 454: launched in 1943, commissioned* 10 May 1943; taken 1945 as a British prize, transferred to the GM/SA; transferred October 1947 to France; stricken 7 Aug 1948, broken up.

M 455: launched 7 Dec 1942, commissioned* 11 Jun 1943. Sunk 30 Jul 1944 at Hamburg, by an aircraft bomb. Raised 26 Aug 1944, sunk again April 1945 at Cuxhaven, in an air attack. Raised, repaired; transferred into the GM/SA; fate unknown.

M 456: launched 3 Mar 1943, commissioned 2 Jul 1943; taken 1945 into the GM/SA; taken 3 Mar 1946 as a USSR prize; became a *T 7* class minesweeper; fate unknown.

M 457, 458: construction contracts not granted.

M 459: launched 31 Jul 1942, commissioned* 7 Dec 1942. Sunk at 1057hrs on 10 Apr 1944 in Narva bay, position 59° 30′N, 27° 5′ 9″E, by a Soviet aircraft bomb; twelve dead.

M 460: launched 27 Jul 1942, commissioned* 6 Feb 1943; taken 1945 as a US prize, transferred to the GM/SA; transferred 11 Oct 1947 to the OMGUS; transferred 4 Jun 1948 to Paulsen & Ivers of Kiel for conversion to a motor ferry; transferred October 1949 to the US Navy; served February 1951 in the US Labour Service Unit B as *M 204*; transferred 30 Aug 1956 to the German Federal navy as *Seeigel*; taken out of service 29 Jan 1960, used March 1960 as the barrack boat *WBM II*, used 28 Jun 1967 as the torpedo defusing ship *Torpedoklarmachstelle II*; sold 4 May 1975 to Motorenwerke Bremerhaven; still in existence in 1982.

M 461: launched 24 Oct 1942, commissioned* 25 Mar 1943; taken 20 Nov 1945 as a USSR prize; fate unknown.

M 462: launched 27 Jan 1943, commissioned* 7 May 1943. Sunk at 1450hrs on 11 Sept 1944 northeast of Skagens Horn, by British aircraft.

M 463: launched 17 Feb 1943, commissioned* 3 Jul 1943. Scuttled and sunk 25 Aug 1944 at Bordeaux, together with *M 262*, *M 304* and *M 363*.

M 464–466: construction contracts not granted.

M 467: launched 9 Jan 1942, commissioned* 31 Oct 1942; taken 1945 into the GM/SA; taken 4 Nov 1945 as a USSR prize; became a *T 7* class minesweeper; fate unknown.

M 468: launched 9 Jul 1942, commissioned* 3 Dec 1942. Sunk at 0402hrs on 12 Aug 1944 west of Namsos, position 64° 29′N, 10° 31′E, by a mine.

M 469: launched 9 Jul 1942, commissioned* 6 Jan 1943. Sunk at 0250hrs on 4 Jul 1944 northwest of Vlieland, position 53° 21′N, 04° 57′E, by a torpedo from a British MTB.

M 470: launched 29 Oct 1942, commissioned* 27 Feb 1943; taken 1945 into the GM/SA; taken 29 Nov 1945 as a USSR prize; became a *T 7* class minesweeper; fate unknown.

M 471: launched 29 Oct 1942, commissioned* 12 Apr 1943. Sunk at 1735hrs on 25 Apr 1943 at Den Helder roads, by an aircraft bomb.

M 472–474: construction contracts not granted.

M 475: launched 29 Aug 1942, commissioned* 23 Dec 1942; taken 1945 as a British prize, transferred to the GM/SA; transferred 1947 to France; stricken 21 Aug 1948, used as the hulk *Q 111*, still in existence in 1956.

M 476: launched 3 Oct 1942, commissioned* 20 Mar 1943; taken 1945 as a British prize, transferred into the GM/SA; transferred 1947 to France; stricken 7 Aug 1948, used as the hulk *Q 88*, broken up in 1956.

M 477–482: construction contracts not granted.

M 483: launched 16 May 1942, commissioned* 1 Dec 1942. Sunk at 0614hrs on 15 Jun 1943 in the vicinity of the Channel Islands, by an aircraft bomb.

M 484: launched 25 Aug 1942, commissioned* 20 Jan 1943; taken 1945 into the GM/SA; taken 9 Dec 1945 as a USSR prize; became a *T 7* class minesweeper; fate unknown.

M 485: construction contract not granted.

M 486: launched in 1942, commissioned* 3 Dec 1942. Sunk at 0040hrs on 6 Aug 1944 in the vicinity of Les Sables d'Olonne, in an engagement with the British cruiser *Bellona* and destroyers *Tartar*, *Ashanti* and *Haida*, and the Canadian destroyer *Iroquois*, together with *M 263* and *SG 3*.

M 487, 488: construction contracts not granted.

M 489: launched 28 Aug 1942, commissioned* 15 May 1943. Sunk 23 Dec 1944 at 2110hrs 1nm south of Mosterhavn, Bomlofjord, by two torpedoes from Norwegian MTBs; forty-six dead.

M 490–494: construction contracts not granted.

M 495: launched 4 Sept 1942, commissioned* 11 Mar 1943; taken 1945 as a US prize, transferred to the GM/SA; transferred to the GM/SA; transferred October 1947 to France; cannibalised, broken up.

M 496: launched 12 Jan 1943, commissioned* 7 Jun 1943; taken 1945 into the GM/SA; taken 24 Nov 1945 as a USSR prize; became a *T 7* class minesweeper; fate unknown.

M 497–501: construction contracts not granted.

*These M-boats carried out active minesweeping duties at some stage in their careers.

M 601 class (1943 Type)

Construction

Laid down as 1943 (1942) minesweepers (official design 1942, adapted from the M-1940 design by the addition of ten extra frames, increasing overall length by 5.5m). The block construction system suggested by AG 'Neptun', Rostock, with each block weighing 3–5 tonnes and assembly work spread over eleven dockyards, was reorganised at the suggestion of Dr Rodin of Schichau, Königsberg, into a system of prefabricated section construction; this reorganisation entailed some 9 months' design work at the Engineering Office East (IBO) of the Reichs Ministry for Armaments and War Production. Planned production was for one boat per dockyard per week for two dockyards.

The prefabricated sections were as follows:

Section 1   Aftership from stern to 120mm forward of frame 30
Section 2   Crew accommodation up to 430mm forward of frame 53
Section 3   Engine room up to 120mm forward of frame 70/73
Section 4   Boiler room up to 120mm forward of frame 98
Section 5   Foreship up to stem
Section 6   Deck, bridge
Section 7   Upper deck superstructure

Sub-assemblies (eight to ten per section) were transported by rail to the assembly companies in-

M-boat 1943: *M 601–1050*

land, where three to five sections of each type were assembled on wagons. At the same rate, assembled sections were transferred to the slips or fitting out berths for final assembly. The planned production timetable was 3–4 weeks for the manufacture of a section, 1 week for assembly up to launch, 2 weeks for fitting out, and 1 week for

Name	Builder (construction no)	Built	Cost in Marks (000s)	Displacement (t = tonnes T = tons)	Length (m)	Breadth (m)	Draught (m)	Power (hp)	Revs (rpm)	Speed (kts)	Range (nm/kts)	Coal (t)	Oil (t)
M 601–800	Neptun*			821T max 668t des 582T std	67.75 oa 63.10 cwl	9.00 8.60	2.68 max 2.27 des 1.92 std	2709ihp max 2400ihp des 2150 shp des	250 max 230 des	17.0 max 16.5des	4000/10 3600/11	136 +20	—
M 801–1000	Schichau*			”	”	”	”	”	”	”	”	”	—
M 1001–1050	Korneu- burg*†			”	”	”	”	”	”	”	”	”	—

* Construction contracts were originally granted as follows on 26 Nov 1942: *M 601–604* Neptun (535–538), *M 661–667* Elsfleth (253–259), *M 751, 752* LMG (436, 437); and as follows on 7 May 1943: *M 621–628* Atlas (376–383), *M 641–646* Unterweser (–), *M 681–684* K & M (–), *M 701–708* Rickmers (247–254), *M 731–734* Nobiskrug (532–535), *M 771–773* Lindenau (89–91), *M 781–783* Meyer (435, 446, 447) and *M 791, 792* Ottens (–). After the decision had been taken to build the boats in sections, construction work was concentrated in the assembly yards given in the table; AG Neptun gave the new construction numbers 539–562 to the vessels reassigned to its yard.
† It was intended to transfer the assembly of these vessels to Deutsche Werke, Toulon, from April 1944.

trials. Delays caused by war conditions were up to 6 months or more.

Transverse frame steel construction, welded (thirteen watertight compartments, double bottom 87 per cent); hard chine bow, tug stern. Armour: bridge and boiler room 10mm Ww (soft) steel. Depth 3.65m. Four main types were built: 1. Standard minesweeper with full barrage weapons fit; 2. Submarine hunter with reduced sweeping gear and an enhanced fit of depth charges (7 × 21 depth charges); 3. Torpedo carrier (see below); 4. Torpedo recovery boat for training.

Propulsion

Engines and boilers as for *M 261–501*. The electrical installation consisted of two 40kW diesel generators and one 100kW turbo generator, giving 180kW, 220V; the mine protection or KFRG installation incorporated two 40kW diesel generators (= 60V). Two rudders.

Armament

Two 10.5cm/45 AA guns (300 rounds), two 3.7cm AA guns (4000 rounds), eight 2cm AA guns (16,000 rounds), one 7.3cm Föhn rocket launcher and twenty-four mines. The torpedo carrier versions were fitted with two 53.3cm fixed deck-mounted TT (number of torpedoes not known), one each side on the upper deck; the torpedo recovery versions carried only one 3.7cm AA gun and four 2cm AA guns, and had space aft for 16–17 training torpedoes.

Handling

Extremely good seaboats, very manoeuvrable and responsive.

Complement

Crew: 6/101 (plus 3/8 as flotilla flagship). Boats: one motor pinnace, one yawl, two inflatable boats.

Notes

Colour scheme grey overall, with camouflage. After construction of the prototype boats *M 601* and *801* production continued using the reorganised construction system. It was planned to transfer construction of the original type to Dutch yards.

Careers

M 601: launched 31 Aug 1944, commissioned* 22 Nov 1944; British prize 1945; transferred to the GM/SA; broken up in Britain in 1948.

M 602: launched 21 Oct 1944, commissioned* 14 Dec 1944; subsequent career as for *M 601*.

M 603: launched 2 Nov 1944, commissioned* 31 Dec 1944; subsequent career as for *M 601*.

M 604: launched 10 Nov 1944, commissioned* 18 Jan 1945; subsequent career as for *M 601*.

M 605: launched 13 Dec 1944, commissioned* 3 Feb 1945; subsequent career as for *M 601*.

M 606: launched 20 Dec 1944, commissioned 16 Mar 1945; US prize 1945; transferred to the GM/SA; transferred 4 Nov 1947 to OMGUS; transferred to Eisen & Metall, Hamburg, as a barrack ship, 9 Jun 1948; returned to US Navy 29 Aug 1949; broken up in 1950 at Ghent.

M 607: launched 30 Dec 1944, commissioned* 16 Mar 1945; US prize 1945; transferred to the GM/SA; transferred 14 Nov 1947 to OMGUS; sold on 19 Feb 1948 to the Hapag Seebärdienst Project as *Hörnum*; sold 27 Oct 1949 to Ivers Linie AG, Kiel, and converted to a steam ferry under the name *Christian Ivers*; sold in 1954 to Kiel Roads GmbH as *Hanne Scarlet*, on charter to Denmark, and in 1962 to Agostino Lauro and converted to the motor ferry *Salvatore Lauro*; sold in 1975 to Libore Lauro SaS under the same name; still in service in 1982.

M 608: Launched 20 Jan 1945, commissioned* 20 Mar 1945; fate as for *M 607*, under the names *Amrum*, *Harald Ivers* and *Lilli Scarlet*, then became the Greek *Elena P* in 1964; still in service in 1982.

M 609: launched 29 Jan 1945, commissioned* 27 Mar 1945; British prize 1945; transferred to the GM/SA; transferred 14 Nov 1947 to OMGUS; sunk in 1947 at Finkenwerder (details unknown); broken up at Hamburg in 1948.

M 610: launched 27 Feb 1945, commissioned 5 Oct 1945 as a US prize; transferred to the GM/SA; transferred 14 Nov 1947 to OMGUS; sold 10 Feb 1948 to Norddeutscher Lloyd, Bremen; conversion

to a motor ferry was planned, but she was considered unsuitable; broken up in 1950 at Ghent.

M 611: launched 12 Mar 1945, commissioned in 1945 as a US prize; transferred to the GM/SA; transferred 14 Nov 1947 to OMGUS; sold in February 1948 to Norddeutscher Lloyd, Bremen; in service from 26 May 1948 as the steam harbour ferry *Wangerooge*; laid up 1950; transferred 8 Oct 1951 to US Labor Service Unit B as *M 206*; transferred 15 Aug 1956 to the Federal German Navy as *Seeschlange*; out of service from 13 Feb 1960, and became the barrack boat *WBM IV*; stricken 29 May 1967; finally expended as a target ship for the naval air arm.

M 612: launched 23 Mar 1945, commissioned 1 Apr 1945 (eleven crew members shot for mutiny!); taken as a British prize 1945; transferred to the GM/SA; broken up in Britain in 1948.

M 613–616: all launched in 1945 and commissioned shortly before completion; probably scuttled 1945–6 in the vicinity of Rostock.

M 617–633: assembly not completed.

M 634–666: section production not completed.

M 667–800: production not begun.

M 801: launched 9 Sept 1944, commissioned* 3 Dec 1944; US prize 1945; transferred to the GM/SA; transferred 14 Nov 1947 to OMGUS; transferred in February 1948 to DAPG, Hamburg, for planned conversion to a barrack ship; returned to OMGUS 9 Mar 1949; sold 20 Jul 1949 to Italy and became the Italian *Gazzela*; served as a training ship from 1960; stricken 1967.

M 802: launched 29 Sep 1944, commissioned 4 Jan 1945. Sunk 3 Apr 1945 in berth 14 at the Germaniawerke Yard, Kiel, by US bombs.

M 803: launched 19 Oct 1944, commissioned* 17 Jan 1945; US prize 1945; transferred to the GM/SA; transferred 14 Nov 1947 to OMGUS; transferred in February 1948 to L Nimitz for planned conversion to a barrack ship; returned to OMGUS 9 Mar 1949; sold 20 Jul 1949 to Italy and became the Italian *Daino*; served as a survey ship from 1960; stricken 1966.

M 804: launched 1 Nov 1944, commissioned* 25

Jan 1945. Sunk 11 Mar 1945 at Kiel-Mönkeberg by US bombs.

M 805: launched 9 Nov 1944, commissioned* 26 Jan 1945. Sunk 11 Mar 1945 at Heikendorfer Bay, Kiel, by US bombs.

M 806: launched 21 Nov 1944; taken as a British prize before completion; transferred to the GM/SA; fate unknown.

M 807: launched 13 Jan 1945; towed to Rostock in January 1945, approximately 99 per cent complete; USSR prize; fate unknown.

M 808: launched in 1945; fate as for M 807.

M 809–813: 90, 88, 85, 65 and 45 per cent complete on the assembly wagons.

M 814–816: sub-assembly production not completed.

M 817–886: sub-assembly production begun or preparations made.

M 887–1000: construction contracts not granted.

M 1001–1009: construction contracts granted to Korneuburg works, Vienna, but transferred after April 1944 to Deutsche Werke, Toulon (formerly the French state dockyard); construction not started.

M 1010–1050: construction contracts not granted.

*These M-boats carried out active minesweeping duties at some stage in their careers.

Foreign minesweepers (1939–1945)

M 551 class (ex-Dutch)

Name	Builder (construction no)	Built	Cost in Marks (000s)	Displacement (t = tonnes T = tons)	Length (m)	Breadth (m)	Draught (m)	Power (hp)	Revs (rpm)	Speed (kts)	Range (nm/kts)	Coal (t)	Oil (t)
M 551	Smit, P (547)	1939–40	1100 Dfl	620T max 502t des 460T std	55.82 oa 55.80 cwl	8.11 7.80	2.68 fwd	1657ihp max 1600ihp		15,3 max 15.0 des	4700/11 1600/15	—	114
M 552 (mod)	" (507) Nederland SB	1936–37 1941	"	"	"	"	"	"		"	"	—	"
M 553 (mod)	Gusto, (715) Nederland SB	1936–37 1941	"	"	"	"	"	"		"	"	—	"

Construction
Laid down as Dutch minesweepers (*Mijnenveger*) of the *Jan van Amstel* class (1936 design). Transverse frame steel construction. Depth 3.90m.

Propulsion
Two vertical 3-cylinder triple expansion engines in one engine room (two 3-bladed screws, 1.85m diameter). Two Yarrow boilers (four fireboxes, 16.2 atmospheres forced, 320sq m) in one boiler room. Electrical installation 31.5kW. One rudder.

Armament
In Dutch service, one 7.5cm/55 AA gun (100 rounds), four 12.7mm AA guns (6000 rounds) and forty mines. *M 551*: one 7.5cm/55 AA gun (number of rounds unknown). [*M 552* and *553* as converted to torpedo recovery boats were fitted with three 2cm AA guns (number of rounds unknown) and mounts for seven torpedoes.]

Complement
Crew: 4/55 (3/43 in Dutch service). Boats: one motor boat, one yawl.

Notes
Colour scheme grey. *M 552* and *553* were rebuilt after 1940 as torpedo recovery and defusing boats, with light tripod masts and torpedo mounts in place of the after &.5mm gun.]

M 551 (ex Willem van Ewijck) (1944).

M 552 (ex Pieter Florisz) and M 553 (ex Abraham van der Hulst) as security boats (1941). Mrva

Careers

M 551: launched 18 Apr 1940 as *Willem van Ewijck*, taken as a German prize 14 May 1940, almost complete; accepted 26 Aug 1940 as the German *MH 1*; transferred to Emden 30 Aug 1940 and commissioned as *M 551*. Returned to the Netherlands in May 1945 for repairs at the Rijkswerft, Willemsoord; in service 15 Aug 1946 as *Abraham van der Hulst* (*MV 2*, *M 802*); became the netlayer *A 928* in 1952; stricken 1961 and used from February 1962 as a training hulk for the Sea Cadet Corps at Maassluis; out of service 18 Apr 1969; broken up by Hendrik-Ido-Ambacht.

M 552: launched 11 May 1937 as *Pieter Florisz*, commissioned 13 Sept 1937; scuttled 14 May 1940 at Medemblik on the IJsselmeer, in position 52° 46′N, 05° 07′E. Raised 12 Aug 1940 as a German prize; repaired during 1941 as the torpedo recovery boat *M 552*. Returned to the Netherlands in May 1945, and recommissioned in August 1946 as *Pieter Florisz* (*MV 4*, *M 804*); became the netlayer *A 926* in 1952; stricken 1961 and used from February 1962 as a training hulk for the Sea Cadet Corps at IJmuiden; out of service by Sept 1976; broken up by Hendrik-Ido-Ambacht.

M 553: launched 31 May 1937 as *Abraham van der Hulst*, commissioned 11 Oct 1937; scuttled 14 May 1940 at Enkhuizen on the IJsselmeer, in position 52° 42′N, 05° 19′E. Raised in August 1940 as a German prize, and repaired during 1941 as the torpedo recovery boat *M 553*. Sunk 21 Apr 1944 west of Brüsterort by a mine. Raised 20 Jul 1944 and transferred to Gotenhafen, later to Stettin, for repairs. Sunk 30 Aug 1944 at Gollnow Dockyard, Stettin, after being completely burnt out by a bomb.

MA 1 class (ex-Danish)

Name	Builder (construction no)	Built	Cost in Marks (000s)	Displacement (t = tonnes T = tons)	Length (m)	Breadth (m)	Draught (m)	Power (hp)	Revs (rpm)	Speed (kts)	Range (nm/kts)	Coal (t)	Oil (t)
MA 1–6	Copenhagen 161–163, 171–173)	1938–42		315T max 274T des	53.79 oa 51.50 pp	6.32	1.98	2200shp des		19 des	1035/15	—	30

Construction

Laid down as Danish minesweepers (*Mine strygere*) (1938 design).

Propulsion

One Atlas geared turbine (one screw, approximately 1.90m diameter) in one engine room. One Thornycroft 3-drum watertube boiler (18 atmospheres forced) in one boiler room. Electrical installation consisted of two TV generators and one 110V diesel generator. One rudder.

Armament

One or two 7.5cm/50 PK guns (number of rounds unknown), one 3.7cm AA gun (number of rounds unknown), two 8.6cm rocket launchers (number of rounds unknown) and thirty mines.

Complement

Crew: 1/47 (4/44 in Danish service). Boats: one whaler, two rafts.

Notes

Colour scheme grey. Fuel consumption was rela-

MA 1 (ex *Sölöven*) and *MA 4–6* (1943).

tively high, so these vessels were not rated highly in German service.

Careers

MA 1: launched 3 Dec 1938 as *Sölöven* (*M 1*), commissioned 10 Jul 1939; taken over by Germany at Korsör on 29 Aug 1943; became the German *MA 1* (*Vs 1201*) in 1943 and *Vs 63* in April 1944; returned to Denmark in May 1945 as *Sölöven*; broken up in 1959.

MA 2: launched 16 Feb 1939 as *Söbjörnen* (*M 2*), commissioned 8 Sept 1939; scuttled 29 Aug 1943 at Holmen. Raised but never in German service as *MA 2*; broken up 1944–45 at Bradbaenken.

MA 3: launched 18 Jul 1939 as *Söulven* (*M 3*), commissioned 17 Jun 1940; fate as for *MA 2*.

MA 4: launched 11 Apr 1942 as *Sörridderen* (*M 4*), commissioned 25 Sept 1942; career as for *MA 1*, but under the German names *MA 4* (*Vs 1202*) and *Vs 64*; stricken 1958 and broken up in 1962.

MA 5: launched 30 Apr 1942 as *Söhesten* (*M 5*), commissioned 6 Jul 1943; taken over by Germany 29 Aug 1943 at Kalundborg; became the German *MA 5* (*Vs 1203*) in 1943 and *Vs 65* in April 1944; damaged by a mine in November 1944 and transferred to Königsberg for repair; not repaired; transferred to Swinemünde and later towed to Brunsbüttelkoog; returned to Denmark 22 Nov 1945 without 7.5cm and rotor; repaired at Copenhagen and returned to service as *Söhesten*; stricken 1958; broken up 1959.

MA 6: launched 16 May 1942 as *Söhunden* (*M 6*); accepted by the Danish Navy 17 Nov 1942, but not commissioned because of fuel shortages; scuttled at Holmen 29 Aug 1943. Raised and repaired as the German *MA 6* (*Vs 1204*), and *Vs 66* in April 1944; returned to Denmark in May 1945 as *Söhunden*; stricken 1958, broken up 1962.

M 1226 class (ex-Italian)

Name	Builder (construction no)	Built	Cost in Marks (000s)	Displacement (t = tonnes T = tons)	Length (m)	Breadth (m)	Draught (m)	Power (hp)	Revs (rpm)	Speed (kts)	Range (nm/kts)	Coal (t)	Oil (t)
M 1226	Tosi	1916–17		217t max 156t des	35.52 oa 33.15 pp	5.88	2.11	964ihp max 950ihp des		14.04 max 14.0 des	750/14	—	
M 1227	Castellamare	1916–17		201t max	33.35 oa 33.15 pp	5.82	2.17	800ihp des		12.0 des	600/12	—	
M 1228	,,	1917–18		201t max	36.52 oa 33.15 pp	5.82	2.14	881ihp max 750ihp des		13.4 max 14.0 des	650/11	—	
M 1229	,,	1919		207t max 182t des	33.15 pp	5.82	2.22	864ihp max 750ihp des		14.0 max 14.0 des	660/10.5	—	
TR 106	Pattison	1919–22		221 max	38.06 oa 35.07 pp	6.00	1.96	816ihp max 750ihp des		12.9 max 14.0 des	740/12	—	

Construction

Laid down as Italian minesweepers (*Rimorchiatori dragamine*, later *Regio dragamine*) (naval design, but *RD 9* to a dockyard design). Tug-style construction.

Propulsion

One vertical 3-cylinder triple expansion engine (one 3–bladed screw, diameter unknown) in one engine room. One Thornycroft WR boiler (details unknown), probably also in the engine room. Electrical installation details unknown. One rudder.

Armament

One 7.6cm/40 AA gun (number of rounds unknown), one 2cm Oerlikon AA gun (*M 1227, 1228*) or two 6.5mm machine guns. *TR 106* was fitted with one 7.6cm/40 AA gun, two 3.7cm Breda AA guns, six 2cm AA guns, two 1.5cm AA guns and two 1.3cm Breda AA guns.

Complement

Crew: unknown (total 22 in Italian service). Boats: one yawl.

Notes

These were obsolete vessels, ineffective against up to date acoustic and magnetic mines. Old destroyer

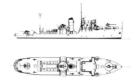

TR 106 (ex *RD 49*) (1944). *Mrva*

or cruiser engines were originally intended for *RD 49*, as for the preceding four vessels (in the case of *RD 49*, the intended engine was the former centre engine of the torpedo cruiser *Tripoli*). After bad experience with *RD 45–48*, *RD 49* was the only vessel actually fitted with the replacement engine. [During rebuilding in 1944 the forecastle was lengthened to provide extra accommodation, and a new bridge house was added above.]

Careers

M 1226: launched 2 Feb 1917 as *RD 9*, commissioned 1 Jul 1917; taken as a German prize 9 Sept 1943 in Piraeus Harbour; commissioned 10 Sept 1943 for the Attica coastal defence flotilla; became *M 1226* in the 12th Minesweeper Flotilla B-Group in December 1943. Sunk 11 Jan 1944 at Piraeus, in position 37° 57′N, 23° 38′E, by bombs; five dead.

M 1227: launched 22 Apr 1917 as *RD 17*, commissioned 2 May 1917; taken as a German prize 9 Sept 1943 in Piraeus Harbour; commissioned 10 Sept 1943 for the Attica coastal defence flotilla; became *M 1227* in the 12th Minesweeper Flotilla B-Group in December 1943. Probably sunk in 1945.

M 1228: launched 15 May 1918 as *RD 26*, commissioned 7 Jun 1918; taken as a German prize 9 Sept 1943 in Piraeus Harbour; commissioned 10 Sept 1943 for the Attica coastal defence flotilla; became *M 1228* in the 12th Minesweeper Flotilla B-Group in December 1943. Sunk in 1944, probably at La Spezia.

M 1229: launched 17 Jul 1919 as *RD 35*, commissioned 29 Aug 1919; taken as a German prize 13 Sept 1943 in Syra Harbour by *GA 41*; commissioned 16 Sept 1943 for the Attica coastal defence flotilla; became *M 1229* in the 12th Minesweeper Flotilla B-Group in December 1943. Sunk in 1944, probably in the Aegean.

TR 106: launched 24 Nov 1921 as *RD 49*, commissioned 3 Mar 1922; scuttled 9 Sept 1943 in the La Spezia drydock; raised and repaired as an escort boat for the 1st Transport Flotilla (Genoa). Scuttled 23 Apr 1945 at Genoa.

Motor minesweepers 1915–1943

F 1 class

Name	Builder (construction no)	Built	Cost in Marks (000s)	Displacement (t = tonnes T = tons)	Length (m)	Breadth (m)	Draught (m)	Power (hp)	Revs (rpm)	Speed (kts)	Range (nm/kts)	Coal (t)	Oil (t)
F 1–15	*		191–244	c20t max 18t des	16.50 oa	4.00†	1.05	120ehp max		10.0 max	250/11	—	3
F 16–39	‡		698–730	c21t max 19t des	17.50 oa	,,	,,	120 to 130ehp		10.0 to 11.0 max	,,	—	,,
F 40–75	**		860–1086	,,	,,	,,	,,	,,	,,	,,	,,	—	,,

* Builders and construction numbers as follows: *F 1–4* Heidtmann, *F 5–8* Nalgo, *F 9–11* von Hacht, *F 12* Waap, *F 13, 14* von Hacht, *F 15* Heidtman.
† Breadth overall (over rubbing strakes) was about 0.20m greater.
‡ Builders and construction numbers as follows: *F 16–19* Lürssen, *F 20–23* Heidtman, *F 24–27* von Hacht, *F 28–30* Havighorst, *F 31* Kremer (442), *F 32–34* Oltmann, *F 35, 36* Oertz, *F 37, 38* A & R (742, 743), *F 39* Schlichting.
** Builders and construction numbers as follows: *F 40, 41* Havighorst, *F 42, 43* Kremer (448, 447), *F 44, 45* Waap, *F 46, 47* Heidtmann, *F 48–51* von Hacht, *F 52–54* Roland, *F 55,* Lürssen, *F 56–59,* A & R (749, 750, 767, 768), *F 60–62* Oltmann, *F 63* Schuldt, *F 64, 65* von Hacht, *F 66, 67* Havighorst, *F 68* Oltmann, *F 69, 70* Schuldt, *F 71* Oltmann, *F 72, 73* Lürssen, *F 74, 75* Kremer (484, 485).

Construction
Laid down as shallow draught motor minesweepers (official design 1915). Transverse frame oak diagonal carvel construction.

Propulsion
Two Benz-Daimler-Hanomag 4-cylinder 4-stroke petrol engines (two 4-bladed screws, 0.65m diameter) in the engine room. One Bosch 12V generator and batteries. One rudder.

Armament
One machine gun; later **F 40** boats each had one Rev machine gun; [around 1916 **F 5**, **6**, **11** and others temporarily had one 45cm deck-mounted TT from **T 148**]; six mines.

Handling
Seaworthy up to Beaufort scale 5 and 6. Could be used with lightweight equipment.

Complement
Crew: 0/7. No boats.

Notes
Colour scheme no 9. Up to 1916 boats were fitted with one funnel.

Careers
All boats up to 1919–20 were commissioned as autonomous minesweeping boats, and were later given the same designation in the Reichsmarine though they also served as barrage and service vessels.

Documentary evidence on date stricken or released is incomplete as most reports were filed without a boat number, especially from police, customs and private owners; full information on identity and fate was the exception rather than the rule. This applies particularly to vessels sold abroad, where many were procured for smuggling or use as yachts. Official lists for the RWS (Reichs Water Police), police, customs and similar boats usually include no dimensions, year of construction, building dockyards or similar information to aid identification.

F 1: launched 1915. Stricken 22 Oct 1920.

F 2: launched 1915. Sunk 7 Nov 1916 north of Samel in the Irben Straits, by a mine.

F 3: launched 1915. Sunk 24 Oct 1917 north of Muhu Island, position approx 58° 36′N, 23° 13′E, by a mine.

F 4–6: launched 1915. Stricken 22 Oct 1920; apparently sunk in 1920.

F 7: launched 1915, commissioned as *RWS Kiel 20* in 1921, as *RWS F 7* in 1925; sold to the Electrical Apparatus Co (Gelap) as *Gisela* in 1926; commissioned by the Reichsmarine as *F 7* in 1928; became the Navy School training boat *Aegir* 31 Mar 1931; became *R 113* in Sept 1939.

F 8: launched 1915. Stricken 22 Oct 1920; sold.

F 9: launched 1915. Sunk 4 Oct 1918 in the North Sea near Hubert-Gatt siren buoy, position 53° 35′N, 06° 21′E, by explosion and fire; salvaged by the Reichsmarine 1920; served as the *RWS E 5*, and as the police boat *Emden* in 1925.

F 10: launched 1915, commissioned as the *RWS Kiel* in 1920, the *RWS F 10* at Hamburg in 1925; served with the Reichsmarine as a service boat at Wilhelmshaven in 1926.

F 11: launched 1915, commissioned as *RWS Stettin 23* in 1920, became *FRW F 11* at Stettin in 1925, and *F 11* in the Reichsmarine in 1928. Stricken 31 Mar 1931; served with the Mürwik naval school as *Odin* until 1945.

F 12: launched 1915. Stricken 22 Oct 1920.

F 13: launched 1915. Stricken 22 Oct 1920; served as the police boat *SW 5* at Stettin in the 1930s, and as *HM 18* in 1940.

F 11 (1916); *F5* and *F6* were similar. *Mrva*

F 15 (1915); *F 10* was similar. *Mrva*

F 20 (1917); *F 25*, was similar, and *F 16–19, 23, 24, 26, 27, 29, 30* and *32–43* were similar but without the foremast. *Mrva*

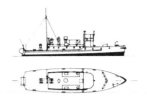

F 38 (1917); *F 22, 28* and *31* were similar. *Mrva*

F 56–59 (1918); *F 44–55* and *60–75* were similar. *Mrva*

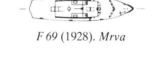

F 69 (1928). *Mrva*

F 14: launched 1915; served as *RWS B 5* in 1920, and the police boat *Bremen 2* in 1925.

F 15: launched 1915, served as the *RWS Hamburg 16* in 1920, the *RWS F 15* in 1925, and again in 1928.

F 16: launched in 1917; interned 15 Nov 1918 at Hellevoetsluis, position 51° 26′N, 03° 51′E; delivered to Belgium and served as the motor boat *V 1 Roi Albert* until the dissolution of the Belgian Navy in 1927, then with the Royal Yacht Club at Brussels as the motor yacht *Vadrouville*.

F 17: launched 1917, commissioned as *RWS Hamburg 15* in 1920, as *RWS F 17* at Hamburg in 1925, and as *F 17* in the Reichsmarine in 1928. Stricken 1 Apr 1935.

F 18: see *F 16*; served in Belgium as *V 2 Reine Elisabeth in* 1927.

F 19: see *F 16*; served in Belgium as *V 3 Prince Leopold* in 1927.

F 20: launched 1917, commissioned as *RWS Kiel 5* in 1920, *RWS F 20* at Kiel in 1925, in the Reichsmarine as *F 20* in 1928. Stricken 31 Mar 1931; sold to Kiel for 475M.

F 21: launched 1917, commissioned as *RWS Stettin 24* in 1920, *RWS F 21* at Stettin in 1925, and again in 1928.

F 22: launched 1917, sold to Holland in Dec 1919.

F 23: launched 1917, commissioned as *RWS Stettin 2* in 1920; served with the Altona water police as *Altona 1* in 1931.

F 24: launched 1917. Sold Dec 1919 to Delfzijl.

F 25: launched 1917, commissioned as *RWS Hamburg 2* in 1920; served as *Police School 4* at Spandau in 1929.

F 26: launched 1917. Sold Dec 1919 to Delfzijl.

F 27: launched 1917, commissioned as *RWS Hamburg 9* in 1920, *RWS Hamburg 1* in 1925, and *RWS Königsberg 1* in 1931.

F 28: launched 1917. Sold Dec 1919 to Delfzijl.

F 29: see *F 16*; served in Belgium as *V 4* in 1927.

F 30: see *F 16*; served in Belgium as *V 5 Chevalier Casaert*, 1927.

F 31: launched 1917. Sold Dec 1919 to Delfzijl.

F 32: launched 1917. Sunk 29 Mar 1918 at 1220hrs in the North Sea near Schiermonnikoog, position 53° 41′N, 06° 14′E, by a mine; seven dead.

F 33: see *F 16*; served in Belgium as *V 6 Roi Leopold I* in 1927.

F 34: launched 1917, commissioned as *RWS Stettin 25* in Nov 1921, as *RWS F 34* at Stettin in 1925, and as *Loki* at the Hansa ocean sports club in 1928.

F 35: see *F 16*; served in Belgium as *V 7 Roi Leopold II* in 1927.

F 36: see *F 16*; served in Belgium as *V 8 Princesse Marie-Jose* in 1927.

F 37: launched in 1917; served as *RWS Königsberg 3* in 1920, *RWS Pillau 1* in 1927, *RWS Elbing 1* in 1929, *RWS Tilsit 1* in 1930, *Elbing 1* in 1931, and *H 532* in 1940.

F 38: launched 1917. Stricken 22 Oct 1920; sold 23 Jun 1921 to Hamburg.

F 39: launched 1917; served as *RWS Tilsit 7* in 1920, *RWS Rossitten 1* in 1925, *RWS Pillau 2* in 1927, *RWS Pillau 1* in 1929, *RWS Tilsit 2* in 1929. Sold 21 Dec 1939 to Königsberg.

F 40: launched 1918, became the *F 16*; served in Belgium as the *V 9 Dinant* in 1927.

F 41: launched 1918. Stricken 22 Oct 1920; sold 23 Jun 1921 for 180,000M to Hamburg.

F 42: launched 1918. Sold Dec 1919 to Delfzijl.

F 43: launched 1918; served as *RWS Hamburg 21* in 1920, *RWS Hamburg 3* in 1925, *Altona I* in 1931, and *H 107* in 1939.

F 44: launched 1918; served as *RWS Stettin 26* in 1920, *RWS F 44* in 1925, and in 1928.

F 45: launched 1918. Stricken 22 Oct 1920.

F 46: launched 1918; served as *RWS Tilsit 18* and *RWS Rossitten 2* in 1920, with the Reichsmarine as *F 46* in 1928. Stricken 31 Mar 1931; sold to Kiel for 475M.

F 47: launched 1918; served as *RWS Stettin 27* in 1920, *RWS F 47* at Stettin in 1925, and in 1928.

F 48: see *F 16*; served in Belgium as *V 10* in 1927.

F 49: launched 1918. Stricken 22 Oct 1920; sold 24 Sept 1921 to customs for 130,000M to serve as *Sperber* at Emden.

F 50: launched 1918. Stricken 22 Oct 1920.

F 51: see *F 49*; served with the Customs service as *Seiler* at Husum, at Kiel in 1925, at Fehmarn in 1929, at Amrum in 1931, at Husum in 1933, and as *H 106* in 1939; repaired, then served with the main customs office at Husum in 1947.

F 52: launched 1918; served as *RWS E 1* in 1920, *RWS F 52* in 1925, with the Reichsmarine as the service boat *Nordholz* in 1928. Stricken 31 Mar 1931; sold 28 Apr 1933 to Kiel.

F53: launched 1918; served as *RWS Kiel 10* in 1920, *RWS F 53* at Kiel in 1925; with customs at Heiligenhafen, as *Schill* at Swinemünde customs in 1926, as reserve in 1932; served 1940 in Operation Sealion; became *V 6111* in 1941, returned 1 Mar 1944.

F 54: see *F 49*; served as *Geier* with customs at Sylt, at Flensburg in 1925, at Kiel in 1932. Sold 1934.

F 55: launched 1918; served as *RWS Kiel 11* in 1920, *RWS F 55* at Kiel in 1925; transferred to Senckenberg Research Institute 24 May 1932.

F 56: launched 1918; see *F 16*; served in Belgium as *V 11* in 1927.

F 57: launched 1918; see *F 16*; served in Belgium as *V 12* in 1927.

F 58: launched 1918; served as *RWS E 4* in 1920, *RWS Emden 1* in 1925.

F 59: see *F 49*; served with customs as *Habicht* at

Amrum, at Kiel in 1931. Sold to Hamburg as a private yacht in 1934.

F 60: launched 1918; served as *RWS Kiel 4* in 1920, *RWS Kiel 1* in 1925.

F 61: launched 1918; served as *RWS Kiel 2* in 1920, *RWS Brunsbüttelkoog 1* in 1927–29, and *RWS Kiel 2* in 1931.

F 62: launched 1918; served as *RWS Stettin 28* in 1920, *RWS Stettin 3* in 1925, with the Reichsmarine as *F 62* in 1928. Stricken 31 Mar 1931; sold as the barrack boat *SW 1* at Rostock in 1932.

F 63: launched 1918. Stricken 22 Oct 1920; served as *Vineta* at Kiel arsenal in 1935; with the SA naval standards 77 at Berlin in the 1930s; still in existence in 1939.

F 64: launched in 1919; served with the Reichsmarine. Stricken 13 Jun 1922.

F 65: launched 1919; served with the Reichsmarine. Stricken 13 Jun 1922; sold 30 Oct 1922 for 400,000M to Molocue (Portuguese Mozambique).

F 66: launched 1919; served with the Reichsmarine, and from 1 Jan 1924 as the traffic boat *Pollux*; sold 23 Apr 1932 to Wilhelmshaven.

F 67: launched 1919; served with the Reichsmarine, and as *Heete* during harbour construction at Wilhelmshaven in 1923; still in existence in 1939.

F 68: launched 1919; served with the Reichsmarine. Stricken 13 Jun 1922; sold.

F 69: launched 1919; served with the Reichs-marine; see *F 49*; served as *Adler* with customs at Sylt, at Fehmarn in 1926, with the Reichsmarine as *F 69* in 1928. Stricken 1 Apr 1935.

F 70: launched 1919; served with the Reichsmarine; served as *RWS Stettin 1* in Feb 1920, as *Stettin 1* with the Stettin water police in 1931; as served in Operation Sealion as *B 122 Mo* in 1940; became *HM 03*; served as *SW 1 Stettin* police boat from 1 Dec 1942 at WSP Command, Ostland.

F 71: launched 1919; served with the Reichsmarine; served as *RWS B 4* Feb 1920, *RWS F 71* in 1925, with the Reichsmarine as *F 71* in 1928. Stricken 31 Mar 1931; sold for 1315M to Kiel.

F 72: launched 1919; served with the Reichsmarine; served as the service boat *Castor* 1 Jan 1924; sold to Oldenburg 23 Apr 1932.

F 73: launched 1919; served in the Reichsmarine; served at the Cuxhaven garrison 1 Jan 1924; became the service boat *Sirius*.

F 74: launched 1919; served in the Reichsmarine. Stricken 22 Oct 1920; sold.

F 75: launched 1919; served in the Reichsmarine; served at Cuxhaven garrison until 1926.

The following vessels have also been identified as (unspecified) former F-boats:

Nord 16; served Feb 1922 in the RWS Mark-Nord region (F-number between *F 40* and *F 75*).

Undine (motor yacht) reported 1930 at Havel, near Wannsee.

Falke (motor vessel) reported 1939 at Lübeck (laid down in Hamburg 1927).

Freya II (motor harbour ferry) reported 1939 at Langeoog (laid down in Vegesack 1918), presumably *F 72* or *F 73*; served 8 Aug 1940 in Operation Sealion; purchased 16 Jul 1941 by the Kriegsmarine. Sunk 26 Aug 1943 northwest of Rottum, position 53° 33′N, 06° 34′E, by a mine.

Hilligenlei (motor vessel) reported 1939 at Langeness having received new Grauhöft-Kappeln engine in 1935; served 27 Jul 1940 in Operation Sealion as *D 19 Mo*. Sunk.

Rena Alice (motor yacht) reported at Kiel 1939 having been converted in 1922 at Hamburg to 160hp; belonged 1939 to the Oberfischmeister (Senior Fishing Harbourmaster) at Altona.

Hannover (further details unknown).

Holstein; served 1940 in Operation Sealion, see flotilla 24 Jun.

Nordsee (*F 1 (4)*); served 1939 with the Marine-SA-Brigade 2 in the North Sea; served 29 Aug 1940 in Operation Sealion; used 12 Sept 1941 as a sea commander's service boat at Calais; stricken 24 Aug 1944, taken to Klahn dockyard, Spandau.

Pidder Lüng; reported 1932 with J Dethlefsen, Pellworm; and in 1935 with Neue Pellwormer Dampfschiff Ges.

One boat (either *F 1* or *F 4*) was sold 1920 to the Oberfischmeister at Kiel; later presumably became *Nordsee* (see above).

R 1 class (1930–33 Types)

Name	Builder (construction no)	Built	Cost in Marks (000s)	Displacement (t = tonnes T = tons)	Length (m)	Breadth (m)	Draught (m)	Power (hp)	Revs (rpm)	Speed (kts)	Range (nm/kts)	Coal (t)	Oil (t)
R 1	Lürssen (12280)	1930–31			24.50 oa 24.00 cwl	4.38	1.22 max	714ehp max 700ehp des		17.0 des	800/13	—	4
R 2	A & R (2655)	1932–33		43.5t max	24.50 oa 24.10 cwl	4.38	1.53	750ehp des		20.0 des		—	
R 3–5	„ (2719–2721)	1932		46.2t max	26.50 oa 26.10 cwl	4.38	1.58	714ehp max 700ehp des		19.5 des		—	
R 6, 7	„ (2744, 2745)	1933		47.6t max	„	„	1.55	750ehp des		„		—	
R 8	Lürssen (12390)	1934			27.80 oa 27.45 cwl	4.50	1.12 max 1.06 des	750ehp des		16.5 des		—	4.9
R 9–14	A & R (2810–2815)	„		52.5t max	27.75 oa 27.35 cwl	4.38	1.36 max 1.28 des	770ehp des		19.8 des		—	4.4
R 15, 16	Schlichting (792, 793)	„		„	„	„	„	„		„		—	„

Construction

Laid down as motor minesweepers, officially as barrage practice vessels (*R 1* designed in 1930 as a 'fast diesel tug'; *R 2* was a counter-design by Abeking & Rasmussen in 1930; *R 3–5* were designed in 1931, *R 6–16* in 1933). Transverse and longitudinal frame steel-light alloy-mahogany double diagonal carvel composite construction (nine watertight compartments, eight in *R 1*). The first sixteen boats were built with a traditional hull, with a half-height forecastle over the forward third of the hull, and a midship superstructure of equal height for engine and accommodation. The rubbing strake was extended forward to about 4m short of the stem. Depth *F 1* 1.95m; *R 2* 2.08m; *R 8* 2.35m; all others 2.15m. Each boat completed as a minesweeper or an escort boat.

Propulsion

Two MWM RS 127 Su 6-cylinder 4-stroke diesel engines (*R 2* two Maybach diesel engines; *R 6–7* two Linke-Hoffmann diesel engines with reduction gearbox (two 3-bladed screws, 0.85m diameter, *R 1* 0.96m diameter) in one engine room. One 110V 10kW diesel generator. One rudder.

R 8 was an exception, with two DWK 6-cylinder four-stroke diesel engines (two Voith-Schneider propellers, 1.50m diameter), and no rudder.

Armament

One [later four] 2cm AA guns (2000 [4000] rounds), plus in some cases up to ten mines.

Handling

Seaworthy and serviceable up to Beaufort scale 6/7; manoeuvred and turned well. The Voith-Schneider propellers made *R 8* 10 per cent slower than the other vessels with conventional screws and rudders, but had the advantage of giving maximum possible manoeuvring capability in a minefield.

Complement

Crew: 1/14 or 0/18. Boats: one inflatable.

Notes

Colour scheme no 9 and camouflage. [*R 10* was rebuilt in Nov 1944 with a round bulge at the bow, two MWM RHS 230 Su 6-cylinder 4-stroke diesels after basic repairs.]

Careers

R 1: launched 9 Apr 1931, commissioned 20 Apr 1931; transferred to Toulon 24 Nov 1943; severely damaged by an aircraft bomb; stricken 11 Dec 1943; used as an experimental hulk, transferred to Eckernförde Jul 1945.

R 2: launched 1 Nov 1933; stricken in February 1945; broken up.

R 3: launched 11 May 1932; transferred to Toulon 24 Nov 1943; severely damaged by an aircraft bomb; stricken; wreck transferred to Pola. Sunk in April 1945.

R 4: launched 25 May 1932. Sunk 22 Feb 1945 off Albona, position 45° 05′N, 14° 10′E, by an aircraft bomb; stricken, wreck transferred to Pola and scuttled in April 1945.

R 5: launched 18 Jun 1932. Sank 3 Jan 1940 in the Baltic off Stolpmünde after suffering ice damage and being stranded.

R 6: launched 29 Sept 1933. Sunk 13 Aug 1943 at 1235hrs off Civitavecchia, position 42° 02′N, 11° 35′N, by an aircraft bomb; three dead.

R 7: launched 30 Sept 1933. Sunk 9 Sept 1943 at Salerno, position 40° 40′N, 14° 45′E, after stranding on 8 Sept; salvaged.

R 8: launched 30 Nov 1933, commissioned 12 Jan 1934; stranded 2 May 1945 in the Tagliamento estuary, position 45° 39′N, 13° 06′E.

R 9: launched 11 Apr 1934. Sunk 2 Aug 1942 in the Bay of Bardia by an aircraft bomb, together with *R 11*.

R 10: launched 9 May 1934. Sunk 24 Mar 1943 at 1330hrs near Ferryville, position 37° 09′N, 09° 49′E, following an explosion on ss *Umbrino* after an air raid; raised in May 1943, [fitted with new engines], and recommissioned 12 Nov 1944. Stranded and sunk 2 May 1945 in the Tagliamento estuary, position 45° 39′N, 13° 06′E.

R 11: launched 27 Jun 1934. Sunk 2 Aug 1942 in the Bay of Bardia, by an aircraft bomb, together with *R 9*.

R 12: launched 28 Jun 1934. Sunk 5 Sept 1944 at 0550hrs in the Adriatic, position 45° 26′ 5″N, 13° 25′ 4″E, by a mine; ten dead.

R 13: launched 19 Jul 1934. Sunk 9 Sept 1943 at Salerno, position 40° 40′N, 14° 45′E; used as a tug for *R 7*.

R 14: launched 6 Sept 1934. Sunk 16 Mar 1945 at Monfalcone dockyard, position 45° 49′N, 13° 32′E, by an aircraft bomb.

R 15: launched 3 May 1934. Sunk 12 Aug 1944 at 1430hrs in a collision while entering Sebenico with *S 629*; severely damaged; repaired and recommissioned. Sunk in the Adriatic 16 Apr 1945 by torpedoes from British MTBs.

R 16: launched 23 May 1934. Stranded and sunk 2 May 1945 in the Tagliamento estuary, position 45° 39′N, 13° 09′E; with *R 8* and *R 10*.

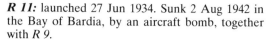

R 1 (1931). Mrva

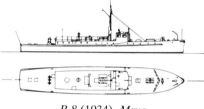

R 8 (1934). Mrva

R 1 (1933). Mrva

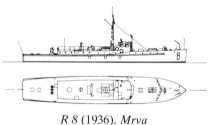

R 8 (1936). Mrva

R 2 (1933). Mrva

Hawse pipe on *R 15* and *R 16*.

R 9–16 (1936); initially all boats were without the upper (forecastle deck) rubbing strake; fenders werefitted on R 9 only. Mrva

R 3–7 (1933). Mrva

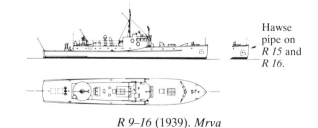

Hawse pipe on *R 15* and *R 16*.

R 9–16 (1939). Mrva

R 17 class (1934 Type)

Name	Builder (construction no)	Built	Cost in Marks (000s)	Displacement (t = tonnes T = tons)	Length (m)	Breadth (m)	Draught (m)	Power (hp)	Revs (rpm)	Speed (kts)	Range (nm/kts)	Coal (t)	Oil (t)
R 17	Schlichting (798)	1935		120t max	36.90 oa 36.00 cwl	5.44	1.38 max 1.30 des	1836ehp max 1800ehp des	600 des	21.2 max 21.0 des	900/15	—	10.8
R 18–20	A & R (2874–2876)	”		”	”	”	”	”	”	”	”	—	”

Construction

Laid down as motor minesweepers (designed in 1934). Transverse and longitudinal frame steel-light alloy-mahogany double diagonal carvel composite construction (nine watertight compartments). Later boats had a flat, shallow hull and long central midship superstructure; this was the first series-produced type with Voith-Schneider propellers. Depth 2.92m. Each boat completed as a minesweeper or an escort boat.

Propulsion

Two MAN 8-cylinder 4-stroke diesel engines with 2:1 reduction gearbox in one engine room (two Voith-Schneider propellers, 1.80m diameter). One 110V 15kW diesel generator.

Armament

Two 2cm AA guns (2000 rounds); up to twelve mines.

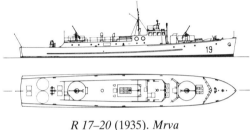

R 17–20 (1935). Mrva

Handling

Manoeuvred well, turned extremely tightly but threw up a high wake. Approximately 10 per cent slower than boats with conventional propellers and rudders.

Complement

Crew: 1/15 or 1/16. Boats: one inflatable.

Notes

Colour scheme no 9 and camouflage.

Careers

R 17: launched 26 Oct 1935. Sunk 10 Apr 1940 at Horten, position 59° 25′, 10° 29′E, by gunfire from the Norwegian minelayer *Olaf Tryggvason*.

R 18: launched 29 Aug 1935; served in the US Labor Service Unit B; taken 1 Dec 1945 as a Danish prize in poor condition; not commissioned; returned to Allies in 1947. Broken up in Britain.

R 19: launched 16 Oct 1935. Sunk 16 Sept 1943 at 1610hrs at Nantes, position 47° 13′N, 01° 34′W, by an aircraft bomb.

R 20: launched 14 Dec 1935. Sunk 16 Aug 1944 in the vicinity of Sylt, by a German mine; nine dead.

R 21 class (1936–42 Types)

Construction

Laid down as motor minesweepers (designed 1936, 1939 and 1942). Transverse and longitudinal frame steel-light alloy-mahogany double diagonal carvel composite construction (nine watertight compartments). Flush deck, hard chine foreship. Depth 3.45m; after *R 41* 3.12m; after *R 130* 3.52m. Each boat completed as a minesweeper or an escort boat.

Propulsion

Two MAN 8-cylinder 4-stroke diesel engines, except *R 41–48*, which had two MWM 6-cylinder 4-stroke diesel engines with 2:1 reduction gearbox, in one engine room (two Voith-Schneider propellers, 1.80m diameter). One 110V 15kW diesel generator.

Armament

Two [six] 2cm AA guns (2000 [6000] rounds); *R 108* and all boats after *R 112* had one 3.7cm AA gun (1000 rounds); three [six] 2cm AA guns (3000 [6000] rounds); [after March 1944 all surviving ves-

sels (for example, *R 69*, *R 83* and *R 76*) were fitted with one 8.6cm rocket launcher.

Handling

Manoeuvred well, turned extremely tightly; suffered some speed loss compared with boats with conventional propellers and rudders.

Complement

Crew: *R 21–24* 0/21 or 1/26; *R 41–129* 1/29 or 2/36; *R 130–150* 3/38. Boats: two inflatables.

Notes

Colour scheme no 9 and camouflage.

Careers

R 21: launched 17 Nov 1937; served in the US Labor Service Unit B; taken as a British prize, broken up.

R 22: launched 28 Oct 1937; taken 13 Oct 1947 as a US prize; sold 17 Jun 1948 to J Knecht of Bremen as the motor vessel *Ostfriesland III*; renamed *Twist* 18 Mar 1952; sold 5 Apr 1954 for breaking up.

R 23: launched 12 Jan 1938; served in the US Labor Service Unit B; taken 26 Oct 1945 as a USSR prize.

R 24: launched 22 Dec 1937; served in the US Labor Service Unit B; taken 1 Dec 1947 as a US prize; [transferred to OMGUS] for various charters. Sunk 16 May 1949 at Bremen old harbour after springing a leak; raised and used as a kitchen facility; wreck returned May 1950 to the US Navy.

R 41: launched 16 Apr 1940. Sunk 19 Jun 1943 in the Seine Estuary, in the vicinity of Barfleur, by torpedo from a British MTB.

R 42: launched 22 May 1940. Sunk after colliding with a wreck 11 Feb 1942 in the Channel, in the vicinity of Ambleteuse, position 50° 49′N, 01° 37′E; no casualties.

R 43: launched 9 Jun 1940; taken out of service 5 Dec 1944; taken as a US prize; served in the GM/SA; transferred 31 Oct 1946 to the OMGUS at Kiel, and in Sept 1949 to the US Army BPE.

R 44: launched 19 Mar 1940. Sunk 23 Jan 1943 at

Name	Builder (construction no)	Built	Cost in Marks (000s)	Displacement (t = tonnes T = tons)	Length (m)	Breadth (m)	Draught (m)	Power (hp)	Revs (rpm)	Speed (kts)	Range (nm/kts)	Coal (t)	Oil (t)
R 21	A & R (2977)	1937–38		123.6t max	37.00 oa 36.00 cwl	5.77	1.38 max 1.35 des	2200ehp des	600 des	23.1 max 21.0 des		—	
R 22, 23	A & R (2978, 2979)	,,		,,	,,	,,	,,	1836ehp max 1800ehp des	,,	,,		—	
R 24	Schlichting (815)	,,		,,	,,	,,	,,	,,	,,	,,		—	
R 41–43	,, (971–973)	1940		135t max 125t des	37.80 oa 36.80 cwl	5.82	1.51 max 1.40 des	1800ehp des	600 des	20.0 des	900/15	—	11.1
R 44–101	A & R (3350–3354, 3372–3377, 3408, 3409, 3392–3407, 3412–3427, 3444–3451, 3431–3435)	1940–42		,,	,,	,,	,,	,,	,,	,,	,,	—	,,,,
R 102–129s	,, (3521–3536, 3586–3597)	1942–42		,,	38.60 oa 36.80 cwl	,,	,,	,,	,,	,,	,,	—	,,
R 130–150	,, (3701–3708, 3760–3772)	1943		155t max 150t des	41.05 oa 38.60 cwl	5.80	1.67 max 1.60 des	2155ehp max 1800ehp des	731 max 600 des	19.8 max 19.0 des	,,	—	11.0

1430hrs off Brest, position 48° 23'N, 04° 30'W, by a British aircraft bomb.

R 45: launched 28 Mar 1940. Sunk 9 May 1942 in the vicinity of Dunkirk, west of Ambleteuse, position 50° 49'N, 01° 36'E, in collision with *Raule*; wreck brought in.

R 46: launched 19 Apr 1940. Sunk 26 Jun 1944 off Le Havre, position 49° 29'N, 00° 06'E, by an explosion caused by a German mine on board.

R 47: launched 19 Apr 1940; served in the GM/SA; taken out of service 5 Dec 1947; taken as a British prize; broken up.

R 48: launched 30 Apr 1940; remainder of career as for *R 47*.

R 49: launched 5 Jun 1940; served in the GM/SA; taken out of service 21 Nov 1947; taken as a British prize; broken up.

R 50: launched 15 Jun 1940. Sunk 13 Jun 1944 in the vicinity of Trouville, position 49° 22'N, 00° 05'E, by a German shallow water mine; no casualties.

R 51: launched 6 Jul 1940. Sunk 15 Jun 1944 in the English Channel by a mine; raised. Sunk 22 Aug 1944 off Rouen by an aircraft bomb.

R 52: launched 7 Aug 1940. Damaged 25 Feb 1944 at 2000hrs in Dieppe harbour, position 49° 56'N, 01° 05'E, by an aircraft bomb; stricken; served in the GM/SA; taken 1947 as a US prize, transferred in Sept 1949 to the US Army BPE.

R 53: launched 8 Aug 1940; served in the GM/SA; taken 20 Dec 1945 as a USSR prize.

R 54: launched 23 Aug 1940. Sunk 16 Dec 1943 at 1031hrs northwest of Anholt, by a mine; no casualties.

R 55: launched 11 Sept 1940; served in the GM/SA; taken 1947 as a US prize, sold 24 Jun 1948 to K Kuss of Oldenburg as the restaurant *Stadt Oldenburg*; sold 3 Dec 1951 to the Federation of German Scouts at Bremerhaven as living accommodation; sold 4 Jan 1954 to Lemwerder for breaking up; broken up 1954.

R 56: launched 28 Sept 1940. Sunk 9 Dec 1943 off north coast of Norway by an aircraft bomb; raised, recommissioned. Sunk 8 Dec 1944 off Bomlofjord by gunfire from a British fighter-bomber.

R 57: launched 10 Oct 1940. Sunk in Drontheim fjord, date and position unknown, in a collision with *U 1163*; broken up.

R 58: launched 25 Oct 1940. Sunk 9 Sept 1941 west of Kronstadt, position 59° 59'N, 29° 45'E, by a mine; raised and recommissioned in 1943; served in the GM/SA; taken 20 Dec 1945 as a USSR prize.

R 59: launched 9 Nov 1940. Sunk 3 Apr 1945 at Kiel by US bombs.

R 60: launched 21 Nov 1940. Sunk 14 Sept 1941 at 0230hrs in Helsinki East dock, position 60° 10'N, 24° 57'E, by sabotage; sixty-one dead.

R 61: launched 6 Dec 1940. Remainder of career as for *R 60*.

R 62: launched 19 Dec 1940. Remainder of career as for *R 60*.

R 63: launched 15 Jan 1941; served in the GM/SA; taken 20 Dec 1945 as a USSR prize.

R 64: launched 20 Jan 1941. Sunk 28 Dec 1943 south of Honningsvaag, position 70° 54' 5"N, 25° 55' 5"E, by a mine; sixteen dead.

R 65: launched 5 Feb 1941; served in the GM/SA; taken 26 Oct 1945 as a USSR prize.

R 66: launched 22 Feb 1941. Sunk 15 Sept 1942 in the Gulf of Finland, in the vicinity of Halli island, position 60° 20'N, 27° 50'E, by a Soviet mine.

R 67: launched 6 Mar 1941; served in the GM/SA; taken 1 Dec 1947 as a US prize; became the motor ferry *Helligenlei* at Hapag 27 May 1948; transferred 23 Nov 1950 to Schiffges Jade of Wilhelmshaven as the motor ferry *Rüstringen*; served 15 Sept 1953 in the GM/SA as the *USN 130*, and in the German Federal Navy 30 Oct 1956 as *Wega*; used 2 Mar 1962 as the barrack boat *WBR XII*, with the Münster naval cadets in 1967 as *Friedrich Lührmann*. Sunk by fire Jul 1978.

R 68: launched 19 Mar 1941; served in the GM/SA; taken 1 Dec 1947 as US prize, served 1948 in the Rhine flotilla as *US 13 Tiger*; transferred 8 Jun 1948 to the Ostdeutsche Dampfsch AG (East German Steamship Co) in Hamburg as the Rhine tug *Tiger*; served 30 Jun 1951 in the US Labor Service Unit B, became *USN 143*; served 16 Nov 1956 in the German Federal navy as *Pegasus*; taken out of service 28 Apr 1961, used as the barrack boat *WBR VI*; stricken 1 Dec 1969; became the motor vessel *Thetis III* 7 May 1973. Sunk 6 Mar 1980 in Hamburg coal harbour; raised, broken up.

R 69: launched 29 Mar 1941. Sunk 10 Apr 1945 in the vicinity of Hela, by Soviet aircraft.

R 70: launched 10 Apr 1941. Sunk 11 Aug 1944 at 2356hrs in the Gulf of Finland, in the vicinity of Halli island, position 60° 20'N, 27° 50'E, 7–10nm south of Pukkio, by a Soviet mine; twenty-one dead.

R 71: launched 25 Apr 1941; served in the GM/SA; taken 5 Dec 1947 as a US prize, transferred 1948 to Bremen as a barrack ship, became *Martha II* in Apr 1951. Sunk 6 Apr 1953 off Bremen in Europa harbour; raised, broken up Jun 1953.

R 72: launched 8 May 1941. Sunk 3 Apr 1945 off Kiel by US bombs.

R 73: launched 21 May 1941. Sunk 14 Jun 1944 at 2321hrs in the Gulf of Finland in the enlarged 'Sea urchin' barrage, position 57° 36′ 5″N, 27° 13′ 2″E, by a German mine; one dead.

R 74: launched 5 Jun 1941. Sunk 12 Mar 1943 at 1827hrs in the vicinity of Boulogne, position 50° 44′N, 01° 36′E, by a mine.

R 75: launched 15 Jun 1941. Sunk 22 Jan 1944 at 1856hrs 1.4nm east of Hela, in a collision with *U 350*.

R 76: launched 26 Jun 1941. Sunk 15 Sept 1944 in the vicinity of Suursaari, position 60° 05′N, 26° 58′E, by Finnish gunfire; stranded; raised 1944, repaired; served in the GM/SA; taken 1 Dec 1947 as a US prize, served in the Rhine flotilla as *US Leopard*, transferred 27 May 1948 to Ostdeutsche Dampfsch AG in Hamburg as the Rhine tug *Leopard*; served in the US Labor Service Unit B 15 Sept 1953 as *USN 145*; served 30 Oct 1956 in the German Federal navy as *Atair*; taken out of service 15 Apr 1960, became *WBR V*, stricken 2 Oct 1970; sold 15 Dec 1970 to the sea sports club at Büsum; broken up 1976.

R 77: launched 8 Oct 1942. Sunk 8 Oct 1942 off Dunkirk, position 51° 02′N, 02° 22′E, by a mine, while escorting *HSK 7* (*Komet*), together with *R 82* and *R 86*.

R 78: launched 31 Jul 1941. Remaining career as for *R 77*.

R 79: launched 8 Aug 1941. Sunk 23 Jun 1944 off Boulogne, position 50° 44′N, 01° 36′E, by two aircraft rockets.

R 80: launched 22 Aug 1941. Sunk 11 Sept 1944 off Hoofdplaat, position 51° 22′N, 02° 40′E, by an aircraft bomb.

R 81: launched 1 Sept 1941. Sunk 16 Jun 1944 at 0100hrs in the vicinity of Boulogne, position 50° 44′N, 01° 36′E, by a British aircraft bomb.

R 82: launched 11 Sept 1941. Sunk 8 Oct 1942 off Dunkirk, position 51° 02′N, 02° 22′E, by a mine, while escorting *HSK 7* (*Komet*) (see *R 77*, *R 78* and *R 86*).

R 83: launched 21 Sept 1941; served in the GM/SA, taken as a British prize 21 Nov 1947; broken up.

R 84: launched 2 Oct 1941. Sunk 20 Aug 1943 in the vicinity of Boulogne, position 50° 44′N, 01° 36′E, by an aircraft bomb and gunfire.

R 85: launched 11 Oct 1941. Sunk 17 Jun 1945 in the vicinity of Dordrecht, position 51° 49′N, 04° 40′E, by an expolosion in the sweeping gear.

R 86: launched 2 Nov 1941. Sunk 8 Oct 1942 off Dunkirk, position 51° 02′N, 01° 22′E, by a mine while escorting *HSK 7* (*Komet*) (see *R 77*, *R 78* and *R 82*).

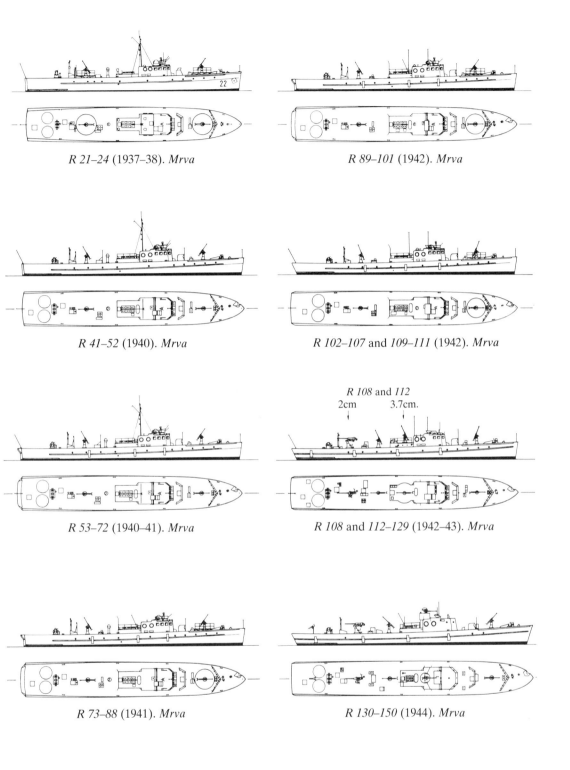

R 21–24 (1937–38). *Mrva*

R 89–101 (1942). *Mrva*

R 41–52 (1940). *Mrva*

R 102–107 and 109–111 (1942). *Mrva*

R 53–72 (1940–41). *Mrva*

R 108 and 112
2cm   3.7cm.

R 108 and 112–129 (1942–43). *Mrva*

R 73–88 (1941). *Mrva*

R 130–150 (1944). *Mrva*

R 87: launched 6 Nov 1941; served in the GM/SA; taken 4 Nov 1945 as a USSR prize.

R 88: launched 19 Nov 1941. Sunk 8 May 1945 in the Kaiser Wilhelm canal.

R 89: launched 6 Dec 1941. Sunk 10 Aug 1944 at 1950hrs at Lepsoe in the vicinity of Aalesund, by a munitions explosion during an air raid.

R 90: launched 16 Dec 1941; served in the GM/SA; taken 9 Jan 1946 as a USSR prize.

R 91: launched 31 Dec 1941; served in the GM/SA; taken 29 Nov 1947 as a US prize, transferred 22 Jun 1948 to the Nord Taucherbetrieb (North German Diving Co) at Lübeck as a barrack boat, trans-

ferred 8 Jul 1949 to H Fleck of Duisburg as a Rhine tug but not used; served in the US Labor Service Unit B 15 Sept 1953 as *USN 11*; transferred 16 Nov 1956 to the German Federal navy as *Aldebaran*; stricken 23 Apr 1970, used as a motor yacht 1976.

R 92: launched 10 Jan 1942. Sunk 15 Jun 1944 at 2300hrs off Boulogne, position 50° 44′N, 01° 36′E, by British bombs, together with *R 125* and *R 129*.

R 93: launched 21 Jan 1942. Sunk 23 Sept 1943 off Dunkirk, position 51° 02′N, 02° 22′E, by a mine.

R 94: launched 4 Mar 1942. Sunk 6 Sept 1943 in the English Channel, by a mine.

R 95: launched 28 Feb 1944. Sunk 12 Jun 1944, in the vicinity of Gravelines, position 50° 59′N, 02° 07′E, by a mine.

R 96: launched 14 Mar 1942; served in the GM/SA; taken 26 Nov 1947 as a US prize; sold to Peglow-Kreutzer AG of Hamburg as an experimental ship for electric sea fishing; sold 30 Jun 1953 to the Fish Products Co at Lewes, Delaware (same purpose).

R 97: launched 21 Mar 1942. Sunk 13 Jun 1944, in the vicinity of Boulogne, position 50° 44′N, 01° 36′E, by an aircraft rocket.

R 98: launched 27 Mar 1942; served in the GM/SA; taken 26 Nov 1947 as a US prize; sold 29 Jun 1948 to F Burde of Bremen as the motor vessel *Mars*; became unserviceable and used 11 Jul 1951 as a barrack ship; broken up 1955.

R 99: launched 11 Apr 1942; served in the GM/SA; taken 26 Nov 1947 as a US prize; served in the Rhine flotilla as *US 23 Panther*; sold 28 May 1948 to Ostdeutsche Dampfsch AG in Hamburg as the Rhine tug *Panther*; served 15 Sept 1953 in the US Labor Service Unit B as *USN 148*; transferred 30 Oct 1956 to the German Federal navy as *Algol*; taken out of service 28 Apr 1961, used as the barrack boat *WBR VIII*; transferred in the 1970s to the Duisburg naval fellowship as *Graf Spee*; broken up 1977.

R 100: launched 19 Apr 1942; served in the GM/SA; taken 16 Nov 1947 as a US prize; sold 15 Jun 1948 to F Gaffling of Kutenhausen as the motor vessel *Maria-Angela*. Grounded and sunk 17 Dec 1951 in the vicinity of Blexen, Unterweser.

R 101: launched 6 May 1942; served in the GM/SA; taken 26 Nov 1947 as a US prize, transferred 30 Jun 1949 to H Fleck of Duisburg as a Rhine tug, but not used; served 30 Jun 1951 in the US Labor Service Unit B as *USN 149*; transferred 11 Dec 1956 to the German Federal navy as *UW 4*; taken out of service 1 Apr 1969; stricken 20 Jul 1970, transferred to the Nienburg naval fellowship as the barrack boat *Niedersachsen*.

R 102: launched 23 May 1942; served in the GM/SA; taken 26 Nov 1947 as a US prize; sold 16 Jun 1948 to Nord Taucherbetrieb, Lübeck, as a barrack boat, then 10 Sept 1949 to A van Holt of Hamburg as a Rhine tug; returned 15 Sept 1953 to the US Navy.

R 103: launched 3 Jun 1942; served in the GM/SA; taken 4 Nov 1945 as a USSR prize.

R 104: launched 16 Jun 1942. Sunk 4 May 1945 in the Kaiser Wilhelm Canal.

R 105: launched 27 Jun 1942; served in the GM/SA; taken 4 Nov 1945 as a USSR prize.

R 106: launched 10 Jul 1942. Sunk 15 Aug 1942 in Gulf of Finland 15nm west of Hungerburg, position 59° 30′N, 28° 03′E, by Soviet bombs.

R 107: launched 4 Aug 1942; served in the GM/SA; taken 4 Nov 1945 as a USSR prize.

R 108: launched 15 Aug 1942. Sunk 16 Apr 1944, in the vicinity of Terschelling, position 53° 22′N, 05° 21′E, in a collision with *R 229*.

R 109: launched 30 Aug 1942. Sunk 26 Nov 1942 west of Fécamp, position 49° 46′N, 00° 21′E, by a German mine.

R 110: launched 12 Sept 1942. Sunk 10 Jun 1944 off the Hook of Holland, position 52° 05′N, 04° 03′E, by a mine.

R 111: launched 27 Sept 1942. Sunk 5 Jul 1944 at 0520hrs off Vlieland island, position 53° 18′N, 05° 00′E, by a British aircraft bomb and gunfire.

R 112: launched 11 Oct 1942. Sunk 2 Jun 1945 off the Altenbruch roads in a collision; broken up.

R 113: launched 29 Oct 1942; served in the GM/SA; taken 20 Dec 1945 as a USSR prize.

R 114: launched 8 Nov 1942. Struck 26 Apr 1943 by a mine between Dunkirk and Calais, sank 27 Apr during a towing operation.

R 115: launched 19 Nov 1942; served in the GM/SA; taken 5 Dec 1947 as a British prize, used as the experimental boat *ML 6115* at Portsmouth; broken up 1954.

R 116: launched 8 Dec 1942. Sunk 29 May 1944 at 0405hrs in the vicinity of Calais, position 45° 10′N, 67° 17′W, by a mine.

R 117: launched 19 Dec 1942; served in the GM/SA; taken 26 Nov 1947 as a US prize, transferred 28 May 1948 to A Zedler of Lübeck as a barrack ship, bought in Jan 1955.

R 118: launched 9 Jan 1943; served in the GM/SA; taken 1945 as a US prize. Sunk 21 Jan 1947 in Kiel bay due to ice pressure.

R 119: launched 21 Jan 1943. Sunk 3 Apr 1945 at Kiel by US bombs.

R 120: launched 17 Feb 1943; served in the GM/SA; taken 1 Dec 1947 as a US prize, transferred 29 Jun 1948 to the Münster Waterways Directorate as a barrack ship; transferred 18 Oct 1949 to W Schnaas of Neuwied, where conversion to the Rhine tug *Dorothea* was begun; served 15 Sept 1953 in the US Labor Service Unit B as *USN 139*; transferred to the German Federal navy as *Skorpion*; taken out of service 3 Aug 1962, used as the barrack boat *WBR XVI*; transferred 1 Jul 1974 to the naval fellowship at Borkum as the barrack boat *Skorpion*.

R 121: launched 11 Mar 1943; remained in Norway after May 1945.

R 122: launched 19 Mar 1943; served in the GM/SA; taken 20 Dec 1945 as a USSR prize.

R 123: launched 1 May 1943. Sunk 29 May 1944 at 0250hrs, in the vicinity of Le Havre, position 49° 29′N, 00° 06′E, by bombs.

R 124: launched 8 May 1943; served in the GM/SA; taken 20 Dec 1945 as a USSR prize.

R 125: launched 28 May 1943. Sunk 15 Jun 1944 at 2300hrs, off Boulogne, position 50° 44′N, 01° 36′E, by British bombs, together with *R 92* and *R 129*.

R 126: launched 22 Jun 1943. Sunk 14 Apr 1945 in the Great Belt, by a mine.

R 127: launched 2 Jul 1943; served in the GM/SA; taken 1 Dec 1947 as a US prize, transferred 29 Jul 1949 to H Fleck of Duisburg as a Rhine tug; served 15 Sept 1953 in the US Labour Service Unit B as *USN 141*, transferred to the German Federal navy as *Deneb*; taken out of service 28 Jul 1961, used as the barrack boat *WBR VII*, transferred 20 Jun 1968 to the naval fellowship at Frankfurt am Main for use as living accommodation.

R 128: launched 10 Jul 1943; served in the GM/SA; taken 1 Dec 1947 as a US prize; transferred 28 May 1948 to A Zedler of Lübeck as a barrack boat; transferred 17 Oct 1949 to W Schnaas of Neuwied as the Rhine tug *Annegret*; served 15 Sept 1953 in the US Labor Service Unit B as *USN 151*, transferred 16 Nov 1956 to the German Federal navy as *Arkturus*; taken out of service 31 May 1963, used as the barrack boat *WBR XVII*, used 1968 as the target ship *Moritz 2*. Sunk 14 Mar 1968 at Wilhelmshaven naval arsenal by fire, wreck scuttled in 1969.

R 129: launched 12 Aug 1943. Sunk 15 Jun 1944 at 2300hrs off Boulogne, position 50° 44′N, 01° 36′E, by British bombs, together with *R 92* and *R 125*.

R 25 class (1937–43 Types)

Construction

Laid down as motor minesweepers (designed 1937, 1940, 1942 and 1943). Transverse and longitudinal frame steel-light alloy-mahogany double diagonal carvel composite construction (eight watertight compartments), known as the *R 401* type. *R 212* was further developed after the enforced cessation of Voith-Schneider propeller installation to simplify production. These were flush deck vessels. Depth *R 25–40* 3.13m; *R 401* and following vessels 3.22m. Each boat completed as a minesweeper or an escort boat.

Propulsion

Two MWM RS 163 Su 6-cylinder 4-stroke diesel engines, after *R 151* with supercharging and 2:1 reduction gearbox, in one engine room (two 3-bladed screws, 0.90m or 1.15m diameter). One 110V 15kW diesel generator. *R 25–40* had two rudders, three after *R 151*. *R 239* was used as a test boat for the new KHD RT 12 M 133 12-cylinder 2-stroke diesel engine (see also *MZ 1*).

Armament

R 25–40 and *151–217* had two 2cm AA guns (2000 rounds); up to ten mines; an additional 3.7cm AA gun (1000 rounds) was fitted later.

R 218–300 had one 3.7cm AA gun (1000 rounds); three [six] 2cm AA guns (3000 [6000] rounds); up to twelve mines.

Name	Builder (construction no)	Built	Cost in Marks (000s)	Displacement (t = tonnes T = tons)	Length (m)	Breadth (m)	Draught (m)	Power (hp)	Revs (rpm)	Speed (kts)	Range (nm/kts)	Coal (t)	Oil (t)
R 25, 26, 38–40	Schlichting (849, 850, 938–940)	1938–39	617 each	126t max 110t des	35.40 oa 34.40 cwl	5.55	1.42 max 1.40 des	1836ehp max 1800ehp des	600 des	23.5 des	1100/15	—	10.0
R 27–34	A & R (3141–3144, 3235, 3236, 3220, 3221)	,,	,,	,,	,,	,,	,,	,,	,,	,,	,,	—	,,
R 151–193	Burmester (B) (2440–2447, 2454–2480, 2506–2513)	1940–42		,,	,,	,,	1.50 max 1.38 des	1800ehp des	,,	,,	,,	—	,,
R 194–199, 206, 207	Burmester (S) (3001–3008)	1942–43		128t max 110t des	36.20 oa 34.40 cwl	,,	1.50 max 1.40 des	,,	,,	,,	,,	—	,,
R 200–205, 208–217	Burmester (B) (2770–2775, 2762–2769, 2776, 2777)	,,		,,	,,	,,	,,	,,	,,	,,	,,	—	,,
R 218–233, 238, 240–247, 254–263, 288–300	,, (2801–2816, 2821, 2823–2830, 2861–2874, 2876–2888)	1943–45		148t max 140t des	39.35 oa 36.80 cwl	5.72	1.61 max 1.50 des	2550ehp max 2500ehp des	,,	22.5 max 21.0 des	1000/15	—	15.0
R 234–237, 248–253, 264–287	Burmester (S) (2817–2820, 2831–2836, 3020–3043)	,,		,,	,,	,,	,,	,,	,,	,,	,,	—	,,
R 239	Burmester (B) (2822)	,,		,,	,,	,,	,,	2300ehp max 2400ehp des	,,	,,	,,	—	,,
R 401–425	A & R (3801–3818, 3901–3907)	1944–45		150t max 140t des	,,	,,	1.65 max 1.50 des	2800ehp des		25.0 des	,,	—	,,
R 426–430	,, (3908–3912)	—		,,	,,	,,	,,	,,		,,	,,	—	,,
R 431–498	,, (3913–3980)	—		,,	,,	,,	,,	,,		,,	,,	—	16.2
R 501–514, 531–545	Burmester (B) (2889–2917)	—		148t max 140t des	,,	,,	1.61 max 1.50 des	2500ehp des	600 des	21.0 des	,,	—	(15)
R 515–530	Burmester (S) (3044–3059)	—		,,	,,	,,	,,	,,	,,	,,	,,	—	,,

R 401–430 had one 3.7cm AA gun (1000 rounds); six 2cm AA guns (6000 rounds); two 8.6cm rocket launchers; up to twelve mines.

R 431 onwards had four 3cm AA guns (rounds unknown); two 8.6cm rocket launchers; up to twelve mines.

Complement

Crew: *R 25–40* 1/19; *R 151–217* 1/28 or 1/30; *R 218–300* 1/28 or 2/38; *R 401–498* 1/32 or 2/35. Boats: inflatables.

Notes

Colour scheme no 9 and camouflage.

All R-boats were allotted to sweeper flotillas after commissioning; some served after 1945 in the GM/SA up to about 1947; some served after 1951 in the US Labor Service Unit B. Of the ships which the Tripartite Naval Commission (TNC) allotted to the USA as prizes after 1945, some remained in Germany. They were chartered *en bloc* by the Office of the Military Government United States (OMGUS) to the Federal government or its predecessor, which in turn signed charter treaties with German shipping companies. On the occasion of the visit of Federal Chancellor Dr Konrad Adenauer to the USA in 1952 the OMGUS vessels were returned to the Federal government free of charge. Some of them were then used for government purposes, others sold to charter companies.

Careers

R 25: launched 8 Jul 1938; served in the GM/SA; taken 30 Jun 1946 as a USSR prize.

R 26: launched 3 Aug 1938; served in the GM/SA; taken 1 Dec 1945 as a Danish prize; broken up 1948 at Odense.

R 27: launched 11 May 1938. Sunk 11 Apr 1944 at 1730hrs in the Pillau-Königsberg channel, by an aircraft bomb.

R 28: launched 25 May 1938; served in the GM/SA; taken 29 May 1946 as a USSR prize.

R 29: launched 22 Jun 1938. Sunk 15 Sept 1944 in the Gulf of Finland, north of Suursaari, position

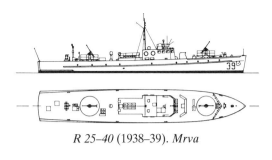

R 25–40 (1938–39). *Mrva*

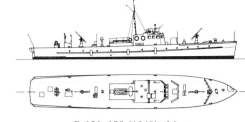

R 151–158 (1940). *Mrva*

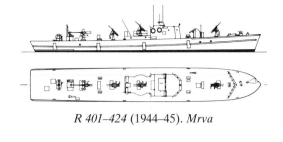

R 401–424 (1944–45). *Mrva*

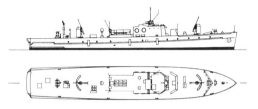

R 25–40 late war appearance. *Mrva*

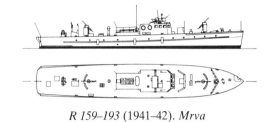

R 159–193 (1941–42). *Mrva*

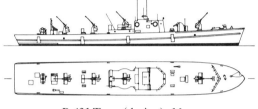

R 431 Type (design). *Mrva*

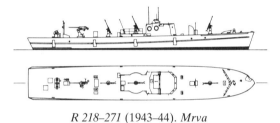

R 218–271 (1943–44). *Mrva*

60° 06'N, 26° 58'E, by a torpedo from the Finnish *Taisto 5*.

R 30: launched 17 Aug 1938. Sunk 23 Sept 1943 at 1250hrs near Kerch, position 45° 21'N, 36° 29'E, by Soviet aircraft bombs.

R 31: launched 21 Sept 1938. Sank 19 Feb 1944 near Pillau-Peyse after suffering ice damage; raised and recommissioned; served in the GM/SA taken 21 Nov 1947 as a British prize; broken up.

R 32: launched 27 Oct 1938. Sunk 13 Nov 1944 off Egersund, position 58° 26'N, 06° 00'E, by aircraft gunfire; raised, recommissioned; served in the GM/SA; taken 1 Dec 1945 as a Danish prize; returned 1947 to the Allies; broken up in Britain.

R 33: launched 1 Feb 1939. Sunk 19 Jul 1943 off Jalta, position 44° 30'N, 34° 10'E, by a Soviet bomb; burned out.

R 34: launched 22 Feb 1939. Sunk 10 Aug 1944 at 0130hrs in the Aegean, in the vicinity of Milos, position 36° 42'N, 24° 27'E, after being struck by a crashed aircraft.

R 35: launched 25 Mar 1939. Sunk 2 Oct 1943 off Feodosia, position 45° 02'N, 35° 24'E, by an aircraft bomb; raised, repaired. Sunk 30 Aug 1944 near Varna, position 43° 11'N, 27° 57'E.

R 36: launched 12 Jul 1939. Sunk 29 Apr 1943 at 1715hrs, north of Constanta, position 44° 18' 4"N, 28° 49' 4"E, by a German mine; no casualties; brought in 1–15 Jun 1943 by *R 165* to Linz-Danube; broken up.

R 37: launched 15 Nov 1939. Sunk 20 Aug 1944 off Constanta, position 44° 10'N, 28° 41'E.

R 38: launched 2 Feb 1939. Sunk 27 Aug 1944 in the Aegean, west of Paros, position 37° 05'N, 25° 08'E, by a mine.

R 39: launched 15 Mar 1939. Sunk 17 Feb 1944 at 1119hrs at Tyrrhenis, west of Ercole, by an aircraft bomb; no casualties.

R 40: launched 5 May 1939. Sunk 7 Mar 1943 at

1912hrs in the vicinity of Boulogne, by a mine; wreck towed in, stricken 19 Apr 1943 for cannibalisation.

R 130: launched 5 Nov 1943; served in the GM/SA; taken 26 Nov 1947 as a US prize, transferred 18 Jun 1948 to the Waterways and Machinery Office at Minden as the barrack ship *VLSWO 232*; transferred 28 Aug 1954 to Verden for use as the *Störtebeker* youth hostel; transferred 1959 to the Roland dockyard at Bremen as a barrack ship.

R 131: launched 26 Nov 1943. Sunk 21 Feb 1944 at 0930hrs southwest of Den Helder, position 52° 55'N, 04° 26'E, by an aircraft bomb; wreck part-raised.

R 132: launched 11 Jan 1944; served in the GM/SA; taken 1 Nov 1947 as a US prize, transferred 1 Jan 1948 to the minesweeping group at Cuxhaven as *R 132*; served 1 Jul 1951 in the US Labor Service Unit B as *USN 132*; transferred 5 Jun 1956 to the German Federal navy as *Orion*; taken out of service 19 Jan 1962, used as the barrack boat *WBR IX*, transferred 18 Dec 1968 to the naval fellowship at Aschaffenburg as the barrack boat *Orion*.

R 133: launched 15 Jan 1944; served in the GM/SA; taken 1 Nov 1947 as a US prize; transferred 1 Jan 1948 to the minesweeping group at Cuxhaven as *R 133*; served 1 Jul 1951 in the US Labor Service Unit B as *USN 133*, transferred 19 Jun 1956 to the

German Federal navy as *Capella*; used 20 Feb 1959 as a stationary training boat, stricken 1969; transferred Feb 1973 to Fritz Daler of Bremerhaven as the barrack boat *Osmagasca*; stranded and partly burnt out at Bremerhaven in 1980.

R 134: launched 26 Jan 1944; served in the GM/SA; taken 1 Nov 1947 as a US prize; transferred 1 Jan 1948 to the minesweeping group at Cuxhaven as *R 134*; served 1 Jul 1951 in the US Labor Service Unit B as *USN 134*; transferred 5 Jun 1956 to the German Federal navy as *Merkur*; taken out of service 31 Oct 1968, damaged by fire 1969, repaired 1970, transferred 1 Aug 1970 to the naval cadets at Büsum as the barrack boat *Cord Widderick*; broken up 1976.

R 135: launched 9 Feb 1944; served in the GM/SA; taken 1 Nov 1947 as a US prize; transferred 1 Jan 1948 to the minesweeping group at Cuxhaven as *R 135*; served 1 Jul 1951 in the US Labor Service Unit B as *USN 135*; transferred 5 Jun 1956 to the German Federal navy as *Rigel*; taken out of service 8 Dec 1961; used as the barrack boat *WBR X*; stricken 30 Sept 1966.

R 136: launched 24 Feb 1944; served in the GM/SA; taken 1 Nov 1947 as a US prize, transferred 1 Jan 1948 to the minesweeping group at Cuxhaven as *R 136*; served 1 Jul 1951 in the US Labor Service Unit B as *USN 136*, transferred to the German Federal navy as *Mars*; taken out of service 20 Feb 1959, used as the barrack boat *WBR II*; sprung a leak 15 Apr 1966 while on tow from Helgoland, brought in to Wilhelmshaven, broken up.

R 137: launched 23 Mar 1944; served in the GM/SA; taken 1 Nov 1947 as a US prize; transferred 1 Jan 1948 to the minesweeping group at Cuxhaven as *R 137*; served 1 Jul 1951 in the US Labor Service Unit B as *USN 137*; transferred 31 Jul 1956 to the German Federal navy as *Regulus*; used 1 Aug 1961 as the training boat *AT 1*; stricken 16 Jan 1964, used Jul 1967 as the target ship *Moritz 1*. Burnt out and sunk 14 Mar 1968 at Wilhelmshaven naval arsenal.

R 138: launched 7 Apr 1944; served in the GM/SA; taken 1 Nov 1947 as a US prize; transferred 1 Jan 1948 to the minesweeping group at Cuxhaven as *R 138*; served 1 Jul 1951 in the US Labor Service Unit B as *USN 138*; transferred 19 Jun 1956 to the German Federal navy as *Castor*; taken out of service 23 Feb 1962, used as the barrack boat *WBR XI*, transferred 19 Sept 1969 to Wilhelmshaven as the barrack boat *Schlicktau*; broken up 1978.

R 139: launched 21 Apr 1944. Sunk 18 Jul 1944 at 2316hrs off Norderney, position 54° N, 07° 37′E, by aircraft rockets causing an explosion in the munitions chamber.

R 140: launched 26 May 1944; served in the GM/SA; taken 1 Nov 1947 as a US prize; transferred 1 Jan 1948 to the minesweeping group at Cuxhaven as *R 140*; served 1 Jul 1951 in the US Labor Service Unit B as *USN 140*; transferred 19 Jun 1956 to the German Federal navy as *Pollux*; taken out of service 20 Feb 1959, used as the barrack boat *WBR III*; stricken 13 Aug 1970.

R 141: launched 3 Jun 1944. Sunk 24 Jun 1944 in the Unterweser Slip, Wesermünde, by bombs.

R 142: launched 17 Jun 1944; served in the GM/SA; taken 1 Jan 1947 as a US prize; transferred 1 Jan 1948 to the minesweeping group at Cuxhaven as *R 142*; served 1 Jul 1951 in the US Labor Service Unit B as *USN 142*; transferred 31 Jul 1956 to the German Federal navy as *Spica*; taken out of service 20 Feb 1959, used as the barrack boat *WBR IV*; taken 1970 to the Modersitzki dockyard, Maasholm; burnt out 1 Feb 1979.

R 143: launched 24 Jun 1944; taken 1945 as a British prize.

R 144: launched 1 Jul 1944; served in the GM/SA; taken 1 Nov 1947 as a US prize; transferred 1 Jan 1948 to the minesweeping group at Cuxhaven as *R 144*; served 1 Jul 1951 in the US Labor Service Unit B as *USN 144*; transferred 5 Jun 1956 to the German Federal navy as *Sirius*; taken out of service 20 Feb 1959, used as the barrack boat *WBR I*; stricken 25 Mar 1968, broken up 1972.

R 145: launched 15 Jul 1944. Sunk 26 Mar 1945 at 1220hrs off Libau, position 56° 31′N, 20° 58′E, by a Soviet aircraft torpedo and gunfire.

R 146: launched 10 Aug 1944; served in the GM/SA; taken 1 Nov 1947 as a US prize; transferred 1 Jan 1948 to the minesweeping group at Cuxhaven as *R 146*; served 1 Jul 1951 in the US Labor Service Unit B as *USN 146*; transferred 31 Jul 1956 to the German Federal navy as *Jupiter*; used 20 Feb 1959 as the training boat *OT 1*, transferred 17 Nov 1969 to the naval fellowhip at Neuss, used 3 Oct 1970 as the living accommodation *Pulchra Nussia*.

R 147: launched 9 Sept 1944; served in the GM/SA; taken 1 Nov 1947 as a US prize; transferred 1 Jan 1948 to the minesweeping group at Cuxhaven as *R 147*; served 1 Jul 1951 in the US Labor Service Unit B as *USN 147*; transferred 31 Jul 1956 to the German Federal navy as *Saturn*; taken out of service 30 Nov 1961, used as the barrack boat *WBR XIII*, later used as a fire and leak security training hulk; transferred 8 Nov 1972 to the seamen's school at Travemünde as a practice hulk.

R 148: launched 21 Oct 1944; served in the GM/SA; taken 1945 as a US prize, used in experiments.

R 149: accepted 29 Nov 1944; taken 4 Nov 1945 as a USSR prize.

R 150: accepted 22 Jan 1945; served in the GM/SA; taken 1 Dec 1947 as a US prize; transferred 16 Jun 1948 to Nord Taucherbetrieb, Lübeck, for use as a diving boat; transferred 5 Sept 1949 to A van Holt of Hamburg as a Rhine tug; served 15 Sept 1953 in the US Labor Service Unit B as *USN 150*; transferred 11 Dec 1956 to the German Federal navy as the training boat *UW 5*; taken out of service 28 Apr 1967; transferred 1967 to the naval cadets at Kiel as the barrack boat *Schleswig-Holstein*; transferred Nov 1979 to Eberhardt dockyard, Arnis.

R 151: launched 18 Jul 1940. Sunk 21 Oct 1944 at 0633hrs in the vicinity of Vardö-Makkauer, by Soviet bombs.

R 152: launched 2 Aug 1940; served in the GM/SA; taken 1 Dec 1945 as a Danish prize, became the Danish *MR 152*; broken up 1951.

R 153: launched 28 Aug 1940; taken 1945 as a British prize; served in the GM/SA; transferred 1 Dec 1945 to Denmark as *MR 153* in poor condition, not recommissioned; returned 1947 to Britain, broken up.

R 154: launched 13 Sept 1940; served in the GM/SA; taken 1 Dec 1945 as a Danish prize, became the Danish *MR 154*, renamed *Asnaes* 1951; transferred 1961 to N J Nomikos of Piraeus as the motor ferry *Arion*.

R 155: launched 3 Oct 1940; served in the GM/SA; taken 1 Dec 1945 as a Danish prize, became the Danish *MR 155*, renamed *Bognaes* 1951; stricken 1957, transferred 1961 to N J Nomikos of Piraeus, as the motor ferry *Faethon*.

R 156: launched 23 Oct 1940; served in the GM/SA; taken 1 Dec 1945 as a Danish prize, became the Danish *MR 156*, renamed *Dyrnaes* in 1951; stricken 1957, used as a target ship.

R 157: launched 13 Nov 1940; served in the GM/SA; taken 1 Dec 1945 as a Danish prize, became the Danish *MR 157*, renamed *Egenaes* 1951; wrecked Jan 1961, broken up.

R 158: launched 28 Nov 1940; collided 21 Sept 1941 north of Hammerfest with *Togo* (ex *Otra*), grounded. Sunk 5 Oct 1941 during a towing attempt, position 70° 41′N 23° 40′E.

R 159: launched 14 Dec 1940; damaged May 1945, remained in Norway.

R 160: launched 4 Jan 1941; served in the GM/SA; taken 1 Nov 1945 as a Danish prize, became the Danish *MR 160*; transferred 1948 to Britain.

R 161: launched 22 Jan 1941. Sunk 30 Mar 1944 at 1505hrs in Livorno industrial harbour, position 43° 33′N, 10° 17′E, by bombs; number of dead unknown.

R 162: launched 7 Feb 1941. Sunk 25 Apr 1945 at Genoa, position 44° 24′N, 08° 54′E.

R 163: launched 5 Mar 1941. Sunk 30 Aug 1944 at Varna, position 43° 11′N, 27° 57′E.

R 164: launched 20 Mar 1941. Remaining career as for *R 163*.

R 165: launched 4 Apr 1941. Remaining career as for *R 163*.

R 166: launched 24 Apr 1941. Remaining career as for *R 163*.

R 167: launched 10 May 1941; served in the GM/SA; taken 19 Nov 1947 as a British prize; became the Danish *MR 167* 27 Jul 1949, renamed *Helgenaes* 1951, broken up 1961.

R 168: launched 29 May 1941; served in the GM/SA; taken 19 Nov 1947 as a British prize; became the Danish *MR 148* 12 Dec 1949, renamed *Lynaes* 1951, broken up 1962.

R 169: launched 13 Jun 1941. Sunk 26 Jul 1941 off Windau, Irben straits, position 57° 24′N, 21° 33′E, by Soviet bombs.

R 170: launched 2 Jul 1941; served in the GM/SA; taken 19 Nov 1947 as a Danish prize, became the Danish *MR 170*; not recommissioned due to poor condition; broken up 1948.

R 171: launched 19 Jul 1941. Sunk 17 Sept 1944 in the North Sea, position 53° 53′ 95″N, 08° 01′ 5″E, by running into a wreck.

R 172: launched 7 Aug 1941; served in the GM/SA; used as a barrack boat; taken out of service 5 Dec 1947; broken up 1948.

R 173: launched 23 Aug 1941; served in the GM/SA; taken 1 Dec 1945 as a Danish prize, became the Danish *MR 173*, broken up 1951.

R 174: launched 11 Sept 1941; served in the GM/SA; taken 19 Nov 1947 as a Danish prize, became the Danish *MR 174*, renamed *Rinkenaes* 1951; broken up Jun 1955.

R 175: launched 1 Oct 1941; served in the GM/SA; taken 19 Nov 1947 as a Danish prize, became the Danish *MR 175*, not recommissioned due to poor condition; broken up 1948.

R 176: launched 23 Oct 1941; served in the GM/SA; taken 19 Nov 1947 as a Danish prize, became the Danish *MR 176*, not recommissioned due to poor condition; broken up.

R 177: launched 6 Nov 1941. Sunk 28 Feb 1945 off Stolpmünde by a mine; ten dead.

R 178: launched 26 Nov 1941. Sunk 12 Sept 1944 at Saloniki, position 40° 38′N, 22° 57′E.

R 179: launched 11 Dec 1941. Sunk 15 May 1944 in the approach to Le Havre, position 49° 29′N, 00° 05′E, by a mine.

R 180: launched 30 Dec 1941. Sunk 2 Jul 1944 at 0255hrs near Fécamp, position 49° 46′N, 00° 20′E, in battle with British MGBs.

R 181: launched 21 Jan 1942; served in the GM/SA; taken 26 Nov 1947 as a Danish prize, became the Danish *MR 181*.

R 182: launched 27 Mar 1942. Sunk 15 Jun 1944 off Le Havre, position 49° 29′N, 00° 06′E, by bombs; raised. Sunk 16 Aug 1944 at Charton in the vicinity of Paris.

R 183: launched 2 Apr 1942; damaged May 1945, remained in Norway.

R 184: launched 17 Apr 1942. Rammed and sunk 16 Aug 1942 off Calais by the British *MGB 330*.

R 185: launched 26 Apr 1942. Sunk 31 Oct 1944 at Saloniki, position 40° 38′N, 22° 57′E.

R 186: launched 16 May 1942. Sunk 25 Jul 1943 at 1615hrs in the vicinity of Spadafora, position

38° 16′ 7″N, 15° 28′ 8″E, in an explosion following an air raid at 1512hrs; two dead.

R 187: launched 29 May 1942. Severely damaged 23 Feb 1944 in the vicinity of Rogoznica, by eleven fighter-bombers; one dead. Towed in, sunk 26 Feb 1944 in Pola dock by an aircraft bomb; raised. Stranded 2 May 1945 in Tagliamento estuary, taken as a Yugoslavian prize.

R 188: launched 11 Jun 1942. Sunk 27 Mar 1944 at 0938hrs in the bay of Povlje, position 43° 20′ 4″N, 16° 17′ 5″E, by bombs.

R 189: launched 24 Jun 1942. Sunk 25 Apr 1945 at Genoa, position 44° 24′N, 08° 54′E.

R 190: launched 11 Jul 1942. Sunk 20 May 1944 at 0610hrs in the Straits of Otranto, by an aircraft bomb; number of dead unknown.

R 191: launched 1 Aug 1942. Sunk 29 Mar 1944 at Sebenico after aircraft gunfire damage and fire; finally sunk 27 Mar 1944 at 1000hrs in Povlje Bay (see *R 188*).

R 192: launched 21 Aug 1942. Sunk 6 Apr 1944 at 0205hrs west of Cecina, position 45° 39′N, 10° 29′E, by gunfire from two British MGBs; seven dead.

R 193: launched 6 Sept 1942. Sunk 30 Aug 1944 at Stettin, by bombs.

R 194: launched 13 Jan 1942. Sunk 29 Feb 1944 at 0930hrs in the vicinity of Cape Stylos, Corfu, position 39° 41′N, 19° 59′E, by an explosion following fighter-bomber attack; seven dead.

R 195: launched 22 Apr 1942. Sunk 31 Oct 1944 at Saloniki, position 40° 38′N, 22° 57′E.

R 196: launched 13 Sept 1942. Sunk 30 Aug 1944 at Varna, position 43° 11′N, 27° 57′E.

R 197: launched 27 Oct 1942. Remainder of career as for *R 196*.

R 198: launched 17 Dec 1942. Sunk 25 Apr 1945 at Genoa, position 44° 24′N, 08° 54′E.

R 199: launched 4 Mar 1943. Remainder of career as for *R 198*.

R 200: launched 26 Feb 1943. Sunk 17 Feb 1944 at 1600hrs at Porto Ercole, position 42° 23′N, 11° 13′E, by an aircraft bomb, stranded; raised 16 Mar 1944, recommissioned 20 Jul 1944, stranded 31 Aug 1944 at 2237hrs in the vicinity of Stefano S, position 40° 50′N, 13° 15′E, by aircraft rockets; number of dead unknown; wreck sunk 15 Sept 1944; blown up.

R 201: launched 13 Mar 1943. Sunk 28 Jan 1944 at 0828hrs in the vicinity of San Stefano, position 42° 26′ 8″N, 11° 04′ 8″E, by bombs; one dead.

R 202: launched 7 Apr 1943. Sunk 5 Feb 1945 at Arendal, position 58° 28′N, 08° 47′E, after an explosion in the engine room.

R 203: launched 27 Jun 1943. Severely damaged 2 Oct 1943 at Feodosia, by bombs; twelve dead. Sunk 25 Aug 1944 at Constanta, position 44° 10′N, 28° 41′E.

R 204: launched 27 Jun 1943. Sunk 11 Apr 1944 at 1050hrs at Feodosia, position 45° 02′N, 35° 24′E, by two Soviet aircraft bombs; two dead.

R 205: launched 17 Jul 1943. Sunk 1 Oct 1943 in the Irben straits, northwest of Domesnaes, by a mine; three dead. Raised, recommissioned. Sunk 25 Aug 1944 at Constanta, position 44° 10′N, 28° 41′E.

R 206: accepted 23 Apr 1943. Sunk 30 Aug 1944 at Varna, position 43° 11′N, 27° 57′E.

R 207: launched 13 Aug 1943. Remainder of career as for *R 206*.

R 208: launched 21 Sept 1942. Damaged 23 Apr 1944 in the Danube 1464.8km, in the vicinity of Batta, with the motor tug *Fritz*, by an aircraft mine; both ships sunk.

R 209: launched 16 Oct 1942. Sunk 30 Aug 1944 at Varna, position 43° 11′N, 27° 57′E.

R 210: launched 29 Oct 1942. Severely damaged 18 May 1944 south of Corfu, position 39° 16′ 8″N, 20° 20′ 3″E, in a collision with *Mal 5*. Sunk 30 Oct 1944 at Thessaloniki, position 40° 38′N, 22° 57′E.

R 211: launched 17 Nov 1942. Sunk 30 Oct 1944 at Thessaloniki, position 40° 38′N, 22° 57′E.

R 212: launched 2 Dec 1942. Sunk 24 Apr 1945 at Genoa, position 44° 24′N, 08° 54′E.

R 213: launched 15 Jan 1943. Sunk 16 Aug 1944 at Charton in the vicinity of Paris (see *R 182* and *R 217*).

R 214: launched 28 Jan 1943; served in the GM/SA; taken 21 Sept 1945 as a Danish prize, became the Danish *MR 214*; broken up 1951.

R 215: launched 5 Feb 1943. Attacked by fighter-bombers, burnt out, stranded, and sunk 13 May 1944 at 1922hrs south of Chiavari, position 49° 19′N, 09° 20′E; five dead.

R 216: launched 4 Aug 1943. Sunk 30 Aug 1944 at Varna, position 43° 11′N, 27° 57′E.

R 217: launched 25 Jun 1943. Sunk 16 Aug 1944 at Charton in the vicinity of Paris (see *R 182* and *R 213*).

R 218: launched 24 Jul 1943. Sunk 19 Aug 1944 in the Channel, in the vicinity of Cape Antifer, by torpedo and gunfire from British MTBs.

R 219: launched 14 Aug 1943. Sunk 24 Aug 1944 at Dieppe harbour entrance, position 49° 56′N, 01° 04′E, by fighter bombers following an engagement with British MTBs.

R 220: launched 12 Oct 1943; served in the GM/SA; taken 22 Nov 1947 as a Dutch prize, and renamed *Walcheren*; sold 1 Feb 1957 for breaking up.

R 221: launched 27 Sept 1943. Sunk 6 Jun 1944 at Blainville, position 49° 04′N, 01° 35′W, by an aircraft bomb.

R 222: launched 13 Oct 1943. Sunk 21 Feb 1944 east of Schleimünde, by a mine.

R 223: launched 29 Oct 1943; taken out of service in Norway Dec 1944; broken up 1945.

R 224: launched 16 Dec 1943. Sunk 6 Jul 1944 at Le Havre, position 49° 29′N, 00° 06′E, by sabotage; raised, recommissioned. Sunk April 1945 at Swinemünde by bombs.

R 225: launched 7 Jan 1944; served in the GM/SA; taken 3 Sept 1945 as a Danish prize, became *MR 225*; transferred 1947 to Britain, broken up.

R 226: launched 27 Jan 1944; served in the GM/SA; taken 29 Sept 1945 as a Danish prize, became the Danish *MR 226*; broken up 1950.

R 227: launched 9 Feb 1944. Sunk 18 Mar 1945 at 1340hrs in the vicinity of Stolpebank between Scholpin and Rixhöft, by Soviet aircraft bombs and gunfire.

R 228: launched 22 Feb 1944; served in the GM/SA. Sunk 9 Aug 1945 in the Kattegat, position 57° 27′ 6″N, 11° 24′ 8″E, after and explosion in the minesweeping equipment; two dead.

R 229: launched 29 Feb 1944; served in the GM/SA; taken 3 Sept 1945 as a Danish prize, became the Danish *MR 229*; broken up 1951.

R 230: launched 14 Mar 1944; served in the GM/SA; taken 3 Sept 1945 as a Danish prize, became the Danish *MR 230*, renamed *Stigsnaes* in 1951; broken up 1961.

R 231: launched 30 Mar 1944. Fate unknown.

R 232: launched 13 Apr 1944. Sunk 15 Jun 1944 at 2300hrs off Boulogne, position 50° 44′N, 01° 36′E, by bombs.

R 233: launched 27 Apr 1944; served in the GM/SA; taken 3 Sept 1945 as a Danish prize, became the Danish *MR 233*, not recommissioned due to poor condition; broken up 1948.

R 234: launched 8 Oct 1943, served in the GM/SA; taken 26 Oct 1945 as a USSR prize*.

R 235: launched 23 Dec 1943. Sunk 8 Sept 1944 during transfer from Belgium to Holland.

R 236: launched 1 Feb 1944; served in the GM/SA; taken 9 Sept 1945 as a Danish prize, became the Danish *MR 236*; renamed *Trellenaes* in 1951, transferred 1961 to N J Nomikos of Piraeus, as the motor ferry *Dedalos*.

R 237: launched 12 Mar 1944. Sunk 15 Jun 1944 at Boulogne, by bombs.

R 238: launched 11 May 1944; served in the GM/SA; taken 3 Sept 1945 as a USSR prize*.

R 239: launched 18 Jun 1944. Sunk 2 Mar 1945 at Hamburg, by bombs.

R 240: launched 20 Jun 1944; served in the GM/SA: taken 22 Nov 1947 as a Dutch prize, named *Goeree*; sold 1959 for breaking up.

R 241: launched 20 Jun 1944; served in the GM/SA; taken 22 Nov 1947 as a US prize, transferred 27 May 1948 to J A Reinecke of Hamburg, as a workshop hulk; engines used in the tankers *Alsen* and *Fehmarn*; hull sold 22 May 1951 to E Kohse of Heilbronn, for conversion to a sauna ship, then 22 Dec 1953 to H Budde & Co of Bremen for breaking up.

R 242: launched 8 Jul 1944; served in the GM/SA; taken 3 Sept 1945 as a Danish prize, became the Danish *MR 242*; renamed *Vornaes* in 1951, broken up 1960.

R 243: launched 20 Jul 1944. Sunk 12 Mar 1945 northeast of Swinemünde, by US bombs.

R 244: launched 30 Jul 1944; served in the GM/SA; taken 22 Jan 1947 as a Dutch prize, became the Dutch *Schouwen*; sold 1 Feb 1957 for breaking up.

R245: launched 18 Aug 1944; served in the GM/SA; taken 15 Nov 1945 as a USSR prize*.

R 246: launched 8 Sept 1944; served in the GM/SA; taken 29 Nov 1947 as a Dutch prize, became the Dutch *Schiermonnikoog*; sold 1 Feb 1957 for breaking up.

R 247: launched 13 Sept 1944. Sunk 4 May 1945 in the Kaiser Wilhelm canal.

R 248: launched 13 Jun 1944. Sunk 30 Aug 1944 at Varna, position 43° 11′N, 27° 57′E.

R 249: launched 19 May 1944; served in the GM/SA; taken 24 Nov 1947 as a US prize, transferred 1949 to P Witton of Minden, as the barrack ship *Gabel-Jürge*; sold 1959 for breaking up.

R 250: launched 24 Jun 1944. Sunk 25 Oct 1944 at Bassfjord, by bombs.

R 251: accepted 19 Jul 1944; originally planned for release to Romania; served in the GM/SA; taken 22 Nov 1947 as a Dutch prize, became the Dutch *Urk*; sold 1 Feb 1957 for breaking up.

R 252: launched 9 Dec 1944. Remainder of career as for *R 251*, except *R 252* was renamed *Stortemelk* by the Dutch.

R 253: launched 31 Aug 1944; served in the GM/SA; taken 27 Nov 1947 as a US prize; transferred 16 Jun 1948 to W Kirchner of Minden as the motor vessel *Silesia*; transferred 22 Dec 1953 to A Thyselius of Bremen for breaking up.

R 254: launched 22 Sept 1944; served in the GM/SA; taken 26 Oct 1945 as a USSR prize*.

R 255: launched 4 Oct 1944; served in the GM/SA; taken 22 Nov 1947 as a Dutch prize, renamed *Schulpengat*; sold 1 Feb 1957 for breaking up.

R 256: launched 18 Oct 1944. Sunk 2 Apr 1945 east of Bornholm, position 53° 07′N, 14° 56′E, in a collision with *T 11* after sustaining bomb damage.

R 257: accepted 21 Nov 1944; served in the GM/SA; taken 4 Nov 1945 as a USSR prize*.

R 258: accepted 31 Oct 1944; served in the GM/SA; taken 26 Oct 1945 as a USSR prize*.

R 259: accepted 11 Nov 1944; served in the GM/SA; taken 3 Sept 1945 as a Danish prize, renamed *MR 259*, not recommissioned due to poor condition; transferred 1947 to Britain, broken up.

R 260: accepted 22 Dec 1944. Sunk 26 Mar 1945 west of Polangen, position 55° 55′N, 21° 03′E, by Soviet torpedo boats.

R 261: accepted 16 Jan 1945. Sunk 3 Apr 1945 at Kiel by US bombs.

R 262: accepted 29 Jan 1945; served in the GM/SA; taken 17 Jan 1946 as a USSR prize*.

R 263: launched 1 Mar 1945; renamed *M 263* in Denmark 24 Sept 1945, not recommissioned due to poor condition; transferred to Britain, broken up.

R 264: launched 4 Oct 1944; served in the GM/SA; taken 27 Nov 1947 as a US prize, transferred 29 Jun 1948 to A Zeiske of Bremen as the motor vessel *Ilse*; still in use in 1955.

R 265: launched 31 Oct 1944; served in the GM/SA; taken 20 Dec 1945 as a USSR prize*.

R 266: launched 21 Nov 1944; served in the GM/SA; taken 27 Nov 1947 as a US prize; transferred 10 Apr 1949 to E Wilk of Oldenburg as the Rhine tug *Rewo II*; served 15 Sept 1953 in the US Labor Service Unit B as *USN 152*, transferred 21 Jan 1957 to the German Federal navy as *AT 1*; stricken 15 Feb 1961, transferred to a ship security training

group. Burnt out and sunk 31 Jul 1968 at Kiel Naval Arsenal.

R 267: accepted 24 Jan 1945; served in the GM/SA; taken 27 Nov 1947 as a US prize; transferred 1949 to Wurzel, Minden, as a barrack boat; broken up 1958.

R 268: launched 18 Dec 1944; served in the GM/SA; taken 25 Nov 1947 as a Dutch prize, renamed *Malzwin*; sold 1 Feb 1957 for breaking up.

R 269: launched 8 Mar 1945; served in the GM/SA; taken 20 Dec 1945 as a USSR prize*.

R 270: launched Feb 1945; served in the GM/SA; taken 20 Nov 1945 as a USSR prize*.

R 271: construction began 9 Feb 1945 at Travemünde but was not completed; broken up.

R 272–276: Destroyed 12 Mar 1945 on the stocks at Swinemünde by bombing; one boat was completed as the Polish *OP–201*.

R 277–287: Not built.

R 288: accepted 24 Feb 1945; served in the GM/SA; taken 15 Nov 1945 as a USSR prize*.

R 289: accepted 9 Mar 1945. Remainder of career as for *R 288*.

R 290: accepted 22 Mar 1945; served in the GM/SA; taken 22 Nov 1947 as a Dutch prize, renamed *Vlieter*; sold 1 Feb 1957 for breaking up.

R 291–300: Construction begun; broken up after capitulation.

R 401: launched 28 Sept 1944; served in the GM/SA; taken 29 Nov 1947 as a US prize; transferred 16 Jun 1948 to Behrendt & Schulte of Bremen as the motor vessel *Koralle*; transferred 16 Nov 1948 to W Schultz of Duisburg.

R 402: launched 10 Oct 1944. Sunk 22 Dec 1944 at 0934hrs north northwest of Feiestein, by a mine; thirteen dead.

R 403: launched 22 Oct 1944; served in the GM/SA; taken 27 Nov 1947 as a US prize, transferred 26 May 1948 to E Albrecht of Bonn as a planned motor ferry; transferred 17 Mar 1949 to W Schultz of Duisburg as the Rhine tug *W.S. 1*, renamed *Atoll* 4 Jan 1950.

R 404: launched 27 Oct 1944; served in the GM/SA 27 Nov 1944; taken as a US prize 27 Nov 1947, transferred 26 May 1948 to E Albrecht of Bonn as the motor ferry *Libelle*, transferred 21 Jan 1949 to Gebr Luwen of Duisburg as a barrack hulk.

R 405: accepted 31 Oct 1944; served in the GM/SA; taken 27 Nov 1947 as a US prize, transferred 30 Jun 1948 to R Wolter of Hamburg as the motor vessel *Hanna*; still in use in March 1954.

R 406: accepted 7 Nov 1944; served in the GM/SA; taken 27 Nov 1947 as a US prize; transferred 27 May 1948 to Schiff Ges Jade of Wilhelmshaven as the motor passenger ferry *Arngast*; served 15 Sept 1953 in the US Labor Service Unit B as *USN 154*, served in the German Federal navy as *OT 1*; stricken 20 Feb 1959, broken up.

R 407: launched 15 Nov 1944; served in the GM/SA; taken 27 Nov 1947 as a US prize; transferred 15 Jun 1948 to E Wilk of Oldenburg as the Rhine tug *Rewo*, renamed *Rewo I* 12 Aug 1949; served 15 Sept 1953 in the US Labor Service Unit B as *USN 153*; served 21 Jan 1957 in the German Federal

navy as *AT 2*; stricken 18 Jan 1963, used as a target ship for naval aircraft.

R 408: accepted 22 Nov 1944; served in the GM/SA; taken 27 Nov 1947 as a US prize; transferred 19 May 1948 to DDG Hansa of Bremen as the motor passenger vessel *Hansa VI*; served 15 Sept 1953 in the US Labor Service Unit B as *USN 155*; served 11 Dec 1956 in the German Federal navy as *UW 6*; stricken 11 Jan 1963, converted to the power supply boat *Stromer*, broken up at Kiel 1977.

R 409: launched 1 Dec 1944; taken 26 Oct 1945 as a USSR prize.

R 410: launched 10 Dec 1944; taken 4 Nov 1945 as a USSR prize.

R 411: accepted 20 Dec 1944; taken 4 Nov 1945 as a USSR prize.

R 412: accepted 29 Dec 1944; taken 1 Dec 1945 as a USSR prize.

R 413: accepted 10 Jan 1945; taken 1 Dec 1945 as a USSR prize.

R 415: launched 1 Feb 1945; taken 1 Dec 1945 as a USSR prize.

R 416: launched 7 Feb 1945; taken 1 Dec 1945 as a USSR prize.

R 417: launched 14 Feb 1945; taken 4 Nov 1945 as a USSR prize.

R 418: launched 21 Feb 1945; taken 15 Nov 1945 as a USSR prize.

R 419: launched 28 Feb 1945; taken 1 Dec 1945 as a USSR prize.

R 420: planned acceptance 3 Mar 1945 (unknown whether acceptance was carried out); taken 24 Nov 1945 as a USSR prize.

R 421: planned acceptance 10 Mar 1945; taken 15 Nov 1945 as USSR prize.

R 422: planned acceptance 17 Mar 1945; served in the GM/SA; taken 15 Nov 1945 as a USSR prize.

R 423: planned acceptance 24 Mar 1945; taken 15 Nov 1945 as a USSR prize.

R 424: planned acceptance 1 Apr 1945; not commissioned until Feb 1946 for service in the GM/SA; taken 22 Nov 1947 as a Dutch prize, renamed *Roompot*; sold 1 Feb 1957 for breaking up.

R 425–427: construction begun, broken up after capitulation.

R 428–473: contract granted 7 Dec 1943, cancelled before construction began.

R 474–498: contract granted 6 Oct 1944, cancelled before construction began.

R 501–525: contract granted 26 Jun 1944, cancelled before construction began.

R 526–545: contract granted 6 Oct 1944, cancelled before construction began.

*Of the vessels *R 234, 245, 254, 258, 262, 265, 269, 270, 288* and *289*, six boats, among them the Soviet *CK 514*, were sent to the East German Sea Police; *511* to *516* were renamed after 1955 *811* to *816*. After 1956 they were replaced by new minesweepers of the *Schwalbe* type. One boat was used in 1956 to 1958 as the training boat *Freundschaft* at the GST/Naval School at Greifswald-Wieck; and was broken up there in 1958. Vessel *811* was scuttled in about 1957–58 in the Adlergrund with a cargo of gas shells.

R 301 class (1942 Type)

Name	Builder (construction no)	Built	Cost in Marks (000s)	Displacement (t = tonnes T = tons)	Length (m)	Breadth (m)	Draught (m)	Power (hp)	Revs (rpm)	Speed (kts)	Range (nm/kts)	Coal (t)	Oil (t)
R 301–312	A & R (3620–3631)	1943–44		184t or 177t max 175t des	41.04 oa 38.60 cwl	6.00	1.88 max 1.80 des	3825ehp max 3750ehp des	620 des	23.5 max 25.0 des	716/20	—	15.8

Construction

Laid down as escort motor minesweepers (*Geleit-Räumboote*) *GR 301–320*, type design by Obering H Docter and the dockyard in 1942, official designation *Räumboote* (minesweeping boats). Composite construction, as for predecessors (nine watertight compartments). Depth 3.50m.

Construction

Three MWM RS 163 Su supercharged 6-cylinder 4-stroke diesel engines with reduction gearbox, in 1 + 1 engine rooms (three 3-bladed screws, 1.3 to 0.95m diameter). One 110V 15kW diesel generator. Two [three] rudders.

Armament

One 3.7cm AA gun (2000 rounds); three [seven] 2cm AA guns (4500 and more rounds); two 53.3cm torpedo release tubes, one 6cm signal rocket launcher, two 8.6cm rocket launchers; in some cases up to sixteen mines.

Handling

Improved seakeeping compared with earlier minesweepers, but the top speed of 23.5 knots did not meet expectations.

Complement

Crew: 1/37 to 1/41. Boats: four inflatable dinghies.

Notes

Colour scheme no 9 and camouflage. Boats after R 307 had a larger magazine.

Careers

R 301: launched 5 Jun 1943. Sunk 16 Oct 1944 off Vardø, position 70° 23′N, 31° 07′E, by an aircraft torpedo.

R 302: launched 21 Jun 1943; served in the GM/SA; taken 17 Nov 1945 as a USSR prize.

R 303: launched 26 Aug 1943; served in the GM/SA; taken 17 Nov 1945 as a USSR prize.

R 304: launched 15 Sept 1943. Sunk 6 Sept 1944 at 0130hrs off Egerøy, position 58° 25′N, 05° 57′E, by a mine.

R 305: launched 8 Oct 1943; served in the GM/SA; taken 17 Nov 1945 as a USSR prize.

R 306: launched 17 Nov 1943. Sunk 13 Dec 1943 at Kiel by US bombs; raised, cannibalised 5 Feb 1944.

R 307: launched 1 Mar 1944; served in the GM/SA; taken 17 Nov 1945 as a USSR prize.

R 308: launched 31 Mar 1944; served in the GM/SA; taken 17 Nov 1945 as a USSR prize.

R 309: launched 30 Apr 1944; transferred 3 May 1945 to Sogne, severely damaged after a grounding, taken out of service; repaired May 1945 in Bergen, later cannibalised for replacement parts.

R 310: launched 10 Jun 1944; served in the GM/SA; taken 17 Nov 1945 as a USSR prize.

R 311: launched 26 Jul 1944; served in the GM/SA; taken 17 Nov 1945 as a USSR prize.

R 312: launched 30 Aug 1944; served in the GM/SA; taken 17 Nov 1945 as a USSR prize.

R 313–320: decision made 6 Dec 1943 not to complete.

R 321–400: construction not begun.

The following drawings show the appearance of the boats as supplied by the dockyards. Conversions carried out in wartime, such as the installation of splinter guards on the wheelhouse, fenders, stern launching stages, shields for 2cm AA guns, removal of masts, etc, are not shown.

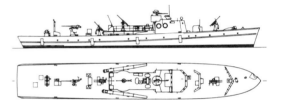

R 302 (1943); *R 301* and *303–306* were similar. *Mrva*

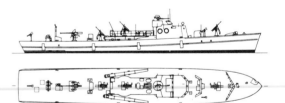

R 310 (1944); *R 307–309, 311* and *312* were similar. *Mrva*

MZ 1 class

Name	Builder (construction no)	Built	Cost in Marks (000s)	Displacement (t = tonnes T = tons)	Length (m)	Breadth (m)	Draught (m)	Power (hp)	Revs (rpm)	Speed (kts)	Range (nm/kts)	Coal (t)	Oil (t)
MZ 1–12	*	1944–45		315t max 285t des 327 max (mod)	52.00 oa 50.00 cwl	8.30	2.10 max 2.00 des	1090ehp max 1200ehp des	682 max 700 des	13.6 max 14.0 des	1000/13.6 2100/12	—	17.5

* See details under Construction.

Construction

Laid down as multi-purpose motor boats (*Mehr-Zweckboote*) for minesweeping, escort and submarine hunting duties (official design 1943). Transverse frame steel construction (eight watertight compartments) with hard chine over almost 100 per cent of the hull length for simplified, large-scale production, including non-shipbuilding companies, in some cases using sectional methods. The bridge, steering position and bulwarks were lightly armoured. Depth 4.0m.

Propulsion

One KHD RD 12 M 133 12-cylinder 2-stroke diesel engine with reversing gearbox (one 3-bladed screw, 0.97m diameter later 1.3m diameter) in the engine room; two 110V 15kW diesel generators; steam and coke oven heating with a four to five day coke supply. One rudder.

Armament

Two Uk 8.8cm/45 guns, (number of rounds unknown); one 3.7cm AA gun; three 8.6cm rocket launchers; eight 2cm AA guns; two 53.3cm TT, fixed installation in forecastle.

Complement

Crew: 2/51. Boats: one cutter; only inflatable boats and rafts after 1945.

Notes

Colour scheme no 9. Additional requirements laid down by the Barrage Test Command (SEK) in the course of trials increased displacement by 42t to a total of 327t, despite the abandonment of the origi-

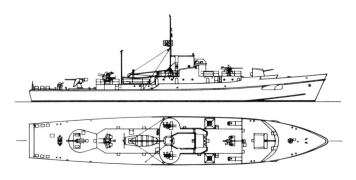

MZ 1 (1944). *Mrva*

nal cutter and derrick. The armament was over-generous and out of proportion to the power system and speed. The new 2-stroke engine, factory-rated at 1200hp at 700 nominal rpm, produced only 1150hp at a maximum speed of 682rpm. The engine was installed without long-term testing as the trials boat *R 239* was lost before the testing period finished. [Remaining ships of the type were to be extended by 5m with a resultant increase in displacement to 365/405/465t. The planned power system was the Lentz uniform expansion steam engine, producing 1040shp at 14 knots, with a range of 1500nm at 14 knots.] These changes in planning should be considered in conjunction with the contract histories, as follows:

MZ 1: Contract granted 24 May 1943 to H C Stülcken, construction no 816.

MZ 2–12: Contract granted initially 5 Jun 1943 to G H H/Rhine dockyard at Walsum, then *MZ 2–4* were transferred to H C Stülcken, construction nos 817–819. After 13 Dec 1943 the final contract was granted to Flenderwerke at Lübeck, construction nos 371–381.

Careers

MZ 1: launched 16 Apr 1944, commissioned 29 Aug 1944; underwent trials Oct 1944 to Jan 1945 at Kiel; underwent trials at SEK; engine tested Mar 1945; tests planned Apr 1945 for warship construction; taken 1945 as a British prize.

MZ 2–4: Broken up on the stocks after 17 Apr 1946.

MZ 5–12: Construction not begun.

Auxiliary motor minesweepers (1939–1945)

R 111 group

Name	Builder (construction no)	Built	Cost in Marks (000s)	Gross tonnage	Length (m)	Breadth (m)	Draught (m)	Power (hp)	Revs (rpm)	Speed (kts)	Range (nm/kts)	Coal (t)	Oil (t)
R 111	Eckmanns	1936		58gt	22.53 oa 19.74 cwl	6.08	2.64	120ehp max					
R 112	Peters (420)	1935		54gt	20.50 oa 18.96 cwl	5.76	2.74	100ehp max					
R 113		1893		43gt	21.50 oa 18.51 cwl	5.96	2.02	85ehp max					
R 114		1890		37gt	21.00 oa 17.68 cwl	5.65	1.85	120ehp max					
R 115	Sietas	1904		40gt	22.00 oa 18.02 cwl	6.06	2.14	90ehp max					
R 116	Behrens	1895		43gt	21.50 oa 17.61 cwl	5.72	2.16	85ehp max	350				
R 117	Sietas	1889		44gt	21.50 oa 19.40 cwl	5.98	2.05	90ehp max	350				
R 118	,,	1894		41gt	21.00 oa 18.40 cwl	5.57	2.13	120ehp max					

Construction

Laid down as Finkenwerder motor fishing cutters of wood construction. Depth approx 3.45m.

Propulsion

R 111, 112: one Deutz 3-cylinder 4-stroke diesel engine; R 113, 115: one DWK 3-cylinder 4-stroke diesel engine; R 116, 117: one HMG (Hanseatic Engine Co, Bergedorf) 2-cylinder 2-stroke diesel engine, type 2D33, consumption 170g/shp); R 114, 118: one BuB diesel engine (one screw, diameter unknown). One rudder.

Armament

One machine gun.

Handling

Very good seakeeping as ocean-going fishing cutters; dry conditions.

Complement

Crew unknown. Boats: one inflatable.

Notes

Peacetime colour scheme (black outboard, wheelhouse, masts, etc., natural wood).

Careers

R 111: built in 1936 as the motor fishing cutter J C Wriede H.F. 330 for Hans Wriede, Hamburg-Finkenwerder; commissioned as R 111 4 Sept 1939, H 219 1940; served 20 May 1940 in Operation Sealion preparations; became M 3270 in 1940, M 3431 in Jun 1941, returned 10 Jan 1945; became H C Wriede for B Fayje, Hamburg-Finkenwerder, in 1968; became the motor yacht CC Consul for B Eifels, Hamburg, in 1974; still in use 1 Jan 1983.

R 112: launched 14 Aug 1935 as the motor fishing cutter Brix Hansen H.F. 324, for Captain H Barghusen, at Hamburg-Finkenwerder; commissioned as R 112 7 Sept 1939, M 3271 Oct 1940, M 3432 Jun 1941; returned 5 Jun 1945. Sunk 20 Jan 1960 in Helgoland harbour after springing a leak; raised; sold in 1961 to H Riepenhausen, Hamburg, and 1966 to H Engel; still in use 1 Jan 1981.

R 113: built in 1893 as the motor fishing cutter Diamant H.F. 59 for J J Meyer, Hamburg-Finkenwerder; owned as Diamant H.F. 59 by Karl Giese in 1937; commissioned as R 113 7 Sept 1939; served 1940 in Operation Sealion preparations; became M 3272 1940, M 3433 Jun 1941; returned 28 Jun 1945; sold 1952 to L F Demmer, Hamburg-Finkenwerder, owned as the motor yacht Diamant by J Bierek, Büsum, in 1953; sold in 1957 to H Runge, Neustadt/Holst; sold in 1972 to Anna Runge, Neustadt/Holst; still in use 1 Jan 1983.

R 114: built in 1890 as the motor fishing cutter Martha H.F. 206 for Joh Schaper, Neuenfelde; became the motor fishing cutter Martha H.F. 365 for Peter Loop, Hamburg-Finkenwerder; commissioned as R 114 4 Sept 1939; served 1940 in Operation Sealion preparations; became M 3273 Jun 1940, M 3434 Jun 1941; kept 20 Jun 1945 at Esbjerg; returned 28 Jun 1945; sold 1951 to T Tonjes, Hamburg-Finkenwerder, owned 1953 as the motor yacht Martha by A von Meyer, Hamburg; still in use 1983.

R 115: built in 1904 as the motor fishing cutter *Seeadler H.F. 263* for Rudolf Holst, Hamburg-Finkenwerder; commissioned as *R 115* 4 Sept 1939; served 1940 in Operation Sealion preparations; became *M 3274* Oct 1940, *M 3435* Jun 1941; returned 28 Jun 1945; sold in 1957 to Gertrud Mewes, Hamburg-Finkenwerder; broken up 1962.

R 116: built in 1895 as the motor fishing cutter *Presto H.F. 39* for Paul Barghusen, Hamburg-Finkenwerder; commissioned as *R 116* 7 Sept 1939; served 1940 in Operation Sealion preparations; became *M 3275* 18 Oct 1940, *M 3436* Jun 1941; returned 28 Jun 1945; taken out of register 1961.

R 117: built in 1889 as the motor fishing cutter *Landrath Küster H.F. 231* for Rudolf Reimers, Hamburg-Finkenwerder; commissioned as *R 117* 7 Sept 1939; served 1940 in Operation Sealion preparations; became *M 3276* Jun 1940, *M 3437* Jun 1941; returned 28 Jun 1945; became *NC 440*; became the motor vessel *Freddy Quinn* in 1971, serving as a training ship for sea cadets at Cuxhaven.

R 118: built in 1894 as the motor fishing cutter *Amor H.F. 30* for Karl Simonsen, Hamburg-Finkenwerder; commissioned as *R 118* 15 Sept 1939; served 1940 in Operation Sealion preparations; became *M 3277* Jun 1940, *M 3438* Jun 1941; returned 28 June 1945; taken out of register 1963.

Small minesweepers and mine launches 1938

MR 1 class

Name	Builder (construction no)	Built	Cost in Marks (000s)	Displacement (t = tonnes T = tons)	Length (m)	Breadth (m)	Draught (m)	Power (hp)	Revs (rpm)	Speed (kts)	Range (nm/kts)	Coal (t)	Oil (t)
MR 1–4, 8–9	A & R (3303–3308)	1938–39	240	23t max	18.50 oa 17.10 cwl	4.20	1.00	350ehp max 300ehp des		18.0 max 12.0 des	450/18	—	
MR 5–7	Roland (550–552)	1938–42	”	”	”	”	”	”		”	”	—	

Construction

Laid down as medium-sized minesweepers (*Mittlere Räumboote*) for mobilisation, official design by Obering H Docter, 1938. Transverse and longitudinal frame steel-light alloy-mahogany double carvel composite construction. Depth 2.65m.

Propulsion

1938 plans included two Deutz DM engines of 175shp each; from Feb 1939 *MR 7–9* had two Daimler-Benz DM engines, all others had two Kämper 6-cylinder diesel engines (three 3-bladed screws, 0.6 diameter). Electrical system details unknown. One rudder.

Armament

Two machine guns; six depth charges.

Complement

Crew of *MR 1–6*: 0/6; after *MR 7*, 0/8.

MR 1–4 (1938). Mrva

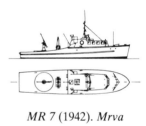
MR 7 (1942). Mrva

Careers

MR 1–4: commissioned 1938 as training boats for Kiel barrage school.

MR 5–6: not built.

MR 7: commissioned 1942 as a sound detector boat for *LS 5* and *6*; served from October 1942 as a group leader boat in the FZ Group, Danube Flotilla; transferred 1 Jul 1943 to the 30th Escort Flotilla. Sunk 6 Jun 1944 at km 1742 in the Danube, at Komaron, by a mine.

MR 8–9: contract cancelled shortly after the outbreak of war.

KR 1 class

Name	Builder (construction no)	Built	Cost in Marks (000s)	Displacement (t = tonnes T = tons)	Length (m)	Breadth (m)	Draught (m)	Power (hp)	Revs (rpm)	Speed (kts)	Range (nm/kts)	Coal (t)	Oil (t)
KR 1, 2	A & R (3300, 3301)	1938		11.3t max	13.50 oa 13.00 cwl	3.44	0.99 max 0.90 des	170ehp max	1500 max	11.5 max		—	
KR 3	Roland (549)			13.3t max	13.53 oa 13.03 cwl	3.48	0.91	150ehp max	1600 max	12.0 max	175/12	—	0.6

Construction

Laid down as small minesweeping boats (*Kleine Räumboote*) intended as prototype launches for a planned *MR* ship, type design by Obering H Docter, 1938. *KR 1* was of transverse and longitudinal frame light alloy construction; *K 2* of mahogany double carvel construction on frames, with synthetic resin glue; *KR 3* was of steel-light alloy-mahogany double carvel composite construction. Depth *KR 1–2* 2.10m; *KR 3* 2.35m.

Propulsion

KR 1–2: two Kämper L 4 D 12 4-cylinder diesel engines (two 3-bladed screws, 0.45m diameter);

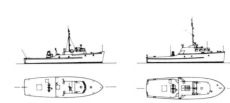

KR 1 (1938). *Mrva*   *KR 3* (1938). *Mrva*

two rudders with rotating Kort Nozzles. *KR 3*: two Deutz SA 6 M 516 6-cylinder diesel engines (two 3-bladed screws, 0.45m diameter); two rudders.

Handling

KR 1 and *2* not satisfactory due to the Kort Nozzle/rudder combination which resulted in reduced speed (10 knots in *KR 1*, and 9.8 knots in *KR 2* compared with an 11.5 knot requirement).

Careers

Taken 1938 to the SEK for trials; *KR 2* still serving in the GM/SA in Jan 1946. Remaining careers unknown.

River minesweepers 1938

FR 1 class

Name	Builder (construction no)	Built	Cost in Marks (000s)	Displacement (t = tonnes T = tons)	Length (m)	Breadth (m)	Draught (m)	Power (hp)	Revs (rpm)	Speed (kts)	Range (nm/kts)	Coal (t)	Oil (t)
FR 1–6	Lürssen (12793–12798)	1938		21t max	15.42 oa	3.30	0.80	260ehp max				—	1.0
(mod)	Linz	1939	0.140	27t max	17.42 oa	"	0.85	300ehp		13.0 max		—	"
FR 7–12	Lürssen (12799–12804)	1939		27t max	17.42 oa	3.30	0.85	300ehp max		13.0 max		—	1.0

Construction

Laid down as river minesweepers (*Fluss-Räumboote*), type design by Obering H Docter, various modifications in 1938. Planned as pure steel boats; a later requirement for 8–10mm armour on the steering position and engine room sides/deck and a rotating AA gun turret meant a design change to transverse and longitudinal frame construction in galvanised sheet steel for the underwater hull (six watertight compartments), and light alloy above water. [The stern was extended by 2m at Linz in 1939.] *FR 7* was built with an extension at Vegesack. Depth 2.20m.

Propulsion

Two Kämper 6-cylinder diesel engines (two 3-bladed screws, diameter unknown). Electrical system details unknown. Two rudders.

Armament

One 2cm AA gun (1500 rounds); after 1943 one 13mm turret machine gun and, aft, one 15mm machine gun without shield; [in winter 1943–44 it was planned to replace the MG 39 with an MG 151 with shield].

Handling

Very crank before being lengthened, due to increased weight; *FR 1* capsized after her transfer to the Danube [the design was satisfactory after the conversion].

Complement

Crew 1/8 or 0/10. Boats: one inflatable.

Notes

Colour scheme no 9.

Careers

The flotilla boats on the Danube were transferred via the Main-Ludwigs canal.

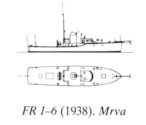

FR 1–6 (1938). *Mrva*

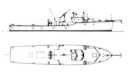

FR 1–12 (1942). *Mrva*

FR 1: launched and commissioned 1 Sept 1938; had a second period in service after her conversion 9 Dec 1938; taken 1945 as a US prize; sold in 1948 to the Schiermak Chocolate Factory, Regensburg, as the motor tug *Bagdad*; sold in 1951 to Main.

FR 2: launched 19 Sept 1938, commissioned 22 Sept 1938. Scuttled 26 Oct 1944 at km 1462 on the Danube, at Dunaszekcso.

FR 3: launched 3 Oct 1938, commissioned 6 Oct 1938; taken 1945 as a US prize; sold in June 1948 to Bayerische Lloyd as the motor tug *Brigach*; sold Nov 1965 for breaking up.

FR 4: launched 17 Oct 1938, commissioned 28 Oct 1938; taken as a US prize for the IWD Danube Branch, Transport Division; served 1951 in the Lower Bavaria Water Police, at Oberpfalz, as *WS 17*; sold 8 Nov 1955 to Bayerische Lloyd as the motor tug *Brenz*; broken up 1968.

FR 5: launched 8 Nov 1938, commissioned 15 Nov 1938. Sunk 6 Sept 1941 at 1200hrs in the Occacov estuary, position 45° 27′ 20″N, 29° 46′ 09″E, by a mine; raised, repaired and recommissioned. Scuttled in May 1945 at km 2201 on the Danube, at Engelhartszell.

FR 6: launched 21 Nov 1938, commissioned 14 Dec 1938. Sunk 6 Sept 1941 at 1200 hrs in the Occacov estuary, position 45° 27′ 20″N, 29° 46′ 06″E, together with *FR 5*, by a mine; eight dead.

FR 7: launched 1 Mar 1939, commissioned 11 Mar 1939; taken 1945 as a US prize for the IWD Danube Branch, Transport Division; transferred 1947 to Austrian Customs; sold in 1951 to G Schwarz of Mauthausen as the motor tug *Pragstein*.

FR 8: launched 8 Apr 1939, commissioned 12 Apr 1939. Sunk May 1945 at km 2079 on the Danube, at Grein.

FR 9: launched 20 May 1939, commissioned 24 May 1939; taken 1945 as a US prize; sold in 1947 to Kiesbaggerei Josef Arndorfer of Straubing, as the motor tug *Josef*.

FR 10: launched 15 Jun 1939, commissioned 21 Jun 1939; taken 1945 as a US prize; sold 2 Jun 1948 to Bayerische Lloyd as the motor tug *Brege*, broken up Sept 1966.

FR 11: launched 12 Aug 1939, commissioned 16 Aug 1939. Sunk 7 Oct 1944 at km 1216 on the Danube after stranding on the Banat side between Semli and the Theiss estuary and coming under fire from Soviet tanks; one dead.

FR 12: launched 21 Sept 1939, commissioned 26 Sept 1939. Sunk 11 Oct 1939 at 1110hrs 200m off the outer pair of buoys in the Kilia estuary entrance at Bugaz, by a mine; no casualties.

FHR 1

Name	Builder (construction no)	Built	Cost in Marks (000s)	Displacement (t = tonnes T = tons)	Length (m)	Breadth (m)	Draught (m)	Power (hp)	Revs (rpm)	Speed (kts)	Range (nm/kts)	Coal (t)	Oil (t)
FHR 1 (mod)	Deggendorf (26)	1925 1938	25	14t max	19.4 oa	3.00	0.80	100ehp max				—	

Construction

Laid down as a motor passenger and tug boat, designed by the Deggendorfer dockyard in 1925, converted 1928; steel construction with a tug type stern and long superstructure. Depth 1.40m.

Propulsion

One Simmering-Graz-Pauker SF 6 6-cylinder diesel engine (one screw, diameter unknown). One rudder.

Armament

One machine gun.

Complement

Crew 0/6. Boats: one inflatable.

Notes

Purchased 1938 by the Kriegsmarine for testing as a prototype for the construction of auxiliary river minesweeping boats (*Fluss-Hilfs-Räumboote*) for the Danube, in competition with the Austrian 14t

FHR 1 (ex *Paul*) (1938–39). *Mrva*

FHR 2–6 (1939). *Mrva*

tug *Drau*. [The original BMW M. 4. A. 12 engine (120hp at 1500rpm) was exchanged for the Simmering engine as on *Drau*.]

Career

Launched 1925, commissioned 27 Jun 1925 as the motor passenger liner *Deggendorf* by Niederbayerische Donau-Personenschiffahrt AG (Lower Bavarian Danube Passenger Shipping Co); converted 1928 to the traction ship *Paul*; purchased 1938 by the Kriegsmarine, and converted to the auxiliary minesweeping boat *FHR 1*, for the Danube Flotilla; served again from October 1939 as the tug and workboat *Paul*, then from 1944 with the IMRDD (Danube Minesweeper Inspectorate); taken 1945 as a US prize, returned to the Deggendorfer dockyard; owned from 1948 by Fa G Schwarz of Mauthausen as the motor tug *Paul*.

FHR 2 class

Name	Builder (construction no)	Built	Cost in Marks (000s)	Displacement (t = tonnes T = tons)	Length (m)	Breadth (m)	Draught (m)	Power (hp)	Revs (rpm)	Speed (kts)	Range (nm/kts)	Coal (t)	Oil (t)
FHR 2–6	Hitzler (98–102)	1938		13.5t max	15.00 oa	3.00	0.90	100ehp max		13.0 max		—	

Construction

Laid down as river minesweepers (*Fluss-Hilfs-Räumboote*) for the Danube, designed 1938, based on the *FHR 1* but with transom stern and a shorter superstructure, steel construction. Depth 1.40m.

Propulsion

One Kämper 6-cylinder diesel engine (one screw, diameter unknown). One rudder.

Armament

One machine gun; [two or three quadruple L/22 AA guns planned].

Complement

Crew 0/6. Boats: one inflatable.

Careers

FHR 2–6: transfer to Romania was planned in 1940 but not carried out; *FHR 4* was launched in the 1940s and sunk in the Danube by a mine; *FHR 2, 3, 5* and *6* were taken in October 1944 as USSR prizes.

Foreign motor minesweepers (1939–1945)

RA 3 class (ex-French)

Name	Builder (construction no)	Built	Cost in Marks (000s)	Displacement (t = tonnes T = tons)	Length (m)	Breadth (m)	Draught (m)	Power (hp)	Revs (rpm)	Speed (kts)	Range (nm/kts)	Coal (t)	Oil (t)
RA 3	CM (H)	1940–43		137T max 114t des 107T std	37.10 oa	5.66	1.95	1836ehp max		15.5 max	1200/9 700/13	—	5.5
RA 4–5	CNN	1940–		,,	,,	,,	,,	,,		,,	,,		,,
RA 1–2	CM (H)	1940–42		160T max 126T std	37.40 oa	5.53	2.40	1836ehp max		15.5 max	1100/10 700/13	—	6.5
RA 6–8	CM (H)*	1942–43		,,	,,	,,	,,	,,		,,	,,		,,

* Taken over by Aug. Normand, Le Havre, at the end of 1942.

Construction
Laid down as minesweepers, designed in France 1938, adapted 1940 after the German occupation. *RA 1–2* and *6–8* were of transverse and longitudinal frame steel construction; the German redesign for *RA 6–8*, in mahogany on modified lines and based on the wooden vessels *RA 3–5*, was not carried out.

Propulsion
Fitted with two MAN 6-cylinder 4-stroke diesel engines with reversing gearbox (two screws of unknown diameter); one 110V 10kW diesel generator. One rudder.

Armament
One 3.7cm AA gun (2000 rounds); three 2cm AA guns (3000 rounds).

Complement
Crew 1/38 or 0/39. Boats: two inflatables.

Careers
CH 17–19, 46–48: Construction was scarcely begun when France was occupied; they were built under German command, planned as exchange units for the French navy; a transfer after Jan 1942 to naval Group South was planned but not carried out.

RA 1 (CH 44): launched 10 Jun 1940, commissioned 20 Jan 1942; Sunk 18 Oct 1944 at 2315hrs northeast of Ostend, position 51° 15′N, 02° 56′E, by a mine; recovered and used as an experimental ship; taken Jan 1946 as British prize at Kiel, renamed *RN 602*; returned 1946 to France, not commissioned; broken up.

RA 2 (CH 45): launched in 1941, commissioned Mar 1942. Sunk 9 Nov 1942 at approx 1540hrs at Le Havre, position 49° 29′N, 00° 06′E, by an aircraft bomb; raised, repaired. Sunk 18 Oct 1944 at 2358hrs northeast of Ostende, position 51° 13′N, 02° 52′E, by a mine; no casualties.

RA 3 (CH 17): accepted 28 Apr 1943; returned 1945 to France; became the Syrian *Tarek Ben Said* in 1952.

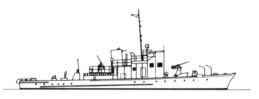

RA 3 (ex CH 17) (1943). Mrva

RA 4 (CH 18): commissioned 31 Oct 1942. Scuttled 16 Aug 1944 at Paris.

RA 5 (CH 19): incomplete on the stocks in 1944 and scuttled at Fécamp. Completed 1946 as *CH 705*, became *P 705*; stricken 2 Jun 1954 as *Q 09*.

RA 6 (CH 46): launched 24 Oct 1942, commissioned 5 Aug 1943. Sunk 16 Aug 1944 at Paris.

RA 7 (CH 47): launched 1943, commissioned 7 Sept 1943. Scuttled 16 Aug 1944 at Paris.

RA 8 (CH 48): launched 8 Jul 1943, accepted 27 Oct 1943. Scuttled 16 Aug 1944 at Paris.

RA 9 (ex-British)

Construction
Laid down in Britain as a motor launch, design by the Admiralty in 1940. Round bilge mahogany double diagonal carvel construction, part of a series built from prefabricated parts (seven watertight compartments); lightly armoured deck. Depth unknown; freeboard amidships 2.13m.

Propulsion
Two Hall-Scott petrol engines (two screws, diameter unknown); one Stuart auxiliary 24V engine for the electrical system. Two rudders.

Name	Builder (construction no)	Built	Cost in Marks (000s)	Displacement (t = tonnes T = tons)	Length (m)	Breadth (m)	Draught (m)	Power (hp)	Revs (rpm)	Speed (kts)	Range (nm/kts)	Coal (t)	Oil (t)
RA 9	Solent	1941		82t max 65t des	34.13 oa	5.57	1.45 max 1.14 des	1290ehp max 1200ehp des	2200 max 1800 des	20.0 max 16.7 des	2500/10 990/15	—	8.8

Armament

One 3.7cm AA gun (rounds unknown); three 2cm AA guns (rounds unknown).

Handling

Usable up to about Beaufort 5.

Complement

Crew 0/17. Boats: one inflatable.

Career

Launched 1941, commissioned 1941 in Britain as *ML 306*; taken 28 Mar 1942 as a German prize at St Nazaire, commissioned as *RA 9*. Sunk 15 Jun 1944 at 0300hrs at Le Havre, position 49° 29′N, 00° 06′E, by bombs from British aircraft, together with *Falke*, *Möwe*, *Jaguar*, *PA 1* and *PA 2*, ten S boats and others.

RA 10 (ex-British)

Name	Builder (construction no)	Built	Cost in Marks (000s)	Displacement (t = tonnes T = tons)	Length (m)	Breadth (m)	Draught (m)	Power (hp)	Revs (rpm)	Speed (kts)	Range (nm/kts)	Coal (t)	Oil (t)
RA 10	Elco	1942		45t max	24.46 oa 23.47 cwl	6.27	1.22	4050ehp max 3600ehp des		45.0 max 40.0 des	240/45	—	8

Construction

Laid down in the USA as a motor torpedo boat type Elco 77, a development of a British Power Boat design by Scott-Paine.

Propulsion

Fitted with three Packard 12-cylinder petrol engines (three screws, 0.7m diameter).

Armament

One 2m AA gun (rounds unknown), four 12.7cm machine guns (rounds unknown), two 53.3cm TT.

Complement

Crew 12 to 14. Boats: one inflatable.

Notes

Conversion was planned for Operation Rice Harvest in which the Packard petrol engines were to be replaced by MAS engines, two 50hp outboard motors added, one motor yawl with davit or derrick, one African canoe, a special sail rig, and FuMB and FuMG radar in place of the UK radio direction finder.

Career

Launched 1942 in the USA as *PT 56*, commissioned 2 Mar 1942 via the Lend-Lease programme in Britain as *BTP 8*, later becoming *MTB 314*; taken 14 Sept 1942 as a German prize off Tobruk by *R 10* and commissioned Sept 1942 as a fast submarine hunter; planned service Mar 1943 for Operation Rice Harvest, an attack with the 6th Minesweeper Flotilla on merchant shipping off the West African coast by Brandenburg Special Forces units. Sunk 30 Apr 1943 at 1400hrs off La Goulette, position 36° 48′N, 10° 19′E, by aircraft bombs; six dead.

RA 11 (ex-British)

Name	Builder (construction no)	Built	Cost in Marks (000s)	Displacement (t = tonnes T = tons)	Length (m)	Breadth (m)	Draught (m)	Power (hp)	Revs (rpm)	Speed (kts)	Range (nm/kts)	Coal (t)	Oil (t)
RA 11	C & N	1942		95T max	35.66 oa 33.53 cwl	5.79	1.30 max 1.14 des	3000ehp des		23.0 max 20.0 des	2000/11	—	19.1

Construction

Laid down in Britain as a Motor Gun Boat, design by Camper & Nicholson in 1939 for Turkey. Round bilge double diagonal carvel construction on steel frames (six watertight compartments). One Ford 110V petrol generator. Depth unknown.

Propulsion

Three Davey Paxman diesel engines (three screws, diameter unknown).

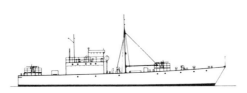

RA 11 (ex Master Standfast) (1943–44). Mrva

Armament

Two 2cm AA guns (rounds unknown); four machine guns.

Complement

Crew: 21 in British service. Boats: one inflatable.

Notes

Converted after the outbreak of war, to British account, together with four sister boats, as blockade breakers for the transport of vital goods between Sweden and Britain, with a 45t hold instead of the original crew accommodation which was provided as an additional deck superstructure; top speed was 23/20 knots instead of 30/27 planned for the type.

Career

Launched 1942, commissioned 1942 in Britain as *Master Standfast* (*ex-MGB 508*). Captured 2 Nov 1943 off Lysekil by *V 1606*; commissioned 10 Nov 1943 in German service as *RA 11* for the Special Operations Group North (for service against Brit-

ish merchant S-boats); transferred 1944 to KMA Kiel for submarine support in Norway; taken May 1945 as a British prize, became the motor yacht *Master Standfast*; served in the late 1940s as a motor ferry on the Rhine; broken up late 1951.

KJ 25 (ex-British)

Name	Builder (construction no)	Built	Cost in Marks (000s)	Displacement (t = tonnes T = tons)	Length (m)	Breadth (m)	Draught (m)	Power (hp)	Revs (rpm)	Speed (kts)	Range (nm/kts)	Coal (t)	Oil (t)
KJ 25	McGruer			54T max	21.94 oa	4.57	1.32 max	300ehp des		11.0 max	2000/10	—	5.7

Construction

Laid down in Britain as a Harbour Defence Motor Launch, Admiralty design 1939–40. Round bilge mahogany double diagonal carvel construction with a lightly armoured upper bridge. Depth unknown.

Propulsion

Fitted with two Gardner diesel engines (two screws, diameter unknown) and one Stuart 24V auxiliary engine for the electrical system. Two rudders.

KJ 25 (ex *HDML 1381*) (1944). *Mrva*

Armament

One 2-pounder (rounds unknown), four machine guns, one Holman projector, eight depth charges or Oropesa minesweeping equipment.

Complement

Crew: 2/8 in British service. Boats: rafts only.

Notes

Colour scheme no 9.

Career

Launched in the 1940s in Britain as *HDML 1381*; taken 26 Aug 1944 off Sirina island, in the Dodecanese, as a German prize; renamed *KJ 25* in German service; used by the Rhodes Coastal Patrol; returned May 1945 to the Royal Navy in the Aegean.

RA 51 class (ex-Dutch)

Name	Builder (construction no)	Built	Cost in Marks (000s)	Displacement (t = tonnes T = tons)	Length (m)	Breadth (m)	Draught (m)	Power (hp)	Revs (rpm)	Speed (kts)	Range (nm/kts)	Coal (t)	Oil (t)
RA 51–56	De Vries (Am) (1604–1607, 1740–1741)	1940		51.3t des	23.04 oa 22.00 cwl	4.50 4.38	1.30 max 1.10 des	220ehp max 200ehp des	1350 max 1250 des	11.0 max 10.0 des		—	6

Construction

Laid down as the Dutch minesweepers (*Mijnenveegboten*) *Mv I–IV, XI, XII*, Dutch design by Scheltema de Here in 1939. Transverse frame steel construction (eight watertight compartments, double bottom approx 80 per cent). Depth 2.36m.

Propulsion

Two Kromhout 8-cylinder diesel engines with 2:1 Brevo reversing gearbox (two 4-bladed screws, 2.00m diameter), one Kromhout-Smit 220V 6kW diesel generator. One rudder.

Armament

Plans included one Dutch 4cm AA gun aft, one German 3.7cm AA gun (1000 rounds) and three 2cm AA guns (4000 rounds).

Handling

Very easy handling, excellent manoeuvrability and responsiveness.

Complement

Crew unknown. Boats: two inflatables.

Careers

RA 51: underwent dockyard trials 19 Jun 1940, in service 29 Aug 1940 as *RH 1*, 15 Dec 1940 as *R 201*, 20 Sept 1941 as *RA 51*, Apr 1944 as *G 3181*, Aug 1944 as *SM 221*. Sunk 24 Aug 1944 at Constanta, position 44° 10′N, 28° 41′E.

RA 52: Accepted 29 Aug 1940 as *RH 2*, renamed *R 202* 15 Dec 1940, *RA 52* 15 Oct 1941, *G 3181* Apr

1944, *SM 222* Aug 1944. Sunk 29 Aug 1944 at Varna, position 43° 11′N, 27° 57′E.

RA 53: accepted 23 Sept 1940 as *RH 3*, renamed *R 203* 15 Dec 1940, *RA 53* 20 Nov 1941. Sunk Aug 1941 in the Irben Straits, by a mine.

•*RA 54:* accepted 17 Oct 1940 as *RH 4*, renamed *R 204* 15 Dec 1940, *RA 54* 10 Dec 1941, *G 3181* Apr 1944, *SM 224* Aug 1944.

RA 55: accepted 20 Nov 1940 as *RH 5*, renamed *R 205* 15 Dec 1940, *RA 55* 1941. Sunk Aug 1941 in the Irben Straits, by a mine.

RA 56: accepted 10 Dec 1940 as *R 206*, renamed *RA 56* 1941, *G 3181* Apr 1944, *SM 223* Aug 1944. Sunk 29 Aug 1944 at Varna, position 43° 11′N, 27° 57′E.

RA 101 class (Danish-built)

Name	Builder (construction no)	Built	Cost in Marks (000s)	Displacement (t = tonnes T = tons)	Length (m)	Breadth (m)	Draught (m)	Power (hp)	Revs (rpm)	Speed (kts)	Range (nm/kts)	Coal (t)	Oil (t)
RA 101–105	Rasmussen (185–189)	1943–44		77.4t max 69.9t des	28.85 oa 27.35 cwl	4.40	1.45	786ehp max 714ehp des	1003 max 900 des	15.5 max 14.5 des	650/9	—	5.5
RA 106–112	" (246–252)	1944–45		85t max	30.00 oa 28.40 cwl	4.61	1.45	714ehp des	896 max 900 des	14.6 max 14.5 des	650/8	—	6

Construction

Laid down in Denmark under German instructions as minesweepers (*Räumboote, Ausland*), design 1942 from *R 9–16*. Composite construction similar to *R 17* (nine watertight compartments), flush deck vessels. Depth 2.81m.

Propulsion

Fitted with two MWM RS 127 Su (after *RA 106* RHS 230 Su) 6-cylinder 4-stroke diesel engines in one engine room (two 3-bladed screws, 0.95 diameter; after *RA 106*, 0.92m diameter). One 110V 10kW diesel generator. One rudder.

Armament

Two 2cm AA guns (2000 rounds); in some cases six mines.

Handling

Extremely good seakeeping.

Complement

Crew 0/18. Boats: two inflatables.

Notes

Colour scheme no 9 and camouflage. *RA 101–105* had internal ballast installed after delivery to improve stability.

Careers

RA 101: launched 1 Jun 1943; taken May 1945 as a British prize, renamed *Codling*, renamed *Sparrowhawk* 1946; served in the FCS Lower Rhine; taken out of service 31 Mar 1949 at Travemünde.*

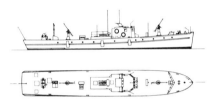

RA 101–105 (1943); *RA 106–112* were similar.
Mrva

RA 102: launched 8 Jul 1943; taken 1945 as a British prize, served in the GM/SA as *RW 102*; taken 25 Apr 1946 as a USSR prize.

RA 103: launched 4 Sept 1943; taken 1945 as a British prize, served with the NCSO, renamed *Swallow* 1946, served in the FCS Lower Rhine; transferred 1949 to the Customs Border Guard Sea Inspectorate; stricken 1950.*

RA 104: launched 19 Nov 1943; taken 1945 as a British prize, renamed *RN 104*, then *Seagull* in 1946; served in the FCS Lower Rhine, and 1949 in the Customs Border Guard Sea Inspectorate as *Seeadler*, at Bremerhaven.*

RA 105: accepted 1 Apr 1944; taken 1945 as a British prize, renamed *Mackerel*.*

RA 106: launched 16 Jul 1944; taken 1945 as a British prize, served in the GM/SA as *Skate*; served 1946 in the US Navy; sold 2 Mar 1948 to the Water-

ways and Machinery Office at Minden as a barrack boat; sold 13 Mar 1950 to P Müller of Neuwied as the Rhine tug *Buran*; still in use Nov 1954.

RA 107: launched 16 Jul 1944; taken 1945 as a British prize, renamed *Herring*; served in the GM/SA, served 1946 in the US Navy; sold 21 Apr 1948 to the Waterways and Machinery Office at Minden as a barrack boat; sold 7 Dec 1949 to W Buchholz of Lorch as a Rhine tug, and 11 Mar 1952 to J Pawliczek of Münster as the tug *Heimat II*. Sunk 1959, raised, broken up 1962.

RA 108: launched 29 Aug 1944; taken 1945 as a British prize; served in the GM/SA.

RA 109: accepted 14 Oct 1944; taken 1945 as a British prize, renamed *Shrimp*; served 1946 in the US Navy as *USN 28*; sold 25 May 1948 to C Jansen of Bremen as the motor vessel *Friesland*, and 19 Nov 1950 to H Labrecht of Duisburg as a Rhine tug; still in service in April 1954.

RA 110: launched Nov 1944; taken 1945 as a British prize, renamed *RW 110*; served in the GM/SA.

RA 111: launched 27 Jan 1945; taken 17 Jan 1946 as a USSR prize.

RA 112: launched 4 Mar 1945; taken 1 Dec 1945 as a USSR prize.

*One boat from *RA 101, 103–105* was converted in the late 1950s to a motor passenger vessel at Druten, Holland; she was later transferred to Ludwigsburger Verkehrs AG (Ludwigsburg Transport Co); owned Mar 1963 by W Schaal of Cuxhaven as *Christiane*; owned 1966 by the Flensburger Personenschiffahrt GmbH (Flensburg Passenger Shipping Co) as *Engelsby*; owned 1968 by Hampel of Laboe as *Lachs*; burned out 1969, broken up.

RA 201 class (Norwegian-built)

Name	Builder (construction no)	Built	Cost in Marks (000s)	Displacement (t = tonnes T = tons)	Length (m)	Breadth (m)	Draught (m)	Power (hp)	Revs (rpm)	Speed (kts)	Range (nm/kts)	Coal (t)	Oil (t)
RA 201–204	M & K	1940–43		35t max	25.00 oa	4.50	1.40			14.0		—	

Construction

Ordered in 1940 without a Kriegsmarine contract to motor yacht designs and plans by Capt H Bartels.

Armament

Fitted with two 2cm AA guns (2000 rounds).

Complement

Crew 0/18 or 1/21. Boats: one inflatable.

Careers

An unauthorised contract was granted by Capt H Bartels in 1940, without the knowledge of Kriegsmarine officials, for which redress was demanded, conceded and carried out.

RA 201: launched 1942, commissioned 1943 as *M 5401*; served in the GM/SA; destroyed before November 1947, according to OMGUS documents, reason unknown.

RA 202: launched 1942, commissioned 1943 as *M 5402*; served in the GM/SA; transferred 1946 to Norway; fate unknown.

RA 203: launched 1943, commissioned 1943; served in the GM/SA; destroyed before November 1947, according to OMGUS documents, reason unknown.

RA 204: launched 1943, commissioned 1943; served in the GM/SA; taken 29 Mar 1946 as a USSR prize.

MS 2 class (ex-Danish)

Name	Builder (construction no)	Built	Cost in Marks (000s)	Displacement (t = tonnes T = tons)	Length (m)	Breadth (m)	Draught (m)	Power (hp)	Revs (rpm)	Speed (kts)	Range (nm/kts)	Coal (t)	Oil (t)
MS 2, 5	Holbaek	1941		74t max 70t des	24.60 oa 24.38 cwl	4.88	1.50 max 1.30 des	220ehp max 200ehp des			11.0 max 10.0 des	1133/10	—
MS 3, 8	Lilleö	„		„	„	„	„	„			„	„	—
MS 6, 10	Ring	„		„	„	„	„	„			„	„	—

Construction

Laid down in Denmark as minesweeping boats (*Minestryger*), Danish design 1940. Wooden vessels. Depth unknown.

Propulsion

Fitted with one B & W Alpha 344 VO diesel engine (one screw, diameter unknown).

Armament

One 2cm AA gun (rounds unknown), one or two machine guns.

Handling

Good economical vessels.

Complement

Crew 9–10. Boats: one yawl.

Careers

The following boats were requisitioned 29 Aug 1943 together with the remainder of the Danish fleet:

MS 2: launched 19 Apr 1941, commissioned 1 Aug 1941 in Denmark as *MS 2*; transferred 29Aug 1943 by Germany to Kalundborg; commissioned 28 Nov 1943 in to the Coastal Defence Flotilla, Great Belt; renamed *Vs 1211* 20 Jan 1944, returned 9 Jun 1945 to the Danish Navy at Nyborg; renamed *Askö* 1951, *Y 386* 1962; served 1964 in the Naval Home Guard as *MHV 81*.

MS 3: launched 21 May 1941, commissioned in Denmark as *MS 3*; captured at 0545hrs on 29 Aug 1943 at Köge roads by *M 42*; commissioned by Germany 30 Sept 1943 as *Vs 119*, later *Vs 820*; returned Jun 1945 to the Danish Navy at Flensburg; renamed *Baagö* 1951, *Y 387* 1962; served 1964 in the Naval Home Guard as *MHV 84*.

MS 5: launched 13 Jun 1941, commissioned 18 Aug 1941 in Denmark as *MS 5*; transferred 29 Aug 1943 by Germany to Nyborg, recommissioned 5 Nov 1943 into the Coastal Defence Flotilla, Great Belt; renamed *Vs 1212* 1944; returned Jun 1945 to the Danish navy, renamed *Enö* 1951, *Y 388* 1962; served 1965 in the Naval Home Guard as *MHV 82*.

MS 6: launched 13 Jun 1941, commissioned 22 Oct 1941 in Denmark as *MS 6*; captured 29 Aug 1943 by German forces at Nyborg, and commissioned 5 Nov 1943 into the Coastal Defence Flotilla, Great Belt; renamed *VS 1213* 20 Jan 1944; returned Jun 1945 to the Danish navy at Flensburg, renamed *Faenö* 1951; served Feb 1960 in the Naval Home Guard as *DMH 69*, in 1964 as *MHV 69*, and in 1974 as *MHV 80*.

MS 8: launched 22 Jul 1941, commissioned 22 Oct 1941 in Denmark as *MS 8*. Sunk 29 Aug 1943 at Copenhagen-Holmen; raised, repaired, recommissioned by Germany 1944; returned May 1945 to the Danish navy at Copenhagen, renamed *Lyö* 1951. *Y 390* 1962; served 1965 in the Naval Home Guard as *MHV 86*.

MS 10: launched 28 Aug 1941, commissioned 13 Dec 1941 in Denmark as *MS 10*. Sunk 29 Aug 1943 at Copenhagen-Holmen; raised, recommissioned by Germany 1944; returned Jun 1945 to the Danish navy, renamed *Strynö* 1951; stricken 30 Jun 1956, sold to W J Bröndholm as the motor passenger vessel *Kollund*; sold 17 Oct 1966 to Willi Freter of Heiligenhafen as the *Hecht I*, became *Hecht II* 1968; sold 1970 to the Germania Shipping Co at Laboe as *Orion I*. Sunk 24 Feb 1975 at Kieler Förde in collision with st *Texaco Ohio*.

RA 254 class (ex-Italian)

Construction

Laid down in Italy as VAS boats (*Motovedette antisommergibili*), second and third series, fitted out as submarine-hunters and -destroyers, Italian dockyard design by Baglietto/Ansaldo in 1941. The second series was of composite construction (twelve watertight compartments); the third series of transverse frame steel construction with transom stern; after *RA 265* they had a composite construction, hard chine. Depth 2.80m.

Propulsion

Fitted with three engines on three screw shafts: *RA 254–257* had three Fiat 12-cylinder diesel engines, ex-Littorina (12/12); all others were planned originally for three newly developed Ansaldo Q 172 12-cylinder diesel engines (170/12); eventually they were fitted with the same engines as for *RA 261–262* (second series), namely with two Carraro 8-cylinder D/300 petrol engines (300hp each) as cruise engines plus one Isotta Fraschini 8-cylinder ASM 183 petrol engine on the centre shaft, but with reversing gearbox. After *RA 265* the class had three diesel engines made by Cie Lilloise de Moteurs (500hp each) (three 3-bladed screws, approx 0.9m diameter).

Armament

The second series were fitted with two 2cm AA guns (rounds unknown), ten depth charges; the third series had one 3.7cm/54 Breda AA gun (rounds unknown), three 2cm AA guns (rounds unknown); two 45cm TT; six depth charges.

Handling

Usable up to about Beaufort 5.

Complement

Crew approx 26. Boats: inflatables only.

Name	Builder (construction no)	Built	Cost in Marks (000s)	Displacement (t = tonnes T = tons)	Length (m)	Breadth (m)	Draught (m)	Power (hp)	Revs (rpm)	Speed (kts)	Range (nm/kts)	Coal (t)	Oil (t)
RA 254–257	Ansaldo (G–V)	1942–44		94.5T max 92.5t des	34.10 oa	5.00	2.1 max 1.4 des	1100ehp des		18.0 max	900/14 500/18	—	9
RA 251–253, 258–260, 263, 264	,,	,,		94.5T max 92.0t des	,,	,,	,,	1100ehp des +600ehp des		19.0 max	400/19 1000/13*	—	8
RA 265–268	Prometeo	1943–		92.0t des	34.10 oa	5.00		1500ehp des					
RA ( ), 261, 262	Baglietto	1943–	3000 Lire each	68.5t max	28.0 oa	4.30	1.77 max 1.33 des	1100ehp des +600ehp des		21.0 max	440/20 1260/14*	—	8.9
(mod)		1943		72t max						20.0 max 14.0 des			

* Cruising engines only.

Notes

After February 1943 all vessels were re-equipped as *Motovedette per il dragaggio veloce* (fast minesweeping boats), beginning with *VAS 232*; torpedo tubes were landed and the submarine hunter equipment reduced. The vessels were not highly rated in German service due to their lack of heating (contributing to severe crew sickness problems), to the fact that they were without cooking facilities, had unreliable engines after 1000–2000hrs, high fuel consumption, and a maximum permissible speed of 10 knots; these boats also had no mine protection system.

Careers

All boats fell into German hands as a result of the Italian capitulation; some were incomplete due to supply problems. Until 7 January 1944 only *RA 255* was serviceable; later the petrol boats *RA 251*, *252* and *257* were used as submarine hunters, with improvised Italian sonars.

RA 251: launched 28 Jan 1943, commissioned 17 Aug 1943 as *VAS 306*; transferred 9 Sept 1943 by Germany to Genoa, commissioned in German service 13 Oct 1943. Sunk 22 Aug 1944 at 2020hrs at Juan Bay, position 43° 34′N, 07° 04′E.

RA 252: launched 24 Dec 1942, commissioned 25 Jun 1943 as *VAS 305*; transferred 9 Sept 1943 by Germany to Livorno, commissioned in German service in October 1943; transferred 1944 to the Marina RSI as *VAS 252*. Sunk 25 Apr 1945 at San Pier d'Arena, position 44° 25′N, 08° 54′E.

RA 253: launched 26 Jan 1943; fitting out at Genoa-Voltri, transferred to Germany 9 Sept 1943, commissioned in German service 9 Nov 1943. In collision 25 Aug 1944 with MFP *F 767* at Cape Noli, one dead, and severely damaged; sent to Genoa to repairs, released to the Marina RSI, renamed *VAS 253*. Sunk 25 Apr 1945 off Genoa, position 44° 24′N, 08° 54′E.

RA 254: launched 17 Jul 1942, commissioned 22 Sept 1942 as *VAS 301*; transferred 9 Sept 1943 by Germany to Genoa, commissioned in German service in 1943. Sunk 25 Apr 1945 at Genoa, position 44° 24′N, 08° 54′E.

RA 255: launched 17 Oct 1942, commissioned 27 Jan 1943 as *VAS 304*; transferred 9 Sept 1943 by Germany to Genoa, commissioned in German service in 1943. Sunk 21 Aug 1944 at 0147hrs in the Gulf of Genoa, position 44° 20′N, 08° 30′E, in an engagement with British units, together with *RA 259*.

RA 256: launched 6 Oct 1942, commissioned 23 Nov 1942 as *VAS 303*; transferred 9 Sept 1943 by Germany to Civitavecchia, commissioned in German service 18 Oct 1943. Badly damaged 30 Mar 1944 at 1515hrs off Livorno, position 43° 33′N, 10° 17′E, by bombs; stricken 21 Jun 1944 as irreparable.

RA 257: launched 16 Sept 1942, commissioned 2 Nov 1942 as *VAS 302*; transferred 9 Sept 1943 by Germany to Civitavecchia, commissioned in German service in 1943. Badly damaged 2 Aug 1944 at 1200hrs at Genoa, position 44° 24′N 08° 54′E, by bombs, and beached for cannibalisation.

RA 258: launched 20 May 1943, fitting out at Genoa-Voltri, taken 9 Sept 1943 by Germany, commissioned in German service 21 Mar 1944. Sunk 25 Apr 1945 at Genoa.

RA 259: launched 21 May 1943, fitting out at Genoa-Voltri, taken 9 Sept 1943 by Germany, commissioned in German service 1 Jun 1944. Sunk 21 Aug 1944 at 0600hrs in the Gulf of Genoa, position approx 44° 20′N, 08° 30′E, in an engagement with British units, together with *RA 255*.

RA 260: launched 13 Apr 1943, fitting out at Genoa-Voltri; taken 9 Sept 1943 by Germany, commissioned in German service 3 Aug 1944. Ran aground 10 Aug 1944 off Cape Mortula due to a navigational error; scuttled there 2 Sept 1944.

RA 261: launched 1943. Sunk 9 Sept 1943 at Porto Venere, La Spezia; raised 1943 and commissioned as *RA 261*. Sunk 5 Sept 1944 at Genoa, by bombs; thirteen dead.

RA 262: launched 1943, commissioned 1943 as *VAS 239*; captured 9 Sept 1943 off Legnana by German units; commissioning as *RA 262* was planned, but she was sunk at 2340hrs on 5 Sept 1944 off Genoa, position 44° 24′N, 08° 54′E, by bombs; raised, not repaired. Sunk 25 Apr 1945 at San Pier d'Arena, position 44° 25′N, 08° 54′E.

RA 263: launched 9 Feb 1943, accepted 9 Dec 1943 as *RA 263*; not serviceable, used 16 May 1944 as the training boat *VAS 263* at the Anti-submarine School at Varignano, Marina RSL; served 1 Oct 1944 as the submarine hunter *VAS 263*. Sunk 25 Apr 1945 at Genoa.

RA 264: launched 20 May 1943, fitting out at Genoa-Voltri; commissioned by Germany. Sunk 25 Apr 1945 at Genoa.

RA 265–268: requisitioned at Prometeo dockyard; construction continued under German command, for planned completion early in 1945. Scuttled or destroyed 25 Apr 1945, when Genoa was evacuated.

RA . . . (ex-VAS 232): launched 1942, commissioned 22 Dec 1942 as *VAS 232*; captured 17 Sept 1943 by Germany at Portoferraio (Elba), not serviceable; transferred to the 6th Minesweeper and 22nd Submarine Hunter Flotilla for cannibalisation. Sunk 1945 at Elba.

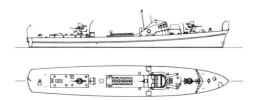

RA 251–260, 263 and *264* (ex VAS boats) (1943–44). *Mrva*

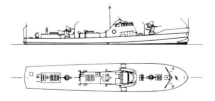

RA 261 and *262* (ex *VAS 236* AND *239*) (1943–44). *Mrva*

RD 101 class (ex-Italian)

Name	Builder (construction no)	Built	Cost in Marks (000s)	Displacement (t = tonnes T = tons)	Length (m)	Breadth (m)	Draught (m)	Power (hp)	Revs (rpm)	Speed (kts)	Range (nm/kts)	Coal (t)	Oil (t)
RD 101–114	Baglietto	1943–		110t max 101t des 94t std	34.00 oa	5.80	1.50 max 1.40 des	2300ehp *		17.0	2000/13	-	10
RD 115–122	CRDA (M) (1474–1481)	"		"	"	"	"	"		"	"	—	"
RD 127–134	Celli (431–438)	"		"	"	"	"	"		"	"	—	"
RD 135	OTO (L)												
RD 136, 140	Picchiotti				as above								
RD 141, 146	Soriente												
RD 147–149	Costaguta								*				

* *RD 113* and *149* 2000ehp as completed.

Construction

Laid down in Italy as RDV boats (*Motodragamine veloci*), Italian Navy design 1942. Transverse frame steel construction. Depth unknown.

Propulsion

Fitted with two Isotta-Fraschini petrol engines, type ASM 183 ADI/D, 1150shp each (two 3-bladed screws, diameter unknown); *RDV 113* and *149* were completed 1945 with four Fiat diesel engines, type V 1612, 500shp each (four 3-bladed screws, diameter unknown).

Armament

One 2cm AA gun (rounds unknown).

Handling

Similar to the German R-boats.

Complement

Crew 24. Boats: inflatables only.

Careers

After the Italian capitulation the boats were requisitioned at the dockyards; continued construction for the navy was planned.

RD 101: commissioned 18 Nov 1944. Scuttled 24 Apr 1945 at Genoa, position 44° 24′N, 08° 54′E.

RD 102: scuttled incomplete on 24 Apr 1945 at Genoa-Varazze; raised, renamed *DV 102* by Italy, *DV III* 1949, *DV 401* 1954, broken up 1958.

RD 103: scuttled incomplete on 24 Apr 1945 at Genoa-Varazze; raised, renamed *DV 103* by Italy, *DV 112* 1949, *DV 402* 1954, broken up 1958.

RD 104: scuttled incomplete on 24 Apr 1945 at Genoa-Varazze; raised, renamed *DV 104* by Italy, *DV 114* 1949, *DV 403* 1953, broken up 1959.

RD 105: scuttled incomplete on 24 Apr 1945 at Genoa-Varazze; raised, renamed *DV 105* by Italy, *DV 115* 1949, *DV 404* 1954, broken up 1954.

RD 106–108: scuttled incomplete on 24 Apr 1945 at Genoa-Varazze.

RD 109: commissioned 29 Mar 1944. Scuttled 24 Apr 1945 at Genoa.

RD 110: commissioned 23 May 1944. Burnt out 3 Jun 1944 at 0302hrs in the Bay of Cecina, 43° 18′N, 10° 29′E, after being driven on to a beach by fighter-bombers.

RD 111: commissioned 3 Sept 1944; served in the 11th Minesweeper Flotilla, later the 22nd Submarine Hunter Flotilla. Scuttled 24 Apr 1945 at Genoa.

RD 112: commissioned 12 Jan 1945. Scuttled 24 Apr 1945 at Genoa.

RD 113: incomplete; commissioned 2 Sept 1945 the Italian as *DV 113*, became the *DV 408* survey vessel in 1954; stricken 1965.

RD 114: incomplete, at Genoa-Varazze; broken up after 1945.

RD 115: commissioned 16 Mar 1945. Sunk 16 Mar 1945 in the Monfalcone dockyard canal, position 45° 49′N, 13° 32′E, by bombs.

RD 116: commissioned 1944. Scuttled 2 May 1945 in the Tagliamento estuary, position 45° 39′N, 13° 06′E.

RD 117–122: incomplete at Monfalcone; broken up after 1945. (Construction of *RDV 123–126* was not begun.)

RD 127: commissioned Apr 1945. Blown up 30 Apr 1945 at Monfalcone, position 45° 49′N, 13° 32′E.

RD 128: almost complete. Blown up 30 Apr 1945 at Monfalcone, position 45° 49′N, 13° 32′E.

RD 129–130: under construction. Blown up 30 Apr 1945 at Monfalcone, position 45° 49′N, 13° 32′E.

RD 131–134: Construction continued 1948 as lagoon tugs, but after 1 Jun 1949 these vessels were commissioned as minesweepers *DV 121–124*, and *DV 411–414* in 1954; stricken 1959.

RD 135: incomplete; scuttled in April 1945 at Livorno, position 43° 33′N, 10° 17′E; raised, planned for conversion to a lagoon tug in 1948, but not completed.

RD 136: incomplete. Scuttled in April 1945 at Limite sul Arno. (Construction of *RDV 137–139* not begun.)

RD 140: incomplete. Scuttled in April 1945 at Limite sul Arno (a construction contract for *RDV 141* was taken over only nominally in September 1943 by the Kriegsmarine, due to the evacuation of Salerno).

RDV 142–145: construction not begun.

RDV 146: construction contract was taken over only nominally in September 1943 by the Kriegsmarine, due to the evacuation of Salerno.

RD 147: launched 15 Dec 1944. Scuttled 25 Apr 1945 at Genoa.

RD 148: incomplete at Genoa-Voltri; completed 1946 by Italy as *DV 148*; became *DV 125* in 1949, *DV 415* in 1954; broken up 1958.

RD 149: incomplete at Genoa-Voltri; completed 1945 by Italy as *DV 149*, *DV 116* 1949, *DV 409* survey vessel 1954; stricken 1965.

Of the ships which the Tripartite Naval Commission (TNC) allotted to the USA as prizes after 1945, some remained in Germany. They were chartered en bloc by the OMGUS to the Federal government or its predecessor, which in turn signed charter treaties with German shipping companies. On the occasion of the visit of Federal Chancellor Dr Konrad Adenauer to the USA in 1952, the OMGUS vessels were returned to the Federal government free of charge. Some of them were then used for government purposes, others sold to charter companies.

Mine transport and minelayers 1859–1943

Mines were first used in the German navy in the 1870–71 war, when pendant mines were used to seal the Kiel Förde, the Jade, the Elbe and the Weser. Each mine was laid by two dredging barges, lighters, or similar vessels, coupled catamaran-style and using their cargo handling gear. After the war various categories of mine vessel began to be developed, and after 1894 non-pendant mines (C/77 CA) became available for the ships listed below.

Non-powered mine barges Initially these were converted former fleet units, but later new vessels were built. Mines were laid using the vessels' loading gear and mine yawls or cutters.

Defensive minelayers These were powered tug-like vessels for transporting a small number of mines and for manoeuvring the mine barges. This system was evidently successful, and remained in use into World War II, its last application being the use of net tenders to manoeuvre net layers (see pages 199–213).

Mine transports and mine research ships
Offensive minelayers In wartime this category was strengthened considerably by re-equipping merchant ships (in particular bathing steamers, ferries and small passenger ships) as auxiliary mine dispersal steamers and mine ships.

Mine barges

Name	Builder (construction nos)	Built	Gross tonnage	Displacement (t = tonnes T = tons)	Length (m)	Breadth (m)	Draught (m)	Hull depth (m)	Power (hp)	Speed (kts)	Range (nm/kts)	Coal (t)	Oil (t)
Minenprahm No 1 (W)* (mod)	Zieske	1859–60 1872–82	165gt	(283t max) (237t des)	41.20 oa 38.00 cwl	6.69	2.20						
Minenprahm No 2 (W)	Lübke	"	"	"	"	"	"						
Minenprahm No 3 (W)	Klawitter												
Minenprahm No 4 (W)	Zieske				as above								
Minenprahm No 1 (K)	Nüscke (G) (89)												
Minenprahm No 2 (K)	Liegnitz												
Minenprahm No 1 (W) ex Basilisk (mod)	KWD	1861–62 1875	200gt	(422t max) (353t des)	43.28 oa 41.02 cwl	6.96	2.35 fwd 2.67 aft						–
MP I, II		c1885		c85 max	31.70 oa	8.00			–	–	–	–	–
MP III, IV		1879–81			c25.00 oa	6.50			–	–	–	–	–
MW I, II	Neptun (379, 380)	1916–17	509gt	673t max 563t des	53.10 oa 50.50 cwl	9.30	2.30	3.45	371ihp max 350ihp des	9.5 max 9.5 des	1190/7	37	–

Mine barge No 1: launched 14 Feb 1860 as steam gunboat second rate *Wespe* (see vol 1, pages 132–3); stricken 19 Mar 1872; converted to *Mine barge No 1* in 1873; served at Wilhelmshaven; replaced in 1878.

Mine barge No 2: launched 14 Feb 1860 as steam gunboat second rate *Pfeil* (see vol 1, pages 132–3); stricken 19 Mar 1872; converted to *Mine barge No 2* in 1873; served at Wilhelmshaven; fate unknown.

Mine barge No 3: launched 14 Feb 1860 as steam gunboat second rate *Fuchs* (see vol 1, pages 132–3); stricken 14 Nov 1882; converted to *Mine barge No 3* in 1884; served at Wilhelmshaven; fate unknown.

Mine barge No 4: launched 14 Feb 1860 as steam gunboat second rate *Tiger* (see vol 1, pages 132–3); stricken 9 Jan 1877; converted to *Mine barge No 4* in 1887; served at Wilhelmshaven; fate unknown.

Mine barge No 1: launched 14 Feb 1860 as steam gunboat second rate *Schwalbe* (see vol 1, pages 132–3); stricken 19 Mar 1872, converted to *Mine barge No 1* in 1872; served at Kiel; fate unknown.

Mine barge No 2: launched 29 Apr 1860 as steam gunboat second rate *Wolf* (see vol 1, pages 132–3); stricken 26 Sept 1875; used as a coal barge at Danzig; converted to *Mine barge No 2* in 1878; served at Kiel. Sunk in the Kiel-Wiek area 4 Aug 1884 by a live torpedo fired from the torpedo test ship *Blücher*; raised and broken up.

Mine barge No 1: launched 20 Aug 1862 as steam gunboat first rate *Basilisk* (see vol 1, pages 133–4); stricken 28 Dec 1876; became *Mine barge B* in 1877, and *Mine barge No 1* 20 Mar 1878; served at Wilhelmshaven; still in service in 1912; fate unknown.

MP I: launched in 1885, commissioned as a North Sea mine barge at Cuxhaven in 1885; used by the barrage vessel division, Kiel, in 1917; became *MP 1* in 1923; served with the SVK in 1935; used as a mine barge at Ostende in September 1940. Sunk at Kiel-Hindenburgufer in 1945 and broken up.

MP II: launched 1885, commissioned as a North Sea mine barge at Cuxhaven in 1885; used by the barrage vessel division, Kiel, in 1917; became *MP 2* 'in 1923; served with 1st Navy AA from 12 Jul 1939; became barrage barge in March 1941 with the Swinemünde Barrage Cadets; used as a barrage barge in January 1942 by the Barrage Guard Flotilla; fate unknown.

MP III: launched 1879, commissioned as a Baltic mine barge at Friedrichsort in 1879; became *MP 3* in 1923; used as a barrage barge by the 1st Navy AA in 1939; used as a barrage barge from 21 May 1941 by the Pillau Barrage Cadet B group; fate unknown.

MP IV: launched 1881, commissioned as a Baltic

mine barge at Friedrichsort in 1881; became *MP 4* in 1923; served in 1936 as the starter ship *Undine* at the Berlin Olympic Games; fate unknown.

MW I: launched 5 Jan 1917, commissioned as mine barge *MW 1* 15 Apr 1917; served at the mine depot, Wilhelmshaven; became *MW 1* in 1923, and transport vessel *Heppens* in 1924; became *MT 1* 22 Oct 1930 and used as a barrage training vessel; taken as USSR prize *Nautafon* 8 Feb 1946.

MW II: launched 15 Mar 1917, commissioned as mine barge *MW II* 9 Aug 1917; served at the mine depot, Wilhelmshaven; became *MW 2* in 1923, and transport vessel *Mariensiel* in 1924; became barrage training vessel *MT 2* 22 Oct 1930; served from January 1942 as a barrack ship with the 8th Minesweeper Flotilla; transferred to the GM/SA in 1945, taken as a US prize 15 Aug 1947, and transferred to OMGUS; used as a barrack ship from 13 Jan 1948 by Eisen & Metall; transferred to Capt Dressler, Brake, for planned conversion to a motor vessel; sold into private ownership in February 1954, but broken up after 1955.

MP I and II (c1900). Mrva

MP III and IV (c1900). Mrva

MT 2 (ex Mariensiel, ex MW II) and MT 1 (ex Heppens, ex MW I) (1935). Mrva

Name	Type and construction	Propulsion	Armament	Complement
Mine barge No 1–4 (W), *1 2* (K) and *1* (W)	Mine barge.	Engine.	50 mines	
MP I, II	North Sea mine barge.	–	50 mines; five mine yawls or cutters for minelaying; four booms [mine rails and launching ramps for C/A mines fitted after 1898].	3 + 30 (boat crews) [1/34]
MP III, IV	Baltic mine barge.	–	50 mines; one boom [mine rails and launching ramps for C/A mines fitted after 1898].	[1/34]
MW I, II	Mine barge. Transverse frame steel construction; five watertight compartments; depth 3.45m.	Two vertical 3-cylinder triple expansion engines (two 3-bladed screws, 1.8m diameter); 1 + 1 Marine boilers (4 fireboxes, 16atm forced). One rudder.	Number of mines unknown; three booms.	1/46 to 1/52

Defensive minelayers

The designation of defensive minelayers varied according to the vessels' allotment to individual mine depots. It comprised the initial letter of the depot concerned, plus the running number in the depot's stock. The 1922 assignation of vessels to

the Imperial Water Police (RWS) was evidently only an administrative measure. To date, no evidence has been found of these vessels' service in the RWS.

After January 1923 all vessels were reclassified

as 'barrage training vessels', and carried the uniform designation C plus a running number, without further reference to their station.

Name	Builder (construction nos)	Built	Gross tonnage	Displacement (t = tonnes T = tons)	Length (m)	Breadth (m)	Draught (m)	Hull depth (m)	Power (hp)	Speed (kts)	Range (nm/kts)	Coal (t)	Oil (t)
Minenleger 1–3	Waltjen (14–16)	1871		24t max	14.60 oa	3.22	1.80		60ihp des	7.7 des			–
Minenleger 4–6	Devrient	1871–72		34t max	20.30 oa	3.30	1.90		250ihp des	8.0 des			–
Minenleger 4 (ex *Rival*)	Vulcan (S) (71)	1873–74	131gt	146t max	30.50 oa 28.90 cwl	5.25	1.98 fwd		„ des	9.5 des			–
F 2–6		1874	33gt						80ihp des				–
W 1–4	Übigau (351, 359, 352, 360)	1902	c60gt	102t max 88t des	18.36 oa 16.90 cwl	4.80	2.14 fwd 1.75 aft		155ihp max 120ihp des	9.0 max 8.0 des		10	–
C 1–5	„ (931, 933–935, 932)	1905–06	67gt	„	18.33 oa 16.88 cwl	5.00	2.14 fwd 1.66 aft		155ihp max 130ihp des	9.0 des		„	–
C 6, 7	Meyer (226, 227)	1907	62gt	111t max 97t des	20.47 oa 18.44 cwl	5.24	2.26 fwd 1.75 aft		155ihp max 140ihp des	„		12	–
G 4, C 8, W 5, C1	„ (234–237)	1908–09	„	„	„	„	„		„	„		„	–
C 3, C 4, C 2	„ (242–244)	1909	„	„	„	„	„		„	„		„	–
C 10, 11	„ (287, 299)	1913–14	„	„	„	„	„		„	„		„	–
C 3, C 5, C 9, W 6	„ (318–321)	1915	c62gt	„	18.80 cwl	5.30	1.64 aft		155ihp max 150ihp des	9.0 des		„	–
C 21–24	Flensburg (374–377)	1938		117t max 96t des	22.90 oa 21.70 cwl	5.80	2.09 max 1.80 des	2.78m	225ihp des	„		–	21
C 25–28	Oelkers (504–507)	1941–43	101gt	146t max 130t des	27.10 oa 24.80 cwl	6.00	2.20 max 2.17 des	3.50m	518ehp max 465ehp des	12.0 max 11.8 des		–	11
C 29–31	De Vries (AL)	1943–		150t max 130t des	26.78 oa 21.38 cwl	6.04	2.47 max 2.08 des	„	„	10.0 des		–	11.4
C 32–34	Botje*	1943	„	„	„	„	„	„	„	„		–	„

* From April 1943 construction of *C 34* was taken over by van Diepen.

Careers

Minelayers 1–3: launched 1871, commissioned Sept 1872 as Waltjen-type spar torpedo boats (see vol 1, page 149); became *Minelayers 1–3* 15 Dec 1875; used for harbour defence at Wilhelmshaven; used on the Kiel barrage 8 Jul 1881 (possibly identical to *F 2–6*, see below); fates unknown.

Minelayer 4: launched 1871, commissioned May 1872 as a Devrient-type spar torpedo boat (see vol 1, page 149); became *Minelayer 4* 15 Dec 1875; used for harbour defence at Wilhelmshaven; replaced by *Minelayer 4* (ex-*Rival*) in 1881 (see below).

Minelayers 5, 6: launched 1871, commissioned Jul/Nov 1872 as Devrient-type spar torpedo boats (see vol 1, page 149); became *Minelayers 5, 6* 15 Dec 1875; used for harbour defence at Wilhelmshaven; replaced by new vessels after 1902.

Minelayer 4: launched 2 Sept 1874, commissioned 14 Dec 1874 as torpedo steamer *Rival* (see vol 1, page 150); became *Minelayer 4* 8 Jul 1881; used for harbour defence at Wilhelmshaven; stricken 1884; became steam tug *Rival*; broken up at Wilhelmshaven 15 Jan 1916.

F 2–6: possibly launched in 1874 and commissioned that year for service as minelayers and mine yawl tugs in the North Sea; transferred to the Friedrichsort mine depot in 1906 as *F 2–6*; still in service in 1917; fates unknown.

W 1: launched 1902, commissioned in 1902; served with the Naval Depot Inspectorate, Wilhelmshaven, as *W 1*; fate unknown.

W 2: launched 1902, commissioned in 1902; served with the Naval Depot Inspectorate, Wilhelmshaven, as *W 2*; fate unknown.

W 3: launched 1902, commissioned in 1902; served with the Naval Depot Inspectorate, Wilhelmshaven, as *W 3*; fate unknown.

W 4: launched 1902, commissioned in 1902; served with the Naval Depot Inspectorate, Wilhelmshaven, as *W 4*; fate unknown.

C 1: launched 1905, commissioned 3 April 1906 as *C 1*; served with 4th AA at Cuxhaven; became *G 1* 31 Mar 1909; served with 3rd AA at Geestemünde; transferred to the Weser Barrage Vessel Division 1

Aug 1914, to the Mine Research Command on 27 Jan 1918, and to the Geestemünde Mine Depot 21 Feb 1920; converted to a steam tug between 27 May and 1 Aug 1920 (superstructure reduced in height to 3.8m, and folding funnel fitted); operated under civil charter 1920–1923 (inland shipping); underwent major repairs after 1 Jan 1924 as barrage training vessel *C 1* in Wilhelmshaven Naval Dockyard; converted to gunnery training boat *Ulan* 14 Jul 1934; served with a coastal defence flotilla; stricken 26 Jan 1939; broken up.

C 2: launched 1905, commissioned 29 May 1906 as *C 2*; served with 4th AA at Cuxhaven; transferred to the Geestemünde Mine Depot as *G 2* 22 Jan 1910, and to the Weser Barrage Vessel Division 1 Aug 1914; transferred to the Geestemünde Mine Depot 4 Feb 1918; converted to a steam tug between 26 May and 11 Jul 1920 (as *C 1*); operated under civil charter 1920–1924 (inland shipping); converted to barrage training vessel *C 2* 8 Feb 1934, at Wilhelmshaven Naval Dockyard; possibly became *C 8* after 1934; fate unknown.

C 3: launched in April 1906, commissioned in May 1906 as *C 3*; served at the Cuxhaven Mine Depot; became *F 1* in 1908, and served at Friedrichsort Mine Depot; served from 1917 with the Kiel Barrage Vessel Division; became the Imperial Water Police vessel *No 1* from January 1922, and barrage training vessel *C 15* in January 1923; stricken in February 1932.

C 4: launched in 1906, commissioned in May 1906 as *C 4* for the Cuxhaven Mine Depot; became barrage practice vessel *C 7* in January 1923; stricken in February 1932 and sold to WSA Bremen as the steamship *Priel*.

C 5: launched in 1906, commissioned in May 1906 as *C 5* for the Cuxhaven Mine Depot; became *F 7* in about 1908, and served at the Friedrichsort Mine Depot; served from 1917 with the Kiel Barrage Vessel Division; became the Imperial Water Police vessel *No 13* in January 1922; became barrage training vessel *C 16* in January 1923; stricken in the 1920s, and sold to WSD Stettin as the steam tug *Swante*; taken over by the UAS in 1939; taken as a

US prize in 1945 under OMGUS control; became the steam tug *Assistent II* 24 Jan 1947 for Fehner, Lemwerder; sold into private ownership 5 Nov 1954; fate unknown.

C 6: launched in 1907, commissioned in March 1908 as *C 6* for the Cuxhaven Mine Depot; served as the Imperial Water Police vessel *No 16* from January 1922; became barrage training vessel *C 9* in January 1923; used for anti-submarine training by the UAS in 1939; taken as a USSR prize 17 June 1946.

C 7: launched in 1907, commissioned in April 1908 as *C 7* for the Cuxhaven Mine Depot; served as the Imperial Water Police vessel *No 17* from January 1922; became barrage training vessel *C 10* in January 1923; transferred to a coastal defence flotilla 26 Jan 1939; taken as a US prize 1945 under OMGUS control; transferred as the steam tug *Henry* 4 Jun 1947 to Hermann Lutter, Bremen, then on 17 Dec 1948 to E Weber, Bremen; returned to OMGUS 19 Jun 1950, defunct; probably broken up.

Name	Type and construction	Propulsion	Armament	Complement
Minelayer 1–3	Defensive minelayer.	One vertical 2-cylinder single expansion engine (one 4-bladed screw, 1.5m diameter), one cylindrical boiler (4atm forced).	Number of mines unknown.	6
Minelayer 4–6	Defensive minelayer.	One vertical 2-cylinder single expansion engine (one 4-bladed screw, 1.7m diameter), one cylindrical boiler (4atm forced).	Number of mines unknown.	6
Minelayer 4 (ex *Rival*)	Defensive minelayer.	Two inclined oscillating 2-cylinder double expansion engines (two side paddle wheels, 3.8m diameter), one locomotive boiler (1.8atm forced).	Number of mines unknown.	
F 2–6	Defensive minelayer.		Number of mines unknown.	
W 1–4	Defensive minelayer.	One vertical 2-cylinder single expansion engine (one 3-bladed screw), one cylindrical boiler (9atm forced).	8 mines.	1/5–0/7
C 1–5	Defensive minelayer.	One vertical 2-cylinder single expansion engine (one 4-bladed screw), one cylindrical boiler (9.2atm forced).	8 mines.	0/7
C 6, 7, G 4, C 8, W 5, C 1, 3, C 4, 2, 10, 11, C 3, 5, 9, W 6	Defensive minelayer.	One vertical 2-cylinder single expansion engine (one 3-bladed screw), one cylindrical boiler (9atm forced).	10 mines.	1/5–0/8
C 21–24	Barrage training vessel; depth 2.78m.	One vertical 4-cylinder double compound engine (one 4-bladed screw, 1.35m diameter), one watertube boiler.	One 2cm AA gun (planned).	1/6–0/12
C 25–28	Barrage training vessel; depth 3.50m.	One Wumag 6-cylinder 4-stroke diesel engine (one 4-bladed screw, 1.6m diameter).	One 2cm AA gun (planned).	0/12
C 29–34	Barrage training vessel; depth 3.50m.	One Wumag 6-cylinder 4-stroke diesel engine (one screw).	One 2cm AA gun (planned).	0/12

C2 (1905); *C 1, 3, 4* and *G 1–6* were similar. *Mrva*   *C 13* (1930); *C 8–12* and *14* (ex *C 5–11*) were similar. *Mrva*   *C15* (1930); *C 16* was similar. *Mrva*   *Tapfer* (ex *C 11*) (1940). *Mrva*

C 21–24 (1938). *Mrva*   *C 25–28* (1942). *Mrva*   *C 29–34* (1943). *Mrva*

G 4: launched in 1909, commissioned in 1910 for the Geestemünde Mine Depot; transferred to Wilhelmshaven Mine Depot in October 1919; served as the Imperial Water Police vessel *No 15* from January 1922; became barrage training vessel *C 4* in January 1923; stricken in March 1932.

C 8: launched in 1908, commissioned in March 1909 for the Cuxhaven Mine Depot; transferred to the SUK in October 1919; served as the Imperial Water Police vessel *No 19* from January 1922; became barrage training vessel *C 11* in January 1923; became the steam tender *Tapfer* in 1941; converted to a remote control minesweeping tug 27 May 1941, and served with the 19th Minesweeper Flotilla; became *Vs 1015* in 1942; served with the GM/SA 3rd Minesweeping Division, in 1945; fate unknown.

W 5: launched in 1909, commissioned in 1909 for the Wilhelmshaven Mine Depot; became *G 3* in 1910 at the Geestemünde Mine Depot, then *W 5* at the Wilhelmshaven Mine Depot later in the decade; served as the Imperial Water Police vessel *No 14* from January 1922; became barrage training vessel *C 3* in January 1923; still in existence in 1938; fate unknown.

C 1: launched in 1908, commissioned in March 1909 for the Cuxhaven Mine Depot; served as the Imperial Water Police vessel *No 18* from January 1922; became barrage training vessel *C 5* in January 1923; transferred to the UAS in 1939; fate unknown.

C 3: launched in 1909, commissioned in February 1910 for the Cuxhaven Mine Depot. Sunk by a mine in the Elbe estuary at 0718hrs on 19 Oct 1914, position 53° 54N, 08° 42′ 5″E; six dead (all crew lost).

C 4: launched in 1909, commissioned in February 1910 for the Cuxhaven Mine Depot; replaced in 1923; fate unknown.

C 2: launched in 1909, commissioned in February 1910 for the Cuxhaven Mine Depot; served as the Imperial Water Police vessel *No 22* from January 1922; became barrage training Vessel *C 6* in January 1923; stricken in March 1932.

C 10: launched in 1913, commissioned in September 1913 for the Cuxhaven Mine Depot; served as the Imperial Water Police vessel *No 25* from January 1922; became barrage training vessel *C 13* in January 1923; became the steam tender *Scharf* 5 Jul 1938; sold to a private owner in Hamburg 1 Aug 1945; fate unknown.

C 11: launched in 1914, commissioned in May 1914 for the Cuxhaven Mine Depot; served as the Imperial Water Police vessel *No 26* from January 1922, became barrage training vessel *C 14* in January 1923; served with a coastal defence flotilla in 1938; taken as a USSR prize 17 Jun 1946.

C 3: launched in 1915, commissiond in 1915 for the Cuxhaven Mine Depot; replaced in 1923; fate unknown.

C 5: launched in 1915, commissioned in 1915 for the Cuxhaven Mine Depot; served as the Imperial Water Police vessel *No 28* from January 1922; became barrage training vessel *C 8* in January 1923; stricken in 1934.

C 9: launched in 1915, commissioned in July 1915 for the Cuxhaven Mine Depot; served as the Imperial Water Policy vessel *No 21* from January 1922; became barrage training vessel *C 12* in January 1923; stricken in February 1932.

W 6: launched in 1915, commissioned 1 Sept 1915 for the Wilhelmshaven Mine Depot; served as the Imperial Water Police vessel *Kiel 1* from January 1922; fate unknown.

C 21: launched 3 Mar 1938, commissioned 16 Jun 1938 for the SVK, Kiel; at Kappeln in May 1945; fate unknown.

C 22: launched 22 Mar 1938, commissioned 19 Jul 1938 for the SVK, Kiel; to GM/SA 1945; became steam tug *Pedoy* in 1949 for F Dahmen of Duisburg; sold in 1954; fate unknown.

C 23: launched 14 Apr 1938, commissioned 9 Aug 1938 for the SVK, Kiel; at Kappeln in May 1945; fate unknown.

C 24: launched 6 May 1938, commissioned 29 Aug 1938 for the SVK, Kiel; fate unknown.

C 25: launched 12 Dec 1941, commissioned 28 Nov 1942 for the SVK, Kiel; served with the 6th Minesweeper Flotilla in 1943; taken as a French prize in 1945; became the buoy layer *B 275*; converted to the survey tender *Crabe* in 1948; stricken in the 1950s.

C 26: launched 30 Apr 1942, commissioned 12 Feb 1943 for the SVK group, Kiel; taken as a USSR prize 12 Dec 1945; fate unknown.

C 27: launched 21 Sept 1942, commissioned 23 Apr 1943 for the SVK, Kiel; taken as a French prize in 1945; became the buoy layer *B 261*; converted to survey tender *Tourteau* in 1948; stricken 1957 as *O 83*; fate unknown.

C 28: launched 7 Apr 1943, commissioned 7 Oct 1943 for the SVK, Kiel; taken as a British prize in 1945; renamed *Diver*; transferred to the Netherlands as *Bandia* in 1952; transferred to Italy as *Permia* 1956; still in existence in 1962; fate unknown.

C 29: launched 1943, commissioned 20 Jun 1943 for the SVK, Kiel. Sunk by a mine in the Kiel Förde 18 May 1944.

C 30: launched 1943, commissioned 25 Sept 1943 for the SVK, Kiel; taken as a British prize in 1945 and renamed *Dipper*; broken up in the 1950s.

C 31: not completed; completed as Dutch pilot boat *Zeezwaluw* 31 Aug 1946.

C 32: launched 1943, commissioned 29 Jun 1943 for the SVK, Kiel; converted to motor tug *Karen* for Jürgen Blöchert, Flensburg, in 1949; transferred to East Germany through a Kiel company in Sept/Oct 1950 to the port authority in Rostock to become the motor tug *Aktivist*; with VEB Ship Salvage after 1952, used for diving and other operations; converted to a motor passenger vessel in 1970, as *Aktivist*, with the VEB Weiss Flotte; in service up to 1984.

C 33: launched 1943, commissioned 14 Jul 1943 for the SVK, Kiel; transferred to the 3rd Minesweeping Group, GM/SA, in Denmark in 1945; to OMGUS 7 Dec 1947; converted to the motor tug *Bardenfleth* for URAG 21 Jun 1949; broken up by Eckhardt & Co, Hamburg, after 8 Apr 1969.

C 34: launched 1943, commissioned 20 Sept 1943 for the EKK; transferred to the 1st Minesweeping Division, GM/SA, in 1945; converted to the motor tug *Rechtenfleth* for URAG 21 Jun 1949; broken up by Eckhardt & Co, Hamburg, after 23 Oct 1967.

Sumary of defensive minelayers, later barrage training vessels

C 1 (1905) became G 1 1909, etc
C 1 (1908) became C 5 1923, etc
C 2 (1905) became G 2 1910, etc
C 2 (1909) became C 6 1923, etc
C 3 (1906) became F 1 1908, etc
C 3 (1909) sunk 19 Oct 1914
C 3 (1915) (*Ersatz C 3*) probably stricken before
  1923
C 3 (1909) ex G 3
C 4 (1906) became C 7 1923, etc
C 4 (1909) details unknown
C 4 (1908) ex G 4
C 5 (1906) became F 7, etc
C 5 (1915) became C 8 1923, etc
C 5 (1908) ex C 1
C 6 (1907) became C 9 1923, etc
C 6 (1909) ex C 2
C 7 (1907) became C 10 1923, etc

C 7 (1909) ex C 4
C 8 (1908) became C 11 1923, etc
C 8 (1915) ex C 5
C 9 (1915) became C 12 1923, etc
C 9 (1907) ex C 6
C 10 (1913) became C 13 1923, etc
C 10 (1907) ex C 7
C 11 (1908) ex C 8
C 12 (1915) ex C 9
C 13 (1913) ex C 10
C 14 (1913) ex C 11
C 15 (1906) ex F 1
C 16 (1906) ex F 7

Friedrichsort mine depot
F 1 (1906) ex C 3
F 2 (1874) still available 1917
F 3 (1874) still available 1917

F 4 (1874) still available 1917
F 5 (1874) still available 1917
F 6 (1874) still available 1917
F 7 (1906) ex C 5

Geestemünde mine depot
G 1 (1905) ex C 1
G 2 (1905) ex C 2
G 3 (1909) ex W 5
G 4 (1909) became C 3 1923, etc

Wilhelmshaven mine depot
W 1 (1902) fate unknown
W 2 (1902) fate unknown
W 3 (1902) fate unknown
W 4 (1902) fate unknown
W 5 (1909) became G 3 1910, etc
W 6 (1915) fate unknown

Mine transports and mine research vessels

Name	Builder (construction nos)	Built	Gross tonnage	Displacement (t = tonnes T = tons)	Length (m)	Breadth (m)	Draught (m)	Hull depth (m)	Power (hp)	Speed (kts)	Range (nm/kts)	Coal (t)	Oil (t)
Rhein	Vulcan (S) (55)	1867	353gt	482t max 398t des	47.10 oa 44.00 cwl	6.01	3.24		273ihp max 200ihp des	9.7 max 9.0 des	1410/7	39	–
Pelikan (mod)	KWW (12) „	1889–91 1908	1821gt	2424t max 2364t des	84.20 oa* 80.90 cwl	11.7*	4.28 fwd 5.14 aft	7.90m	3072ihp max 3000ihp des	15.3 max 15.0 des	4200/10	410 max 311 des	–

* Length over mine-launching platform 85.00m; breadth over bridge wings 13.10m.

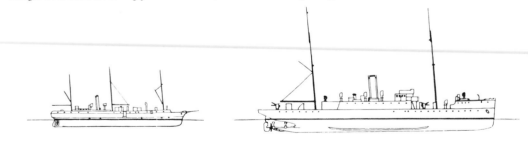

Rhein (1910).   *Pelikan* (1910).

Notes

Pelikan: designed and built as a transport steamer for the relief crews of warships stationed overseas. Her rôle was changed before completion, since such a service was considered unnecessary.

Before 1907 she had no upper bridge forward; after that year the searchlights were 5m further forward than shown in the drawing. The after deckhouse extension was replaced by an engine room skylight 1m high.

Name	Type and construction	Propulsion	Armament	Complement
Rhein	Steam ship, transverse frame iron construction, one deck (4 watertight compartments).	One vertical 2-cylinder single expansion engine (one 3-bladed screw, 2.5m diameter), one trunk boiler (3 fireboxes, 5atm forced).	Two 3.7cm machine guns, 100 mines.	1/80 [0/50]
Pelikan	Steam ship, transverse and longitudinal frame steel construction, one deck (11 watertight compartments); depth 7.9m.	Two vertical 3-cylinder triple expansion engines (two 3-bladed screws, 3.5m diameter), two cylindrical double-ended boilers (12 fireboxes, 12atm forced, 710sq m).	Four 8.8cm/30 guns (900 [539] rounds), 400 mines.	8/187 [11/189]

In 1916 the after deckhouse was extended to 1.5m behind the mainmast and a 10m long upper superstructure deck was added, with a searchlight mounted on the after edge. After 1908 an upper deck mine-launching position was added. The vessel was nicknamed 'Pelischiff' (Peliship) after Kaiser Wilhelm II was alleged to have remarked 'There are no barges in my navy!', since her correct name suggested a barge (*Kahn* means 'barge' in German).

Careers

Rhein: launched 7 Sept 1867, commissioned 17 Oct 1867 as a transport vessel. Converted to a mine dispersal steamer in 1883, became a mine training ship in 1888, and a mine experiment ship in 1896.

Stricken 24 Jun 1911, used as a training and workshop hulk for mine hunters at Cuxhaven. Sold to Rönnebek 11 Aug 1920 and converted to a barge.

Pelikan: launched 29 Jul 1890, commissioned 15 Oct 1891 as a guard and research ship for the Baltic. Converted to mine experiment ship 1 Nov 1895.

Offensive minelayers

Name	Builder (construction no)	Built	Cost in Marks (000s)	Displacement (t = tonnes T = tons)	Length (m)	Breadth (m)	Draught (m)	Power (hp)	Revs (rpm)	Speed (kts)	Range (nm/kts)	Coal (t)	Oil (t)
Nautilus (mod)	Weser (152) KWK	1905–07 1909–10	2879	2345t max 1975t des*	98.20 oa 90.20 cwl 100.90 oa (mod)	11.20	4.42 fwd 4.54 aft	6638ihp max 6600ihp des	188 max 180 des	20.8 max 20.0 des	3530/9	490 max 200 des	–
Albatross (mod)	„ (162) KWK	1907–08 1910–11	3014	2506t max 2208t des*	100.90 oa 96.60 cwl	11.50	4.40 fwd 4.57 aft	5963ihp max 6600ihp des	169 max 160 des	20.2 max 20.0 des	3680/9	526 max 200 des	–

* *Nautilus* 1693gt, 816nt; *Albatross* 1780gt, 981nt.

Construction

Laid down as mine steamers *A* and *B* (official designs 1904 and 1905). Transverse and longitudinal steel construction (nine watertight compartments, double bottom 60 per cent); depth 7.21/7.43m. Immersion increased by 1cm per 6.17/6.92t. Trim moment 3150/3740m–t.

Propulsion

Two vertical 3-cylinder triple expansion engines (two 4-bladed screws, 3.2m diameter) in two engine rooms, four marine-type boilers (eight fireboxes, 15atm forced, 1,525sq m) in 1 + 1 + 1 (or 1 + 1 in *Albatross*) boiler rooms. Two turbo generators, 110V, 90kW. One rudder.

Armament

Eight 8cm/35 QF guns (2000 rounds), range 9100m [*Nautilus* 1918, four 2cm AA guns and 24 machine guns, plus, for landing operations, two 7.6cm guns, four mine launchers and two flamethrowers]. *Nautilus* 186 + 205 mines; *Albatross* 288 mines.

Handling

Quite good sea boats, but with weather helm, and suffering from severe drift. Manoeuvred and turned well.

Complement

Crew: 10/191; 11/197. Boats: two picket boats, one launch, two yawls, one dinghy.

Notes

Colour scheme No 9. After conversion upper deck mine-launching positions replaced those originally located on the mine deck. *Nautilus* had her stern overhang increased by 2.7m, making her new length overall 100.9m. The after deckhouse with a searchlight platform was removed and a new searchlight platform was installed on the mainmast 13m above the CWL. The superstructure deck was extended to aft of the mainmast.

Careers

Nautilus: launched 28 Aug 1906, commissioned 19

Mar 1907 for mine training. Converted to a mine cruiser for coastal defence in 1914; stricken at Kiel 21 Mar 1919; used as a store ship after 1921 for Didea, Bremen; became *Hulk I* after 1 Jan 1923, then *Hulk A* with the Training Inspectorate at Bremerhaven from 1 Apr 1928. Sold 18 Aug 1928 for 180,000M; broken up at Copenhagen.

Albatross: launched 23 Oct 1907, commissioned 19 May 1908 for mine training. Converted to mine cruiser 1914. Sunk 2 Jul 1915 at 0812hrs off Gotland, position 57° 25′N, 18° 57′E, after running aground under gunfire from the Russian cruisers *Admiral Makarolev*, *Baja*, *Bogatyr* and *Oleg*; 28 dead. Salvaged and towed to Farösund; interned at Oskarshamn 1 Oct 1915; returned to Kiel in January 1919; out of service 23 Jan 1919 and stricken 21 Mar 1921; sold for 900,000M and broken up at Hamburg in 1921.

Mine steamers *C* and *D*: see mine cruisers *Brummer and Bremse*, vol 1, pages 140–141.

Minelayer *Lauting* will be covered in a future volume.

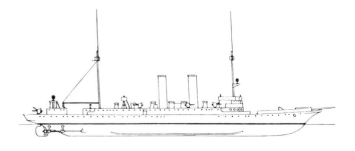
Nautilus (1910).

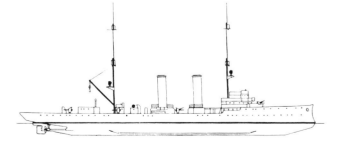
Albatross (1914).

Auxiliary minelayers 1914–1945

Auxiliary minelayers 1914–1918 and (*) 1939–1945 (I)

Name	Builder (construction nos)	Built	Gross tonnage	Displacement (t = tonnes T = tons)	Length (m)	Breadth (m)	Draught (m)	Hull depth (m)	Power (hp)	Speed (kts)	Range and fuel (nm/kts/t)	Owner
Apollo	SAG (132)	1883	634gt		50.99 cwl	7.88	5.48		300ihp des	9.5 des		D G Neptun, Bremen
Dahlström	Howaldt (K) (153)	1887	73gt		24.08 cwl	6.09	2.41		120ihp des	11.3 des		Neue Dampfer Co, Kiel
Deutschland (mod as Stralsund*)	Vulcan (S) (292)	1909 1940	2847gt 2972gt†	c4200t max	113.80 oa 108.00 cwl	16.26	4.90	7.26	5000ihp des	16.5 des	/15/210 + 160 (coal)	Königl. Preussische Eisenbahn-Direktion/ Deutsche Reichsbahn, Stettin
Preussen	” (293)	”	”	”	”	”	”	”	”	”	”	”
Hertha*	Oderwerke (547)	1905	1257gt 1221gt†		81.90 oa 76.28 cwl	10.35	4.11	4.30	2600ihp des	16.0 des	815/15/110 (coal)	J F Braeunlich GmbH, Stettin
Kaiser* (mod) (mod)	Vulcan (S)	” 1914 1922	1916gt 1912gt†	1920t max	96.30 oa 92.23 cwl	11.70	2.97	4.05	6000shp at 560rpm des 3000shp at 375rpm des	20.0 des 16.0 des	2380/12 248 (coal)	Hamburg-Amerika Linie, Hamburg
Königin Luise	” (344)	1913	2163gt	2160t max	94.00 oa 89.80 cwl	12.20	3.30	4.85	6500shp des	20.0 des		”
Odin* (mod)	Oderwerke (526)	1902 1907	1177gt 1137gt†		77.60 oa 72.11 cwl	10.34	4.09		2300ihp des	16.0 des	850/15/	J F Braeunlich GmbH, Stettin

† As in 1939.

Careers

Apollo: launched Jul 1883, commissioned 6 Aug 1914 as auxiliary mine dispersal steamer *E*, North Sea. Used only as mine and munitions transport vessel because of inadequate speed. 16 Oct 1914 out of service, returned. Sunk by drift ice at Steindeich, Pagensand, 17 Feb 1917; raised 25 Sept 1917 and repaired. Became *Harald* in 1919, and Italian *Araldo* in 1923. Severely damaged after collision at Malaga 13 Dec 1928; broken up.

Dahlström: launched 1887, commissioned 27 Oct 1914 as an auxiliary mine dispersal steamer at Kiel; no service. Became a service vessel with the Barrage Transport Division at Kiel 3 Nov 1914; returned 26 Nov 1918; became the steam tug *Condor*, still in existence in 1939; fate unknown.

Deutschland: launched 17 Feb 1909, commissioned 4 Aug 1914 as auxiliary mine dispersal steamer in the Baltic; returned 16 Nov 1919: served as Sassnitz-Trelleborg railway ferry; intended for Operation Sealion, 23 Aug 1940, and renamed *Stralsund* but saw no service after being hit by an aircraft bomb at Le Havre 25 Sept 1940; out of service at Stettin 7 Nov 1940; returned to service as the railway ferry *Deutschland*; converted to hospital transport ship 20 Jan 1945; taken as Soviet prize 12 Mar 1946, renamed *Anvia*; broken up 1960?

Hertha: launched in April 1905, hired 1 Aug 1914 for use as auxiliary hospital ship *E*, commissioned 10 Sept 1914 as an auxiliary mine dispersal steamer

Name	Type and construction	Propulsion	Armament	Complement
Apollo	Steam ship, 2 decks.	One vertical 3-cylinder triple expansion engine. One screw, one cylindrical boiler.	Two 3.7cm machine guns (400 rounds), number of mines unknown.	(14)
Dahlström	Steam ferry, 1 deck.	One compound engine, one screw, one cylindrical boiler.	20 mines.	(13)
Deutschland, Preussen	Steam ferry, railway ferry, 2 decks (7 watertight compartments); depth 7.26m.	Two vertical 3-cylinder triple expansion engines (two 4-bladed screws, 3.6m diameter), four cylindrical boilers (12atm forced).	Four 8.8cm/40 guns, two 5cm QF guns,* two 8.8cm AA guns (400 rounds), [ten 2cm AA guns, one 3.7cm AA gun from December 1944*], 420 mines.	
*Hertha**	Steam ferry (sea bathing ship), 2 decks (5 watertight compartments); depth 4.30m.	Two vertical 3-cylinder triple expansion engines (two 4-bladed screws, 2.6m diameter), two cylindrical boilers (12atm forced).	Two 3.7cm machine guns (400 rounds), 130 mines.	(54)
*Kaiser**	Turbine ferry [sea bathing ship], 2 decks (7 watertight compartments); depth 4.05m.	Two sets AEG turbines (two 4-bladed screws, 1.9/[2.3]m diameter), four watertube boilers (14atm forced), [two Marine-type boilers after 1922].	Two 8.8cm/40 QF guns (260 rounds), 180 mines, *two 8.8cm/75 guns; two 3.7cm AA guns, eight 2cm AA guns, [one 8.8cm AA gun, one 3.7cm AA gun, ten 2cm AA guns four 1944], 200 mines.	10/200 [8/158] (98)
Königin Luise	Turbine ferry [sea bathing ship], 2 decks (8 watertight compartments); depth 4.85m.	Two sets AEG turbines with Föttinger transformer (two 4-bladed screws, 2.24m diameter), two Marine-type boilers (14atm forced).	Two 3.7cm machine guns (400 rounds), 180, 200* mines.	5/115 (86)
*Odin**	Steam ferry [sea bathing ship], 2 decks (5 watertight compartments); depth 6.34m.	Two vertical 3-cylinder triple expansion engines (two 4-bladed screws, 2.6m diameter), two cylindrical boilers (12atm forced).	Two 3.7cm machine guns (400 rounds), 130 mines; *two 3.7cm AA guns (1,200 rounds), 120 mines.	(55)

* Weapons and other equipment shipped at artillery and mine depots at Cuxhaven and Friedrichsort near Kiel.

in the Baltic; returned to Baltic bathing service 18 Jul 1919; converted to a submarine barrack and targt ship with the 25th submarine flotilla 5 Oct 1939. Taken as a Greek prize 17 Sept 1945 and renamed *Heimara*; sunk by a mine in the vicinity of Piraeus 19 Jan 1947, position approx 38°N, 14° 50′E.

Kaiser: launched 8 Apr 1905, chartered 1906 as an experimental fleet turbine ship. Employed as an auxiliary mine dispersal steamer for patrol duties with the Elbe flotilla in August 1914; taken as British prize in 1919; re-purchased 23 Sept 1921 and used as a sea bathing vessel; became a KM barrack ship at Hamburg in 1938; converted to a mine ship 28 Aug 1939; commissioned 6 Sept 1939; transferred to the barrage experimental group 1 Oct 1943, for use as an experimental ship; returned to use as mine ship Aug 1944; taken as British prize at Bremerhaven in 1945; became Soviet prize 22 Aug 1945 and renamed *Nekrasov*; became Polish *Beniowski* Apr 1947; broken up 1954.

Königin Luise: launched 8 May 1913, commissioned 3 Aug 1914 as an auxiliary mine dispersal steamer B. Sunk in the Thames estuary at 1320hrs on 5 Aug 1914 by gunfire from the British cruiser *Amphion* and a destroyer, position 51° 52′N, 02° 30′E; 77 dead.

Odin: launched 8 Feb 1902, commissioned Sept 1914 as auxiliary mine dispersal steamer in the Bal-

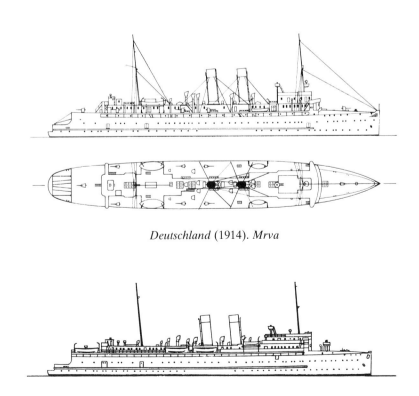

Deutschland (1914). *Mrva*

Preussen (1914).

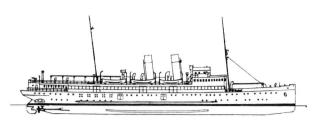

Königin Luise (1914).

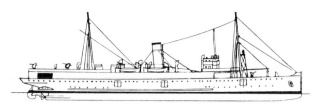

Kaiser (1914).

tic; returned 1918; taken as British prize 14 Mar 1919, and re-purchased 1920 for sea bathing service. Converted to a target and guard ship for submarine training 1 Sept 1939; used as a tender for the Technical Training Group, operational submarines, from March 1942; sunk in Danzig Bay 7 Aug 1944 by a torpedo from a German U-boat; position and casualties unknown.

Preussen: launched 3 Apr 1909, commissioned 5 Aug 1914 to serve as auxiliary mine dispersal steamer in the North Sea; no service. Returned 15 Aug 1914 to railway ferry service; stranded in a snowstorm and sunk at Teufelsgrund, in the vicinity of Rügen, 10 Dec 1937; raised Jan 1938 and repaired; converted to a hospital transport ship 8 Nov 1944; returned 5 Jan 1945; taken as a USSR

prize at Lübeck 21 Mar 1946 and renamed *Krilyon*; converted to a steam passenger vessel for the Vladivostok-Kamchatka service around 1951; out of service in 1975 and serving as barrack ship for harbour construction at Wrangel Bay in the vicinity of Vladivostok. Still in existence at Vostochny, 1980.

Auxiliary minelayers 1914–1918 and (*) 1939–1945 (II)

Name	Builder (construction nos)	Built	Gross tonnage	Displacement (t = tonnes T = tons)	Length (m)	Breadth (m)	Draught (m)	Hull depth (m)	Power (hp)	Speed (kts)	Range and fuel (nm/kts/t)	Owner
Primus	Howaldt (K) (463)	1907	297gt		30.00 oa 24.10 pp	10.50	3.51	4.41	350ihp des	8.0 des	1170 (coal)	Kiel Town
Prinz Adalbert	" (297)	1895	699gt		66.88 oa 63.18 cwl	8.74	3.71	4.12	1300ihp des	13.0 des		Sartori & Berger, Kiel
Prinz Sigismund	" (350)	1899	697gt		66.20 oa 62.67 cwl	8.72	3.78	4.19	1430ihp des	"		"
Prinz Waldemar	" (266)	1893	660gt		66.00 oa 62.18 cwl	8.48	3.70	4.09	1170ihp des	"		"
*Rügen**	Oderwerke (644)	1914	1894gt 2170gt†		95.20 oa 89.70 cwl	11.60	4.21	6.61	3200ihp des	16.0 des	1700/15/ 340 (coal)	Th Gribel KG a A, Stettin
Senta	Hawthorn Leslie	1905	4077gt		120.40 oa 115.90 cwl	14.93	7.60	7.81	4200ihp des	10.0 des		T Law & Co, Glasgow
Silvana	Howaldt (K) (321)	1897	804gt		66.20 oa 62.68 cwl	9.00	3.91	4.12	1400ihp des	13.0 des		Hamburg-Amerika Linie, Hamburg
Wotan	CNA (37)	1908	3390gt		109.80 oa 105.50 cwl	14.63	5.82	7.84	1750ihp des	8.0 des		Wotan Schiffahrts GmbH, Hamburg

† As in 1939.

Careers

Primus: launched 1907, commissioned 3 Aug 1914 as an auxiliary mine dispersal steamer at Kiel; returned 28 Dec 1914; used as a canal ferry at Brunsbüttel in 1945, and around 1969–70 serving as a working barge with a marine construction company at Loos; fate unknown.

Prinz Adalbert: launched 17 Mar 1895, commis-

sioned 3 Aug 1914 as an auxiliary mine dispersal steamer B in the Baltic; returned 22 Nov 1918; became *Bürgermeister Smidt* in 1924; broken up 1929.

Prinz Sigismund: launched 24 Apr 1899, commissioned 14 Aug 1914 as an auxiliary mine dispersal steamer A in the Baltic; became leader ship in the Barrage Vessel Division at Kiel 19 Jul 1918; returned 2 Dec 1918; became the Greek *Elli*

Daskalaki 1925; renamed *Elli Toyia* 1933; renamed *Euboea* 1933; broken up 1937.

Prinz Waldemar: launched Feb 1893, commissioned 2 Aug 1914 as an auxiliary mine dispersal steamer in the Baltic; no service; returned 15 Sept 1914; to service with a patrol half-flotilla, Kiel, 25 Mar 1915; returned 26 Nov 1918; renamed *Kronprinzessin Cecilie* 1924; broken up 1929.

Name	Type and construction	Propulsion	Armament	Complement
Primus	Steam ferry, 1 deck (7 watertight compartments); depth 4.41m.	One vertical 3-cylinder triple expansion engine (two 4-bladed screws, 2.5m diameter), two cylindrical boilers (13atm forced).	60 mines.	
Prinz Adalbert	Steam ferry, 2 decks (7 watertight compartments); depth 4.12m.	Two vertical 3-cylinder triple expansion engines (two 3-bladed screws, 3.4m diameter), four cylindrical boilers (12.5atm forced).	Two 3.7cm machine guns (400 rounds), 80 + 90† mines.	(28)
Prinz Sigismund	Steam ferry, 2 decks (8 watertight compartments); depth 4.19m.	Two vertical 3-cylinder triple expansion engines (two 3-bladed screws, 3.4m diameter), four cylindrical boilers (12.5atm forced).	Two 3.7cm machine guns (400 rounds), 80 + 90† mines.	(27)
Prinz Waldemar	Steam ferry, 2 decks (6 watertight compartments); depth 4.09m.	Two vertical 3-cylinder triple expansion engines (two 3-bladed screws, 3.4m diameter), two cylindrical boilers (12.5atm forced).	Two 3.7cm machine guns (400 rounds), 80 mines.	(23)
*Rügen**	Steam ferry, 2 decks (7 watertight compartments); depth 6.61m.	Two vertical 3-cylinder triple expansion engines (two 3-bladed screws, 4.6m diameter), three cylindrical boilers (13atm forced).	Two 3.7cm machine guns (400 rounds), 153 mines, *two 3.7cm AA guns (1,200 rounds), 120 mines.	(45) 58
Senta	Steam ship, 2 decks (7 watertight compartments); depth 7.81m.	One vertical 3-cylinder triple expansion engine (one 4-bladed screw, 5.9m diameter), two cylindrical boilers (12.6atm forced).	Two 8.8cm/40 QF guns (260 rounds), approx 200 mines.	(42)
Silvana	Steam ferry, 2 decks (7 watertight compartments); depth 4.12m.	Two vertical 3-cylinder triple expansion engines (two 3-bladed screws, 3.4m diameter), four cylindrical boilers (12.5atm forced).	Two 3.7cm machine guns (400 rounds), 80–100 mines.	(48)
Wotan	Steam ship, 2 decks (7 watertight compartments); depth 7.84m.	One vertical 3-cylinder triple expansion engine (one 4-bladed screw), three cylindrical boilers (13atm forced).	320 mines.	(28)

* Weapons and other equipment shipped at the artillery and mine depots at Cuxhaven and Friedrichsort near Kiel.
† In the former saloon, used as mine storage space.

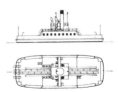

Primus (1914). *Mrva*

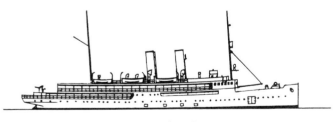

Rügen (1915).

Rügen: launched 21 Feb 1914, commissioned 21 Nov 1914 as an auxiliary mine dispersal steamer in the Baltic; converted to a barrack ship for submarine training, 4 Jul 1918; taken as British prize, 14 Mar 1919, but not accepted; returned 17 Apr 1919 to the sea bathing service; used as hospital ship in the North Sea from 25 Sept 1939, and in the Baltic in 1942. Out of service 20 Sept 1945; taken as Soviet prize 11 Mar 1946 and renamed *Ivan Susanin*; stricken 1960.

Senta: launched 1905 as the cargo steamer *Duns Law*; upon outbreak of war detained at Nordenham 4 Aug 1914; served as an auxiliary ship with the North Sea Patrol Group 1914; auxiliary mine dispersal steamer in the Baltic 13 Feb 1917; returned 16 Dec 1918; renamed *Ravensworth* 1919; broken up 1929.

Silvana: launched 4 Apr 1897, commissioned 5 Aug 1914 as an auxiliary mine dispersal steamer in the Baltic; no service; returned Nov 1914; became leader ship of a Baltic convoy escort flotilla (*Hs 19, 49, 71* and *74*) Mar 1915; served with a patrol half-flotilla in the Baltic 1 Mar 1918; returned 30 Nov 1918; taken as a French prize 1919; repurchased 1920; broken up 1924.

Wotan: launched 28 Apr 1908 as the cargo steamer *St Johann*; renamed *Oswiga* 1912; renamed *Wotan* 1915; start of conversion 6 Apr 1916; commissioned 14 Aug 1916 as an auxiliary mine dispersal steamer for the Baltic; returned 17 Apr 1917; taken as British prize 3 Apr 1919; became Italian *Wotan* 1926, British *Berkdale* 1927, Latvian *Everolanda* 1933, Soviet *Everolanda* 1940; renamed *Janis Rainis* 1960; broken up in the USSR 1967.

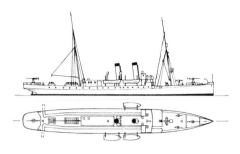

Prinz Adalbert (1914); *Prinz Sigismund* and *Prinz Waldemar* were similar. *Mrva*

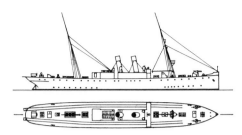

Silvana (1914). *Mrva*

Mine hulks and storage vessels 1914–1918

Comet: launched 15 Nov 1892, ex-aviso (see vol 1, page 96); used as a mine hulk at Emden after 1913; broken up at Hamburg 1921.

Condor: launched 23 Feb 1892, ex-fourth rate cruiser (see vol 1, pages 97–98), 1628t, no engines, 34-man military crew plus ten-man civilian crew; used as a mine hulk at Kiel-Friedrichsort in 1916; stricken 18 Nov 1920; broken up at Hamburg 1921.

Greif: launched 29 Jul 1886, ex-light cruiser (aviso) (see vol 1, page 93); became a mine storage hulk at Kiel-Heikendorf in 1917; broken up at Hamburg 1921.

Prinzess Wilhelm: launched 22 Sept 1887, ex-light cruiser (cruiser corvette) (see vol 1, pages 94–95); used as a mine storage hulk at Danzig from Feb 1914, then at Kiel and later at Wilhelmshaven; broken up at Wilhelmshaven 1922.

Seeadler: launched 2 Feb 1892, ex-fourth rate cruiser (see vol 1, pages 97–98); became a mine storage ship at Vareler Tief from 16 Sept 1915; sunk in Jade bay after an explosion on 19 Apr 1917, position 53° 29'N, 08° 12'E; no casualties.

Alsleben: launched 1909 as a cargo steamer for the Saaleschiffahrt shipping company of Hamburg; 299ldt, 51.42 × 6.00m, 300ihp, 11kts, two screws, 9 plus 1 men; served at the Friedrichsort Mine Depot; returned; converted to a motor vessel 1927; taken as Soviet prize 1945.

Antonie: launch date unknown; inland towing barge, owner Hackert; 713ldt, 3 plus 1 men; served at the Friedrichsort mine depot, dates unknown.

Blau: launch date unknown; inland towing barge, owner Karl Blau; 567ldt, 3 plus 1 men; served at the Friedrichsort mine depot, dates unknown.

City of Leeds: launched 8 Jun 1903 as a cargo/ passenger steamer for The Great Central Railway, Grimsby; 1349gt, 78.18 × 10.50m, 2500ihp, 16kts, 55 men; detained at Hamburg upon outbreak of war 4 Aug 1914; served at the Friedrichsort Mine Depot from 1914, as not serviceable; returned 20 Jan 1919, broken up at Blyth 1936.

Colchester: launched 1889 as a cargo steamer for the Great Eastern Railway Co, Harwich; 964gt, 85.54 × 9.45m, 14kts; taken as a prize by *V 47* and *V 67* in the North Sea 21 Sept 1916 and taken to Zeebrugge; used as a mine storage ship at Bruges from 1916; transferred to the Baltic Sept 1917; provisions steamer at Oesel 8 Nov 1917; stranded and sank at Laboe 2 Mar 1918; raised; returned 1919 but not repaired; broken up.

Diplomat: launch date unknown, inland towing barge, owner Michaelis; 705ldt, 3 plus 1 men; served at the Friedrichsort mine depot, dates unknown.

Esther: launch date unknown, Russian schooner; seized by Germany on the occupation of Libau; no other information available.

Frieda: launch date unknown, steam ship for Steffen Sohst, Kiel; 75gt; served at the Friedrichsort mine depot, dates unknown.

Fulda: launched 1899 as a sea lighter for Hapag, Hamburg; 738gt, 1200ldt, no engine, 8 plus 2 men; served at the Friedrichsort mine depot, dates unknown; returned 1919; still in existence in 1928; fate unknown.

HK 20: launch date unknown; iron barge; prize ship, two men; transferred to Port Captain, Libau, dates unknown.

HK 22: launch date unknown, iron barge; prize ship, one man; served at the mine depot, Libau, dates unknown.

Henriette: launch date unknown, inland towing barge, owner Otto Briest sen; 628ldt, 3 plus 1 men; served at the Friedrichsort mine depot, dates unknown.

Johannes: launch date unknown, Russian schooner; seized by Germany on the occupation of Libau; transferred to Port Captain, Libau, dates unknown.

Mariechen I: launch date unknown, inland towing barge, owner Otto Peters; 767ldt, 3 plus 1 men; served at the Friedrichsort mine depot, dates unknown.

Mariechen II: launch date unknown, inland towing barge, owner Otto Briest jun; 582ldt, 3 plus 1 men; served at the Friedrichsort mine depot, dates unknown.

Mosel: launched 1901 as a sea lighter for Hapag, Hamburg; 740gt, 1200ldt, no engine, 9 plus 2 men; served at the Friedrichsort mine depot, dates unknown.

Ottilie: launch date unknown, inland towing barge, owner Rüsske; 569ldt, 3 plus 1 men; served at the Friedrichsort mine depot, dates unknown.

Rhein: launched 1899 as a sea lighter for Hapag, Hamburg; 739gt, 1200ldt, no engine, 8 plus 2 men; served at the Friedrichsort mine depot, dates unknown. Returned 1919; in existence in 1928; fate unknown.

Saratow: launched 1888 as a steam ship for the Russian North-West Shipping Co, Libau; taken as a prize while serving as a Russian blockship at Libau, 8 May 1915; 1679gt, 79.55 × 10.39m, 850ihp, 10kts, 16 men; transferred to Port Captain, Libau, 1915; became the Latvian *Saratov* 1921; stranded and sank at Libau 14 Jan 1923.

Schulze: launch date unknown, inland towing barge, owner Wilhelm Schulze; 707ldt, 3 plus 1 men; served at the Friedrichsort mine depot, dates unknown.

Stitterich: launch date unknown, inland towing barge, owner Wilhelm Stitterich; 747ldt, 3 plus 1 men; served at the Friedrichsort mine depot, dates unknown.

Waterploeg: launched 1910 as a galleas for H Sloots, Groningen; 140gt, 30.35 × 5.99 × 2.18m; taken as a prize 4 Aug 1918; served at the Friedrichsort mine depot.

Werra: launched 1900 as a sea lighter for Hapag, Hamburg; 734gt, 1200ldt, no engine, 8 plus 2 men; served at the Friedrichsort mine depot, dates unknown, returned 1919; still in existence in 1928; fate unknown.

Mine hulk *Seeadler* (1915). *Mrva*

Mine transports and minelayers 1920–1945

From 1920 to 1935 no units intended exclusively as minelayers were designed for the German fleet. Destroyers (24 to 60 mines), torpedo boats (20 to 50 mines), M boats (30 mines), R boats (6 to 12 mines) and S boats (4 to 8 mines) were intended to assume this task in the event of mobilisation.

In addition, it was intended that the artillery training ships *Brummer* and *Bremse* and the aviso *Grille* would be fitted out as minelayers.

The first attempt to procure minelayers occurred in 1936–37, when a bid was made to purchase four mine ships belonging to the Spanish fleet. When these efforts failed, a design was drawn up for service in the Baltic-northern North Sea region. These ships were included in the Z plan, but with a low priority rating.

A class offensive minelayers

Name	Builder (construction no)	Built	Cost in Marks (000s)	Displacement (t = tonnes T = tons)	Length (m)	Breadth (m)	Draught (m)	Power (hp)	Revs (rpm)	Speed (kts)	Range (nm/kts)	Coal (t)	Oil (t)
A, C	Deschimag S* (625, 626)	1938–	10,000	6380t max 5750t des	152.00 oa 145.00 cwl	16.20	5.42 max 4.68 des	40,000shp des	330	28.0 des	–	–	770 max 580 des
E, F	Howaldt (H) (798, 799)	”	”	”	”	”	”	”	”	”	–		”

* From May 1943 construction of *C* was transferred to DWA (construction no 270).

Construction
Laid down as mine ships *A*, *C*, *E*, *F* (official design 1937–38); transverse frame steel construction (16 watertight compartments, double bottom approx 73%). The armour comprised 20mm WH (hard) steel outer plating in way of the mine launching equipment (frames 0–10); depth 11.45m.

Propulsion
Two sets of Deschimag turbines (two screws, 3.4m diameter) in 1 + 1 engine rooms; four Wagner high-pressure boilers (45atm forced, 400°) in 1 + 1 boiler rooms; two turbo generators; one rudder.

Armament
Eight 10.5cm QF guns (3200 rounds); eight 3.7cm AA guns (8000 rounds); 400 EMC mines

Complement
Crew: 19/422, later reduced to 320. Boats: one launch, one pinnace, one cutter, two yawls, one dinghy.

Notes
One ship's aircraft with catapult and landing sail was planned, but this was abandoned in 1938 in favour of doubled gun armament.

Careers
A: contract granted 4 Jul 1938; intended completion according to the Z Plan was 1 Jul 1941; cancelled Sept 1939.

C: contract granted 4 Jul 1938; transferred to Deutsche Werft, Hamburg, 4 May 1939; intended completion 1 Jun 1942; cancelled Sept 1939.

E: contract granted 12 May 1939; intended completion according to the Z Plan was 1 Jul 1942; cancelled Sept 1939.

F: contract granted 12 May 1939; intended completion according to the Z Plan was 1 Jan 1943; cancelled Sept 1939.

Contracts were awarded for the gunnery training ships *B* and *D*, and the cadet training ships *G* and *H*, built to the same design. In the event of mobilisation these ships were also to be fitted with mine rails.

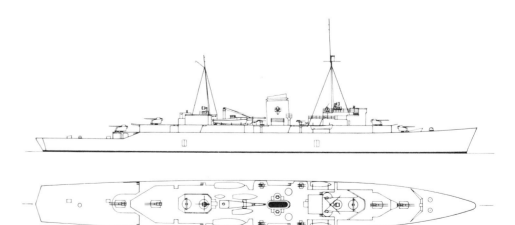

Mine ships *A*, *C*, *E* and *F* (1938 design). *Mrva*

Mine transports

Name	Builder (construction nos)	Built	Gross tonnage	Displacement (t = tonnes T = tons)	Length (m)	Breadth (m)	Draught (m)	Hull depth (m)	Power (hp)	Speed (kts)	Range (nm/kts)	Coal (t)	Oil (t)
Lauting	Oderwerke	1934	867gt	1253t max	56.70 oa 53.30 cwl	10.41	4.41	5.21	450ehp des	9.5 max 7.9 des	3000/9	–	35.2
Rhein	,, (777)	,,	899gt	,,	,,	,,	,,	,,	,,	,,	,,	–	,,
Otter	Schichau (E) (1292)	1935	902gt	1220t max	56.70 oa 53.00 cwl	10.40	,,	,,	,,	9.5 max	,,	–	
Irben	,, (1351)	1936	900gt	1158t max	,,	10.38	,,	,,	,,	,,	,,	–	

Careers

Lauting: launched 1934, commissioned 1934 as a mine transporter at the Wilhelmshaven Arsenal; served under the Commodore, mine ships, from 20 Aug 1943; served with the GM/SA 1945; taken as a US prize and transferred to OMGUS 8 Dec 1947; became motor vessel *Lauting* for HAL, Hamburg, 23 Jan 1948; sold into private ownership 4 Jun 1954; owned by Emder Verkehrs AG 1956; sold to Schulte & Bruns, Emden, 1960; sold to HP Vith of Flensburg as *Alnor* Oct 1961; to Greece as *Kadiani* 1969; sunk 16 Mar 1969 in a storm, in the vicinity of Flamborough Head, position 55° 49′N, 02° 07′E.

Rhein: launched 1934, commissioned 1934 as a mine transporter for the Wilhelmshaven Arsenal; served under the Commodore, mine ships, from 20 Aug 1943; served with the GM/SA 1945; taken as a US prize and transferred to OMGUS, Dec 1947; became motor vessel *Klaus Leonhardt* for Leonhardt & Blumberg, Hamburg, 23 May 1949; renamed *Uhlenhorst* for Johannes Ick, Hamburg, 1950; broken up Nov 1964.

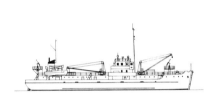

Irben (1940). *Mrva*

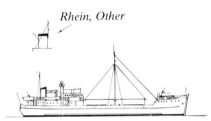

Rhein, Other

Lauting (1943); *other* and *Rhein* were similar. *Mrva*

Otter: launched 1934, commissioned 1934 as a mine transporter for the Cuxhaven Arsenal; served under the Commodore, mine ships, from 10 Apr 1943. Sunk by a mine explosion at 1730hrs on 20 Jun 1944 in vicinity of Kotka, after being hit by a bomb from a Soviet aircraft, position 60° 28′N, 26° 56′E; casualties unknown. Raised and repaired; became Finnish motor vessel *Anita* in 1950; became Swedish *Portos* in 1956; Italian *Pupi* in 1964; renamed *Lilion* 1966; broken up 1982.

Irben: launched 1936, commissioned 1936 as a mine transporter for the Cuxhaven Arsenal; served under the Commodore, mine ships, from 10 Apr 1943. Sunk at Kiel-Mönkeberg by bombs from a US aircraft on 3 Apr 1945; wreck broken up.

Name	Type and construction	Propulsion	Armament	Complement
Lauting, Rhein	Mine transporter, 2 decks; depth 5.21m.	One Sulzer 4-cylinder 2-stroke diesel engine (one 4-bladed screw, 2.4m diameter).	Four 2cm AA guns, 300–370 mines.	4/39
Otter, Irben	Mine transporter, 2 decks; depth 5.21m.	One Sulzer 4-cylinder 2-stroke diesel engine (one 4-bladed screw, 2.4m diameter). *Otter* [one MWN 6-cylinder 4-stroke diesel engine from 1941].	Four 2cm AA guns; 300–370 mines (*Otter*); 240 mines (*Irben*).	2/38

Foreign minelayers (1939–1945)

Ex-Norwegian minelayers

Name	Builder (construction no)	Built	Displacement (t = tonnes T = tons)	Length (m)	Breadth (m)	Draught (m)	Hull depth (m)	Power (hp)	Speed (kts)	Range (nm/kts)	Coal (t)	Oil (t)
Brummer (II)	Hovedverft (119)	1931–34	1860t max 1763t des 1596t std	97.30 oa 92.50 cwl	11.45	4.03 max 3.60 des	7.19	6000shp + 1400ehp des	22.0 max 19.0 des	3000/14	–	200 max
Kamerun, Togo	Nylands	1939	370t max 320t des	52.10 oa 50.90 cwl	7.05	2.00 max 1.83 des		900ihp des	12.0 max (13.5 des)	1400/9	–	
Laugen, Glommen	Akers	1916–17	380t max 335t des	43.30 oa 41.90 cwl	8.45	1.89		170ihp des	9.5 des		21	–
Tyr	Hovedverft (67)	1887	294t max 270t des	31.80 oa 28.00 cwl	8.60	2.20	2.45	450ihp max 400ihp des	10.5 max 10.0 des	750/8	22	–
Gor	" (64)	1884	280t max 268t des	31.80 oa 30.00 cwl	"	2.10		420ihp max 450ihp des	10.0 max 10.5 des	800/10	"	–
Nor, Brage, Vidar	Hovedverft (57, 58, 60)	1878–82	270t max 255t des	29.00 oa	7.90	2.00		230ihp max 200ihp des	10.0 max 8.0 des	600/8	"	–
Vale, Uller	" (54, 55)	1874–76	250t max 238t des	27.00 oa	"	2.10 fwd 1.90 aft		210ihp max 200ihp des	8.0 des	"	"	–

Career

Brummer (II): launched 21 Dec 1932, commissioned 21 Jun 1934 as the Norwegian minelayer *Olav Tryggvason*; surrendered intact at Horten 9 Apr 1940; commissioned as German minelayer *Albatross* 11 Apr 1940; renamed mine ship *Brummer* (II) 16 May 1940; severely damaged in a US air raid while in dock V at Deutsche Werke Kiel 3 Apr 1945, and left irreparable; wreck broken up 1945–48.

Kamerun: launched 1939, commissioned 1940 as the Norwegian mine sweeper *Rauma*; surrendered damaged at Horten 9 Apr 1940; commissioned as minelayer and patrol boat *Kamerun (NO 01)* 18 Apr 1940, for the Oslo Harbour Defence Flotilla; became *V 5908* in 1941; serviceable at Horten in May 1945; taken over by the GM/SA; returned in 1947; stricken 1963.

Togo: launched 5 Aug 1939, commissioned 1940 as the Norwegian minesweeper *Otra*; captured at Filtvet by the torpedo boat *Möwe* 9 Apr 1940; commissioned 10 Apr 1940 as minelayer and patrol boat *Togo*; became *NO 02* in the Oslo Harbour Defence Flotilla 16 Apr 1940; became *V 5908* 25 Mar 1941; later served at *NT 05*, then *V 6512*; serviceable at Untereidet in May 1945; taken over by the GM/SA; returned 1947; stricken 1963.

Laugen: launched 1916, commissioned 1917 as the Norwegian minelayer *Laugen*; surrendred intact at Melsomvik 14 Apr 1940; commissioned 27 Mar 1941 as *NN 05* for service on the U-boat mine barrage in the Narvik region; serviceable at the Harstad naval base in May 1945; returned; stricken 1950; late sold and converted to motor ferry *Rosenberg VI*; when under ownership of Moss Rosenberg Verft AS, was condemned 2 May 1979 and later sunk by gunfire off west coast of Norway during a naval exercise.

Glommen: launched 1916, commissioned 1917 as the Norwegian minelayer *Glommen*; surrendered intact at Melsomvik 14 Apr 1940; commissioned as a U-boat tender in Drontheimfjord 27 Jul 1940; served as a minelayer in the Kirkenes region from 25 Mar 1941 as *NKi 01*; sunk in Drontheimfjord by an aircraft bomb, 17 Nov 1944.

Tyr: launched 16 Mar 1887, commissioned 1887 as a Norwegian second rate gunboat; served as submarine tender from 14 Apr 1910; converted to a minelayer 1914; taken as a German prize at Storsund 20 Apr 1940; commissioned 1 May 1940 as a minelayer for the Bergen Harbour Defence Flotilla (together with *Uller*); returned May 1945; stricken, converted to a crane barge; sold to Bergen owners 1951, converted to cargo vessel and renamed *Bjorn-West*; converted to ferry 1953; sold 1987 to owner at Haugesund; still in service.

Gor: launched 7 May 1884, commissioned 1885 as a Norwegian second rate gunboat; converted to a minelayer 1911–13; surrendered at Kjelkenes to *M 1* and *S 12* 13 May 1940; commissioned as a loading ship for U-boat batteries; converted to steam production ship for torpedo boats at Bergen 1940–41; returned May 1945; stricken 1946; sold and converted to an oil lighter; broken up.

Vidar: launched 31 Jan 1882, commissioned 1882 as a Norwegian second rate gunboat; converted to a minelayer 1911–13; surrendered intact at

Melsomvik 14 Apr 1940; commissioned 1940 as *NK 31* to serve as a minelayer in the Kristiansand S Harbour Defence Flotilla; under repair at Kristiansand S May 1945; returned; stricken 1947; sold; fate unknown.

Brage: launched 1 Nov 1878, commissioned 1879 as a Norwegian second rate gunboat; converted to a minelayer 1911–13; surrendered at Melsomvik 14 Apr 1940; service unknown; returned Apr 1945; stricken.

Nor: launched 23 Oct 1878, commissioned 1879 as a Norwegian second rate gunboat; converted to a minelayer 1911–13; surrendered intact at Melsomvik 14 Apr 1940; at the KM dockyard at Horten during 1941–42; returned May 1945; stricken 1949; sold and converted to motor salvage vessel *Flatholm* (144gt); still in service as a lighter in 1984.

Uller: launched 24 Jul 1876, commissioned 1877 as Norwegian second rate gunboat; converted to a minelayer 1911–13; surrendered at Vallensviken, Bergen, 9 Apr 1940; commissioned 12 Apr 1940 as a minelayer for the Bergen Harbour Defence Flotilla, with crew of *Hanonia* (see page 000); suffered bomb damage at Storakersundet 1 May 1940, and was run aground and burnt out at Torsholmen in the Sognefjord, position 61° 06′N, 05° 04′ 06″E.

Vale: launched 14 Apr 1874, commissioned 1874 as a Norwegian second rate gunboat; converted to a minelayer 1911–13; surrendered at Kjelkenes to *M 1* and *S 12* 13 May 1940; converted to a steam production ship at Bergen 1940–41; became a steam tug for the Bergen harbourmaster in 1943; returned 1945, stricken.

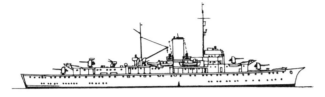

Brummer (ex *Olav Tryggvason*) (1941).

Kamerun (ex *Rauma*) and *Togo* (ex *Otra*) (1941).

Name	Type and construction	Propulsion	Armament	Complement
Brummer (II)	Minelayer; depth 7.19m.	Two sets Laval turbines with gear transmission two Sulzer 8-cylinder four-stroke diesel engines (cruise), (two 3-bladed screws, 2.6m diameter), three watertube boilers (20atm forced).	Four 12.7cm/45 QF guns, two 3.7cm AA guns, four 2cm AA guns [three 10.5 AA guns, two 3.7cm AA guns, ten 2cm AA guns after summer 1943], 280 mines.	168
Kamerun, Togo	Minesweeper.	Two vertical 3-cylinder triple expansion engines (two 3-bladed screws), one watertube boiler.	Two 7.6cm Bofors AA guns, two 2cm AA guns, two AA machine guns, number of mines unknown.	2/16 (23)
Laugen, Glommen	Minelayer.	One vertical 3-cylinder triple expansion engine (one 3-bladed screw, 1.8m diameter), one cylindrical boiler (14atm forced).	Two 7.6cm Bofors AA guns, 50 mines.	0/38
Tyr	Minelayer; depth 2.45m.	Two vertical 3-cylinder triple expansion engines (two 3-bladed screws), two cylindrical boilers (6.5atm forced).	One 12cm QF gun, two AA machine guns, 20 mines.	(44)
Gor	Minelayer; depth 2.95m.	Two vertical 3-cylinder triple expansion engines (two 3-bladed screws), two boilers.	One 7.6cm Bofors gun, two 3.7cm AA guns, 20 mines.	(45)
Nor, Brage, Vidar	Minelayer.	Two vertical 3-cylinder triple expansion engines (two 3-bladed screws), two boilers.	One 4.7cm gun, two 3.7cm AA guns, 20 mines.	0/16 (38)
Vale, Uller	Minelayer.	Two vertical 3-cylinder triple expansion engines (two 3-bladed screws), two boilers.	Two 3.7cm QF guns, 20 mines.	(41)

Ex-Yugoslav minelayers

Careers

Drache: launched 22 Jun 1929 as Yugoslav repair ship *Zmaj*; suffered an engine room fire in the vicinity of Vlissingen on 9 Sept 1929 during transfer voyage; returned to Hamburg for repair; second trials and delivery voyage 20 Aug 1930; taken as German prize at Split 17 Apr 1941; commissioned 1941 as Luftwaffe aircraft salvage ship *Drache*; served as a troop transporter under the Admiral, Aegean, from 25 Nov 1941; converted to a minelayer Apr–Aug 1942 (aircraft crane removed, funnel mantled, mine rails installed); commissioned 26 Nov 1942; set on fire in Vathi harbour, Samos, by

Name	Builder (construction no)	Built	Displacement (t = tonnes T = tons)	Length (m)	Breadth (m)	Draught (m)	Hull depth (m)	Power (hp)	Speed (kts)	Range (nm/kts)	Coal (t)	Oil (t)
Drache	DWA; Reiherstieg (118)	1929–31	1870T max	76.50 cwl	13.70	4.00 max 3.51 des		3260shp max 3000shp des	15.0 des	4000/	–	
(mod)	(Trieste)	1942										
Pasman	Jadranska	1931	142t max 130t des 125t std	30.0 oa	8.0	1.60		280ihp des	9.0 des			–

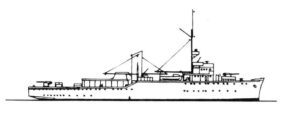

Drache (ex *Zmaj*) (1943).

low-level aircraft strafing at 1525hrs on 22 Sept 1944, position 37° 45′N, 26° 59′E. Sunk at 1725hrs after an internal explosion, total loss; 11 dead.

Pasman: launched 1931 as Yugoslav minelayer *Mosor*; taken as an Italian prize at Sibenik 22 Apr 1941; commissioned as *Pasman*; taken over at Sibenik by the crew of the Siebel ferry *SF 193* on 20 Dec 1943; sunk in Kozja Draga bay, Ist island, on 5 Jan 1944, after running aground in fog while on transfer to Pola for fitting out; crew captured by *NB 3* (partisan fleet); stricken 13 Jan 1944 as a total loss; wreck broken up 1954.

Name	Type and construction	Propulsion	Armament	Complement
Drache	Aircraft salvage ship, 2 decks.	Two MAN 8-cylinder 4-stroke diesel engines (two screws).	Two 10.5cm AA guns, five 3.7cm AA guns, six 2cm AA guns; [two 8.8cm AA guns, five 3.7cm AA guns, thirteen 2cm AA guns, from 1944; one helicopter (Jan–Feb 1943)], 120 EMC mines.	
Pasman	Minelayer (Italian *Albona* type).	Two vertical 3-cylinder triple expansion engines (two screws).	One 4.7cm/44 gun, number of mines unknown.	26 German + 4 Croat

Miscellaneous foreign minelaying vessels

Careers

Fasana: launched 29 Sept 1924, commissioned 26 Mar 1925 as the Italian minelayer *Fasana*; taken as a German prize at San Rocco dockyard, Trieste, 10 Sept 1943; commissioned 20 Apr 1944 for the 11th Security Division; returned Jul 1945; stricken 1 Sept 1950.

Kehrwieder: launched 24 Jul 1918, commissioned 20 Sept 1918 as German minesweeper *M 120* (see page 118); sold to Italy 15 Dec 1921, and became minesweeping boat *Abastro*; converted to minelayer *Cotrone* in 1925; taken over by German forces at La Spezia 9 Sept 1943; commissioned 2 Oct 1943 as minelayer *Kehrwieder* (*G 702*) for the 3rd Escort Flotilla. Sunk in dock 4, La Spezia, at 1340hrs on 19 May 1944 in an aerial attack; raised Mar 1947, repaired and returned to service as Italian merchant navy training ship *Garaventa*; stricken Sept 1968 and broken up.

Oldenburg: launched 8 May 1934, commissioned 22 Feb 1934 as *Garigliano*, an Italian water tanker with minelaying equipment; damaged at Maddalena 13 Sept 1943, and taken over by German forces as *F 844*; commissioned as *Dwarsläufer* for the 3rd Escort Flotilla 25 Nov 1943; became mine ship *Oldenburg* Feb 1944; engine burned out by an aircraft bomb at La Spezia at 0900hrs on 12 May 1944; repaired Oct–Nov 1944; scuttled at Genoa 25 Apr 1945; raised 1946 and returned to Italian service as *Garigliano*; stricken 1 Apr 1952 and broken up.

Vallelunga: launched 28 May 1924, commissioned 15 Dec 1924 as Italian mine and munitions transporter *Vallelunga*; scuttled at La Spezia 9 Sept 1943; raised Oct 1943, repaired and commissioned 31 Mar 1944 as a harbour minelayer for Genoa;

Oldenburg (ex *Garigliano*) (1944). *Mrva*

Vallelunga and *Westmark* (ex *Panigaglia*) (1943).

Name	Type and construction	Propulsion	Armament	Complement
Fasana	Minelayer.	Two Fiat 2-stroke diesel engines (two 3-bladed screws, 1.4m diameter), [two new diesel engines installed Nov 1944].	One 7.6cm QF gun (200 rounds), six 2cm guns, 180 mines.	66
Kehrwieder	Minelayer; depth 3.27m.	Two vertical 3-cylinder triple expansion engines (two 3-bladed screws, 1.97 diameter), two Marine-type boilers.	One 3.7cm AA gun, five 2cm Oerlikon AA guns (eight planned), three AA machine guns (four planned), 24–44 mines.	3/63
Oldenburg	Water carrier.	Two Fiat 6-cylinder 2-stroke diesel engines (two 3-bladed screws, 2.1m diameter).	Two 3.7cm AA guns, 14 2cm AA guns, 136 PS mines – 145 mines.	
Vallelunga, Westmark	Munition transporter; depth 3.35m.	Two vertical 3-cylinder triple expansion engines (two 3-bladed screws, 2.1m diameter), two Thornycroft watertube boilers (15atm forced).	30–35 mines.	
Albona, Laurana, Rovigno	Minelayer, ex Austro-Hungarian mine tender, 1 deck (3 watertight compartments); depth 2.1m.	Two vertical 2-cylinder double expansion engines (two 3-bladed screws, 1.4m diameter), one Yarrow watertube boiler (13.5atm forced).	Two 7.6cm QF guns, six 2cm AA guns, 20–34 mines.	19 (27)
Alula, Gallipoli, Otranto	Escort gunboat; depth 3.0–3.3m.	One vertical 3-cylinder triple expansion engine (one screw), one cylindrical boiler.	Two 7.6cm QF guns; (one 3.7cm gun only in *Alula*), 30 mines.	0/24

Name	Builder (construction no)	Built	Displacement (t = tonnes T = tons)	Length (m)	Breadth (m)	Draught (m)	Hull depth (m)	Power (hp)	Speed (kts)	Range (nm/kts)	Coal (t)	Oil (t)
Fasana	Castellamare	1924	705T max 652t des 530T std	66.32 oa 58.59 cwl	9.75 9.30	2.00 max 1.90 des		700ehp max 700ehp des	6.0 max 10.0 des	700/10	–	20
Kehrwieder	Neptun (433)	1918	606T max 525t des 515T std	59.40 oa 56.10 cwl	7.40	2.40 fwd 2.30 aft	3.27	(1600ihp des)	8.0 max (14.0 des)	2400/10	130	–
Oldenburg	Tirreno	1933–34	1141T max 1055t des	66.12 cwl	10.05	4.20 max 3.10 des		600shp max	7.0 max		–	36
Vallelunga	San Giorgio	1921–24	1071T max 970t des 916T std	56.24 oa 52.51 cwl	9.00	3.00	3.35	1400ihp des	8.0 max (11.0 des)		143	–
Albona	Danubius	1917–20	121t max 113t des	31.80 oa 29.40 cwl	6.52	1.40	2.10	280ihp des	9.0 max 11.0 des		–	4
Laurana	”	”	”	”	”	”	”	”	”		–	”
Rovigno	”	”	”	”	”	”	”	”	”		–	”
Alula	Seikishi	1912	430t max	40.10 pp	6.49			480ihp max	7.0 max (13.0 des)			–
Gallipoli	Osaka I W	1911	400t max 310t des	36.04 oa 33.80 cwl	6.72	2.80	3.00 to 3.30	340ihp max	7.0 max (11.0 des)	2000/8		–
Otranto	Smith's Dock (474)	1911	385t max 350t des 290t std	(36.00 oa) 33.84 cwl	6.38	2.70	3.00 to 3.30	550ihp max	9.0 max (10.0 des)	2000/8		–

sunk at Genoa at 1100hrs on 28 May 1944 following an explosion after being hit by an aircraft bomb; number of casualties unknown.

Westmark: launched 10 Jul 1923, commissioned 15 Dec 1924 as Italian mine and munitions transporter *Panigaglia*; taken over by German forces 8 Sept 1943 at La Spezia. Sunk in the bay of La Spezia by an aircraft bomb Oct 1943; raised 11 Jan–20 Apr 1944, repaired and commissioned 28 Sept 1944 as mine ship *Westmark*; scuttled at La Spezia 29 Apr 1945; raised 1946 and returned; sank in San Stefano harbour after an accidental explosion 1 Jul 1947.

Albona: launched 20 Jul 1918 as Austro-

Hungarian mine tender *MT 130*; completed by the dockyard on its own account after Nov 1918; purchased 3 Jan 1920 by the Italian navy as minesweeper *RD 58*; became minelayer *Albona* 2 Jul 1921; with *Gallipoli, Otranto* and *Rovigno* on minelaying service in the Cyclades 9 Sept 1943; entered Syros harbour and surrendered to German navy 10 Sept 1943; became *Netztender 57* (net tender) with the Net Barrage Flotilla South; scuttled at Saloniki 31 Oct 1944.

Laurana: launched 24 Aug 1918 as Austro-Hungarian mine tender *MT 131*; completed by the dockyard on its own account after Nov 1918; purchased 7 Feb 1920 by Italian navy as minesweeper *RD 59*; became minelayer *Laurana* 2 Jul 1921; taken over by German forces at Venice 11 Sept 1943; commissioned 4 Oct 1943 as an Adriatic mine storage ship; served as a harbour minelayer at Trieste from 30 Sept 1944. Sunk at Trieste by a British aircraft bomb 20 Feb 1945; number of casualties unknown; wreck broken up 1949.

Rovigno: launched 28 Sept 1918 as Austro-Hungarian mine tender *MT 132*; completed by the dockyard on its own account after Nov 1918; purchased 16 Jul 1920 by Italian navy as minesweeper *RD 60*; became minelayer *Rovigno* 2 Jul 1921; fate from 9 Sept 1943 as for *Albona*, but became *Netztender 56*.

Alula: launched 1912 as Japanese steam fishing boat *Sekijo Maru*; purchased by Italian navy in 1916 and commissioned 1 Feb 1917 as minesweeper *G 23*; became gunboat *Alula* 2 Jun 1921; taken over by German forces at Piraeus 9 Sept 1943, and commissioned 10 Sept 1943 as a minelayer with the Attika Coastal Defence Flotilla; transferred to the 12th Minesweeping Flotilla, B group, as *M 1221* Dec 1943; became *GA 77* in 1944; scuttled at Saloniki 31 Oct 1944.

Gallipoli: launched 1911 as Japanese steam fishing boat *Hakata Maru No 8*; purchased by Italian navy in 1916 and commissioned 1 Feb 1917 as minesweeper *G 31*; became gunboat *Gallipoli* 15 Oct 1923; on minelaying service in the Cyclades with *Otranto, Albona,* and *Rovigno* 9 Sept 1943; entered Syros harbour and surrendered to the German navy 10 Sept 1943; commissioned 16 Sept 1943 as a minelayer for the Attika Coastal Defence Flotilla; transferred to the 12th Minesweeping Flotilla, B group, as *M 1222* Dec 1943; became *GA 79* in 1944; scuttled at Saloniki 31 Oct 1944.

Otranto: launched 1911 as steam fishing boat *Mariveles*, later Japanese steam fishing boat *Suniya Maru*; purchased by Italian navy in 1916 and commissioned 15 May 1917 as minesweeper *G 36*; became gunboat *Otranto* 15 Oct 1923; on minelaying service in the Cyclades with *Gallipoli, Albona,* and *Rovigno* 9 Sept 1943; entered Hermoupolis, Syros, and surrendered to the German navy 13 Sept 1943; commissioned 16 Sept 1943 as a minelayer for the Attika Coastal Defence Flotilla; transferred to the 12th Minesweeping Flotilla, B group, as *M 1223* Dec 1943; became *GA 78* in 1944; scuttled at Saloniki 31 Oct 1944.

Mine ships 1939–1945

Mine ships (I)

Name	Builder (construction nos)	Built	Gross tonnage	Displacement (t = tonnes T = tons)	Length (m)	Breadth (m)	Draught (m)	Hull depth (m)	Power (hp)	Speed (kts)	Range and fuel (nm/kts/t)	Owner
Adjutant	Smith's Dock (1050)	1937	354gt		42.80 oa 40.97 cwl	8.02	3.47	4.47	1600ihp max	14.0 max	5000/14/112 oil	Hvalfanger-selsk. 'Polaris' AS, Larvik
Barbara	John Brown	1908	2345gt	c1900t max	104.50 oa 100.90 cwl	13.16	3.70	5.37	9500shp max	19.0 max	/ /191 coal	LNER, Harwich
Brandenburg	FCM (S)	1936	3894gt		106.70 oa 101.70 cwl	15.00	5.70	7.85	4800shp max	15.0 max		Chargeurs Reunis, Le Havre
Bulgaria	WR Co	1894	1108gt		77.80 oa 73.30 cwl	10.21	5.77	6.33	1200ihp des		/ /170 coal	Soc. Commerciale Bulgare de Navigation à Vapeur, Varna

Careers

Adjutant: launched 1937 as *Pol IX*; taken as a prize by the armed merchant cruiser *Pinguin* 14 Jan 1941; served as tender *Adjutant* from 10 Feb 1941; fitted out as an auxiliary mine ship from 24 May 1941 (with weapons from *Pinguin* and a range finder from the prize motor passenger liner *Rangitane*), operating off New Zealand; scuttled after engine failure at 1600hrs on 1 Jul 1941 near Chatham Island, by gunfire from *Pinguin*.

Barbara: launched 1908 as turbine ferry *Munich*; renamed *St Denis* later; scuttled at Rotterdam 12 May 1940; raised; in German hands 1 Nov 1940, conversion to a mine ship planned, but engine and other machinery unserviceable; served as a barrack ship at Kiel until 1949, then broken up.

Brandenburg: launched 1936 as *Kita*; taken over in the south of France 18 Dec 1942; planned as *SG 8*

Name	Type and construction	Propulsion	Armament	Complement
Adjutant	Whaler (3 watertight compartments); depth 4.47m.	One vertical 3-cylinder triple expansion engine (one 4-bladed screw), one watertube boiler (15.8atm forced).	One 6cm/18 boat gun (260 rounds), two 2cm AA guns (2000 rounds), 20 TMB mines.	2/14
Barbara	Turbine ferry, 2 decks + shelter deck; depth 5.37m.	Three sets Parsons turbines (three 4-bladed screws), two Thornycroft boilers (14atm forced).	Number of mines unknown.	(60)
Brandenburg	Turbine fruit carrier, 4 hatches, 2 decks + shelter deck; depth 7.85m.	Two geared turbines (two 4-bladed screws, 5.2m diameter), three Prudhon-Capus oil-fired boilers (16atm forced).	Three 10.5cm/45 QF guns, three 3.7cm AA guns, eighteen 2cm AA guns, six depth charge launchers (100 rounds), 225 EMC mines, 260 UMB mines.	
Bulgaria	Steam ship (spar decker), (5 watertight compartments); depth 6.33m.	One vertical 3-cylinder triple expansion engine (one 4-bladed screw, 4.7m diameter), two cylindrical boilers (7atm forced).	Number of mines unknown.	84

Feb/Mar 1943; commissioned as mine ship 1 May 1943. Sunk at 1647hrs on 21 Sept 1943 in the vicinity of Capraia, position 43° 06′ 5″N, 10° 01′ 2″E, by a torpedo from the British submarine *Unseen*; 25 dead.

Bulgaria: launched Aug 1894 as *Bulgaria*; commissioned 16 Mar 1942. Sunk at 1523hrs on 8 Oct 1943 south of Amorgos, position approx 36° 46′, 25° 51′, by a torpedo from the British submarine *Unruly*; 39 dead.

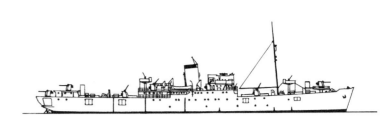

Brandenburg (ex *Kita*) (1943).

Mine ships (II)

Name	Builder (construction nos)	Built	Gross tonnage	Displacement (t = tonnes T = tons)	Length (m)	Breadth (m)	Draught (m)	Hull depth (m)	Power (hp)	Speed (kts)	Range and fuel (nm/kts/t)	Owner
Cobra (mod)	Vulcan (657) Howaldt (H)	1926 1939	2131gt	2760t max	87.41 oa 82.40 cwl	12.22	2.97	6.20	3600shp max	17.0 max	2180/17/196 oil	Hamburg-Amerika-Linie Hamburg
Cyrnos	Weser (873)	1929	2406gt	3230t max	94.50 oa 89.30 cwl	12.52	5.80 max 5.20 des	7.64	3700ehp max 3300ehp des	16.1 max 15.0 des	/ /108 oil	Cie de Navigation Fraissinet, Marseille
Dietrich von Bern	Bacino (121)	1934	984gt		66.70 oa 62.20 cwl	9.85	3.62	4.04	915ihp max (1470ihp des)	8.0 max (13.5 des)		SA di Nav. 'La Meridionale'
Doggerbank	H & W (686 G)	1926	5154gt		133.70 oa 128.10 cwl	16.41	7.80	8.07	2300shp max	11.0 max	/ /1030 oil	Bank Line Ltd, Glasgow
Elsass (mod)	FCM (L) Schelde	1930 1942	2687gt*	3648t max	103.50 oa 99.40 cwl	13.72	3.70	7.62	14,260shp max 10,000 shp des	23.3 max 19.5 des	1500/19/	SA de Gérance et d'Armement, Le Havre

* German measurement.

Careers

Cobra: launched 14 Jan 1926, commissioned 26 Aug 1939; capsized and sunk in a US air raid on the Gusto dockyard near Schiedam at 1700hrs on 27 Aug 1942; four dead; wreck broken up.

Cyrnos: launched 21 Mar 1929 as a French motor passenger vessel; became French patrol ship *P 2* 1940; taken as a German prize Aug 1940; commissioned 1 May 1943 as *SG 13* (see vol 1, page 236) damaged by an aircraft bomb 83nm south of Naples at 1820hrs on 11 Jul 1943; towed in to La Ciotat 4 Aug 1943; converted to a minelayer after 13 Oct 1943 and commissioned in 1944; scuttled at Marseille 24 Aug 1944; raised Apr 1945 and repaired; in service as *Cyrnos* 1947; broken up Nov 1966.

Dietrich von Bern: launched 1934 as Italian steam ferry *Mazara*; converted to Italian auxiliary cruiser and minelayer *D 24* 18 Sept 1940; taken as a German prize 9 Sept 1943; commissioned 2 Apr 1944; sunk at 2250hrs on 13 Aug 1944 off Genoa, position 44° 24′N, 08° 57′E by British bombs; one dead; later raised and repaired as steam ferry *Mazara*; broken up in Italy 1965.

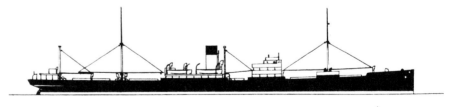

Doggerbank (ex *Speybank*) (1942).

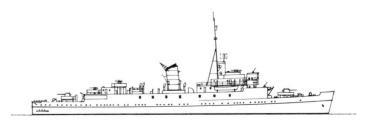

Elsass (ex *Cote d'Azur*) (1943). *Mrva*

Name	Type and construction	Propulsion	Armament	Complement
Cobra	Turbine ferry (see bathing ship), 2 decks (9 watertight compartments); depth 6.20m.	Two sets geared turbines (two 4-bladed screws), two marine-type boilers (14atm forced).	Two 8.8cm AA guns (400 rounds), one 3.7cm gun, two 2cm AA guns, 150 EMC mines.	(78) approx. 200
Cyrnos (SG 13)	Motor passenger vessel, 2 decks + shelter deck (9 watertight compartments); depth 7.64m.	Two MAN 6-cylinder 2-stroke diesel engines (two 4-bladed screws).	Three 10.5cm/65 guns, four 3.7cm AA guns, sixteen 2cm AA guns, 220 mines.	194
Dietrich von Bern	Steam ferry, 2 decks + shelter deck; depth 4.04m.	One vertical 3-cylinder triple expansion engine (one 4-bladed screw), two cylindrical boilers (15atm forced).	Two 7.6cm QF guns, two 3.7cm Breda AA guns, eight 2cm Scotti AA guns, four AA machine guns.	
Doggerbank (Schiff 53)	Motor vessel, (2) decks (8 watertight compartments); depth 8.07m.	Two Harland & Wolff 6-cylinder 4-stroke diesel engines (two 4-bladed screws, 5.8m diameter).	One 10.5cm/45 QF gun, two 2cm AA guns, 155 EMC mines, 55 EMF mines, 70 TMB mines.	
Elsass	Turbine ferry (14 watertight compartments), 2 decks + shelter deck; depth 7.62m.	Two sets Parsons geared turbines (two 3-bladed screws, 2.9m diameter), four Babcock-Wilcox boilers (17 atm forced).	Two 10.5cm AA guns, 16 2cm AA guns, helicopter (temporarily), 150 UMB–180 EMC mines.	1/208 (+ 46 helicopter crew).

Doggerbank: launched Apr 1926 as *Speybank*; taken as a prize by *Atlantis* 31 Jan 1941; returned to France disguised as the British freighter *Springbank*; converted; served Mar and Apr 1942 as an auxiliary warship (including minelaying operations off Cape Town) in the interim, then served as a blockade breaker to and from Japan. Sunk in error in the mid-Atlantic, position 29° 10′N, 34° 10′W, 4 Mar 1943 by a torpedo from German U-boat *U 43* because she had returned from Japan a month too early; number of casualties unknown. As a U-boat support ship she carried 50 torpedoes and 70 TMB mines.

Elsass: launched 1930 as *Cote d'Azur*; sunk 27 May

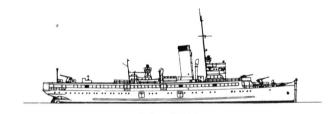

Cobra (1940).

1940 in vicinity of Dunkirk, position 51° 03′N, 02° 24′E, by bombs from German aircraft; raised Jan 1941 and repaired; converted to barrack ship *Elsass* in 1942 and commissioned 18 Oct 1942;

served from 2 Sept to 19 Nov 1943 as a helicopter training ship, and also in Feb 1944. Sunk at 0429hrs on 5 Jan 1945 east of Samsö, position 55° 43′N, 10° 40′E, by a German mine; 87 dead.

Mine ships (III)

Careers

Hanonia: launched Oct 1900 as Russian steam ship *Alexei Gorisinov*; sold to Sweden as *Drott* 1904; renamed *Smaland* 1917; sold to Finland as *Hanø* 1934; sold to Estonia as *Hanonia* 1939; taken as a prize by *U 34* off Norway, 24 Sept 1939; commissioned 2 Mar 1940 as mine ship *Schiff II*; became *Schiff III* 2 Apr 1940; grounded in Soerfjord 11 Apr 1940; salvaged 12 Apr 1940 and repaired; served as a mine storage ship for the Bergen Barrage Arsenal from 9 Jul 1942; probably sunk in the Baltic before the end of the war.

Hansestadt Danzig: launched 17 Mar 1926, commissioned 30 Aug 1939; sunk at 1908hrs on 9 Jul 1941 south of Ölandsund Östbygrund, position 56° 12′N, 16° 17′E, by a Swedish mine together with *Preussen* (see page 189) and *Tannenberg* (see page 191); 9 dead; wreck broken up in 1952.

Hansestadt Danzig: launched 1937 as Norwegian motor ferry *Peter Wessel*; purchased by the Kriegsmarine Aug 1939; commissioned as troop transporter 30 Aug 1939; transferred to the control of the Commodore, mine ships 12 Dec 1944, and con-

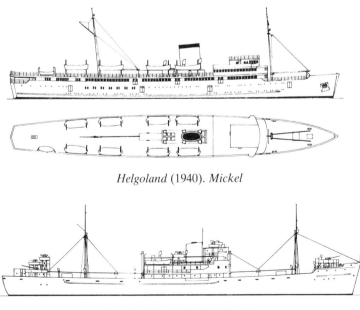

Helgoland (1940). *Mickel*

Kiebitz (ex *Ramb III*) (1944). *Mrva*

Name	Builder (construction nos)	Built	Gross tonnage	Displacement (t = tonnes T = tons)	Length (m)	Breadth (m)	Draught (m)	Hull depth (m)	Power (hp)	Speed (kts)	Range and fuel (nm/kts/t)	Owner
Hanonia (mod)	Grangemouth (208) Stülcken	1900 1939–40	1813gt*		85.16 oa 83.34 cwl	12.90	5.13	6.05	1000ihp des	6.0 max (8.0 des)	/ /423 coal	N Lopato, Karessaare
Hansestadt Danzig (mod)	Vulcan (678) Oderwerke	1926 1939	2431gt		90.50 cwl	11.70	c4.50	5.80	6400shp max	20.0 max	2000/16/	Reichs-verkehrs-ministerium, Stettin (Norddeut-scher Lloyd)
Hansestadt Danzig (ex Peter Wessel)	Aalborg (56)	1937	1415gt		72.55 oa 68.00 cwl	13.00	4.40	4.90	2560ehp max	15.5 max	1200/15/109 oil	Norsk-Dansk Turistraart AS, Larvik
Helgoland	Lindenau	1939	2947gt	3545t max	(113.00 oa) 106.50 cwl	13.20	3.50	4.80	4400shp max 4000shp des	17.0 max 16.0 des	2000/16/200 oil	Hamburg-Amerika-Linie, Hamburg
Juminda	OTO (G) (249)	1928	742gt	850t max	59.22 oa 56.13 cwl	8.61		5.92		8.0 max	700/8/117 coal	SA Nav. Toscana, Livorno
Kiebitz (mod)	Ansaldo (GS) STT	1938 1943	3667gt	5182T des	123.60 oa 116.80 cwl	15.0	4.95	7.53	7200ehp max	19.5 max 17.0 des	/ /446 oil	Regia Azienda Monopolio Banane, Genoa

* German measurement.

verted to a mine ship; commissioned 1 Feb 1945 (no mine service); returned to Norway as *Peter Wessel* 1945; sold to Italy as *Jollyemme* 1968; broken up at La Spezia 1981.

Helgoland launched 6 May 1939, commission planned 1939, but the Voith-Schneider installation was defective, so she was used as a barrack ship at Cuxhaven; transferred to the GM/SA 2nd Mine-sweeping Division 1945; burned out at Cuxhaven 18 Mar 1946; released to England 11 Jul 1947; scuttled with gas munitions 1948.

Juminda: launched 1929 as Italian steam passenger vessel *Elbano Gasperi*; served as Italian service steamer and auxiliary minelayer *F 8*; taken over by German forces at La Spezia 9 Sept 1943; commissioned 27 Sept 1943; renamed *Juminda* 30 Sept 1943; sunk at 0145hrs on 29 Oct 1943 2nm west of

Name	Type and construction	Propulsion	Armament	Complement
Hanonia	Steam ship, 1 deck; depth 6.05m.	One vertical 3-cylinder triple expansion engine (one 4-bladed screw), 2 boilers.	Three AA machine guns, 144 mines.	
Hansestadt Danzig	Motor passenger vessel, 2 decks + shelter deck; depth 5.8m.	Two Vulcan 10-cylinder 4-stroke diesel engines (two 3-bladed screws, 2.5m diameter).	Two 8.8cm AA guns, four 3.7cm AA guns, six 2cm AA guns, 360 mines.	(83) 10/200
Hansestadt Danzig (ex-*Peter Wessel*)	Motor ferry, 2 decks + shelter deck; depth 4.90m.	Two Atlas 7-cylinder 2-stroke diesel engines (two 4-bladed screws).	Two 3.7cm AA guns, 180 mines.	(30)
Helgoland	Turbine ferry, 2 decks + shelter deck; depth 4.80m.	Two sets AEG turbines, one diesel generator (3500V), one AEG electric motor, two La Mont boilers, two Voith-Schneider propulsion units with six blades, 1.8m long.	320 mines (planned).	(90)
Juminda	Steam passenger vessel; depth 5.92m.	One vertical 3-cylinder triple expansion engine (one screw), three flame tube boilers.	Four AA machine guns, two 3.7cm AA guns (planned), four 2cm AA guns, four 2cm Oerlikon AA guns, 62 Italian CR mines.	22
Kiebitz	Motor fruit carrier, 2 decks + shelter deck; depth 7.53m.	Two Fiat 9-cylinder 2-stroke diesel engines (two 4-bladed screws).	Three 12cm guns, one 3.7cm AA gun, five 2cm AA guns, four AA machine guns, 240 EMC mines (from July 1944).	3/64

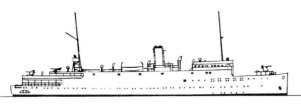

Hansestadt Danzig (1940); *Preussen* was similar.

Kaiser (1940). *Mrva*

San Stefano, position 42° 27′N, 11° 05′E, by two torpedoes from British MTBs; six dead.

Kiebitz: launched 1938 at Italian motor fruit carrier *Ramb III*; became Italian auxiliary cruiser *D 29* 11 Jun 1940; damaged by a torpedo in Benghazi harbour 30 May 1941, and returned to Trieste for repair; taken over by German forces at Trieste and repairs completed with German armaments; temporarily commissioned as a troop transporter Nov 1943; served as a mine ship, without gyro compass, etc, from 15 Feb 1944, with further fitting out performed after first service. Burnt out and sunk at 2030hrs on 5 Nov 1944 at Fiume, by three bombs from American aircraft; 25 dead. Raised by Yugoslavia; in service from 1950 as Yugoslav training ship and state yacht *Galeb*; still in existence in 1984.

Mine ships (IV)

Name	Builder (construction nos)	Built	Gross tonnage	Displacement (t = tonnes T = tons)	Length (m)	Breadth (m)	Draught (m)	Hull depth (m)	Power (hp)	Speed (kts)	Range and fuel (nm/kts/t)	Owner
Königin Luise	Howaldt (H) (731)	1934	2399gt	3373t max	93.50 oa 87.98 cwl	12.80	3.60	6.46	4500shp max	17.0 max	4000/17/167 oil	Hamburg-Amerika-Linie, Hamburg
Kuckuck	Quarnaro (223)	1943	3162gt	4570t max	116.90 oa 104.00 cwl	15.20	6.39	6.60	6300shp max 4375shp des	17.0 max 14.0 des	/ /170 oil	Tirrenia SA Nav., Naples
La France	Wiborg	1909	699gt*		57.92 oa 55.70 cwl	8.36	3.99	4.75		9.0 max		AS La France (O G Gjessens), Skudesnes
Linz	Danzig†	1940	3374gt		104.20 oa 98.50 cwl	13.92	6.85	8.10	4800ehp max	16.0 max	5760/15/199 oil	Norddeutscher Lloyd, Bremen
Lothringen (mod)	FCM (H)	1941 1942	2434gt	1975t max	94.50 oa 93.60 cwl	12.10	3.15	7.10	22,000shp max	24.0 max 22.0 des	/ /163 oil	SNCF, Dieppe

* German measurement.
† Completed by Odense Staalskibsvaeft, 1943.

Careers

Königin Luise: launched 10 Apr 1934, commissioned 13 Sept 1939. Sunk at 1711hrs on 25 Sept 1941 near Helsinki, position 60° 07′N, 24° 56′E by a Soviet mine; 77 dead. Raised 1947 and broken up.

Kuckuck: requisitioned on stocks at Fiume 9 Sept 1943, commissioned 26 Sept 1944. Sunk at Fiume on 5 Nov 1944: by British bombs; number of casualties unknown. Raised in 1948 and repaired; became Yugoslavian motor vessel *Locchi* in 1950, and *Učka* after 1951; grounded at Tripoli, Libya, 6 Jan 1978; sold to Brodospas, Split, for breaking up.

La France: launched Jul 1909 as Norwegian steam ship *La France*; taken as a German prize 1940; served as a mine storage ship under the control of the Admiral North Coast from 3 Jul 1940; served with the Kirkenes Sea Defence Command from Mar 1941. Capsized and sunk in shallow water near Skudesnes, position 59° 08′N, 05° 18′E, by a rocket attack. Raised post-war and repaired; named *King* in 1949; renamed *Magnhild* in 1950; became Costa Rican *Pandora* 1955; renamed *Pandokrator* 1957; sold to Greece as *Mihalis* 1963; still in service 1989.

Linz: launched as a motor vessel; transferred to Denmark for completion as a mine ship; sabotaged at the Odense dockyard 27 Jul 1943, the entire engine and electrical installation being rendered

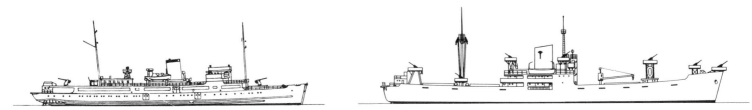

Königin Luise (1940).

Kuckuck (ex *Vitorio Locchi*) (1944). *Mickel*

Linz (1944). *Mrva*

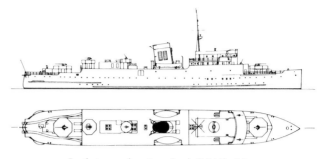

Lothringen (ex *Londres*) (1944). *Mrva*

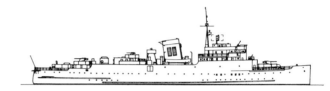

Lothringen (ex *Londres*) (1944, after
rearmament). *Mrva*

unusable owing to water penetration; nevertheless
commissioned 3 Aug 1943 and towed to Stettin for
repairs 16 Aug 1943; serviceable by Jan 1944; taken
as British prize 8 Jul 1945; became motor ferry
Empire Wansbeck on Hook of Holland–Harwich
service; became Greek *Esperos* 1962; broken up in
Spain 1980.

Lothringen: taken as a prize in France while still on
the stocks, Jun 1940; launched 19 Dec 1941 and
commissioned as a mine ship for the West Group,
1942; served as a target ship for submarines 1943;
converted to a mine ship May 1944, and in service
from 24 Jun 1944; returned 17 Nov 1945; sold to
Britain as *Londres* 1951; became Greek *Ionion II*
1963; renamed *Sofoclis Venizelos* 1964. Burned out
and sunk in Piraeus harbour 14 Apr 1966.

Name	Type and construction	Propulsion	Armament	Complement
Königin Luise	Motor ferry (sea bathing ship), (10 watertight compartments), 2 decks + shelter deck; depth 6.46m.	Two MAN 4-cylinder 4-stroke diesel engines (two 4-bladed screws, 2.1m diameter).	Two 8.8cm AA guns (400 rounds), one 3.7cm AA gun (3000 rounds), two 2cm AA guns, 240 mines.	8/172
Kuckuck	Motor vessel, 1 deck (6 watertight compartments); depth 6.60m.	Two Ansaldo 8-cylinder 2-stroke diesel engines (two 4-bladed screws, 4.2m diameter).	Two 7.6cm AA guns, four 2cm AA guns (final armament as planned was three 10.5cm/45 QF guns, six 3.7cm/83 QF guns, four 3.7cm AA guns, 18 2cm AA guns, eight 8.6cm rocket launchers), 290 EMC mines.	2/54
La France	Steam ship; depth 4.75m.	One vertical 3-cylinder triple expansion engine (one screw), boilers unknown.	137 Norwegian mines, 300 explosive buoys.	
Linz	Motor vessel, 2 decks (7 watertight compartments); depth 8.10m.	One MAN 6-cylinder 2-stroke diesel engine (one 4-bladed screw, 4.5m diameter).	Two 10.5cm AA guns, two 3.7cm AA guns, fourteen 2cm AA guns, 340 mines.	10/202
Lothringen	Turbine ferry, 2 decks + shelter deck; depth 7.10m.	Two sets Parsons geared turbines (two 4-bladed screws, 2.8m diameter), two Penhoët watertube boilers (27atm forced).	Two 8.8cm/45 AA guns (800 rounds), two 3.7cm AA guns (4000 rounds), three 2cm AA guns (6000 rounds), 200 EMC mines.	Approx 175

Mine ships (V)

Careers

Marienburg: incomplete at Stettin May 1945; taken
as USSR prize and completed at Wismar in 1953 as
Soviet *Lensoviet*; renamed *Abhazija* 1962; broken
up in Barcelona, Spain, after Mar 1980.

Niedersachsen: launched 1934; served as French
Guyane (ex *Dora*); transferred to Italy 4 Dec 1942

as *Acqui*; taken over by the German 3rd Escort
Flotilla 12 Dec 1943; named *Niedersachsen* 20 Dec
1943. Sunk at 1723hrs on 15 Feb 1944 near Toulon,
position 43° 02' 6"N, 06° 01' 7"E, by a torpedo from
the British submarine *Upstart*; 12 dead.

Nymphe: launched 11 Aug 1916 as German minesweeper *M 42* (see page ?); converted to steam

ferry *Nymphe* 1922; transferred to France as *La
Nymphe* 1923; served as French minesweeper
AD 204 1939–40; planned conversion to anti-
submarine training vessel *Nymphe* Apr 1944, but
became a mine ship in May 1944; scuttled Apr
1945, time and place unknown.

Ostmark: launched 1932 as French ferry *Cote*

Name	Builder (construction nos)	Built	Gross tonnage	Displacement (t = tonnes T = tons)	Length (m)	Breadth (m)	Draught (m)	Hull depth (m)	Power (hp)	Speed (kts)	Range and fuel (nm/kts/t)	Owner
(Marienburg)	Oderwerke (807)	1939*	6200gt		138.00 oa 131.20 cwl	18.50		8.13	8000shp max	18.0 max		Reichs-verkehrs-ministerium, Stettin
Niedersachsen	B & W (607)	1934	1794gt		86.71 cwl	12.62	5.80	4.62	2100ehp max	13.0 max 10.0 des	/ /495 oil	Cie Générale d'Armement Maritimes, Rouen
Nymphe	Vulkan (V) (604)	1916	452gt	1020t max 600t des	58.41 oa 56.10 cwl	7.30	2.25	3.40	1800ihp max 1600ihp des	16.5 max 12.0 des	2000/14/115 coal	SA des Bains de Mer et du Cercle des Etrangers de Monaco
Ostmark (mod)	FCM (H) Germania	1932 1942	3047gt	3648t max	103.50 oa 99.40 cwl	13.72	3.70	7.62	13,000shp max 9000shp des	23.0 max 19.5 des	1500/19/	SA de Gérance & d'Armement, Le Havre
Passat	Blythswood (11)	1926	8998gt	c14,000t max	148.70 oa 143.30 cwl	18.95	8.93	10.80	3100shp max	11.0 max	/ /1158 oil	A F Klaveness & Co, Oslo
Pommern (mod)	Framnes La Ciotat	1939	2956gt		102.70 oa 98.32 cwl	14.14	4.90	6.00	3950shp max 3325shp des	17.5 max 16.0 des		Cie Générale Trans-atlantique, Le Havre
Preussen (mod)	Oderwerke (725) "	1926 1940	2529gt		93.60 oa 90.40 cwl	11.69		5.97	6400shp max 10,000shp max†	16.0 max 20.0 max†	2900/16/195 oil	Reichs-verkehrs-ministerium, Stettin

* Uncompleted until 1953.

† With superchargers (removed in June 1940 due to development problems, for a saving of 6t in displacement).

Niedersachsen (ex *Guyane*) (1944).   *Ostmark* (ex *Cote d'Argent*) (1943). *Mrva*

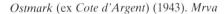

d'Argent; taken as a prize in France 30 Jul 1940; converted after a fire to a barrack ship with the 42nd and 44th Minesweeper Flotillas 30 Mar 1941; commissioned 15 Oct 1941 as 2nd command flagship; served as a target ship for KG 40 (for torpedo-bomber pilot training) from Feb 1942. Sunk by British bombs 21 Apr 1945 west of Anholt, exact position unknown; 109 dead.

Passat: launched 21 Oct 1925 as Norwegian motor tanker *Storstad*; taken as a prize by *Pinguin* on 7 Oct 1940, position 15° 07′S, 67° approx E; commissioned 12 Oct 1940 as an auxiliary mine ship; served as reconnaissance ship *Storstad* from 16 Nov 1940; transferred to Bordeaux, 27 Feb 1941 for duties with Fleet Training, North; severely damaged at Pauillac before leaving port by British bombs on 2 Sept 1942; out of service 4 May 1943, and released for cannibalisation; wreck scuttled at Nantes 11 Aug 1944, then raised and broken up.

Pommern: launched 1939 as motor fruit carrier *Belain d'Esnambuc*; taken over by French navy in 1939; requisitioned by KM as *Flora 1* 16 Dec 1942; conversion to *SG 7* was planned for Feb/Mar 1943; converted to a mine ship after 30 Jan 1943 and in service from May 1943. Sunk at 0845hrs on 5 Oct 1943 1.5nm south of San Remo, position 43° 47′N, 07° 51′E, by an Italian mine; 20 dead.

Preussen: launched Mar 1926, commissioned 3 Sept 1939. Sunk at 1840hrs on 9 Jul 1941 south of Ölandsund Östbygrund, position 56° 12′N, 16° 17′E, by Swedish mines, along with *Hansestadt Danzig* (see page 185) and *Tannenberg* (see page 191); four dead; wreck broken up 1958.

Name	Type and construction	Propulsion	Armament	Complement
(Marienburg)	Turbine ferry; depth 8.13m.	Two geared turbines with electrical transmission (two 4-bladed screws), one watertube boiler.	300 mines.	
Niedersachsen	Motor fruit carrier, 2 decks + shelter deck, (7 watertight compartments); depth 4.62m.	One B&W 2-stroke diesel engine (one 3-bladed screw, 3.8m diameter).	Two 10.5cm/45 AA guns, two 6.9cm AA guns, twelve 2cm AA guns, 260 mines.	5/169
Nymphe	Steam ferry (minesweeper), 1 deck (8 watertight compartments); depth 3.40m.	Two vertical 3-cylinder triple expansion engines (two 4-bladed screws, 1.9m diameter), two Marine-type boilers (16atm forced).	One 9cm QF gun, two 3.7cm AA guns, four 2cm AA guns, two AA machine guns, 30–42 (P5) mines.	1/39
Ostmark	Turbine ferry, 2 decks + shelter deck (14 watertight compartments); depth 7.62m.	Two sets Parsons geared turbines (two 3-bladed screws, 2.9m diameter), four Babcock-Wilcox watertube boilers (18.2atm forced).	Two 10.5cm/45 QF guns (226 rounds), four 4cm AA guns, two 3.7cm QF guns, four 2cm AA guns (planned final armament was two 10.5cm/45 QF guns, nine 4cm AA guns, sixteen 2cm AA guns, two 7.3cm rocket launchers), 240 mines.	240
Passat	Motor tanker, 2 decks; depth 10.80m.	Two Kincaid 6-cylinder 4-stroke diesel engines (two 4-bladed screws).	Two AA machine guns, 110 mines.	3/34
Pommern	Motor fruit carrier.	One Sulzer 7-cylinder 2-stroke diesel engine (one 4-bladed screw).	Three 10.5cm QF guns, six 3.7cm guns, sixteen 2cm AA guns, six depth charge launchers (100 rounds), 195 (EMC/EMF) – 204 (UMB) mines.	
Preussen	Motor passenger vessel, 2 decks; depth 5.97m.	Two MAN 10-cylinder 4-stroke diesel engines (two 3-bladed screws, 2.50m diameter).	Two 8.8cm/45 AA guns, 400 mines.	Approx 10/200 (83)

Mine ships (VI)

Careers

Roland: launched 16 Mar 1927, commissioned 24 Aug 1939 as mine ship *A*, under the Commodore of Torpedo Boats, West. Sunk at 2241hrs on 21 Apr 1944 near Narva, position 59° 43′ 12″N, 27° 28′ 2″E, by a mine; approximately 235 dead.

Romania: taken over from Romania Mar 1942, planned as a hospital ship; served as a torpedo boat escort ship, 1st S-boat Flotilla, from 6 Dec 1942; became a mine ship, Black Sea, from 3 Nov 1943; set on fire by Soviet bombs while on passage from Sevastopol to Constanta on 11 May 1944, position unknown; sunk following a munitions explosion at 0710hrs on 12 May 1944; number of casualties unknown.

San Giorgio: taken over by German forces at Ancona in Sept 1943, commissioned as *G 106* 9 Oct 1943 for the 11th Training Flotilla. Stranded and sunk in a Bora storm at Punta della Maestre on 12 Feb 1944, position unknown; raised, returned and broken up.

Schildkröte: launched 1931 as motor ferry *Pollux,* renamed *André Constant* 1935, *Georges et Henri* 1937 and *Courdannes* 1939; commissioned Jun 1944 for the 3rd Coastal Defence Division; returned 1945, still in existence 1968. Fate unknown.

Schwerin: launched 15 Apr 1926, commissioned 22 Aug 1940 for Operation Sealion; returned 25 Nov 1940 and used for railway ferry service. Sunk 20 Feb 1944 in Rostock harbour by British bombs; raised 20 Oct 1944 and moved to Warnemünde as a store hulk 14 Nov 1944; broken up after 23 Aug 1948.

Skagerrak: taken over by German forces May 1940; commissioned 17 Aug 1940 for Operation Sealion; used as a target ship for the 27th U-boat

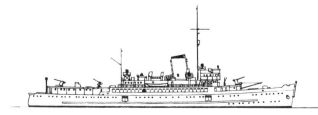

Roland (1940).

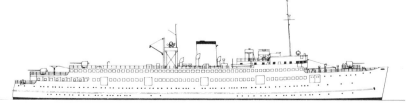

Tannenberg (1940). *Mrva*

Name	Builder (construction nos)	Built	Gross tonnage	Displacement (t = tonnes T = tons)	Length (m)	Breadth (m)	Draught (m)	Hull depth (m)	Power (hp)	Speed (kts)	Range and fuel (nm/kts/t)	Owner
Roland (mod)	Tecklenborg (414) Vegesack	1927 1939	2436gt		90.82 oa 86.80 cwl	13.04	3.40 max 3.07 des	3.86	4850shp max	18.0 max	2100/18/242 oil	Nord-deutscher-Lloyd, Bremen
Romania	ACL	1904	3152gt		108.70 cwl	12.73	5.46	8.39	7200ihp max 7000ihp des	18.0 max 18.0 des		Servicul Maritime Romanul, Constanta
San Giorgio (mod)	STT Breda	1914 1944	364gt		c57.00 oa 53.14 cwl	7.46	2.52	3.50		8.0 max		'Istria-Trieste' SA di Navig., Trieste
Schildkröte	Bodewes	1931	240gt		37.87 cwl	7.19	2.45	2.70	200ehp max	7.0 max		Soc. des Ciments 'La Couronne', Boulogne
Schwerin (mod)	Schichau (E) (470) Kröger	1926 1940	3133gt		107.20 oa 101.80 cwl	18.00	4.20	5.99	4400ihp max 4200ihp des	18.0 max 15.5 des	600/15.5/80 oil	Deutsche Reichsbahn, Warnemünde
Skagerrak (mod)	Aalborg (61) B & W	1939 1943	1281gt		70.70 oa 65.21 cwl	11.57	4.02	5.03	5000shp max	17.0 max	/ /268 oil	Christian-sand D/S, Christian-sand
Tannenberg (mod)	Oderwerke (780) „	1935 1939	5504gt		129.60 oa 121.30 cwl	15.54	7.59	8.33	12,000shp max	20.0 max	2000/20/265 oil	Reichs-verkehrs-ministerium, Stettin

Name	Type and construction	Propulsion	Armament	Complement
Roland	Turbine ferry (sea bathing ship), 2 decks + shelter deck (8 watertight compartments); depth 3.86m.	Two geared turbines (two 3-bladed screws, 2.30m diameter), two Marine-type boilers (16atm forced).	Two 8.8cm AA guns (400 rounds), one 3.7cm AA gun, two 2cm AA guns, 233 UMA mines.	Approx 240 (68)
Romania	Steam passenger vessel, 2 decks + shelter deck (6 watertight compartments); depth 8.39m.	Two vertical 3-cylinder triple expansion engines (two 4-bladed screws), five cylindrical boilers (12.6atm forced).	Four 2cm AA guns, 80 mines.	
San Giorgio	Steam ferry; depth 3.50m.	One vertical 3-cylinder triple expansion engine (one 4-bladed screw), four boilers (14.5atm forced).	Four 2cm AA guns, 18 mines.	
Schildkröte	Motor ferry, 1 deck (4 watertight compartments); depth 2.70m.	One Kromhout 4-cylinder 2-stroke diesel engine (one screw).	67 KMA mines.	
Schwerin	Steam ferry, 2 decks + shelter deck; depth 5.99m.	Two vertical 3-cylinder triple expansion engines (two 4-bladed screws), four boilers (14.5atm forced).	Two 8.8cm AA guns, (400 rounds), six 2cm AA guns, 280 mines.	
Skagerrak	Motor ferry, 2 decks + shelter deck; depth 5.03m.	Two B&W 10-cylinder 2-stroke diesel engines (two 4-bladed screws).	Two 3.7cm AA guns, four 2cm AA guns, four AA machine guns, 118 EMC mines.	127
Tannenberg	Turbine ferry, 3 decks; depth 8.33m.	Two sets Wagner-Schichau geared turbines (two 4-bladed screws, 3.14m diameter), two Marine-type boilers (70atm forced).	Three 15cm/45 QF guns, four 3.7cm AA guns, six 2cm AA guns, 383 (EMD) – 460 mines.	(114)

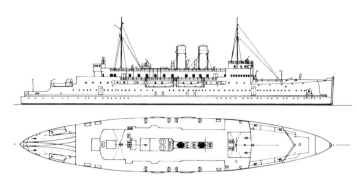

Schwerin (1940). *Mrva*   *Skagerrak* (ex *Skagerrak I*) (1943). *Mickel*

Flotilla from 20 Aug 1942; modification of the stern was undertaken Jul–Nov 1943, with the addition of 96t of fixed ballast. Sunk at 1142hrs on 20 Jan 1944 west of Egeroy, position 50° 19′ 8″N, 06° 01′ 01″E, by a British aerial torpedo; seven dead.

Tannenberg: launched 16 Mar 1935, commissioned 2 Sept 1939; served as training ship *B 1* from 30 May 1940; became flotilla flagship for the Commodore, Mine Ships 1 Sept 1940. Sunk at 1840hrs on 9 Jul 1941 south of Ölandsund Östbygrund,

position 56° 12′N, 16° 17′E, by Swedish mines, along with *Hansestadt Danzig* (see page 185) and *Preussen* (see page 189); ten dead; wreck broken up 1952.

Mine ships (VII)

Name	Builder (construction nos)	Built	Gross tonnage	Displacement (t = tonnes T = tons)	Length (m)	Breadth (m)	Draught (m)	Hull depth (m)	Power (hp)	Speed (kts)	Range and fuel (nm/kts/t)	Owner
Ulm (mod)	Danzig (78) Stülcken	1938 1940–42	3071gt		102.50 oa 98.00 cwl	13.87	6.40	8.79	3950shp max	16.0 max	11,000/10/ 445 to 390 oil	Norddeutscher Lloyd, Bremen
Versailles (mod)	FCM (H) Rickmers (G)	1919 1941	2156gt		95.00 oa 90.85 cwl	11.03	3.21 max 2.80 des	6.82	15,000shp des	17.0 max (23.0 des)	2475/18/230 oil	SNCF, Dieppe
Wullenwever	„	1912	1882gt		93.10 oa 89.41 cwl	10.54	5.00 max 3.20 des	6.53	9000shp max	22.0 max	1000/15/97 oil	„
Xanten (mod)	Oderwerke (682) Linz	1919 1941–42		201t max 176t des	43.00 oa 41.80 cwl	6.00	1.85 max 1.70 des	2.29	600ihp des	8.9 max (14 des)	640/9/35 coal	Zuckerfabrik Smarda, Giurgiu
Zeus	STT (767)	1928	2423gt	3100t max	89.03 oa 83.97 cwl	12.65	4.98	5.21	4200shp max	14.0 max	/ /100 oil	'Adriatica' SA di Navig., Venice

Careers

Togo: commissioned 18 Aug 1940 for Operation Sealion, etc; refitted as a commerce raider from 16 Jun 1941.

Ulm: launched Nov 1937 as *Rapide*, completed as *Ulm* 1938; requisitioned 18 Mar 1940 and disguised as an Olsen liner; first operational service was against shipping on the Dover–Thames route; later converted by HC Stülcken Sohn, Hamburg. Burnt out and sunk 31 Jul 1940; raised and repaired Aug 1940, and returned to service 25 Nov 1941 as a 2nd command Flagship. Scuttled and sunk at 2345hrs on 25 Aug 1942 150nm east of Bear Island, position 74° 45′N, 26° 50′E, after sustaining serious damage in action against the British destroyers *Marne*, *Martin* and *Onslaught*; 141 dead.

Versailles: launched 1919, commissioned Jul 1921 as Channel ferry *Versailles*; taken as a prize at Nantes Aug 1940; served as a barrack ship with the 42nd Minesweeper Flotilla from 6 Nov 1940; served from 19 Mar 1941 with Mine Ship Group, West; out of service, inoperable, 24 Jan 1942; transferred to the SVK and used as a barrack ship from 18 Jul 1942; returned 1945 and broken up 1947–48.

Wullenwever: launched 1912, commissioned Sept 1912 as English Channel ferry *Rouen*; taken as a prize at Bordeaux 30 Aug 1940; in service as *Schiff 50* from 24 Mar 1941, converted after Jun 1941; served from Jul 1941 as a research vessel with the NVK. Sunk by a mine in the Baltic 25 Apr 1943, position unknown; raised Aug 1943, repaired and

returned 1945; stricken 22 Mar 1946; broken up at Dieppe in 1949.

Xanten: launched 1919 as *FM 36* (see page 000); stricken 31 Dec 1919; became Romanian steam ferry *Socrates*; purchased Oct 1941 by KM; became mineship *Xanten* 21 Oct 1941, and *UJ 116* in 1942; scuttled in the vicinity of Constanta 25 Aug 1944.

Zeus: launched 1928 as motor passenger liner *Francesco Morosini*; became Italian auxiliary cruiser/minelayer *D 12* 26 Jun 1940; taken over by German forces at Piraeus 18 Sept 1943; scuttled at Saloniki 30 Oct 1944 after being bombed by British aircraft; number of casualties unknown; wreck broken up in 1952.

Name	Type and construction	Propulsion	Armament	Complement
Togo	(to be covered in a future volume)			
Ulm	Motor fruit carrier, 2 decks + shelter deck; depth 8.79m.	One MAN 6-cylinder 2-stroke diesel engine (one 4-bladed screw).	One 10.5cm QF gun, one 3.7cm AA gun, four 2cm AA guns, 355 (UMB) – 482 (EMC) mines.	10/193 (55)
Versailles	Turbine ferry, 3 decks + shelter deck; depth 8.79m.	Two sets Parsons geared turbines (two 4-bladed screws, 2.8m diameter), four Penhoët watertube boilers (15atm forced).	Two 2cm AA guns, 111 mines.	
Wullenwever	Turbine ferry, 2 decks (11 watertight compartments); depth 6.53m.	Three sets Parsons turbines (three 3-bladed screws, 2.6m diameter) four watertube boilers (12atm forced).	Four 2cm AA guns (two 8.8cm guns, 125 EMC mines planned as an auxiliary mine ship).	2/92 (33)
Xanten	Steam ferry (ex minesweeper), 1 deck (4 watertight compartments; depth 2.29m.	Two vertical 3-cylinder triple expansion engines (two 3-bladed screws, 1.4m diameter), one [two after March 1943] Marine-type boilers.	Two 2cm AA guns, 20 mines, [3.7cm AA guns fitted October 1942 (number unknown)].	
Zeus	Motor passenger vessel, 3 decks; depth 5.21m.	Two Fiat 6-cylinder 2-stroke diesel engines (two 4-bladed screws).	Two 12cm QF guns, four 3.7cm AA guns, nineteen 2cm AA guns, 240 mines.	

Togo (1940. *Mrva*

Wullenwever (ex *Rouen*) (1941); *Skarpion* (ex *Newhaven*) was similar.

Ulm (1941). *Mrva*

Versailles (1941). *Mickel*

Zeus (ex *Francesco Morosini*) (1944). *Mrva*

Xanten (ex *Socrates*, ex *FM 36*) (1941). *Mrva*

Net vessels 1900–1918

Net storage and handling vessels

Name	Builder (construction nos)	Built	Gross tonnage	Displacement (t = tonnes T = tons)	Length (m)	Breadth (m)	Draught (m)	Hull depth (m)	Power (hp)	Speed (kts)	Range and fuel (nm/kts/t)	Owner
Burgfried	Stephenson (58)	1899	4822gt		114.60 oa 113.90 cwl	15.30	8.30	9.20		8.5		Scotia SS Co Ltd, Liverpool
Eskimo	Earle's (556)	1910	3326gt	c6300t max	106.10 oa 100.90 cwl	13.80	6.60	7.77	2800ihp max	c14.0 max		T Wilson's Sons & Co, Hull
(mod)	Oderwerke	1916										
Glückauf	Weser (129)	1901	736gt		66.00 oa 62.80	12.70	2.60	3.80	100ihp max	c12.0 max		Nord-deutscher Lloyd, Bremen
(mod)		1916										
Rossall	Gray (492)	1895	2739gt	c5800t max	100.40 oa 95.60 cwl	12.80	6.10	7.52	850ihp max	c9.0 max		Galbraith, Pembroke & Co, London (embargo ship)

Careers

Burgfried: launched 1899 as the British steamship *Montauk Point*; detained at Hamburg upon the outbreak of war 4 Aug 1914; store ship at Hamburg, 1915; net store ship with the Baltic Net Barrage Group, 25 Nov 1916; returned 17 Jan 1919; became Norwegian *Snefond*, 1919; Danish *Stillehavet*, 1919; to Germany with Continental Shipping Company as *Carlsfeld*, 1923; renamed *Omega* with Reederei AG of 1896, Hamburg, 1923; broken up 1926.

Eskimo: launched 9 Apr 1910 as British steamship *Eskimo*; taken as German prize by the auxiliary cruiser *Vineta* in the vicinity of Risor on 27 Jul 1916 and taken to Swinemünde; to navy 13 Nov 1916, converted by the removal of after mast, wheelhouse and engine room skylight to create a working deck; commissioned 4 Mar 1917 as a net and leader ship with the Baltic Net Barrage Group; returned 21 Jan 1919; became French *Eskimo* (Cie Paquet) 1924; fate unknown.

Glückauf: launched 3 Apr 1909 as steam ferry *Glückauf*; joined blockade vessel division, Jade, 3 Aug 1914; leader ship, North Sea Net Barrage Group, 10 Dec 1915; escort flotilla, 1 Sept 1918; returned 1919, became German steamship *Glückauf* (Norddeutscher Lloyd, Bremen); be-

Name	Type and construction	Propulsion	Armament	Complement
Burgfried	Steam ship; depth 9.20m.	One vertical 3-cylinder triple expansion engine (one screw), two cylindrical boilers.	–	
Eskimo	Steam ship, 3 decks (9 [later 12] watertight compartments); depth 7.77m.	Two vertical 4-cylinder quadruple expansion engines (two 4-bladed screws, 5.3m diameter), four cylindrical boilers (15atm forced).	Four 8.8cm/45 guns.	3/146 (5/72)
Glückauf	Steam ferry, 1 deck + shelter deck (5 watertight compartments); depth 3.80m.	Two vertical 3-cylinder triple expansion engines (two 4-bladed screws), two cylindrical boilers (12.5atm forced).	Two 5.2cm/55 guns.	3/42 (4/13)
Rossall	Steam ship, 1 deck (6 watertight compartments); depth 7.52m.	One vertical 3-cylinder triple expansion engine (one 4-bladed screw).	Two 8.8cm/45 guns.	6/127

came French *Altas* with France & Canada Cie., 1927; broken up 1935.

Rossall: launched 26 Jan 1895 as British steamship *Rossall*; detained at Bremerhaven 1 Aug 1914; returned and became British *Pinot* Jul 1920; became Italian *Lucia* (Sicula Carboni) Jul 1923; broken up 1935.

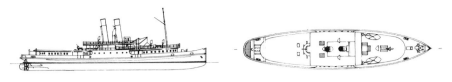

Glückauf (1915). *Mickel*

Net lighters

Name	Builder (construction nos)	Built	Gross tonnage	Displacement (t = tonnes T = tons)	Length (m)	Breadth (m)	Draught (m)	Hull depth (m)	Power (hp)	Speed (kts)	Range and fuel (nm/kts/t)	Owner
M.N.L. I	Meyer (127)	1897	597gt	900t max	55.00 cwl	9.00	3.60 fwd 1.90 aft	4.20	—	—	—	Norddeutscher Lloyd, Bremen
M.N.L. II	Tecklenborg (157)	”	562gt	”	57.50 oa 55.00 cwl	9.30	1.90 aft	4.00	—	—	—	”
M.N.L. III	” (158)	”	563gt	”	”	”	”	”	—	—	—	”
M.N.L. VI	” (166)	1898	570gt	”	”	”	”	”	—	—	—	”
M.N.L. VII	” (167)	”	”	”	”	”	”	”	—	—	—	”
M.N.L. IV	Kralingen	1899	622gt						—	—	—	DDG Hansa, Bremen
M.N.L. V (ex *L*)	”	”	”						—	—	—	”
M.N.L. V (ex *N*)	Vuijk	1905	628gt		53.00 cwl	9.00			—	—	—	”

Careers

M.N.L. I: launched 1897 as sea-going lighter *NDL 88*; purchased by the navy 4 Dec 1915 and commissioned 16 Dec 1915 as navy net lighter (Marine-Netzleichter) *M.N.L. I* with the Baltic Net Barrage Group; became *Netzleichter I* at Kiel, 1 Dec 1922; to first naval gunnery division 12 Jul 1939; to Net Barrage Group I, 6 Sept 1939; out of service 21 Sept 1940; barrack ship, Net Barrage Group centre, 1 Jun 1941; sunk by an aircraft bomb and burned out, 26/27 Aug 1944.

M.N.L. VI (ex *NDL 93*) (1918); M.N.L. I and VII were similar. Mickel *M.N.L. VI*

M.N.L. II: launched 1897 as sea-going lighter *NDL 89*; purchased by navy 4 Dec 1915; commissioned 26 Jan 1916 as *M.N.L. II* with the Baltic Net Barrage Group; released for delivery to Allies 17 Jun 1920, but turned down; became *Netzleichter II* at Kiel, 6 Jun 1922; renamed *Netzleichter 2*, 4 Jul 1933; to harbour captain, Pillau, 14 Aug 1939; Net Barrage Group I, 6 Sept 1939; renamed *Netzleger V*,

Name	Type and construction	Propulsion	Armament	Complement
M.N.L. I	Sea-going lighter (5 watertight compartments); depth 4.2m.	No engines; 1 auxiliary boiler, 47t coal.	None.	0/49–0/51 (of which 0/7–0/11 permanent).
M.N.L. II, III, VI, VII	Sea-going lighter (5 watertight compartments); depth 4.0m.	”	”	”
M.N.L. IV, V	Sea-going lighter (5 watertight compartments).	”	”	”
M.N.L. V (ex *N*)	Sea-going lighter (5 watertight compartments; depth 5.70m.	”	”	”

1 Jan 1941, with Net Barrage Group Centre; GM/SA 1945/46; taken as US prize 1947; from Bremerhaven to Belgium 7 May 1947; probably broken up.

M.N.L. III: launched 1897 as sea-going lighter *NDL 90*; commissioned 29 Jan 1916 as *M.N.L. III* with the Baltic Net Barrage Group; returned 3 Apr 1919 as *NDL 90*; became *Vs 112* in 1942; became floating workshop *Vs 62*; GM/SA 1945. No further details.

M.N.L. VI: launched 1898 as sea-going lighter *NDL 93*; purchased by navy 7 Nov 1915; became *Netzleichter I* with the North Sea Net Barrage Group 10 Dec 1915; became *M.N.L. VI* with the Baltic Net Barrage Group, 21 Oct 1918; released for delivery to Allies 8 Oct 1920, but turned down; became *Netzleichter III* at Kiel 6 Jun 1922; renamed *Netzleichter 3*, 4 Jul 1933. No further details.

M.N.L. VII: launched 1898 as sea-going lighter *NDL 94*; became *Netzleichter II* with the Net Barrage Group North, 23 Jan 1916; became *M.N.L. VII* with the Baltic Net Barrage Group 29 Jan 1918; returned 9 Apr 1919 as *NDL 94*; transport ship store, Hamburg, 1941; returned 1945; still in service 1953. No further details.

M.N.L. IV: launched 1899 as sea-going lighter *M*; became *M.N.L. IV* with the Baltic Net Barrage Group, 9 Mar 1917; returned 31 Jan 1920. No further details.

M.N.L. V: launched 1899 as sea-going lighter *L*; became *M.N.L. V* with the Baltic Net Barrage Group, 23 Apr 1917; sunk 28 Sept 1917. No further details.

M.N.L. V: launched 1905 as sea-going lighter *N*; became *M.N.L. V* with the Baltic Net Barrage Group, Oct 1917; returned 7 Apr 1919 as sea-going lighter *N*; still in existence 1928.

Net transports

Name	Type and construction	Propulsion	Armament	Complement
Adolph	Steam tug, 1 deck; depth 3.55m.	One vertical 3-cylinder triple expansion engine (one screw), one cylindrical boiler.	None.	
Amerika	Steam tug, 1 deck; depth 3.9m.	One vertical 3-cylinder triple expansion engine (one screw), one cylindrical boiler (153sq m, 13.5atm forced).	None.	0/14
Bremerhaven	Steam tug, 1 deck; depth 3.00m.	One vertical 3-cylinder triple expansion engine (one screw), one cylindrical boiler (90sq m, 12atm forced).	None.	0/12
Carl Dantziger	Steam tug, 1 deck; depth 3.20m.	One 2-cylinder compound engine (one screw), one cylindrical boiler.	None.	0/12
Fairplay V	Steam tug, 1 deck; depth 3.46m.	One vertical 2-cylinder compound engine (one screw), one cylindrical boiler (118sq m, 10.5atm forced).	Two machine guns.	0/13
Fairplay XI	Steam tug, 1 deck; depth 3.05m.	One vertical 2-cylinder compound engine (one screw), one cylindrical boiler (94sq m, 10.5atm forced).	None.	0/12
Kehrewieder	Steam ferry, 1 deck; depth 3.40m.	One vertical 4-cylinder double compound engine (two side paddle wheels), one cylindrical boiler.	One 8.8cm gun.	
Saturn	Steam tug, 1 deck; depth 3.50m.	One vertical 3-cylinder triple expansion engine (one screw), one cylindrical boiler (108sq m, 7.5atm forced).	None.	0/24
Seeadler	Steam ferry, 1 deck; depth 4.60m.	Two vertical 3-cylinder triple expansion engines (2 screws), four cylindrical boilers.	Three 5.2cm guns.	1/36
Sirius	Steam tug, 1 deck; depth 3.95m.	One vertical 3-cylinder triple expansion engine (one screw), one cylindrical boiler (162sq m, 13.5atm forced).	Two 3.7cm machine guns.	0/22
Wilhelm Wrede	Steam tug, 1 deck; depth 3.50m.	One vertical 3-cylinder triple expansion engine (one screw), one boiler.	None.	0/13

Name	Builder (construction nos)	Built	Gross tonnage	Displacement (t = tonnes T = tons)	Length (m)	Breadth (m)	Draught (m)	Hull depth (m)	Power (hp)	Speed (kts)	Range and fuel (nm/kts/t)	Owner
Adolp	Gips	1912	155gt	305t max	29.46 oa	6.40		3.55				Habermann & Guekes AG, Kiel
Amerika	Atlas (97)	,,	176gt		30.67 oa	6.80	3.35 fwd 3.05 aft	3.99	525ihp max*	11.2		DDG Hansa, Bremen
Bremerhaven	Seebeck (219)	1904	80gt		23.60 oa	5.54	2.57	3.00	380ihp max 280ihp des	11.0 des	946/11/24 coal	Schleppschiff-Ges. Unterweser, Bremen.
Carl Dantziger	SMF (529)	1913	93gt		22.46 oa	5.71	2.87	3.20	430ihp max 380ihp des	10.0 des	/ /30 coal	B W Wessels, Emden
Fairplay V	Stülcken (191)	1901	102gt		25.20 oa	5.64	3.18	3.46	510ihp max 425ihp des	11.0 des	980/10/35 coal	C Tiedemann/ Pauls & Blohm KG, Hamburg
Fairplay XI	SMF (524)	1912	74gt		21.17 oa	5.43	2.82	3.05	347ihp max 320ihp des	10.5 max	500/10/16 coal	,,
Kehrewieder	Tecklenborg (103)	1890	477gt		56.45	7.14		3.40	750ihp	11.7 max 11.0 des		Norddeutscher Lloyd, Bremen
Saturn	Seebeck (66)	1893	120gt		29.35 oa	5.68	3.16	3.50	350ihp max 30ihp des	9.0 des	600/9/27 coal	,,
Seeadler	,, (121)	1897	541gt		51.50 oa 50.06 cwl	8.00	3.05	4.60	1000ihp max 950ihp des	13.5		,,
Sirius	Frerichs (137)	1907	196gt		32.90 oa	7.04	3.44	3.95	760ihp max 500ihp des	11.0 max 6.0 des	1200/10/ 60 coal	,,
Wilhelm Wrede	SMF	1914	215gt		36.01 oa 34.10 cwl	7.01	3.28	3.50	700ihp max			Schrader & Wrede, Hamburg

*120rpm max.

Careers

Adolph: launched 1912 as steam tug *Adolph*; blockade service vessel Hever *A* from 23 Sept 1915; net vessel with the Baltic Net Barrage Group from 5 May 1917; sunk in Kiel bay on 19 May 1917, following collision with the steamship *Askania*.

Amerika: launched 19 Oct 1912, commissioned 17 Dec 1912 as steam tug *Amerika*; with blockade vessel division from 4 Aug 1914; net vessel with Net Barrage Group North from 14 Apr 1916; with Ems patrol flotilla from 17 Apr 1918; Jade ship blockade, Jul 1918; returned 28 Nov 1918; became Swedish *O.A. Melin* in 1926; renamed *Stronggrogg* in 1947; broken up in 1962.

Bremerhaven: launched 1904 as steam tug *Bremerhaven*; to HM division, Ems, 19 Oct 1914; net vessel with the Baltic Net Barrage Group from 16 Dec 1915; returned 7 Apr 1919; in vessel pool, Weser, 4 Mar 1939; Operation Sealion tug *C .. S* in 1940; KM dockyard Wilhelmshaven, 194?; KM dockyard Drontheim, 194?; returned 13 Jun 1945; sunk by a mine at Bremerhaven on 6 Oct 1945, five dead.

Carl Dantziger: launched 1913, commissioned May 1913 as steam tug *Carl Dantziger*; blockade service vessel with Ems blockade division from 1 Aug 1914; net vessel with Baltic Net Barrage Group from 4 Feb 1916; returned 28 Aug 1919; broken up in Holland 1959.

Fairplay V: launched 1901 as steam tug *Fairplay V*; net vessel with Baltic Net Barrage Group from 14 Dec 1916; patrol half-flotilla West from 18 Jan 1917; with blockade vessel division, Weser, from 27 Aug 1917; returned 11 Feb 1919; KM dockyard Kiel, 5 Sept 1939; Operation Sealion tug *D .. S*, 1940; returned 9 Sept 1945; broken up Dec 1957.

Fairplay XI: launched 1912 as steam tug *Fairplay XI*; with blockade vessel division, Jade, from 5 Sept 1914; net vessel with Baltic Net Barrage Group from 17 Jun 1916; returned 28 May 1919; earmarked for Operation Sealion as tug, 1940; returned, broken up Jul 1964.

Kehrewieder: launched 1890 as sea bathing tender

Kehrewieder; net vessel with the Baltic Net Barrage Group from 9 Mar 1917; returned 3 Apr 1919; sold to H. Peters dockyard, Wewelsfleth, in May 1920, for breaking up?

Saturn: launched 1893 as steam tug *Saturn*; hunting boat, HM division, Wilhelmshaven, from 6 Oct 1914; net vessel with Net Barrage Group North from 10 Dec 1915; with blockade vessel division at Borkum from 22 Sept 1917; returned, renamed *Johannes Westphal* with Sieg & Co., Danzig, 1919; earmarked for Operation Sealion as tug, 1940; returned 3 Jun 1945; became Polish steam tug *Slon* in 1947, with harbour authorities at Gdansk; broken up in 1962.

Seeadler: launched Jan 1897, commissioned 1 May 1897 as sea bathing tender, Helgoland-Sylt; external transit ship with the Jade blockade vessel division from 2 Aug 1914; experimental vessel with the technical trial commission at Kiel from 15 Oct 1915; net vessel with the Baltic Net Barrage Group from 16 Dec 1915; with harbour defence flotilla from 11 May 1917; net vessel with the Baltic Net Barrage Group from 23 Jan 1918; returned 3 Apr 1919; became steam tug *Seewolf* (Schuchmann) 1924; to Portuguese Colonial Department 1926; renamed *Infante Dom Henrique* in 1935; broken up in 1939.

Sirius: launched 1907 as steam tug *Sirius*; with HM division Wilhelmshaven from 7 Aug 1914; experimental vessel with the technical trial commission at Kiel from 18 Oct 1915; net vessel with the Baltic Net Barrage Group from 16 Dec 1915; returned 2 Jun 1919; with Net Barrage Group from 13 Oct 1939; became *Netztender 15* with Net Barrage Group Centre, from 21 Mar 1941; sunk at Reval on 25 Nov 1943 after collision with motor vessel *Gotenland*, position 59° 24′N, 24° 45′E, one dead; raised 2 Dec 1944, and repaired; to Towage Office, Kiel, 1945; taken as US prize 25 Apr 1946, OMGUS; on charter to Norddeutscher Lloyd, Bremen, from 23 Feb 1948; returned to US Navy, Bremerhaven, 23 May 1950. No further details.

Wilhelm Wrede: launched 1914 as steam tug *Wilhelm Wrede*; with blockade vessel division, Elbe, from 1 Aug 1914; net vessel with Baltic Net Barrage Group from 5 May 1917; returned 5 Apr 1919; renamed *Zeus* with Bugsier Reed. & Bergungs AG of Hamburg in 1919; became Portuguese *Milhafre* in 1930; became Italian *Tenax* in 1936; sunk east of Sicily on 6 Aug 1943 after being bombed and strafed by aircraft, position 38° 26′N, 15° 54′E.

Net repair vessels

Name	Builder (construction nos)	Built	Gross tonnage	Displacement (t = tonnes T = tons)	Length (m)	Breadth (m)	Draught (m)	Hull depth (m)	Power (hp)	Speed (kts)	Range and fuel (nm/kts/t)	Owner
Alma	Thyen	1907	147gt		28.63 oa	6.50	3.11	3.28	110ihp max	6.0 max	2880/6/16 coal	Leerer Herings-fischerei AG, Leer
Ella	Cassens (24)	1908	166gt		30.18 oa	7.00	3.08	3.28	10ihp max	,,	,,	,,
Tony	,,	1906	144gt		28.58 oa	6.52	2.99	,,	120ihp max	7.0 max	,,	,,

Careers

Alma: launched 1907 as steam lugger *Alma*; net repair lugger with the Baltic Net Barrage Group from 31 Aug 1918; returned 9 Dec 1918; later renamed *Stella* for the Trop. Hai und Grossfischreederei GmbH of Hamburg; fate unknown.

Ella: launched Mar 1908 as steam lugger *Ella*; chartered 10 Dec 1915; conversion completed 23 Feb 1916; commissioned 19 May 1917 as net repair lugger with the Baltic Net Barrage Group; returned 16 Dec 1918; North Station from 14 Jul 1940; became *Vs 129* with coastal defence flotilla group D, Flensburg, from 20 Mar 1941; became *Sperrwachschiff 3* with blockade command, Western Baltic/Kiel guard flotilla from 14 Nov 1942; later became *DWo 77* with coastal defence flotilla, Western Baltic; returned 16 Aug 1945; fate unknown.

Tony: launched May 1906 as steam lugger; temporarily to first submarine hunter flotilla 17–21 Dec 1915, but proved unsuitable; net repair lugger with the Baltic Net Barrage Group from 19 Jun 1917; returned 9 Dec 1918; became *V 1231* in 1942; returned 1945; became motor vessel *Luise Raabe* (Fritz Raabe) 1950; served as salvage ship *Luise Raabe* with Werner Armbrust of Kiel from 1951; became *Gesa* with H. Breckwoldt of Flensburg, 1955; broken up 1964.

Name	Type and construction	Propulsion	Armament	Complement
Alma, Ella, Tony	Steam lugger, 1 deck; depth 3.28m.	One vertical 2-cylinder compound engine (one screw), one cylindrical boiler (44sq m, 10atm forced; *Tony* 38sq m, 9atm forced).	None.	(16)

Net vessels 1939–1945

Netlayers (I)

Name	Builder (construction nos)	Built	Gross tonnage	Displacement (t = tonnes T = tons)	Length (m)	Breadth (m)	Draught (m)	Hull depth (m)	Power (hp)	Speed (kts)	Range and fuel (nm/kts/t)	Owner
Valencia	Neptun (374)	1922	3096gt	c5600t max	103.04 oa	15.03	6.76	9.60	1550ihp max	11.0 max	13,610/10/ 1260 coal	Robert M Slomen, jr, Hamburg
Genna (mod)	Flensburg (420) DWA	1930 1939	1949gt	c3200t max	90.36 oa	13.03	4.95	5.79	1600ihp max	12.0 max	8750/12/	,,
*Netzleichler 1 (ex M.N.L. 1)**												
Netzleger I (mod)	Rickmers (B) (209) Stülcken	1939 1940–41	2042gt		98.60 oa 91.33 cwl	13.05	5.33	7.86	1350ihp max	,,	10,000/12/ 507 coal	Argo-Reederei Richard Adler & Co, Bremen

* See page 195.

Careers

Valencia: launched Aug 1922, commissioned Oct 1922 as steamship *Valencia*; commissioned as net layer with Net Barrage Group I 6 Sept 1939; struck mine and sunk in the north entrance to The Sound on 5 Jun 1940, stranded; raised 16 Jun 1940 and brought into Copenhagen; out of service; returned 3 Nov 1940; repaired at Nakskov; sunk in the vicinity of Maloy on 1 Feb 1944 after hitting a mine, position 61° 55′N, 05° 08′E, stranded; raised

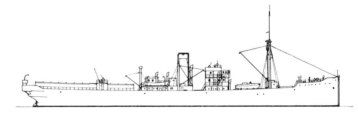

Valencia (1940). *Mrva*

Name	Type and construction	Propulsion	Armament	Complement
Valencia	Steam ship, 2 decks; depth 9.60m.	One vertical 3-cylinder triple expansion engine (one screw), two cylindrical boilers (396sq m, 13.5atm forced).	Four 2cm AA guns, 128 lengths 24m net.	5/143
Genua	Steam ship, 1 deck; depth 5.79m.	One vertical 4-cylinder double compound engine (one 3-bladed screw), two boilers (404sq m, 14atm forced).	Four 2cm AA guns, 77 lengths 24m net, 23 lengths 16m net.	5/157
Netzleichter 1	See page 195.			
Netzleger I	Steam ship; depth 7.86m.	One vertical 4-cylinder double compound engine with waste steam turbine (one screw), two cylindrical boilers (340sq m, 16atm forced).	One 7.5cm gun, two 3.7cm AA guns, four 2cm AA guns.	152/160

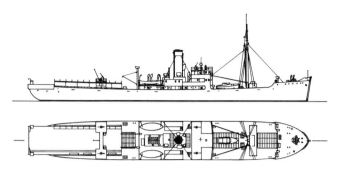

Genua (1940). *Mrva*

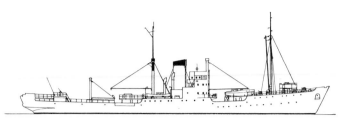

Netzleger I (ex *Franz E. Schütte*) (1943). *Mrva*

194? and repaired, became Norwegian *Skittland*; became Danish *Ulla* 1954; became German *Senior* with Ahrenkiel & Bene of Hamburg in 1956; became Lebanese *Senior* in 1960; broken up in 1962.

Genua: launched 11 Jul 1930, commissioned 6 Oct 1930 as steamship *Genua*; converted after 4 Sept

1939 for Net Barrage Group I; commissioned 14 Sept 1939; sunk at Egersund at 0105hrs on 14 Oct 1940 by a torpedo from the British destroyer *Cossack*, position 58° 26′N, 05° 40′E, 78 dead.

Netzleger I: launched 22 Apr 1939, commissioned 11 Jul 1939 as steamship *Franz E. Schütte*; became

Operation Sealion transporter *RO 35* from 11 Aug 1940; converted to net layer after 15 Oct 1940, as replacement for *Genua*; commissioned 3 May 1941 as *Netzleger I* with Net Barrage Group Centre; GM/SA 1945, first minesweeper division; USSR prize 19 Feb 1946, became training ship *Lena*; broken up about 1960.

Netlayers (II)

Name	Builder (construction nos)	Built	Gross tonnage	Displacement (t = tonnes T = tons)	Length (m)	Breadth (m)	Draught (m)	Hull depth (m)	Power (hp)	Speed (kts)	Range and fuel (nm/kts/t)	Owner
Netzleger II	Flensburg (433)	1936	2474gt	3327t max	88.40 oa 83.82 cwl	13.55	5.87	7.30	1300ihp max	12.0 max	11,340/11/ 846 coal	Sauber & Co, Hamburg
(mod)	(Aarhus)											
Netzleger III	Unterweser (271)	1939	1100gt	3065t max	76.00 oa 69.94 cwl	10.55	4.25	5.80	1100ehp max	14.0 max	5000/14/ 100 oil	D G Neptun, Bremen
(mod)	B & W	1940										
Netzleger III	Finnboda (304)	1922	1573gt		82.56 oa	12.53	4.75	7.77	1000ehp max	10.0 max	20,000/10/ 476 oil	Stockholms Rederi AB Svea, Stockholm
Netzleger IV	Neptun (463)	1936	1246gt	c3160t max	75.10 oa 73.50 cwl	10.57	4.31	4.90	1100ehp max	12.0 max	6300/12/ 100 oil	DG Neptun, Bremen
Netzleger V	*	1897										
Netzleger VI (Seeleichter 25/41)	Wärtsilä (787)	1942	2270gt		93.00 oa 87.60 cwl	13.46	3.80	6.30	—	—	—	(Kriegsmarine new construction)
Netzleger VII	Howaldt (K) (426)	1905	672gt		64.00 oa	10.29	3.13		600ihp max	8.0 max		A Dunin-Slepse, Galati
(mod)	(Piraeus)	1941–42										

* See page 195.

Careers

Netzleger II: launched 3 Nov 1936, commissioned 30 Dec 1936 as steamship *Herman Sauber*; converted for Net Barrage Group after Mar 1941; commissioned 12 Oct 1941 as *Netzleger II* for Net Barrage Group North; with German minesweeping

group, Norway, 1945; released to USSR 28 Mar 1946; broken up about 1956.

Netzleger III: launched 29 Jun 1939, commissioned Nov 1939 as motor vessel *Uranus*; converted for Net Barrage Group I after 23 Jul 1940 as replacement for *Valencia*; commissioned as *Netzleger III*

5 Apr 1941 for Net Barrage Group West; sunk by an aircraft bomb in the vicinity of Ile de Batz at 1515hrs on 30 Jul 1942, position approx. 48° 45′N, 04° 02′W.

Netzleger III: launched 1922 as Swedish motor vessel *Frost*; declared prize at Bordeaux 18 Sept

Name	Type and construction	Propulsion	Armament	Complement
Netzleger II	Steam ship, 1 deck; depth 7.30m.	One vertical 3-cylinder triple expansion engine (one screw), two cylindrical boilers (390sq m, 15atm forced).	One 7.5cm gun, two 3.7cm AA guns, four 2cm AA guns.	110–158
Netzleger III (ex *Uranus*)	Motor vessel, 1 deck; depth 5.80m.	Two Krupp-Germania 6-cylinder 4-stroke diesel engines (two 4-bladed screws).	Two 3.7cm AA guns, two 2cm AA guns.	90
Netzleger III (ex *Hendrik Fisser*)	Motor vessel, 1 deck + shelter deck; depth 7.77m.	Two Atlas 4-cylinder 2-stroke diesel engines (two screws).	One 7.5cm gun, four 2cm AA guns, two heavy machine guns.	
Netzleger IV	Motor vessel, 1 deck; depth 4.90m.	Two MAN 6-cylinder 4-stroke diesel engines (two 4-bladed screws).	Four 3.7cm AA guns, seven 2cm AA guns [nine 2cm AA guns, 1944].	82–90
Netzleger V	See page 195.			
Netzleger VI	Lighter, depth 6.30m.	No engines; 1 boiler (50sq m, 10atm forced).	Four 2cm AA guns [later seven 2cm AA guns]; 1 buoy boat.	110–124
Netzleger VII	Steam ship, 1 deck.	Two vertical 3-cylinder triple expansion engines (two screws).	One 10.52cm gun, two 3.7 AA guns, six 2cm AA guns.	2/138

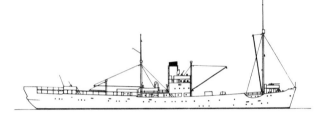

Netzleger II (ex Herman Sauber) (1942). Mrva

Netzleger III (ex Hendrik Fisser, ex Frost) (1944).
Mrva

Netzleger IV (ex Najade) (1940.

Netzleger VII (Piräus) (ex Ville de Toulon) (1944).
Mrva

1940; taken over by German Reich against compensation payment of 300,000 RM, 27 May 1941, renamed *Hendrik Fisser*; converted for Net Barrage Group after 30 Sept 1942; commissioned as *Netzleger III* 3 Dec 1942 for Net Barrage Group West; scuttled in Bordeaux as block ship on 2 Aug 1944, position 44° 50′N, 00° 34′W; raised 1946 and resold by French government to A/B Svea, repaired at Antwerp; renamed *Fjord*; became German *Fjordmöwe* 1955, with H. Krohn of Travemünde; on Swedish charter as *Fjorden* 1959; became Greek *Kassos* in 1964; laid up 1971.

Netzleger IV: launched Nov 1936, commissioned Mar 1937 as motor vessel *Najade*; converted after 10 May 1940 as a replacement for *Netzleichter 1*

and *2*; commissioned 18 Sept 1940 with Net Barrage Group I; with Net Barrage Group Centre from 1 Apr 1942; GM/SA, 1945; taken as Belgian prize 1 Feb 1946, renamed *Irene Marie*; became German *Rimberg* with E. Jacob of Flensburg, 1956; became Greek *Sophia T.* 1960; sunk in Sea of Marmara on 9 Dec 1961, position 40° 35′N, 27° 34′E.

Netzleger V: see page 195.

Netzleger VI (Genua): Soviet heavy lighter contract; taken over by KM in 1941 as sea-going lighter *25/41* before construction was started. Launched 27 Jun 1942, commissioned 25 Nov 1942 as *Netzleger VI (Genua)*, with Net Barrage Group North; GM/SA, 1945; taken as US prize, OMGUS, 1 Nov 1947; to Norway 8 Mar 1948; became motor

vessel *Emil Berger* with A. Zedler of Lübeck, 1951; became Greek *Santa Paola* 1969; became Cypriot *Nijitas* 1974; still in service in 1976.

Netzleger VII (Piräus): launched 1905 as Russian steamship *Elpidifor*; Russian mine hunter *T 230* from Nov 1916; to Danzig as *Ville de Toulon*, 1922; became French *Ville de Toulon* in 1936; requisitioned 1941; commissioned 1 Apr 1942 as *Netzleger VII (Piräus)* with Net Barrage Group South; scuttled at Saloniki 30 Oct 1944, position 40° 38′N, 22° 57′E; raised 1947; became Greek *Mariella* 1948; renamed *Marti* 1953; sunk in the vicinity of Sarayburnu, in the Marmara Sea, on 9 Aug 1953; raised 1957 and repaired, became Turkish *Sefer*; broken up at Istanbul in 1970.

Netlayers (III)

Name	Builder (construction nos)	Built	Gross tonnage	Displacement (t = tonnes T = tons)	Length (m)	Breadth (m)	Draught (m)	Hull depth (m)	Power (hp)	Speed (kts)	Range and fuel (nm/kts/t)	Owner
Netzleger VIII	Wärtsilä (788)	1942	2270gt	c3000t max	92.70 oa 87.60 cwl	13.46	3.80	6.30	—	—	—	(Kriegs-marine new con-struction)
Netzleger IX	” (794)	1943	228gt	”	”	”	”	”	900ehp max	10.0 max	/ /81 oil	”
Netzleger X	” (795)	1944	c2300gt	”	”	”	”	”	”	”	”	”
Netzleger XI	R & F (199)	1905	997gt	1163t max	66.50 oa	10.08	3.96	4.57	1000ihp max	10.0 max	/ /140 coal	P Cottar-opoulos & G Theophy-lactos, Marseille
Netzleger XII	(Salamis)	1934	125gt		24.25 oa	8.20	3.19			7.0 max		D Mer-kouris, Piraeus
Netzleger XIII	Howaldt (K) (670)	1926	1419gt		74.94 oa	11.55	4.39	5.11	650ihp max	9.0 max		Srenska Lloyd, Göteborg
Netzleger XIV	(Piraeus)	1943–44								c14.0 max		
Netzleger XV	NNS (13)	1924	135gt		30.51 oa	5.42	2.10	2.20	90ehp max	7.0 max		Wwe. J Boerma, Groningen

Careers

Netzleger VIII (Eggeroe): Soviet heavy lighter contract; taken over by KM in 1941 as sea lighter *26/41* before building was started; launched 1 Aug 1942, commissioned as *Netzleger VIII (Eggeroe)* 22 May 1943, for NVEK Test Command; out of service at Travemünde Jan 1945, disarmed; taken as British prize, Flensburg, May 1945; transferred to USSR 28 Dec 1945. Fate unknown.

Netzleger IX (Gemma): Soviet heavy lighter con-tract; taken over by KM in 1941 as sea lighter *32/41* before building was started; launched 11 Dec 1943, commissioned as *Netzleger IX (Gemma)* 17 Jul 1944, for NVEK; severely damaged by a bomb from a British aircraft at Gotenhafen on 18 Dec 1944; following emergency repairs transferred

Name	Type and construction	Propulsion	Armament	Complement
Netzleger VIII	Lighter; depth 6.30m.	No engines; one boiler (50sq m, 10atm forced).	One 4cm Bofors gun, six 2cm AA guns [eleven 2cm AA guns, 1944].	120/124
Netzleger IX, X	Motor vessel; depth 6.30m.	One Wumag 8 SW 55 diesel engine (one screw).	Two 3.7cm AA guns, six 2cm AA guns.	3/109
Netzleger XI	Steam ship, 1 deck; depth 4.57m.	One vertical 3-cylinder triple expansion engine (one screw), two cylindrical boilers (308sq m, 12atm forced).		
Netzleger XII	Motor vessel, 1 deck.	One Humboldt-Deutz 2-cylinder 2-stroke diesel engine (one screw).	One 3.7cm AA gun, two 2cm AA guns.	23
Netzleger XIII	Steam ship, 1 deck; depth 5.11m.	One vertical 3-cylinder triple expansion engine (one screw), two cylindrical boilers (202sq m, 13atm forced).	One 8.8cm gun, four 3.7cm AA guns, two 2cm AA guns.	6/118
Netzleger XIV	Motor vessel, 1 deck.	One diesel engine (one screw).	One 8.8cm gun, one 3.7cm AA gun, six 2cm AA guns.	2/42
Netzleger XV	Motor vessel, 1 deck; depth 2.20m.	One Brons 2-cylinder 4-stroke diesel engine (one screw).	One 3.7cm AA gun, two 2cm AA guns.	36

One quadraple 2cm gun from 1944 (see *NL VII*).

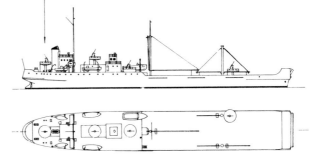

Netzleger VI (Genna) (1943). *Mrva*

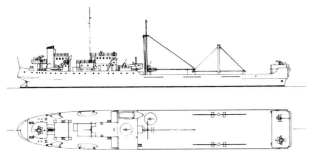

Netzleger VIII (Eggeroe) (1944). *Mrva*

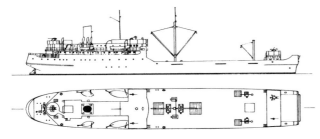

Netzleger IX (Gemma) (1944); *Netzleger X (Weststern)* was similar. *Mrva*

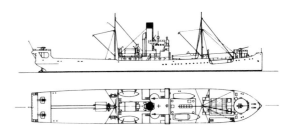

Netzleger XIII (ex Deime, ex Gallia) (1945). *Mrva*

from Danzig to Sassnitz as an emigrant transporter; finally to Sonderburg for cannibalisation and breaking up.

Netzleger X (Weststern): Soviet heavy lighter contract; taken over by KM in 1941 as sea lighter *33/41* before building was started; launched 15 Jul 1944, but released incomplete on 13 Sept 1944 as net lighter and transferred to Sonderburg. After Feb 1945 fitted out for Net Barrage Group Centre by crew of *Netzleger IX (Gemma)*, using dismantled parts from Schumann dockyard; no service. Transferred to Bremerhaven 10 Oct 1946; to Norway 1947; renamed *Norvest* 1948; became Dutch *Le Maire* 1951; to Hong Kong as *Dartford* 1960; broken up at Shanghai Oct 1968.

Netzleger XI: launched May 1905 as the British steamship *Ploussa*; renamed *Glentaise* in the 1920s; renamed *Antrim Coast* 1930; became French *Regina Pacis* 1933; renamed *Prado* 1937; from 1939 to 15 Oct 1940 served as French auxiliary mine hunter

AD 372; requisitioned for Net Barrage Group West in 1942; named *Netzleger XI* 19 Feb 1943, assigned to Net Barrage Group West on south coast of France; finally completed 12 Apr 1943; scuttled at Marseille Aug 1944.

Netzleger XII: launched 1934 as Greek motor sailing boat *Adroniki*; later became motor vessel *Salamis*; taken as German prize 1941: *11 V 3*, 11th coastal defence flotilla; converted to net layer 1943, and commissioned as *Netzleger XII* 18 Jul 1943, assigned to Net Barrage Group South; sunk in the Aegean by a torpedo from the French submarine *Curie* on 2 Oct 1944, position unknown, nine dead.

Netzleger XIII: launched Dec 1925 as steamship *Orion* for Heinrich Schmidt of Flensburg; became Swedish *Gallia* in 1931; taken as prize at Bergen 9 Apr 1940; converted to network ship from 19 Nov to 21 Nov 1940 and commissioned as *Deime* 21 Dec 1940, assigned to Net Barrage Group I; converted to net layer mid-1943 and commissioned as *Netzleger XIII* 26 Oct 1943, assigned to Net Bar-

rage Group North; at Drontheim with German minesweeping group North 10 May 1945; became French *Retiaire* 1947; stricken 12 Feb 1952; broken up 1960.

Netzleger XIV (Ares): launched as unidentified motor vessel, date unknown; seized for Net Barrage Group South in mid-1943; commissioned as *Netzleger XIV (Ares)* Aug 1944; scuttled at Saloniki in Oct 1944, position 40° 38′N, 22° 57′E.

Netzleger XV: launched 1924 as Dutch motor vessel *Antilope*; seized at Rotterdam 8 Apr 1942 for Black Sea service and purchased for 3,100 Hfl, transported overland to the Danube; commissioned for Dnieper coastal shipping Mar 1943; converted May to Oct 1943, commissioned as *Netzleger XV* on 10 Feb 1944 and assigned to Net Barrage Group Black Sea; run aground in the vicinity of Sfîntu Gheorghe 25 Feb 1944; towed off 3 Mar 1944, but sunk 5 Mar 1944 in the vicinity of Constanta while under tow by *Grafenau*.

Netlayers (IV)

Name	Builder (construction nos)	Built	Gross tonnage	Displacement (t = tonnes T = tons)	Length (m)	Breadth (m)	Draught (m)	Hull depth (m)	Power (hp)	Speed (kts)	Range and fuel (nm/kts)	Owner
Netzleger XVI	Smith's Dock (623)	1899	846gt		68.58 oa	9.75	3.66	3.96	460ihp max			D E Moscho-mas & J A Fassoulis, Piraeus

Name	Type and construction	Propulsion	Armament	Complement
Netzleger XVI	Steam ship, 1 deck; depth 3.96m.	One vertical 3-cylinder triple expansion engine (one screw), one water tube boiler (138sq m, 11atm forced).	–	–

Career

Launched 1899 as Greek steamship *Panaghia Vagliano*; later renamed *Cadmos*, then *Aspasia Nomikos*; renamed *Leros* 1936; seized for Net Barrage Group South in mid-1943; sunk by an aircraft bomb at Piraeus on 11 Jan 1944, during conversion to net layer, raised Jan 1944; incomplete Oct 1944, scuttled.

Net tenders

Name	Builder (construction nos)	Built	Gross tonnage	Displacement (t = tonnes T = tons)	Length (m)	Breadth (m)	Draught (m)	Hull depth (m)	Power (hp)	Speed (kts)	Range and fuel (nm/kts/t)	Owner
NT 6	Zaanland (430)	1941	497gt		54.59 oa 52.23 cwl	8.72	3.35	3.71	550ehp max	9.0 max	/ /65 oil	NV Rederij Pavo (NV Houthandel v/h W Pout), Zaandam
NT 6	Deschimag S (579)	1937	354gt		40.52 oa	8.03	4.32	4.60	1300ihp max			Walter Ram Neusser Öl-Werke AG, Bremen
(mod)	NDL	1939										
NT 8	,, (580)	,,	,,		,,	,,	,,	,,	,,			,,
NT 9	Bodewes (309)	1940	394gt		46.66 oa 43.78 cwl	7.97	2.82	3.27		9.0 max		NV Tankrederij 'Obo', Rotterdam
NT 10	,, (318)	1941	484gt		52.85 oa 49.30 cwl	8.66	3.17	3.60	450ehp max	,,	/ /44.5 oil	Rederij Ponto, Zaandam
NT 11	De Haan (210)		390gt		50.45 oa 47.55 cwl	7.93	2.77	4.81		,,		Weber & Wagenburg, Rotterdam
NT 12	Noord (581)	,,	489gt		54.99 oa 52.07 cwl	8.06	3.30		735ehp max	,,		H Stinnes, Rotterdam
NT 13	Niestern (226)	,,	395gt		57.92 oa	8.56	3.16	4.93	525ehp max	9.5 max		J Muthert, Groningen
NT 14	Vulcan (H) (679 (H197))	1920	341gt		38.71 oa	8.15	3.85	4.50	995ihp max 700ihp des	12.0 max 11.0 des	3830/11/ 170 coal	Bugsier-, Reederei- und Bergungs AG, Hamburg
NT 15	*											

Name	Builder (construction nos)	Built	Gross tonnage	Displacement (t = tonnes T = tons)	Length (m)	Breadth (m)	Draught (m)	Hull depth (m)	Power (hp)	Speed (kts)	Range and fuel (nm/kts/t)	Owner
NT 16	Oelkers (417)	1922	169gt		31.67 oa	6.98	3.75	3.98	650ihp max 450ihp des		/ /75 coal	Petersen & Alpers, Hamburg
NT 17, NT 19	LMG (128, 127)	1914	108gt		25.23 oa	6.05	2.97	3.27	430ihp max 320ihp des	10.0 max	2160/10/ 60 coal	,,
NT 18	Neptun (274)	1907	94gt		23.96 oa	6.03	2.40	2.85	485ehp max 350ehp des	11.3 max 10.0 des	2160/10/ 12 oil	Neue Dampfer Co AG, Kiel
NT 20	Howaldt (K) (711)	1930	160gt		31.42 oa 29.14 cwl	6.92	3.24	3.80	750ehp max 550ehp des	11.0 max	4700/11/ 34 oil	
NT 21	Vulcain	1903	146gt		27.66 oa	6.40	3.25	3.88	600ihp max	10.0 max	1680/10/ 70 coal	Fairplay Schlepp-dampf-schiffs-Reederei Richard Borchardt, Hamburg
NT 23	Fullerton (128)	1896	149gt		30.48 oa	6.48	2.60	3.08	600ihp max 550ihp des	11.0 max 9.0 des	1500/9/45 coal	Cie de Commerce 'Les Tuyaux Bleus', Bordeaux
NT 24		1943–44	400gt		37.70 oa	6.00				9.5 max		(Kriegs-marine new con-struction)
NT 25, NT 26, NT 46, NT 59	Wärtsilä (766, 767, 771, 773)	1941–42	530gt		49.90 oa 46.05 cwl	9.58	4.15	4.70	1600ihp max	11.0 max		(Kriegs-marine new con-struction taken over from Soviet tug designs)
NT 27	Boele (158)	1927			27.00	5.55	1.62	2.18	300ihp max 275ihp des	10.0 max	/ /30 coal	Scheep-vaart Mij Jega Wouters, Antwerp
NT 28, NT 29	ACL	1933	462gt	728t max	51.80 oa 46.60 cwl	9.30	3.30 max 2.60 des	4.10	1000ehp max	11.0 max	1500/10/ 30 oil	Service de Phare et Balises, Le Verdon/ La Rochelle
NT 30, NT 31	(Bordeaux)	1931	80gt		20.50 oa	5.75	1.65 max 1.50 des		105ehp max	8.0 max	/ /4 oil	Ponts et Chaus-sées, Brest
NT 32	Paans	1912	61gt		17.35 oa	4.90	1.85 fwd 1.50 aft	1.93	,,	7.6 max	1368/7/4.5 oil	Slepboot-reederij JJ Oud-akker, Enk-huizen

Name	Builder (construction nos)	Built	Gross tonnage	Displacement (t = tonnes T = tons)	Length (m)	Breadth (m)	Draught (m)	Hull depth (m)	Power (hp)	Speed (kts)	Range and fuel (nm/kts/t)	Owner
NT 33	de Jong	1930	50gt		20.12	5.07	2.00 max 1.50 des	1.85	245ehp max 200ehp des	8.8 max	/ /8.5 oil	J A v Alphen, Rotterdam
NT 38	Dubigeon	1925	96gt		21.33	5.62	3.34	3.75	750ihp max 600ihp des	9.0 max 8.0 des	/ /30 coal	Cie Cahmbon, Marseille
NT 41	Sachsenberg (984)	1928	108gt		25.55	5.50	2.10 max 1.70 des		575ehp max 400ehp des	10.0 max	2000/10/ 11 oil	Ste. Générale de Navigation sur la Haute Seine et les Canaux du Centre, Paris
NT 43	SPCN (3513)	1940	382gt	506t max	47.76	8.35	3.00			10.0 max		Marine Nationale Française
NT 44	" (3406)	1938	396gt	487t max	47.30 oa					"		"
NT 55	" (3694)	1943		516t max	47.75 oa	8.35	3.00			"		"
NT 47	Wärtsilä (286)	1942	530gt		49.00 oa 45.15 cwl	9.10	3.17	4.00	960ihp max 600ihp des	11.0 max	/ /98 coal	(Kriegsmarine new construction)
NT 48	Smit, L (899)	1939	118gt		27.46 oa	6.48	2.79		750ehp max			Breejen & van den Bout, Berg en Dal
NT 49	Foxhol (46)	1938	385gt		42.70	7.75	2.77					H Damhof, Hoogezand
NT 51	Atlas (257)	1929	188gt		27.81 oa 27.50 cwl	7.29	3.30	3.95	980ihp max 650ihp des	11.5 des	1000/11/ 45 coal	Unterweser Reederei AG, Bremen
NT 52	SMF (523)	1912	227gt		37.26 oa	7.08	3.36	4.25	850ihp max	12.0 max	2200/12/ 107 coal	Bugsier-, Reederei- und Bergungs- AG, Hamburg
NT 54	Arsenal Brest	1919	400gt	40.20 oa	8.00	4.00			1000ihp max 700ihp des	10.0 max 9.0 des		Marine Nationale Française
NT 56, NT 57	†											
NT ( ) (ex FR 92, ex Perseverante)		1932	350gt	458t max					500ihp max	8.0 max		Marine Nationale Française

* See *Sirius*, page 198.
† See *Rovigno, Albona*, page 181.

Name	Type and construction	Propulsion	Armament	Complement
NT 6	Motor vessel, 1 deck; depth 3.71m.	One Atlas MaK 6-cylinder 4-stroke diesel engine (one screw).		
NT 7	Whaler, 1 deck; depth 4.60m.	One vertical 3-cylinder triple expansion engine (one screw), one cylindrical boiler (310sq m, 15.5atm forced).	Two 2cm AA guns.	0/28
NT 9	Motor vessel, 1 deck; depth 3.27m.	One Werkspoor 6-cylinder 4-stroke diesel engine (one screw).	Two 2cm AA guns (4000 rounds), one heavy machine gun (9000 rounds).	1/42
NT 10	Motor vessel, 1 deck; depth 3.60m.	One MaK 8-cylinder 4-stroke diesel engine (one screw).		0/39
NT 11	Motor vessel, 1 deck + shelter deck; depth 4.81m.	One KHD 7-cylinder 4-stroke diesel engine (one screw).	Two 2cm AA guns.	0/42
NT 12	Motor vessel, 1 deck; depth 4.81m.	One Bolnes 6-cylinder 2-stroke diesel engine (one screw).	Two 2cm AA guns planned.	0/22
NT 13	Motor vessel, 1 deck + shelter deck; depth 4.93m.	One MAN 8-cylinder 4-stroke diesel engine (one screw).	Two 2cm AA guns (4000 rounds), one machine gun (9000 rounds).	1/42
NT 14	Steam tug, 1 deck; depth 4.50m.	One vertical 3-cylinder triple expansion engine (one screw), one cylindrical boiler (198sq m, 13atm forced).		0/21
NT 15	See page 198.			
NT 16	Steam tug, 1 deck; depth 3.98m.	One vertical 3-cylinder triple expansion engine (one screw), one cylindrical boiler (130sq m, 13.5atm forced).		
NT 17	Steam tug, 1 deck; depth 3.27m.	One vertical 3-cylinder triple expansion engine (one screw), one cylindrical boiler (110sq m, 12.5atm forced).		(8)
NT 18	Motor tug, 1 deck; depth 2.85m.	One DWK 8-cylinder 4-stroke diesel engine (one screw).		13
NT 20	Motor tug, 1 deck; depth 3.80m.	One Linke-Hofmann-Busch 7-cylinder 4-stroke diesel engine (one screw).		(8)
NT 21	Steam tug, 1 deck; depth 3.88m.	One vertical 3-cylinder triple expansion engine (one screw), one cylindrical boiler (108sq m, 13atm forced).		0/20
NT 23	Steam tug, 1 deck (6 watertight compartments); depth 3.08m.	One 2-cylinder compound engine (one screw), one cylindrical boiler (154sq m, 9atm forced).		0/11
NT 24	Motor vessel.	One diesel engine (one screw).	Four 2cm AA guns.	0/35
NT 25, 26, 46, 59	Steam tug, 1 deck; depth 4.70m.	One vertical 3-cylinder triple expansion engine (one screw), two cylindrical boilers (280sq m, 16atm forced).	Two 2cm AA guns.	1/30
NT 27	Steam tug, 1 deck; depth 2.81m.	One vertical 3-cylinder triple expansion engine (one screw), one boiler.		

Name	Type and construction	Propulsion	Armament	Complement
NT 28	Diesel-electric buoy layer, 1 deck, (10 watertight compartments); depth 4.10m.	Two MAN 6-cylinder 4-stroke diesel engines, two screw motors (two screws).	One 2cm AA gun.	12–16
NT 30	Motor buoy layer, 1 deck.	One diesel engine (one screw).	One 2cm AA gun.	0/7
NT 32	Motor tug, 1 deck; depth 1.93m.	One diesel engine (one screw).		
NT 33	Motor tug, 1 deck; depth 1.85m.	One Deutz 4-cylinder diesel engine (one screw).		
NT 38	Steam tug, 1 deck (4 watertight compartments); depth 3.75m.	One vertical 3-cylinder triple expansion engine (one screw), one cylindrical boiler (185sq m, 13atm forced).		
NT 41	Motor tug, 1 deck.	One 4-stroke Deutz diesel engine (one screw).		0/7
NT 43	Gabare.		One 5.7cm gun, one 2cm AA gun.	0/36
NT 47	Steam tug, 1 deck; depth 4.00m.	Two vertical 3-cylinder triple expansion engines (two screws), two cylindrical boilers (242sq m, 15atm forced).		23
NT 48	Motor tug, 1 deck.	One Bolnes 6-cylinder 4-stroke diesel engine (one screw).		
NT 49	Motor vessel, 1 deck.	One Brons 4-cylinder 2-stroke diesel engine (one screw).		
NT 51	Steam tug, 1 deck; depth 3.95m.	One vertical 3-cylinder triple expansion engine (one screw), one boiler (175sq m, 13.5 atm forced).		1/20
NT 52	Steam tug, 1 deck; depth 4.25m.	One 2-cylinder compound engine (one screw), one cylindrical boiler (191sq m, 11.5atm forced).		0/22
NT 54	Steam tug, 1 deck.			
NT 56, 57	See page 181.			
NT ( ) (ex *FR 92*)	Steam gabare			

Careers

NT 6: launched 1941 as Dutch motor vessel *Pavo*; commissioned as *NT 6*, 3 Mar 1942; GM/SA 1945; taken as US prize Nov 1947, OMGUS; returned as motor vessel *Pavo*; became German *Bertz* for Schepers of Haren, 1960; became Greek *Anna* 1970; Broken up 1983.

NT 7: launched 9 Jun 1937 as whaler *Rau VII*; commissioned as *Netztender I* 26 Oct 1939, assigned to Net Barrage Group I; with special group 5, 'Weserübung' from 1 Apr to 10 May 1940; to Net Barrage Group North as *NT 7* 1 Apr 1942; to German minesweeping group, Norway, May 1945; taken as Norwegian prize May 1947, renamed *Thorgrim*; released to USSR Feb 1948. Fate unknown.

NT 8: launched 19 Jun 1937 as whaler *Rau VIII*; commissioned as *Netztender II* 26 Oct 1939, assigned to Net Barrage Group I; with special group 5, 'Weserübung; from 1 Apr to 10 May 1940; to Net

Barrage Group North as *NT 8* 1 Apr 1942; to German minesweeping group, Norway, May 1945; taken as Norwegian prize May 1948; sold and converted to whaler 1948 and renamed *Polarbris 1*; sold 1966, converted to fishing vessel, and renamed *Lem Senior*; sold 1981, converted to offshore safety/standby vessel and renamed *Blue Safe*; sold to Britain 1988 and renamed *Grampian Osprey*. Still in service 1991.

NT 9: launched 1940 as Dutch motor vessel *Huybrecht*, completed as *Zetetica*; commissioned with Net Barrage Group I on 11 Oct 1941; became *NT 9* with Net Barrage Group West 1 Apr 1942; scuttled Jun 1944; raised, repaired and re-engined by 1948, became Dutch motor vessel *Leny*; became Italian *Pasquale Camalich* 1960; renamed *Rocco Madonna* 1966; became Panamanian *Rina* 1975; renamed *Aspis* 1976; became Cypriot *Trader* 1978; became Panamanian *Maria M.1* 1982. Still in service 1990.

NT 10: under construction as Dutch motor vessel *Ponto*; purchased by KM on 21 May 1941 and launched as *NT 10* Jun 1941; commissioned 11 Oct 1941 with Net Barrage Group I; to Net Barrage Group North 1 Apr 1942; returned 1945, became Dutch motor vessel *Ponto*; renamed *Ameland* 1965; renamed *Udo* 1968; became German *Hans B.* 1970; became *Neermoor* with S. Bojen of Neermoor, 1970; still in service 1976. Believed broken up about 1985.

NT 11: launched Feb 1941 as Dutch motor vessel *Bestevaer*; commissioned 10 Apr 1942 as *NT 11* with Net Barrage Group West; scuttled at Cherbourg Jun 1944, position 49° 38'N, 01° 38'E, raised, repaired, became motor vessel *Bestevaer*; became Danish *Else Priva* 1959; renamed *Jatile* 1984. Still in service 1991.

NT 12: launched Feb 1941 as Dutch motor vessel *Hast V*; seized 30 Jun 1941; commissioned 23 Oct 1941 with Net Barrage Group I; became *NT 12*

with Net Barrage Group North 1 Apr 1942; returned 1945, motor vessel *Hast V*; became German *Margitta J* (H. Janssen) 1959; became *Andrea I* with W. Oltmann Jr., Elsfleth, 1962; broken up 1964.

NT 13: launched Jun 1941 as Dutch motor vessel *Batavier*; commissioned as *NT 13* 29 May 1942 with Net Barrage Group Centre, temporarily serving as net layer in Aarhus group, with laying equipment above bow; specialised for repair work after 1944 by installation of third derrick on foremast; GM/SA 1945; returned 26 Jan 1946, and reverted to motor vessel *Batavier*; became Finnish *Tatu* 1972; broken up 1985.

NT 14: launched 8 Aug 1920 and commissioned Nov 1920 as steam tug *Adana*, (Hamburg-Amerika-Linie); renamed *Simson* Nov 1927; with Net Barrage Group I from 6 Sept 1939; became *NT 14* with Net Barrage Group North on 1 Apr 1942; sunk by a mine in the vicinity of Great Wrangel, Gulf of Finland, on 15 Apr 1943 during salvaging of *M ..*, position unknown, 19 dead.

NT 16: launched 1922 as steam tug *Adolf*; commissioned Oct 1939 with Net Barrage Group I; became *NT 16* with Net Barrage Group Centre 1 Apr 1942; sunk by a mine in Ebeltoft Bay, Kattegat, 17 Oct 1942, position unknown, five dead.

NT 17: launched 1914 as steam tug *Falkenstein* (NDC); renamed *Stubbenhuk* with Petersen & Alpers 1930; commissioned 6 Sept 1939 with Net Barrage Group I; became *NT 17* with Net Barrage Group Centre 1 Apr 1942; capsized in storm and sunk in Gulf of Finland on 18 Apr 1943 when net load collapsed, position unknown, no casualties.

NT 18: launched 1907 as steam ferry *Süd* (NDC); became motor tug *Bülk* 1935; commissioned 6 Sept 1939 with Net Barrage Group I; became *NT 18* with Net Barrage Group Centre 1 Apr 1942; Net Barrage Group North Sea, Mar 1944; GM/SA 1945, tender; returned 15 Sept 1947; sold to Holland 1964. Fate unknown.

NT 19: launched 1914 as steam tug *Jaegersburg* (NDC); became *Steinhöft* with Petersen & Alpers 1929; commissioned 6 Sept 1939 with Net Barrage Group I; became *NT 19* with Net Barrage Group Centre 1 Apr 1942; tug office Kiel, RN, Sept 1945; returned 1945; renamed *Joachim* with Johannsen & Sohn, Lübeck, 1952; broken up 1956.

NT 20: launched 1930 as motor tug *Stein*; commissioned 6 Sept 1939 with Net Barrage Group I; became *NT 20* with Net Barrage Group Centre 1 Apr 1942; with German minesweeping group, Denmark, 1945; returned 1947; became Dutch *Temi III* 1964; became Cypriot *Pirahna 2* 1975; became Kuwaiti *Nowres I* 1977. Still in service 1990.

NT 21: launched 1903 as steam tug *Vulcain I*; completed for URAG as *Vegesack*; renamed *Johannes Schupp* 1927; renamed *Fairplay XVIII* 1932; commissioned 1 Dec 1939 with Net Barrage Group I; became *NT 21* with Net Barrage Group North 1 Apr 1942; USSR prize 16 Apr 1946. Fate unknown.

NT 23 (Argus): launched 1896 as French steam tug *Dona Catalina*; later renamed *Perigord*; Operation Sealion tug at Hako, St Nazaire 10 Jun 1940; became *NT 23 (Argus)* with Net Barrage Group West 27 Jun 1941; sunk by a mine at Paimboeuf, Loire, 26/27 Nov 1942; raised 14 Dec 1942; Net Barrage Group Atlantic Coast, Oct 1943; returned as *Perigord* 1945; broken up 1956.

NT 24: launched 1943, commissioned 19 Feb 1944 as *NT 24 (Hans (Bussenius*))*, assigned to Net Barrage Group Centre; to Holland late 1945. Fate unknown.

NT 25: launched 25 Sept 1941, commissioned 8 Jul 1942 as *NT 25 (Hugo (Heinke))** assigned to NVEK; Net Barrage Group Centre Mar 1944; GM/SA 1945; taken as Norwegian prize 194?; became motor tanker *Polarsirkel* 1950; became sealer *Polarsirkel* 1953; renamed *Asbjörn* 1970; broken up 1974.

NT 26: launched 1 Nov 1941, commissioned 1 Jul 1942 as *NT 26 (Otto (Eichler*))*, assigned to Net Barrage Group Centre; to Net Barrage Group North 1 Aug 1942; GM/SA 1945, fate unknown.

NT 27 (Jupiter): launched 1927 as Dutch steam tug *Jega*; Operation Sealion tug *R 20 S* Aug 1940; became *B 110 S* 1940; became *NT 27 (Jupiter)* with Net Barrage Group West, Jul 1942; later became *Wacht am Rhein III*, then Dutch *Damco 14*; motor tug 1962; later renamed *Susanna G.*, then *Ilmar* then *Taurus*; still in existence in 1984.

NT 28 (Planet): launched 1933 as French buoy layer *Charles Ribière*; sunk west of Talais Buoy, Gironde, on 30 May 1942, after striking a mine, stranded; raised by KM 1942; commissioned 21 Aug 1942 as *NT 28 (Planet)*; assigned to Net Barrage Group West; sunk by three rocket bombs at Tancarville lock in the Seine estuary at 1110hrs on 7 May 1944; raised, wreck sunk by an aircraft bomb at Le Havre at around 1900hrs on 2 Aug 1944, during a large-scale attack.

NT 29 (Saturn): launched 1933 as French buoy layer *Charles Babin*; commissioned 23 Aug 1942 as *NT 29 (Saturn)*; assigned to Net Barrage Group West; sunk by an aircraft bomb in La Pallice outer harbour 16 Sept 1942, position unknown; raised and repaired; sunk in the vicinity of Boulogne by an aircraft bomb 18 Jun 1944.

NT 30 (Wega): launched 1931 as French buoy layer *Fromrust*; commissioned Oct 1942 as *NT 30 (Wega)*; assigned to Net Barrage Group West; sunk in western region Jun 1944.

NT 31 (Aldebaran): launched 1931 as French buoy layer *Gradlon*; commissioned 10 Jan 1943 as *NT 31 (Aldebaran)*; assigned to Net Barrage Group West; pilot command, Trouville, 16 Feb 1943; scuttled in western region Jun 1944.

NT 32 (Castor): launched 1912 as Dutch motor tug *Mina*; renamed *Tema* 13 Jun 1939; Operation Sealion tug *R 85 S* Aug 1940; *D 119 S* 194?; commissioned 12 Sept 1942 as *NT 32 (Castor)*; assigned to Net Barrage Group West; sunk in western region Jun 1944.

NT 33 (Pollux): launched 1930 as Dutch motor tug *St. John*; Operation Sealion tug *R 66 S* Aug 1940; *D 116 S* 1940; commissioned 12 Sept 1942 as *NT 33 (Pollux)*; assigned to Net Barrage Group West; returned 1945 as *St. John*; still in existence 1983.

*These vessels were intended to be named after members of the Net Barrage Group who had died in the sinking of the net layer *Genua*. Approval was granted only for the use of first names.

Summary of net tenders 1939–1945

Number	Vessel type	Name
1		*IO 81 (FW19)*
2		*FW 20 (ex Copri II)*
3		
4		
5		
6	motor ship	*Pavo*
7	whaling ship	*Rau VII*
8	"	*Rau VIII*
9	motor ship	*Zetetica*
10	"	*Ponto*
11	"	*Bestevaer*
12	"	*Hast V*
13	"	*Batavier*
14	steam tug	*Simson*
15	"	*Sirius*
16	"	*Adolf*
17	"	*Stubbenhuk*
18	motor tug	*Bülk*
19	steam tug	*Steinhöft*
20	motor tug	*Stein*
21	steam tug	*Fairplay XVIII*
22	steam tug	*Paul*
24	motor ship	*Hans (Bussenius)*
25	steam tug	*Hugo (Heinke)*
26	"	*Otto (Eichler)*
27	"	*Jupiter (ex Jega)*
28	buoy layer	*Plant (ex Charles Ribière)*
29	"	*Saturn (ex Charles Babin)*
30	"	*Wega (ex Fromrust)*
31	"	*Aldebaran (ex Gradlon)*
32	steam tug	*Castor (ex Tema)*
33	"	*Pollux (ex St. John)*
34	motor fishing cutter	*Suda*
35	"	*Volos*
36	"	*Sofia*
37	buoy layer	*Orion*
38	steam tug	*Hecht (ex Marseillais 4)*
39	"	*Paardenplaat*
40	"	*Welplaat*
41	motor tug	*Loriot*
42		
43	buoy layer	*Wal (ex Agissante)*
44	"	*Prudente*
45	motor tug	*Schollevaer*
46	steam tug	*Rabaul*
47	"	*Korsfjord*
48	"	*Mico*
49	motor ship	*Hoop*
50		
51	steam tug	*Elsfleth*
52	"	*Titan*
53	"	*Taucher O. Walf II*
54	"	*Lutteur*
55	buoy layer	*Mordante*
56	minelayer	*Rovigno*
57	"	*Albona*
58	motor fishing cutter	*Kissa*
59	steam tug	*Polangen*
60		
61		
(66)	buoy layer	*FR 92 (ex Perseverante)*

NT 38 (Hecht): launched 1925 as French steam tug *Marseillais 4*; commissioned 1 Apr 1942 as *NT 38 (Hecht)*; assigned to Net Barrage Group West, French south coast; sunk Marseille Jun 1944.

NT 41: launched 1928 as French motor tug *Loriot*; commissioned 23 Mar 1942 as *NT 41*, assigned to Net Barrage Group West; French navy tug *R 2* 1945; to Office National de la Navigation as inland tug 16 May 1945; fate unknown.

NT 43 (Wal): launched 19 Jul 1940, commissioned 13 Jan 1941 as French net tender *Agissante*; scuttled Toulon 27 Nov 1942; raised 7 Jan 1943 and commissioned 31 May 1943 as *NT 43 (Wal)*, assigned to Net Barrage Group West, French south coast; scuttled Marseille Aug 1944; raised, repaired 1947; out of service as *Q 333* Nov 1961; stricken 28 Feb 1963; fate unknown.

NT 44: launched 1936 as French net tender *Prudente*; scuttled Marseille 27 Nov 1942; raised 17 Feb 1943, repaired and commissioned Aug 1943 as *NT 44*, assigned to Net Barrage Group West, French south coast; sunk at north pier, Monaco harbour, 14 Dec 1943, while laying torpedo blockade nets, by a torpedo from the British submarine *Untiring*; two dead.

NT 46: launched 5 Aug 1942 as steam tug *Rabaul* (KM); commissioned 12 Mar 1943 as *NT 46*, assigned to Net Barrage Group North; taken as US prize 1945; German *Ludwig Plate*, WSD Bremen, 1946; broken up Bremerhaven Feb 1946.

NT 47: launched 1942 as steam tug *Korsfjord* (KM); commissioned 13 Mar 1943 as *NT 47*, assigned to Net Barrage Group Centre; tug office Kiel, RN, 1945; became German *Corsar* with Controll Co, Hamburg, Jun 1948; became Indian *Azad* 10 Oct 1951; still in existence 1968.

NT 48: launched 1939 as Dutch motor tug *Mico*; *NT 48* with Net Barrage Group North Sea 1942; returned as *Mico* 1945; became Belgian *Baron de Mere* 1946; became Dutch *Jan M.* 1977.

NT 49: launched 1938 as Dutch motor vessel *Hoop*; commissioned 15 Jul 1942 as *NT 49*, assigned to Net Barrage Group Holland; sunk by a mine in the Skagerrak, 22 Aug 1944, position unknown.

NT 51: launched 7 Mar 1929 as steam tug *Elsfleth*; vessel pool Wilhelmshaven, 4 Sept to 31 Dec 1939; Operation Sealion tug 11 Aug 1940; KM dockyard Drontheim 1 Jan 1943; became *NT 51* 9 Mar 1944, assigned to Net Barrage Group North; returned 28 Feb 1946; renamed *Ernst* with Louis Meyer, Hamburg, 11 Aug 1960; broken up 1970.

NT 52: launched 1912 as steam tug *Lucia Wrede*; renamed *Titan* 1919; KM dockyard Kiel 28 Aug 1939; Operation Sealion tug 1940; converted 15

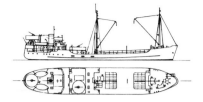

NT 24 (Hans (Bussenius)) (1944). Mrva

NT 16 (ex Adolf) (1940). Mrva

NT 25 (Hugo) (1942); NT 26 (otto), NT 46 (Rabaul) and NT 59 (ex Polangen) were similar. Mrva

Apr 1943 to Apr 1944; commissioned as *NT 52* on 5 Apr 1944, assigned to Net Barrage Group Centre; Net Barrage Flotilla North 1945; returned 4 Dec 1945 as *Titan*; broken up after 1 Feb 1952.

NT 54: launched 1919 as French navy tug *Lutteur*; scuttled 18 Jun 1940; raised and repaired as *V 1801* (inadequate range!); Operation Sealion tug *O 22 S* 2 Oct 1940; became *NT 54* 1 May 1944, with Net Barrage Group North Sea; returned 1945; stricken 24 Oct 1951.

NT 55: launched 16 Mar 1943 as French net tender *Mordante*; planned for Net Barrage Group South as replacement for *NT 44* (ex *Prudente*), but not completed; scuttled Marseille Aug 1944; raised May 1945 but not repaired; stricken 27 Jun 1949.

NT 59: launched 28 Nov 1942, commissioned 17 May 1943 as KM tug *Polangen*, (Mast Libau); became *NT 59* Jun 1944, assigned to Net Barrage Group Centre; taken as French prize 1945, navy tug *Infatigable* at Cherbourg; still in existence 1967.

NT ( ): launched 1932 as French net tender *Perseverante*; became Italian *FR 92* 1942; taken over by KM in Toulon 9 Sept 1943; transferred from

Genoa to La Spezia Jun 1944 for fastest possible adaptation, but not completed; scuttled Genoa 23 Apr 1945; raised 9 Nov 1945, repaired at Toulon; fate unknown.

In the case of the following net tenders, either no definite identification has been made or there is inadequate technical data:

NT 1 (ex IO 81) (FW 19): (FW was the designation for the German guard flotilla, Varna). Net Barrage Group, Varna, 30 Apr 1944; fate unknown.

NT 2 (ex Copri II) (FW 20): in Net Barrage Group, Varna, 30 Apr 1944; scuttled at sea between 1 May and 15 Jun 1944 after failure of both engines.

NT 22: ex Dutch steam tug *Paul* or *Part*; commissioned 27 Jun 1941 for Net Barrage Group West; became *NT 22* 1 Apr 1942, with Net Barrage Group West; scuttled in Western Region Jun 1944.

NT 34 (Suda): ex motor fishing cutter, 60gt; one 3.7cm AA gun; one 2cm AA gun; commissioned as *NT 34* 1 Apr 1942, assigned to Net Barrage Group South; sunk by an aircraft bomb in the vicinity of Volos, 13 Sept 1944.

NT 35 (Volos): ex motor fishing cutter, 12gt; one 2cm AA gun; commissioned 1 Apr 1942 as *NT 35*, assigned to Net Barrage Group South; scuttled at Saloniki Oct 1944.

NT 36: ex Greek motor fishing cutter *Sofia*, 60gt; 7kts; one 3.7cm AA gun; one 2cm AA gun; commissioned 1 Apr 1942 as *NT 36*, assigned to Net Barrage Group South; scuttled in Psytallia Bay, in the vicinity of Piraeus, Oct 1944, after engine failure.

NT 37 (Orion): ex French buoy layer, with Net Barrage Group West 20 Sept 1943; sunk in western region Jun 1944.

NT 39: ex Dutch steam tug *Paardenplaat*; Net Barrage Group North Sea 1945; returned?

NT 40: ex Dutch steam tug *Welplaat*; details unknown.

NT 45: ex Dutch motor tug *Schollevaer*; commissioned 1939, 148gt; late 1943 with Net Barrage Group North Sea; possibly returned 1945.

NT 53: launched 1938 as steam tug *Taucher O. Wulf II*; commissioned 25 Jun 1942 as *NT 59*, assigned to Net Barrage Group Holland; details unknown.

NT 58: ex motor fishing cutter *Kissa*, Net Barrage Group South; sunk by an aircraft bomb at Piraeus, Oct 1944.

NT 61 (ex NSG 1): scuttled at Saloniki Oct 1944.

Net Barrage Group workboats

Careers

Arbeitsboot 1: launch date unknown, commissioned 24 Aug 1939 as harbour defence boat *H 127*; Operation Sealion 1940; commissioned 17 Aug

1940, with Net barrage Group I; Net Barrage Group Centre 1 Jan 1941; sunk by an aircraft bomb at Reval, 24 Mar 1944; raised, repaired at Reval 28 Mar to 29 Jul 1944; GM/SA, Net Barrage Group

Denmark as *A 1*; returned 194?, became motor fishing cutter *LÜ 104*.

Arbeitsboot 2: launched 1933, commissioned 13

Name (type)	Builder	Built	Gross tonnage	Length (m)	Breadth (m)	Draught (m)	Engines	Power (hp)	Speed (kts)	Owner
Arbeitsboot 1 (motor fishing cutter)			12gt				1 diesel	15ehp max		Chr G W Mahrt, Eckernförde
Arbeitsboot 2 (motor fishing cutter)	Mathiesen	1933	14gt	12.90 oa	4.50	1.80	,,	50ehp		Peter Mahrt, Eckernförde
Arbeitsboot 13 (motor tug)		1931	30gt	14.60 oa	4.50	1.90	,,	160ehp max	8.0 max	Soc. de Traveaux et Industrie Maritime Estier & Co
Arbeitsboot 14 (steam tug)	CNM	1926	38gt	16.20 oa	4.30	2.90	1 compound	150ihp max	8.50	Soc. Gen. de Transbordements Maritimes, Marseille
Arbeitsboot 15 (motor tug)	Claparède	1922	27gt	14.50 oa	3.80	2.60	1 diesel	150ihp max	,,	,,
Arbeitsboot 16 (motor tug)	(Arles)	1930	14gt	11.20 oa	3.80	1.60	,,	80ehp max	7.0 max	Enterprises Maritimes et Commerciales, Marseille
Arbeitsboot 17 (motor tug)	(Marseille)	1933	9gt	940 oa	3.30	1.80	,,	70ehp max	6.0 max	,,
Arbeitsboot 20 (motor tug)	Bekkum	1923		11.30 oa	2.80	0.80	1 petrol	40ehp max		Soc. Dumez, Paris
Arbeitsbot 21 (motor tug)	Kromhout			12.80 oa	3,.10	0.60	1 glow plug	60ehp max	7.0 max	Gentrale Suika, Amsterdam
Arbeitsboot 22 (motor tug)	Seijmonsberger		4gt	13.20 oa	3.50	0.70	1 glow plug	44ehp max	8.0 max	Boesel, Amsterdam
Arbeitsboot 27 (motor tug)		1926	20gt	14.80 oa	4.30	1.80	1 diesel	80ehp max	10.0 max	Enterprise Jean Negri et Fils, Marseille
Arbeitsbot 28 (motor tug)			10gt				,,	50ehp max	5.5 max	,,
Arbeitsboot 30 (motor fishing cutter)	Tømmerup	1931	30gt				,,	93ehp max		Danish navy
Arbeitsboot 31 (motor fishing cutter)	Nipper	1929	28gt	15.30 oa	4.60	2.00	,,	68ehp max		,,
Arbeitsboot 32 (motor fishing cutter)	,,	,,	31gt	15.50 oa	4.90	,,	,,	71ehp max	9.0 max	,,
Arbeitsboot 33 (motor fishing cutter)	,,	1931	26gt	15.30 oa	4.50	1.90	,,	113ehp max	7.0 max	,,
Arbeitsboot 34 (motor fishing cutter)	Christoffersen	1939	27gt	18.10 oa	5.00	2.30	,,	87ehp max	,,	,,
Arbeitsboot 39 (motor fishing cutter)	(Travemünde)	1912	3.6gt	8.70 oa	3.0	1.0	,,	20ehp max		Hans Westphal, Travemünde
Arbeitsboot 41 (motor fishing cutter)		1926	15gt	13.90 oa	4.90	1.90	,,	120ehp max		Willi Köhn, Kolberg
Arbeitsboot 42 (motor fishing cutter)		1939	21gt	13.00 oa	4.80	1.80	,,	70ehp max		Johannes Spiering, Sager
(Arbeitsboot 43) (motor fishing cutter)		1938	16gt	13.40 oa	4.60	,,	,,	90ehp max		Karl Walkows, Leba
Arbeitsboot 43 (*Vorwärts*) (motor fishing cutter)	(Wollin)	1926	,,	15.00 oa	,,	,,	,,	75ehp max	8.0 max	Alfred Greinke, Leba
Arbeitsboot ( ) (*Herman Fischer*) (motor fishing cutter)			28gt	14.90 oa	4.20	2.00	,,	,,		Bernhard Stöven, Cuxhaven
Arbeitsboot ( ) (*Serveaux 14*) (motor tug)	(Netherlands)	1930		18.50 oa	4.60	1.90	,,	155ehp max	6.0 max	Soc. Gen. de Transbordements Maritimes, Marseille

Sept 1939 as harbour defence boat *H 130*; Operation Sealion 1940; commissioned 17 Aug 1940, with Net Barrage Group I; Net Barrage Group Centre 1 Jan 1941; returned 1945. Fate unknown.

Arbeitsboot 3: launched 1935 as motor fishing cutter *STO 36*, Joh Birkenhagen, Stolpmünde; 112gt; blockade pilot group East 29 Jun 1940; Net Barrage Group I 1940; Net Barrage Group Centre 1 Jan 1941; sunk at Reval 24 Mar 1944, position 59° 26′N, 24° 46′E.

Arbeitsboot 4: launch date unknown, motor fishing cutter *Forscher (SAG 4)*, Paul Gnewuch, Sager; pilot boat, guard ship group, eastern sea routes, 7 Sept 1939; blockade pilot group East, 1940; Net Barrage Group I, 1940; Net Barrage Group centre 1 Jan 1941; GM/SA, Net Barrage Group Denmark, 1945; returned 18 Dec 1945. Fate unknown.

Arbeitsboot 5: launched 1940, French motor fishing cutter *L'Avenir des Cadets (CC 2699)*, 48gt; commissioned 27 Jun 1941, Net Barrage Group West; sunk at Bordeaux 1945; raised, became auxiliary buoy layer *Fregate* 1950; lobster boat 1967. Fate unknown.

Arbeitsboot 6: launch date unknown, French motor fishing cutter *Lieutenant Mege*; commissioned 27 Jun 1941, Net Barrage Group West (St Jean de Luz).

Arbeitsboot 7: launched 1939, French motor fishing cutter *St. Augustine (CC 2678)*, 37gt; commissioned 27 Jun 1941, Net Barrage Group West.

Arbeitsboot 8: launched 1936, French motor fishing cutter *Eh Pourquoi Pas (CC2563)*, 35gt; commissioned 27 Jun 1941, Net Barrage Group West.

Arbeitsboot 9: launched 1933, French motor fishing cutter *Rospigo (CC2275)* 51gt; commissioned 27 Jun 1941, Net Barrage Group West.

Arbeitsboot 10: launch date unknown, French motor fishing cutter *La Junon*; commissioned 27 Jun 1941, Net Barrage Group West (Le Verdon).

Arbeitsboot 11: launched 1937, French motor fishing cutter *Myosotis (CC2607)*, 45gt; commissioned 27 Jun 1941, Net Barrage Group West; returned 1945; sunk 40 nautical miles west of Quessant, Nov 1947.

Arbeitsboot 12: launched 1934, French motor fishing cutter *Ça M'Suffit (CC2345)*, 39gt; commissioned 27 Jun 1941, Net Barrage Group West; sunk at Brest 1944.

Arbeitsboot 13: launched 1931, commissioned 19 Feb 1943, Net Barrage Group West, sub-group French south coast; scuttled at Marseille 1944; raised, sold in 1961.

Arbeitsboot 14: launched 1926, commissioned 19 Feb 1943, Net Barrage Group West, sub-group French south coast (Marseille).

Arbeitsboot 15: launched 1922, commissioned 19 Feb 1943, Net Barrage Group West, sub-group French south coast; scuttled in La Joliette dock, Marseille, Aug 1944.

Arbeitsboot 16: launched 1930, commissioned 1 Aug 1943, Net Barrage Group West.

Arbeitsboot 17: launched 1933, commissioned 1 Aug 1943, Net Barrage Group West.

Arbeitsboot 18: launch date unknown, French motor tug (?) *Entremar 6*; commissioned 1 Aug 1943, Net Barrage Group West (Cherbourg).

Arbeitsboot 19: launch date unknown, French motor tug (?) *Cachelot 2*; commissioned 1 Aug 1943, Net Barrage Group West (Cherbourg).

Arbeitsboot 20: launched 1923 as Dutch motor tug *Di Tijd Zal't Leeren V*; later became French *Dominique*; commissioned 1 Aug 1943, Net Blockade Group West, French south coast group (Marseille).

Arbeitsboot 21: launch date unknown. *C 227 Mo*; Operation Sealion, 2 Jul 1940; commissioned 9 Apr 1943, Net Barrage Group West.

Arbeitsboot 22: launch date unknown. *C 231 Mo*; 5th Flotilla Operation Sealion; 18th training flotilla Fecamp, 194?; Rotterdam naval office 30 Dec 1942; commissioned 9 Apr 1943, Net Barrage Group West; sunk at Boulogne by an aircraft bomb, 17 Jun 1944, position 50° 43′N, 01° 35′E.

Arbeitsboot 23: launch date unknown; French *Verrault*; *C 232 Mo*, Operation Sealion, 1940; commissioned 2 Apr 1943, Net Barrage Group West.

Arbeitsboot 24: launched 1933 as French motor fishing cutter *Petit Joseph (L3726)*, 46gt; commissioned 14 Apr 1943, Net Barrage Group West (Lorient).

Arbeitsboot 25: launch date unknown, French motor fishing cutter *Petit Quinquin*; commissioned 1 Aug 1943, Net Barrage Group West (St. Jean de Luz).

Arbeitsboot 26: launched 1939, French motor fishing cutter *Goizeko Izarra (BA 989)* commissioned 1 Aug 1943, Net Barrage Group West (St. Jean de Luz).

Arbeitsboot 27: launched 1926, commissioned 1 Aug 1943, Net Barrage Group West, French south coast group (Marseille); scuttled at Marseille Aug 1944, broken up.

Arbeitsboot 28: launch date unknown, commissioned 1 Aug 1943, Net Barrage Group West.

Arbeitsboot 29: launch date unknown, Danish motor fishing cutter *P 11*; commissioned 12 Oct 1943, Net Barrage Group Centre; at Travemünde 1 Oct 1944. Fate unknown.

Arbeitsboot 30: launched 1931, commissioned 12 Oct 1943, Net Barrage Group Centre; returned 1945, Danish fleet; motor fishing cutter *Nordsøen* 195?.

Arbeitsboot 31: launched 1929, *P 24* in Danish mine hunter service May 1942; taken over by KM at Horsens 29 Aug 1943; commissioned 12 Oct 1943, Net Barrage Group Centre; returned 1945, Danish fleet; *Y 349* 1 Apr 1951; *DMH 61* 1 Sept 1958; *MHV 61* 1960; still in existence 1982.

Arbeitsboot 32: launched 1929, *P 33* in Danish mine hunter service Nov 1942; taken over by KM at Køoge 29 Aug 1943, commissioned, Net Barrage Group Centre; returned 1945, Danish fleet; *Y 357* 1 Apr 1951; *DMH 64* 1 Sept 1958; *MHV 64* 1960; still in service 1982.

Arbeitsboot 33: launched 1931, *P 36* in Danish mine hunter service Apr 1943; taken over by KM at Holmen/Copenhagen 29 Aug 1943, commissioned, Net Barrage Group centre; returned 1945, Danish fleet; *Y 360* 1 Apr 1951; stricken 1965, became mo-

Summary of net barrage workboats

Number	Vessel type	Name
1	motor fishing cutter	*ECKE 16*
2	”	*Nordstern (ECKE 40)*
3	”	*STO 36*
4	”	*Forscher (SAG 4)*
5	”	*L'Avenir des Cadets (CC 2699, French)*
6	”	*Lieutenant Mee*, French
7	”	*St Augustine (CC 2678, French)*
8	”	*Eh Pourquoi Pas (CC 2563, French)*
9	”	*Rospico (CC 2275, French)*
10	”	*La Junon*, French
11	”	*Myosotis (CC 2607, French)*
12	”	*Ça M'Suffit (CC 2345, French)*
13	motor tug	*Rigel*, French
14	steam tug	*Serveaux 13*, French
15	motor tug	*Branly*, French
16	”	*Somarco VI*, French
17	”	*Somarco VII*, French
18	tug	*Entremar 6*, French
19	tug	*Cachelot 2*, French
20	motor tug	*Dominique*, French
21	”	*C.S.M 8*, Dutch
22	”	*Piet*, Dutch
23		*Verrault*, French
24	motor fishing cutter	*Petit Joseph (L 3326, French)*
25	”	*Petit Quinquin*, French
26	”	*Goizeko Izarra (BA 989, French)*
27	motor tug	*Marins Negri*, French
28	”	*Simbad*, French
29	motor fishing cutter	*P 11*, Danish
30	”	*Nordsøen (P 23, Danish)*
31	”	*Mette (P 24, Danish)*
32	”	*Jonna (P 33, Danish)*
33	”	*Just Bruun (P 36, Danish)*
34	”	*Helene (P 38, Danish)*
35	”	*Gertrud (TRA 11)*
36		
37		
38		
39	”	*Ingrid (TRA 12)*
40		
41	”	*Arantes (KOL 34)*
42	”	*Falke (SAG 48)*
43	”	*Vorwärts (LEBA 57/ LEBA 48)*
44		
45		*N.S.G. 2*

tor fishing cutter *Lilli Jane*; renamed *Lene Meng* 1974; still in service 1980.

Arbeitsboot 34: launched 1939, *P 38* in Danish mine hunter service Jun 1943; taken over by KM at Holmen/Copenhagen 29 Aug 1943, commissioned, Net Barrage Group Centre; returned 1945, Danish fleet; still in existence 1955.

Arbeitsboot 35: launch date unknown, motor fishing cutter *Gertrud TRA 11 (ex Edelweiss)*, Wilm. Schmöde jr. Travemünde, one diesel engine; 36 PSe; observation group, Baltic routes, Korsör, Apr to 9 Sept 1939; Operation Sealion 15 Aug to 25 Nov 1940; commissioned 3 Apr 1944, Net Barrage Group Centre; returned 17 Oct 1945.

Arbeitsboot 39: launched 1912, commissioned 3 Apr 1944, Net Barrage Group Centre (Travemünde); out of service 29 Jun 1945; returned 17 Oct 1945.

Arbeitsboot 41: launched 1926, commissioned 20 Aug 1944, Net Barrage Group Centre (Travemünde); returned 9 Jul 1945, and renamed *TRA 34*.

Arbeitsboot 42: launched 1939; transfer boat, blockade pilot service, Sund, 1939; Net Barrage Group Centre 26 Aug 1944; returned 17 Oct 1945, and renamed *LUF 187* (Travemünde).

Arbeitsboot 43: launched 1938, planned for Net Barrage Group Centre (Kiel), 20 Aug 1944; not commissioned, unserviceable; returned 26 Aug 1944.

Arbeitsboot 43: launched 1926, commissioned 28 Aug 1944, Net Barrage Group Centre (Kiel); returned 14 Nov 1945.

Arbeitsboot 45(?) (N.S.G. 2) scuttled at Saloniki, Oct 1944.

Arbeitsboot ( ): launch date unknown, motor fishing cutter *Hermann Fischer (PC 286)*; Operation Sealion, 16 Aug to 7 Sept 1940; commissioned 25 May 1944 as workboat and supply boat, Net Barrage Group North Sea (German Bight).

Arbeitsboot ( ): launch date unknown, motor boat *Møre*, Lars Klauseleh, Aalesund; 25gt; commissioned 20 Oct 1941, Net Barrage Group North.

Arbeitsboot ( ): launched 1934, French motor fishing cutter *Etoile (BA 187)*; B Termel, Ciboure St Jean, 6gt, 17ehp; commissioned 17 Dec 1942, Net Barrage Group West (Gironde).

Arbeitsboot ( ): launched 1930, French motor tug *Serveaux 14*; seized for Net Barrage Group West, sub-group French south coast, 22 Dec 1942.

The following vessels also saw service in the Net Barrage Group, but only fragmentary information is available on them:

Hans Otto (depot ship): Launched 1897, sea-going lighter, Joh Ed Schupp, Hamburg; 643gt, 1070t, no engine; commissioned 8 Aug 1941, Net Barrage Group Centre; storage lighter, Libau, 1 Apr 1942; sunk by an aircraft bomb at Kiel, Jun 1943, stranded; raised, repaired 25 Aug 1945, returned.

Netzprahm I (net barge): commissioned 1 Aug 1943, Net Barrage Group West, sub-group French south coast (Marseille); sunk Jun 1944.

Netzprahm II (ex *S.A. 28*): dredging barge, WSA Cuxhaven; taken over 17 Jan 1944, under conversion at Brake in Mar 1944 for net Barrage Group North Sea; completion planned for Jul 1944; fate unknown.

Netzprahm III (ex *Antonietta*): launch date unknown, Dutch lighter; commissioned 1941 for Net Barrage Group West; Net Barrage Group Holland 1942; Net Barrage Group North Sea Nov 1943; returned from Vlaardingen to the German Bight Oct 1944; fate unknown.

Netzleichter I (tender): commissioned 1941, Net Barrage Group Centre.

Netzleichter III (ex lighter *Ibis*): Net Barrage Group North Sea.

Net tug *P 2:* Net Barrage Group South/Aegean.

Net tug *P 300:* Net Barrage Group South/Aegean, scuttled 1944.

Control boats *1–8:* Net Barrage Group West; all sunk Jun 1944 (?).

Barrage vessels 1914–1919

Barrage lighters

All barrage lighters belonged to Norddeutscher Lloyd stock, Bremen. Specifications of the lighters *3* to *41*, which were built before 1882, have not been established to date. All lighters were devoid of engines, and most were fitted with one 3.7cm machine gun. Numbers *85*, *143* and *157* carried one searchlight.

Careers

NDL 3: barrage lighter in Hubert-Plate channel, 5 Jun 1916; Barrage Vessel Group Ems, 18 Dec 1916; returned 25 Nov 1918; Bremen naval office 1945.

NDL 7: ship barrage, Ems, 9 Jun 1916; returned 11 Nov 1916; air barrage, Borkum, 7 Mar to 2 Oct 1940; KM dockyard Wilhelmshaven, 17 May 1941; returned 11 Dec 1943.

NDL 7: ship barrage, Ems, 9 Jun 1916; returned 11 Nov 1916; air barrage, Borkum, 7 Mar to 2 Oct 1940; KM dockyard Wilhelmshaven, 17 May 1941; returned 11 Dec 1943.

NDL 9: ship barrage, Ems, 12 Jun 1916; returned 6 Nov 1916.

NDL 11: ship barrage, Ems, 12 Jun 1916; returned 1 Dec 1916.

NDL 13: ship barrage, Elbe, 10 Feb 1916; returned 18 Apr 1918; barrage experimental group, Kiel, 11 Sept 1943; sunk.

NDL 15: ship barrage, Elbe, 17 Mar 1915; returned 22 Apr 1918; Bremerhaven naval office 194?.

NDL 17: ship barrage, Elbe, 18 Feb 1915; returned 17 Apr 1918.

NDL 19: ship barrage, Elbe, 18 Feb 1915; returned 22 Apr 1918.

NDL 23: ship barrage, Elbe, 10 Feb 1916; returned 11 Apr 1918.

NDL 31: ship barrage, Elbe, 17 Mar 1915; returned 15 Apr 1918.

NDL 32: ship barrage, Elbe, 17 Mar 1915; returned 17 Apr 1918.

NDL 33: ship barrage, Elbe, 10 Feb 1916; returned 11 Apr 1918.

NDL 34: ship barrage, Elbe, 17 Mar 1915; returned 27 Nov 1917.

NDL 35: ship barrage, Elbe, 10 Feb 1916; returned 8 Apr 1918.

NDL 37: ship barrage, Ems, 9 Jun 1916; returned 11 Nov 1916.

NDL 38: ship barrage, Ems, 14 Jun 1916; returned 19 Oct 1916; office ship, 12th minesweeping flotilla, 22 Jul 1918; returned 15 Dec 1919.

NDL 39: ship barrage, Ems, 5 Jun 1916; returned 28 Nov 1916; office ship, 12th minesweeping flotilla, 22 Jul 1918; returned 14 Jan 1919.

NDL 40: ship barrage, Ems, 14 Jun 1916; returned 16 Nov 1916; office ship, 4th minesweeping flotilla, 1918; returned 28 Aug 1919.

NDL 41: ship barrage, Elbe, 10 Feb 1916; returned 24 Apr 1918.

NDL 43: ship barrage, Jade, 2 Jan 1915; returned 10 Dec 1918.

NDL 45: ship barrage, Jade, 24 Dec 1914; returned 9 Jan 1919.

NDL 46: barrage lighter in the Hubert-Plate breakthrough, 18 Jun 1916; barrage vessel division, Ems, 18 Dec 1916; returned 19 Nov 1918.

NDL 47: barrage lighter in the Hubert-Plate breakthrough, 13 Jun 1916; barrage vessel division, Ems, 18 Dec 1916; returned 11 Jan 1919.

NDL 48: barrage lighter in the Hubert-Plate breakthrough, 13 Jun 1916; barrage vessel division, Ems, 18 Dec 1916; returned 18 Nov 1918.

NDL 49: ship barrage, Jade, 24 Dec 1914; returned 10 Dec 1918.

NDL 50: ship barrage, Jade, 2 Jan 1915; returned 24 Apr 1919.

NDL 51: ship barrage, Jade, 2 Jan 1915; returned 13 Dec 1918.

NDL 52: ship barrage, Jade, 2 Jan 1915; returned 27 Nov 1916.

NDL 53: ship barrage, Elbe, 16 Nov 1914; ship barrage, Jade, 9 May 1918; returned 13 Dec 1918.

NDL 54: ship barrage, Elbe, 1 Nov 1914; ship blockade, Jade, 9 May 1918; returned 22 Dec 1919.

NDL 55: ship barrage, Jade, 24 Dec 1914; returned 12 Dec 1918.

NDL 56: ship barrage, Ems, 9 Jun 1916; returned 17 Jan 1917.

NDL 57: ship barrage, Jade, 2 Jan 1915; returned 9 Dec 1918.

NDL 58: ship barrage, Jade, 24 Dec 1914; returned 14 Dec 1918.

NDL 59: ship barrage, Jade, 2 Jan 1915; returned 13 Dec 1918.

NDL 60: ship barrage, Jade, 2 Jan 1915; returned 9 Dec 1918.

NDL 61: ship barrage, Ems, 9 Jun 1916; returned 16 Nov 1916.

NDL 62: ship barrage, Jade, 24 Dec 1914; returned 20 Dec 1918.

NDL 63: ship barrage, Jade, 2 Jan 1915; returned 3 Jan 1919.

NDL 64: ship barrage, Jade, 2 Jan 1915; returned 27 Nov 1916; Bremerhaven Naval Equipment Store 15 Mar 1941; Cuxhaven Barrage Arsenal, 1944; returned; broken up at Köhlbrand dockyard, Hamburg, 1952.

NDL 65: ship barrage, Elbe, 1 Nov 1914; returned 18 Apr 1918.

NDL 66: ship barrage, Jade, 2 Jan 1915; returned 18 Dec 1918.

NDL 67: ship barrage, Elbe, 1 Nov 1914; returned 8 Apr 1918.

NDL 68: ship barrage, Elbe, 16 Nov 1914; returned 26 Apr 1918.

NDL 71: ship barrage, Jade, 2 Jan 1915; returned 10 Dec 1918.

NDL 72: ship barrage, Elbe, 1 Nov 1914; returned 20 Apr 1918.

NDL 73: ship barrage, Ems, 12 Jun 1916; returned 30 Sept 1916.

NDL 74: ship barrage, Jade, 2 Jan 1915; returned 5 Dec 1918.

NDL 75: ship barrage, Jade, 2 Jan 1915; returned 28 Dec 1918.

NDL 76: ship barrage, Jade, 2 Jan 1915; returned 11 Dec 1918.

NDL 79: ship barrage, Jade, 17 Feb 1915; returned 10 Nov 1916; still in existence 1955.

NDL 81: ship barrage, Jade, 2 Jan 1915; returned 20 Jan 1918.

NDL 82: ship barrage, Jade, 12 Jun 1916; returned 22 Dec 1918.

NDL 83: ship barrage, Jade, 2 Jan 1915; returned 14 Dec 1918.

NDL 84: ship barrage, Jade, 2 Jan 1915; returned 18 Dec 1918.

NDL 85: ship barrage, Jade, 4 Jul 1916; returned 18 Sept 1919; still in existence 1939.

Name	Builder (construction nos)	Built	Gross tonnage	Length between perpendiculars (m)	Breadth (m)	Hull depth (m)
NDL 43, 45, 46	(Bremen)	1882	221gt			
NDL 47, 48	Meyer (14, 15)	"	226gt	38.12	7..32	2.95
NDL 49–51	(Bremerhaven)	1883	220gt			
NDL 52–54	Ulrichs (106a–c)	"	238gt	38.17		
NDL 55–60	Meyer (20–25)	1883–84	225gt	44.00	7.32	3.01
NDL 61–66	Tecklenborg (70–75)	1887–88	235gt	38.00	7.30	3.30
NDL 67, 68, 71, 72	Meyer (53, 54, 57, 58)	1889	229gt	38.18	7.32	3.01
NDL 73–76	" (65–68)	1890	269gt	44.30	"	"
NDL 79	" (117)	1896	398gt	50.60	8.00	3.40
NDL 81, 82	Wencke, FW	1896–97	266gt	44.30	7.32	3.02
NDL 83, 84	Tecklenborg (152, 153)	1897	280gt	"	"	"
NDL 85	Meyer (120	"	442gt	55.00	8.00	3.40
NDL 88–90	*					
NDL 92	Vuijk	1898	407gt			
NDL 93–94	*					
NDL 97	Bodewes (102)	1900	391gt	50.34	8.37	3.24
NDL 103, 104	Vuijk	"	399gt			
NDL 109	"	1902	411gt			
NDL 111, 113, 114	v d Kuijl	1902–03	279gt			
NDL 126	Vuijk	1906	284gt	50.00	8.00	3.40
NDL 130, 131	Lühring (83, 84)	1906–07	285gt	44.30	7.32	3.02
NDL 143	NMA (40)	1907	389gt	50.0	8.00	3.40
NDL 149, 150, 152	Wilminck	1912	293gt	44.30	7.37	3.02
NDL 151, 153, 154	Lühring (123–125)	"	287gt	44.29	7.32	"
NDL 156	Wilminck	1913	414gt	50.68	8.03	3.54
NDL 157, 158	Vuijk	"	407gt	50.42	"	3.50
NDL 160, 161	Wilminck	"	418gt	51.78	8.02	3.47
NDL 170, 171	Atlas (112, 113)	1914	404gt	40.38	8.04	3.52

* See page 195.

NDL 88–90: see page 195.

NDL 92: ship barrage, Jade, 9 Jun 1916; returned 27 Oct 1916; Imperial dockyard Danzig, 23 Nov 1916; returned 2 Jul 1919.

NDL 93–94: see page 195.

NDL 97: barrage lighter in the Hubert-Plate breakthrough, 8 Jun 1916; barrage vessel division, Ems, 18 Dec 1916; returned 2 Dec 1918.

NDL 103: ship barrage, Ems, 9 Jun 1916, returned 7 Oct 1916.

NDL 104: ship barrage, Ems, 14 Jun 1916; returned 2 Dec 1916; salvage lighter for *Rheinland*, 1918; sunk in the Baltic at 1130hrs on 4 Jun 1918, position 59° 54′N, 10° 55′E, stranded; raised. Fate unknown.

NDL 109: ship barrage, Ems, 5 Jun 1916; returned 23 Oct 1916.

NDL 111: ship barrage, Jade, 2 Jan 1915; returned 11 Dec 1918.

NDL 113: ship barrage, Jade, 2 Jan 1915; returned 16 Sept 1916.

NDL 114: ship barrage, Jade, 2 Jan 1915; returned 14 Dec 1918; Wesermünde Naval Equipment Store, 20 Oct 1939; air barrage, Jade, 2nd harbour defence flotilla, 6 Mar 1940; KM dockyard Kiel, 10 Jun 1942.

NDL 126: ship barrage, Jade, 2 Jan 1915; returned 12 Dec 1918; Wesermünde supply office, 25 Sept 1939; Cuxhaven Barrage Arsenal, 8 Mar 1944.

NDL 130: ship barrage, Jade, 2 Jan 1915; returned 14 Dec 1918; Wesermünde vessel pool, 1939; returned.

NDL 131: ship barrage, Ems, 14 Jun 1916; returned 27 Oct 1916.

NDL 143: ship barrage, Jade, 4 Jul 1916; returned 22 Nov 1918.

NDL 149: ship barrage, Jade, 2 Jan 1915; returned 24 Apr 1919; air barrage, Jade, 2nd harbour defence flotilla, 4 May 1940; floating workshop at Drontheim, 1942; Swinemünde naval equipment and repair store, 22 Jul 1943; steam supply barge.

NDL 150: ship barrage, Jade, 23 Jan 1915; returned 22 Feb 1917; Emden Naval Equipment Store, 3 Sept 1939; returned 1945; still in existence 1956.

NDL 151: ship barrage, Jade, 15 Feb 1915; returned 19 Mar 1919; air barrage, Jade, 2nd harbour defence flotilla, 7 May 1940; Emden Naval Equipment Store, 25 Jun 1941; returned 1 Nov 1945.

NDL 152: ship barrage, Jade, 15 Feb 1915; returned 22 Dec 1918.

NDL 153: ship barrage, Jade, 15 Feb 1915; net barrage division, Baltic, 1916; returned 21 Feb 1919; net barrage vessel *AL*, barrage command, Pillau, 23 Feb 1940; GM/SA 1945; returned 8 Dec 1945, broken up Nov 1967.

NDL 154: ship barrage, Jade, 23 Jan 1915; returned 17 Mar 1919; became blockade breach lighter *Ost I* (31 men) 9 Dec 1939; became *H 241* 12 Apr 1940; barrage barge, Kiel harbour defence flotilla, Dec 1942; became *DW 41* with explosives group, Kiel, Jun 1943; sunk in the Jade 1944, position 53° 44′ 10″N, 08° 03′ 3″E.

NDL 156: ship barrage, Ems, 5 Jun 1916; returned 3 Nov 1916; Mast Emden 3 Sept 1939; returned 8 Aug 1944; still in existence 1965.

NDL 157: ship barrage, Jade, 4 Jan 1915; returned 8 Dec 1918; still in existence 1956.

NDL 158: ship barrage, Jade, 18 Nov 1915; returned 9 Aug 1918; transport ship store, Hamburg, 9 Jan 1941; returned 17 Feb 1941.

NDL 160: ship barrage, Ems, 5 Jun 1916; returned 2 Oct 1916; barrage vessel division, Elbe, 25 Apr 1918; returned 24 Dec 1918; still in existence 1939.

NDL 161: ship barrage, Jade, 24 Dec 1914; returned 20 Sept 1916.

NDL 170: barrage lighter, Hubert-Plate breakthrough, 18 Dec 1916; returned 11 Jan 1919; became barrage lighter *West 1*, 6 Dec 1939; became *Sperrfahrzeug 31*, 1940; became *H 240* Apr 1940; became *DW 40*; GM/SA, 2nd minesweeping division 1945–47; returned 1947; still in existence 1965.

NDL 171: ship barrage, Ems, 5 Jun 1916; returned 23 Jul 1916; transport ship store, Hamburg, 9 Jan 1941; returned 17 Feb 1941; still in existence 1965.

Barrage vessels

Name	Type and construction	Propulsion	Armament	Complement
Alexandra	Steam ship, 1 deck (6 watertight compartments); depth 4.95m.	One 3-cylinder triple expansion engine (one screw), two boilers (310sq m, 14atm forced).	Four 10.5cm guns.	(18)
Ariadne	Steam ship, 2 decks; depth 5.28m.	One 3-cylinder triple expansion engine (one screw), two boilers (124sq m, 12atm forced).	One 3.7cm machine gun, two depth charges.	(13)
Donar	Steam icebreaker; depth 4.55m.	One 2-cylinder compound engine (one 4-bladed screw, 3.30m diameter), two boilers (305sq m, 8.5atm forced).	–	(11)
Egeria	Steam ship, 1 deck; depth 5.28m.	One 3-cylinder triple expansion engine (one screw), one boiler (115sq m, 12atm forced).	One 5.2cm QF gun, one 3.7cm machine gun, three depth charges; searchlight.	(13)
Möwe	Steam ship, 2 decks; depth 6.40m.	One 3-cylinder triple expansion engine (one screw), two boilers.	Two 8.8cm guns; searchlight.	20
Neptun	Steam ship, 1 deck; depth 4.20m.	One 3-cylinder triple expansion engine (one screw), one boiler (130sq m, 12atm forced).	One 8.8cm gun, one 3.7cm machine gun; one searchlight.	(14)
Pax	Steam ship, 1 deck; depth 4.10m.	One 2-cylinder compound engine (one screw), one boiler (120sq m, 7.5atm forced).	One 3.7cm machine gun, three depth charges.	(12)

Name	Type and construction	Propulsion	Armament	Complement
Poseidon	Steam fisheries research ship; depth 4.50m.	Two 2-cylinder compound engines (one screw), two boilers (190sq m, 8atm forced).	One 5.2cm gun, two 3.7cm machine guns; one searchlight.	(17)
Ralum	Steam ship, 1 deck; depth 3.45m.	One 3-cylinder triple expansion engine (one screw), one boiler.	Two 3.7 machine guns, three depth charges.	
Saturn	Steam ship, 2 decks; depth 3.35m.	One 2-cylinder compound engine (one screw), one boiler.	One 3.7cm machine gun, three depth charges.	(12)
Schwan	Steam ship, 2 decks; depth 6.40m.	One 3-cylinder triple expansion engine (one screw), two boilers (276sq m, 14atm forced).	Two 8.8cm guns; one searchlight.	(19)
Seelotse	Steam ferry, 1 deck; depth 3.60m.	One 2-cylinder compound engine (one screw), one boiler (115sq m, 9.5atm forced).	Two 3.7cm machine guns; one searchlight.	(5)
Seestern	Steam ferry; depth 4.00m.	One 3-cylinder triple expansion engine (one screw), one boiler (172sq m, 12.5atm forced).	Two 3.7cm machine guns; one searchlight.	
Themis	Steam ship, 1 deck; depth 3.53m.	One 2-cylinder compound engine (one screw), one boiler (95sq m, 7atm forced).	One 3.7cm machine gun, three depth charges.	(12)
Victoria	Steam ship, 1 deck; depth 4.15m.	One 3-cylinder triple expansion engine (one screw), one boiler (130sq m, 12atm forced).	One 8.8cm gun, one 3.7cm machine gun, four depth charges; one searchlight.	(12)

Careers

Alexandra: launched 18 Mar 1909, commissioned 16 May 1909 as steamship *Alexandra*; commissioned 6 Dec 1915 as submarine decoy *Hilfsschiffe A Alexandra*; light barrage ship, The Sound, 20 Dec 1917; returned 26 Nov 1918; taken as British prize, 29 Jun 1920; renamed *Arbroath* 1921; became Canadian *Gaspesia* 1922; renamed *North Voyageur* 1946; to Honduras 1949; sunk in the Guyana basin as a result of water penetration on 22 Oct 1950, position approx 10°N, 52° 25′W.

Ariadne: launched May 1898, commissioned 15 Jul 1898 as steamship *Ariadne*; leader ship Oster-Ems, barrage vessel, Ems division, 1914; returned 1919; taken as Norwegian prize, 29 Oct 1945, renamed *Pollnes*; lost on voyage from Bodø to Dublin after 7 Jan 1947.

Donar: launched 28 Jul 1892 as icebreaker *Donar*; internal transit ship, barrage vessel, Weser division, 5 Aug 1914; tender with the High Seas Fleet, 29 Jan 1917; tender with Libau harbour captain 20 Mar 1917; returned 1919; Operation Sealion, 23 Aug to 10 Dec 1940; KM dockyard Wilhelmshaven 20 Jul 1942; dredging service in the vicinity of Korsör; returned 7 Jan 1943; tug office, Kiel, 1946; taken as US prize 1947, and on charter to WSD Bremen; transferred back 12 Apr 1950; broken up at Bremerhaven 1964.

Egeria: launched Apr 1898 as steamship *Egeria*; reserve barrage ship for Ems and Jade, 14 Feb 1916; returned 29 Nov 1918; severely damaged by an aircraft bomb at Hamburg, 20 Mar 1945; broken up 1945.

Möwe: launched 22 Dec 1912 as steamship *Möwe*; barrage ship in ship barrage, Jade, 23 Mar 1915; returned 30 Nov 1918; became French *Marechal Gallieni* in 1926; broken up at Bombay in 1954.

Neptun: launched Dec 1911 as steamship *Neptun*; commissioned 26 Apr 1916 as guard ship with ship barrage, Jade; returned 12 Sept 1919; stranded and sunk at Skalleriff, Kattegat, 29 Dec 1939.

Pax: launched May 1893 as steamship *Pax*; guard ship with ship barrage, Jade, 25 Mar 1916; returned 30 Aug 1916; sunk at Hamburg by an aircraft bomb, 8 Apr 1945.

Poseidon: launched 1902 as fisheries research ship *Poseidon*; external transit ship, barrage vessel, Weser division, 5 Aug 1914; leader boat, patrol flotilla, Ems, 14 Nov 1917; returned 11 Dec 1918; Reichs post research ship, 1938; became navigation training ship *Rigel* at Gotenhafen, 7 Oct 1943; taken as USSR prize 4 Nov 1945. Fate unknown.

Ralum: launched 1914 as steamship *Ralum*; inner transit ship, barrage vessel, Elbe division, 7 Mar 1916; guard ship with ship barrage, Jade, 3 Apr 1918; returned 5 Dec 1918; became British in 1930 (home port Suva, in the Fiji islands); still in existence 1935. Fate unknown.

Saturn: launched before 1911 as steamship *Saturn*; guard ship with ship barrage, Jade, 6 Nov 1916; returned 4 Apr 1918; sunk in Weser estuary after springing a leak, 28 Dec 1921.

Schwan: launched 11 Sept 1907 as steamship *Schwan*; barrage ship, Ems, 10 Jun 1916; returned 26 Nov 1916; stranded and sunk in the vicinity of Bodø on 28 Jan 1918, position 63° 16′N, 21° 56′E; raised and repaired; taken as British prize 1920; repurchased 1921; renamed *Pinguin* (Argo Reederei) 1938; to naval air group, Stettin, 3 Sept 1939; pilot steamer with barrage group East, 14 Dec 1939; barrage pilot ship, barrage command Kiel, 1 Jul 1940; guard ship 13 Apr 1941; barrage pilot ship, pilot command Wilhelmshaven, 6 Mar 1945; returned 1945; broken up at Hamburg in 1954.

Seelotse: launched Jul 1908 as steam ferry *Seelotse*; searchlight ship 5 Aug 1914; barrage vessel, Elbe division; coastal region office V, 18 Apr 1918; returned 1919; became *Bürgermeister Lafrenz* with Fehmarn Line, 1921; became *Flamingo* with the Förde-Reederei GmbH, 1951; broken up by Harmstorff, Lübeck, in 1967.

Seestern: launched 1914 as steam ferry *Seestern*; external transit ship, 3 Aug 1914; barrage vessel, Elbe division; returned 5 Dec 1918; became steam tug *Seeschlepper* 1919; sold to Stinnes 1923, stricken from register.

Themis: launched Apr 1891 as steamship *Themis*; guard ship 22 Mar 1916; ship barrage, Jade; returned 12 Nov 1918; renamed *Elbing IX* with Zedler, Elbing, 1 Nov 1939; sunk in the vicinity of Swinemünde on 6 Nov 1942 by a torpedo from the Soviet submarine *L 3*.

Victoria: launched May 1911, commissioned 11 Jun 1911 as steamship *Victoria*; guard ship with ship barrage, Jade, 18 Apr 1916; returned 1917; to W. Ritscher, Moorburg, Aug 1954 for breaking up.

Name	Builder (construction nos)	Built	Gross tonnage	Length (m)	Breadth (m)	Draught (m)	Hull depth (m)	Power (hp)	Speed (kts)	Range and fuel (nm/kts/t)	Owner
Alexandra	NEptun (28)	1909	1123gt	69.02 oa 62.32 cwl	9.79	4.72	4.95	1000ihp max	11.5 max		Riga-Lübecker Dampfschiffs-Ges, Lübeck
Ariadne	Seebeck (G) (128)	1898	621gt	51.97 oa	8.28	3.67	5.28	400ihp max	8.5 max		DSG 'Neptun', Bremen
Donar	BSV (201)	1892	522gt	45.50 oa 43.20 cwl	10.50	3.40	4.55	1000ihp max	11.0 max		Bremen State Authorities, Bremen
Egeria	Vulkan (V) (419)	1898	627gt	51.85 oa	8.24	4.56	5.28	350ihp max	8.5 max		DSG 'Neptun', Bremen
Möwc	Seebeck (G) (328)	1912	1251gt	73.59 oa	10.96	3.96	6.40	1350ihp max	12.0 max		DSG 'Argo', Bremen
Neptun	Weser (188)	1911	659gt	61.70 oa 54.90	8.60	3.90	4.20	350ihp max	8.0 max		DSG 'Neptun', Bremen
Pax	„ (106)	1893	513gt	48.48 oa	7.97	3.63	4.10	300ihp max	8.5 max		„
Poseidon	Vulkan (V) (454)	1902	481gt	49.00 oa 45.50 cwl	9.10	3.63	4.50	500ihp max	11.0 max		Deutscher Seefischverein, Hannover
Ralum	Lemm	1914	356gt	40.23 oa	7.21			260ihp max			Hamburgische Südsee AG, Hamburg
Saturn	Koch (42)	1891	467gt	48.51 oa	7.83		3.35	250ihp max			DSG 'Neptun', Bremen
Schwan	Neptun (271)	1907	1212gt	76.20 oa 73.39 cwl	10.33	3.57	6.40	1000ihp max	12.5 max		DSG 'Argo', Bremen
Seelotse	SMF (497)	1908	150gt	36.08 oa 31.08 cwl	6.52			410ihp max	10.0 max		Cuxhaven-Brunsbüttel Dampfer-AG, Cuxhaven
Seestern	Meyer (309)	1914	343gt	40.00 oa	7.80	2.64	4.00	500ihp max			„
Themis	Evers	1891	467gross	48.51 oa	7.29	3.35	3.53m	250ihp max			DSG 'Neptun', Bremen
Victoria	Wester (179)	1911	660gt	54.90 oa	8.60	3.92	4.15m	350ihp max	8.0 max		„

Foreign barrage vessels

Careers

Atle Jarl: launched Feb 1904 as British steamship *Navarre*; later became Norwegian *Atle Jarl*; taken as German prize in the North Sea by *U 78*, 21 Oct 1916; barrage handling ship with the Kiel Barrage Division, 26 Sept 1917; barrack and store ship, mine research commission, 20 Jul 1918; became German *Barbara* with Globus Reederei of Bremen, 1922; became Yugoslav *Morava* 1925; became French *Soussien*, 1934; became Italian *Rastrello* 1937; sunk at Naples by an aircraft bomb on 16 Jun 1940, position 40° 50'N, 14° 60'E.

Bothnia: launched Oct 1899 as Russian steamship *Bothnia*; detained at Hamburg 1 Aug 1914; light barrage ship, The Sound, 5 Feb 1916; sunk south of Dragør by a mine at 0908hrs on 5 Dec 1917, position 55° 31'N, 12° 30'E, two dead.

Brilliant: launched Nov 1903 as Norwegian steamship *Brilliant*; taken as German prize by *U 38* approx 40 nautical miles west of Horns reef, position 55° 22'N, 5° 10'E, on 18 Apr 1915; guard vessel, barrage vessel, Ems division, 16 Jun 1916; ship barrage, Jade, 13 Jul 1918; collier for mine hunter groups, sea transport department, 1919; war prisoners transporter in the Mediterranean, 1921; sold 1922, became German steamship *Brunhilde* (Retzlaff, Stettin); renamed *Eduard Geiss* with Geiss, Stolpmülde, 1930; sunk by an aircraft bomb in the vicinity of Borkum, 6 May 1944.

Glyndwr: launched Oct 1904 as British steamship *Craigronald*; renamed *Glyndwr* 1911; detained at Memel 4 Aug 1914; aircraft support ship 16 Dec 1914; severely damaged by a mine in the vicinity of Lyserort on 4 Jun 1915; out of service for basic repairs 23 Jun 1915; light blockade ship, The Sound 2 Sept 1916; returned 20 Jan 1919; renamed *Arkenside* 1920; became Greek *Matheos* 1921; renamed *Agia Varvara* 1937; broken up 1959.

Listrac: launched 1907 as French steamship *Listrac*; detained at Hamburg 4 Aug 1914; barrage breach ship, Aarösund division, 1 May 1916; benzol transporter, Ems supply centre, 16 Sept 1918; returned 19 Jan 1919; to French navy 1939; requisi-

Name	Builder (construction nos)	Built	Gross tonnage	Length (m)	Breadth (m)	Draught (m)	Hull depth (m)	Power (hp)	Speed (kts)	Range and fuel (nm/kts/t)	Owner
Alte Jarl	Irvine	1904	1249gt	69.88 oa	10.42	4.32	5.21	1050ihp max			Det Nordenfjeldske Dampskipsselsk., Trondheim
Bothnia	M & N (166)	1899	1349gt	70.10 oa	10.12	4.60	5.26				Wasa Nordsjoe Angf. AB, Wasa
Brilliant	Nylands (139)	1903	1459gt	71.36 oa 70.62 cwl	10.73	5.50	6.62	700ihp max	9.0 max		Acties Bonheur, Christiania
Glyndwr	Rodger (380)	1904	2425gt	100.70 oa 95.60 cwl	13.40	5.80	6.18	1600ihp max	10.0 max		Scarisbrick SS Co Ltd, Cardiff
Listrac	FCM (H) (319)	1907	778gt	59.74 oa	8.43	3.68	4.45		11.0 max		Worms & Cie, Le Havre
Saxon	Harkness (143)	1898	495gt	49.73 oa	7.93	3.91	3.96				F W Smyth, London

tioned by Great Britain at Portsmouth on 3 Jul 1940; sunk off Dundee by a torpedo on 11 Oct 1940, position 56° 25′N, 02° 05′W, fatalities not known.

Saxon: launched Nov 1898 as British steamship *Saxon*; detained at Hamburg 4 Aug 1914; barrage breach ship, Aarösund division, 1 May 1916; benzol transporter 16 Sept 1918; returned 5 Dec 1918;

renamed *George*, became Greek *Georgios Koniordos*; renamed *Vivi* 1940; still in existence 1947; fate unknown.

Name	Type and construction	Propulsion	Armament	Complement
Atle Jarl	Steam ship, 1 deck + shelter deck; depth 5.21m.	One 3-cylinder triple expansion engine (one screw), two boilers.		52
Bothnia	Steam ship, 1 deck (5 watertight compartments; depth 5.26m.	One 3-cylinder triple expansion engine (one screw), two boilers (192sq m, 11.5atm forced).	Two 8.8cm guns; two searchlights.	
Brilliant	Steam ship, 1 deck + shelter deck; depth 6.62m.	One 3-cylinder triple expansion engine (one screw), one boiler.	Two 8.8cm guns; one searchlight.	(15)
Glyndwr	Steam ship, 1 deck (6 watertight compartments); depth 6.18m.	One 3-cylinder triple expansion engine (one 4-bladed screw, 5.20m diameter), two cylindrical boilers (392sq m, 12.5atm forced).	Two 10.5cm/45 guns, four 3.7cm machine guns; two searchlights.	4/87
Listrac	Steam ship, 1 deck; depth 4.45m.	One 3-cylinder triple expansion engine (one screw), one boiler.		

Barrage tugs, transports and inspection vessels

Careers

Adolph, Amerika: see page 196.

Arion: launched 1900 as steam tug *Arion*; search boat, HM division, Wilhelmshaven, 21 Aug 1914; barrage vessel, Wester-Ems C, 28 Feb 1918; returned 15 Nov 1918; Emden vessel pool 3 Sept 1939; Operation Sealion tug *O 10 S*, Aug 1940; scuttled at Gironde 23 Aug 1944.

Arrakan: launched Jul 1892 as steam tug *Arrakan*; barrage marker ship, barrage vessel division, Jade, 3 Aug 1914; returned 13 Mar 1915; sold to Midgard Deutsche Seeverkehrs AG, Nordenham, 1916, and renamed *Nordenham III*; search boat, HM division, Geestemünde, 8 May 1916; returned 27 Feb 1917; renamed *Unverzagt* with Wagner, Weser-

münde, around 1937; naval equipment store, Bremerhaven, 4 Sept 1939; returned 2 Jun 1944; broken up at Hamburg in 1957.

Athlet: launched in 1880 as steam tug *Athlet*; barrage service vessel with the Barrage Vessel Group Elbe, 5 Aug 1914; returned 9 Aug 1914; Imperial dockyard Wilhelmshaven, 13 Sept 1914; returned 18 Jan 1915; sold in 1929, probably broken up.

Blexen: launched in 1912 as steam tug *Blexen*; barrage vessel with the Barrage Vessel Group Jade, 3 Aug 1914; tug and routine steamer, Imperial dockyard Wilhelmshaven, 22 Oct 1914; returned 1918; Operation Sealion tug 12 Aug 1940; returned 24 Dec 1940; became *Geeste* (URAG) in 1963; replaced 1966.

Blitz: launched 1889 as customs boat *Blitz*; customs office Geestemünde; became steam tug *Blitz* Mar 1914; barrage service vessel Alte Ems B with the Barrage Vessel Group Ems, 27 Dec 1915; inspection vessel Emden outer harbour A, Mar 1918; returned 21 Nov 1918; sold 1927, became inland ship *Lina*. Fate unknown.

Brunshausen: launched 1 Nov 1897, commissioned 2 Jan 1898 as steam tug *Brunshausen*; barrage service vessel Oster-Ems C with the Barrage Vessel Group Ems, 1 Aug 1914; scuttled at Libau at 1700hrs on 26 Sept 1917, position 56° 32′N, 20° 58′E; raised and repaired; returned 16 Nov 1918; sold to KM in 1938 and renamed *Helgoland*, with harbour construction office, Helgoland; sunk at Helgoland by an aircraft bomb in 1944.

Name	Builder (construction nos)	Built	Gross tonnage	Length (m)	Breadth (m)	Draught (m)	Hull depth (m)	Power (hp)	Speed (kts)	Range and fuel (nm/kts/t)	Owner
Adolph, Amerika	*										
Arion	Seebeck (157)	1900	123gt	29.14 oa	5.95	3.20	3.50	495ihp max	10.5 max		Norddeutscher Lloyd, Bremen
Arrakan, Pegu	Rickmers (W) (89, 88)	1892	78gt	24.60 oa	5.17		2.68	180ihp max			Reiswerk Rickmers mbH, Bremen
Athlet	J & S (129)	1880	114gt	25.84 oa	5.70		3.64	335ihp max			Verein. Bugsier- & Frachtschiffges., Hamburg
Blexen, Farge	Wiemann (152, 151)	1912	81gt	23.50 oa	5.33	2.44	2.59	380ihp max	10.0	/ /20 coal	Schleppschiffahrts-AG 'Unterweser', Bremen
Blitz	Tecklenborg (92)	1889	77gt	22.50 oa	4.50	2.40		200ihp max	11.0 max		,,
Brunshausen	Seebeck (127)	1897	230gt	37.50 oa 35.32 cwl	6.86	3.10	4.05	600ihp max	,,		Hamburg-Amerika-Linie, Hamburg
Bülk	Howaldt (K) (384)	1901	154gt	30.68 oa	6.42		3.72	450ihp max	,,		Neue Dampfer Co, Kiel
Castor	Wilminck	1906	80gt	24.14 oa	5.20	2.70	3.50	360ihp max	10.0 max	900/10/18 coal	Norddeutscher Lloyd, Bremen
Cornelie Wessels	SMF (491)	1908	132gt	12.12 oa	6.11	3.25	3.65	400ihp max	12.0 max	/ /60 coal	P W Wessels Wwe., Emden
Cyclop	HWD	,,	151gt	29.26 oa	6.10		3.20	220ihp max			Norddeutscher Lloyd, Bremen
Daressalam, Lome	Stülcken (319, 321)	1906	113gt	22.91 oa	5.92		3.81	500ihp max	9.0 max		Woermann-Linie, Hamburg
Dia Aubel	SMF	1911	99gt	24.16 oa	5.61		3.40	325ihp max	10.0 max		P W Wessels Wwe., Emden
Diana	Oelkers (375)	,,	59gt	19.50 oa	5.20	2.30	2.75	245ihp max	8.0 max	/ /16 coal	Neue Schleppschiffahrt Louis Meyer, Hamburg
Diomedes	Stülcken (162)	1899	169gt	30.50 oa	6.28		4.34	450ihp max	11.0 max	1800/11/55 coal	Petersen & Alpers, Hamburg
Fairplay I	SMF	1895	66gt	20.84 oa	5.08	2.74	2.96	330ihp max	10.0 max	530/10/	C Tiedmann/Pauls & Blohm KG, Hamburg
Fairplay V	*										
Fairplay VIII	Oderwerke (592—	1907	90gt	24.10	5.87	2.90	3.20	350ihp max	10.5 max	640/10/	,,
Fairplay IX	SMF (514)	1910	74gt	21.17 oa	5.42	2.82	3.05	350ihp max	,,	640/10/	
Fairplay X	,, (522)	1911	159gt	31.18 oa	6.92	2.98	3.85	615ihp max			,,
Fairplay XI	*										
Gebr. Wrede	SMF (333)	1894	139gt	29.19 oa	5.98	2.10		470ihp max	11.0 max		Schrader & Wrede, Hamburg
Geestemünde	Vulkan (V) (516)	1908	107gt	25.70 oa	6.02		3.25	500ihp max	,,	1890/11/52 coal	Schleppschiffahrts-AG 'Unterweser', Bremen

Name	Builder (construction nos)	Built	Gross tonnage	Length (m)	Breadth (m)	Draught (m)	Hull depth (m)	Power (hp)	Speed (kts)	Range and fuel (nm/kts/t)	Owner
Gladiator	SMF (294)	1891	208gt	33.11 oa	6.60		4.0	500ihp max			Verein. Bugsier- & Frachtschiffges., Hamburg
Goliath	" (464)	1907	63gt	18.84 oa	5.20		2.79	220ihp max	10.0 max		"
Greif	Klawitter (216)	1898	68gt	24.97 oa	5.02	2.40	2.74	"	"		Bremer Schleppschiff-Ges., Bremen
Helgoland	Tecklenborg (107)	1891	203gt	35.00 oa	6.74	3.73	4.07	450ihp max	11.0 max	900/11/	DDG 'Hansa', Bremen
Hemmoor II	SMF (528)	1910	7gt	21.00 oa	5.50		2.95	320ihp max			Portland-Cement-Fabrik 'Hem-Moor'
Johan Reinicke II	Oelkers (400)	1913	79gt	24.40 oa	5.72	2.75	2.98	350ihp max	10.0 max	2440/10.68 coal	Joh A Reinicke, Hamburg
Krautsand	Brandenburg (152)	1901	253gt	35.08 oa	7.30		4.09	600ihp max	11.0 max		Hamburg-Amerika-Linie, Hamburg
Kuhwaerder	Neptun (186)	1899	132gt	24.54 oa	5.79	3.35	3.71	400ihp max	10.5 max		"
Lucia Wrede	SMF (523)	1912	227gt	37.26 oa	7.08	3.36	4.25	850ihp max	12.0 max	2200/12/ 107 coal	Schrader & Wrede, Hamburg
Mars	Seebeck (192)	1902	74gt	23.98 oa	5.80	2.78	3.00	250ihp max			Norddeutscher Lloyd, Bremen
Mercur	" (105)	1895	124gt	29.17 oa	5.76		3.50	325ihp max			"
Möwe	Jürgens (197)	1891	152gt	29.93 oa	5.85		3.31	420ihp max	10.0 max		Nordischer Bergungsverein, Hamburg
Neufahr-wasser	Vulkan (V) (536)	1910	261gt	35.42 oa	7.28		4.32	600ihp max	11.0 max		Schleppschiffahrts-AG 'Unterweser', Bremen
Nordenham I	Drewes	1907	80gt	25.25 oa	5.70	2.61	3.28	270ihp max	9.0 max	650/9/20 coal	'Midgard' Deutsche Seeverkehrs-AG, Nordenham
Nordstern	NMA (80)	1911	157gt	29.96 oa	6.63	2.80	3.60	700ihp max	10.0 max	1500/10/50 coal	Norddeutscher Lloyd, Bremen
Papenburg II	Meyer (179)	1903	59gt	20.13 oa	5.30	1.65	2.30	250ihp max			Papenburger Schleppdampf-schiffsreederei, Papenburg
Peter Wessels	SMF	"	135gt	27.14 oa	6.12	3.20	3.64	400ihp max	12.0 max	3100/12/60 coal	P W Wessels Wwe., Emden
Reiher	Jürgens (198)	1891	132gt	26.62 oa	5.85		3.34	440ihp max	10.0 max	1230/10/40 coal	Norddeutscher Bergungsverein, Hamburg
Rhein-Ems IV	Meyer (185)	1904	58gt	20.17 oa	5.20	1.70	2.30	250ihp max			Verein. Bugsier- & Frachtschiffges., Hamburg
Roland	Klawitter (378)	1913	248gt	33.96 oa	7.39		4.45				A & H Klasen, Papenburg-Halte
Botesand	Chalmers (144)	1906	128gt	29.64 oa	5.80	2.97		450ihp max			Schleppschiffahrts-AG 'Unterweser', Bremen
Saturn	*										

Name	Builder (construction nos)	Built	Gross tonnage	Length (m)	Breadth (m)	Draught (m)	Hull depth (m)	Power (hp)	Speed (kts)	Range and fuel (nm/kts/t)	Owner
Simson	Wencke, B (73)	1892	213gt	32.77 oa	6.55	2.99	2.98	540ihp max		512/9/ 20 coal	Verein. Bugsier- & Frachtschiffges., Hamburg
Stein	Howaldt (K) (414)	1904	256gt	34.28 oa	7.92		3.84	685ihp max	12.0 max		Neue Dampfer Co, Kiel
Telegraph	Brandenburg	1890	147gt	27.30 oa	5.96		5.07	40ihp max			Verein. Bugsier- & Frachtschiffges., Hamburg
Terscheling	J & S (260)	1890	135gt	29.17oa	5.83		3.42	320ihp max			Schrader & Wrede, Hamburg
Triton	Seebeck (158)	1900	123gt	29.15 oa	5.89	3.20	3.50	”	10.5 max	1000/10.5/ 32 coal	Norddeutscher Lloyd, Bremen
Unterweser 8	” (153)	”	46gt	20.45 oa	4.50	1.57	2.20	125ihp max	8.0 max		Schleppschiffahrts-AG 'Unterweser', Bremen
Unterweser 16	” (54)	1892	54gt	21.60 oa	4.60	2.20	2.50	160ihp max			”
Vegesack	Vulcain	1903	146gt	27.66 oa	6.40	3.25	3.88	600ihp max	10.0 max	1680/10/70 coal	”
Vesta	Drewes	1907	77gt	24.16 oa	5.20		2.55	380ihp max	”	650/10/ 16.5 coal	Norddeutscher Lloyd, Bremen
Vulcan	Seebeck (115)	1896	124gt	29.16 oa	5.75	3.22	3.50	500ihp max	12.0 max	1260/12/35 oil	”
W. Th. Stratmann	Stülcken (358)	1907	102gt	24.34 oa	5.65	3.20	3.53	400ihp max	11.0 max	1960/11/60 coal	Petersen & Alpers, Hamburg
Willy Charles	Oelkers (384)	1911	73gt	23.60 oa	5.64	2.70	3.10	575ihp max	”	1300/11/40 coal	”

* See page 196.

Bülk: launched in 1901 as steam tug *Bülk*; barrage service vessel with the Barrage Vessel Group Kiel, 8 Aug 1914; tender park, Kiel, 29 Nov 1918; returned 1919 and renamed *Wolf* with coastal transport AG; renamed *Max Trees I* in the 1920s; became Belgian *Assistant* then sold to French ownership in the 1930s; fate unknown.

Castor: launched in 1906 as steam tug *Castor*; barrage service vessel on the Jade ship barrage 19 Mar 1915; returned 9 Dec 1915; naval equipment store, Wesermünde, 5 Mar 1939; returned 24 Sept 1943; broken up by Eisen & Metall of Hamburg in 1952.

Cornelie Wessels: launched 1908 as steam tug *Cornelie Wessels*; barrage service vessel Wester-Ems A with the Barrage Vessel Group Ems, 1 Aug 1914; returned 19 Nov 1918; Operation Sealion tug, 19 Aug 1940; returned 28 Jan 1941; renamed *Kormoran* with Gebr Beckedorf in 1952; broken up in 1956.

Cyclop: launched in 1908 as steam tug *Cyclop*; HM Group Ems, 1 Aug 1914; returned 4 Sept 1915; barrage service vessel Jade B, 3 Dec 1915; HM division Wilhelmshaven, 28 Jul 1917; Ems tender, 5 Nov 1917; returned 1918. Fate unknown.

Daressalam: launched in Aug 1906 as steam tug *Daressalam*; barrage service vessel with the Barrage Vessel Group Weser, 2 Aug 1914; returned 25 Feb 1919; capsized and sunk in storm on 22 Dec 1935, on passage from Beira to Chinde, position 18° 46′S, 37° 22′E.

Dia Aubel: launched in 1911 as steam tug *Dia Aubel*; barrage service vessel 1 Aug 1914; returned 29 Aug 1915; patrol flotilla, Ems, 24 Jun 1916; tender, 5 Nov 1917; returned 1918; Operation Sealion tug 11 Aug 1940; returned 28 Oct 1940; broken up in Holland in 1953.

Diana: launched in June 1911 and commissioned 19 Aug 1911 as steam tug *Diana*; ship barrage, Elbe, 1 Aug 1914; tender, 13 Jun 1918; returned 4 Jan 1919; renamed *Walter* 16 Jul 1934; served as inland ship after 9 Sept 1937; Operation Sealion tug Aug 1940; naval equipment store, Cuxhaven, 1944; returned 1945; sold to A Ritscher of Hamburg on 31 Mar 1964, and then sold on to Holland for breaking up.

Diomedes: launched in 1899 as steam tug *Diomedes*; barrage service vessel with the Barrage Vessel Group Jade, 8 Oct 1914; boat department, Flanders, 2 Apr 1915; scuttled at Zeebrugge on 15 Oct 1918.

Emil: launched in 1913 and commissioned 3 Feb 1914 as steam tug *Emil*; barrage service vessel, west coast, 3 Aug 1914; returned 16 Oct 1915; tender, 13 Jun 1918; returned 1 Jan 1919; lengthened to 24.8m in 1937; KM dockyard Wilhelmshaven, 6 Sept 1939; Operation Sealion tug Aug 1940; returned 5 Jun 1945; renamed *Steamer* with Eckelmann of Hamburg, 30 Apr 1969, planned as paddle boat; to O Schmidt of Hamburg for breaking up, 25 May 1976.

Fairplay I: launched in 1895 as steam tug *Fairplay*; renamed *Fairplay I* in 1898; Barrage Vessel Group Jade, 9 Sept 1914; service steamer, 1st squadron, Nov 1916; returned; on the Coastal Defence list, 5 Sept 1939; KM dockyard Wilhelmshaven, 11 Oct 1939; Gotenhafen Naval Equipment Store, 1943; returned 7 Jul 1945; renamed *Richard* with Eisen & Metall of Hamburg in 1951; broken up in Nov 1953.

Fairplay V: see page ???.

Fairplay VIII: launched in 1907 as steam tug *Fairplay VIII*, boat 5 with HM division, Cuxhaven, 4 Aug 1914; barrage service vessel Elbe C, 4 Mar 1918; returned 8 Feb 1919; Operation Sealion tug, 28 Aug 1940; Laboe Coastal Defence, 30 Nov 1944; Channel guard department, Holtenau, 3 Feb 1945; returned 21 Jul 1945; replaced in 1962; fate unknown.

Fairplay IX: launched in 1910 as steam tug *Fairplay IX*; boat 9 with HM division, Cuxhaven, 4 Aug 1914; barrage service vessel Elbe F, 4 Mar 1918; returned 5 Feb 1919; Cuxhaven Naval Equipment Store, 31 Oct 1939; returned 10 Jul 1945; broken up by Harmstorff, Lübeck, Sept 1966.

Fairplay X: launched 22 Nov 1911 and commissioned 12 Jan 1912 as steam tug *Fairplay X*; barrage service vessel Elbe C, ship barrage, Elbe, 1 Aug 1914; barrage service vessel Elbe D, 11 Nov 1916; returned 22 Feb 1919; became British *Fairplay One*, 11 Aug 1938; became German *Fairplay XX*, 5 Oct 1950; underwent major rebuild as a motor tug in 1951, and renamed *Fairplay I*; became Italian *Duro*, 27 May 1964. Fate unknown.

Fairplay XI: see page 196.

Farge: launched in 1912 as steam tug *Farge*; search boat, HM Group Ems, 31 Jul 1914; returned 13 Oct 1914; barrage service vessel Jade A, 7 Jan 1916; returned 21 Nov 1918; sold in 1933. Fate unknown.

Gebr. Wrede: launched 1894 as steam tug *Gebr. Wrede*; barrage vessel Elbe *B*; returned 2 Dec 1918; renamed *Vulcan* in 1919; became Polish *Tyran* in 1928; taken as German prize; fate unknown.

Neufahrwasser: Gotenhafen Torpedo Trials Station, 25 Nov 1940; stricken and broken up as beyond repair, 16 Jan 1941.

Geestemünde: launched in 1908 as steam tug *Geestemünde*; Barrage Vessel Group Weser, 11 Aug 1914; patrol half-flotilla West, 27 Jan 1917; supply base Warnemünde 20 Dec 1918; returned 1919; KM dockyard Wilhelmshaven, 11 Nov 1939; Operation Sealion tug, 12 Aug 1940; returned 21 Dec 1940; renamed *Blumenthal* in 1951; broken up in 1963.

Gladiator: launched in 1891 as steam tug *Gladiator*; barrage service vessel Hever A, 20 Nov 1914; shipping department 20 Sept 1915; returned; sunk in the vicinity of Gjedser on 16 Apr 1928 after a collision.

Goliath: launched in 1907 as steam tug *Goliath*; Barrage Vessel Group Elbe, 1 Aug 1914; returned 6 Aug 1914; tender, 5 Nov 1917; returned; became *Oliva* at Danzig, 1937; fate unknown.

Greif: launched in 1898 as steam tug *Greif*; Barrage Vessel Group Jade, 1 May 1916; Barrage Vessel Group Weser, 1917; tender, Ems, 1 Dec 1917; returned 1918.

Helgoland: launched in Mar 1891 as steam tug *Helgoland*; barrage pilot steamer with Barrage Vessel Group Weser, 4 Aug 1914; barrage service vessel Oster-Ems B, 28 Apr 1916; barrage service vessel Oster-Ems A, 1918; returned 5 Apr 1919; became *H 105*, 22 Aug 1939; became barrage guard ship *Sperrwachschiff 5*, 6 Oct 1939; became *DWo 65* 1 Jun 1943; became *Vs 156* 20 Dec 1943; returned 5 Jun 1945, as steam tug *Silbermöwe*; broken up in Nov 1951.

Hemmoor II: launched in 1910 as steam tug *Hemmoor II*; Imperial dockyard Wilhelmshaven, 17 Sept 1914; observation vessel with Barrage Vessel Group Ems, 5 Jun 1916; returned 13 Dec 1918. Fate unknown.

Johann Reinicke II: launched in Aug 1913 as steam tug *Johann Reinicke II*; barrage service vessel Lister Tief *A*, 31 Jul 1914; returhned 5 Dec 1918; renamed *Vorsetzen* with Petersen & Alpers of Hamburg, 14 Jul 1924; KM dockyard Wilhelmshaven, 5 Sept 1939; Operation Sealion tug *O .. S*, Aug 1940; naval equipment and repair store, Memel, Apr 1943; returned 5 Jun 1945; broken up by Eckardt & Co. of Hamburg in May 1957.

Krautsand: launched 28 Nov 1901 as steam tug

Krautsand; Barrage Vessel Group, Elbe, 2 Aug 1914; sunk in the North Sea by a mine on 2 Oct 1916, position 54° 11′N, 07° 43′E, six dead.

Kuhwaerder: launched 22 Sept 1899 as steam tug *Kuhwaerder*; barrage service vessel Vortrapp Tief, 2 Aug 1914; barrage service vessel Oster-Ems C, Sept 1917; Barrage Vessel Group Weser, 20 Jan 1918; returned 14 Dec 1918; renamed *Kuhwärder* in 1923; renamed *Neptun* for J Fritzen of Stettin, 5 Dec 1935; Operation Sealion tug 12 Aug 1940; returned 11 Nov 1940; broken up in 1952.

Lome: launched in Oct 1906 as steam tug *Lome*; barrage service vessel with Barrage Vessel Group Elbe, 1 Aug 1914; returned 24 Jul 1915; tender, harbour captain, Windau, 1917; returned 1920; renamed *Rovuma* (Deutsche-Ost-Afrika Linie), 1 Oct 1921; stranded and sunk in the vicinity of Pebane on 16 Jul 1924.

Lucia Wrede: launched in 1912 as steam tug *Lucia Wrede*; at Imperial dockyard Wilhelmshaven, 8 Sept 1914; searchlight ship with Barrage Vessel Group Jade, 16 Sept 1914; sold by owner to Imperial dockyard, Danzig, 13 Mar 1915; returned 1919 as tug *Titan*; KM dockyard, Kiel, 28 Aug 1939; Operation Sealion tug Aug 1940; became *NT 52* in 1944, see pages ???–???.

Mars: launched in 1902 as steam tug *Mars*; search boat with HM Group Ems, 31 Jul 1914; service vessel, ship barrage, Jade, 5 Nov 1915; returned 31 Dec 1918; fate unknown.

Mercur: launched in 1895 as steam tug *Mercur*; barrage service vessel Jade A, 3 Aug 1914; ship barrage, Jade, 10 Apr 1917; returned 16 Dec 1918; released to Great Britain at Methil, 11 Sept 1945; fate unknown.

Möwe: launched in 1895 as steam tug *Möwe*; ship barrage, Jade, 1 Aug 1914; returned 1 Jun 1915; fate unknown.

Neufahrwasser: launched in 1910 and commissioned in May 1910 as steam tug *Neufahrwasser*; barrage service vessel with Barrage Vessel Group Weser, 4 Aug 1914; sunk by a mine at Wangerooge, 13 Jul 1917, position 54° 09′N, 07°E 37′, 23 dead.

Nordenham I: launched in 1907 as Dutch steam tug *Admiral de Ruyter*; became German *Nordenham* in 191?; Barrage Vessel Group Ems, 5 Aug 1914; renamed *Nordenham I* in 1916; II half-flotilla, patrol flotilla, Ems, 15 Jun 1917; tender, Ems, 20 Jan 1918; returned 1918; Operation Sealion tug 2 Aug 1940; returned 15 May 1941; MBSK centre, 1 Feb 1945; returned 18 Aug 1945; broken up in 1953.

Nordstern: launched 23 Oct 1911 and commissioned 16 Nov 1911 as steam tug *Nordstern*; service vessel with ship barrage, Jade, 15 Mar 1915; returned 13 May 1919; became *Sperrfahrzeug 58* with Barrage Group North Sea station, 22 Apr 1940; later became *H 247*; *DW 47* 1943; returned 1945; renamed *Claus* for Johannsen of Lübeck in 1955; broken up by Harmstorff, Lübeck, in Jun 1967.

Papenburg II: launched in 1903 as steam tug *Papenburg II*; HM Group Ems, 1 Aug 1914; returned 19 Oct 1914; inspection vessel, Emden outer harbour B, 17 Jan 1916; returned 2 Aug 1918; renamed *Helgoland* for Duis, Westerhauderfehn; still in existence in 1939.

Pegu: launched in 1892 as steam tug *Pegu*; barrage marker ship, barrage vessel division, Jade, 3 Aug 1914; search boat, HM Group Geestemünde, 12 Mar 1915; returned 6 Dec 1916; sold to 'Midgard', Deutsche Seeverkehrs AG; renamed *Nordenham II*. Fate unknown.

Peter Wessels: launched in 1903 as steam tug *Peter Wessels*; barrage service vessel Wester-Ems B, 2 Aug 1914; returned 15 Apr 1919; naval equipment store, Emden, 3 Sept 1939; Operation Sealion tug, Aug 1940; sunk by a mine in the Ems, 2 Sept 1941, position 53° 41′ 34″N, 06° 39′ 25″E.

Reiher: launched in 1891 as steam tug *Reiher*; service vessel with ship barrage, Elbe, 1 Aug 1914; tender, 24 Apr 1918; returned 1918; KM dockyard, Kiel, 1939; sunk by an aircraft bomb while in berth 4 at Deutsche Werke Kiel in 1945; raised; repaired; stranded and sunk in the vicinity of Scharhörn, 23 Dec 1947.

Rhein-Ems IV: launched in 1904 as steam tug *Rhein-Ems IV*; HM Group Ems, 2 Aug 1914; patrol vessel for upper Ems, 28 Feb 1916; inspection vessel, Emden inner harbour, 1918; returned 18 Nov 1918; renamed *Deike* with Sloman of Hamburg, 18 Mar 1923; inland ship, 22 Dec 1926; fate unknown.

Roland: launched in 1913 as steam tug *Roland*; barrage service vessel Elbe *A*, 1 Aug 1914; returned 4 Dec 1918; lost in North Sea 23 Oct 1921.

Rotesand: launched in Aug 1906 as British steam tug *Douglas II*; became German *Rotesand* in May 1907; Imperial dockyard Wilhelmshaven, 13 Sept 1914; ship barrage, Jade, 1915; became Swedish *Holmen II* 18 Dec 1919; broken up in 1959.

Saturn: see page 196.

Simson: launched in 1892 as steam tug *Simson*; barrage service vessel Elbe *D*, 3 Aug 1914; barrage service vessel Elbe *E*, 11 Nov 1916; returned 1 Apr 1919; became Polish *Sambor* 12 Dec 1926; became Danzig *Union* (Sieg) 1927; renamed *Ernst* in 1937; with naval office, Bremen, Emden branch (special duties) 9 Aug 1940; returned 31 Oct 1940; became Polish *Centaur* 13 Dec 1947; replaced 1966; fate unknown.

Stein: launched in 1904 as steam tug *Stein*; service vessel for the Barrage Vessel Group Kiel, 1914; returned 1919; became British *Herwit*, 1929; still in existence in 1941.

Telegraph: launched in 1890 as steam tug *Telegraph*; barrage marker ship, Elbe *II*; 1 Aug 1914; barrage marker ship Elbe *I*, Jan 1917; returned 23 Nov 1918; renamed *Perseus* in 1919; renamed *Norderney* with Ems Schlepper AG in 1925; still in Emden in Jun 1945; fate unknown.

Terschelling: launched in 1890 as steam tug *Terschelling*; barrage marker ship Elbe *I*, 6 Aug 1914; tender, 7 Jan 1917; returned 1919; renamed *Lux* in 1923; broken up in 1935.

Triton: launched in 1900 as steam tug *Triton*; search boat, HM division, Wilhelmshaven, 9 Aug 1914; service boat for the Barrage Vessel Group Weser, 6 Apr 1918; returned 18 Nov 1918; Operation Sealion tug, 20 Aug 1940; returned 4 Jan 1941; ice assistance Group North, 9 Feb 1942; returned 1 Jun 1942; broken up by Eisen & Metall of Hamburg in 1954.

Unterweser 8: launched in 1900 as steam tug *Unterweser 8*; barrage tug for the Barrage Vessel Group Weser, 5 Aug 1914; torpedo dockyard 8 Mar 1916; returned; sold in 1928; fate unknown.

Unterweser 16: launched in 1892 as steam tug *Germania*; renamed *Unterweser 16* in 1901; barrage service vessel for the Barrage Vessel Group Weser, 4 Aug 1914; returned 18 Aug 1914; search boat, HM division, Geestemünde, 29 Mar 1916; returned 1920; sold in 1930; fate unknown.

Vegesack: launched in 1903 as Belgian steam tug *Vulcan I*; became German *Vegesack* in Mar 1905; barrage service vessel for the Barrage Vessel Group Weser, 4 Aug 1914; shipping department, 23 Jul 1915; returned 1918–19; renamed *Johannes Schupp* in 1927; renamed *Fairplay XVIII* in 1932; net tender, 1 Dec 1939; see page 204.

Vesta: launched in 1907 as steam tug *Vesta*; barrage service vessel for the Barrage Vessel Group Weser, 23 Aug 1914; tender, Kiel, 11 Sept 1918; returned 1919; Naval Equipment Store, Emden, 3

Sept 1939; returned 12 Oct 1943; broken up by Eisen & Metall of Hamburg in 1954.

Vulcan: launched in 1896 as steam tug *Vulcan*; barrage service vessel Hever *B*, 6 Oct 1914; patrol flotilla, Jade/Weser, 4 Apr 1918; returned 27 Nov 1918; renamed *Nordenham XII* (Midgard) in 1928; Seelöwe tug, Aug 1940; tug on lower Weser, 1947/48; returned, broken up in 1955.

W. Th. Stratmann: launched in 1907 as steam tug *W. Th. Stratmann*; barrage service vessel Lister Tief *B*, 3 Aug 1914; tender, 9 Nov 1917; returned 1 Jan 1919; KM dockyard Wilhelmshaven, 6 Sept 1939; Operation Sealion tug, Aug 1940; KM dockyard Drontheim, 3 Apr 1941; taken as Soviet prize off Oslo in 1945; became Polish *Sztorm*, 16 Jun 1946; renamed *Cyclop* 21 May 1947; broken up in Oct 1952.

Willy Charles: launched in 1911 and commissioned 18 Jan 1912 as steam tug *Willy Charles*; barrage service vessel west coast, 31 Jul 1914; returned 1 Dec 1914; tender, 191?; returned 1 Jan 1919; KM dockyard Wilhelmshaven, 6 Sept 1939; Operation

Sealion tug, Aug 1940; naval equipment store, Stavanger, 1941; returned 28 Oct 1945; converted to diesel-electric tug in 1960; renamed *Falke* with Possehl, Lübeck, 5 Jun 1969; still in existence in 1982.

Only fragmentary information is available on the following barrage tugs:

Alexander: Lehnkering & Co, Emden: inspection vessel, Emden outer harbour *A*, 14 Jan 1916; returned 15 Mar 1918; KM dockyard Wilhelmshaven/Emden, 20 May 1942; to Munster Water Police, 12 Oct 1942; fate unknown.

Hugo Stinnes (2): Hugo Stinnes, Hamburg; 60gt; 250ihp, 10kts, six men: service vessel with the Barrage Vessel Group Kiel, 1914; returned 28 Nov 1918; further details unknown.

Trollö: (prize ship?) 150ihp, one 3.7cm machine gun: inspection vessel Paapsand South with the Barrage Vessel Group Ems 1 Apr 1916; inspection vessel Emden inner harbour, 1918; to Reichs evaluation office, 31 Oct 1919; fate unknown.

Name	Type and construction	Propulsion	Armament	Complement
Adolph, Amerika	See page 196, net vessels.			
Arion	Depth 3.50m.	One 3-cylinder triple expansion engine, one boiler (111sq m, 12.5atm forced).	One 3.7cm machine gun.	(9)
Arrakan, Pegu	Depth 2.63m.	One 2-cylinder compound engine, one boiler (68sq m, 8atm forced).		(5)
Athlet	Depth 3.64m.	One 2-cylinder compound engine, one boiler.		(8)
Blexen, Farge	Depth 2.59m.	One 3-cylinder triple expansion engine, one boiler (110sq m, 12atm forced).		5
Blitz			One 3.7cm machine gun.	
Brunshausen	Depth 4.05m.	One 2-cylinder compound engine, one boiler.	One 3.7cm machine gun, two depth charges.	(9)
Bülk	Depth 3.72m.	One 2-cylinder compound engine, one boiler.		(8)
Castor	Depth 3.50m.	One 3-cylinder triple expansion engine, one boiler (77sq m, 13atm forced).		(7)
Cornelie Wessels	Depth 3.65m.	One 4-cylinder double compound engine, one boiler (115sq m, 9atm forced).	One 3.7cm machine gun, two depth charges.	(8)
Cyclop	Depth 3.20m.	One 3-cylinder triple expansion engine, one boiler.	One 3.7cm machine gun.	
Daressalam, Lome	Depth 3.81m.	One 2-cylinder compound engine, one boiler.	–	9
Dia Aubel	Depth 3.40m.	One 2-cylinder compound engine, one boiler (95sq m, 9.5atm forced).		(5)
Diana	Depth 2.75m.	One 2-cylinder compound engine, one boiler (65sq m, 11atm forced).	–	(7)
Diomedes	Depth 4.34m.	One 3-cylinder triple expansion engine, one boiler.		(9)

Name	Type and construction	Propulsion	Armament	Complement
Emil	Depth 3.20m.	One 2-cylinder compound engine, one boiler (116sq m, 11atm forced).		(10)
Fairplay I	Depth 2.96m.	One 2-cylinder compound engine, one boiler (72sq m, 8.5atm forced).		(6)
Fairplay V	See page 196.			
Fairplay VIII	Depth 3.20m.	One 2-cylinder compound engine, one boiler (96sq m, 12atm forced).	–	(5)
Fairplay IX	Depth 3.05m.	One 2-cylinder compound engine, one boiler (86sq m, 10.5atm forced).	–	(6)
Fairplay X	Depth 3.85m.	One 3-cylinder triple expansion engine, one boiler.	One 3.7cm machine gun, two depth charges.	(9)
Fairplay XI	See page 196.			
Gebr. Wrede		One 2-cylinder compound engine, one boiler (102sq m, 8.5atm forced).	One 3.7cm machine gun, two depth charges.	(8)
Geestemünde	Depth 3.25m.	One 3-cylinder triple expansion engine, one boiler (100sq m, 12.5atm forced).		(7)
Gladiator	Depth 4.00m.	One 2-cylinder compound engine, one boiler.	One 3.7 cm machine gun.	(9)
Goliath	Depth 2.79m.	One 2-cylinder compound engine, one boiler (74sq m, 10atm forced).		(5)
Greif	Depth 2.74m.	One 3-cylinder triple expansion engine, one boiler.	One 3.7cm machine gun.	(6)
Helgoland	Depth 4.07m.	One 2-cylinder compound engine, one boiler (164sq m, 7.5atm forced).	One 3.7cm machine gun, one depth charge.	(7)
Hemmoor II	Depth 2.95m.	One 2-cylinder compound engine, one boiler.	One 3.7cm machine gun.	(5)
Johann Reinicke II	Depth 2.98m.	One 2-cylinder compound engine, one boiler (92sq m, 11atm forced).	One 3.7cm machine gun.	5
Krautsand	Depth 4.09m.	One 2-cylinder compound engine, one boiler.		(10)
Kuhwaerder	Depth 3.71m.	One 2-cylinder compound engine, one boiler (126sq m, 8atm forced).	One 3.7cm machine gun.	(7)
Lucia Wrede	Depth 4.25m.	One 2-cylinder compound engine, one boiler (191sq m, 11.5atm forced).	One searchlight.	12
Mars	Depth 3.00m.	One 3-cylinder triple expansion engine, one boiler.	One 3.7cm machine gun.	(7)
Mercur	Depth 3.50m.	One 3-cylinder triple expansion engine, one boiler (101sq m, 12atm forced).	One 3.7cm machine gun.	(9)
Möwe	Depth 3.31m.	One 2-cylinder compound engine, one boiler.		(9)
Neufahrwasser	Depth 4.32m.			(10)

Name	Type and construction	Propulsion	Armament	Complement
Nordenham I	Depth 3.28m.	One 3-cylinder triple expansion engine, one boiler (90sq m, 13atm forced).	One 3.7cm machine gun, two depth charges.	5
Nordstern	Depth 3.60m.	One 3-cylinder triple expansion engine, one boiler (145sq m, 13.5atm forced).	One 3.7cm machine gun.	(9)
Papenbug II	Depth 2.30m.	One 2-cylinder compound engine, one boiler (80sq m, 9atm forced).	–	(4)
Peter Wessels	Depth 3.64m.	One 2-cylinder compound engine, one boiler (120sq m, 9atm forced).	One 3.7cm machine gun, two depth charges.	(8)
Reiher	Depth 3.34m.	One 2-cylinder compound engine, one boiler (114sq m, 9atm forced).	–	(8) 11
Rhein-Ems IV	Depth 2.30m.	One 2-cylinder compound engine, one boiler (80sq m, 9atm forced).	–	(4)
Roland	Depth 4.45m.	One 3-cylinder triple expansion engine, one boiler.	One 3.7cm machine gun, one depth charge.	
Rotesand		One 3-cylinder triple expansion engine, one boiler.	One 3.7cm machine gun.	(9)
Saturn	See page 196.			
Simson	Depth 2.98m.	One 2-cylinder compound engine, one boiler (108sq m, 10atm forced).	One 3.7cm machine gun, two depth charges.	(9) 4
Stein	Depth 3.84m.	One 3-cylinder triple expansion engine, two boilers.		(9) 12
Telegraph	Depth 4.07m.	One 2-cylinder compound engine, one boiler (102sq m, 7atm forced).	One 3.7cm machine gun.	(8)
Terschelling	Depth 3.42m.	One 2-cylinder compound engine, one boiler.	One 3.7cm machine gun.	(8)
Triton	Depth 3.50m.	One 3-cylinder triple expansion engine, one boiler (111sq m, 12.5atm forced).	–	(9) 8
Unterweser	Depth 2.20m.	One 2-cylinder compound engine, one boiler (8atm forced).		(4)
Unterweser 16	Depth 2.50m.	One 2-cylinder compound engine, one boiler.		(5)
Vegesack	Depth 3.88m.	One 3-cylinder triple expansion engine, one boiler (108sq m, 13atm forced).		(8)
Vesta	Depth 2.55m.	One 3-cylinder triple expansion engine, one boiler (89sq m, 13atm forced).	One 3.7cm machine gun.	(7) 6
Vulcan	Depth 3.50m.	One 3-cylinder triple expansion engine, one boiler (110sq m, 12atm forced).	One 3.7cm machine gun.	(9)
W. Th. Stratmann	Depth 3.53m.	One 2-cylinder compound engine, one boiler (100sq m, 10atm forced).	One 3.7cm machine gun.	(7) 5
Willy Charles	Depth 3.10m.	One 2-cylinder compound engine, one boiler (116sq m, 11atm forced).		(5) 4

Miscellaneous barrage vessels

Name	Builder (construction nos)	Built	Gross tonnage	Length (m)	Breadth (m)	Draught (m)	Hull depth (m)	Power (hp)	Speed (kts)	Range and fuel (nm/kts/t)	Owner
Balder	SMF (349)	1896	162gt	36.75 oa	6.16	2.99	3.08	250ihp max	10.0 max		Verein. Flensburg-Ekensunder und Sonderburger DSG, Flensburg
Bötticher	Howaldt (169)	1888	58gt	20.80 oa	5.25	2.06		80ihp max			Neue Dampfer Co, Kiel
Condor	SMF (486)	1907	182gt	33.64 oa	7.01	3.00	4.00	450ihp max	10.0 max	1224/10/40 coal	Dampfschiff-Ges. Ostseebäder-dienst, Kiel
Dahlström	*										
Herzog Friedrich	SMF	1901	81gt	25.75	5.10	2.48	2.55	150ihp max			Schleswig-Kappeler-Dampfschiff-Ges., Schleswig
Köhlbrand	Reiherstieg (379)	1890	152gt	33.78	6.08	2.72	2.10	260ihp max	9.0 max		Wachsmuth & Krogmann, Hamburg
Kraetke	Howaldt (K)	1903	61gt	21.72	5.71	2.14		120ihp max	„		Neue Dampfer Co, Kiel
Oldenburg	Frerichs (241)	1911	428gt	45.41	9.98		3.96	720ihp max			Weserschiffs-Ges., Oldenburg
Scharhörn	SMF (496)	1907	125gt	41.80	6.80	2.62	3.65	800ihp max			State of Hamburg
Weser								100ihp max			Weserschiff-Ges., Oldenburg
Wodan	BSB	1889	71gt	27.00 oa	6.40	2.60	2.98	300ihp max	9.0 max		State of Bremen

* See page 170.

Careers

Balder: launched 28 Apr 1896 as steam passenger vessel *Balder*; barrage pilot steamer, 5 Aug 1914; returned 14 Oct 1916; barrage service vessel Jade B, 29 Oct 1917; returned 12 Dec 1918; became Danish *Balder* (Sønderburg DS) 1920; renamed *Turisten* 2 Feb 1949; became cattle transporter *Spekulanten* 31 Oct 1950; broken up in 1954.

Bötticher: launched in 1888 as steam ferry *Bötticher*; barrage service vessel with the Barrage Vessel Group Kiel, 14 Aug 1914; returned 18 Oct 1914; sold to Aug Blume, Rendsburg, in 1918; became French *Docteur Roux*, date unknown; renamed *Chassiron* in 1939; sunk in the English Channel by a torpedo, 19 Dec 1940.

Condor: launched in 1907 as steam passenger vessel *Condor*; barrage service vessel with the Barrage Vessel Group Kiel, 5 Aug 1914; returned 16 Aug 1914; became *Vs 59*, 26 Jan 1943; returned 30 Nov 1945; broken up in 1951.

Dahlström: see page 170.

Herzog Friedrich: launched in 1901 as steam passenger vessel *Herzog Friedrich*; barrage service vessel with the Barrage Vessel Group Kiel, 5 Aug 1914; returned 17 Dec 1914; renamed *Victoria* (Hansen) 1938; experimental ship for listening and radar apparatus, 1939; tender for *Scharnhorst*, 1940; grounded and sunk near Bellevue Bridge, Kiel, during air raid Mar 1944; raised and repaired 1948/49, renamed *Viktoria*; purchased by German Federal navy in 1958, converted in 1959; commissioned as *Viktoria (Y 808)* 1 Dec 1960; barrage weapons experimental site; naval troop experimental command, 1965; out of service 30 Sept 1970; sold 31 Jan 1971, floating DJH *Pirat*, Neuhaus/Oste.

Köhlbrand: launched 1890 as steam ferry *Köhlbrand*; patrol flotilla Wilhelmshaven 1914; inspection vessel Wattum South with the Barrage Vessel Group Ems, 27 Mar 1918; returned 5 Dec 1918; renamed *Sachsen*, then *Bismarck*, then *Nymphe* (Piper, Stettin); still in existence in 1939; fate unknown.

Kraetke: launched in 1903 as steam ferry *Kraetke*; barrage service vessel with the Barrage Vessel Group Kiel, 19 Oct 1914; Imperial dockyard Kiel; returned 1918, sold to Stralsund and converted to steam fishing boat *Kraetke* (Fielitz, Moorburg); still in existence in 1933.

Oldenburg: launched 1911 as steam passenger vessel *Oldenburg*; transit ship Schillig with the Barrage Vessel Group Jade, 18 Aug 1915; returned 21 Nov 1918; renamed *Senator Petersen* (Hadag) 1920; renamed *Dietrich Eckart* 1934; renamed *Senator Petersen* 1946; motor ferry 1957; sold to Sweden (A/B Nordø, Oskarshamn) 16 Jun 1967; still in existence in 1973.

Scharhörn: launched in 1907 as survey steamer *Schaarhörn*, later renamed *Scharhörn*; leader boat, HM Group Cuxhaven, 4 Aug 1914; inspection vessel Alte Ems, 16 Mar 1918; barrack and support ship for workers and soldiers' council, 15 Nov 1918; returned 4 Feb 1919; laid up until 1925; then survey and excursion ship; renamed *Johannes Cars* (H Repeter, Cuxhaven) 15 Jan 1972 and planned as museum ship; sold to Scotland 30 Aug 1973; still in existence at Newcastle-upon-Tyne in Feb 1982.

Weser: launch date unknown; inspection vessel, Wattum North, 1914; barrage service vessel Alte Ems A with the Barrage Vessel Group Ems, 1 Feb 1915; returned 25 Nov 1918; fate unknown.

Wodan: launched 1889 as icebreaker *Wodan*; barrage service vessel with the Barrage Vessel Group Weser, 6 Apr 1916; tender, High Seas Fleet, 29 Jan 1917; returned 10 Feb 1917; Operation Sealion tug 23 Aug 1940; returned 21 Nov 1940; broken up by Eisen & Metall, Hamburg, around 1955.

The following fishing steamers also saw service in the Barrage Vessel Groups:

Deutschland, Franz, Grossadmiral von Köster, H H Meyer, Johann Hinrich, Max, Otto Fricke, Prinz Leopold, Schleswig, Senator Mummsen, Sonderburg, Theda.

Name	Type and construction	Propulsion	Armament	Complement
Balder	Steam passenger vessel; depth 3.08m.	One 2-cylinder compound engine, one boiler (75sq m, 8.5atm forced).	One 3.7cm machine gun.	(8)
Bötticher	Steam ferry.	One 2-cylinder compound engine, one boiler.		(3)
Condor	Steam passenger vessel; depth 4.00m.	One 3-cylinder triple expansion engine, one boiler (129sq m, 13atm forced).		(9)
Dahlström	See page 170, minelayers.			
Herzog Friedrich	Steam passenger vessel; depth 2.55m.	One 2-cylinder compound engine, one boiler (53sq m, 9atm forced).		(6)
Köhlbrand	Steam ferry; depth 2.10m.	One 2-cylinder compound engine, one boiler (7atm forced).	One 3.7cm machine gun.	(10)
Kraetke	Steam ferry.	One 2-cylinder compound engine, one boiler.		(3)
Oldenburg	Steam passenger vessel; depth 3.96m.	Two 3-cylinder triple expansion engines.	One 5.2cm gun; two 3.7cm machine guns.	(11)
Scharhörn	Steam survey steamer; depth 3.65m.	Two 3-cylinder triple expansion engines, one boiler (186sq m, 14atm forced).	One 3.7cm machine gun.	(8)
Weser	Steam ferry.	One 2-cylinder compound engine, one boiler.	One 3.7cm machine gun.	
Wodan	Steam icebreaker; depth 2.98m.	One 2-cylinder compound engine (one 4-bladed screw, 1.97m diameter), two boilers (128sq m, 7atm forced).		

Summary of barrage service vessels etc with special designations

Barrage service vessel Jade A	*Mercur/Farge*
„ „ „ Jade B	*Cyclop/Balder*
Barrage service vessel Elbe A	*Roland*
„ „ „ Elbe B	*Gebr. Wrede*
„ „ „ Elbe C	*Fairplay X/Fairplay VIII*
„ „ „ Elbe D	*Simson/Fairplay X*
„ „ „ Elbe E	*Simson*
„ „ „ Elbe F	*Fairplay IX*
Barrage service vessel Western Ems A	*Cornelie Wessels*
„ „ „ Ems B	*Peter Wessels*
„ „ „ Ems C	*Arion*
„ „ „ Eastern Ems A	steam fishing boat *H.H. Meyer/Helgoland*
„ „ „ Ems B	*Helgoland(?)*/steam fishing boat *Grossadmiral von Köster*
„ „ „ Ems C	*Brunshausen/Kuhwaerder*
„ „ „ Alte Ems A	steam ferry *Weser*
„ „ „ Alte Ems B	*Blitz*
Barrage service vessel Lister Deep A	*Johann Reinicke II*
„ „ „ Lister Deep B	*W. Th. Stratmann*/steam fishing boat *Max*/steam fishing boat *H.H. Meyer*
Barrage service vessel Vortrapp Deep	*Kuhwaerder*
„ „ „ Hever A	*Gladiator/Adolph*
„ „ „ Hever B	*Vulcan*
Blockade marker ship, Elbe I	*Terschelling/Telegraph*
„ „ „ II	*Telegraph*
Experimental vessel, Emden outer harbour A	*Alexander/Blitz*
„ „ „ B	*Papenburg II*

Barrage vessels 1939–1945

Barrage tugs and patrol vessels

Name	Builder (construction nos)	Built	Gross tonnage	Length (m)	Breadth (m)	Draught (m)	Hull depth (m)	Power (hp)	Speed (kts)	Range and fuel (nm/kts/t)	Owner
Adler (M.S. I)	Union (250)	1928	62gt	21.24 oa	5.65	1.94	2.40	330ehp max	9.0 max	/ /3.9 oil	WSD Königsberg/ Wasser-strassenamt Pillan
Geheimrat Mau	Schichau (E)	1908	160gt	30.30 oa	5.90	2.20	2.60	350ihp max	10.0 max	700/10/18 coal	Hafenbauamt Kolberg
Georgswärder	Oelkers (421)	1923	96gt	25.48 oa	6.10	3.08	3.20	500ihp max	„		Lütgens & Reimers, Hamburg
Herman	Union (211)	1925	63gt	23.73 oa	5.83	2.30	2.50	325ihp max	„	330/10/10 coal	Wischke & Reimers, Königsberg
Kuhwärder	SMF	1919	„	18.83 oa	5.22	2.70		250ihp max	9.5 max	1000/9/22 coal	Lütgens & Reimers, Hamburg
Nordstern	*										
Saspe	K & P	1912	98gt	23.95 oa	5.52	2.57		350ihp max	10.0 max	800/10/30 coal	Bugsier-, Reederei- und Bergungs- GmbH, Danzig
Simson	J & S (495)	1882	104gt	26.09 oa	6.43	2.92	2.98	380ihp max	„	512/9/20 coal	Wischke & Reimers, Königsberg
Sophie Wessels	Boon	1902	41gt	18.56 oa	4.32	2.00		150ihp max	8.0 max	/ /10 coal	P W Wessels Wwe., Emden
Wilhelmine	Körner	1905	64gt	19.46 oa	5.01		2.45	250ihp max			Petersen & Alpers, Hamburg
Wotan	(Netherlands)	„	(32gt)	24.69 oa	5.55	1.95	2.30	250ihp max	10.0 max	600/10/15 coal	C L Bieber, Memel

* See page 219.

Careers

Adler (M.S.I.): launched in 1928 as motor tug *Adler*; barrage tug, Barrage Command Pillau, 26 May 1941; under charter as tug, 1946–48; returned to Hamburg Water Police 16 Mar 1948; renamed *Kollmar*; sold in Jun 1979 via A Ritscher, Hamburg, to Holland for breaking up.

Geheimrat Mau: launched in 1908 as tug and excursion steamer *Geheimrat Mau*; barrage guard steamer, Barrage Command Swinemünde, 11 Jun 1941; became leader boat *DPK 03* in 1943; later became *Vs 203*; probably returned 1945.

Georgswärder: launched in 1923 and commissioned 21 Jun 1923 as steam tug *Georgswärder*; KM dockyard Kiel, 3 Sept 1939; Seelöwe tug, Aug 1940; barrage guard steamer, Barrage Patrol Group Swinemünde, 20 Jan 1942; later naval equipment and repair store, Pillau; returned 16 Nov 1945; renamed *Jean Louis* (Louis Meyer, Hamburg) 2 May 1957; converted to motor tug in 1962; became Dutch *Baanjard* in 1982; renamed *Savanna* (Dutch) 1986. Still in service 1989.

Hermann: launched in 1925 as steam tug *Hermann*; became *Sperrfahrzeug 54* 19 Aug 1939; Operation Sealion tug, 10 Aug 1940; returned 30 Jan 1941; RN tug office, Kiel, Sept 1945.

Kuhwärder: launched 1919 as steam tug *Westfälisches Kohlenkontor X*; renamed *Daukos* (DAL/ Kosmos, Hamburg) 1923; renamed *Export* (Lütgens & Reimers) 1926; renamed *Kuhwärder* 1937; became *Sperrfahrzeug 12*, Barrage Command Kiel, 5 Sept 1939; later renamed; returned 5 Jun 1945; broken up at Hamburg in 1954.

Nordstern: see page 219.

Saspe: launched in 1912 as steam tug *Ostsee*; re-named *Theseus* 1919; renamed *Saspe* 1931; became *Sperrfahrzeug 57*, 30 Aug 1939; sunk by a mine 2nm east of Den Helder on 15 Dec 1940, position 52° 57′N, 04° 20′E; raised, repaired; sunk by an aircraft bomb at Gotenhafen on 9 Oct 1943; raised; taken as USSR prize, 11 May 1945; fate unknown.

Simson: launched in 1882 as steam tug *Simson*; became *Sperrfahrzeug 53*, Baltic, 25 Sept 1939; later barrage pilot steamer, Pillau; sunk at Pillau by an aircraft bomb, 15 Apr 1945.

Sophie Wessels: launched in 1902 as steam tug *Sophie Wessels*; KM dockyard Wilhelmshaven 1 Nov 1940; returned 10 Nov 1941; barrage tug at Emden, 13 Oct 1942; returned 30 Dec 1942; same service 29 Jul 1944; returned 28 Oct 1944; broken up in the Netherlands in 1955.

Wilhelmine: launched in 1905 as steam tug

Johannes Körner III; renamed *Wilhelmine* in 1908; became *Sperrfahrzeug 13*, 30 Aug 1939; later renamed; returned 1945, broken up in 1955.

Wotan: launched in 1905 as steam tug *Wotan*; bar-

rage tug, Barrage Command Memel, 18 Jun 1941; transferred to the Naval Equipment and Repair Store, Pillau; sunk in the Zeeland barrage by a German mine, 13 Apr 1945.

Name	Type and construction	Propulsion	Complement
Adler (M.S.I.)	Motor tug; depth 2.40m.	One four-stroke Deutz diesel engine.	(6)
Geheimrat Mau	Tug and excursion steamer; depth 2.60m.	One 3-cylinder triple expansion engine, one boiler.	(8)
Georgswärder	Steam tug; depth 3.20m.	One 2-cylinder compound engine, one boiler (130sq m, 12atm forced).	(5)
Hermann	Steam tug; depth 2.50m.	One 3-cylinder triple expansion engine, one boiler (89sq m, 13atm forced).	(4)
Kuhwärder	Steam tug.	One 2-cylinder compound engine, one boiler.	
Nordstern	See page 219.		
Saspe	Steam tug.	One 3-cylinder triple expansion engine, one boiler (97sq m, 13atm forced).	(8)
Simson	Steam tug; depth 2.98m.	One 2-cylinder compound engine, one boiler (108sq m, 10atm forced).	(6)
Sophie Wessels	Steam tug.	One-cylinder compound engine, one boiler.	(5)
Wilhelmine	Steam tug; depth 2.45m.	One 2-cylinder compound engine, one boiler (70sq m, 11atm forced).	(4)
Wotan	Steam tug; depth 2.30m.	One 3-cylinder triple expansion engine, one boiler.	(4)

Barrage lighters

Al (ex **NDL 153**)**:** see page 214.

Memel: Barrage Command Memel, 1941; no further details known.

Mitte: 33 men; commissioned 17 Jul 1941, Barrage Group Kiel; 4th Guard Flotilla Sept 1944; no further details known.

M P 2: see page 163.

M P 3: see page 163.

Ost I (ex **NDL 154**)**:** 31–33 men; Barrage Com-

mand Pillau, 1 Jan 1939; *H 241* 1940; harbour defence flotilla, Kiel, 1 Feb 1942; Barrage Group Kiel, *DW 41*, Jun 1943; sunk in Schillig roads, 1944, position 53° 44′ 17″N, 08° 03′ 32″E, wreck still in existence in 1949.

West (ex **NDL 170**)**:** see page 214.

Within the Barrage Groups and Barrage Commands, the following luggers were also used as balloon carriers: *Auerhahn, Geier, Gross-Friedrichsburg, Kuckuck, Marabu, Norden, Taube* and *Zaunkönig*.

Glossary of builders and dockyards

Abbreviation	Builder/Dockyard
A & R	Yacht & Bootswerft Abeking & Rassmussen, Lemwerder
Aalborg	Aalborg Vaerft AS, Aalborg
ACL	Ateliers et Chantiers de la Loire, St Nazaire
Akers	A/S Akers Mekaniske Verkstad, Oslo
Ansaldo (GS)	Ansaldo SA, Genoa-Sestri Ponente
Ansaldo (GV)	Ansaldo-Cantieri Cerusa, Genoa-Voltri
Ansaldo (L)	SA Ansaldo San Giorgio del Muggiano, La Spezia
Arsenal Brest	Arsenal de la Marine Nationale Française, Brest
Arsenale Taranto	R Arsenale, Taranto
Atlas	Atlas-Werke AG, Bremen
Augustin-Normand	Ateliers et Chantiers Augustin-Normand, Le Havre
B & V	Blohm & Voss (later Blohm & Voss AG), Hamburg
B & W	A/S Burmeister & Wain's Maskin- & Skibsbyggeri, Copenhagen
Bacino	Cantieri Navale Bacino, Palermo
Baglietto	Baglietto Varazze Navalmeccanica, Castellamare
Baltic	Baltic Yard, St Petersburg (Petrograd)
Bekkum	J V Bekkum, Purmerend
Blythswood	Blythswood Shipbuilding Co Ltd, Glasgow
Bodewes	NV Scheepswerven Gebr Bodewes, Hasselt (also NV Bodewes Scheepswerven, Martenshoek)
Boele	P Boele, Slikkerveer
Boele's	Boele's Scheepswerven & Maschinefabriek NV, Bolnes
Boon	Boon, Hoogezand
Botje	Botje Ensign & Co, Groningen
Brandenburg	H Brandenburg Werft, Hamburg
Breda	Cantieri Navali Breda, Mestre
BSB	Bremer Schiffbauges, Bremen
BSV	Bremer Schiffbauges, Vegesack
Burmester (B)	Burmester, Burg Lesum
Burmester (S)	Burmester, Swinemünde
C & N	Camper & Nicholson, Gosport
Cassens	C Cassens, Emden
Castellamare	Cantieri di Castellamare di Stabia
Celli	Celli, Venice
Chalmers	W Chalmers & Co, Rutherglen
Chatham	HM Dockyard, Chatham
Christoffersen	J Christoffersen, Nordby
Claparède	Claparède, Argenteuil
CM (M)	Chantiers de la Mediterranée, Le Havre
CNA	Chantiers Navales Anversois, Hoboken
CNM	Chantiers Navales et Chaudronniers du Midi, Marseille
CNN	Chantiers Navales de Normandie, Fécamp
Copenhagen	State Dockyard, Copenhagen
Costaguta	Costaguta, Genoa-Voltri
CRDA (M)	Cantieri Riuniti dell'Adriatico, Monfalcone
Danubius	Cantieri Danubius SA, Porto Recanati
Danzig	Danziger Werft AG, Danzig
De Haan	De Haan & Oerlemans Scheepsbouw, Heusden
De Jong	Scheeps- & Maschinefabriek A de Jong, Vlaardingen
De Schelde	NV Koninklijke Mij 'De Schelde', Vlissingen
De Vries (Al)	De Vries-Lentsch, Alphen a/d Rijn
De Vries (Am)	De Vries-Lentsch, Amsterdam
Deggendorf	Deggendorfer Werft & Eisenbau Ges, Deggendorf
Deschimag S	Deutsche Schiff und Maschinenbau AG (Seebeck Yard), Bremen
Deschimag W	Deutsche Schiff und Maschinenbau AG (AG Weser), Bremen
Devrient	Devrient & Co, Danzig
Drewes	J Drewes & Co, Gideon
Dubigeon	Ateliers et Chantiers Dubigeon, Nantes
DWA	Deutsche Werft AG, Hamburg
DWK	Deutsche Werke AG, Kiel
Earle	Earle's Shipbuilding & Engineering Co Ltd, Hull
Eckmans	Eckmans Werft, Hamburg-Finkenwärder
Elco	Electric Boat Co, Bayonne NY
Elsfleth	Elsflether Werft AG, Elsfleth
Evers	G Evers, Lübeck
FCM (S)	Forges et Chantiers de la Méditerranée, La Seyne
FCM (H)	Forges et Chantiers de la Méditerranée, Le Havre
Finnboda	Finnboda Varf AB, Stockholm
Flender	Flender-Werke AG, Lübeck-Siems
Flensburg	Flensburger Schiffsbau-Ges, Flensburg
Foxhol	NV Scheepswerf 'Foxhol', Foxhol
Framnes	A/S Framnæs Mekaniske Verksted, Sandefjord
Frerichs	J Frerichs & Co, Einswerden
Fullerton	John Fullerton & Co, Paisley
Gebr Pot	NV Scheepswerf Gebr Pot, Bolnes
Germania	Fried. Krupp Germaniawerft AG, Kiel
Gips	C Gips & Zonen, Dordrecht
Grangemouth	Grangemouth Dockyard Co Ltd, Grangemouth
Gray	Wm Gray & Co Ltd, West Hartlepool
Gusto	NV Werf Gusto v/h Firma A F Smulders, Schiedam
H & W	Harland & Wolff Ltd, Govan
Hansa	Hansawerft, Tönning
Harkness	W Harkness & Son Ltd, Stockton-on-Tees
Hawthorn Leslie	R & W Hawthorn, Leslie & Co Ltd, Hebburn, Newcastle-upon-Tyne
Hitzler	J G Hitzler Schiffswerf, Regensburg

Holbaek	Holbaek Skibs & Baadebyggeri, Korsør	Nederland SB	Nederlandse Scheepsbouw Mij, Amsterdam
Hollersche	Hollersche Carlshütte, Rendsburg	Neptun	AG Neptun, Rostock
Hovedwerft	Marinens Hovedwerft, Horten	Niestern	Scheepswerven Gebr Niestern, Delfzijl
Howaldt	Gebrüder Howaldt, Kiel (forerunner to Howaldt (K) etc)	Nikolayev	State Yard, Nikolayev
		Nipper	Brod Nipper, Skagen
Howaldt (H)	Howaldtswerke Hamburg AG, Hamburg	NDL	Norddeutscher Lloyd Technical Establishment, Bremen
Howaldt (K)	Howaldtswerke AG, Kiel	NMA	Norddeutsche Maschinen- und Armaturenfabrik, Bremen
HWD	Hong Kong & Whampoa Dock Co Ltd, Kowloon, Hong Kong	NNS	Noord Nederlandse Scheepswerven NV, Groningen
Irvine	Irvine's Shipbuilding & Dry Docks Co Ltd, Middleton	Nobiskrug	Werft Nobiskrug, Rendsburg
J & S	Schiffswerft Janssen & Schmilinsky AG, Hamburg	Noord	Werf De Noord, Alblasserdam
Jadranska	Jadranska Brodogradilista, Kraljevica	Nordsee	Nordseewerke, Emden
		Nüscke (G)	A E Nüscke, Grabow
John Brown	John Brown & Co Ltd, Clydebank	Nüscke (S)	Nüscke & Co AG, Stettin
Jürgens	Chr Jürgens & Co, Hamburg	Nylands	Nylands Mekaniske Verkstad, Oslo
K & M	Norderwerft Köser & Meyer, Hamburg	Odense	Odense Staalskibsvaerft A/S, Odense
K & P	J Const Kievitz & A Pannevis, Dordrecht	Oderwerke	Stettiner Oderwerke AG, Stettin
Klawitter	Klawitter, Danzig	Oelkers	Johann Oelkers KG, Hamburg
Klöckner	Klöckner, Ulm		
KMW	Kriegsmarinewerft, Wilhelmshaven	Osaka I W	Osaka Iron Works, Osaka
		OTO (G)	Cantieri Odero Terni Orlando, Genoa
Koch	Henry Koch, Lübeck		
Körner	J A Körner, Hamburg	OTO (L)	Cantieri Odero Terni Orlando, Livorno
Korneuburg	Schiffswerft Korneuburg AG, Vienna	OTO (M)	Cantieri Odero Terni Orlando, Muggiano
Kremer	D W Kremer Sohn, Elmshorn		
Kröger	Kröger, Warnemünde	Ottens	Ottensener Eisenwerke AG, Hamburg
Kromhout	Kromhout, Amsterdam		
KWB	Kaiserliche Werft, Bruges	Paans	Paans-Roodevaart, Moerdijk
KWD	Kaiserliche Werft, Danzig (formerly Königliche Werft, Danzig)	Pattison	Cantieri Pattison, Naples
		Peters	Hugo Peters, Beidenfleth
		Picchiotti	Picchiotti, Limite sull'Arno
KWK	Kaiserliche Werft, Kiel	Prometeo	Cantieri Prometeo, Genoa
KWW	Kaiserliche Werft, Wilhelmshaven	Quarnaro	Cantieri Navali del Quarnaro, Fiume
L & B	Lange & Böker, Reval	R & F	Ramage & Ferguson Ltd, Leith
Lemm	F Lemm, Boitzenburg		
Liegnitz	Liegnitz, Grabow	Rasmussen	Rasmussen-Werft, Svendborg
Lilleö	Lilleö Skibsvaerft, Korsør		
Lindenau	Lindenau, Memel	Reiherstieg	Reiherstieg Schiffswerft, Hamburg
Linz	Linzer Schiffswerft, Linz		
LMG	Lübecker Maschinenbau-Ges, Lübeck	Rickmers (B)	Rickmers-Werft AG, Bremerhaven
Lübke	Lübke, Wolgast	Rickmers (G)	Rickmers Reismühlen & Schiffbau AG, Geestemünde
Lühring	C Lühring Schiffswerft & Trockendock, Kirchhammelwarden	Rickmers (W)	Rickmers-Werft AG, Wesermünde
Lürssen	Fr Lürssen Werft GmbH & Co, Vegesack	Ring	J Ring Andersen Traeskibsvaerft, Svendborg
M & M	Murdoch & Murray Ltd, Port Glasgow	Rodger	A Rodger & Co Ltd, Port Glasgow
M & K	Mjellem & Karlsen A/S, Bergen	Roland	Roland-Werft, Hemslingen
		Rotterdam DD	Rotterdamse Droogdok Mij NV, Rotterdam
Mathiesen	Mathiesen, Arnis		
McGruer	McGruer, Clynder	Russud	Russud, Nikolayev
Meyer	Jos L Meyer, Papenburg	S & H	Schweffel & Howaldt, Kiel
Mützelfeld	Mützelfeldtwerft GmbH, Cuxhaven	SAG	Stettiner AG (formerly Müller & Holberg), Stetten
Nederland Dok	Nederlandse Dok & Scheepsbouw Mij NV, Amsterdam	Sachsenberg	Gebrüder Sachsenberg, Rosslau (Elbe)

San Giorgio	Societá Fiat 'San Giorgio', La Spezia-Muggiano
San Rocco	San Rocco, Trieste
Schelde	Scheldewerft, Vlissingen
Schichau (D)	F Schichau GmbH, Danzig
Schichau (E)	F Schichau Gmbh, Elbing
Schlichting	Schlichting-Werft, Travemünde
Seebeck	G Seebeck AG, Geestemünde
Seijmonsberg	Fa S Seijmonsbergen Werf 'Concordia', Amsterdam
Seikishi	Seikishi Ono, Osaka
Sietas	J J Sietas Schiffswerft, Cranz-Neuenfelde
SMF	Schiffswerft & Maschinen Fabrik (formerly Janssen & Schmilinsky), Hamburg
Smit, J & K	J & K Smit's Scheepswerf, Kinderdijk
Smit, L	NV L Smit & Zoon Scheepsen Werktuig Bouw, Kinderdijk
Smit, P	NV Maschinefabrieken, Scheepswerf van P Smit Jr, Rotterdam
Smith's Dock	Smith's Dock Ltd, Middlesbrough and North Shields
Solent	Solent Shipyard, Salisbury Green
Soriente	Soriente, Salerno
SPCN	Societé Provençale de Construction Navale, La Ciotat
Stephenson	R Stephenson & Co Ltd, Newcastle-upon-Tyne
STT	Stabilimento Tecnico Triestino, Trieste
Stülcken	H C Stülcken Sohn, Hamburg
Tecklenborg	J C Tecklenborg AG, Geestemünde
Thormählen	Thormählen, Elmshorn
Thyen	G H Thyen, Brake
Tirreno	Cantieri del Tirreno, Riva Trigoso
Tømmerup	A & K A Tømmerup, Hobro
Tosi	Cantieri Franco Tosi, Taranto
Übigau	Dresdner Maschinenfabrik & Schiffswerft 'Übigau', Dresden
Ulrichs	H F Ulrichs, Fähr (Vegesack)
Union	Union-Giesserei, Königsberg
Unterweser	Schiffbau-Ges Unterweser AG, Bremerhaven
v d Giessen	C v d Giessen & Zonens Scheepswerven, Krimpen a/d IJssel
v d Kuijl	M van der Kuijl, Slikkerveer
van Diepen	NV Scheepswerf Gebr van Diepen, Waterhuizen
Vegesack	Vegesacker Werft, Vegesack
Verschure	Verschure & Co's Scheepswerf & Maschinefabriek NV, Amsterdam
Vickers C	Canadian Vickers Ltd, Montreal

Vuijk	A Vuijk & Zonen, Capelle a/d IJssel	Walter	H Walter GmbH	Wilton	Dok & Werf Mij Wilton-Fijenoord NV, Schiedam
Vulcain	SA Le Vulcain Belge, Hoboken	Waltjen	Waltjen & Co, Bremen	Wollheim	Caesar Wollheim, Breslau
Vulcan (H)	AG Vulcan, Hamburg	Wärtsilä	Wärtsilä-Koncernen, Crichton-Vulkan, Turku/Åbo	Worms	Ateliers et Chantiers de La Seine-Maritime (Chantiers Worms), Le Trait
Vulcan (S)	Stettiner Maschinenbau AG Vulcan, Stettin	Wencke, F W	F W Wencke, Bremerhaven	WR Co	Wigham Richardson & Co Ltd, Newcastle-upon-Tyne
Vulkan (B)	Bremer Vulkan, AG, Bremen	Wencke, B	B Wencke Söhne, Hamburg		
		Weser	AG Weser, Bremen	Zaanland	NV Zaanlandse Scheepsbouw Mij, Zaandam
Vulkan (V)	Bremer Vulkan AG, Vegesack (Bremer Vulcan Schiffbau & Maschinenfabrik up to 1939)	Wiborg	N Wiborg, Fevig	Zieske	Zieske, Stettin
		Wiemann	Gebr Wiemann, Brandenburg		
		Wilmink	J Th Wilmink & Co, Groningen		

Index